THE CHRISTIAN FAITH

THE CHRISTIAN FAITH

IN THE
DOCTRINAL DOCUMENTS OF THE CATHOLIC CHURCH

REVISED EDITION
EDITED BY

J. NEUNER, S.J. & J. DUPUIS, S.J.

COLLINS

Collins Liturgical Publications
187 Piccadilly, London W1V 9DA

Collins Liturgical Australia
55 Clarence St Sydney PO Box 3023 Sydney 2001

ISBN 0 00 599706 2

This edition first published by Theological Publications in India,
St Peter's Seminary, Malleswaram West PO, Bangalore 560 055.
© 1982 Theological Publications in India

Not for sale in S.E. Asia or in Africa except S. Africa

First published by Collins, 1983

Manufactured in Great Britain by Collins, Glasgow

FOREWORD

The origin of this book goes back as far as 1938 to the first publication in German of the Church's doctrinal documents edited by J. Neuner and H. Roos under the title *Der Glaube der Kirche in den Urkunden der Lehrverkündigung.* Later editions of that book were prepared by K. Rahner, the two editors being prevented by circumstances from pursuing their work. An English translation of the sixth edition of the work was brought out by Mercier Press, Cork, Ireland, in 1967, under the title *The Teaching of the Catholic Church.* In 1969 the Mercier Press licensed an Indian edition of the book. This was mostly a reprint of the English edition; except for a few modifications and additions, it innovated only by appending to each chapter a survey of the doctrine of the Second Vatican Council.

The profound changes in theological thinking characteristic of recent years have, however, made it desirable to produce a new edition of the Church's doctrinal documents. Not only was an up-dating of the material required in order to include some characteristic texts of Vatican II and post-conciliar documents; it seemed also necessary to leave out some texts which have lost their relevance while re-introducing others. The introductions to the chapters had to be re-written in the light of the Council's doctrine; those to the various documents had to be revised in the light of recent scholarship. Translations needed amending and have in many cases been done anew. Most of all, it seemed opportune to introduce new chapters so as to cover some important fields of modern theology.

This work has enlisted the collaboration of professors belonging to the two theological faculties of Vidyajyoti, Institute of Religious Studies, Delhi, and of Jnana-Deepa, Institute of Philosphy and Religion, Pune. Individual chapters were prepared by the following authors: Symbols and Professions of Faith, Chapters VI, XI, XII, XIII, XV: J. Dupuis; Chapters I, III, VII, XVI: J. Neuner; Chapter II: R. Van de Walle; Chapters IV, V: P. De Letter; Chapters VIII, IX: J. Lerch; Chapter X: G. Gispert-Sauch; Chapters XIV, XVII, XX: G. Gilleman; Chapters XVIII, XXII: G. Lobo; Chapters XIX, XXIII: A. Bermejo; Chapter XXI: F. Timmermans. The coordination and unification of the chapters is the work of the two editors. The responsibility for the book in its present form lies therefore with them only. The editors wish to express their gratitude to the authors for their co-operation.

Since the first edition of the forerunner of this book in 1938 other publications of Church documents have appeared in various languages. It is in the nature of these works that they are all inter-related and mutually dependent as regards the selection and arrangement of texts as well as the evaluation and interpretation of the documents provided in various introductions and notes. As other collections have derived some help from the predecessor of the present book, it has in turn drawn some inspiration from them. Mention may be made of G. Dumeige, *La Foi Catholique*, Paris 1969. Above all, however, it is on the new edition of the *Enchiridion Symbolorum, Definitionum et Declarationum de Rebus Fidei et Morum* first made by A. Schönmetzer in 1962 that every new collection of doctrinal documents necessarily depends as its main source. The editors gratefully acknowledge the help derived by them from these various sources.

J. NEUNER — J. DUPUIS

TABLE OF CONTENTS

INTRODUCTION TO THE FIRST EDITION   XXV

INTRODUCTION TO THE FOURTH REVISED AND ENLARGED
   EDITION
                                 XXXIV

SYMBOLS AND PROFESSIONS OF FAITH   1

The Dèr-Balizeh Papyrus   3
The Apostolic Tradition of Hippolytus (c. 215-217)   3
The Symbol of St Ambrose (ob. 397)   4
The Symbol of Rufinus (c. 404)   4
The Symbol of the Roman Order of baptism   4
The Symbol of Eusebius   5
The First General Council of Nicaea
   Symbol of Nicaea (325)   5
The Symbol of Cyril of Jerusalem (c. 348)   6
The Symbol of Epiphanius (374)   7
The First General Council of Constantinople
   Symbol of Constantinople (381)   8
The "Faith of Damasus"   10
The Pseudo-Athanasian Symbol Quicumque   11
The Eleventh Council of Toledo
   Symbol of faith (675)   13
The Fourth Lateran General Council
   Symbol of Lateran (1215)   13
The Second General Council of Lyons
   "Profession of faith of Michael Palaeologus" (1274) 16
The profession of faith of Pius IV
   Bull Iniunctum Nobis (1564)   20
The profession of faith of Paul VI (1968)   22

CHAPTER I : REVELATION AND FAITH   31

Promise signed by L. E. Bautain (1844)   36
The 4th proposition signed by A. Bonnetty (1855)   36
Pius IX, Encyclical Letter Qui Pluribus (1846)   36
id., Syllabus of condemned errors (1864)   39
The First Vatican General Council
   Dogmatic Constitution Dei Filius on the Catholic
   Faith (1870)   40

Errors of A. Rosmini-Serbati condemned by the Holy
  Office (1887)   48
Oath againt the errors of Modernism (1910)   48
Pius XII, Encyclical Letter *Humani Generis* (1950)   52
The Second Vatican General Council
      Dogmatic Constitution *Dei Verbum* (1965)   54
      Pastoral Constitution *Gaudium et Spes* (1965)   56
Paul VI, Encyclical Letter *Ecclesiam suam* (1964)   57
Declaration *Mysterium Ecclesiae* of the S. Congregation for
      the doctrine of the faith (1973)   59
John Paul II, Apostolic Constitution *Sapientia*
      Christiana (1979)   61
id., Address to Scientists (1980)   62

CHAPTER II : TRADITION AND SCRIPTURE   67

The Council of Laodicea (360?)   70
Innocent I, Letter *Consulenti Tibi* to Exsuperius,
      bishop of Toulouse (405)   70
Gelasius I, Decree of Gelasius   70
The Second General Council of Constantinople
      Profession of Faith (553)   70
The Council of Lateran (649)   71
The Second General Council of Nicaea (787)   71
Leo IX, Letter *Congratulamur Vehementer* to Peter,
      patriarch of Antioch (1053)   71
The General Council of Florence
      Decree for the Jacobites (1442)   72
The Council of Paris (*Senonense)* (1528)   72
The General Council of Trent
      Decree on sacred books and on traditions to be
      received (1546)   72
The First Vatican General Council
      Dogmatic Constitution *Dei Filius* on the Catholic
      Faith (1870)   75
Leo XIII, Encyclical Letter *Providentissimus Deus* (1893) 76
Decree *Lamentabili* of the Holy Office (1907). Articles
      of Modernism condemned.   79
Benedict XV, Encyclical Letter *Spiritus Paraclitus* (1920) 80
Pius XII, Encyclical Letter *Divino Afflante Spiritu* (1943) 82
Letter of the Biblical Commission to Cardinal Suhard,
      Archbishop of Paris (1948)   84

Pius XII, Encyclical Letter *Humani Generis* (1950)   85
Instruction of the Biblical Commission *Sancta Mater*
     Ecclesia (1964)   86
The Second Vatican General Council
     Dogmatic Constitution *Dei Verbum* (1965)   88
S. Congregation for Catholic education on Theological
     Formation of Future Priests (1976)   92

CHAPTER III : THE TRIUNE GOD   95

Dionysius, Letter to Dionysius of Alexandria (262)   98
The First General Council of Nicaea
     Symbol of Nicaea (325)   99
The First General Council of Constantinople
     Symbol of Constantinople (381)   99
The Council of Rome
     "Tome of Damasus" (382)   100
The Pseudo-Athanasian Symbol *Quicumque*   102
The Eleventh Council of Toledo
     Symbol of faith (675)   102
The Fourth Lateran General Council (1215)   106
The Second General Council of Lyons
     Constitution on the Blessed Trinity and on the
     Catholic Faith (1274)   109
The General Council of Florence
     Decree for the Greeks (1439)   110
     Decree for the Jacobites (1442)   110
The First Vatican General Council
     Dogmatic Constitution *Dei Filius* on the Catholic
     Faith (1870)   111
The Second Vatican General Council   112
Declaration *Mysterium Filii Dei* of the S. Congregation for
     the doctrine of the faith (1972)   113

CHAPTER IV : MAN AND THE WORLD   115

The Council of Constantinople
     Anathematisms against the Origenists (543)   118
The Council of Braga
     Anathematisms against the Priscillianists (561)   118
Innocent III, Profession of faith prescribed to the
     Waldensians (1208)   119

The Fourth Lateran General Council
    Symbol of Lateran (1215) — 120
The General Council of Vienna (1311-1312) — 120
John XXII, Errors of Eckhart on the relation between
    God and world and man (1329) — 121
Benedict XII, Libellus *Cum Dudum* (1341) — 122
The General Council of Florence
    Decree for the Jacobites (1442) — 122
The Fifth Lateran General Council
    Bull *Apostolici Regiminis* (1513) — 122
Pius IX, *Syllabus* of condemned errors (1864) — 123
The First Vatican General Council
    Dogmatic Constitution *Dei Filius* on the Catholic
    Faith (1870) — 124
Pius XII, Encyclical Letter *Humani Generis* (1950) — 125
The Second Vatican General Council — 126
    Pastoral Constitution *Gaudium et Spes* (1965) — 126
    Declaration *Nostra Aetate* (1965) — 128
John Paul II, Address to the Third General Assembly of
    Latin American Bishops (1979) — 128
id., Encyclical Letter *Redemptor Hominis* — 129

CHAPTER V : ORIGINAL JUSTICE AND FALL — 133

The Sixteenth Council of Carthage (418) — 135
The *Indiculus* (between 435 and 422) — 135
The Second Council of Orange (529) — 136
Innocent III, Letter to Humbert, archbishop of Arles (1201) — 136
The General Council of Trent
    Decree on original sin (1546) — 137
Pius V, Bull *Ex Omnibus Afflictionibus* (1567)
    Condemned propositions of Michael de Bay — 140
The Second Vatican General Council — 140
Paul VI, Address to theologians at the Symposium on
    original sin (1966) — 141
John Paul II, Encyclical Letter *Redemptor Hominis* (1979) — 141

CHAPTER VI : JESUS CHRIST THE SAVIOUR — 143

The First General Council of Nicaea
    Symbol of Nicaea (325) — 146
The First General Council of Constantinople
    Symbol of Constantinople (381) — 146

The Council of Rome
    "Tome of Damasus" (382)   147
The General Council of Ephesus (431)
    Second Letter of Cyril of Alexandria to Nestorius   148
    The Twelve Anathematisms of Cyril against Nestorius   149
The formula of union between Cyril of Alexandria and the
    bishops of Antioch (433)   151
Leo I, Letter to Flavian of Constantinople (499)   151
The General Council of Chalcedon
    Symbol of Chalcedon (451)   153
John II, Letter to the Senate of Constantinople (534)   155
The Council of Constantinople
    Anathematisms against the Origenists (543)   156
Vigilius, *Constitutum I* (553)   156
The Second General Council of Constantinople
    Anathematisms against the three chapters (553)   158
Gregory the Great, Letter to Eulogius, patriarch of
    Alexandria (600)   164
The Council of Lateran (649)   165
The Eleventh Council of Toledo
    Symbol of Faith (675)   168
The Third General Council of Constantinople
    Definition on the two wills and actions in Christ (681)   172
Hadrian I, Letter *Si Tamen Licet* addressed to the Spanish
    bishops (793)   173
The Council of Friuli
    Profession of faith (796 or 797)   174
Innocent III, Profession of faith prescribed to the
    Waldensians (1208)   175
The Fourth Lateran General Council
    Symbol of Lateran (1215)   176
The Second General Council of Lyons
    "Profession of faith of Michael Palaeologus" (1274)   176
Clement VI, Jubilee Bull *Unigenitus Dei Filius* (1343)   176
The General Council of Florence
    Decree for the Jacobites (1442)   177
The General Council of Trent
    Decree on Justification (1547)   178
Paul IV, Constitution *Cum Quorumdam Hominum* (1555)   178
Pius VI, Constitution *Auctorem Fidei* (1794)   179

Decree *Lamentabili* of the Holy Office (1907). Articles of
    Modernism condemned   180
Decree of the Holy Office (1918)   181
Pius XI, Encyclical Letter *Quas Primas* (1925)   182
id., Encyclical Letter *Miserentissimus Redemptor* (1928)   183
Pius XII, Encyclical Letter *Mystici Corporis* (1943)   185
id., Encyclical Letter *Sempiternus Rex* (1951)   186
id., Encyclical Letter *Haurietis Aquas* (1956)   187
The Second Vatican General Council
    Pastoral Constitution *Gaudium et Spes* (1965)   191
Declaration *Mysterium Filii Dei* of the S. Congregation
    for the doctrine of the faith (1972)   192
Paul VI, Apostolic Exhortation *Evangelii Nuntiandi* (1975)   193
John Paul II, Address to the Third General Assembly of
    Latin American Bishops (1979)   194
id., Encyclical Letter *Redemptor Hominis* (1979)   197

CHAPTER VII : THE MOTHER OF THE SAVIOUR   199

The General Council of Ephesus (431)   201
John II, Letter to the Senate of Constantinople (534)   201
The Council of Lateran (649)   201
Sixtus IV, Constitution *Cum Praeexcelsa* (1477)   201
The General Council of Trent
    Decree on original sin (1546)   203
    Decree on justification (1547)   203
Paul IV, Constitution *Cum Quorumdam Hominum* (1555)   203
Pius V, Bull *Ex Omnibus Afflictionibus* (1567).
    Condemned propositions of Michael de Bay   204
Pius IX, Bull *Ineffabilis Deus* (1854)   204
Leo XIII, Encyclical Letter *Octobri Mense* (1891)   205
Pius XII, Apostolic Constitution *Munificentissimus*
    Deus (1950)   206
The Second Vatican General Council   207
    Dogmatic Constitution *Lumen Gentium* (1964)   208
Paul VI, Apostolic Exhortation *Marialis Cultus* (1974)   210

CHAPTER VIII : THE CHURCH   213

Innocent I, Letter *In Requirendis* to the African Bishops (417) 216
The Fourth Lateran General Council
    Symbol of Lateran (1215)   216

The Second General Council of Lyons
   "Profession of faith of Michael Palaeologus" (1274)   217
Boniface VIII, Bull *Unam Sanctam* (1302)   217
John XXII, Condemnation of errors of Marsilius of Padua
   on the constitution of the Church (1327)   218
The General Council of Constance
   Decree *Haec Sancta* (1415)   219
   Condemnation of the errors of Wyclif and Hus (1415)   220
The General Council of Florence
   Decree for the Greeks (1439)   222
   Decree for the Jacobites (1442)   222
Leo X, Bull *Exsurge Domine* (1520). Errors of Luther
   condemned   223
Pius VI, Constitution *Auctorem Fidei* (1794)   223
Pius IX, Allocution *Singulari Quadam* (1854)   223
id.; Encyclical Letter *Quanto Conficiamur Moerore* (1863)   224
id., Encyclical Letter *Quanta Cura* (1864)   225
The First Vatican General Council
   Dogmatic Constitution *Dei Filius* on the Catholic
   Faith (1870)   226
   Dogmatic Constitution *Pastor Aeternus* on the
   Church of Christ (1870)   226
Collective Declaration by the German Hierarchy (1875)   234
Decree *Lamentabili* of the Holy Office (1907). Articles of
   modernism condemned   235
Pius XII, Encyclical Letter *Mystici Corporis* (1943)   236
Letter of the Holy Office to the Archbishop of Boston (1949)   240
Pius XII, Encyclical Letter *Humani Generis* (150)   243
The Second Vatican General Council   244
   Dogmatic Constitution *Lumen Gentium* (1964)   244
Declaration *Mysterium Ecclesiae* of the S. Congregation
   for the doctrine of the faith (1973)   247
Paul VI, Apostolic Exhortation *Evangelii Nuntiandi* (1975)   249
John Paul II, Encyclical Letter *Redemptor Hominis* (1979)   250

CHAPTER IX : THE CHURCH AND THE CHURCHES   253

Pius IX, Letter *Iam Vos Omnes* to Protestants and other
   non-Catholic (1868)   257
id., Encyclical Letter *Quartus Supra* to the Armenians (1873)   257
Leo XII, Encyclical Letter *Praeclara Gratulationis* (1894)   258

Pius XI, Encyclical Letter *Mortalium Animos* (1928)   259
Instruction *Ecclesia Catholica* of the Holy Office (1949)   260
The Second Vatican General Council
    Decree *Unitatis Redintegratio* (1964)   261
Post-Conciliar Documents on Ecumenism   265
Statement by the Secretariat for Promoting Christian Unity,
    In Quibus Rerum Circumstantiis (1972)   267
John Paul II, Discourse at the Liturgy in St George's
    at Phanar (1979)   268
id., Homily to the Diaspora Catholics at Osnabrück (1980)   270
id., Address to the Evangelical Church Council of
    Germany (1980)   271
id., Address to the German Episcopal Conference (1980)   272

CHAPTER X : THE CHURCH AND THE WORLD RELIGIONS   273

The Second General Council of Nicaea (787)   276
Gregory VII, Letter to Anzir, King of Mauritania (1076)   276
The General Council of Florence
    Decree for the Jacobites (1442)   277
Leo XII, Encyclical Letter *Ubi Primum* (1824)   279
Gregory XVI, Encyclical Letter *Mirari Nos Arbitramur*
    (1832)   280
Pius IX, Encyclical Letter *Qui Pluribus* (1846)   280
id., Allocution *Singulari Quadam* (1854)   281
id., Encyclical Letter *Quanto Conficiamur Moerore* (1863)   282
id., *Syllabus* of condemned errors (1864)   283
Leo XIII, Encyclical Letter *Immortale Dei* (1885)   284
The First Plenary Council of India (1950)   285
The Second Vatican General Council
    Dogmatic Constitution *Lumen Gentium* (1964)   287
    Declaration *Nostra Aetate* (1965)   288
    Decree *Ad Gentes* (1965)   289
    Pastoral Constitution *Gaudium et Spes* (1965)   291
Paul VI, Encyclical Letter *Ecclesiam Suam* (1964)   292
id., Address to representatives of various religions (1964)   293
id., Letter *Africarum Terrarum* to the hierarchy and the
    peoples of Africa (1967)   294
id., Radio-Message to the governments and peoples of
    Asia (1970)   296
id., Apostolic Exhortation *Evangelii Nuntiandi* (1975)   296

John Paul II, Encyclical Letter *Redemptor Hominis* (1979)   298
id., Message to the People of Asia (1981)   299

CHAPTER XI : THE CHURCH AND THE MISSIONS   301

The First General Council of Nicaea (325)   304
Gregory the Great, Letter to Abbot Mellitus   304
The Fourth Lateran General Council (1215)   305
The General Council of Vienna (1311-1312)   306
The General Council of Basel
    Decree on Jews and Neophytes (1434)   307
Instruction of the S. Congregation *de Propaganda Fide* to
    the vicars apostolic of Tonkin and Cochinchina (1659)   308
Benedict XV, Apostolic Letter *Maximum Illud* (1919)   310
Pius XI, Encyclical Letter *Rerum Ecclesiae* (1926)   313
Pius XII, Encyclical Letter *Summi Pontificatus* (1939)   315
id., Address to the directors of Pontifical Mission Works
    (1944)   316
id., Christmas Message (1945)   317
id., Encyclical Letter *Evangelii Praecones* (1951)   318
id., Encyclical Letter *Fidei Donum* (1957)   320
John XXIII, Encyclical Letter *Princeps Pastorum* (1959)   320
The Second Vatican General Council   322
    Dogmatic Constitution *Lumen Gentium* (1964)   324
    Decree *Ad Gentes* (1965)   324
    Pastoral Constitution *Gaudium et Spes* (1965)   327
Paul VI, Mission Sunday Message (1970)   328
id., Apostolic Exhortation *Evangelii Nuntiandi* (1975)   330
John Paul II, Address to Workmen in São-Paulo (1980)   332

CHAPTER XII : CHRISTIAN WORSHIP   335

The Fourth Lateran General Council (1215)   337
The General Council of Trent
    Decree on teaching and preaching the word of God
    (1546)   338
Pius IX, Encyclical Letter *Amantissimus* (1862)   339
Leo XIII, Constitution *Orientalium Dignitas* (1894)   339
Pius X, Motu Proprio *Tra Le Sollecitudini* (1903)   340
id., Decree *Sacra Tridentina* (1905)   340
id., Apostolic Constitution *Tradita Ab Antiquis* (1912)   341
Pius XI, Encyclical Letter *Quas Primas* (1925)   342

id., Apostolic Constitution *Divini Cultus* (1928)   343
id., Letter *Missionalium Rerum* (1937)   343
Pius XII, Encyclical Letter *Mystici Corporis* (1943)   344
id., Encyclical Letter *Mediator Dei* (1947)   345
id., Encyclical Letter *Musicae Sacrae Disciplina* (1955)   349
id., Discourse at the international Congress on Pastoral
    Liturgy (1956)   350
Instruction of the S. Congregation of rites on sacred music
    and the sacred liturgy (1958)   350
The Second Vatican General Council
    Constitution *Sacrosanctum Concilium* (1963)   351
    Decree *Orientalium Ecclesiarum* (1964)   354
Post-Conciliar Documents on Sacred Liturgy   355
John Paul II, Address to the Bishops of Zaïre (1980)   356

APPENDIX : ON THE CULT OF SAINTS AND SACRED IMAGES   358

The Second General Council of Nicaea
    Definition on sacred images (787)   359
The Fourth General Council of Contantinople (869-870)   360
Martin V, Bull *Inter Cunctas* (1418)   360
The General Council of Trent
    Decree on the invocation, the veneration and the relics
    of saints and on sacred images (1563)   361
The Second Vatican General Council
    Constitution *Sacrosanctum Concilium* (1963)   363
Paul VI, Apostolic Exhortation *Evangelii Nuntiandi* (1975)   363

CHAPTER XIII : THE SACRAMENTS OF THE CHURCH   365

Innocent III, Profession of faith prescribed to the
    Waldensians (1208)   367
The Second General Council of Lyons
    "Profession of faith of Michael Palaeologus" (1274)   367
The General Council of Constance
    Condemnation of the errors of Wyclif and Hus (1415)   367
Martin V, Bull *Inter Cunctas* (1418)   368
The General Council of Florence
    Decree for the Armenians (1439)   368
Leo X, Bull *Exsurge Domine* (1520). Errors of Luther
    condemned   370
The General Council of Trent
    Decree on the sacraments (1547)   370

Doctrine on communion under both species and
on communion of little children (1562)   373
Decree of the Holy Office (1690). Jansenist errors
condemned   373
Decree *Lamentabili* of the Holy Office (1907). Articles
of Modernism condemned   374
Pius X, Encyclical Letter *Pascendi* (1907)   374
Pius XII, Encyclical Letter *Mystici Corporis* (1943)   375
id., Encyclical Letter *Mediator Dei* (1947)   377
The Second Vatican General Council   378
Constitution *Sacrosantum Concilium* (1963)   379
Paul VI, Apostolic Exhortation *Evangelii Nuntiandi* (1975)   380

CHAPTER XIV : BAPTISM AND CONFIRMATION   383

Stephen I, Letter to Cyprian, bishop of Carthage (256)   386
The Council of Elvira (c. 300-303)   386
The First General Council of Nicaea (325)   386
Siricius, Letter to Himerius, bishop of Tarragona (385)   387
Innocent I, Letter to Decentius, bishop of Gubbio (416)   387
The Sixteenth Council of Carthage (418)   388
Innocent II, Letter to the bishop of Cremonia   388
Innocent III, Letter to Humbert, archbishop of Arles (1201)   389
id., Profession of faith prescribed to the Waldensians (1208)   390
The General Council of Florence
Decree for the Armenians (1439)   390
Decree for the Jacobites (1442)   392
The General Council of Trent
Canons on the sacrament of baptism (1547)   392
Canons on the sacrament of confirmation (1547) 394
Decree *Lamentabili* of the Holy Office (1907). Articles
of modernism condemned   395
Pius XII, Decree *Spiritus Sancti Munera* on the minister of
confirmation (1946)   396
The Second Vatican General Council   396
Dogmatic Constitution *Lumen Gentium* (1964)   397
Decree *Apostolicam Actuositatem* (1965)   397
Directory Concerning Ecumenical Matters, *Ad Totam
Ecclesiam* (1967)   398
Paul VI, Apostolic Constitution *Divinae Consortium
Naturae* (1971)   399

Instruction on Infant Baptism, *Pastoralis Actio,* of the
    S. Congregation for the doctrine of the faith (1980)   400

CHAPTER XV : THE EUCHARIST   403

The Council of Rome
    Oath of Berengar of Tours (1079)   407
Innocent III, Letter *Cum Marthae Circa* to John,
    former archbishop of Lyons (1202)   407
id., Profession of faith prescribed to the Waldensians (1208)   409
The Fourth Lateran General Council
    Symbol of Lateran (1215)   409
The General Council of Constance
    Decree on communion under the species of
    bread alone (1415)   409
Martin V, Bull *Inter Cunctas* (1418)   410
The General Council of Florence
    Decree for the Greeks (1439)   411
    Decree for the Armenians (1439)   411
The General Council of Trent
    Decree on the most Holy Eucharist (1551)   413
    Doctrine on communion under both species and
    on communion of little children (1562)   421
    Doctrine on the most Holy Sacrifice of the Mass (1562)   423
Pius XII, Encyclical Letter *Mystici Corporis* (1943)   428
id., Encyclical Letter *Mediator Dei* (1947)   430
id., Encyclical Letter *Humani Generis* (1950)   431
id., Discourse at the International Congress on Pastoral
    Liturgy (1956)   432
The Second Vatican General Council   433
    Constitution *Sacrosanctum Concilium* (1963)   435
    Dogmatic Constitution *Lumen Gentium* (1964)   436
Paul VI, Encyclical Letter *Mysterium Fidei* (1965)   436
Instruction *Encharisticum Mysterium* of the
    S. Congregation of rites (1967)   438
General Instruction on the Roman Missal of the
    S. Congregation for divine worship (1970)   441
John Paul II, Letter to All the Bishops of the Church,
    Dominicae Cenae (1980)   442
id., Homily at the Inaugural Mass of the National Eucharistic
    Congress at Fortaleza (1980)   443

CHAPTER XVI : RECONCILIATION AND THE ANOINTING
        OF THE SICK   445

The First General Council of Nicaea (325)   449
Innocent I, Letter to Decentius, bishop of Gubbio (416)   449
Celestine I, Letter to the bishops of Vienna and
        Narbonne (428)   450
Leo I, Letter to Theodore, bishop of Frejus (452)   451
id., Letter to the bishops of Roman rural districts (459)   451
The Third Council of Toledo (589)   452
The Fourth Lateran General Council (1215)   453
The General Council of Constance
        Condemnation of the errors of Wyclif and Hus (1415) 453
Martin V, Bull Inter Cunctas (1418)   454
The General Council of Florence
        Decree for the Armenians (1439)   454
Leo X, Bull Exsurge Domine (1520). Errors of Luther
        condemned   455
The General Council of Trent
        Doctrine on the sacrament of penance (1551)   457
        Doctrine on the sacrament of extreme unction (1551) 465
        Canons on the sacrament of penance (1551)   468
        Canons concerning extreme unction (1551)   470
Decree Lamentabili of the Holy Office (1907). Articles of
        Modernism condemned   471
Benedict XV, Apostolic Letter Sodalitatem Nostrae
        Dominae (1921)   472
Pius XII, Encyclical Letter Mystici Corporis (1943)   472
The Second Vatican General Council   473
        Constitution Sacrosanctum Concilium (1963)   474
        Dogmatic Constitution Lumen Gentium (1964)   475
Paul VI, Apostolic Constitution Sacram Unctionem
        Infirmorum (1972)   475
The New Ordo Paenitentiae (1973)   476
John Paul II, Encyclical Letter Redemptor Hominis (1979)   478

APPENDIX: INDULGENCES

Clement VI, Jubilee Bull Unigenitus Dei Filius (1343)   482
Martin V, Bull Inter Cunctas (1418)   483
Leo X, Bull Exsurge Domine (1520). Errors of Luther
        condemned   483

The General Council of Trent
 Decree on indulgences (1563)   484
Paul VI, Apostolic Constitution *Indulgentiarum Doctrina*
 (1967)   485

CHAPTER XVII: ORDER   489

Clement I, Letter to the Corinthians (*c.* 96)   492
Gregory I, Letter to the bishops of Georgia (*c.* 601)   493
Innocent III, Profession of faith prescribed to the
 Waldensians (1208)   493
Boniface IX, Bull *Sacrae Religionis* (1400)   493
The General Council of Florence
 Decree for the Armenians (1439)   494
The General Council of Trent
 Doctrine on the sacrament of Order (1563)   495
Leo XIII, Bull *Apostolicae Curae* on Anglican Ordina-
 tions (1896)   499
Decree *Lamentabili* of the Holy Office (1907). Articles of
 Modernism condemned   502
Pius XII, Apostolic Constitution *Episcopalis
 Consecrationis* (1944)   502
id., Encyclical Letter *Mediator Dei* (1947)   502
id., Apostolic Constitution *Sacramentum Ordinis* (1947)   506
The Second Vatican General Council   507
 Dogmatic Constitution *Lumen Gentium* (1964)   509
 Decree Ad Gentes (1965)   512
Paul VI, Motu Proprio *Sacrum Diaconatus Ordinem* (1967)   512
id., Encyclical Letter *Sacerdotalis Coelibatus* (1967)   512
id., Apostolic Constitution *Pontificalis Romani* (1968)   513
The Third Synod of Bishops in Rome
 De Sacerdotio Ministeriali (1971)   513
Paul VI, Apostolic Letter *Ministeria Quaedam* (1972)   515
id., Apostolic Letter *Ad Pascendum* (1972)   516
Declaration *Mysterium Ecclesiae* of the S. Congregation
 for the doctrine of the faith (1973)   516
Paul VI, Apostolic Exhortation *Evangelii Nuntiandi* (1975)   517
Declaration of the S. Congregation for the doctrine of the
 faith, *Inter Insigniores* (1976)   518
John Paul II, Letter to All the Priests of the Church (1979)   520
id., Homily at the Conclusion of the Particular Synod of
 the Dutch Bishops in Rome (1980)   521

CHAPTER XVIII: MATRIMONY   523

Alexander III, Letter to the archbishop of Salerno   526
Innocent III, Profession of faith prescribed to the
    Waldensians (1208)   526
The General Council of Florence
    Decree for the Armenians (1439)   526
The General Council of Trent
    Doctrine on the sacrament of matrimony (1563)   527
Leo XIII, Encyclical Letter *Arcanum Divinae Sapientiae*
    (1880)   530
Pius XI, Encyclical Letter *Casti Connubii* (1930)   531
The Second Vatican General Council   534
    Dogmatic Constitution *Lumen Gentium* (1964)   534
    Pastoral Constitution *Gaudium et Spes* (1965)   535
Paul VI, Encyclical Letter *Humanae Vitae* (1968)   537
Decree *Circa Impotentiam* of the S. Congregation for
    the doctrine of the faith (1977)   537
John Paul II, Apostolic Exhortation *Familiaris Consortio*
    (1981)   538

CHAPTER XIX: THE LIFE OF GRACE   541

The Sixteenth Council of Carthage (418)   544
The *Indiculus* (between 435 and 442)   546
The Second Council of Orange (529)   549
Leo X, Bull *Exsurge Domine* (1520). Errors of Luther
    condemned   553
The General Council of Trent
    Decree on Justification (1547)   554
Pius V, Bull *Ex Omnibus Afflictionibus* (1567).
    Condemned propositions of Michael de Bay   571
Innocent X, Constitution *Cum Occasione* (1653). Errors of
    Cornelius Jansen condemned   573
Clement XI, Constitution *Unigenitus Dei Filius* (1713).
    Propositions of Pasquier Quesnel condemned   574
Leo XIII, Encyclical Letter *Divinum Illud* (1897)   576
Pius XII, Encyclical Letter *Mystici Corporis* (1943)   577
The Second Vatican General Council   579
    Dogmatic Constitution *Lumen Gentium* (1964)   580

CHAPTER XX: PRINCIPLES OF CHRISTIAN LIFE   583

John XXII, Bull *Ad Conditorem* (1322)   586
The General Council of Trent
   Decree on Justification (1547)   586
Errors of laxist morality condemned by the Holy Office
   (1665)   586
Errors of laxist morality condemned by the Holy
   Office (1679)   586
Innocent XI, Constitution *Caelestis Pastor* (1687).
   Propostions of Michael Molinos condemned   587
Decree of the Holy Office (24 Aug. 1690)   588
Decree of the Holy Office (7 Dec. 1690). Jansenist
   errors condemned   588
Pius IX, *Syllabus* of condemned errors (1864)   588
Leo XIII, Encyclical Letter *Libertas Praestantissimum* (1888) 589
id., Letter *Testem Benevolentiae* to Cardinal Gibbons,
   Archbishop of Baltimore (1899)   591
Pius XI, Encyclical Letter *Quadragesimo Anno* (1931)   593
Pius XII, Encyclical Letter *Summi Pontificatus* (1939)   593
id., Encyclical Letter *Mystici Corporis* (1943)   594
Instruction of the Holy Office on "Situation Ethics" (1956) 595
John XXIII, Encyclical Letter *Pacem in Terris* (1963)   596
The Second Vatican General Council   600
   Dogmatic Constitution *Lumen Gentium* (1964)   602
   Declaration *Dignitatis Humanae* (1965)   604
   Pastoral Constitution *Gaudium et Spes* (1965)   605
Declaration *De Persona Humana* of the S. Congregation
   for the doctrine of the faith (1975)   609
John Paul II, Encyclical *Redemptor Hominis* (1979)   609

CHAPTER XXI: THE SOCIAL DOCTRINE OF THE CHURCH   611

Leo XIII, Encyclical Letter *Rerum Novarum* (1891)   616
Pius XI, Encyclical Letter *Quadragesimo Anno* (1931)   618
Pius XII, Discourse on the fiftieth anniversary of
   Rerum Novarum (1941)   621
John XXIII, Encyclical Letter *Mater et Magistra* (1961)   622
id., Encyclical Letter *Pacem in Terris* (1963)   627
The Second Vatican General Council
   Pastoral Constitution *Gaudium et Spes* (1965)   632
Paul VI, Encyclical Letter *Populorum Progressio* (1967)   634

id., Apostolic Letter *Octogesima Adveniens* (1971)   640
The Third Synod of Bishops in Rome
 De Iustitia in Mundo (1971)   645
Paul VI, Bull of Induction of the Holy Year 1975 (1974)   649
The Fourth Synod of Bishops in Rome
 De Evangelizatione Mundi Hodierni (1974)   649
Paul VI, Apostolic Exhortation *Evangelii Nuntiandi* (1975)   650
John Paul II, Encyclical Letter *Redemptor Hominis* (1979)   652
id., Encyclical Letter *Dives in Misericordia* (1980)   653
id., Encyclical Letter *Laborem Exercens* (1981)   654
id., Apostolic Exhortation *Familiaris Consortio* (1981)   657

CHAPTER XXII: SEXUAL ORDER AND RESPECT FOR LIFE   659

Errors of laxist morality condemned by the Holy Office
 (1679)   662
Pius XI, Encyclical Letter *Casti Connubii* (1930)   662
Pius XII, Allocution to midwives (1951)   665
id., Allocution to the second world congress of fertility
 and sterility (1956)   666
The Second Vatican General Council
 Pastoral Constitution *Gaudium et Spes* (1965)   667
Paul VI, Encyclical Letter *Humanae Vitae* (1968)   670
Declaration *De Abortu Procurato* of the S. Congregation
 for the doctrine of the faith (1974)   672
Declaration *De Persona Humana* of the S. Congregation
 for the doctrine of the faith (1975)   674
Declaration on Euthanasia of the S. Congregation for
 the doctrine of the faith (1980)   676
John Paul II, Apostolic Exhortation *Familiaris Consortio*
 (1981)   678

CHAPTER XXIII: CHRISTIAN FULFILMENT   679

The Council of Constantinople
 Anathematisms against the Origenists (543)   682
The Eleventh Council of Toledo
 Symbol of faith (675)   682
The Fourth Lateran General Council
 Symbol of Lateran (1215)   683
The Second General Council of Lyons
 "Profession of faith of Michael Palaeologus" (1274)   683

Benedict XII, Constitution *Benedictus Deus* (1336)   684
The General Council of Florence
    Decree for the Greeks (1439)   685
The General Council of Trent
    Decree on purgatory (1563)   686
The Second Vatican General Council   687
    Dogmatic Constitution *Lumen Gentium* (1964)   688
    Pastoral Constitution *Gaudium et Spes* (1965)   690
Letter of the S. Congregation for the doctrine of the
    faith on Certain Questions Concerning Eschatology
    (1979)   691

CHRONOLOGICAL TABLE OF DOCUMENTS   697

BIBLICAL INDEX   709

ANALYTICAL AND ONOMASTIC INDEX

CONCORDANCE WITH DENZINGER-SCHÖNMETZER

INTRODUCTION TO THE FIRST EDITION

Catholic theology must be taught "in the light of faith and under the guidance of the Church's teaching authority" *(OT 16)*. It must be solidly anchored in the word of God, "which ought to be, as it were, the soul of all theology" *(ibid.)*. But reflection on divine revelation is not the private pursuit of individuals; it is a task entrusted by Jesus Christ to the Church herself, which she must perform under the vigilance of the teaching office established by Him as the custodian of His word. Keeping it faithfully and transmitting it through her living Tradition, guided by it as by her ultimate norm, the Church has grown through the centuries in her awareness of the content of the deposit of faith committed to her. The responsibility of her teaching office consists in authentically declaring the divine deposit, in expanding and in interpreting it through the centuries in accordance with the changing conditions of the times and the specific needs of each generation. Thanks to this charism of interpretation, the same message endures through the centuries of Christianity, ever true to itself and capable of reaching out to the contemporary world of every age.

To ensure continuity in the task of proclaiming the revealed word to the modern world, this is the function of the doctrinal documents issued by the Church through the centuries; this shows their indispensable place in a study of theology that wishes to be at once creative and faithful to the past. The Church's living Tradition today is the sum total of twenty centuries of Christian faith and life, and this no attempt at presenting the Christian message to modern man can afford to ignore. An accurate reading, however, of Church documents requires a keen theological discernment, capable of evaluating their content and of distinguishing in them elements of lasting value from others that time has rendered obsolete.

The deep significance of doctrinal documents lies in the authoritative guidance which they have provided in the past and still provide today for the correct understanding of divine revelation. In the course of history the Church has rejected errors which tended to disfigure the word of God and to evacuate the Christian message; she has done so with a sure instinct for the implications of the deposit entrusted to her. As her consciousness grew, she has unfolded what was latent in the message and, as circumstances required, she has

expressed it in more articulate formulations. Her solemn pronouncements of faith give authentic expression to the unchanging word of
God; in their deep meaning and intention they remain valid for all
times and can never be contradicted by new enunciations.

This is not to say that an absolute value necessarily attaches to
the traditional concepts of ancient formulations. For the revealed
truth lies beyond human concepts, all of which are essentially inadequate to express it fully. No matter how deeply traditional and
founded on authoritative teaching they may be, these concepts are
but pointers to a mystery which they can never encompass and
whose content they can never exhaust. The definitions even of the
early Councils intend no more than to indicate a direction along
which the Christian mystery can appropriately be thought. They are
not last but first words; not boundaries but signposts. St Thomas
Aquinas knew that "the act of faith is directed not to an enunciation
but to the reality" that lies beyond it.[1] Never exhausted by any
formulation, this reality remains always open to new and deeper
insights.

Human concepts, moreover, fall under the law of historical evolution, and this imposes on them a further unavoidable limitation. As
their meaning evolves in the course of time, faithfulness to the
intention of ancient formulations may at a later period recommend
the use of new concepts. For, as every human discourse, the expression of the Church's faith is subject to the law of change inherent to
human language.

Our own times have become more deeply aware of this twofold
limitation that affects the discourse of the Church's faith. Under the
impulse given it by Pope John XXIII,[2] the Second Vatican Council
has reminded theologians that "the deposit of faith, that is the truths
contained in it, are one thing, the manner of formulating these truths,
while keeping the same sense and meaning, is another" (GS 62). To
discern the intention of the faith through the concepts in which it is
formulated, to recognise in its various expressions—all of which are
conditioned by space and time—the faith of all times and of all places,
is the task of the interpreter of doctrine.

Besides, and more important than, the limitations inherent in
human language are those derived from the historical situation of the

----

1. *Summa Theologica*, II, II, 1, 2, ad 2.

2. *Discourse on the opening day of the Second Vatican Council*, Cf. *AAS* 54 (1962)
792.

documents which affects their docrine. This is in itself historically conditioned. The documents of the Church are occasional pronouncements, usually intended to meet the challenge of definite errors. The historical circumstances in which they were written called for emphasising those elements of the faith which were being threatened. The need for emphasis, however, is by nature little conducive to a harmonious and well-poised formulation of doctrine. The formulation is the more easily selective and one-sided as the documents bear more deeply the stamp of current controversies. In the process full justice is not always done to other facets of the revealed message nor are the truths expressed always properly focussed. Much less do the documents present a complete account of the Christian message. In fact, its most intimate core is rarely touched upon by them; this is taken for granted rather than explicitly stated. And, while the correct conceptual enunciation of the mysteries of the faith is stressed and officially formulated, little is said about knowing the one true God and Jesus Christ whom He has sent *(cf. Jn 17.3)* as constituting the essence of the Christian life, and about the radical demand made on the Christian to follow Christ in the mystery of His death and resurrection.

In the history of the Church's General Councils Vatican II is, perhaps, the first to be almost entirely free of controversial overtones; this is why, though less doctrinal than pastoral in purpose, it has succeeded better than its predecessors in establishing the balance between complementary aspects of the faith. It is significant to observe that the last Council points to a "hierarchy" of the truths contained in Catholic doctrine, which is based on "their different relationship to the foundation of the Christian faith" *(UR 11)*, and advocates a "fraternal rivalry" by which all Christians "will be spurred on to a deeper knowledge and a clearer expression of the unfathomable riches of Christ" *(ibid.)*. In the same direction, Vatican II also recognises more clearly than did the ancient Councils of union the full legitimacy of differences between East and West in the theological enunciation of doctrine—which "diverse theological formulations are often to be considered as mutually complementary rather than conflicting" *(UR 17)*. By these words the Council states the principle of legitimate pluralism in the expression of the faith—a principle which in past centuries has often been overlooked.

What has been said above goes to show that the theological interpretation of Church documents is a delicate task. Their doctrinal value must be assessed; this is done in two ways. It may first be asked what claim the nature of a document makes to be an expression of the most fundamental data of the Christian faith. From this point of view the Symbols and Professions of Faith of ancient origin hold a privileged position. Hence the prominence given to them in this book, where they are treated in the first place and where an effort is made to follow their historical development. Distinct from the question of the relationship of truths to the fundamental data of the Christian faith is the question of the degree of authority with which any document pronounces on matters connected with it. It is important to discern to what extent the teaching authority of the Church is involved in each text.

All statements in which the legitimate authority of the Church pronounces on matters pertaining to the divine revelation demand an inner assent on the part of the members of the Church. But not all have the same value. Only the universal authority, including General Councils and Popes, can make final pronouncements. The criterion by which to recognise them is the Church's own intention as expressed in each document. The concrete application of this principle, however, is a delicate matter, for the Church's precise intention is not always easily discerned. Modern historical criticism has brought to light the fact that not every proposition censured with *Anathema* implies a definition of the truth contradictorily opposed. Not all documents of General Councils, not even all their canons, are proposed as infallible definitions. The precise dogmatic value of documents remains in many cases open to question. In such cases the irrevocability of propositions is to be ascertained and cannot be presumed. Other texts, which by themselves make no claim to infallibility, have through the subsequent approbation of the Roman Pontiffs or through the general acceptance which they have received from the Church, acquired a high degree of authority. Where the need arises, this volume indicates the doctrinal value of documents in the measure in which it can at present be prudently assessed.

A note of caution must be added as regards the judicious use that must be made of any collection of doctrinal texts. The danger of using such a collection in too mechanical a manner has been pointed out in recent years. It easily leads to what has been stamped as "Denzinger theology"—a theology in which creativity and personal appropriation of the message are stifled by the repetition of trite formulas. The fact is then overlooked that, while no theology can afford to ignore the heritage of the past, neither can it forego its obligation to contribute to a deeper assimilation of the revealed truth. In this task its main point of reference remains the word of God. Such a theology, moreover, tends to isolate the documents from the ideological context in which they arose and from the life of the Church at the particular period during which they were written. The result is that formulations the precise meaning of which must be discovered against their historical background, tend to be treated as parts of a timeless system of doctrine. In addition, little attention is paid to the fact that a collection is made up of documents hailing from sources of vastly different doctrinal authority, ranging from General Councils to papal encyclicals and decrees of the Roman Congregations. In the process, the Church's teaching office itself is wrongly treated as a uniform, monolithic thing, as a supra-temporal structure disengaged from her socio-historical reality. It is therefore supremely important to counteract the impression that the presentation in one collection of sources of vastly different origin and doctrinal value may easily create, by relating each document to its historical context and ascertaining its precise authority.

In an essay on "The Correct Use of Denzinger",[1] Y. Congar, while recognising the merits of the *Enchiridion* on which every collection of Church documents in modern times has been based, also points to some serious deficiencies. Most important among these is the fact that the *Enchiridion* is sometimes unduly selective. Some texts have been truncated with the result that only one aspect of the truth expressed in particular documents has been preserved, complementary aspects also mentioned in the texts being lost sight of. Such a grievous omission occurs in the declaration of the Roman primacy made by the Council of Florence in its *Decree for the Greeks,* where Denzinger omits the complementary declaration made by the same document of the traditional privileges of the Oriental patriarchates. The same author observes with satisfaction that the recent edition of the *Enchiridion* provided by A. Schön-metzer makes good most of these losses. Yet, even in its present form the *Enchiridion* is not altogether without blemish. The extraordinary magisterium of the General Councils and of papal definitions finds in it its due place; prominence is also rightly given to those particular Councils which in the course of time have acquired much authority through papal confirmation or the broad acceptance mostly of the Western Church. The material representing the Church's ordinary magisterium is, however, too exclusively limited

---

1. Y. CONGAR, *Situation et tâches de la théologie* (Paris 1967) 111-133.

to its Roman expression, with special emphasis on papal encyclicals, while other organs of the same ordinary magisterium are not sufficiently heard. Y. Congar recognises that to supplement this deficiency much work would need to be done, which would require enlisting the collaboration of an international team of scholars. This remains a task for the future.

It was beyond the scope of the present work and beyond the means at the disposal of the editors to improve much on Denzinger-Schönmetzer in this direction. The main novel feature of the work lies elsewhere. In the last decades some areas of theological studies to which in the past little attention had been paid have received new emphasis, and other new fields have emerged. To cope with this broadened theological interest, the scope of the book has been widened beyond the frame-work of traditional treatises and new chapters have been added. These include: "The Church and the World Religions", "The Church and the Missions", "Christian Worship ". Moreover, it was also found desirable to cover some areas of Christian morality never included before in collections of Church documents in modern languages. In the vast field of Christian living a strict selection had, however, to be made; some tipics have been selected because of the growing importance they have received in recent years. They fall under three chapters: "Principles of Christian Life", "The Social Doctrine of the Church", "Sexual Order and Respect for Life". These limitations notwithstanding, the enlarged material and broadened scope of this new book justify its new title. *The Christian Faith* extends here not only to orthodoxy but to orthopraxy as well; it is viewed in all its dimensions and related to the realities of the modern world.

Widening the scope of the book implied enlarging the volume which has grown to a size considerably greater than its predecessor, *The Teaching of the Catholic Church*. Severe limits were therefore imposed on the editors as regards the selection of the material related to the new topics. Only such texts could be included as have played an important role in the development of the doctrine and through which this development can be followed. Texts of a different nature, for instance liturgical texts or other witnesses of the Church's faith and practice, had to be left out of consideration. By and large, the principle of selection remains the same as in the other chapters. Apart from a few significant entries from the ordinary magisterium of local Churches, the stress remains on the Church's central teaching authority.

Other original features of the book have been mentioned in the Foreword. They are all parts of a general up-dating, in approach and content, which the important movement of return to the sources and of new theological reflection, characteristic of recent years, have made necessary. Ten years ago, this movement led to the Second Vatican Council, and the Council itself has given it a new point of departure. Prominence had therefore to be given to the Council's doctrine, in which the great theological themes are solidly based on the universal data of Scripture and Tradition and presented in relation to the life of the Church. To let the new orientation proper to Vatican II stand out against the background of previous documents, quoting extensive passages was not required in view of the fact that every theological student has access to the complete collection of the conciliar documents. In the case of the Council's ecclesiological doctrine, to make a judicious selection was found impracticable; for other topics important key-passages are explicitly quoted. But the Council's doctrine is in all cases presented by way of synthetic introductions following the order of the various chapters, with ample references to the Council documents.

It is hoped that this new book, with its original features, enlarged material and broadened scope, will provide students of theology with an instrument better fitted to help them perceive all the dimensions of the Christian faith. It is also hoped that it will foster doctrinal clarity and a keen sense of the historical unfolding of Catholic doctrine through the centuries, both of which are of vital importance for our time.

Scripture quotations occurring in the documents are normally given according to the *Revised Standard Version;* this rule is, however, purposely departed from wherever the intention of the documents is clearly to argue from the Vulgate text. The translation of excerpts of some papal encyclicals is borrowed from, or based upon, the text provided by the *Catholic Truth Society,* London; that of the documents of the Second Vatican Council is mostly based on the text published by *The Clergy Monthly.* This dependence on previous translations is herewith gratefully acknowledged. To the introduction to each chapter an analytical table of its main points of doctrine is appended for easy reference to the relevant texts. A chronological table of documents, a biblical index and an analytical and onomastic index are given at the end of the volume. The volume closes with a concordance with the other editions of Church documents mentioned in this introduction.

KEY TO NUMBERS

Each chapter has its key number followed by the numbers of the successive texts. Thus the texts of the first chapter have the numbers 101, 102, etc., those of the second chapter the numbers 201, 202, etc. In this way the number of each text indicates the chapter to which it belongs. The Symbols and Professions of Faith, which are placed at the beginning and form a unit by themsleves, have no key number, but only serial numbers: 1, 2, etc. The numbers of the volume are printed in heavy Roman type in the margin. For the sake of easy reference to the original Greek or Latin, the corresponding numbers in Denzinger-Schönmetzer are added for all texts found in that collection; these are printed in italics. For documents which are not found in Denzinger-Schönmetzer the sources are indicated in the introductions to the texts.

Numbers of the volume printed between brackets ( ) indicate either documents which are not quoted but to which an introduction is given, or parts of documents which are not quoted but only summarised. For texts quoted elsewhere in the volume cross-references are given. Both in the introductions to the documents and in the texts, cross-references indicate the numbers of this volume; *i* following a number refers to the introduction to that number. For documents not quoted in the volume, references are given to their numbers in Denzinger-Schönmetzer *(DS)*. Numbers between square brackets [ ] indicate condemned propositions. A system of sub-numbers has been introduced; these are not always continuous, but indicate, for the sake of easy reference, the serial numbers of the propositions contained in the document quoted.

ABBREVIATIONS FOR SOURCES

AAS	*Acta Apostolicae Sedis*, Rome, 1909...
ASS	*Acta Sanctae Sedis*, Rome, 1865-1908.
Acta	refers to the *Acta* of a particular Pope.
COD	*Canciliorum Oecumenicorum Decreta*, Freiburg im Breisgau, 1962.
Mansi	J.D. Mansi, *Sacrorum Conciliorum nova et amplissima collectio*, Florence, 1759....
PG	*Patrologia Graeca*, ed. J.P. Migne, Paris, 1857-1866.
PL	*Patrologia Latina*, ed. J.P. Migne, Paris, 1844-1855.

DS   H. Denzinger-A. Schönmetzer, *Enchiridion Symbolorum, Definitionum et Declarationum de rebus fidei et morum*, Freiburg im Breisgau, 1965.

D   H. Denzinger, *Enchiridion Symbolorum, Definitionum et Declarationum de rebus fidei et morum*, Freiburg im Breisgau, 1953.

ABBREVIATIONS FOR THE DOCUMENTS OF
THE SECOND VATICAN COUNCIL

AA   *Apostolicam Actuositatem*, Decree on the apostolate of the laity.

AG   *Ad Gentes*, Decree on the missionary activity of the Church.

CD   *Christus Dominus*, Decree on the pastoral office of bishops in the Church.

DH   *Dignitatis Humanae*, Declaration on religious freedom.

DV   *Dei Verbum*, Dogmatic Constitution on divine revelation.

GE   *Gravissimum Educationis*, Declaration on Christian education.

GS   *Gaudium et Spes*, Pastoral Constitution on the Church in the modern world.

IM   *Inter Mirifica*, Decree on mass communications media.

LG   *Lumen Gentium*, Dogmatic Constitution on the Church.

NA   *Nostra Aetate*, Declaration on the relationship of the Church to non-Christian religions.

OE   *Orientalium Ecclesiarum*, Decree on the Catholic Oriental Churches.

OT   *Optatam Totius*, Decree on priestly formation.

PC   *Perfectae Caritatis*, Decree on the adaptation and renewal of the religious life.

PO   *Presbyterorum Ordinis*, Decree on the ministry and life of priests.

SC   *Sacrosanctum Concilium*, Constitution on the Sacred Liturgy.

UR   *Unitatis Redintegratio*, Decree on Ecumenism.

INTRODUCTION TO THE FOURTH REVISED AND ENLARGED EDITION

In the second and third editions of *The Christian Faith* (1976 and 1978) only a few texts were added; they were placed in an appendix so that the body of the book might remain unchanged. Nine years, however, after the first edition, the updating of this collection of Church documents demands more serious reflection. Not only must some recent doctrinal documents be added, but the trends prevailing in the official teaching of the Church in our time must be made perceptible. Hence this revised and enlarged edition.

A prevailing trend in recent documents of the magisterium is a deep sense of responsibility on the part of the hierarchy to protect the substance of the Christian faith from erosion under the influence of modern sciences and secularising tendencies. Hence an increasing concern about the way theology needs to be taught: on the one hand, the legitimate freedom of theological sciences is recognised; on the other hand, the accountability of modern theologians to the Christian people who expect guidance from them, is stressed. This pastoral concern for the faithful is predominant even in documents which of their nature are primarily doctrinal, such as those on the nature of the Church, infallibility, life after death. It is even more pronounced in documents dealing with Christian practice: evangelisation, social ethics, the sexual order, the administration of the sacraments, the vast range of problems related to ecumenism.

In view of this growing concern for the faith of the people it would be misleading to confine a documentation of the Church's magisterium to official pronouncements by the central authority. Orientations, at times important, are also given in a less official manner, in addresses of the Pope, in homilies and audiences. In such documents, doctrine, concern for the people and a preoccupation to meet the problems of today are blended together. The range of these less official pronouncements is immense. One needs only think of the pastoral journeys of the Pope to various countries and of some important speeches he made on these occasions on vital issues. The style of such statements is obviously less concise and at times less precise than that of the classical documents to which we are used. Yet they have great bearing on the Christian life and show the relevance of the Christian message for our time. It is obviously beyond the scope of this book to account for all such statements; still a collection of doctrinal documents would be found inadequate if it were to bypass them entirely. Those have been introduced in various chapters which appeared especially significant.

In the Introduction to the First Edition we noted that the Church's ordinary magisterium has in the past been too easily reduced to its Roman expression and that other organs of the same have not been sufficiently heard. The remark remains valid today. To do justice to the various forms of the ordinary magisterium would demand, in particular, that important pronouncements by episcopal conferences and their various federations be taken into account. This remains even now beyond the scope of this book. It would require enlisting the collaboration of an international team of scholars and in the process the book would grow to a disproportionate size. In broadening the representation of the ordinary magisterium we have been forced to limit ourselves to the Synods of Bishops in Rome which today are a privileged expression of the collegial responsibility of the bishops.

The need was felt for a revision of some of the material included in previous editions: a few documents have been left out (without alteration in serial numbers) which seem less relevant today; some introductions have been reworked for the sake of greater accuracy. Some chapters have undergone a more serious revision. This is especially true of the chapter on "The Social Doctrine of the Church". The editors are grateful to Frs G. Lobo, G. Gispert-Sauch, A. Bermejo and R. Van de Walle for their help in revising some of the chapters.

Previous editions included a concordance with three other collections of documents. The concordance has now been reduced to Denzinger-Schönmetzer, *Enchiridion Symbolorum, Definitionum et Declarationum de Rebus Fidei et Morum.* Reference to Denzinger's *Enchiridion* is no longer required. Similarly, there seems to be no need any more to include references to the predecessor of this book, Neuner-Roos, *The Teaching of the Catholic Church,* which has now been replaced for nearly ten years.

We hope that this revised and enlarged edition will meet the needs of our readers, both professors and students.

J. NEUNER—J. DUPUIS

The earliest profession of faith in the apostolic Church is Christological. It is expressed in three concise formulas: 'Jesus is the Christ' (cf. Acts 2.36; 10.36; Col. 2.6); 'Jesus is the Lord' (1 Cor. 12.3; Rom. 10.9; cf. Acts 2.36; Phil. 2.11); 'Jesus is the Son of God' (cf. Acts 9.20; 13.33; Rom. 1.4; Heb. 4.14). Soon it received a more ample development in which the Christ-event, the central event of salvation history, is progressively elaborated upon (1 Cor. 15.3-4; Phil. 2.6-11; 1 Tim. 3.16). A further development in the life of the apostolic Church is the introduction of a Trinitarian profession of faith. This is a natural evolution, for the Trinitarian confession was latent in the Christological (cf. Acts 2.33) and implied in the early kerygma (cf. Acts 2.14-39; 3.12-26; 4.8-12; 5.29-32; 10.34-43; 13.16-41). The Trinitarian profession of faith in the New Testament is best witnessed to by Mt. 28.19-20 and 2 Cor. 13.13; it corresponds to the Trinitarian teaching of the Apostles (cf. Eph. 1.3-14).

The post-apostolic Church inherited this double expression of the Christian faith, the Trinitarian and the Christological in its elaborate form. The "Apostles' Creed"—called thus by Rufinus and St Ambrose in the fourth century—seems to result from the amalgamation of the two; hence the more evolved form of its second article referring to Christ. The legendary tradition according to which the "Apostles' Creed", made up of twelve articles, would have been composed by the apostles themselves, has long been exploded. Yet, though not composed by the apostles, the "Apostles' Creed" can legitimately be considered to represent their faith. Its origin can be reconstituted by having recourse to early documents. Among these only a few are mentioned here; they have been selected because of their historical importance in the development of the symbol of the apostles. A papyrus found at Dêr-Balizeh has preserved a purely Trinitarian profession of faith. The Apostolic Tradition of Hippolytus contains a baptismal profession of faith, Trinitarian in structure but with a more ample Christological development. The Trinitarian formula goes back to 2 Cor. 13.13 and Mt. 28.19; the Christological development to 1 Cor. 15.3-6 and 1 Cor. 12.3.

The early professions of faith result, therefore, from the merger of two enunciations, one Trinitarian and one Christological, both of which are based on the New Testament. All the early Creeds have the same structure; all share the same perspective. They are centred not on dogmatic truths, but on the economy of salvation with its Trinitarian rhythm as exposed by St Paul in Eph. 1.3-14. The three articles of the faith correspond to three periods of this history; the three are marked by the work proper to one of the three persons: creation is assigned to the Father, redemption to Christ, sanctification to the Holy Spirit. Initiated by the Father, the history of salvation culminates in the Christ-event; the effects of the Christ-event are operative during the Church era through the working of the Holy Spirit.

To those primitive data, later Creeds have in the course of the centuries added such further precisions as concrete circumstances made necessary to maintain the primitive faith. These later additions are meant to high-light some aspects of the faith; they do not alter it. Nor do they obscure the fundamental vision of the Symbol, which through the centuries remains linked to the history of salvation and bears the mark of its Trinitarian character.

THE DER-BALIZEH PAPYRUS

Discovered in Upper Egypt in the sixth century, this document represents a fourth century liturgy; but the Symbol contained in it goes back to a much earlier date, probably to the end of the second century. Its Trinitarian form expands Mt. 28.19; it contains no elaborate Christological development.

Cf. G. ROBERTS – B. CAPELLE, *An Early Euchologion. The Dêr-Balizeh Papyrus* (London 1940) 32.

1. I believe in God, the Father almighty,

2. and in His only-begotten Son, Jesus Christ,

and in the Holy Spirit, and in the resurrection of the flesh [in *(en)* the] Holy Catholic Church.

THE APOSTOLIC TRADITION OF HIPPOLYTUS (c. 215-217)

Written at Rome in the early third century, probably by a Syrian priest, the Apostolic Tradition *(21) contains a baptismal liturgy. The sacrament is administered with a threefold profession of faith, accompanied by a threefold immersion. The minister of the sacrament asks three questions, corresponding to the three articles of the faith; to each question the baptizant answers: "I believe". Taken as a unit, this baptismal profession represents a Symbol of faith, the structure of which is Trinitarian. The second article contains an elaborate Christological development.*

Cf. B. BOTTE, *La Tradition Apostolique de Saint Hippolyte. Essai de reconstitution* (Münster 1963) 48-50.

2 Do you believe in God, the Father almighty?

10 Do you believe in Jesus Christ, the Son of God, who was born of the Virgin Mary by the Holy Spirit, has been crucified under Pontius Pilate, died [and was buried], who, on the third day rose again, alive, from the dead, ascended into heaven and took His seat at the right hand of the Father, and shall come to judge the living and the dead?

Do you believe in the Holy Church and the resurrection of the body in the Holy Spirit?[1]

---

1. "Credis in Spiritu et sanctam Ecclesiam et carnis resurrectionem". The object of faith seems to be that the present era in the history of salvation, viz. the Church-era leading to the parousia, is the time of the economy of the Holy Spirit: Do you believe that the Church (lives) in the Holy Spirit and that the resurrection of the dead (takes place) in Him? Cf. P. NAUTIN, *Je crois à l'Esprit Saint dans la Sainte Eglise pour la résurrection de la chair* (Paris 1947) 67. This interpretation is corroborated by another version of the text of Hippolytus: "Do you believe in the Holy Spirit, the source of goodness and life, who makes all things clean in the Holy Church"? (BOTTE, *l. c.* 50).

THE SYMBOL OF ST AMBROSE (*ob.* 397)

St Ambrose seems to have been the first to refer to the Symbol of faith as "Symbol of the Apostles". He explains it in an opuscule called Explanation of the Symbol, the text of which he probably dictated to a scribe. The author refers to it also as the "Symbol of Rome". This is not intended to mean that the text coincides strictly with that in use in Rome (cf. n. 5), but that the content is substantially the same. The text of the Symbol can be reconstituted by joining together the articles interspersed by St Ambrose's explanations.

3   I believe in God, the Father almighty,

13   And in Jesus Christ, His only Son, our Lord, who was born of the Virgin Mary by the Holy Spirit, who suffered under Pontius Pilate, died and was buried. On the third day He rose again from the dead. He ascended into heaven, and is seated at the right hand of the Father, wherefrom He shall come to judge the living and the dead.

And in the Holy Spirit, the Holy Church, the forgiveness of sins and the resurrection of the body.

THE SYMBOL OF RUFINUS (*c.* 404)

Rufinus too makes reference to the "Symbol of the Apostles". While writing c. 404 to explain the text used in Aquilaea, he gives an account of its few divergences from the text accepted in Rome (cf. n. 5). Unlike the Ambrosian text (cf. n. 3), that of Rufinus contains the reference to Christ's descent to the dead.

4   I believe in God, the Father almighty, invisible and impass-
16   ible,

And in Jesus Christ, His only Son, our Lord, who was born of the Virgin Mary by the Holy Spirit, was crucified under Pontius Pilate and was buried. He went down to the dead *(ad inferna).* On the third day He rose again from the dead. He ascended into heaven, and is seated at the right hand of the Father. From there He shall come to judge the living and the dead.

And in the Holy Spirit, the Holy Church, the forgiveness of sins and the resurrection of the body.

THE SYMBOL OF THE ROMAN ORDER OF BAPTISM

This is the form of the "Symbol of the Apostles" accepted in Rome during the tenth century, but already previously recognised throughout the Western Church. Ninth century codices witness to its being used in Gaul in the local language. Except for accidental variants, this text of the "Symbol of the Apostles" will thereafter remain traditional in the West. It has both the Trinitarian structure and the large Christological development. Numbers in the text indicate the division in twelve articles, on which is based the legendary tradition which attributes it to the twelve apostles. Proper to the West, this Symbol is unknown to the Eastern Churches. These will always refer to the Creed of Nicaea (cf. nn. 7-8) as the first authoritative Symbol of the Christian faith.

5 I believe in God, the Father almighty, creator of heaven and
30 earth (1).

And in Jesus Christ, His only Son, our Lord (2), who was conceived by the Holy Spirit, born of the Virgin Mary (3), suffered under Pontius Pilate, was crucified, died and was buried; He went down to the dead *(ad inferna)* (4). On the third day He rose again from the dead (5). He ascended to the heavens, and is seated at the right hand of God, the Father almighty (6), wherefrom He shall come again to judge the living and the dead (7).

I believe in the Holy Spirit (8), the Holy Catholic Church, the communion of saints (9), the forgiveness of sins (10), the resurrection of the body (11), and the life everlasting (12).

THE SYMBOL OF EUSEBIUS

In a letter addressed to his diocese (325), Eusebius, bishop of Caesaraea, refers to the profession of faith with which he had been baptised. This testifies to the use of this Symbol around the middle of the third century. Its historical importance consists mostly in the influence it has exercised on the composition of the Symbol of Nicaea (cf. n. 7). The Trinitarian structure is clear: one God, one Lord, one Spirit, refers to Eph. 4.4-6 and 1 Cor. 8.6. The Christological development contains dogmatic affirmations unknown to the Symbol of the Apostles; the third article merely mentions the Holy Spirit.

6 We believe in one God, the Father almighty, the maker of
40 all things visible and invisible.

And in one Lord Jesus Christ, the Word of God, God from God, Light from Light, Life from Life, the only-begotten Son, first born of all creation, begotten from the Father before all ages, through whom all things were made. For our salvation He became flesh and lived as a man, He suffered and rose again on the third day and ascended to the Father. He shall come again in glory to judge the living and the dead.

We believe also in one Holy Spirit.

THE FIRST GENERAL COUNCIL OF NICAEA
SYMBOL OF NICAEA (325)

Convened by Emperor Constantine to affirm the faith against the Arian crisis, the Council of "318 Fathers", from East and West, was held at Nicaea from June 16 to August 25, 325; a representative sent from Rome by Pope Sylvester attended the Council. Arius, a priest in Alexandria (ob. 336) denied the equality of the Son with the Father: the Son was understood to have been created in time by the Father and to have been used by Him as His instrument for the creation of the world. In its Creed the Council solemnly proclaimed the oneness in being ("consubstantiality") of the Son with the Father; to the Symbol is appended a clear condemnation of the Arian errors. Eusebius (ob. 340) himself testifies to the fact that the Symbol of Caesaraea served as basis for the Nicene Creed. Many formulations have been taken over from it; others have been purposely left out because they could lend themselves to an Arian interpretation; others still were added to provide further precisions necessary in the context of the Arian crisis. Though not directly intended as a baptismal Creed, the Symbol of Nicaea exercised a deep influence on the baptismal Creeds of the fourth century.

Cf. I. ORTIZ DE URBINA, *Nicée et Constantinople* (Paris 1963) 69-92.

7 We believe in one God, the Father almighty, maker of all
125 things, visible and invisible.

And in one Lord Jesus Christ, the Son of God, the only-begotten generated from the Father, that is, from the being (*ousia*) of the Father, God from God, Light from Light, true God from true God, begotten, not made, one in being (*homoousios)* with the Father, through whom all things were made, those in heaven and those on earth. For us men and for our salvation He came down, and became flesh, was made man, suffered, and rose again on the third day. He ascended to the heavens and shall come again to judge the living and the dead.

And in the Holy Spirit.

8 As for those who say: "There was a time when He was not"
126 and "Before being begotten He was not", and who declare
that He was made from nothing (*ex ouk ontòn*), or that the Son of God is from a different substance *(hupostasis)* or being *(ousia),* that is, created *(ktistos)* or subject to change and alteration,—(such persons) the Catholic Church condemns.

THE SYMBOL OF CYRIL OF JERUSALEM (c. 348)

It has sometimes been thought that the Symbol of Cyril had served as basis for the Creed of Nicaea. But the closer similarity which exists between some of the expressions of the Eusebian Symbol and the Nicene Creed undermines this assertion. The truth rather seems to be that the Creed of Cyril, in the form in which it has been preserved, has been partly influenced by the Nicene Creed. The term homoousios, *introduced by the Council of Nicaea, is left out because of the Sabellian overtones, which, in the mind of*

Cyril, could be attached to it. The text of the Creed of Cyril has been reconstituted by gleaning from his various Catechetical Instructions (Cat. Myst. VI-XVIII). As in the text of Eusebius, one God, one Lord, one Spirit, goes back to Eph. 4.4-6 and 1 Cor. 8.6. Unlike Eusebius and the Council of Nicaea, Cyril develops at length the economy of the Spirit in the third article of his Creed.

Cf. I. ORTIZ DE URBINA, *Nicée et Constantinople* (Paris 1963) 69-73.

9   We believe in one God, the Father almighty, maker of heaven
41   and earth, of all things visible and invisible.

And in one Lord Jesus Christ, the only-begotten Son of God, generated from the Father, true God before all the ages, through whom all things were made. He [came down, became flesh and] was made man, was crucified [and buried]. He rose again [from the dead] on the third day, and ascended to the heavens, and took His seat at the right hand of the Father. He shall come in glory to judge the living and the dead; to His Kingdom there will be no end.

And in one Holy Spirit, the Paraclete, who has spoken in the prophets, and in one baptism of conversion for the forgiveness of sins, and in one Holy and Catholic Church, and in the resurrection of the body, and the life everlasting.

THE SYMBOL OF EPIPHANIUS (374)

This Symbol is a personal composition of Epiphanius, bishop of Salamis. It exists under two forms, a short form destined to "those who are to receive holy baptism", and a long form for further catechesis. It depends much on the Symbol of Nicaea, whose condemnation of the Arian error it repeats but to which it adds further precisions. Historically, its importance lies in the influence it will exercise at the Council of Constantinople (cf. nn. 12-13). One of its characteristics is its doctrinal affirmations regarding the Holy Spirit. Epiphanius (ob. 403) writes in the context of the already rising trends which deny the divinity of the Holy Spirit. He thus prepares in advance the doctrine of Constantinople. The short form is quoted here because its more precise formulations as regards the divinity of the Spirit will be adopted by the Council of Constantinople. For the long form, cf. DS 44-45.

10   We believe in one God, the Father almighty, maker of hea-
42   ven and earth, of all things visible and invisible.

And in one Lord Jesus Christ, the only-begotten Son of God, generated from the Father before all ages, that is, from the being (*ousia*) of the Father, Light from Light, true God from true God, begotten, not made, one in being (*homoousios*) with the Father, through whom all things were made, those in the heavens and those on earth. For us men and for our salvation He came down from the heavens, and became flesh from the Holy Spirit and the Virgin Mary, and was made man. For our sake too He was crucified under Pontius Pilate, suffered and was buried. On the third day He rose again according to the Scriptures. He ascended to the heavens and is seated at the right hand of the Father. He shall come again in glory to judge the living and the dead; to His Kingdom there will be no end.

And in the Holy Spirit, the Lord (*to Kurion*) and Giver of life, who proceeds (*ekporeuomenon*) from the Father, who together with the Father and the Son is worshipped and glorified, who has spoken through the prophets. (And) in one Holy, Catholic and apostolic Church. We acknowledge one baptism for the forgiveness of sins. We expect the resurrection of the dead and the life of the world to come. Amen.

11   As for those who say: "There was a time when He was not",
43   and "Before being begotten He was not", or who declare that
     He was made from nothing, or that the Son of God is from a different substance or being, or subject to change and alteration,— such persons the Catholic and apostolic Church condemns.

THE FIRST GENERAL COUNCIL OF CONSTANTINOPLE
SYMBOL OF CONSTANTINOPLE (381)

The Council was convened by Emperor Theodosius I to "confirm the faith of Nicaea" and to reaffirm it against the Arian current which had not entirely died out; more particularly the intention was to determine the doctrine of the Holy Spirit—about which Nicaea had remained silent— against various heretical tendencies, notably that of Eunomius and the Macedonians, also called "Pneumatomachs", who denied His divinity. The Council was held from May till July 381. It was composed of "150 Fathers", all from the East. Pope Damasus was not represented. No mention of the Symbol of Constantinople will later be made at Ephesus (431), but Chalcedon (451) will consider it as representing "the faith of the 150 Fathers gathered at Constantinople"; in the West, Constantinople will be regarded as an ecumenical Council only in the sixth century. The post-factum approbation that raises this Byzantine Synod to the rank of General Council extends to its Symbol, and notably to its doctrine of the Holy Spirit. The divinity of the Holy Spirit is proclaimed beyond doubt though in less decisive terms than had been used at Nicaea with regard to the divinity of the Son. The term homoousios *is avoided, probably in an effort to win over the Pneumatomachs. To the Symbol are appended various canons, the first of which condemns various errors against the divinity of the Son and of the Spirit.*

The Symbol of Constantinople, which will only much later (from the 17th century on) be known as the "Nicene-Constantinopolitan Symbol" has not been composed by the Council. It is a revised version of the Symbol of Epiphanius of Salamis, contained in his work Ancoratus *(374); it differs from it in details only. It incorporates many elements of the Symbol of Nicaea and of the apostolic Symbol; some notations seem to be borrowed from the symbol of Cyril of Jerusalem. Though not a new composition made by the Council of Constantinople, the Symbol seems to have been promulgated by the Council. After gaining recognition, it soon acquired greater authority than the Nicene Creed, even in the West. Introduced first in the East in the liturgy of baptism and then in the Mass, it made its way later into the Western liturgy in a slightly different form (cf. DS 150). The original text is given here.*

Cf. I.ORTIZ DE URBINA, *Nicée et Constantinople* (Paris 1963) 182-205.

12   We believe in one God, the Father almighty, maker of
150   heaven and earth, of all things visible and invisible.

And in one Lord Jesus Christ, the only-begotten Son of God, generated from the Father before all ages, Light from Light, true God from true God, begotten, not made, one in being (*homoousios*) with the Father, through whom all things were made. For us men and for our salvation He came down from the heavens, and became flesh from the Holy Spirit and the Virgin Mary and was made man. For our sake too He was crucified under Pontius Pilate, suffered and was buried. On the third day He rose again according to the Scriptures, He ascended to the heavens and is seated at the right hand of the Father. He shall come again in glory to judge the living and the dead; to His Kingdom there will be no end.

And in the Holy Spirit, the Lord (*to Kurion*) and Giver of life, who proceeds (*ekporeuomenon*) from the Father,[1] who together with the Father and the Son is worshipped and glorified, who has spoken through the prophets. (And) in one Holy Catholic and apostolic Church. We acknowledge one baptism for the forgiveness of sins. We expect the resurrection of the dead and the life of the world to come. Amen.

Canon I

13   The faith of the 318 Fathers who gathered at Nicaea of Bithinia
151   may not be adulterated. It remains authoritative and all heresy

---

1. The Latin translation adds "and the Son" *(filioque)*. This addition was first introduced in Spain in the sixth century; it is found in the profession of faith of the third Council of Toledo (589) *(DS 470)*. From Spain, it spread to Gaul and Germany. Under the Carolingian Empire, a Synod of Aachen (809) requested Pope Leo III to have it introduced in the entire Latin Church; the Pope, however, did not acquiesce to this request for fear of imposing a clause added to the traditional text of the Creed. It was introduced in the Roman liturgy of the Mass by Pope Benedict VIII *(ob. 1024)*. The Greeks ignored the *filioque* and denied every right to make any addition to the Creed. The question was later to be discussed between Latins and Greeks at the two union Councils: Lyons II (1274) *(cf. n. 321)* and Florence (1439) *(cf. nn. 322 ff)*.

must be condemned, especially that of the Eunomians or 'Anomaeans' (*anomoioi*), of the Arians or Eudoxians, of the Semi-Arians or Pneumatomachs, of the Sabellians, the Marcellians, the Photinians and the Apollinarists.

THE "FAITH OF DAMASUS"

This profession of faith has sometimes been attributed to Pope Dama-sus (ob. 384) or to St Jerome. In reality, it belongs to the fifth century and seems to have originated from Southern Gaul rather than from Spain. It reflects the more elaborate enunciation of the faith characteristic of the West during that period. Originally, the addition "and from the Son" (et filio) *concerning the procession of the Holy Spirit, was absent; it has been introduced later (cf. n. 12, note).*

14   We believe in one God, the Father almighty,
71   and in our one Lord Jesus Christ, the Son of God,
      and in [one] Holy Spirit, God.

We do not worship and confess three Gods, but one God who is Father and Son and Holy Spirit. He is one God, yet not solitary; He is not at the same time Father to Himself and Son, but the Father is He who begets and the Son He who is begotten. As for the Holy Spirit, He is neither begotten nor unbegotten (*ingenitus*), neither created nor made, but He proceeds from the Father and the Son, being equally eternal and fully equal with the Father and the Son and cooperating with them; for it is written: "By the Word of the Lord the heavens were made", that is, by the Son of God, "and all their host by the breath of His mouth" *(Ps. 33 (32) 6)*; and elsewhere: "When you send forth your Spirit, they are created, and you renew the face of the earth" *(cf. Ps. 104 (103) 30)*. Therefore, in the name of the Father and of the Son and of the Holy Spirit we confess one God, for the term 'God' refers to power, not to personal characteristics *(proprie-tas)*. The proper name for the Father is Father, and the proper name for the Son is Son, and the proper name for the Holy Spirit is Holy Spirit. And in this Trinity we believe that God (is) one because what is of one nature and of one substance and of one power with the Father is from one Father. The Father begets the Son, not by an act of will (*non voluntate*), nor out of necessity, but by nature.

15   In the last times, the Son, who never ceased to be with the
72   Father, came down from the Father to save us and to fulfil the
      Scriptures. He was conceived from the Holy Spirit and born of the Virgin Mary. He assumed body, soul and sensibility, that is. a

complete human nature *(perfectum hominem);* He did not lose what He was, but began to be what He was not, in such a way, however, that He is perfect in His own nature *(in suis)* and truly shares in ours *(in nostris).* For, He who was God has been born as a man, and He who has been born as a man acts as God; and He who acts as God dies as man, and He who dies as man rises again as God. Having conquered the power of death with that body with which He had been born and had suffered and died, He rose again on the third day; He ascended to the Father and is seated at His right hand in the glory which He always has had and always has. We believe that we who have been cleansed in His death and in His blood shall be raised up by Him on the last day in this body in which we now live. It is our hope that we shall receive from Him eternal life, the reward of good merit, or else (we shall receive) the penalty of eternal punishment for sins. Read these words, keep them, subject your soul to this faith. From Christ the Lord you will receive both life and reward.

THE PSEUDO-ATHANASIAN SYMBOL *QUICUMQUE*

This Symbol of faith has, since the seventh century, been wrongly attributed to Athanasius of Alexandria (ob. 373), who had attended the Council of Nicaea as a deacon and had later become the champion of the Nicene faith in the East. In reality, the content of the Symbol clearly shows that it belongs to another time and another environment. It is a didactic summary of doctrine, characterised by the Latin approach to the mystery of the Trinity. Its antithetic formulations are much in the manner of St Augustine. It is an original Latin composition belonging to the end of the fifth century, the author of which remains unknown. It has enjoyed great authority in the Latin Church; its rhythmic character has contributed to its widespread diffusion among various Western Liturgies.

Cf. J. N. D. KELLY, *The Athanasian Creed* (London 1964).

16   Whoever wishes to be saved must, first of all, hold the Catho-
75   lic faith, for, unless he keeps it whole and inviolate, he will
      undoubtedly perish for ever.

Now this is the Catholic faith: We worship one God in the Trinity and the Trinity in unity, without either confusing the persons or dividing the substance; for the person of the Father is one, the Son's is another, the Holy Spirit's another; but the Godhead of Father, Son and Holy Spirit is one, their glory equal, their majesty equally eternal.

Such as the Father is, such is the Son, such also the Holy Spirit; uncreated is the Father, uncreated the Son, uncreated the Holy

Spirit; infinite *(immensus)* is the Father, infinite the Son, infinite the Holy Spirit; eternal is the Father, eternal the Son, eternal the Holy Spirit; yet, they are not three eternal beings but one eternal, just as they are not three uncreated beings or three infinite beings but one uncreated and one infinite. In the same way, almighty is the Father, almighty the Son, almighty the Holy Spirit; yet, they are not three almighty beings but one almighty. Thus, the Father is God, the Son is God, the Holy Spirit is God; yet, they are not three gods but one God. Thus, the Father is Lord, the Son is Lord, the Holy Spirit is Lord; yet, they are not three lords but one Lord. For, as the Christian truth compels us to acknowledge each person distinctly as God and Lord, so too the Catholic religion forbids us to speak of three gods or lords.

The Father has neither been made by anyone, nor is He created or begotten; the Son is from the Father alone, not made nor created but begotten; the Holy Spirit is from the Father and the Son, not made nor created nor begotten, but proceeding. So there is one Father, not three Fathers; one Son, not three Sons; one Holy Spirit, not three Holy Spirits. And in this Trinity there is no before or after, no greater or lesser, but all three persons are equally eternal with each other and fully equal. Thus, in all things, as has already been stated above, both unity in the Trinity and Trinity in the unity must be worshipped. Let him therefore who wishes to be saved think this of the Trinity.

17 For his eternal salvation it is necessary, however that he
76 should also faithfully believe in the incarnation of our Lord
Jesus Christ. Here then is the right faith: We believe and confess that our Lord Jesus Christ, the Son of God, is both and equally God and man. He is God from the substance of the Father, begotten before the ages, and He is man from the substance of a mother, born in time; perfect God and perfect man, composed of a rational soul and a human body; equal to the Father as to His divinity, less than the Father as to His humanity. Although He is God and man, He is nevertheless one Christ, not two; however, not one because the divinity has been changed into a human body, but because the humanity has been assumed into God; entirely one, not by a confusion of substance but by the unity of personhood. For, as a rational soul and a body are a single man, so God and man are one Christ. He suffered for our salvation, went down to the underworld *(ad infernos)*, rose again from the dead on the third day, ascended to

the heavens, is seated at the right hand of the Father, wherefrom He shall come to judge the living and the dead. At His coming all men are to rise again with their bodies and to render an account of their own deeds; those who have done good will go to eternal life, but those who have done evil to eternal fire.

This is the Catholic faith. Unless one believes it faithfully and firmly, he cannot be saved.

THE ELEVENTH COUNCIL OF TOLEDO
SYMBOL OF FAITH (675)

(18) *Begun on Nov. 7, 675, the provincial Synod of Toledo gathered 17 bishops only. Its Symbol of faith, which formerly was wrongly attributed to Eusebius of Vercelli (ob. c. 371), can be considered as the work of the Synod, though its redaction was prepared in advance by the Metropolitan Quiricius, and proposed by him to the Fathers of the Synod for their approval. It borrows from dogmatic statements already formulated in the professions of faith promulgated by previous local Synods held in the same city, especially the fourth Council of Toledo (633) (cf. DS 485) and the Sixth Council of Toledo (638) (cf. DS 490-493). For reference, see also Toledo I (400) (DS 188-190) and Toledo III (589) (DS 470). It also incorporates data from the Pseudo-Athanasian Symbol "Quicumque" (cf. nn. 16-17) and from the great Latin doctors, especially Augustine (354-430). Though never expressly approved by any general Council or any Pope, it has through the centuries received the greatest appreciation as an authentic expression of the Church's doctrine, and remains an important document. Most of its affirmations belong to the doctrine of the faith. Later local Councils of Toledo will draw much upon Toledo XI; such is for instance the case with Toledo XVI (DS 568-575). Just as, and even more than the Symbol "Quicumque", the Symbol of Toledo XI reflects the Latin approach to the basic mysteries of the faith, the Trinity and the incarnation. Its principal merit is that it contains the deepest insights and the clearest formulations ever proposed by any official document in the West, as regards these two mysteries. A short paragraph on the fate of man after death is added. The text on the mystery of the Trinity is found in nn. 308-316; that on the incarnation and the redemption in nn. 628-634; that on the fate of man after death in n. 2302.*

THE FOURTH LATERAN GENERAL COUNCIL
SYMBOL OF LATERAN (1215)

Convened by Pope Innocent III, the fourth General Lateran Council, one of the greatest among the Western Councils, was held in 1215, from Nov. 11 to 30. Its primary task was to meet the challenge of the recent heresies of the Albigensians and the Cathars, the Amalricians and the Waldensians, in particular of Abbot Joachim of Fiore. Some of these heretical currents are more explicitly referred to in subsequent chapters issued by the Council (70 in all); all however are already taken into account in the profession of the "Catholic Faith" which constitutes chapter I. This solemn profession of faith was approved by the Pope. It recalls and on more than one point further explicitates the contents of the Catholic faith. The faith of Nicaea (cf. n. 7) and Constantinople (cf. n. 12) are easily recognizable in the text; so too are the doctrine of Ephesus (cf. nn. 604 ff) and of Chalcedon (cf. nn. 613 ff) as regards the incarnation. The new Symbol seems also to draw upon more recent and more elaborate Symbols of faith: for some Christological developments it is inspired by the Symbol of Toledo XI (cf. nn. 628 ff), from which it also borrows much of its eschatological doctrine (cf. n. 2302). At the same time it takes up in abridged form a previous profession of faith already directed against the errors of the Waldensians (cf. DS 790-797). Its structure remains Trinitarian. One of its characteristic features is the affirmation that God in His unity is the unique principle of creation; similarly, the incarnation is said to be the common work of the entire Trinity. Though in continuity with the ancient tradition, it innovates considerably where the formulation of the mystery of the Church is concerned. Its sacrificial and eucharistic character appears for the first time in a solemn document; this is based on Christ's own priestly function. The Ecclesiology of this profession of faith is essentially sacramental and eucharistic: our sharing in the body and blood of Christ is the foundation of the mystery of communion which is the Church. It also clearly affirms the ministerial priesthood by the exercise of which the Eucharist is present in the Church.

Cf. R. FOREVILLE, *Latran I, II, III, IV* (Paris 1965) 275-286.

Chapter I: On the Catholic Faith

(Definition against the Albigensians and the Cathars)

19   We firmly believe and confess without reservation that there
800   is only one true God, eternal, infinite (*immensus*) and un-
          changeable, incomprehensible, almighty and ineffable, the Father, the Son and the Holy Spirit; three persons indeed but one essence, substance or nature entirely simple. The Father is from no one, the Son from the Father only, and the Holy Spirit equally from both *(pariter ab utroque)*. Without beginning, always and without end, the Father begets, the Son is born and the Holy Spirit proceeds. They are of the same substance (*consubstantiales)* and fully equal, equally almighty and equally eternal. (They are) the one principle of the universe, the creator of all things, visible and invisible, spiritual and corporeal, who by His almighty power from the beginning of time made at once (*simul*) out of nothing both orders of creatures, the spiritual and the corporeal, that is, the angelic and the earthly, and then (*deinde*) the human creature, who as it were shares in both orders, being composed of spirit and body. For the devil and the other demons were indeed created by God naturally good, but they became evil by their own doing. As for man, he sinned at the

suggestion of the devil. This Holy Trinity, undivided according to its common essence and distinct according to the proper characteristics of the persons (*secundum personales proprietates*), communicated the doctrine of salvation to the human race, first through Moses, the holy prophets and its other servants, according to a well ordered disposition of times.

20 Finally, the only-begotten Son of God, Jesus Christ, whose
801 incarnation is the common work of the whole Trinity, conceived from Mary ever Virgin with the co-operation of the Holy Spirit, made true man, composed of a rational soul and a human body, one person in two natures, showed the way of life more clearly. Though immortal and impassible according to His divinity, He, the very same, became passible and mortal according to His humanity. He also suffered and died on the wood of the cross for the salvation of the human race; He went down to the underworld *(ad infernos)*, rose again from the dead and ascended into heaven; but He went down in the soul, rose again in the body and ascended equally in both. He shall come at the end of time to judge the living and the dead and to render to each one according to his works, to the reprobate (*reprobis*) as well as to the elect. All of them will rise again with their own bodies which they now bear, to receive according to their works, whether these have been good or evil, the ones perpetual punishment with the devil and the others everlasting glory with Christ.

21 There is indeed one universal Church of the faithful out-
802 side which no one at all is saved,[1] and in which the priest himself, Jesus Christ, is also the sacrifice *(idem ipse sacerdos est sacrificium Jesus Christus)*. His body and blood are truly contained in the sacrament of the altar under the appearances of bread and wine, the bread being transubstantiated into the body by the divine power and the wine into the blood, to the effect that we receive from what is His in what He has received from what is ours *(ut . . . accipiamus ipsi de suo, quod accepit ipse de nostro)* in order that the mystery of unity may be accomplished. Indeed, no one can perform *(conficere)* this sacrament, except the priest duly ordained according to (the power of) the keys of the Church, which Jesus Christ Himself conceded to the apostles and their successors. The sacrament of baptism (which is celebrated in water at the invocation of God and of the undivided Trinity, viz. the Father, the Son and the

---

1. CYPRIAN OF CARTHAGE, *Letter (73) to Iubaianus*, 21.

Holy Spirit) conduces to the salvation of children as well as of adults when duly conferred by anyone according to the Church's form. If, after receiving baptism, anyone shall have lapsed into sin, he can always be restored through true penance. Not only virgins and the continent *(continentes)*, but also married persons, by pleasing God through right faith and good work, merit to attain to eternal happiness.

THE SECOND GENERAL COUNCIL OF LYONS
"PROFESSION OF FAITH OF MICHAEL PALAEOLOGUS" (1274)

Convened by Pope Gregory X, the second General Council of Lyons was held in six sessions from May 7 to July 17, 1274. Besides reforming the Church, it aimed at bringing to an end the two century old schism between East and West and to bring about the reunion of the Churches. Invited to be personally present at the Council, emperor Michael VIII Palaeologus sent a delegation to Lyons. At the fourth session held on July 6, 1274, what is usually called the "profession of faith of Michael Palaeologus" was read before the Council Fathers. This document was not written at the Council, nor was it accepted by the Greeks as a basis for a doctrinal agreement with the Latins. It was neither promulgated, nor even discussed by the Council Fathers, but simply read from a letter sent by the Byzantine emperor. In this letter, the emperor merely transcribed, without discussion or modification, the text of a profession of faith proposed to him by Pope Clement IV as early as March 4, 1267. In Clement's mind, this profession contained "the faith of the Holy Roman Church", the acceptance of which by the Greeks was the pre-required condition for union. If the emperor personally subscribed to it, this was due to his desire to establish union with Rome.

The text is therefore pre-conciliar. It is composed of two parts. The first part takes up with a few alterations a Trinitarian and Christological profession of faith submitted by Pope Leo IX to Peter, patriarch of Antioch, two centuries earlier (1053), that is one year before the consummation of the Eastern Schism (1054). For the redaction of this profession (cf. DS nn. 680-686), Leo IX had leaned heavily on the Statuta Ecclesiae Antiqua, *a canonical and liturgical compilation made in Southern Gaul towards the end of the fifth century.[1] The second part, written by the theologians of Clement IV, has directly in view the recent discussion with the Greeks; it contrasts abruptly to their "various errors" the current theology of the Latins, mostly as regards the eschatological doctrine, sacramental theology and the primacy of the Roman Church.*

In the first part, the Christological doctrine of Chalcedon (cf. nn. 613 ff) is linked to the section of the Trinitarian profession devoted to the second person. The Trinitarian doctrine reflects strongly the Latin approach to the mystery: the unity of nature is the point of departure for the enunciation of the plurality of persons; the procession of the Holy Spirit is conceived after the Latin tradition. Such a one-sided formulation of the mystery was not conducive to establishing union with the Greeks. In the second part, the text

---

1. Cf. Ch. MUNIER, Les *"Statuta Ecclesiae Antiqua"* (Paris 1960).

of Clement lays stress on the immediate retribution and the nature of purgatory, the two questions raised by the Greeks in the current controversies. But these points are inserted into a complete doctrine of individual eschatology, which will be taken up later by the Council of Florence (cf. nn. 2308 f), and will become classical. A clause on the general judgment is added to mark the agreement which existed between Greeks and Latins on this point.

Cf. H. WOLTER-H. HOLSTEIN, *Lyon I et Lyon II* (Paris 1966) 162-171.

First Part

22   We believe in the Holy Trinity, Father, Son and Holy Spirit,
851   one almighty God; and that in the Trinity the whole Godhead is the same essence *(coessentialis)*, the same substance *(consubstantialis)*, equally eternal and equally almighty, of
one will, one power and majesty. (This Trinity is) the creator of all
things created, from whom, in whom, by whom all things exist in
heaven and on earth, the visible and the invisible, the corporeal and
the spiritual. We believe that each single person in the Trinity is the
one true God, fully and perfectly.

23   We believe in the Son of God, Word of God, eternally born
852   from the Father, of the same substance, equally almighty and
in all things equal to the Father in divinity; born in time, from
the Holy Spirit and from Mary ever Virgin, with a rational soul. He
has two births, one an eternal birth from the Father, the other a
temporal birth from a mother. He is true God and true man, real
(proprium) and perfect in both natures; neither an adoptive son nor
an apparent son, but the one and only Son of God, in and from two
natures, that is, the divine and the human, in the unity of one person.
He is impassible and immortal in His divinity, but in His humanity He
suffered for us and for our salvation a true bodily passion; He died,
was buried, went down to the dead, and on the third day rose again
from the dead by a true bodily resurrection. Forty days after His
resurrection He ascended into heaven with His risen body and His
soul; He is seated at the right hand of God the Father, wherefrom He
shall come to judge the living and the dead and to render to each one
according to his works, whether these have been good or evil.

24   We believe also in the Holy Spirit, fully, perfectly and truly
853   God, proceeding from the Father and the Son, fully equal,
of the same substance, equally almighty and equally eternal
with the Father and the Son in all things. We believe that this Holy

Trinity is not three gods but one only God, almighty, eternal, invisible and immutable.

25   We believe that the Holy Catholic and apostolic Church is
854   the one true Church, in which are given one holy baptism and the true forgiveness of all sins. We believe also in the true resurrection of this body which we now bear, and in the life eternal. We believe also that God, the Lord almighty, is the one author of the New Testament and the Old, of the Law, the Prophets and the Apostles.

855   Such is the true Catholic faith, which in the above mentioned articles the most Holy Roman Church holds and preaches.

Second Part

26   But, because of various errors, introduced by some through
855   ignorance and by others out of malice, she says and preaches: that those who after baptism lapse into sin must not be rebaptised, but obtain pardon for their sins through true penance;

856   that, if, being truly repentant, they die in charity before having satisfied by worthy fruits of penance for their sins of commission and omission, their souls are cleansed after death by purgatorial and purifying penalties, as Brother John has explained to us;[1] and that to alleviate such penalties the acts of intercession *(suffragia)* of the living faithful benefit them, namely the sacrifices of the Mass, prayers, alms and other works of piety which the faithful are wont to do for the other faithful according to the Church's institutions.

857   As for the souls of those who, after having received holy baptism, have incurred no stain of sin whatever, and those souls who, after having contracted the stain of sin, have been cleansed, either while remaining still in their bodies or after having been divested of them as stated above, they are received immediately *(mox)* into heaven.

858   As for the souls of those who die in mortal sin or with original sin only, they go down immediately *(mox)* to hell *(in infernum)*, to be punished however with different punishments.

---

1. This refers to John Parastron, a Franciscan of Greek origin, who acted as mediator between Rome and Byzantium, and was entrusted with the task of conveying to the imperial court and to the patriarchate of Constantinople the Pope's invitation to the Council.

27   The same most Holy Roman Church firmly believes and
859   firmly asserts that nevertheless on the day of Judgment all
men will appear with their bodies before the judgment-seat of
Christ, to render an account of their own deeds *(cf. Rom. 14.10-12)*.

28   The same Holy Roman Church also holds and teaches that
860   there are seven sacraments of the Church: one is baptism,
which has been mentioned above; another is the sacrament of
confirmation which bishops confer by the laying on of hands while
they anoint the reborn; then penance, the Eucharist, the sacrament
of order, matrimony and extreme unction which, according to the
doctrine of the Blessed James,[1] is administered to the sick. The same
Roman Church performs *(conficit)* the sacrament of the Eucharist
with unleavened bread; she holds and teaches that in this sacrament
the bread is truly transubstantiated into the body of our Lord Jesus
Christ, and the wine into His blood. As regards matrimony, she holds
that neither is a man allowed to have several wives at the same time
nor a woman several husbands. But, when a legitimate marriage is
dissolved by the death of one of the spouses, she declares that a
second and afterwards a third wedding are successively licit, if no
other canonical impediment goes against it for any reason.

29   The Holy Roman Church possesses also the highest and full
861   primacy and authority over the universal Catholic Church,
which she recognises in truth and humility to have received
with fulness of power from the Lord Himself in the person of Blessed
Peter, the chief or head of the apostles, of whom the Roman Pontiff is
the successor. And, as she is bound above all to defend the truth of
faith, so too, if any questions should arise regarding the faith, they
must be decided by her judgment. Anyone accused in matters
pertaining to the forum of the Church may appeal to her; and in all
causes within the purview of ecclesiastical enquiry, recourse may be
had to her judgment. To her all the Churches are subject; their
prelates give obedience and reverence to her. Her fulness of power,
moreover, is so firm that she admits the other Churches to a share in
her solicitude. The same Roman Church has honoured many of
those Churches, and chiefly the Patriarchal Churches, with various
privileges, its own prerogative being, however, always observed and
safeguarded both in general Councils and in some other matters.

_____

1. Cf. *James* 5.14-15.

THE PROFESSION OF FAITH OF PIUS IV
BULL *INIUNCTUM NOBIS* (1564)

The Council of Trent (1545-1563), in its "Decree on General Reform" (1563), had legislated that all prelates in the Church would have to make a profession of faith and of obedience to the Roman See. Its formulation was promulgated by Pope Pius IV in the Bull Iniunctum Nobis *(13 November 1564), largely under pressure from St Peter Canisius (ob. 1597). It is often called the "Tridentine Profession of Faith", even though the text was not fixed by the Council; it may more adequately be named the "Profession of Faith of Pius IV". Besides repeating the Symbol of Constantinople (cf. n. 12), it sums up the essential doctrinal elements declared by the Council of Trent against the background of the errors of the Reformation. After the First Vatican General Council (1869-1870), a decree of the "Congregation of the Council" (Jan. 20, 1877)[1] introduced in the text of Pius IV the reference to that Council with regard to the primacy of the Roman Pontiff and his infallible teaching office (cf. n. 37). In 1910, Pius X added to it the anti-Modernist oath (cf. n. 143). In 1967, the Sacred Congregation of the Faith promulgated a new text for the profession of faith to be made by law by various categories of persons.[2] In this new text, the anti-modernist oath is suppressed, while to the Symbol of Constantinople a single paragraph is added, which replaces the previous summary of Tridentine doctrine. This paragraph merely mentions the Church's doctrine of faith in general; it goes on to refer especially to the mystery of the Church, of the sacraments, especially the Mass, and to the primacy of the Roman Pontiff.*

30 I, N., with firm faith believe and profess each and every
1862 article contained in the Symbol of faith which the Holy Roman
Church uses:

[*There follows the text of the Symbol of Constantinople in its Latin form used in the Roman Liturgy: DS 150.*]

31 I most firmly accept and embrace the apostolic and eccle-
1863 siastical traditions, and all other observances and constitu-
tions of the same Church. I likewise accept Holy Scripture according to that sense which Holy Mother Church has held and does hold, to whom it belongs to judge of the true meaning and interpretation of the Sacred Scriptures; I shall never accept or interpret them otherwise than according to the unanimous consent of the Fathers.

32 I also profess that there are truly and properly speaking
1864 seven sacraments of the New Law, instituted by Jesus Christ
our Lord and necessary for the salvation of the human race,

---

1. *ASS* 1877, 71 ff.
2. *AAS* 59 (1967) 1058.

though not all are necessary for each individual person: (they are) baptism, confirmation, the Eucharist, penance, extreme unction, order and matrimony. And (I profess) that they confer grace, and that of these, baptism, confirmation and order cannot be repeated without sacrilege. I also admit and accept the rites received and approved in the Catholic Church for the administration of all the sacraments mentioned above.

33   I embrace and accept each and all the articles defined and
1865   declared by the most Holy Synod of Trent concerning original sin and justification.

34   I also profess that in the Mass there is offered to God a
1866   true sacrifice, properly speaking, which is propitiatory for the living and the dead, and that in the most Holy Sacrament of the Eucharist the body and blood together with the soul and the divinity of our Lord Jesus Christ are truly, really and substantially present, and that there takes place a change *(conversio)* of the whole substance of bread into the body and of the whole substance of wine into the blood; and this change the Catholic Church calls transubstantiation. I also confess that under each species alone *(sub altera tantum specie)* the whole and entire Christ and the true sacrament is received.

35   I steadfastly hold that there is a purgatory, and that the
1867   souls detained there are helped by the acts of intercession *(suffragiis)* of the faithful; likewise, that the saints reigning together with Christ should be venerated and invoked, that they offer prayers to God for us, and that their relics should be venerated. I firmly declare that the images of Christ and of the Mother of God ever Virgin and of the other saints as well are to be kept and preserved, and that due honour and veneration should be given to them. I also affirm that the power of indulgences has been left by Christ to the Church, and that their use is very beneficial to the Christian people.

36   I acknowledge the Holy, Catholic and apostolic, Roman
1868   Church as the mother and the teacher of all the Churches, and I promise and swear true obedience to the Roman Pontiff, successor of Blessed Peter, chief of the apostles, and Vicar of Christ.

37   I unhesitantly accept and profess also all other things trans-
1869   mitted, defined and declared by the sacred canons and

the ecumenical Councils, especially by the most Holy Council of Trent [and by the ecumenical Vatican Council, mostly as regards the primacy of the Roman Pontiff and his infallible teaching authority]. At the same time, all contrary propositions and whatever heresies have been condemned, rejected and anathematised by the Church, I too condemn, reject and anathematise.

38   This true Catholic faith, outside of which no one can be saved,
1870   which of my own accord I now profess and truly hold, I, N.,
         do promise, vow and swear that, with the help of God, I shall most faithfully keep and confess entire and inviolate, to my last breath, and that I shall take care, as far as it lies in my power, that it be held, taught and preached by those under me, or those over whom I have charge by virtue of my office. So help me God and these His Holy Gospels.

THE PROFESSION OF FAITH OF PAUL VI (1968)

On the nineteenth centenary of the martyrdom of the apostles Peter and Paul (June 30, 1968), which marked the end of the "year of faith" (1967-1968) called by him one year earlier, Pope Paul VI closed the liturgical celebration with a "solemn profession of faith". Preoccupied by "the disquiet which at the present time agitates certain quarters with regard to the faith", the Pope considered it his duty to "fulfil the mandate entrusted by Christ to Peter", whose successor he is, "to confirm his brothers in the faith". The Pope expressly declared that, "without being properly speaking a dogmatic definition", his profession of faith "repeats in substance the Creed of Nicaea, with some developments called for by the spiritual condition of our times". Besides the clear reference to the Nicene Symbol, it integrates texts from other solemn documents of the Church, in particular the ecclesiological doctrine of the Second Vatican General Council. Some developments are calculated to re-state clearly the Church's faith against the background of recent controversies. The doctrine on original sin and on the Eucharist are cases in point.[1]

39/1   We believe in one God, Father, Son and Holy Spirit, creator
           of things visible—such as this world in which our brief life runs its course—and of things invisible—such as the pure spirits which are also called angels (*cf. n. 412*)— and creator in each man of his spiritual and immortal soul (*cf. n. 410*).

39/2   We believe that this only God is as absolutely one in His
           infinitely Holy essence as in His other perfections: in His

---

1. Cf. *AAS* 60 (1968) 433-445. The "profession of faith" occupies nn. 8-30 of the text (*ibid.* 436-445). References to the documents of the Second Vatican General Council are given between brackets.

almighty power, His infinite knowledge, His providence,His will and His love. He is 'He who is' as He revealed to Moses (*cf. Ex. 3.14 Vulg.*); He is 'Love', as the apostle John has taught us *(cf. 1 Jn 4.8)*; so that these two names, Being and Love, express ineffably the same divine essence of Him who has wished to make Himself manifest to us, and who, "dwelling in unapproachable light" *(1 Tim. 6.16)*, is in Himself above every name and every created thing and every created intellect. God alone can give us right and full knowledge of Himself, by revealing Himself as Father, Son and Holy Spirit, in whose eternal life we are by grace called to share, here on earth in the obscurity of faith and after death in eternal light. The mutual bonds which from all eternity constitute the three persons, each of whom is one and the same divine Being, constitute the blessed inmost life of the most Holy God, infinitely beyond all that we can humanly understand (*cf. n. 132*). We give thanks, however, to the divine goodness that very many believers can testify with us before men to the unity of God, even though they know not the mystery of the most Holy Trinity.

39/3 We believe then in God who eternally begets the Son; we believe in the Son, the Word of God, who is eternally begotten; we believe in the Holy Spirit, the uncreated person who proceeds from the Father and the Son as their eternal love. Thus, in the three divine persons who are "equally eternal and fully equal" *(cf. n. 16)* the life and beatitude of God, perfectly one, superabound and are consummated in the supreme excellence and glory proper to the uncreated essence, and always "both unity in the Trinity and Trinity in the unity must be worshipped" *(cf. n. 16)*.

39/4 We believe in our Lord Jesus Christ, the Son of God. He is the eternal Word, born of the Father before all ages and of one same substance with the Father, that is one in being with the Father *(homoousios tô Patri) (cf. n. 7);* through Him all things were made. He became flesh from the Virgin Mary by the Holy Spirit and was made man. Therefore, He is "equal to the Father as to His divinity, less than the Father as to His humanity" *(cf. n. 17)*, entirely one "not by a confusion of substance" (which is impossible), "but by the unity of personhood" *(cf. n. 17)*.

39/5 He dwelled among us, full of grace and truth. He proclaimed and established the Kingdom of God, making the Father manifest to us. He gave us His new commandment to love one another as He Himself loved us. He taught us the way of the beatitudes of the Gospel: poverty in spirit, meekness, suffering borne with patience, thirst after justice, mercy, purity of heart, peace-making, persecution suffered for justice sake. He suffered under Pontius Pilate, He, the Lamb of God bearing the sins of the world; He died for us, nailed to the cross, saving us by His redeeming blood. He was buried and, of His own power, rose again on the third day, raising us by His resurrection to that sharing in the divine life which is the life of grace. He ascended into heaven, wherefrom He shall come again, this time in glory, to judge the living and the dead, each according to his merits: those who have responded to the love and goodness of God will go to eternal life, but those who have rejected them to the end will be sentenced to the fire that will never be extinguished. And to His Kingdom there will be no end.

39/6   We believe in the Holy Spirit, the Lord and Giver of life, who together with the Father and the Son is worshipped and glorified. He has spoken through the prophets; He was sent to us by Christ after His resurrection and His ascension to the Father; He enlightens, vivifies, protects and guides the Church; He purifies her members if they do not refuse His grace. His action, which penetrates to the inmost of the soul, enables man to respond to the command of Jesus: "You must be perfect as your heavenly Father is perfect" *(Mt. 5.48).*

39/7   We believe that Mary, who remained ever a Virgin, is the Mother of the Incarnate Word, our God and Saviour Jesus Christ *(cf. nn. 605-606/1),* and that, by reason of her singular election, "she was, in consideration of the merits of her Son, redeemed in a more eminent manner" *(LG 53),* "preserved immune from all stain of original sin" *(cf. n. 709),* and "by an exceptional gift of grace stands far above all other creatures" *(LG 53).*

39/8   Joined by a close and indissoluble bond to the mysteries of the incarnation and redemption *(cf. LG 53, 58, 61),* the Blessed Virgin Mary, the Immaculate, "when the course of her earthly life was finished, was taken up, body and soul, to the glory of heaven" *(cf. n. 715)* and, likened to her Son who rose again from the dead, she received in anticipation the future lot of all the just. We believe that the Holy Mother of God, the new Eve, "Mother of the Church" *(LG 53, 56, 61),* "continues in heaven to exercise her maternal role" with regard to Christ's members, "helping to bring

forth and to increase the divine life in the souls of all the redeemed'
(LG 62).

39/9   We believe that in Adam all have sinned, which means that
the original offence committed by him caused the human
race, common to all, to fall to a state in which it bears the consequences of that offence. This is no longer the state in which the human
nature was at the beginning in our first parents, constituted as they
were in holiness and justice, and in which man was immune from evil
and death. And so, it is human nature so fallen, deprived from the gift
of grace with which it had first been adorned, injured in its own
natural powers and subjected to the dominion of death, that is
communicated to all men; it is in this sense that every man is born in
sin. We therefore hold, with the Council of Trent, that original sin is
transmitted with human nature "by propagation, not by imitation"
and that it "is in all men, proper to each" *(cf. n. 510)*.

39/10   We believe that our Lord Jesus Christ by the sacrifice of
the Cross redeemed us from original sin and all the personal
sins committed by each one of us, so that the word of the apostle is
verified: "Where sin increased, grace abounded all the more" *(Rom.
5.20)*.

39/11   We believe in and confess one baptism instituted by our
Lord Jesus Christ for the forgiveness of sins. Baptism should
be administered even to little children "who of themselves cannot
have yet committed any sin", in order that, though born deprived of
supernatural grace, they may be reborn "of water and the Holy
Spirit" to the divine life in Christ Jesus *(cf. n. 511)*.

39/12   We believe in one, Holy, Catholic and apostolic Church,
built by Jesus Christ on that rock which is Peter. She is the
"Mystical Body of Christ", at once a visible society "provided with
hierarchical organs" and a "spiritual community; the Church on
earth", the pilgrim People of God here below, and "the Church filled
with heavenly blessings"; "the germ and the first fruits of the Kingdom of God", through which the work and the sufferings of redemption are continued throughout human history, and which looks with
all its stength for the perfect accomplishment it will obtain beyond
time in glory *(LG 8, 5)*. In the course of time, the Lord Jesus Christ
forms His Church by means of the sacraments emanating from His
fulness *(LG 7, 11)*. For, by these the Church makes her members
share in the mystery of the death and resurrection of Jesus Christ,

through the grace of the Holy Spirit who gives her life and movement *(SC 5, 6; LG 7, 12, 50)*. She is therefore holy, though having sinners in her midst, because she herself has no other life but the life of grace. If they live by her life, her members are sanctified; if they move away from her life, they fall into sins and disorders that prevent the radiation of her sanctity. This is why she suffers and does penance for those offences, of which she has the power to free her children through the blood of Christ and the gift of the Holy Spirit.

39/13 Heiress of the divine promise and daughter of Abraham according to the Spirit, through that Israel whose sacred Scriptures she lovingly guards, and whose patriarchs and prophets she venerates; founded upon the apostles and faithfully handing down through the centuries their ever-living word and their powers as pastors in the successor of Peter and the bishops in communion with him; perpetually assisted by the Holy Spirit, the Church has the charge of guarding, teaching, explaining and spreading the truth which God revealed dimly to men through the prophets, and then fully in the Lord Jesus. We believe all "that is contained in the word of God, written or handed down, and that the Church proposes for belief as divinely revealed, whether by a solemn decree or by the ordinary and universal teaching office" *(cf. n. 121)*. We believe in the infallibility enjoyed by the successor of Peter when, as pastor and teacher of all the Christians, "he speaks *ex cathedra" (cf. n. 839)* and which "also resides in the episcopal Body when it exericses with him the supreme teaching office" *(LG 25)*.

39/14 We believe that the Church founded by Jesus Christ and for which He prayed is indefectibly one in faith, worship and the bond of hierarchical communion *(LG 8, 18-23; UR 2)*. In the bosom of this Church, the rich variety of liturgical rites and the legitimate diversity of theological and spiritual heritages and of special disciplines, far from "injuring her unity, make it more manifest" *(LG 23; OE 2-6)*.

39/15 Recognising also the existence, "outside the organism" of the Church of Christ of "numerous elements of sanctification and truth which, because they belong to her as her own, call for Catholic unity" *(LG 8)*, and believing in the action of the Holy Spirit who stirs up in the heart of all the disciples of Christ a desire for this unity *(LG 15)*, we entertain the hope that the Christians who do not yet enjoy full communion in one only Church will at last be united in one flock with only one Shepherd.

39/16   We believe that "the Church is necessary for salvation. For, Christ, who is the sole Mediator and the one way to salvation, makes Himself present for us in His Body which is the Church" *(LG 14)*. But the divine design of salvation embraces all men; and those "who without fault on their part do not know the Gospel of Christ and His Church but seek God with a sincere heart, and under the influence of grace endeavour to do His will as recognised through the prompting of their conscience", they too in a number known only to God "can obtain eternal salvation" *(LG 16)*.

39/17   We believe that the Mass, celebrated by the priest representing the person of Christ by virtue of the power received through the sacrament of Order, and offered by him in the name of Christ and of the members of His Mystical Body, is indeed the sacrifice of Calvary rendered sacramentally present on our altars. We believe that, as the bread and wine consecrated by the Lord at the Last Supper were changed into His body and His blood which were soon to be offered for us on the Cross, likewise the bread and wine consecrated by the priest are changed into the body and blood of Christ enthroned gloriously in heaven; and we believe that the mysterious presence of the Lord, under the species which continue to appear to our senses as before, is a true, real and substantial presence *(cf. n. 1526)*.

39/18   Thus, in this sacrament Christ cannot become present otherwise than by the change of the whole substance of bread into His body, and the change of the whole substance of wine into His blood, while only the properties of the bread and wine which our senses perceive remain unchanged. This mysterious change is fittingly and properly named by the Church transubstantiation. Every theological explanation which seeks some understanding of this mystery must, in order to be in accord with Catholic faith, maintain firmly that in the order of reality itself, independently of our mind, the bread and wine have ceased to exist after the consecration, so that it is the adorable body and blood of the Lord Jesus which from then on are really before us under the sacramental species of bread and wine *(cf. nn. 1519, 1527, 1577)*, as the Lord willed it, in order to give Himself to us as food and to bind us together in the unity of His Mystical Body.

39/19   The unique and indivisible existence of the Lord glorious in heaven is not multiplied, but is rendered present by the sacrament in the many places on earth where the eucharistic sacrifice is celebrated. And this existence remains present, after the celebration of the sacrifice, in the Blessed Sacrament which is in the tabernacle as the living heart of our churches. Therefore, it is our sweet duty to honour and adore, in the Blessed Host which our eyes see, the Incarnate Word Himself whom they cannot see and who, yet, without leaving heaven, is made present before us.

39/20 We confess also that the Kingdom of God, begun here on earth in the Church of Christ, is not "of this world" *(Jn 18.36)* whose "form is passing away" *(1 Cor. 7.31)*, and that its proper growth cannot be identified with the progress of civilisation, of science or of human technology, but that it consists in an ever more profound knowledge of the unfathomable riches of Christ, an ever stronger hope of eternal blessings, an ever more ardent response to the love of God, and finally in an ever more abundant diffusion of grace and holiness among men. But it is this same love which impels the Church to be also continuously concerned about the true temporal welfare of men. While she never ceases to remind all her children that "they have not" here on earth "a lasting city" *(Heb. 13.14)*, she also urges them to contribute, each according to his condition of life and his means, to the welfare of their earthly city, to promote justice, peace and fraternal concord among men, to give their help generously to their brothers, especially to the poorest and most unfortunate. The deep solicitude of the Church, the Spouse of Christ, for the needs of men, for their joys and hopes, their griefs and efforts, is therefore nothing other than the desire which strongly urges her to be present to them in order to enlighten them with the light of Christ and to gather and unite them all in Him, their only Saviour. This solicitude can never be understood to mean that the Church conforms herself to the things of this world or that the ardour is lessened with which she expects her Lord and the eternal Kingdom.

39/21 We believe in the life eternal. We believe that the souls of all those who die in the grace of Christ—whether they must still be purified in purgatory, or , from the moment they leave their bodies, Jesus takes them to paradise as He did for the good thief— constitute the People of God beyond death; death will be finally vanquished on the day of the resurrection when these souls will be re-united with their bodies.

39/22 We believe that the multitude of those gathered around Jesus and Mary in paradise forms the Church of heaven, where in the enjoyment of eternal beatitude they see God as He is *(1 Jn 3.2; cf. n. 2305)*, and where they also, in different ways and degrees, are associated with the holy angels in the divine rule exercised by the glorified Christ, by interceding for us and by providing with their brotherly solicitude a powerful help to our infirmity *(LG 49)*.

39/23 We believe in the communion of all the faithful of Christ, those who are pilgrims on earth, the dead who are being purified, and the blessed in heaven, all together forming one Church; and we also believe that in this communion the merciful love of God and His saints is ever turning listening ears to our prayers, as Jesus told us: "Ask and you will receive" *(Jn 16.24)*. Confessing this faith and sustained by this hope, we look forward to the resurrection of the dead and the life of the world to come.

Blessed be God thrice Holy. Amen.

CHAPTER I

REVELATION AND FAITH

It is of the very essence of man that he cannot be reduced to the immediate and limited reality of his empirical existence but experiences himself as confronted with an ultimate reality, the incomprehensible, which is the source of his being and to which he is related in his final destiny. The very fact that he experiences his life as limited and imperfect implies the realisation of a transcendence, an openness to the ultimate reality which we call God.

For the Christian this reality is not the vague horizon of his own earthly existence; Christian existence is based on the belief that God has spoken. The ultimate mystery which is the source of human existence and of all creation has revealed itself as love, unfathomable yet personal, all embracing yet giving a name to every creature. This love makes full claim on man; it gives him a destiny beyond himself, one that comes from God's own freedom and is written in the depth of man's heart.

Man's response to this invitation is faith. Through faith man steps outside the limited world of his experience and reasoning into the realm of the wholly 'other', beyond his own calculation and control.

The entire history of salvation consists in the repeated and ever more radical challenge made to man to commit himself entirely to God's word, to give up his self-reliance and allow himself to be taken up into the incomprehensible mystery of the living God. This total self-commitment is the basic act of the Christian existence.

The failures of Israel and of the Church are in fact failures in faith, not only and not primarily in the sense that certain truths revealed by God are denied, but that man drifts again towards self-reliance and hence becomes a prey to isolation, narrowness of spirit, weakness, darkness and sin. It is at all times man's temptation to build his existence on his work and so to keep his life in his own hands. The Jews asked Jesus: "What must we do to be doing the works of God?" Jesus gives the true answer which it is hard for man to accept: "This is the work of God, that you believe in Him whom He has sent" (Jn 6.28f).

In the bibical perspective revelation and faith comprise the totality of the Christian existence. Theological reflection, however, is concerned mainly with their epistemological aspects. Already the Council of Trent lays stress on the intellectual aspect of faith when it speaks of the faith required for justification: "believing to be true what has been divinely revealed" (cf. n. 1930).

In the 19th century, the reflection on revelation and faith in their relation to natural knowledge became the centre of theological discussion and the focal point of many Church documents. There were, on the one hand, the claims of rationalists who asserted the autonomy of human reason and rejected divine revelation as an arbitrary and degrading interference with man's sovereignty; there was, on the other hand, since Kant, the radical distrust of pure reason, denying the possibility for deductive thinking to arrive at any truth beyond the domain of empirical knowledge. This doctrine shook traditional apologetics to their foundations. New foundations were sought for the reality of religion, mainly in revelation itself, while the rational justification of faith was abandoned. Among these attempts we note Fideism, Traditionalism, and finally Modernism.

Thus the Church documents of the 19th and of the first part of the 20th century answer errors belonging to two opposite trends. They assert, on the one hand, the dignity of human reason and its capability to know the existence of God and to ascertain the historical credentials of the Christian revelation. On the other hand, they insist on the strictly supernatural character of revelation, and on the nature of the faith-commitment as essentially different from an intellectual assent based on rational evidence. They further show the mutual relation between faith and reason.

Going beyond these epistemological problems, the Second Vatican Council places both revelation and faith within the universal context of the Christian existence and thus re-opens the possibility of showing their concrete significance for man and human society.

*   *   *

The main doctrinal points treated in the documents of this chapter are the following:

There are two kinds of religious knowledge, natural by reason, and supernatural by faith: 112/8f, 116f, 126, 131, 137.

Man's natural knowledge of God

Man can come through reason to the knowledge of God: 101, 113,
    115, 143/1, 144, (153);
and of other religious truths: 102, 103.
This knowledge, however, is not intuitive: 141f.

Revelation

God can and does reveal himself to man: 112/2f, 113, 116f, 131, 140.
Through revelation God confirms the natural religious truths: 114f,
    135, 145;
but primarily calls man to participate in His own divine life: 114, 117,
    149;
and gives him the fulness of his human destiny: 106, 149.
God reveals Himself from the beginning of the human race: 150;
in the history of salvation: 150;
and finally in Jesus Christ: 151.
The fact of the divine revelation can be proved with certainty mainly
    through the miracles: 104, 110f, 112/7, 119, 127f, 143/2, 146.
Revelation is not man's own achievement: 108, 112/4.
The content of revelation, being God's own life, remains beyond
    man's comprehension: 112/9, 114, 131f, 137;
it cannot be reduced to a philosophical system: 106, 108, 136;
it is entrusted to the Church: 121, 123, 134, 139f, 143/3.9.11, 238, 836,
    859.
Though it unfolds in history, it remains essentially the same: 108,
    112/5, 136, 139, 143/4.7f.11, 152.

Faith

Man's response to God's revelation is faith: 110f, 118, 143/5, 152.
It is essentially distinct from a natural assent: 110, 112/8, 118, 126.
It is a free assent, involving the whole person: 120, 129, 152;
under the influence of grace: 118, 120, 124, 129, 152, 1930.
It includes the submission of the intellect: 118, 120, 126f, 143/5, 1930.
It is man's duty to respond in faith to God's word: 109, 111, 118, 121,
    125, 130.
Faith is necessary for salvation: 118, 120, 122, 1935.
Though the content of faith consists in the divine mystery, it can and
    must be expressed in systematic language: 105, 147f.

Atheism

It is understandable in the context of a secular culture: (154), 157-
    159;

yet, it must be rejected because it destroys the foundations of human life and society: (154), 155f.

Faith and Reason

No real contradiction can exist between faith and reason: 107, 112/6, 133f, 135, 164.

Faith cannot be contradicted by sound philosophy: 107, 133f, 139, 147;

nor by history: 143/6-12.

Reason is meant to lead to faith and to help penetrating it: 107, 109-111, 132, 135.

Science cannot propose hypotheses contradicting revelation: 112/10f, 134, 138.

Faith and Science

There is no conflict between faith and science: 164-165.
The limits of scientific knowledge: 166.
The right use of science: 167-169.
Science needs faith: 170.

Dogma and Theology

Interpretation of dogma: 160-161.
Dogmatic relativism is excluded: 162.
Theology and Magisterium: 163.

CONDEMNATION OF FIDEISM, TRADITIONALISM, RATIONALISM

Two apparently contradictory trends dominate the theology of revelation in the 19th century: Fideism with its total reliance on revelation and its distrust of human reason, and Rationalism in its various forms which considers natural reason as the only source of human knowledge, and therefore rejects revelation as hostile to man's autonomy and to true human progress. The struggle against these opposite tendencies comes to its climax in the first Vatican General Council. Before this Council, however, the Church had already declared her attitude in a series of documents, four of which are mentioned here.

1. The articles subscribed to by L.E. Bautain (1796–1867), professor in Strasbourg, reckoned as the principal representative of Fideism. Profoundly impressed by Kant's philosophy and by his own experience in returning to the faith, moved also by pastoral reasons, Bautain sought the source of religious and moral knowledge exclusively in divine revelation. He denied the possibility of arriving at a certain knowledge of the existence of God and of the fact of revelation by purely natural powers. To prove his orthodoxy, he was made to subscribe six theses by the Bishop of Strasbourg in 1835 and again, with slight modifications, in 1840 (cf. DS 2751–2756). The most precise disavowal of his doctrines is contained in five theses proposed to him by the Roman Congregation for bishops and regulars in 1844, when he intended to found a congregation of religious. The first four theses, quoted here, are concerned with the problem of reason and faith.

2. Closely related to Fideism were the representatives of Traditionalism: L. de Bonald (ob. 1840), F. de Lamennais (ob. 1854) and A. Bonnetty (ob. 1876). Having the same distrust for human reason, they sought the source of all religious and moral knowledge in human tradition which ultimately goes back to primitive revelation. Bonnetty had to subscribe to four articles proposed to him by the Roman Congregation of the Index (cf. DS 2811–2814). Articles 1 to 3 repeat the articles signed by Bautain and the doctrine of Qui Pluribus *(cf. nn. 106ff). Only article 4 is quoted here; it defends the scholastic method which was attacked by Traditionalism on account of its rational procedure.*

3. Most important among Pius IX's earlier encyclicals is Qui Pluribus, *which is concerned with the controversy around Fideism on the one hand, and Rationalism in the form of Hermesianism, on the other. The two fundamental errors of Hermes (1775–1831), professor of dogmatic theology in Bonn, were: 1) at the beginning of all theological knowledge there is absolute doubt; 2) the grounds for assent to faith are not different from the grounds for assent to natural knowledge; in both cases it is the inner necessity of the human capacity for knowledge which compels assent; this is held necessary in order to preserve human dignity. Thereby, however, the difference between natural and supernatural knowledge is suppressed. The encyclical rejects Rationalism, and positively asserts that there can be no contradiction between faith and reason; it then explains the role of reason in relation to the Christian faith.*

4. In view of the critical situation of the Church, not only with regard to the theological sciences, but in ethical, social, political and other matters as well, Pius IX composed a Syllabus of 80 propositions containing what seemed to be the most dangerous errors of the time (cf. DS 2901–2980); it is joined to the encyclical Quanta cura. *In this syllabus, the Pope condemned among others the errors of Rationalism and of rationalistic trends (Semi-rationalism).*

PROMISE SIGNED BY L. E. BAUTAIN (1844)

We promise today and for the future *never to teach:*

101
2765
1. That one cannot give a true proof for the existence of God by the light of rightly ordained reason only, apart from divine revelation.

102
2766
2. That by reason alone one cannot demonstrate the spirituality and immortality of the soul or any other purely natural, rational or moral truth.

103
2767
3. That by reason alone one cannot have the knowledge of principles or metaphysics as well as of the truths that depend on them, a knowledge totally distinct from supernatural theology which is based on divine revelation.

104
2768
4. That reason cannot acquire a true and full knowledge of the motives of credibility, i.e., of those motives which make the divine revelation evidently credible, such as especially the miracles and prophecies, and in particular the resurrection of Jesus Christ.

THE 4th PROPOSITION SIGNED BY A. BONNETTY (1855)

105
2814
4. The method used by St Thomas, St Bonaventure and after them by other Scholastic theologians does not lead to rationalism, and has not been the cause why philosophy in modern schools moves towards naturalism and pantheism. Hence one should not blame these doctors and teachers for using this method, especially as they did so with the approval or at least the silent consent of the Church.

PIUS IX

ENCYCLICAL LETTER *QUI PLURIBUS* (1846)

(Condemnation of Rationalism)

106
2775
(The enemies of Christianity do not hesitate to teach) that the sacred mysteries of our faith are fictions and human inventions, that the doctrine of the Catholic Church is hostile

to the good and welfare of human society. They do not refrain from renouncing even Christ Himself and God. To mislead people more easily and to deceive mainly the imprudent and the unlearned and to lead them into their own erroneous ways, they claim to be the only ones who know the road to prosperity; they do not hesitate to usurp the name of philosophers as though philosophy, which is totally engaged in the investigation of natural truth, would have to reject what the supreme and merciful God, the author of all nature, has deigned to reveal to men in His singular generosity and mercy so that they should attain true happiness and salvation.

107   Hence they never cease with absurd and fallacious ways
2776   of argumentation to appeal to the power and excellence
        of human reason and to extol it against the holy faith in Christ; they boldly assert that this faith is contrary to reason.

Surely nothing more foolish, more impious, more opposed to reason itself can be imagined. For, though faith is above reason, there can never be found a real contradiction or disagreement between them, as both of them originate from the same source of immutable and eternal truth, from the good and great God, and both so help each other that right reason demonstrates, safeguards and defends the truth of faith, whereas faith frees reason from all errors and through the knowledge of divine things enlightens, strengthens, and perfects it.

108   With similar fallacy these enemies of divine revelation,
2777   while paying supreme homage to human progress, attempt
        with arbitrary and sacrilegious means to introduce this progress into the Catholic religion as though this religion were the work not of God but of men, or a philosophical invention that could be perfected by human means. To those who so deplorably stray away one may apply the verdict with which Tertullian rightly condemned the philosophers of his age "who begot a stoic, platonic, and dialectic (Aristotelian) Christianity."[1] Indeed, as our holy religion is not invented by human reason but mercifully revealed by God to men, everyone can easily see that this religion receives all its strength from the authority of God who has spoken, and can never be deduced or perfected by human reason.

---

1. TERTULLIAN, *De praescriptione haereticorum,* 7, 11.

(Reason leads to faith)

109 It is the duty of human reason with diligence to inquire
2778 into the fact of revelation—lest it be deceived and fall into
error in such an important matter—in order that it may be
assured that God has spoken and that it may offer Him an intelligent
obedience as the apostle wisely teaches *(cf. Rom. 12.1 Vulg.).* For
who would not know, or could not know, that all faith must be given
to God when He speaks, and that nothing corresponds more to
reason than to accept and firmly to adhere to whatever is known to
be revealed by God who can neither err nor deceive?

110 But how many, how wonderful, how lucid are the argu-
2779 ments at hand by which reason ought to be thoroughly convinced that Christ's religion is divine and that "our doctrines
in their entirety have their roots from above, in the Lord of heaven";[2]
that therefore there is nothing more certain than our faith, nothing
safer, nothing more holy, nothing that rests on firmer principles. It is
this faith that is the teacher of life, the guide to salvation, the mother
and nurse of virtues. This faith is confirmed through the birth, the life,
the death, the resurrection, the wisdom, the miracles and prophecies
of its author and fulfiller, Christ Jesus. Everywhere it shines with the
light of its heavenly doctrine; it is enriched through the treasures of
celestial riches; through so many predictions of prophets, through
the splendour of so many miracles, through the constancy of so
many martyrs and the glory of so many saints it shines forth, clear
and sublime. Proclaiming the saving laws of Christ, acquiring ever
greater strength from the most cruel persecutions themselves, it has
spread over the whole earth, on land and sea, from sunrise to sunset
with only the cross as its standard. It has overthrown the fallacy of
idols and dissipated the darkness of errors; it has triumphed over
enemies of every kind; it has illumined all peoples, races and nations,
however barbarous and crude, and no matter how different in their
natural gifts, customs, laws and social structures, with the light of
divine knowledge; it has subjected them to the easy yoke of Christ
Himself *(cf. Mt. 11.30),* announcing peace and good tidings to all. All
this is totally resplendent with such brightness of the divine wisdom
and power that every reflecting mind easily understands that the
Christian faith is God's work.

---

2. JOHN CHRYSOSTOM, *Interpretatio in Is.,* 1, 1.

111   Thus, human reason clearly and manifestly recognises
2780   from these altogether lucid and firm arguments that God is
          the author of this faith. It can proceed no further, but it has
fully to reject, and to rid itself of any difficulty and doubt and offer
total surrender to this faith, because it is assured that, whatever this
faith proposes to man to believe and to do, is given by God.

SYLLABUS OF CONDEMNED ERRORS (1864)

(Errors of Rationalism condemned)

[112/2]   Every influence of God on man and world must be
2902   denied.

[112/3]   Human reason is, without any reference to God, the
2903   sole judge of truth and falsehood, of good and evil; it is
          autonomous, and by its natural powers is sufficient to
assure the welfare of men and nations.

[112/4]   All religious truths originate from the natural power of
2904   human reason. Hence reason is the principal norm by
          which man can and must reach knowledge of whatever
kind of truths.

[112/5]   Divine revelation is imperfect and hence subject to
2905   continual and indefinite progress, which ought to
          correspond to the progress of human reason.

[112/6]   The faith in Christ is detrimental to human reason; and
2906   divine revelation not only is of no use but is even harmful
          to man's perfection.

[112/7]   The prophecies and miracles set forth in the narration
2907   of the Sacred Scriptures are poetical fictions; the
          mysteries of the Christian faith are the outcome of philoso-
phical reflections; in the books of both Testaments mythical tales are
contained; Jesus Christ Himself is a mythical fiction.

(Errors of Semi-rationalism condemned)

[112/8]   Since human reason is on a par with religion itself, theo-
2908   logical disciplines have to be handled in the same man-
          ner as the philosophical ones.

[112/9]   All dogmas of the Christian religion are, without dis-

2909   tinction, the object of natural science or of philosophy; human reason with only historical training can, by means of its natural powers and principles, come to a true understanding of all, even the more obscure dogmas, provided only that such dogmas be proposed to reason as its object.

[112/10] As there is a distinction between the philosopher and
2910   his philosophy, he has the right and the duty to submit himself to the authority which he acknowledges as legitimate; but philosphy neither can nor must submit to any authority.

[112/11] The Church must not only abstain from any interfer-
2911   ence with philosophy; she must also tolerate the errors of philosophy, and leave it to philosophy to correct itself.

THE FIRST VATICAN GENERAL COUNCIL
THIRD SESSION
DOGMATIC CONSTITUTION *DEI FILIUS* ON THE CATHOLIC
FAITH (1870)

To meet the numerous problems of the time, Pope Pius IX summoned the 20th General Council. It met in the Vatican from December 1869 to September 1870. From among the many drafts proposed to the Council only two Constitutions were finalised, the first on the Catholic faith, the second on the primacy and infallibility of the Pope (cf. nn. 818 ff).

In the four chapters of the Constitution on the Catholic Faith and in the corresponding canons, the Church set forth the doctrine against the current errors of the 19th century: materialism, rationalism, pantheism, and also against the dangerous trends of fideism and traditionalism. The first chapter deals with God and creation (cf. nn. 412–413); the second with revelation, its relation to human reason, and the channels of Scripture and Tradition through which revelation is communicated; the third chapter treats of faith, its rational and supernatural foundations and its place in the Christian life; the fourth enters into the complex problems of the relation between faith and reason.

The doctrine of the Council is expressed in terms of 19th century theology. Revelation is presented primarily as the communication of supernatural truth inaccessible to natural reason, and faith as the acceptance of the revealed truth. The Second Vatican Council will later complement this doctrine with a more personalistic approach, according to which revelation appears as the self-communication of God, and faith as the free act of man's response in a commitment of his whole person.

Chapter II: Revelation

(Natural knowledge of God and supernatural revelation)

113   The same Holy Mother Church holds and teaches that

3004   God, the beginning and end of all things, can be known with certainty from the things that were created through the natural light of human reason, for "ever since the creation of the world His invisible nature has been clearly perceived in the things that have been made" *(Rom. 1.20);* but that it pleased His wisdom and bounty to reveal Himself and His eternal decrees in another and a supernatural way, as the apostle says: "In many and various ways God spoke of old to our fathers by the prophets; but in these last days He has spoken to us by the Son" *(Heb. 1.1-2).*

(The necessity of divine revelation)

114   It is to be ascribed to this divine revelation that such *3005*   truths among things divine as of themselves are not beyond human reason can, even in the present condition of mankind, be known by everyone with facility, with firm certitude and with no admixture of error. It is, however, not for this reason that revelation is to be called absolutely necessary, but because God in His infinite goodness has ordained man to a supernatural end, viz.,to share in the good things of God which utterly exceed the intelligence of the human mind, for "no eye has seen, nor ear heard, nor the heart of man conceived, what God prepared for those who love him"*(1 Cor. 2.9).*

(The rest of the chapter is found in n. 216).

Canons on Chapter II

115   1. If anyone says that the One true God, our Creator and *3026*   Lord, cannot be known with certainty with the natural light of human reason through the things that are created, *anathema sit.*

116   2. If anyone says that it is impossible or useless for man *3027*   to be taught through divine revelation about God and the cult to be rendered to Him, *anathema sit.*

117   3. If anyone says that man cannot be called by God to a *3028*   knowledge and perfection that surpasses the natural, but that he can and must by himself, through constant progress, finally arrive at the possession of all that is true and good, *anathema sit.*

Chapter III: Faith

(Definition of faith)

118   Since man is totally dependent upon God, as upon his
3008   Creator and Lord, and since created reason is absolutely
          subject to uncreated truth, we are bound to yield by faith the
full homage of intellect and will to God who reveals Himself. The
Catholic Church professes that this faith, which is the "beginning of
man's salvation" *(cf. n. 1935),* is a supernatural virtue whereby,
inspired and assisted by the grace of God, we believe that what He
has revealed is true, not because the intrinsic truth of things is
recognised by the natural light of reason, but because of the authority of God Himself who reveals them, who can neither err nor
deceive. For faith, as the apostle testifies, is "the assurance of things
hoped for, the conviction of things not seen" *(Heb. 11.1).*

(The rational basis of faith)

119   However, in order that the obedience of our faith be
3009   nevertheless in harmony with reason *(cf. Rom. 12.1),* God
          willed that exterior proofs of His revelation, viz. divine facts,
especially miracles and prophecies, should be joined to the interior
helps of the Holy Spirit; as they manifestly display the omnipotence
and infinite knowledge of God, they are the most certain signs of the
divine revelation, adapted to the intelligence of all men. Therefore
Moses and the prophets, and especially Christ our Lord Himself,
performed many manifest miracles and uttered prophecies; and of
the apostles we read: "They went forth and preached everywhere,
while the Lord worked with them and confirmed the message by the
signs that attended it" *(Mk 16.20);* and again it is written: "We have
the prophetic word made more sure; you will do well to pay attention
to this as to a lamp shining in a dark place" *(2 Pet. 1.19).*

(Faith as God's gift)

120   Though the assent of faith is by no means a blind impulse
3010   of the mind, still no man can "assent to the Gospel mes-
          sage", as is necessary to obtain salvation, "without the illumi-
nation and inspiration of the Holy Spirit, who gives to all joy in
assenting to the truth and believing it" *(cf. n. 1919).* Wherefore faith
itself, even when it is not working through love *(cf. Gal. 5.6),* is in itself
a gift of God, and the act of faith is a work appertaining to salvation,

by which man yields voluntary obedience to God Himself by assenting to and cooperating with grace, which he could resist.

(The object of faith)

121   Further, all those things are to be believed with divine and
3011   Catholic faith which are contained in the word of God,
          written or handed down, and which by the Church, either in
solemn judgment or through her ordinary and universal teaching
office, are proposed for belief as having been divinely revealed.

(The necessity of faith for salvation)

122   Since "without faith it is impossible to please God" *(Heb.*
3012   *11.6)* and to attain to the fellowship of His sons, there-
          fore without faith no one has ever attained justification, nor
will anyone obtain eternal life unless he has persevered in it to the end
(cf. Mt. 10.22; 24.13). However, to enable us to fulfil the obligation to
embrace the true faith and persistently to persevere in it, God has
instituted the Church through His only-begotten Son and has
endowed her with manifest marks of His institution so that she may
be recognised by all men as the guardian and teacher of the revealed
word.

(The Church as guarantee of revelation)

123   To the sole Catholic Church belong all the manifold and
3013   wonderful endowments which by divine disposition are
          meant to put into light the credibility of the Christian faith.
Nay more, the Church by herself, with her marvellous propagation,
eminent holiness and inexhaustible fruitfulness in everything that is
good, with her Catholic unity and invincible stability, is a great and
perpetual motive of credibility and an irrefutable testimony of her
divine mission.

3014   Thus, like a standard lifted up among the nations *(cf. Is.*
          11.12), she invites to herself those who do not yet believe, and
at the same time gives greater assurance to her children that the faith
which they profess rests on solid ground.

(The inner grace as guarantee of faith)

124   To this testimony the efficacious help coming from the
3014   power above is added. For the merciful Lord stirs up and aids
          with His grace those who are wandering astray, that they be

able to "come to the knowledge of the truth" *(1 Tim. 2.4)*, and those whom "He has called out of darkness into His admirable light" *(1 Pet. 2.9)*. He confirms them with His grace that they may persevere in this light, for He deserts none who does not desert Him *(cf. n. 1938)*. Therefore, the condition of those who by the heavenly gift of faith have embraced the Catholic truth, and of those who led by human opinions follow a false religion, is by no means the same. For, those who have received the faith under the teaching authority of the Church can never have a just reason to change this same faith or to call it into question. For this reason, "giving thanks to God the Father who has qualified us to share in the inheritance of the saints in light" *(Col. 1.12)*, let us not neglect so great a salvation, but "looking to Jesus the pioneer and perfecter of our faith" *(Heb. 12.2)*, "let us hold fast the confession of our hope without wavering" *(Heb. 10.23)*.

Canons on Chapter III

125 1. If anyone says that human reason is so independent that *3031* faith cannot be enjoined upon it by God, *anathema sit.*

126 2. If anyone says that divine faith is not distinct from the *3032* natural knowledge of God and of moral truths; that, therefore, for divine faith it is not necessary that the revealed truth be believed on the authority of God who reveals it, *anathema sit.*

127 3. If anyone says that divine revelation cannot be made *3033* credible by outward signs, and that, therefore, men ought to
be moved to faith solely by each one's inner experience or by personal inspiration, *anathema sit.*

128 4. If anyone says that no miracles are possible, and that, *3034* therefore, all accounts of them, even those contained in Holy
Scripture, are to be dismissed as fables and myths; or that miracles can never be recognised with certainty, and that the divine origin of the Christian religion cannot be legitimately proved by them, *anathema sit.*

129 5. If anyone says that the assent to the Christian faith is *3035* not free but is produced with necessity by arguments of
human reason; or that the grace of God is necessary only for that living faith which works by love, *anathema sit.*

130 6. If anyone says that the condition of the faithful and

3036 of those who have not yet attained to the only true faith is the
same, so that Catholics could have a just reason for suspend-
ing their judgment and calling into question the faith which they have
already received under the teaching authority of the Church, until
they have completed a scientific demonstration of the credibility and
truth of their faith, *anathema sit.*

Chapter IV: Faith and Reason

(The twofold order of religious knowledge)

131 The perpetual common belief of the Catholic Church has
3015 held and holds also this: there is a twofold order of
knowledge, distinct not only in its principle but also in its
object; in its principle, because in the one we know by natural reason,
in the other by divine faith; in its object, because apart from what
natural reason can attain, there are proposed to our belief mysteries
that are hidden in God, which can never be known unless they are
revealed by God. Hence the apostle who, on the one hand, testifies
that God is known to the gentiles in the things that have been made
(cf. Rom. 1.20), on the other hand, when speaking about the grace
and truth that came through Jesus Christ *(cf. Jn 1.17),* proclaims:
"We speak the wisdom of God in a mystery, a wisdom which is
hidden, which God ordained before the world unto our glory, which
none of the princes of this world knew.... But to us God has revealed
by His Spirit. For the Spirit searches everything, yea the deep
things of God" *(1 Cor. 2.7-10 Vulg.).* The only-Begotten Himself
praises the Father because He has hidden these things from the wise
and understanding and has revealed them to babes *(cf. Mt. 11.25).*

(Task and limits of reason)

132 Nevertheless, if reason illumined by faith inquires in an
3016 earnest, pious and sober manner, it attains by God's grace a
certain understanding of the mysteries, which is most
fruitful, both from the analogy with the objects of its natural
knowledge and from the connection of these mysteries with one
another and with man's ultimate end. But it never becomes capable
of understanding them in the way it does truths which constitute its
proper object. For divine mysteries by their very nature so excel the
created intellect that, even when they have been communicated in
revelation and received by faith, they remain covered by the veil of
faith itself and shrouded as it were in darkness as long as in this

mortal life "we are away from the Lord; for we walk by faith, not by sight" *(2 Cor. 5.6-7).*

(Faith and reason cannot contradict each other)

133   However, though faith is above reason, there can never be
3017   a real discrepancy between faith and reason, since the
             same God who reveals mysteries and infuses faith has bes-
towed the light of reason on the human mind, and God cannot deny
Himself, nor can truth ever contradict truth. The deceptive appearance of such a contradiction is mainly due to the fact that either the
dogmas of faith have not been understood and expounded according
to the mind of the Church, or that uncertain theories are taken for
verdicts of reason. Thus "we define that every assertion that is
opposed to enlightened faith is utterly false" *(Lateran V: DS 1441).*

134   Further, the Church which, along with the apostolic office
3018   of teaching, received the charge of guarding the deposit of
             faith has also from God the right and the duty to proscribe
what is falsely called knowledge *(cf. 1. Tim. 6.20),* lest anyone be
deceived by philosophy and vain fallacy *(cf. Col. 2.8).* Hence all
believing Christians are not only forbidden to defend as legitimate
conclusions of science such opinions which they realise to be contrary to the doctrine of faith, particularly if they have been condemned by the Church, but they are seriously bound to account
them as errors which put on the fallacious appearance of truth.

(Mutual support of faith and reason)

135   Not only can there be no conflict between faith and reason,
3019   they also support each other since right reason demon-
             strates the foundations of faith and, illumined by its light,
pursues the science of divine things, while faith frees and protects
reason from errors and provides it with manifold insights. It is therefore far remote from the truth to say that the Church opposes the
study of human arts and sciences; on the contrary, she supports and
promotes them in many ways. She does not ignore or despise the
benefits that human life derives from them. Indeed, she confesses: as
they have their origin from God who is the Lord of knowledge *(cf. 1
Sam. 2.3),* so too, if rightly pursued, they lead to God with His grace.
Nor does the Church in any way forbid that these sciences, each in
its sphere, should make use of their own principles and of the method
proper to them. While, however, acknowledging this just freedom, she
seriously warns lest they fall into error by going contrary to the divine

doctrine, or, stepping beyond their own limits, they enter into the sphere of faith and create confusion.

(The development of dogma)

136 For the doctrine of faith which God has revealed has not
3020 been proposed like a philosophical system to be per-
fected by human ingenuity, but has been committed to the spouse of Christ as a divine trust to be faithfully kept and infallibly declared. Hence also that meaning of the sacred dogmas is perpetually to be retained which our Holy Mother Church has once declared, and there must never be a deviation from that meaning on the specious ground and title of a more profound understanding. "Therefore, let there be growth and abundant progress in understanding, knowledge and wisdom, in each and all, in individuals and in the whole Church, at all times and in the progress of ages, but only within the proper limits, i.e., within the same dogma, the same meaning, the same judgment."[1]

Canons on Chapter IV

137 1. If anyone says that in divine revelation no true and
3041 properly so called mysteries are contained but that all dog-
mas of faith can be understood and demonstrated from natural principles by reason, if it is properly trained, *anathema sit.*

138 2. If anyone says that human sciences are to be pursued
3042 with such liberty that their assertions, even if opposed to
revealed doctrine, may be held as true and cannot be proscribed by the Church, *anathema sit.*

139 3. If anyone says that, as science progresses, at times a
3043 sense is to be given to dogmas proposed by the Church,
different from the one which the Church has understood and understands, *anathema sit.*

Epilogue

140 Therefore, in fulfilment of our supreme pastoral office. we
3044 beseech in the love of Jesus Christ, and we command in
the authority of the same God our Saviour, all Christian faithful, and especially those who hold authority or are engaged in

---

1. VINCENT OF LERINS, *Commonitorium primum,* 23.

teaching, to put their zeal and effort in removing and eliminating these errors from the holy Church and in spreading the light of pure faith.

3045   It is, however, not enough to avoid the malice of heresy unless those errors which lead close to it are also carefully avoided. We therefore remind all of their duty to observe also the constitutions and decrees by which such perverse opinions, which are not explicitly enumerated here, are proscribed by this Holy See.

LEO XIII

ERRORS OF A. ROSMINI-SERBATI CONDEMNED BY THE HOLY OFFICE (1887)

Though the orthodoxy of Rosmini (1797–1855) had been questioned during his lifetime, his books were declared free from errors by the Congregation of the Index in 1854. Yet, after his death renewed doubts were raised, and in 1887 the Holy Office condemned 40 propositions taken mainly from his posthumous works. The following two propositions are taken from his Teosofia *(1859), but are too much isolated from their context. They are reproduced here not so much for their historical interest—whether or not they could be understood in an orthodox sense— but because of their significance for our time. Our natural knowledge of God is not intuitive; it is through the limited experience of created things that we have access to God's transcendent mystery.*

[141]   1. In the order of created things there is immediately
3201   manifested to the human intellect something divine in itself, such that it belongs to the divine nature.

[142]   5. The being *(esse)* that man sees must necessarily be
3205   something of the necessary and eternal Being *(entis)*, of the cause that creates, determines, and perfects all contingent beings; and that is God.

PIUS X

OATH AGAINST THE ERRORS OF MODERNISM (1910)

Modernism has become the generic name for the most varied attempts to reconcile the Christian religion with the findings of agnostic philosophy, rationalistic science of history, and in general with all those cultural movements which in their development have progressively become estranged from religion or have set themselves in hostile opposition to it. In this general sense modernism practically covers all the abortive attempts of the nineteenth century to find a satisfactory solution to the problem of revelation and its proofs in the face of modern science and philosophy.

In the technical sense, in which the term is used here, modernism comprises those systems which yielded to the attacks made against the foundations of the Christian faith and, therefore, sought a new basis for religion. This basis no longer consists in absolute philosophical certitudes about God, creation, etc., and in the historical certitudes concerning the event of Jesus Christ and His work, but solely in man's inner self, in the religious experience, and in the power with which this experience asserts itself in the Church and throughout the world in all cultures and ages. Through this interiorisation of religion modernism stands against a religious rationalism, but also against Christianity with its insistence on positive revelation.

After repeated individual initiatives, Pius X finally opposed modernism in an official manner in the decree Lamentabili *(1907) which rejects its most important errors (DS 3401-3466), and in the encyclical* Pascendi *(1907) which contains a wide-ranging exposition of its various doctrines and attempts to systematise them (DS 3475-3500).*

In 1910 the entire body of the clergy involved in pastoral work or in the teaching profession was obliged to take an oath rejecting the essential errors of modernism concerning revelation and tradition. On account of the concise form in which it summarises the modernist errors, this oath, apart from its disciplinary importance, has also considerable doctrinal value as a document of the Church's teaching authority. The formula has been replaced by a short text in 1967 (cf. n. 32i).

143   I firmly embrace and accept each and everything that is
3537   defined, proposed and declared by the infallible teaching
         authority of the Church, and in particular those principal
truths which are directly opposed to the errors of this time.

143/1 First of all, I profess that God, the beginning and the end
3538   of all things, can be known with certainty, and that His
         existence can also be proved through the natural light of
reason from the things that were made *(cf. Rom. 1.20)*, viz., from the
visible works of creation, as the cause from its effects.

143/2 Secondly, I recognise the exterior proofs of revelation,
3539   that is to say, the divine works, mainly the miracles and
         prophecies, as sure signs of the divine origin of the Christian
religion, and I hold that they are well adapted to the understanding of
all ages and of all men, also those of the present time.

143/3 Thirdly, I hold with equally firm faith that the Church, the
3540   guardian and teacher of the revealed word, was person-
         ally *(proxime)* and directly instituted by the true historical
Christ Himself during His life among us, and that it is built upon
Peter, the prince of the apostolic hierarchy and upon his successors
through the ages.

143/4 Fourthly, I sincerely accept the doctrine of the faith which
3541   was handed down to us in the same meaning and always
        with the same purport from the apostles through the
orthodox Fathers. I therefore entirely reject the heretical theory of
the evolution of the dogmas, viz., that they change from one meaning
to another, different from the one which the Church previously held.
I also condemn any error which substitutes to the divine trust left to
the Spouse of Christ to be faithfully guarded by her, a philosophical
system or a creation of human reflection which gradually developed
through human effort and is to be perfected in the future through
indefinite progress.

143/5 Fifthly, I hold with certainty and I sincerely confess that
3542   faith is not a blind impulse of religion welling up from the
        depth of the subconscious under the impulse of the heart and
the inclination of a morally conditioned will, but the genuine assent of
the intellect to a truth which is received from outside "by hearing". In
this assent, given on the authority of the all-truthful God, we hold to
be true what has been said, attested to, and revealed by the personal
God, our Creator and Lord.

143/6 I also submit myself with due respect and I adhere whole-
3543   heartedly to all the condemnations, declarations, and pres-
        cripts contained in the encyclical *Pascendi* and the decree
Lamentabili, particularly those referring to the so-called history of
dogma.

143/7 I also reject the error of those who maintain that the faith
3544   proposed by the Church can be contrary to history, and that
        the Catholic dogmas in the sense in which they are now
understood are irreconcilable with the origins of the Christian religion as they really were.

143/8 I condemn and reject also the conception of those who
3545   say that an educated Christian puts on a double personality,
        the one of a believer, the other of a historian, as though it were
allowed for the historian to hold something contrary to the faith of
the believer or to advance hypotheses from which it would follow
that the dogmas are false or doubtful, provided only that these are
not directly denied.

143/9 Equally I reject any way of judging and interpreting Holy

3546 Scripture which takes no account of the Church's Tradition, of the analogy of faith and the norms laid down by the apostolic See; which adheres to the theories of the rationalists, and presumptuously and rashly accepts textual criticism as the only supreme rule.

143/10 Equally I reject the opinion of those who maintain that
3547 a lecturer or writer on matters of historical theology must discard all preconceived opinions about the supernatural origin of Catholic Tradition or about the promise of divine help to preserve for ever all revealed truth; that the writings of the individual Fathers should be interpreted on purely scientific principles to the exclusion of all sacred authority, with the same freedom of judgment with which any profane document is studied.

143/11 Finally, I profess in general that I am completely adverse
3548 to the error of the Modernists who say that there is nothing divine in the sacred Tradition or—what is still worse— who admit it in a pantheistic sense, which would leave us with a bare and simple fact, on a par with the common facts of history, the fact, namely, that a band of men continued in subsequent ages through their efforts, their solicitude and ingenuity, the school that was started by Christ and His apostles.

143/12 Thus I hold, and shall continue to hold to my last breath,
3549 the faith of the Fathers in the sure charism of truth that is, has been, and always will be in the succession of the bishops from the apostles, for the purpose that not what seems better and more suited according to the culture of each age should be held, but that the absolute and immutable truth, which from the beginning was preached by the apostles, "should never be believed, never be understood, in a different way".[1]

143/13 I promise that I shall keep all this faithfully, wholly, and
3550 sincerely, that I shall keep it inviolate, never deviating from it in teaching or in any way in word or in writing. Thus I promise, thus I swear; so help me God and these holy gospels of God.

---

1. TERTULLIAN, *De praescriptione haereticorum*, 28.

PIUS XII

ENCYCLICAL LETTER *HUMANI GENERIS* (1950)

This encyclical issued on 12 August 1950 by Pius XII constitutes almost a new Syllabus of errors to be rejected; it is concerned with "certain false opinions which threaten to sap the foundation of Catholic teaching", as the encyclical itself describes its theme. It opposes certain theological and philosophical tendencies which had appeared in various places, notably in France (Nouvelle Theologie), *without, however, constituting a new system. The encyclical is correspondingly many-sided.*

Two passages are reproduced here. The first refers to the rational foundations of faith. Pius XII maintains the doctrine of Vatican I about the possibility of giving a rational proof for the philosophical and historical foundations of faith, but he admits the possibility of great subjective obstacles which may prevent their acceptance.

The second text deals with the expression of faith through changing philosophical systems. It admits the limitations of human concepts, but it asserts that the terms in which the divine revelation has been expressed do contain the word of God in a lasting and binding manner. It deplores the rashness with which the formulations of the faith are abandoned by some theologians.

(The rational basis of faith)

144 Though human reason is, strictly speaking, truly capable
3875 by its own natural power and light of attaining to a true and certain knowledge of the one personal God who watches over and controls the world by His providence, and of the natural law written in our hearts by the Creator; yet there are many obstacles which prevent reason from the effective and fruitful use of this inborn faculty. For the truths that refer to God and concern the relations between God and man wholly transcend the visible order of things, and, if they are translated into human action and influence it, they call for self-surrender and abnegation. The human mind, in its turn, is hampered in the attaining of such truths, not only by the impact of the senses and the imagination, but also by disordered appetites which are the consequences of original sin. So it happens that men in such matters easily persuade themselves that what they would not like to be true is false or at least doubtful.

145 Hence we have to admit that divine revelation is morally
3876 necessary in order that such religious and moral truths "as of themselves are not beyond human reason can, even in the present condition of mankind, be known by everyone with facility, with firm certitude and with no admixture of error" *(cf. n. 114).*

146 Difficulties may occur to the human mind also in forming

3876   a firm judgment concerning the credibility of the Catholic
       faith, though we are provided by God with such a wealth of
wonderful exterior signs by which the divine origin of the Christian
religion can be proved with certainty even by the natural light of
reason alone. But a man may be guided by prejudices, he may be
influenced by his passions and his ill intentions, and so he can turn
away from, and resist not only the evidence of the exterior signs
which is plain to the eyes, but also the heavenly inspirations which
God conveys to our minds.

Faith and theological terminology)

147   (Desirous to come as close as possible to the way of think-
3822   ing and speaking of modern systems, some theologians)
       hope that the way is made clear for re-stating dogma in terms
of modern philosophy, of immanentism, idealism, existentialism, or
any other system, according to the needs of the day. As for the
bolder spirits, they assert that this is possible and necessary,
because the mysteries of faith can never be formulated in notions
which adequately express the truth, but only in approximate
notions, which, as they say, are always subject to change, by which the
truth is indicated up to a point, but at the same time necessarily
deformed. Therefore, in their opinion, it is not absurd, rather it is
absolutely necessary, that theology should constantly exchange old
concepts for new ones, in accordance with various philosophies
which it uses as its instruments in the course of time. So theology
would express in a human way the same divine truths in different,
and even to some extent opposite ways, which, however, they
maintain, mean the same thing. They go on to say that the history of
dogma consists in giving an account of the various successive forms
in which revealed truth has been clothed, in accordance with the
various doctrines and theories which developed in the course of
centuries.

148   It will be clear, from all we have been saying, that the
3883   efforts made by these thinkers not merely lead to what is
       called dogmatic 'relativism' but already contain it. Such relati-
vism is strongly fostered by the disrespect they show for the doctrine
commonly handed down, and for the terminology by which it is
expressed. Surely, all are agreed that the terms expressing certain
ideas, as they are used in the schools and even by the teaching
authority of the Church itself, are susceptible of further perfecting
and refining; it is also known that the Church in the use of these

terms has not always been consistent. It is also clear that the Church cannot tie itself to any philosophical system which flourishes for a short time; but what has been built up in a common consensus by Catholic teachers in the course of centuries, in their effort to reach a certain understanding of the dogma, does certainly not rest on such flimsy grounds. It rests on principles and notions which are deduced from a true understanding of created things; in the deduction of these insights the divinely revealed truth, like a star, illumined the human mind through the Church. No wonder, then, that some of these conceptions have not only been used, but even have been sanctioned by ecumenical Councils, so that it is wrong to deviate from them.

THE SECOND VATICAN GENERAL COUNCIL
DOGMATIC CONSTITUTION *DEI VERBUM* (1965)

The Constitution Dei Verbum *is hailed both by Catholics and non-Catholics as one of the most constructive documents of the Council. It shows in a unique way the renewal of theological perspective adopted by the Council Fathers. The first draft, presented in the first session of the Council, was still couched in traditional text-book terminology, with an attitude of defensive apologetics. It was rejected. The final document does include the doctrine of Vatican I, but the perspective has changed. Revelation is presented as God's self-gift to man to make him share in the divine life. In the unfolding of the theme, the Constitution takes into account the biblical research and the findings of modern theology.*

The Constitution deals in 6 chapters: 1) with revelation itself; 2) with its transmission in Tradition; 3) with the inspiration of Holy Scripture ;4) with the revelation of the Old Testament; 5) with the revelation in Jesus Christ; 6) with Holy Scripture in the life of the Church.

Chapter I,2-5, is quoted here. These paragraphs contain the new perspectives on revelation developed by the Council: the nature of revelation (2), its preparatory stages leading to the coming of Jesus Christ (3), the fulness of revelation in Jesus Christ (4), and man's response to revelation in faith (5).

Chapter I: Revelation Itself

(The nature and object of revelation)

149 2. In His goodness and wisdom God chose to reveal Himself and to make known the mystery of His will *(cf. Eph. 1.9)*, by which through Christ, the Word made flesh, men have access in the Holy Spirit to the Father, and they are made partakers of the divine nature *(cf. Eph. 2.18; 2 Pet. 1.4)*. Through this revelation, therefore, the invisible God *(cf. Col. 1.15; 1 Tim. 1.17)*, out of the abundance of

His love, speaks to men as friends *(cf. Ex. 33.11; Jn 15.14-15)* and dwells among them *(cf. Bar. 3.38)*, so that He may invite and receive them into communion with Himself. This plan of revelation is realised by deeds and words intrinsically connected: the deeds wrought by God in the history of salvation manifest and confirm the teaching and the realities signified by the words, while the words themselves declare and explain the deeds and the mystery contained in them. The deepest truth thus revealed both about God and about man's salvation shines out for us in Christ, who is the mediator and at the same time the fulness of all revelation.

(The preparation of the Gospel-Revelation)

150 3. God who creates and sustains all things through the Word *(cf. Jn 1.3)* gives men permanent testimony to Himself in the created things *(cf. Rom. 1.19-20)*. Moreover, wishing to open the way of supernatural salvation, He revealed Himself to our first parents from the very beginning. After their fall he kindled in them the hope of salvation by His promise of redemption *(cf. Gen. 3.15)*. He continued to watch over mankind unceasingly so as to grant eternal life to all who seek salvation through the faithful pursuit of good works *(cf. Rom. 2.6-7)*. In His own time he called Abraham in order to make of him a great nation *(cf. Gen. 12.2)*. After the time of the patriarchs, He taught His people, through Moses and the prophets, to acknowledge Him as the one true living God, provident Father and just Judge, and to wait for the promised Saviour. In this way, down through the centuries, God was preparing the way for the Gospel.

(Jesus Christ is in His person the fulness of revelation)

151 4. After God had spoken in many and various ways through the prophets, "in these last days He has spoken to us by the Son" *(Heb. 1.1-2)*. For he sent His Son, the eternal Word, who enlightens all men, so that He might dwell among men and declare to them the secrets of God *(cf. Jn 1.1-18)*. Jesus Christ, therefore, the Word made flesh, sent as "a man to men",[1] "utters the words of God" *(Jn 3.34)* and accomplishes the work of salvation committed to Him by the Father *(cf. Jn 5.36; 17.4)*. To see Jesus is to see also the Father *(cf. Jn 14.9)*. Jesus, therefore, brings revelation to its final

---

1. *Epistola ad Diognetum*, 8, 4.

perfection by His whole presence and self-manifestation, by His words and deeds, His signs and wonders, particularly by His death and glorious resurrection, and finally by the sending of the Spirit of truth; He confirms with divine testimony the fact of revelation that God is with us to free us from the darkness of sin and death and to raise us up to life eternal.

The Christian dispensation, therefore, being the new and definitive Covenant, will never pass away, and we now await no new public revelation before the glorious manifestation of our Lord Jesus Christ *(cf. 1 Tim. 6.14; Tit. 2.13).*

(Revelation is to be received by faith)

152 5. To God who reveals Himself must be given "the obedience of faith" *(Rom. 16.26; cf. Rom.1.5; 2 Cor. 10.5-6),* by which man freely commits his whole self to God, offering "the full homage of intellect and will to God who reveals Himself" *(cf. n. 118)* and freely assenting to the revelation granted by Him. This faith cannot exist without the prevenient and assisting grace of God and the interior succour of the Holy Spirit, who moves the heart and turns it to God, opens the eyes of the mind, and gives "to all joy in assenting to the truth and in believing it" *(cf. n. 120).* The same Holy Spirit continually perfects the faith by His gifts so as to bring about an ever deeper understanding of revelation.

(The object of revelation)

(153) 6. *(The doctrine of Vatican I is reasserted, concerning man's natural power to know God by reason, the revelation of divine mysteries, and also of truths which by themselves can be the object of natural knowledge) (cf. n. 114).*

PASTORAL CONSTITUTION *GAUDIUM ET SPES* (1965)

(154) *It is characteristic of Vatican II that it places doctrinal questions into the context of actual life. God's revelation and man's response to it must be realised in our modern age of science, secularism and social transformation.* Gaudium et Spes *analyses the attitude of modern man towards God.*

The entire document conceives mankind as a comunity on its "journey to the Kingdom of the Father" (1); it answers man's questions "in the light of Christ, the image of the unseen God" (10). The Constitution vindicates the relevance of revelation and faith for man in his personal life, in society, and in the various spheres of his activities.

Of special significance is the section about modern atheism, i.e., man's refusal to accept God and His revelation. Atheism is considered under the following aspects:

1) The phenomenon of modern atheism: its widespread presence in the modern world with the result that it "must be accounted among the most serious problems of this age"; its various forms, and the reasons for its growing influence (19).

2) Systematic atheism: it claims to liberate the human mind as to make man "the sole artisan and creator of his own history"; to lead to "economic and social emancipation"; to guide man in the building up of the earthly city (20).

3) The Church's attitude: the significance of faith in God for man's personal life and for human society (21).

PAUL VI

ENCYCLICAL LETTER *ECCLESIAM SUAM* (1964)

While the Council through its documents inaugurated a new understanding both of the word of God and of the modern world in which it has to be proclaimed, and so prepared a new approach of the Chuch to human society, Pope Paul VI wrote his first encyclical Ecclesiam Suam *which outlines the renewed attitude of the Church to the world of today.*

Two passages of this encyclical referring to atheism *are quoted here. In fact, they are previous to the corresponding Council texts of* Gaudium et Spes. *The Pope speaks of the "concentric circles" with which the Church must enter into dialogue. The widest of these circles embraces the whole of mankind. It is in this context that the Pope speaks about atheism. The text is found in AAS 56 (1964) 650-653.*

(The destructive power of modern atheism)

155 We realise, however, that in this limitless circle there are many, very many unfortunately, who profess no religion; not a few also, we know, declare that they deny God in various ways. We are aware that some of them proclaim their godlessness openly and uphold it as a programme of human education and political conduct in the futile and fatal conviction that they are setting men free from obsolete and false opinions about life and the world, and put in their place, as they pretend, conceptions that are scientific and in conformity with the needs of modern progress.

156 This, indeed, is the most serious problem of our time. We are firmly convinced that the principles on which the denial of God is based are by their nature utterly erroneous; they are not in keeping with the ultimate and necessary requirements of thought; they deprive the rational order of the world of its true and effective foundations; they do not provide human life with sound judgment to solve problems but with an empty dogma which degrades and saddens it, and destroys at the root any social order which would base itself on it. Thus it does not bring freedom but is the source of the saddest fall, attempting to quench the light of the living God. We shall therefore resist with all our strength the evil assault of this denial; we do so in the supreme cause of truth, in virtue of our sacred duty faithfully to profess Christ and His Gospel, moved by a burning and unshakable love which inspires in us a concern for the fortunes of the human race. We do it in the invincible hope that modern man may feel again impelled, through those religious ideals which the Catholic faith sets before him, to pursue a civilisation that never declines but tends to the natural and supernatural perfection of the human mind, enabled by divine grace to possess temporal goods in peace and honour, and confidently hoping for the attainment of perennial goods.

(The roots of modern atheism)

157   But though we must speak firmly and clearly to preserve and defend religion and the human values which it proclaims and fosters, we are moved by our pastoral office to seek in the heart of the modern atheists the reasons of these disturbances and denial. One can easily see that these reasons are many and complex, so that we must examine them carefully and refute them effectively. Some of them arise from the demand that divine things be presented in a worthier and purer way than is the case in certain imperfect forms of language and worship; we ought to do all in our power to improve them and to make them more transparent so that they may express more adequately the sacred reality of which they are the signs. We see men with an earnest and often noble yearning, with hearts moved by zeal, and burning with ideals of the unattainable, who dream of justice and progress and seek in striving for a social order the attainment of values that to them appear the highest and almost divine. Such ideals for them are a substitute for Him who is the Absolute and Necessary; they testify to the fact that they are in the grip of the longing for that supreme Principle and End that cannot be eradicated from the human heart; it is for us, in the patient and wise exercise of the teaching ministry, to show that all this transcends man's nature as well as is immanent in it.

158   Again we see men accurately using the tools of human reasoning, at times not without some simplification, for the purpose of building up a notion of the whole universe founded on science. This search is all the less reprehensible as it often follows ways of logical procedure not unlike those received in the classical schools and based on a strict discipline of the mind. But, against the will of those who think that in this way they have found a sure support in defending atheism, this discipline impels them through its innate dynamism to proceed to the renewed and definite acknowledgment of the highest God, to a metaphysical and logical system. The atheistic politico-scientist deliberately stops this cogent process of reasoning at a certain point and so extinguishes the sovereign light through which the universe could become intelligible. Who of us would not effectively assist him to come, ultimately, to the realisation of the objective truth of the universe in which the mind is struck by the divine presence and the lips begin to utter humble words of consoling prayers?

159 At times we also find (atheists) of noble sentiments who are impatient with the mediocrity and the self-seeking of large sections of our present human society; they ingeniously borrow from our gospels ways of speaking and phrases, using them to express solidarity, mutual help and compassion. Shall we not be able to trace these words, which express moral values, back to their true source which is Christian?

DECLARATION *MYSTERIUM ECCLESIAE* OF THE
S. CONGREGATION FOR THE DOCTRINE OF THE FAITH
(11 May 1973)

This document on the mystery of the Church is primarily concerned with the charism of infallibility pertaining to the Church's teaching authority (cf. n. 883). While strongly upholding the traditional doctrine of infallibility, it nevertheless recognizes that dogmatic formulas are historically conditioned, with the result that they always remain incomplete and perfectible. This important section of the Declaration begins by acknowledging the "difficulties of various kinds" to which the transmission of divine Revelation is subject: these arise from the very nature of the mysteries of the faith (cf. n. 132); they "also arise from the historical condition that affects the expression of Revelation". With regard to this historical condition, the declaration makes considerations—somewhat novel in an official document—by which the unavoidable inadequacy and perfectibility of dogmatic formulas is brought out, and all of which "have to be taken into account in order that these pronouncements may be properly interpreted". It goes on to expose the important consequences deriving from these considerations as regards the interpretation of dogmatic formulas pronounced by the Church's teaching authority. It notes, however, that, incomplete and perfectible as they may be, these formulas remain true in their meaning; this excludes "dogmatic relativism". The text is found in AAS 65 (1973) 402-404.

(The historical conditioning of dogmatic formulas)

160   With regard to this historical conditioning, it must first be observed that the meaning of the pronouncements of faith depends partly upon the expressive power of the language used at a certain point in time and in particular circumstances. Moreover, it sometimes happens that some dogmatic truth is first expressed incompletely (but not falsely), and at a later date, when considered in a broader context of faith or human knowledge, it receives a fuller and more perfect expression. In addition, when the Church makes new pronouncements, she intends to confirm or clarify what is in some way contained in Sacred Scripture or in previous expressions of Tradition; but at the same time she usually has the intention of solving certain questions or removing certain errors. All these things have to be taken into account in order that these pronouncements may be properly interpreted. Finally, even though the truths which the Church intends to teach through her dogmatic formulas are distinct from the changeable conceptions of the given epoch and can be expressed without them, nevertheless it can sometimes happen that these truths may be enunciated by the Sacred Magisterium in terms that bear traces of such conceptions.

(The interpretation of dogmatic formulas)

161   In view of the above it must be stated that the dogmatic formulas of the Church's Magisterium were from the beginning suitable for communicating revealed truth, and that as they are they remain for ever suitable for communicating this truth to those who interpret them correctly. It does not however follow that everyone of these formulas has always been or will always be so to the same extent. For this reason theologians seek to define exactly the intention of teaching proper to the various formulas, and in carrying out this work they are of considerable assistance to the living Magisterium of the Church, to which they remain subordinated. For this reason also it often happens that ancient dogmatic formulas and others closely connected with them remain living and fruitful in the habitual usage of the Church, but with suitable expository and explanatory additions that maintain and clarify their original meaning. In addition, it has sometimes happened that in this habitual usage of the Church certain of these formulas gave way to new expressions which, proposed and approved by the Sacred Magisterium, presented more clearly or more completely the same meaning.

(Dogmatic relativism is excluded)

162 As for the meaning of dogmatic formulas, this remains ever true and constant in the Church, even when it is expressed with greater clarity or more developed. The faithful.therefore, must shun the opinion, first, that dogmatic formulas (or some category of them) cannot signify truth in a determinate way, but can only offer changeable approximations to it, which to a certain extent distort or alter it; secondly, that these formulas signify the truth only in an indeterminate way, this truth being like a goal that is constantly being sought by means of such approximations. Those who hold such an opinion do not avoid dogmatic relativism and they corrupt the concept of the Church's infallibility relative to the truth to be taught or held in a determinate way.

JOHN PAUL II

APOSTOLIC CONSTITUTION *SAPIENTIA CHRISTIANA* (1979)

The Church's dialogue with modern society, promoted by the Council, necessarily led to an opening of theology towards many spheres of culture and sciences. Theology rightly claims the freedom to investigate new realms in which the message of the Gospel has to be articulated.

Thus the relation of academic freedom in theological research and teaching to the hierarchical magisterium has had to be faced anew. In the Apostolic Constitution which promulgates the new legislation covering ecclesiastical academic studies in Universities and Faculties (29 April 1979), the relationship of academic freedom to ecclesiastical authority is carefully formulated: While "just freedom" is recognised both for teaching and research "within the limits of God's Word", teaching must be carried out in accordance with the Church's magisterium. The reason is that theology is taught in the name of the Church, while research may open out towards new avenues, provided it does so in "deference to the Church's Magisterium" and its function of authoritatively interpreting the Word of God.

(Theology and Magisterium)

163 39, 1. Following the norm of the Second Vatican Council, according to the nature of each faculty:

1) just freedom *(GS 59)* should be acknowledged in research and teaching so that true progress can be obtained in learning and understanding divine truth;

2) at the same time it is clear that:

a) true freedom in teaching is necessarily contained within the limits of God's Word as this is constantly taught by the Church's Magisterium;

b) likewise, true freedom in research is necessarily based

upon firm adherence to God's Word and deference to the Church's Magisterium, whose duty it is to interpret authentically the Word of God.

2. Therefore, in such a weighty matter one must proceed with prudence, with trust and without suspicion, at the same time with judgment and without rashness, especially in teaching, while working to harmonise studiously the necessities of science with the pastoral needs of the People of God.

ADDRESS TO SCIENTISTS

(15 November, 1980)

On November 15th, 1980, Pope John Paul II addressed a gathering of scientists and university students in the Cathedral of Cologne. It was on the feast of St Albert the Great, on the 700th anniversary of his death. In fact the invitation of the Pope to Germany was occasioned by this anniversary and Cologne had been the second home of the Saint. The historic importance of Albert the Great lies in the fact that in the first crucial encounter of secular sciences (Aristotelian philosophy) and traditional faith he took up a position which remains programmatic even today. The Pope used the occasion to propose in a systematic way the relation of science to faith in our time; this has radically changed from suspicion and hostility to complementarity and the recognised need, on both sides, of collaboration in a time of crisis of the scientific-technical culture. The text is found in Osservatore Romano *(English Edition), 24 November, 1980, pp. 6-7.*

(The recognition of science according to Albert the Great)

164 2. The claim to truth of a science based on rationality is recognised; in fact it is accepted in its contents, completed, corrected and developed in its independent rationality. And precisely in this way it becomes the property of the Christian world. In this way the latter sees its own understanding of the world enormously enriched without having to give up any essential element of its tradition, far less the foundation of its faith. For there can be no fundamental conflict between a reason which, in conformity with its own nature which comes from God, is geared to truth and is qualified to know truth, and a faith which refers to the same divine source of all truth.

(The conflicts of the past are deplored)

165 3. Many people... still feel the weight of those notorious conflicts which arose from the interference of religious authorities in the process of the development of scientific knowledge. The

Church remembers this with regret, for today we realise the errors and shortcomings of these ways of proceeding. We can say today that they have been overcome, thanks to the power of persuasion of science, and thanks above all to the work of a scientific theology, which has deepened the understanding of faith and freed it from the conditionings of time.

(The crisis of merely functional science)

166   3. Our culture, in all its areas, is imbued with a science which proceeds in a way that is largely functionalistic. This applies also to the area of values and norms, of spiritual orientation in general. Precisely here science comes up against its own limits. There is talk of a crisis of legitimation of science, nay more, of a crisis of orientation of our whole scientific culture. What is its essence?...

Science alone is not capable of answering the question of meanings; in fact it cannot even set it in the framework of its starting point. And yet this question of meanings cannot tolerate an indefinite postponement of its answer. If widespread confidence in science is disappointed, then the state of mind easily changes into hostility to science. In this space that has remained empty, ideologies suddenly break in. They sometimes behave as if they were "scientific", but they owe their power of persuasion to the urgent need for an answer to the question of meanings and to interest in social and political change. Science that is purely functional, without values and alienated from truth, can enter the service of these ideologies; a reason that is only instrumental runs the risk of losing its freedom....

(The criterion for the right use of science)

167   4. There is no reason to consider technico-scientific culture as opposed to the world of God's creation. It is clear beyond all doubt that technical knowledge can be used for good as well as for evil....Technical science, aimed at the transformation of the world, is justified on the basis of the service it renders man and humanity. ...Man's personal dignity represents the criterion by which all cultural application of technico-scientific knowledge must be judged.

(Science must safeguard man's freedom)

168   4. (Sciences extend also to) the scientific analysis of man and of the world in which he lives, at the social and cultural level. An absolutely incalculable mass of knowledge has thereby come to light, which has repercussions on both public and private life. The social system of modern states, the health and educational system, economic processes and cultural activities are all marked in many ways by the influence of these sciences. But it is important that science should not keep man under its thumb. Also in the culture of technology, man, in conformity with his dignity, must remain free; in fact it must be the meaning of this culture to give him greater freedom.

(Science is bound to truth)

169 5. To be able to influence praxis, (science) must first be determined by truth, and therefore be free for truth. A free science, bound only to truth, does not let itself be reduced to the model of functionalism or any other which limits understanding of scientific rationality....

I do not hesitate at all to see also the science of faith on the horizon of rationality understood in this way. The Church wants independent theological research, which is not identified with the ecclesiastical Magisterium, but which knows it is committed with regard to it in common service of the truth of faith and the People of God. It cannot be ignored that tensions and even conflicts may arise. But this cannot be ignored either as regards the relationship between Church and science. The reason is to be sought in the finiteness of our reason, limited in its extension and therefore exposed to error. Nevertheless we can always hope for a solution of reconciliation, if we take our stand on the ability of this same reason to attain truth.

(Science needs faith)

170 5. In the past precursors of modern science fought against the Church with the slogans: reason, freedom and progress. Today, in view of the crisis with regard to the meaning of science, the multiple threats to its freedom and the doubt about progress, the battle-fronts have been inverted. Today it is the Church that takes up the defence:

—for reason and science, which she recognises as having the ability to attain truth, which legitimises it as a human realisation;

—for the freedom of science, through which the latter possesses its dignity as a human and personal good;

—for progress in the service of a humanity which needs it to safeguard its life and its dignity.

With this task, the Church and all Christians are at the centre of the debate of these times of ours. An adequate solution of the pressing questions about the meaning of human existence, norms of action, and the prospects of a more far-reaching hope, is possible only in the renewed connection between scientific thought and the power of faith in man in search of truth. The pursuit of a new humanism on which the future of the third millennium can be based, will be successful only on condition that scientific knowledge again enters upon a living relationship with the truth revealed to man as God's gift. Man's reason is a grand intrument for knowledge and structuring of the world. It needs, however, in order to realise the whole wealth of human possibilities, to open to the Word of eternal Truth, which became man in Christ.

CHAPTER II

TRADITION AND SCRIPTURE

Divine revelation is God's manifestation in human history and society, realised "in deeds and words" (DV 2). The Old Covenant consists in the election, guidance and mission of the chosen people of Israel; the books of the Old Testament narrate and interpret these events so that in them God's own design for man, and ultimately the unfathomable mystery of the divine life itself, may shine forth. The New Testament is centred on the final event of salvation history, on Jesus Christ; its books contain the earthly life of Jesus of Nazareth, His exaltation, and His continued presence in the Church as the Risen Lord, as the centre of life of all who believe.

Christian revelation is contained in Tradition and Scripture. In a broad sense tradition stands for the collective acceptance and communication of truths and customs in a community; in the specific sense in which the Church documents speak of Tradition, it is the process by which divine revelation, coming from Jesus Christ through the apostles, is communicated and unfolded in the community of the Church; it may also be used for the content of the revelation so communicated. Jesus Himself has entrusted His mission and message to His disciples and has given them the guarantee of His assistance in the fulfilment of their task. So He made the living Church the medium through which His saving message should reach all mankind: "Go therefore and make disciples of all nations... and I am with you always to the close of the age" (Mt. 28.19).

Thus the living Tradition of the Church is the channel through which divine revelation comes to us. Every truth of faith comes to us by way of Tradition. This holds good even for Scripture itself. It is from the earliest Tradition that the sacred books were written, and it is through the living Church that they were recognised as inspired and gathered together in the Bible as the written word of God.

Holy Scripture, however, is more than just the first volume in a series of writings that make up Tradition. It consists of "inspired" books, i.e., books written under the special assistance of the Holy Spirit and therefore teaching "without error the truth which God wanted to be put into the sacred writings for the sake of our salvation" (DV 11). Thus they are the authentic expression of the divine revelation. They are the norm on which all further reflection on the divine revelation and its doctrinal expression are based.

As Holy Scripture grows from Tradition, so it is to be interpreted by it. It is spelled out in the life, worship, and teaching of the Church, under the ecclesiastical authority. Thus, God's word remains alive in the community, and is not confined to a dead letter. The word of God is not subject to free and arbitrary interpretations according to the changing spirit of the times; nor is the Bible merely the occasion whereby God Himself speaks His revealing word to individuals. To interpret it belongs to the Church, for the mission of Jesus Christ is entrusted to her.

The earliest documents of the Church have only very sketchy references to Scripture and Tradition as authoritative and authentic vehicles of revelation. Two main problems stand out in the early centuries. First is the continuity between the Old and New Testaments, against gnostic trends which attributed the Old Testament to a demiurge and only the New Testament to God the Father and His Son, Jesus Christ. The second is the establishment of the canon of inspired books.

It is only in the Council of Trent that the problem of the relation of Scripture to Tradition became prominent, because the Reformers denied the value of Tradition and considered Scripture as the only source of revelation. Without entering into the exact meaning of Tradition, Trent speaks of Scripture and Tradition as two sources of revelation. It is only in the Second Vatican Council that the mutual relation between Scripture and Tradition is clarified and presented in the context of a more comprehensive view of the unfolding of Christian doctrine as a dynamic process within the Christian community.

The more recent documents are mainly concerned with the questions raised by modern Bible criticism and by natural sciences and history. It is the merit of the Second Vatican Council that a predominantly apologetic attitude is replaced by the positive approach to Scripture and Tradition as the medium through which the word of God is constantly present in the Church.

*   *   *

The main points of doctrine contained in this chapter fall under the following headings:

Divine Revelation is contained both in Tradition and Scripture: 31, 39/13, 121, 206, 209, 210, 213, 216, 219, 246, 247.

Tradition transmits the word of God: 31, 143/4.11, 204, 205, 206, 210, 213, 215, 216, 219.

Tradition is found in the teaching of the Fathers, in liturgy, in the doctrine of the Councils: 31, 37, 143/12, 204, 205, 206, 209, 219, 222.

The Bible comprises the books of the Old and New Testaments: (201), (202), (203), 208, 210-213, 216, 218.

The Latin Vulgate is the accepted standard version: 213, 214, 233, 252-254.

The books of the Bible are, with all their parts, inspired and have God as author: 206, 207, 208, 210, 216, 218, 221, 226, 227, 228/9-16, 229, 230, 232, 249.

They contain salvific truth free from error: 128, 216, 226, 227, 228/11-16, 230, 231, 240, 249.

Their inerrancy is not limited to the moral and religious statements: 226, 230, 238.

The Bible is entrusted to the Church and is to be interpreted by her: 31, 39/13, 143/9, 208, 210, 215, 217, 220, 221, 228/1.4, 238, 248.

Its literal sense must be found: 234;

according to the literary genres: 236, 237, 239, 240-245.

The spiritual sense must be ascertained: 235.

The interpretation must be based on Tradition: 143/9, 215, 217, 220-222, 228/23, 238, 250.

Modern sciences are to be used as helps: 223, 232, 234.

There is no ultimate conflict with natural sciences: 223, 226;

nor with history: 223, 225, 228/14.16.24, 231.

The spiritual and theological use of Scripture: 255-257.

The place of Scripture in theology: 258.

THE COUNCIL OF LAODICEA (360?)

(The canon of Scripture)

(201) *(Canon 60 of the Council enumerates the books recognised as Sacred Scripture. Baruch is explicitly mentioned with Jeremiah but Tobit, Judith, Wisdom, Sirach, 1 and 2 Maccabees, and Revelation do not figure on the list).*

INNOCENT I

LETTER *CONSULENTI TIBI* TO EXSUPERIUS, BISHOP OF TOULOUSE (405)

(The canon of Scripture)

(202) *(All the deutero-canonical books of the Old Testament are listed.*
213 *Baruch is not explicitly mentioned but is most probably considered as a part of Jeremiah).*

GELASIUS I (492-496)
DECREE OF GELASIUS (time unknown)

This decree is a compilation of documents the various parts of which pertain to various periods. Its part II on the canon of scriptures goes back in substance to Pope Damasus I (366-384), even though the text as found in the Decree of Gelasius cannot be attributed to the Decree of Damasus (382).

(The canon of Scripture)

(203) *(Judith is placed at times before Esther and Esdra, at times after*
179 *these, and at times is omitted. Baruch is mentioned with Jeremiah,* "cum uno Baruch", *or omitted.)*

THE SECOND GENERAL COUNCIL OF CONSTANTINOPLE

PROFESSION OF FAITH (553)

The ultimate foundation for the inerrant Christian doctrine is not a proof drawn from Holy Scripture alone; still less is it one that is based on theological reasoning. It is the living Tradition itself, inherited from apostolic times. On this Council, see n. 619i and n. 620i.

(Tradition)

204 We profess that we hold and preach the faith which from the beginning was given to the apostles by our great God and Saviour Jesus Christ, and was proclaimed by them to the whole world. The holy Fathers professed, explained and handed on this faith to the holy Church, particularly those Fathers who took part in the four holy Councils which we follow and accept entirely for everything....

THE COUNCIL OF LATERAN (649)

(Tradition)

205 *Canon* 17: Whosoever does not confess, in accordance
517 with the holy Fathers, by word and from the heart, really and in
truth, to the last word, all that has been handed down and proclaimed to the holy, catholic and apostolic Church by the holy Fathers and by the five venerable General Councils, *condemnatus sit*.

THE SECOND GENERAL COUNCIL OF NICAEA (787)

(On ecclesiastical Tradition)

206 Anyone who does not accept the whole of the Church's
609 Tradition, both written and unwritten, *anathema sit*.

LEO IX

LETTER *CONGRATULAMUR VEHEMENTER* TO PETER, PATRIARCH OF ANTIOCH (1053)

The classic formula 'God is the author of both the Old and New Testaments' is taken from the Statuta Ecclesiae Antiqua. *Since the fifth century, the newly consecrated bishops had to profess their belief in the divine authorship of the Old Testament; Marcion had asserted that the Old Testament was inspired by the Devil.*

The formula occurs in most of the official documents on Biblical inspiration:

—*The Creed of Leo IX (1053)*	*(DS 685)*
—*The profession of faith for the Waldensians (1208)*	*(DS 790)*
—*The Council of Lyons (M. Palaeologus) (1274)*	*(DS 854)*
—*The Council of Florence (Jacobites) (1441)*	*(DS 1334)*
—*The Council of Trent (Session IV) (1546)*	*(DS 1501)*
—*The Council of Vatican I (Session III) (1870)*	*(DS 3006)*
—Providentissimus Deus, *Leo XIII (1893)*	*(DS 3293)*
—*The Decree* Lamentabili, *Pius X (1907)*	*(DS 3409)*
—*The Council of Vatican II,* Dei Verbum, *11 (1965)*	

The letter of Pope Leo IX, mentioned here, contains a profession of faith.

(God is the author of Scripture)

207 . . . I also believe that God, the Lord almighty, is the only

685   author of both the Old and the New Testaments, i.e., the Law
       and the Prophets, and the Apostles.

THE GENERAL COUNCIL OF FLORENCE
DECREE FOR THE JACOBITES (1442)

This decree was written in view of the reunion of the Jacobites. It reaffirms that God is the author of both Old and New Testaments, against gnostic ideas which were still surviving. The Jacobites themselves held a number of apocryphal books to be inspired. Hence the list of the canonical books was also included. It will be repeated later by the Council of Trent.

(God is the author of the books of the Old and New Testaments)

208   (The holy Roman Church) professes that one and the
1334   same God is author of the Old and New Testaments, i.e., of
       the Law, the Prophets and the Gospel, because by inspira-
tion of one and the same Holy Spirit the saints of both convenants
have spoken. She accepts and venerates their books....

(There follows the list of canonical books: DS 1335; cf. the Council of Trent: nn. 211-212).

THE COUNCIL OF PARIS (Senonense) (1528)

The Reformers rejected Tradition and adhered to Scripture only, sola Scriptura. This regional Council condemns this teaching in its fifth decree. The text is found in Enchiridion Biblicum (1954), n. 55.

(Some truths which are not explicitly contained in Scripture must be firmly believed)

209   5. There is no doubt that Scripture covers a vast field of
       religious doctrines and expounds them with ineffable profun-
dity. It is nevertheless a pernicious error to think that nothing has to
be believed that is not expressed in Scripture; indeed many traditions have come from Christ through the apostles to later generations and have been transmitted from mouth to mouth by familiar
discourse. All these must be accepted with unshakable conviction,
even though they are not contained explicitly in sacred Scripture.

THE GENERAL COUNCIL OF TRENT
FOURTH SESSION
DECREE ON SACRED BOOKS AND ON TRADITIONS TO BE
RECEIVED (1546)

The Reformers challenged the position of the Church concerning both Scripture and Tradition. As to the Canon of the Bible, already Erasmus of Rotterdam had taught that several parts of the Scripture were not authen-

tic. Martin Luther distinguished three groups of books: first those featuring God's work of salvation (John, Romans, Galatians, Ephesians, 1 Peter and 1 John); secondly other canonical books (Synoptics, Acts, the rest of the Pauline epistles, 2 Peter and 2 John); thirdly non-canonical books (Hebrews, James, Jude, Revelation, various books of the Old Testament).

Tradition as a source of revelation was unanimously rejected by the Refomers.

The Council distinguished between external traditions (fasting, penitential discipline, rituals, etc.) and traditons of faith, i.e., such traditional elements in doctrine, prayer, feasts, etc., which are evidence of a truth of faith as belonging to what the Church has held from apostolic times. They may be transmitted orally or in writing. The Council was not concerned with external traditions, but only with traditions of faith; but it refrained from listing such individual truths in connection with original sin.

The Council also sought in a special decree to counter abuses concerning the use of the Bible. There was no standard version; the text was in many places corrupt; liturgical books often contained incomplete quotations. There was also much arbitrariness in interpretation and preaching. No ecclesiastical approbation was sought for interpretations or new editions.

The decree accepted the Vulgate as the 'authentic' Latin version. In the context, 'authentic' does not refer to the origin or authorship of the sacred books, but to the accuracy of the translation, in the sense that it contains no dogmatic error and reproduces the substance of the written word of God.

The decree further states that the interpretation of Scripture must be in agreement with the Church's Tradition.

(Written books and unwritten traditions)

210
1501

The holy ecumenical and general Council of Trent... has always this purpose in mind that in the Church errors be removed and the purity of the Gospel be preserved. This Gospel was promised of old through the prophets in the Sacred Scriptures; Our Lord Jesus Christ, Son of God, first promulgated it from His own lips; He in turn ordered that it be preached through the apostles to all creatures as the source of all saving truth and rule of conduct. The Council clearly perceives that this truth and rule are contained in the written books and unwritten traditions which have come down to us, having been received by the apostles from the mouth of Christ Himself or from the apostles by the dictation of the Holy Spirit, and have been transmitted as it were from hand to hand. Following, then, the example of the orthodox Fathers, it receives and venerates with the same sense of loyalty and reverence all the books of the Old and New Testaments—for God alone is the author of both—together with all the traditions concerning faith and morals, as coming from the mouth of Christ or being inspired by the Holy Spirit and preserved in continuous succession in the Catholic Church.

(The Canon of Scripture)

211 The Council has thought it proper to insert in this decree
1502 a list of the sacred books, so that no doubt may remain
as to which books are recognised by the Council.
They are the following:

Old Testament: The five books of Moses, i.e., Genesis, Exodus, Leviticus, Numbers, Deuteronomy; Joshua, Judges, Ruth, four books of Kings, two of Chronicles, the first book of Ezra, the second book of Ezra called the book of Nehemiah, Tobit, Judith, Esther, Job, the book of Psalms of David containing 150 psalms, Proverbs, Ecclesiastes, the Song of Songs, Wisdom, Ecclesiasticus, Isaiah, Jeremiah with Baruch, Ezechiel, Daniel, the twelve minor prophets, i.e., Hosea, Joel, Amos, Obadiah, Jonah, Micah, Nahum, Habakkuk, Zephaniah, Haggai, Zachariah and Malachi; two books of Maccabees, i.e., the first and the second.

212 New Testament: The four Gospels according to Matthew,
1503 Mark, Luke and John; the Acts of the apostles written
by Luke the Evangelist; fourteen epistles of the apostle Paul, i.e., to the Romans, two to the Corinthians, to the Galatians, Ephesians, Philippians, Colossians, two to the Thessalonians, two to Timothy, to Titus, Philemon, and the Hebrews; two epistles of the apostle Peter, three of the apostle John, one of the apostle James, one of the apostle Jude, and the Revelation of the apostle John.

213 If anyone does not accept all these books in their entirety,
1504 with all their parts, as they are being read in the Catholic
Church and are contained in the ancient Latin Vulgate edition, as sacred and canonical, and knowingly and deliberately rejects the aforesaid traditions, *anathema sit.*

(The Vulgate as the standard version)

214 Moreover, because the same holy Council thought it very
1506 useful to the Church if it were known which of all the
Latin editions of the sacred books now in circulation is to be regarded as the authentic version, it declares and decrees: This same ancient Vulgate version which has been preserved by the Church for so many centuries is to be regarded as the authentic translation in public readings, disputations, sermons and expositions, and let no one dare or presume to reject it on any grounds.

(The Church as interpreter of Holy Scripture)

215 Furthermore, to restrain irresponsible minds, it decrees
1507 that no one, relying on his own prudence, twist Holy Scripture in matters of faith and morals that pertain to the edifice of
Christian doctrine, according to his own mind, contrary to the
meaning that holy mother the Church has held and holds—since it
belongs to her to judge the true meaning and interpretation of Holy
Scripture—and that no one dare to interpret the Scripture in a way
contrary to the unanimous consensus of the Fathers, even though
such interpretations be not intended for publication.

THE FIRST VATICAN GENERAL COUNCIL

THIRD SESSION
DOGMATIC CONSTITUTION *DEI FILIUS* ON THE
CATHOLIC FAITH (1870)

*In conjunction with the doctrine of revelation, Vatican I had to deal also
with the question of the sources of revelation. It reiterated the doctrine of
Trent concerning Tradition and Scripture and interpreted it in view of
contemporary opinions. It described inspiration against the doctrines of D.
Haneberg who saw in it only a subsequent approbation by the Church and
of J. Jahn who considered it as an external and negative assistance which
guarantees an inerrancy 'in fieri'.*

Chapter II: On Revelation

(Scripture and Tradition as sources of revelation)

216 Further, this supernatural revelation, according to the
3006 universal belief of the Church, declared by the sacred Synod
of Trent, "is contained in the written books and unwritten
traditions which have come down to us, having been received by the
apostles from the mouth of Christ Himself, or from the apostles
themselves by he dictation of the Holy Spirit, and have been transmitted as it were from hand to hand" *(cf. n. 210)*. These books of the
Old and New Testaments are to be received as sacred and canonical
in their integrity, with all their parts, as they are enumerated in the
decree of the said Council and are contained in the ancient Latin
edition of the Vulgate. These the Church holds to be sacred and
canonical, not because, having been carefully composed by mere
human industry, they were afterwards approved by her authority,
nor merely because they contain revelation with no admixture of
error, but because, having been written by the inspiration of the Holy

Spirit, they have God for their author and have been delivered as such to the Church herself.

(Interpretation of Holy Scripture)

217 However, what the holy Council of Trent has laid down
3007 concerning the interpretation of the divine Scripture for the
good purpose of restraining indisciplined minds, has been explained by certain men in a distorted manner. Hence we renew the same decree and declare this to be its sense: In matters of faith and morals, affecting the building up of Christian doctrine, that is to be held as the true sense of Holy Scripture which Holy Mother the Church has held and holds, to whom it belongs to judge of the true sense and interpretation of Holy Scriptures. Therefore no one is allowed to interpret the same Sacred Scripture contrary to this sense, or contrary to the unanimous consent of the Fathers.

Canon 4 to Chapter II

218 If anyone does not receive as sacred and canonical the
3029 books of Holy Scritpture, entire and with all their parts, as
the sacred Synod of Trent has enumerated them, or denies that they have been divinely inspired, *anathema sit.*

Chapter III: On Faith

(Scripture and Tradition contain the divine revelation)

219 ...All those things are to be believed with divine and
3011 Catholic faith which are contained in the word of God,
written or handed down, and which by the Church, either in solemn judgment or through her ordinary and universal teaching office, are proposed for belief as having been divinely revealed.

LEO XIII

ENCYCLICAL LETTER *PROVIDENTISSIMUS DEUS* (1893)

This encyclical on the study of Holy Scripture represents the Church's first far-ranging treatment of the questions raised by modern Bible criticism. Leo XIII unhesitatingly recognises the services rendered by scientific methods of Biblical research and wishes them to be used for a deeper understanding of the sacred books. But the Bible is the word of God and is therefore infallible. Scientific research can never ignore this fact. Therefore, no interpretation can neglect the criteria of faith and tradition.

The encyclical is based on the firm conviction that there can be no contradiction between the word of God and the findings of sciences, provided on both sides men honestly seek the truth and are aware of their own limitations. God who created nature and is the author of Scripture cannot contradict Himself.

(Faith as norm for the interpretation of Scripture)

220 Where the sense of biblical texts has been authoritatively declared, either by the sacred authors themselves under the inspiration of the Holy Spirit, as in many passages of the New Testament, or by the Church assisted by the same Holy Spirit, whether by means of a solemn judgment or by her ordinary and universal authority, it should be the special and religious care of the Catholic interpreter to explain them in the same way and to prove by the help which science supplies that it is the only interpretation which can rightly be approved according to the laws of sound exegesis.

221 In other points the analogy of faith must be followed, and
3283 Catholic doctrine as it has been received from the authority of the Church must be considered as the supreme criterion. For, since it is the same God who is author of the sacred books and of the doctrine handed down by the Church, it is obviously impossible to extract from the former a legitimate interpretation which in any way conflicts with the latter.

(The Catholic interpretation draws from the wealth of Tradition, mainly the Fathers of the Church)

222 The authority of the holy Fathers is very great whenever
3284 they explain unanimously in one and the same manner a biblical testimony as belonging to the doctrine of faith and morals, as "after the apostles they were the ones to plant and water, build, shepherd, and rear the Holy Church in her growth".[1] For, through their consensus it becomes evident that such an explanation has been handed down from the apostles in accordance with the Catholic faith.

(Higher Criticism, and the limits of 'inner criteria')

223 Without foundation and to the detriment of religion a system
3286 has been introduced which parades under the name of higher criticism, according to which the origin, integrity, and

---

1. St Augustine, *Contra Iulianum Pelagianum*, II, 10, 37.

authority of any book can be judged by what is called internal criteria. On the contrary, it is evident that in historical questions, such as the origin and preservation of books, historical testimonies are of greater value than others and should be sought out and weighed with greatest care. On the other hand, internal criteria are generally not important enough to be admitted except as a sort of confirmatory evidence.

(The Bible and natural sciences)

224   No real disagreement can exist between the theologian
3287   and the scientist provided each keeps within his own limits....

3288   If nevertheless there is disagreement,... it should be remembered that the sacred writers, or more truly "the Spirit of God who spoke through them, did not wish to teach men such truths (as the inner structure of visible objects) which do not help any one to salvation";[1] and that, for this reason, rather than trying to provide a scientific exposition of nature, they sometimes describe and treat these matters either in a somewhat figurative language or as the common manner of speech those times required, and indeed still requires nowadays in everyday life, even amongst most learned people.

(Historicity)

225   The same principles can also be transferred to related
3290   branches of knowledge, especially to history.

(Divine origin and inerrancy of Sacred Scripture)

226   It would be utterly impious to limit inspiration to some
3291   portions only of Sacred Scripture or to admit that the sacred author himself has erred. Nor can one tolerate the method of those who extricate themselves from difficulties by allowing without hesitation that divine inspiration extends to matters of faith and morals and to nothing more....

3292   For all the books in their entirety, which the Church receives as sacred and canonical, with all their parts, have been written under the dictation of the Holy Spirit. Now it is utterly impossible that divine inspiration could contain any error; it not only by its

---

1. St Augustine, *De Genesi ad litt.,* II, 9, 20.

nature excludes any error, but excludes and rejects it with the same necessity, as it is impossible that God, the highest Truth, be the author of any error whatsoever.

3293 This is the ancient and constant faith of the Church.

(References are given to the Councils of Florence, Trent, Vatican I).

227 It is futile to argue that the Holy Spirit took men as His
3293 instruments in writing, implying that some error could slip in, not indeed from the principal author, but from the inspired writers. For by His supernatural power He so stimulated and moved them to write, so assisted them while they were writing that they properly conceived in their mind, wished to write down faithfully, and expressed aptly with infallible truth all those things, and only those things, which He Himself ordered; otherwise He could not Himself be the author of the whole of Sacred Scripture.

PIUS X

DECREE *LAMENTABILI* OF THE HOLY OFFICE (1907) ARTICLES OF MODERNISM CONDEMNED

Modernism (cf. n. 143i) subscribed to liberal scriptural sciences in matters of biblical criticism and exegesis. The articles condemned concern the relation of the Church's magisterium to Scripture (1-4), the modernist view on divine inspiration (9-12), and some specific questions (13-24).

[228/1] The ecclesiastical law which requires that books treat-
3401 ing of Holy Scripture be submitted to previous censorship does not apply to workers in the field of criticism or of scientific exegesis of the Old and New Testaments.

[228/4] The Church's teaching office cannot, even by dogmatic
3404 definition, determine the genuine meaning of sacred Scripture.

[228/9] Those who believe that God is really the author of Holy
3409 Scripture show too much simplicity or ignorance.

[228/11] Divine inspiration does not extend to the whole of
3411 Scripture in such a way that each and every part of it is kept free from error.

[228/14] In many of their accounts the Evangelists narrated not so
3414 much the truth as what they thought would—even though it be false—be more helpful to their readers.

[228/15] Until the canon has been defined and established, the
3415 gospels were constantly enlarged and amended;
therefore no more than a slight and uncertain trace of
Christ's teaching has remained.

[228/16] John's narrations are not really historical but a mystical
3416 contemplation of the Gospel. The discourses in his gospel are theological meditations about the mystery of salvation, devoid of historical truth.

[228/23] There can and in fact there does exist conflict between
3423 the facts related by Holy Scripture and the Church's
dogma based upon them. The critic can thus reject as
false things which the Church believes as most certain.

[228/24] An exegete is not to be blamed when he sets up prem-
3424 ises from which it follows that dogmas are historically false or doubtful, provided that he does not directly
deny the dogmas themselves.

BENEDICT XV

ENCYCLICAL LETTER *SPIRITUS PARACLITUS* (1920)

*The occasion for the encyclical was the fifteen-hundredth anniversary of
the death of St Jerome, the great translator and interpreter of Sacred
Scripture. The doctrine developed is essentially that expressed by Leo XIII,
but Benedict XV's main task was to deal with the misinterpretation of the
passage in which his predecessor dealt with the historicity of the inspired
books.*

(Divine inspiration of the Bible)

229 (St Jerome consistently teaches the Catholic doctrine)
3650 that the sacred books are written under the inspiration
of the Holy Spirit, have God for their author, and were as
such entrusted to the Church. Indeed he asserts that the books of
Holy Scripture were written under the inspiration of the Holy Spirit,
by His instruction, stimulus, and even dictation, and were indeed
written and produced by Him. Besides he has no doubts that the
individual writers placed themselves freely at the service of the divine
dictation according to each one's nature and gifts. For he not only
consistently asserts the common features of all sacred writers, viz.,
that in writing they followed the Spirit of God, so that God must be
considered the primary cause of every thought and every sentence
of Scripture, but he also accurately distinguishes the special characteristics of each one.

(Inspiration extends to both religious and profane matters)

230 Recent exegetes distinguish between a primary or religious
3652 and a secondary or profane element in Scripture; while
admitting that divine inspiration applies to every sentence,
even to every word of Holy Scripture, they restrict and narrow down
its effects, especially its absolute truth and inerrancy, to the primary
or religious element. They believe that only what deals with religion is
intended and taught by God in the Scriptures. Everything else that
belongs to profane subjects and serves the revealed doctrine, as it
were as an outer garment of divine truth, was merely permitted and
was left subject to the shortcomings of the writer. No wonder therefore that there are many things in Scripture concerning natural
sciences, history, and the like, which cannot be reconciled with
modern scientific progress....

But it is apparent from the very words of Pope (Leo XIII) how rash
and wrong such contentions are.... He rejected any distinction
between primary and secondary elements, as they are called,
removed all ambiguity, and clearly showed that the opinion of those
who believe that concerning the truth of statements one does not
need to ask what God said so much as why He said it, is very far from
the truth. He likewise taught that the divine inspiration extends to all
parts of Scripture without distinction, and that no error could occur
in the inspired text. "It would be utterly impious to limit inspiration to
some portions only of Sacred Scripture or to admit that the sacred
author himself has erred" *(cf. n. 226)*.

(Historical truth)

231 And those depart no less from the teaching of the Church
3653 ... who hold the view that the historical parts of Holy
Scripture are not based on the absolute truth of facts, but
upon what they call relative truths, and upon the views of ordinary
people. They are even bold enough to argue from the very words of
Pope Leo, for he said that the principles of natural science could be
transferred to historical disciplines *(cf. n. 225)*. Thus they maintain
that, as the sacred writers wrote about natural things according to
their outward appearance, so too, they reported events without
accurate knowledge as they appeared in the eyes of ordinary people
or from the false testimony of others, without indicating the source of
their information or making the accounts of others their own.

Why should we refute with many words this entirely misleading
and false assumption, unjust as it is to our predecessor? Physics has

to do with what is apparent to the senses and must therefore agree with the appearances. But the principal law of history is that the accounts of facts must agree with the facts as they actually occurred. If the false opinion just mentioned were once accepted, how would the truth of the sacred narration still be free from all error, as our predecessor in the whole context of his letter declared that we must believe?

PIUS XII

ENCYCLICAL LETTER *DIVINO AFFLANTE SPIRITU* (1943)

This encyclical is a landmark in modern Catholic exegesis. The knowledge and mastery of biblical and Oriental languages is fostered; the position of the Church with regard to the Latin Vulgate is clarified; Catholic exegetes are encouraged to make proper use of textual criticism and literary analysis of the sacred books, according to literary genres and form criticism; they must attach great importance to the literal meaning without neglecting the 'spiritual' or theological sense of the sacred texts.

(Original texts and the Latin Vulgate version)

232   The exegete must explain the text in the original language which, since it was written by the sacred author himself, has greater weight and authority than even the best translation, either ancient or modern. He will be able to accomplish his task more easily and in a more effective way if to the knowledge of biblical languages he adds a sound skill in literary criticism.

233   As for the decree of the Council of Trent requiring that
3825   the Vulgate be regarded as the authentic Latin version *(cf. n. 214)*, it is common knowledge that this concerns only the Latin Church and her public use of Scriptures, and obviously in no way detracts from the authority and value of the original texts.... This special authority or, as it is called, 'authenticity' which the Council attributes to the Vulgate was not given on account of special critical reasons but rather because of the lawful use the Vulgate had enjoyed in the Church for so many centuries. This long use proves that the Vulgate, as the Church has understood and now understands, is free from all error in matters of faith and morals so that, as the Church herself testifies and confirms, it can be safely quoted, without the least fear of erring, in disputations, public readings, and sermons. Its authenticity is therefore more properly called 'juridical' than 'critical'.

The Tridentine decree does not forbid that translations be made into modern languages, also from the original texts themselves, for the use and benefit of the faithful and the easier understanding of the divine word, as, we know, has already been done in many places laudably and with the approval of the authority of the Church.

(Literal and spiritual meaning)

234   Equipped with knowledge of languages and skill in the tools
3826   of the critical method, the Catholic exegete should under-
        take as his most important task to ascertain and to explain the true meaning of the sacred books. In carrying out this task the exegetes should keep in mind that their chief task must be to discern and determine what is known as the literal sense of the words of the Bible.... Commentators must first and foremost show what is the theological doctrine concerning faith and morals of each book and text....

3827   By giving an interpretation...that is primarily theological,
        they will effectively silence those who assert that in biblical commentaries they find hardly anything to raise their minds to God, nourish their souls and foster their interior life, and therefore main-tain that we must have recourse to a spiritual and so-called mystical interpretation....

235   It is true that not every spiritual sense is excluded from
3828   Sacred Scripture; what was said and done in the Old Testa-
        ment was wisely ordained and disposed by God so that the past would spiritually foreshadow what was to happen in the new covenant of grace. It is therefore the duty of the exegete to discover and explain not only the literal meaning of the words, i.e., that which the sacred writers intended and expressed, but also their spiritual significance, provided it be established that such meaning has been given to them by God Himself. For God alone was able to know this spiritual significance and to reveal it to us. In the gospels our divine Saviour Himself points out and teaches such type of meaning; the apostles, following the example of the Master, make use of it in their preaching and writings; the traditional teaching of the Church con-tinuously gives proof of it; finally the ancient practice of the liturgy bears out this meaning, wherever the well-known saying can be applied in truth: the norm of prayer is the norm of belief *(cf. n. 1913)*. Catholic exegetes should bring this divinely intended spiritual mean-ing to light and propound it with the carefulness that the dignity of the divine word demands. They should be scrupulously careful not to

propose other metaphorical senses as though they were the original meaning of Holy Scripture.

(Literary genres)

236 It is absolutely necessary for the interpreter to go back in *3830* spirit to those remote centuries of the East, and to make proper use of the help given by history, archaeology, ethnology and other sciences, in order to discover what literary forms the writers of those early ages intended to use and did in fact use. For, to express what they had in mind, the ancients of the East did not always avail themselves of the same forms and expressions as we do today; they used those that were current among people of their own time and place. The exegete cannot determine what these were by an a priori judgment but must first make a careful study of ancient literature.... The sacred writers, like the other ancients, use certain arts of exposition and narration, certain idioms known as 'approximations' which are typical of Semitic languages, certain hyperbolic ways of speaking, and certain paradoxes intended for emphasis. The sacred books need not exclude any of the forms of expression that were commonly used in human speech among the ancient peoples, especially of the East, so long as they are not incompatible with God's sanctity and veracity....

In many cases in which the authors are accused of some historical inaccuracy or some inexact recording of certain events, there is in fact nothing else to be found than those customary and characteristic forms of expression or style of narration which were current among people of that time, and were in fact quite legitimately and commonly used. Just impartiality demands that when these are found in the word of God...they should no more be considered as error than when similar expressions are used in everyday speech.

LETTER OF THE BIBLICAL COMMISSION TO CARDINAL SUHARD, ARCHBISHOP OF PARIS (1948)

This letter, written by the secretary, J.M. Vosté, has in fact the authority of a decree of the Biblical Commission; it contains an important application of the above principles (cf. n. 236) to the literary genre of Genesis, chapters 1-11, and stresses the caution needed to decide their historicity. It also somewhat rectifies previous decrees regarding the Mosaic origin of the Pentateuch and accepts "written documents or oral traditions and post-Mosaic modifications and additions".

237 The question of the literary forms of the first eleven chapters
3864 of Genesis is much more complicated and obscure. These
literary forms do not correspond to any of our classic categories and cannot be judged in the light of Graeco-Latin or modern
literary genres. Their historicity can be neither affirmed nor denied
en bloc without unjustifiably applying to them the rules of a literary
genre in which they cannot be classified.... To declare a priori that
the accounts found in them do not contain history in the modern
sense of the word would easily lead to the misunderstanding that
they contain no history in any sense of the word, while they do
actually relate in simple and colourful language, adapted to the
intelligence of less educated men, the fundamental truths underlying
the divine plan of salvation. They are a popular description of the
origins of the human race and of the chosen people.

ENCYCLICAL LETTER *HUMANI GENERIS* (1950)

From this document (cf. n. 144i) two texts referring to Scripture are
quoted here:
    The first text rejects once more the theory of the double meaning of
Scripture, one human and one divine, the former fallible, the latter inerrant.
    The second clarifies the letter to Cardinal Suhard (cf. n. 237) concerning
the historical value of the first eleven chapters of Genesis.

(Interpretation of Scriptural inerrancy)

238 There are some who clearly distort the sense of the definition
3887 laid down by the first Vatican Council as to the divine authorship of the Bible.... They even use misguided language about
the human meaning of the sacred books, under which a divine
meaning is concealed, and claim that only this divine meaning is
infallible. In their interpretation of Scripture they will not take into
consideration the harmony of revealed truths with one another, nor
pay attention to the tradition of the Church.

(Comment on the letter to Cardinal Suhard)

239 It was clearly laid down in that letter that the first eleven
3898 chapters of Genesis... do nevertheless come under the heading of history; in what exact sense, it is for the further study of
the exegete to determine. These chapters have a naïve, symbolic
way of speaking, well suited to the understanding of primitive people.
But they do disclose to us certain important truths, upon which the
attainment of our eternal salvation depends, and they do also give a

popular description of the origin of the human race and of the chosen people. It may be true that the ancient authors of sacred history drew some of their material from current popular stories. So much may be granted. But it must be remembered that they did so under the impulse of divine inspiration which preserved them from all error in selecting and assessing the material they used.

These excerpts from current stories, which are found in the sacred books, must not be put on a level with mere myths, or with legend in general.... In the Old Testament a love of truth and a cult of simplicity shine out in such a way as to put these writers on a distinctly different level from their profane contemporaries.

PAUL VI

INSTRUCTION OF THE BIBLICAL COMMISSION
SANCTA MATER ECCLESIA (1964)

In this Instruction, concerned with the historical truth of the gospels, biblical scholars are encouraged and protected against unfair criticism. The most modern and scientific methods of research are approved, including a sane and balanced Form Criticism (5).

The three stages in which the Gospel message has come down to us is described at length: from Christ's own words and actions to the apostolic preaching, and from the Sitz im Leben of the apostolic Church to the writers of the gospels (6-10).

Besides, the Instruction points out the complexity of many problems of exegesis and insists on the ultimate pastoral purpose of biblical studies: to nourish the spiritual life and to bring men to salvation. The text is found in AAS 56 (1964) 712 ff.

(Form Criticism)

240 5. In appropriate cases the interpreter is free to seek out what sound elements there are in the method of form-history; he can freely make use of these to gain a fuller understanding of the gospels.

(The threefold stage in the formation of the Gospels)

241 6. In order to determine correctly the trustworthiness of what is transmitted in the gospels, the interpreter must take careful note of the three stages of tradition by which the teaching and the life of Jesus came down to us.

242 7. (1) Christ our Lord attached to Himself certain chosen disciples who had followed Him from the beginning, had seen

His works and heard His words, and thus were qualified to become witnesses of His life and teaching. Our Lord, when expounding His teaching by word of mouth, observed the method of reasoning and of expression which were in common use at that time.... He accommodated Himself to the mentality of His hearers, and ensured that His teaching would be deeply impressed on their minds and would easily be retained by the memory of the disciples.

243   8. (2) The apostles, bearing witness to Jesus, proclaimed first and foremost the death and resurrection of the Lord, faithfully recounting His life and words and, as regards the manner of their preaching, taking into account the circumstances of their hearers. After Jesus had risen from the dead, and when His divinity was clearly perceived, the faith of the disciples, far from blotting out the remembrance of the events that had happened, rather consolidated it since their faith was based on what Jesus had done and taught.... Yet, it need not be denied that the apostles, when handing on to their hearers the things which in actual fact the Lord had said and done, did so in the light of that fuller understanding which they enjoyed as the result of being instructed by the glorious events accomplished in Christ, and illumined by the Spirit of Truth.... They made use of such various forms of speech as were adapted to their own purpose and to the mentality of their hearers.

244   9. (3) The apostles took this earliest body of instruction, which had been handed down orally at first and then in writing..., and set it down in the four gospels. In doing so, each of them followed a method suitable to the special purpose which he had in view. They selected certain things out of the many traditions; some they synthetized, some they elaborated in view of the situation of the churches, painstakingly using every means of bringing home to their readers the firm truth in which they had been instructed. For, out of the material which they had received, the sacred authors selected especially those items which were adapted to the various circumstances of the faithful as well as to the end which they themselves had in view; these items they recounted in a manner fitting those circumstances and that end.... In handing on the words and deeds of our Saviour, they explained them..., one Evangelist setting them in one context, another in another.... The truth of the narrative is not affected in the least by the fact that the Evangelists report the sayings or doings of our Lord in a different order or that they use different words to express what He said, not keeping to the letter but nevertheless preserving the sense.

245 10. The result of recent studies has made it clear that the teaching and the life of Jesus were not simply recounted for the purpose of being kept in remembrance, but were 'preached' in such a way as to provide the Church with the foundation on which to build faith and morals.

THE SECOND VATICAN GENERAL COUNCIL
DOGMATIC CONSTITUTION *DEI VERBUM* (1965)

Chapter II: The Transmission of Divine Revelation

This chapter deals with the respective functions of Tradition, Scripture and the teaching office of the Church, in handing down through the ages the events of salvation history.

Revelation is passed on by the heralds of the Gospel, the apostles and their successors (7). 'Sacred Tradition' has its origin from the apostles. The Council is concerned with doctrinal tradition, not with ecclesiastical laws or customs. The emphasis is laid on the active role of the Church and on the development of the content of revelation with the help of the Holy Spirit (8). The vexed question concerning 'two sources' is dealt with in number 9: in a positive way both Scripture and Tradition are presented as two functions within the living historical transmission of truth rather than as static sources of ideas. The controversy on the sufficiency of Scripture alone is thus avoided by situating the problem on a higher plane. The Council does not affirm that Scripture is 'insufficient' in the sense of not containing all matters of faith, but it states that the Church "does not derive her certainty from Scripture alone".

Describing the position of the Church and the magisterium, the Constitution turns against the suspicion that the Roman Church claims, in her teaching, an absolute and arbitrary authority that would be above the word of God (10).

(Sacred Tradition)

246 8. ...The tradition received by the apostles includes everything which contributes to the living of a holy life by the people of God and the increase of their faith; thus the Church, in her teaching, life and worship, perpetuates and hands on to all generations all that she herself is, and all that she believes.

This Tradition, derived from the apostles, progresses in the Church with the help of the Holy Spirit, for there is growth in the understanding both of the realities and of the words handed down. This happens through study and contemplation on the part of the believers who ponder them in their hearts *(cf. Lk. 2.19, 51),* through their intimate penetration of the spiritual realities of their own experience, and through the preaching of those who have received a sure charism of truth together with episcopal succession. Thus the Church tends continually through the centuries towards the fulness of divine truth....

The words of the holy Fathers bear witness to the presence of this life-giving tradition.... It is through the same tradition that the entire canon of the sacred books is known to the Church.... In this way God, who spoke of old, still holds unbroken converse with the spouse of His beloved Son; and the Holy Spirit, through whom the living voice of the Gospel resounds in the Church, and through her in the world, introduces believers into all truth, and makes the word of Christ dwell abundantly in them *(cf. Col. 3.16).*

(Relation between Tradition and Scripture)

247   9. Hence there exists a close connection and communication between Sacred Tradition and Sacred Scripture. For both of them, flowing from the same divine well-spring, in a certain way merge into unity, and tend toward the same end. For Sacred Scripture is the word of God inasmuch as it is consigned to writing under the inspiration of the Holy Spirit, while Sacred Tradition takes the word of God entrusted by Christ the Lord and the Holy Spirit to the apostles, and hands it on to their successors in its integrity, so that, led by the light of the Spirit of truth, they may, in their preaching of this word, preserve it faithfully, explain it and cause it to spread. Consequently, it is not from Sacred Scripture alone that the Church derives her certainty about the whole content of revelation. And so, both Sacred Scripture and Sacred Tradition are to be accepted and venerated with the same sense of loyalty and reverence *(cf. n. 210).*

(Scripture and Tradition in relation to the Church's magisterium)

248   10. ...The office of authentically interpreting the word of God, whether written or handed down, has been entrusted to the living teaching office of the Church alone, whose authority is exercised in the name of Jesus Christ. This teaching office, however, is not above the word of God, but ministers to it, teaching only what has been handed on, listening to this word devoutly, guarding it religiously and expounding it faithfully, by divine commission and with the help of the Holy Spirit; it draws from the one deposit of faith everything which it proposes for belief as divinely revealed.

It is clear therefore that, by God's most wise design, Sacred Tradition, Sacred Scripture and the Church's teaching authority are so linked and so associated together that one cannot stand without the others, and that all together and each in its own way contribute effectively to the salvation of men under the action of the one Holy Spirit.

Chapter III: The Divine Inspiration of Sacred Scripture and its Interpretation

The fact of inspiration is reaffirmed in the words of the First Vatican Council (cf. n. 216), and its process is described as a co-operation between God and the men He chose and 'employed'. Thus, the term 'instrument' is avoided.

Inerrancy is proposed in a new and positive way: the truth of Scripture is not that of natural science or profane history, but "Truth for the sake of our salvation" (11).

The guidance given for the right interpretation of Scripture resumes the guidelines given in previous documents: due attention is to be paid to literary forms, but also to the living Tradition of the whole Church and to the analogy of faith (12).

Finally, the marvellous condescension of God (cf. St John Chrysostom's sunkatabasis) *is compared to the 'kenosis' of the incarnation (13).*

(Inspiration and truth of Holy Scripture)

249   11. ...For the composing of these sacred books God chose men, and while He employed them, they made use of their own powers and abilities, so that with God acting in them and through them, they—as true authors—committed to writing all those things and only those that He wanted (cf. n. 227).

Since therefore everything asserted by the inspired authors or sacred writers must be held to be asserted by the Holy Spirit, it must be acknowledged that the books of Scripture teach firmly, faithfully and without error the truth which God wanted to be consigned to sacred writings for the sake of our salvation....

(Interpretation)

250   12. ...Sacred Scripture must be read and interpreted in the same spirit in which it was written. In order therefore to discover the correct meaning of the sacred texts, no less serious attention must be paid to the content, and unity of the whole of Scripture in the light of the living Tradition of the whole Church and of the analogy of faith.

(God's condescension)

251   13. ...The words of God, expressed in human language, resemble human speech, just as once the Word of the eternal Father, taking to Himself the weak flesh of humanity, became similar to men.

Chapters IV and V: The Old and the New Testaments

After a brief description of Salvation history (14), the Constitution shows the importance of the Old Testament (15) and its relation to the New Testament. According to the saying of St Augustine, "The New Testament lies hidden in the Old and the Old is made manifest in the New"[1] (16).

The New Testament has an excellence of its own (17), especially the gospels which are of apostolic origin (18) and have a historical character; number 19 is a summary of the instruction of the Biblical Commission 'Sancta Mater Ecclesia' (cf. nn. 240-245). The chapter concludes with an extremely brief account of all the other New Testament writings (20).

(Importance of the Old Testament for Christians)

252   15. ...Though these books contain also certain things which are imperfect and merely temporary, they still exhibit a true divine pedagogy.... They give expression to a lively sense of God, contain a storehouse of sublime teachings about God, of saving wisdom about human life, and a wonderful treasury of prayers; in sum, the mystery of our salvation is present in them in a hidden way.

(The unity of the two Testaments)

253   16. ...The books of the Old Testament in their entirety have been assumed into the proclamation of the Gospel, and it is in the New Testament that they acquire and manifest their full significance (cf. Mt. 5.17; Lk. 24.27; Rom. 16.25-26; 2 Cor. 3.14-16). In their turn the Old Testament books shed light on the New Testament and explain it.

(The apostolic origin of the Gospel)

254   18. ...What the apostles preached by the command of Christ, afterwards they and other men of the apostolic circle under the inspiration of the divine Spirit handed on to us in writings which are the foundation of our faith, namely, the four-fold Gospel, according to Matthew, Mark, Luke and John.

---

1. St Augustine, *Quaest. in Hept.*, 2, 73

Chapter VI: Sacred Scripture in the Life of the Church

All preaching must be nourished and governed by Sacred Scripture (21). Suitable translations from the original texts must be made available in the language of the people; when possible, these may be made in collaboration with other Christians (22).

Exegetes and theologians are encouraged in the apostolic use of the Bible (23). Theology must become more and more biblical (24). Finally, the Council recommends guided reading of Holy Scripture as a stimulus to the life in the Spirit (25).

(The importance of Holy Scripture for the Church)

255 21. ...In the sacred books it is the heavenly Father Himself who meets His children with tender love and enters into conversation with them. Now there is such force and efficacy in the word of God that it constitutes strength and support for the Church, and for her children it provides strength of faith, the food of the soul and a pure and unfailing source of the spiritual life.

(The importance of Scripture for theology)

256 24. ...Let the study of the sacred page be as it were the soul of sacred theology. Through the same word of Scripture the ministry of the word, which includes pastoral preaching, catechesis, and all Christian instruction, where the liturgical homily ought to have a privileged place, also must find healthy nourishment and holy growth.

(The reading of Holy Scripture is recommended)

257 26. ...Just as the life of the Church is strengthened through the persistent frequenting of the eucharistic mystery, so also we may hope for a new stimulus for the life of the Spirit from a growing devotion to the word of God which lasts for ever *(Is. 40.8; cf. 1 Pet. 1.23-25).*

PAUL VI

S. CONGREGATION FOR CATHOLIC EDUCATION
THE THEOLOGICAL FORMATION OF FUTURE PRIESTS
(22 February 1976)

This lengthy document, issued by the Sacred Congregation for Catholic Education, has an official character though it is not contained in the Osservatore Romano nor in the Acta Apostolicae Sedis. It was sent to all bishops and Directors of Seminaries. In an important section it outlines the principles to be observed in the teaching of Sacred Scripture, the relation of Scripture to Tradition and its place as the basis of all theological disciplines. The text is found in The Pope Speaks, *Vol. 21 (1976), pp. 365-366.*

(The place of Scripture in theology)

258 79. The basic fact which theological teaching must take into account is that Sacred Scripture is the starting point, the *permanent foundation*, and the life-giving and animating principle of all theology (cf. *DV 24*). The professor of biblical sciences must therefore carry out his mission with the competence and thorough scientific preparation that the importance of his discipline requires. To be faithful to his mission, he must deal, at different levels, with the text, with the event to which the text relates, and with the tradition which communicates and interprets the text. But, while he applies textual, literary and historical analysis, he must also keep alive in the minds of his students an awareness of the unity of the mystery and of God's plan. Since Scripture is passed on to us by the Church and in part came into existence within the Church, it requires to be read and undertood in the light of ecclesiastical tradition.[1]

80. The primordial role of Sacred Scripture determines the nature of its relation to theology and its various disciplines. We must recall here that Sacred Scripture cannot be taken into account in function solely of these disciplines (as though it were but a source of probative texts); on the contrary, theology in its entirety is called upon to help to a better and increasingly profound understanding of the sacred texts, that is, of the dogmatic and moral truths they contain. Consequently, after the introductory questions have been handled, the teaching of Sacred Scripture must culminate in a biblical theology which gives a unified vision of the Christian mystery.

---

1. Cf. Instruction *Sancta Mater Ecclesia*, 21 April 1964, *AAS* 56 (1964) 713f.

CHAPTER III

THE TRIUNE GOD

"This is eternal life that they know thee, the only true God, and Jesus Christ whom thou hast sent" (Jn 17.3). This is how the substance of the Christian life is expressed in Jesus' words according to John's gospel. The core of the Christian message consists in the mystery of Jesus Christ, but Jesus Himself understood His coming as the manifestation of the Father. Through Him all are made to share in the life and light of God. Hence the Christian doctrine about God is the foundation of the Church's faith.

Two series of problems concerning God figure in the documents of the Church from the early times. First among these is the right conception of God as compared to the distorted ideas found in the world surrounding the Christian fold. The Christian conception of God goes back to the Old Testament, is deepened in the revelation of Jesus Christ, and pervades the entire orbit of Christian life, worship and thought. God is one, the only source of all being, the material world included. He comprises all perfection. He is the living God, not an impersonal ground of the world's being, but the free and sovereign source of all salvation. This had to be ascertained as an integral part of the Christian faith against the mythological, pantheistic and dualistic conceptions to which the Christians were constantly exposed. This Christian idea of God is expressed primarily in the liturgy and in the ordinary teaching of the Church; it is also contained in Creeds and doctrinal documents, mostly in brief formulas.

The second series of problems concerns the Holy Trinity. This occupies much more space in the doctrinal texts. The Christian concept of God unfolds itself in the mission and revelation of the Son and the Spirit. Since together with the Father they are truly divine, the unity in God and the mutual relation between the divine persons needs to be clarified. This mystery became from the beginning the object of theological reflection.

From early times Trinitarian theology developed two different approaches. In the patristic theology of the East the idea prevailed that the one God is God the Father, and that the Son and the Spirit share with Him His divine life. This conception had the merit of being based on Scripture, but it could lend itself to misinterpretations. It could lead to subordinationist ideas which, in fact, did spring up in the East and came to a climax with the heresy of Arius. The other conception, prominent in the West, conceived God as the one divine substance, comprising Father, Son and Spirit. In this view, the unity of God and the equality of Father, Son and Spirit were easily safeguarded; but, the basic truth of the oneness of the divine nature could be misunderstood in such a way as to lead to the denial of the real distinction of the three persons. Modalism in its various forms did, in fact, deny this distinction.

The documents of the Church reject the various misguided conceptions of the Trinity in order to preserve the revealed mystery in its integrity. This indeed is the real significance of the Trinitarian Creeds and of the doctrinal precisions added to them by the Councils. They insist, on the one hand, on the oneness of God and on the divinity and full equality of the divine persons, and, on the other hand, on their origin and their mutual distinction from one another. In a later period, when the origin of the Holy Spirit from Father and Son became a major issue between the Eastern and Western Churches, this controversy took an important place in the documents of the Church.

The theological concepts and the terminology used in these documents became more and more technical and at times somewhat involved. This could hardly be avoided in view of the depth of the mystery which they had to convey. It should, however, be borne in mind that the subtlety in reasoning was never meant to rationalise the divine mystery but to preserve its integrity against all rationalistic simplifications. All Trinitarian heresies are such simplifications which, if they were allowed to prevail, would ultimately evacuate the mystery.

*   *   *

The doctrinal points dealt with in this chapter are the following:

The Christian concept of God

There is one personal God: 5-14, 19, 39/1, 306/20, 327-329.
He transcends the world: 327, 330f;
and is of infinite perfections: 19, 39/2, 327.

One God, three persons

In God there are three persons, Father, Son, and Holy Spirit: 1-19, 39/2, 301, 303, 306/21.24, 308, 325.

The three are one undivided Godhead: 16, 19, 22, 39/3, 301, 303, 306/20.24, 308, 311-313, 315, 317-320, 325, 620/1, 627/1.

Each person is fully God: 16, 19, 22, 24, 306/3f.10.24, 312;

the Father: 308;

the Son: 6-14, 23, 302f, 306/3.12.13, 309;

the Holy Spirit: 12, 14, 16, 24, 39/6, 305, 306/1.3.16-18.22f, 310.

The divine persons are distinct from one another: 14, 16, 301, 306/2, 313f, 333;

they are distinct through mutual relationship: 39/2, 313, 325.

The origin of the divine persons

The Father is absolute origin, from Himself: 16, 19, 308, 325f.

The Son is born from the Father, from eternity: 6-19, 23, 39/3-4, 302f, 306/11, 309, 318, 325.

The Holy Spirit proceeds from Father and Son: 14, 16, 19, 23, 39/3, 310, 319, 321–325.

The divine persons are united through mutual indwelling: 316, 326.

The divine actions in the world are common to the three persons: 306/19, 315, 326.

The Trinitarian mystery is revealed in the mission of Son and Spirit for the salvation of men: (332).

DIONYSIUS

LETTER TO DIONYSIUS OF ALEXANDRIA (262)

The Trinitarian doctrine develops in the dialectic between the oneness of God and the distinction of the divine persons. The insistence on the oneness, predominant in the West, finds its extreme form in Sabellianism (Modalism) which denies the real distinction of the divine persons. The insistence on the distinction, prevalent in the East with Origen as primary representative, is in danger of placing the Word on the level of creatures.

Dionysius, bishop of Alexandria about the middle of the 3rd century, was concerned with combating the false doctrine of Sabellius; in the process he put too much emphasis on the real distinction of the divine persons with the result that his opponents accused him of tritheism. This discussion became the occasion for a first important statement on the Trinity by Pope Dionysius, striking the correct balance between the distinction of the divine persons and their unity and equality. This document anticipates already to some extent the Arian controversy.

(Unity and Trinity in God)

301 Next I should rightly speak against those who divide,
112 dismember, and so destroy the divine oneness *(monarchia),*
this most august teaching of the Church of God, into three powers and separate beings *(hupostaseis)* and into three Godheads. For I have heard that among you some preachers and teachers of the divine word hold this opinion which is, so to speak, diametrically opposed to the teaching of Sabellius. It is his (Sabellius') blasphemy that the Son is the Father and vice versa, whereas they somehow preach three gods as they divide the sacred unity into three different beings *(hupostaseis),* entirely separate from each other. The Word of God must necessarily be united with the God of all, and the Holy Spirit must abide and dwell in God; it is also necessary that the divine Trinity be recapitulated and led back to One, as to a supreme point, that is to the almighty God of all things. For the doctrine of the misguided Marcion who cuts and divides the divine Oneness *(monarchia)* into three principles is truly diabolic and does not belong to the true disciples of Christ and to those who accept the discipline of the Saviour. For these know well that, while the Trinity is preached in the divine Scripture, neither in the Old nor in the New Testament three gods are taught.

(The divinity of the Son)

302 Equally guilty are those who believe that the Son is a creature
113 and that the Lord was made in the same way as one of the things that were really made, for the divine Word testifies that

He is born as it is proper and fitting for Him and not created or made. It is indeed not a small but an enormous blasphemy to say that the Lord is in some way made by hand. For if the Son was made there was a time when He was not. But He was always since He is in the Father, as He Himself declares *(cf. Jn 14.10f)*, and since Christ is Word, Wisdom and Power—and, as you know, the divine Scriptures teach that Christ is all that *(cf. Jn 1.14; 1 Cor. 1.24)*—all of which are truly God's powers. Hence, if the Son was made, there was a time when these were not, which would mean that there was a time when God was without them, which is truly absurd....

(Conclusion)

303 Therefore, neither is the admirable and divine unity to be
115 separated into three Godheads, nor is the excellence and supreme greatness of the Lord to be diminished by using the word 'made' *(poiêsis);* but one must believe in God, the almighty Father, in Christ Jesus His Son, and in the Holy Spirit in such a way that the Word is united with the God of all. For He says: "I and the Father are one" *(Jn 10.30)* and "I am in the Father and the Father in me" (Jn 14.11). In this way the divine Trinity and the holy doctrine of the Oneness *(monarchia)* will be preserved in their integrity.

THE FIRST GENERAL COUNCIL OF NICAEA
SYMBOL OF NICAEA (325)

(304) *The Council of Nicaea condemned the heresy of Arius who taught that the second person of the Godhead is not equal to the Father but is created in time. Arius' doctrine is the extreme form of the trend of subordinationism which is not absent among the early Fathers. It connects the Son, through whom all things were made, with the created world in such a way that He is no longer truly God but belongs already to the side of creation.*

The Council is a landmark in the Trinitarian doctrine as it firmly places the Son of God on the side of God. This is the meaning of the key word of the council, 'homoousios', "one in being" with the Father. The question, however, of the positive relation between Father and Son remains here open and is not yet ripe for definition. Hence the struggle regarding the positive meaning of the 'homoousios' *will arise only after the Council. See introduction and text, n. 7.*

THE FIRST GENERAL COUNCIL OF CONSTANTINOPLE
SYMBOL OF CONSTANTINOPLE (381)

The second ecumenical Council, the first of Constantinople, deals with the divinity of the Holy Spirit. All Arians had necessarily denied His divinity as a consequence of their denying the divinity of the Son. Some continued to do so even after the Arian heresy was rejected at Nicaea. It is only after Nicaea that the question of the Holy Spirit came into the orbit of serious theological reflection. The Creed is till today the common formula of faith between East and West.

The text of the Creed is found under n. 12. Here only the passage concerning the Holy Spirit is quoted. It expresses His divinity by His func-tions, mainly by His function of giving the divine life to man. The original text speaks only of the origin of the Holy Spirit from the Father. In the third Council of Toledo (589) the 'Filioque' was added so that the Creed asserts the origin of the Holy Spirit "from the Father and the Son". This addition became the object of the great controversy between the Eastern and Western Churches from the 8th century onwards (cf. n. 12, note 1).

305   (We believe) in the Holy Spirit, the Lord and Giver of life, who
150   proceeds from the Father (and the Son), who together with
          the Father and the Son is worshipped and glorified, who has
spoken through the prophets.

THE COUNCIL OF ROME

"TOME OF DAMASUS" (382)

Shortly after the General Council of Constantinople, Pope Damasus (366-384) called a Council at Rome to renew the condemnation of the errors of the time. Some of these refer to Christology (cf. nn. 603/6ff). Those regarding the Trinity are mainly concerned with the divinity of the Son and of the Holy Spirit.

306/1   We anathematise those who do not with full freedom
153   proclaim that He (the Holy Spirit) is of one power and
            substance with the Father and the Son.

306/2   We likewise anathematise those who follow the error of
154   Sabellius in saying that the Father and the Son are one and
            the same.

306/3   We anathematise Arius and Eunomius who, with equal
155   impiety though in different words, assert that the Son and
            the Holy Spirit are creatures.

306/10 Anyone who denies that the Father is always, the Son is
162   always, and the Holy Spirit is always, is a heretic.

306/11 Anyone who denies that the Son is born of the Father, that
163   is of His divine substance, is a heretic.

306/12 Anyone who denies that the Son of God is true God, as the

164   Father is true God, that He can do all things, knows all things, and is equal to the Father, is a heretic.

306/13   Anyone who says that the Son, while incarnate on earth,
165   was not in heaven with the Father, is a heretic.

306/16   Anyone who denies that the Holy Spirit, like the Son, is
168   really and truly from the Father, of the divine substance, and true God, is a heretic.

306/17   Anyone who denies that the Holy Spirit can do all things,
169   knows all things and is everywhere present, just as the Father and the Son, is a heretic.

306/18   Anyone who says that the Holy Spirit is a creature, or made
170   by the Son, is a heretic.

306/19   Anyone who denies that the Father made all things, that is
171   things visible and invisible, through the Son and the Holy Spirit, is a heretic.

306/20   Anyone who denies that the Father, the Son and the Holy
172   Spirit have one Godhead, one might, one majesty, one power, one glory, one Lordship, one kingdom, one will and truth, is a heretic.

306/21   Anyone who denies that there are three true persons, the
173   Father, the Son and the Holy Spirit, equal, living eternally, containing all things visible and invisible, all-powerful, judging, creating and saving all things, is a heretic.

306/22   Anyone who denies that the Holy Spirit is to be adored by
174   all creatures just as the Son and the Father, is a heretic.

306/23   Anyone who has a correct idea about Father and Son, but
175   not about the Holy Spirit is a heretic, because all heretics who do not think correctly about the Son and the Spirit share in the unbelief of the Jews and pagans.

306/24   If anyone, while saying that the Father is God, that His Son
176   is God and that the Holy Spirit is God, divides them and means (several) gods, and does not say that they are God on account of the one Godhead and might which we believe and know to belong to the Father and the Son and the Holy Spirit; and if he excludes the Son and the Holy Spirit and believes that only the Father is God and this is what he means when he believes in one

God, he is a heretic on all these points and indeed a Jew. For, the name of gods has been dispensed and given by God to the angels and all the saints; but for the Father, the Son and the Holy Spirit, because of their one and equal divinity it is not the name of gods but of God which we are shown and taught to believe; for we are baptised solely in the Father, Son, and Holy Spirit, and not in the name of archangels or angels, as the heretics, the Jews or even the pagans in their blindness.

177   This then is the salvation of Christians, that, believing in the Trinity, that is in Father, Son and Holy Spirit, (and) baptised in it, we must believe without doubt that to it belongs the one and only true Godhead and might, majesty and substance.

THE PSEUDO-ATHANASIAN SYMBOL *QUICUMQUE*

(307) *The classical formula of the Trinitarian faith in the West is the so-called "Athanasian Creed", which belongs to the end of the 5th century. See introduction and text in nn. 16-17.*

THE ELEVENTH COUNCIL OF TOLEDO
SYMBOL OF FAITH (675)

This small local Council, attended by only 17 bishops, has little significance today except for the beautiful confession of faith which was recited at its opening. The official value of this document consists in the fact that in subsequent centuries it was kept in highest regard and considered a genuine expression of the Trinitarian faith; it is one of the important formulas of doctrine. In fact, hardly anywhere is the reflection of the early Church on the Trinitarian mystery and on Christ expressed with such precision and acumen as in this Creed which sums up the tradition of the earlier Councils and patristic theology of the West.

(The divine Trinity)

. **308**   We confess and believe that the holy and ineffable Trinity,
525   Father, Son and Holy Spirit, is one God by nature, of one substance, of one nature as also of one majesty and power.

(The Father)

And we profess that the Father is not begotten, not created, but unbegotten. For He Himself, from whom the Son has received His birth and the Holy Spirit His procession, has His origin from no one. He is therefore the source and origin of the whole Godhead. He Himself is the Father of His own essence, who in an ineffable way has begotten the Son from His ineffable substance. Yet He did not beget something different *(aliud)* from what He Himself is: God has begotten God, light has begotten light. From Him, therefore, is "all fatherhood in heaven and on earth" *(cf. Eph. 3.15 Vulg.)*.

(The Son)

309 We also confess that the Son was born, but not made, from
526   the substance of the Father, without beginning, before all
ages, for at no time did the Father exist without the Son, nor the Son without the Father. Yet the Father is not from the Son, as the Son is from the Father, because the Father was not generated by the Son but the Son by the Father. The Son, therefore, is God from the Father, and the Father is God, but not from the Son. He is indeed the Father of the Son, not God from the Son; but the latter is the Son of the Father and God from the Father. Yet in all things the Son is equal to God the Father, for He has never begun nor ceased to be born. We also believe that He is of one substance with the Father; wherefore He is called *homoousios* with the Father, that is of the same being as the Father, for *homos* in Greek means 'one' and *ousia* means 'being', and joined together they mean 'one in being'. We must believe that the Son is begotten or born not from nothing or from any other substance, but from the womb of the Father, that is from His substance. Therefore the Father is eternal, and the Son is also eternal. If He was always Father, He always had a Son, whose Father He was, and therefore we confess that the Son was born from the Father without beginning. We do not call the same Son of God a part of a divided nature,[1] because He was generated from the Father, but we assert that the perfect Father has begotten the perfect Son, without diminution or division, for it pertains to the Godhead alone not to have an unequal Son. This Son of God is also Son by nature, not by adoption; of Him we must also believe that God the Father begot Him neither by an act of will nor out of necessity, for in God there is no necessity nor does will precede wisdom.

(The Holy Spirit)

310 We also believe that the Holy Spirit, the third person in the
527   Trinity, is God, one and equal with God the Father and the
Son, of one substance and of one nature, not, however, begot-

---

1. Cf. VIGILIUS THAPS., *Contra Arianos, Sabellianos et Photinianos dialogus*, II, 13.

ten nor created but proceeding from both, and that He is the Spirit of both. Of this Holy Spirit, we also believe that He is neither unbegotten nor begotten, for if we called Him unbegotten we would assert two Fathers, or if begotten, we would appear to preach two Sons. Yet He is called the Spirit not of the Father alone, nor of the Son alone, but of both Father and Son. For He does not proceed from the Father to the Son, nor from the Son to sanctify creatures, but He is shown to have proceeded from both at once, because He is known as the love or the sanctity of both. Hence we believe that the Holy Spirit is sent by both, as the Son is sent by the Father. But He is not less than the Father and the Son, in the way in which the Son, on account of the body which He has assumed, testifies that He is less than the Father and the Holy Spirit.

(The oneness in the Trinity)

311   This is the way of speaking about the Holy Trinity as it has
528   been handed down: one must not call it or believe it to be
         threefold, but Trinity. Nor can it properly be said that in the one God there is the Trinity, but the one God is the Trinity. In the relative names of the persons the Father is related to the Son, the Son to the Father, and the Holy Spirit to both. While they are called three persons in view of their relations, we believe in one nature or substance. Although we profess three persons, we do not profess three substances, but one substance and three persons. For the Father is Father not with respect to Himself but to the Son, and the Son is Son not to Himself but in relation to the Father; and likewise the Holy Spirit is not referred to Himself but is related to the Father and the Son, inasmuch as He is called the Spirit of the Father and the Son. So when we say 'God', this does not express a relationship to another, as of the Father to the Son or of the Son to the Father or of the Holy Spirit to the Father and the Son, but 'God' refers to Himself only.

312   For, if we are asked about the single persons, we must confess
529   that each is God. Therefore, we say that the Father is God,
         the Son is God, the Holy Spirit is God, each one distinctly; yet there are not three gods, but one God. Similarly, we say that the Father is almighty, the Son is almighty, the Holy Spirit is almighty, each one distinctly; yet there are not three almighty ones, but one Almighty, as we profess one light and one principle. Hence we confess and believe that each person distinctly is fully God, and the

three persons together are one God. Theirs is an undivided and equal Godhead, majesty and power, which is neither diminished in the single persons nor increased in the three. For it is not less when each person is called God separately, nor is it greater when all three persons are called one God.

313 This Holy Trinity, which is the one true God, is not without
530 number; yet it is not comprised by number, because in the relationships of the persons there appears number, but in the substance of the Godhead nothing is comprised that could be counted. Therefore they imply number only in so far as they are mutually related, but they lack number in so far as they are by themselves *(ad se)*. For this Holy Trinity has so much one name referring to its nature that it cannot be used in the plural with relation to the three persons. This then is, in our faith, the meaning of the saying in Holy Scripture: "Great is our Lord, abundant in power, and of His wisdom there is no number" *(Ps. 147 (146) 5 Vulg.)*.

(The Trinity in the oneness)

314 However, though we have said that these three persons are
530 one God, we are not allowed to say that the same one is the Father who is the Son, or that He is the Son who is the Father, or that He who is the Holy Spirit is either the Father or the Son. For He is not the Father who is the Son, nor is the Son He who is the Father, nor is the Holy Spirit He who is the Father or the Son, even though the Father is that which the Son is, the Son that which the Father is, the Father and the Son that which the Holy Spirit is, that is one God by nature. For, when we say: He who is the Father is not the Son, we refer to the distinction of persons; but when we say: the Father is that which the Son is, the Son that which the Father is, and the Holy Spirit that which the Father is and the Son is, this clearly refers to the nature or substance, whereby God exists since in substance they are one; for we distinguish the persons, but we do not divide the Godhead.

531 Hence, we recognise the Trinity in the distinction of persons and we profess the unity on account of the nature or substance. Thus, the three are one by nature, not as person.

(The undivided Trinity)

315 Nevertheless these three persons are not to be considered

531 separable since, according to our belief, none of them ever existed or acted before another, after another, without another. For they are inseparable both in what they are and in what they do, because, according to our faith, between the Father who generates and the Son who is generated or the Holy Spirit who proceeds, there has not been an interval of time in which the one who generates would precede the one who is generated, or there would be no begotten one to Him who begets, or the Holy Spirit in His proceeding would appear later than Father or Son. For this reason we profess and believe that this Trinity is inseparable and distinct *(inconfusa)*. We say, therefore, of these three persons, as our fore-fathers defined it, that they should be acknowledged, not separated. For if we listen to what Holy Scripture says about Wisdom: "She is a reflection of eternal light" *(Wis. 7.26)*, we see that, as the reflection belongs inseparably to the light, so too, according to our confession, the Son cannot be separated from the Father. Therefore, neither do we confuse these three persons whose nature is one and insepara-ble, nor do we preach that they are in any way separable.

316 The Holy Trinity itself has indeed deigned clearly to reveal it to
532 us: in these names by which He wanted the single persons to be known, it is impossible to understand one person without the other; one cannot conceive of the Father without the Son, nor can the Son be found without the Father. Indeed, the very relation-ship expressed in the personal names forbids us to separate the persons, for, though it does not name them together, it implies them. No one can hear any one of these names without necessarily under-standing also the other.

While then these Three are One and this One Three, each of the persons retains His own characteristics: The Father has eternity without birth; the Son has eternity with birth; the Holy Spirit has procession without birth with eternity.

THE FOURTH LATERAN GENERAL COUNCIL (1215)

More than four hundred bishops answered Pope Innocent III's call to the twelfth General Council held at the Lateran in Rome. Two documents of this Council are significant for the interpretation of the Trinitarian faith. First is the solemn Creed composed for the occasion, directed against the heretical trends of the time, mainly against the Albigensian revolt. It con-tains the basic truths about the Holy Trinity (cf. n. 19).

The second document is a special statement against Abbot Joachim de Fiore (ob. 1202). There had been two main approaches to the understand-

ing of the Trinitarian mystery. According to the one coming mainly from the Eastern Fathers and which is centred on God the Father, God means the Father; Son and Holy Spirit are conceived as participating in His divinity. The second, developed mainly in the West, especially by St Augustine, was centred on the one divine nature which subsists as Father, Son and Holy Spirit. Peter the Lombard had systematised this approach, making the divine essence the centre of his speculation. Joachim de Fiore took up the Eastern trend, and attacked Peter. In doing so he exaggerated the distinction of the divine persons. The Council defends Peter against this false accusation and sanctions the doctrine which became the basis of the Trinitarian speculation of most scholastics.

Chapter II: The Error of Abbot Joachim

317 We condemn and reject the booklet or tract written by Abbot
803 Joachim against Master Peter the Lombard on the unity and
essence of the Trinity, calling him heretical and insane, because in his *Sententiae* he says: "There is one supreme reality, the Father, the Son and the Holy Spirit, which is neither generating, nor born, nor proceeding." Thus, Joachim asserts that he (Peter) does not teach a Trinity but a quaternity in God, viz., three persons and that common essence as a fourth. Joachim clearly professes that there is no such reality which is Father, Son and Holy Spirit; there is no essence or substance or nature, though he agrees that Father, Son and Holy Spirit are one essence, one substance and one nature. But this unity he conceives not as true and proper, but, so to say, as collective and by similitude, just as many people are called one nation, and many faithful one Church, as in the texts: "The multitude of believers had but one heart and one soul" *(Acts 4.32 Vulg.)*, and "he who is united to the Lord becomes one spirit with Him" *(1 Cor. 6.17)*; and again: "He who plants and he who waters are one" *(1 Cor. 3.8)*, and "we all are one body in Christ" *(Rom. 12.5)*; and in the book of Kings: "My people and your people are one" *(cf. Ruth 1.16)*. To support his doctrine he relies mainly on the word which Christ spoke in the Gospel about the faithful: "I will, Father, that they be one in us as we are one, that they may be perfectly one" *(Jn 17.22f)*. This is how he argues: Christ's faithful are one not as one reality which is common to all, but they are one in this way, namely, one Church on account of the unity of the faith, and finally one kingdom on account of the bond of indissoluble charity. So we read in the canonical epistle of the apostle John (as it is found in some codices): "There are three who give testimony in heaven, the Father, the Son and the Holy Spirit, and the three are one" *(1 Jn 5.7 Vulg.)*, and immediately it is

added: "And there are three that give testimony on earth, the spirit, the water and the blood, and these three are one" *(1 Jn 5.8 Vulg.)*.

318 We therefore, with the approval of the Sacred Council, believe
804 and confess with Peter the Lombard that there is one highest, incomprehensible and ineffable reality, which is truly Father, Son, and Holy Spirit; the three persons together, and each person distinctly; therefore in God there is only Trinity, not a quaternity, because each of the persons is that reality, viz., that divine substance, essence or nature which alone is the beginning of all things, apart from which nothing else can be found. This reality is neither generating nor generated, nor proceeding, but it is the Father who generates, the Son who is generated and the Holy Spirit who proceeds, so that there be distinctions between the persons but unity in nature.

319 Hence, though "the Father is one person *(alius)*, the Son
805 another person, and the Holy Spirit another person, yet there is not another reality *(aliud)*",[1] but what the Father is, this very same reality is also the Son, this the Holy Spirit, so that in orthodox Catholic faith we believe them to be of one substance. For the Father gives His substance to the Son, generating Him from eternity, as He Himself testifies: "That which my Father has given me is greater than all" *(Jn 10.29 Vulg.)*. One cannot say that He gave Him a part of His substance and retained a part for Himself, since the substance of the Father is indivisible, being entirely simple. Nor can one say that in generating the Father transferred His substance to the Son, as though He gave it to the Son in such a way as not to retain it for Himself, for so He would have ceased to be substance. It is therefore clear that the Son, being born, received the substance of the Father without any diminution, and thus Father and Son have the same substance. Thus, the Father and the Son and the Holy Spirit who proceeds from both are the same reality.

320 When then He who is the Truth prays to the Father for His
806 faithful "that they may be one in us as we also are one" *(Jn 17.22)*, the word 'one' as applied to the disciples is to be taken in the sense of a union of charity in grace, but in the case of the divine persons in the sense of a unity of identity in nature. In the same way, in another occasion the Truth says: "you must be perfect as your

---

1. Cf. GREGORY OF NAZIANZEN, *Epistola ad Cledonium.*

heavenly Father is perfect" *(Mt. 5.48)*, as though He were saying more explicitly: "you must be perfect" in the perfection of grace "as your heavenly Father is perfect" in the perfection of nature, i.e., each in his own way. For between Creator and creature no similitude can be expressed without implying a greater dissimilitude. Anyone therefore who presumes to defend or approve the opinion or doctrine of the above-mentioned Joachim in this matter should be rejected by all as a heretic.

THE SECOND GENERAL COUNCIL OF LYONS

CONSTITUTION ON THE BLESSED TRINITY AND ON THE CATHOLIC FAITH (1274)

The Council has significance as the first large-scale attempt to bring about the re-union of the Eastern and Western Churches (cf. n. 22i).

For the Trinitarian doctrine, two documents are important: 1) the so-called "Profession of Faith of Michael Palaeologus", a large part of which deals with the Trinitarian mystery (cf. nn. 22-25); 2) the "Constitution on the Holy Trinity and the Catholic Faith", containing the explanation of the Latin doctrine on the origin of the Holy Spirit. Against Eastern misunderstandings it is stated that the origin of the Holy Spirit from Father and Son does not imply a double principle in God. This passage of the Constitution is quoted here.

(On the procession of the Holy Spirit)

321 We confess faithfully and devoutly that the Holy Spirit pro-
850 ceeds eternally from Father and Son, not as from two princi-
ples but from one, not by two spirations but by one only. This the holy Roman Church, the mother and teacher of all the faithful, has so far professed, preached and taught; this she continues to hold, to preach, to profess and to teach. This is the unchangeable and true doctrine of the orthodox Fathers and Doctors, both Latin and Greek. However, some have fallen into various errors out of ignorance of the above indisputable truth. Therefore, in order to forestall such errors, with the approval of the holy Council, we condemn and disapprove those who presume to deny that the Holy Spirit proceeds eternally from Father and Son, or who rashly dare to assert that the Holy Spirit proceeds from Father and Son as from two principles, not from one.

THE GENERAL COUNCIL OF FLORENCE

The 17th General Council, held at Florence, marks the second large-scale attempt to bring about union between the Eastern and the Western

Churches. *It was more successful than Lyons II; yet, again, it had no lasting effect. The Council treated the controversial questions between East and West.*

For the Trinitarian doctrine two documents are important:

1. The Decree for the Greeks (1439): it explains the procession of the Holy Spirit from Father and Son, allowing, however, also the dynamic formula, more in keeping with Eastern thinking, according to which the Spirit proceeds from the Father through the Son. It also defends as legitimate the insertion of the 'Filioque' in the Creed.

2. The Decree for the Jacobites (1442): it is addressed to Syrian Christians and contains an elaborate formulation of the Trinitarian faith, with special emphasis on the procession of the Holy Spirit. It also contains the classical formula, borrowed from St Anselm, that in God everything is one except for the relative opposition of the persons, e.g., between Father and Son. It culminates in the doctrine of the mutual indwelling of the divine persons.

DECREE FOR THE GREEKS (1439)

(On the procession of the Holy Spirit)

322 In the name of the Holy Trinity, Father, Son and Holy Spirit,
1300 with the approval of this sacred universal Council of Florence, we define that this truth of faith must be believed and received by all and that all must profess: the Holy Spirit is eternally from Father and Son; He has His nature and subsistence at once *(simul)* from Father and Son; He proceeds eternally from both as from one principle and through one spiration *(cf. n. 321)*.

323 We declare: When the holy Doctors and Fathers say that the
1301 Holy Spirit proceeds from the Father through the Son, this must be understood in the sense that, as the Father, so also the Son is what the Greeks call 'cause' and the Latins 'principle' of the subsistence of the Holy Spirit. And, since the Father has through generation given to the only-begotten Son everything that belongs to the Father, except being Father, the Son has also eternally from the Father, from whom He is eternally born, that the Holy Spirit proceeds from the Son.

324 Moreover, we define that the explanatory words *'Filioque'*
1302 have been added in the Symbol legitimately and with good reason for the sake of clarifying the truth and under the impact of a real need at that time.

DECREE FOR THE JACOBITES (1442)

325 The holy Roman Church, founded on the word of our Lord

1330   and Saviour, firmly believes, professes and preaches the one true almighty, unchangeable and eternal God, Father, Son and Holy Spirit, one in essence, trine in persons: the Father not begotten, the Son begotten from the Father, and the Holy Spirit proceeding from Father and Son. The Father is not the Son or the Holy Spirit; the Son is not the Father or the Holy Spirit; the Holy Spirit is not the Father or the Son. But, the Father is only the Father, the Son only the Son, the Holy Spirit only the Holy Spirit. The Father alone begot the Son out of His substance; the Son alone was begotten from the Father alone; the Holy Spirit alone proceeds from both Father and Son. These three persons are one God and not three gods, for the three are one substance, one essence, one nature, one Godhead, one infinity, one eternity, and everything (in them) is one where there is no opposition of relationship.[1]

326   "On account of this unity the Father is wholly in the Son and
1331   wholly in the Holy Spirit; the Son wholly in the Father and wholly in the Holy Spirit; the Holy Spirit wholly in the Father and wholly in the Son. None precedes the other in eternity, none exceeds the other in greatness, nor excels the other in power. For it is from eternity and without beginning that the Son has taken His origin from the Father, and from eternity and without beginning that the Holy Spirit proceeds from the Father and the Son."[2]

All that the Father is or has, He has not from another but from Himself; He is the origin without origin. All that the Son is or has, He has from the Father; He is origin from origin. All that the Holy Spirit is or has, He has at once *(simul)* from the Father and the Son. But the Father and the Son are not two origins of the Holy Spirit but one origin, just as Father, Son and Holy Spirit are not three origins of creation but one origin.

THE FIRST VATICAN GENERAL COUNCIL
THIRD SESSION

DOGMATIC CONSTITUTION *DEI FILIUS* ON THE CATHOLIC
FAITH (1870)

In its confrontation with the current errors (cf. n. 113i), the XXth General Council, the first held at the Vatican, had to re-assert the genuine

---

1. This fundamental principle of Trinitarian theology seems to have been first enunciated by St Anselm, *De processione Spiritus Sancti,* 1.

2. Cf. Fulgentius Rusp., *De fide liber ad Petrum,* 1. 4.

Christian concept of God against materialistic and pantheistic trends. The
following text is found at the beginning of the Constitution Dei Filius.

Chapter I: God Creator of All Things

327   The holy, Catholic Roman Church believes and confesses:
3001   there is one God, true and living, Creator and Lord of heaven
          and earth, mighty, eternal, immense, incomprehensible, infi-
nite in His intellect and will and in all perfection. As He is one unique
and spiritual substance, entirely simple and unchangeable, we must
proclaim Him distinct from the world in existence and essence,
blissful in Himself and from Himself, ineffably exalted above all things
that exist or can be conceived besides Him.

Canons on God Creator of All Things

328   1. If anyone denies the one true God, Creator and Lord of
3021   things visible and invisible, *anathema sit.*

329   2. If anyone is not ashamed to assert that nothing exists
3022   besides matter, *anathema sit.*

330   3. If anyone says that the substance and essence of God and
3023   all things is one and the same, *anathema sit.*

331   4. If anyone says that finite beings, the corporeal as well as the
3024   spiritual, or at least the spiritual ones, have emanated from
          the divine substance; or that the divine essence becomes all
things by self-manifestation or self-evolution; or lastly that God is the
universal or indefinite being which, by self-determination, constitutes
the universality of beings, differentiated in genera, species and individuals, *anathema sit.*

THE SECOND VATICAN GENERAL COUNCIL

(332)   *Vatican II did not treat systematically the theme of God and the*
          Trinity. Yet the deeper reflection on man and his situation, on
human society and on man's needs and aspirations in our time, demanded
the re-thinking of man's relation to God. Besides, the new perspectives on
the mystery of salvation, of revelation and the Church, implied a more
elaborate presentation of the Trinitarian mystery and of the missions of the
Son and the Holy Spirit.
          The Trinitarian structure of the entire work of salvation is unfolded in
LG 2-4, with the conclusion, borrowed from St Cyprian, that "the Church is

clearly a people whose unity derives from that of the Father, the Son, and the Holy Spirit." The same perspective is found in AG 2-4, with a special emphasis on the mission of the Church. Moreover, the Trinitarian life is presented as the model and source of the inter-personal relations in human society (GS 24).

PAUL VI

DECLARATION *MYSTERIUM FILII DEI* OF THE
S. CONGREGATION FOR THE DOCTRINE OF THE FAITH
(21 February 1972)

This declaration is primarily concerned with a certain danger, to which recent theological re-thinking has given rise, of presenting Christological formulations which would fall short of the mystery of Christ's person. The mystery of Christ is, however, so intimately connected with the mystery of the Trinity that failures to enunciate one adequately often entail parallel failures as regards the other. This document recalls that, notwithstanding the fact that the mystery of the Trinity has been revealed to us in the history of salvation, God is in Himself triune independently of, and prior to His self-manifestation in history. The eternity of the three persons, and in particular of the Holy Spirit, must be preserved. The pronouncements of the Councils of the Church are quoted to this effect; the document re-affirms that the doctrine "concerning the eternal person of the Holy Spirit belongs to the immutable truth of the Catholic faith" (cf. n. 671). The text is found in AAS 64 (1972) 237 ff.

(Recent errors concerning the most Holy Trinity and especially the Holy Spirit)

333 The opinion that Revelation has left us uncertain about the eternity of the Trinity, and in particular about the eternal existence of the Holy Spirit as a person in God distinct from the Father and the Son, is, therefore, contrary to the faith. It is true that the mystery of the Most Holy Trinity was revealed to us in the economy of salvation, and most of all in Christ Himself who was sent into the world by the Father and together with the Father sends to the People of God the life-giving Spirit. But, by this revelation there is also given to those who believe some knowledge of God's intimate life, in which "the Father who begets, the Son who is born, and the Holy Spirit who proceeds" are "of the same substance and fully equal, equally almighty and equally eternal" (cf. n. 19).

CHAPTER IV

MAN AND THE WORLD

Revelation is God's word addressed to man. It speaks of God in relation to man and the world to make man understand and fulfil the destiny given him in God's plan. This plan of God is centred on Jesus Christ, in whom God wants "to unite all things, things in heaven and things on earth" (Eph. 1.10). From its very beginning creation is ordained towards Jesus Christ. He is "the first-born of all creation.... All things were created through Him and for Him" (Col. 1.15f). Thus, the doctrine of creation belongs to the biblical revelation; from the beginning it has been included in the Christian faith and is found already in the early Creeds.

The theology of creation is concerned not with the scientific understanding of man and the world, though it necessarily had first to be expressed in terms of the contemporary cosmology of the Bible and later of the Middle Ages. It is in fact one of the main concerns of a modern theology of creation to free itself of conceptions which, conditioned as they were by time, appear today antiquated, and to express the revealed truth in terms meaningful to modern man, while, at the same time, asserting anew the basic truths conveyed in the Bible and consistently defended by the Church.

The first, and in fact the oldest concern with regard to the doctrine of creation is the assertion of the one God, Creator of heaven and earth; related to it is the struggle against a dualistic conception of the world. It is incompatible with the biblical and Christian conception of God that the material universe, and consequently also the human body, be excluded from God's creation and considered as evil, as originating from the realm of darkness; hence the Church's relentless condemnation of the various forms of Manichaeism right into the Middle Ages.

At the same time the Church has always insisted on God's transcendence, on His freedom in creating man and the world. God's intimate union with His creatures notwithstanding, the dividing line between the infinite and the finite may never be blurred. Hence the rejection of various forms of pantheism, of an explanation of the world through emanation, and, in our own time, of a material conception of evolution which would exclude God's creative action and freedom.

As to man, it is the sacred duty of the Church throughout the ages to defend his spiritual nature and his destiny reaching beyond the material processes of nature; this is why her doctrine lays emphasis on man's spiritual soul originated from God, and on his freedom. At the same time man is one, in body and soul; his spiritual destiny may not be divorced from his concrete human life. It is not man's soul only, but the whole human person, and in him the whole created world which must find their fulfilment in God. Hence the Church's repeated condemnation of theories which tend to separate body and soul.

In recent theology, formulated in the Second Vatican Council and post-Conciliar documents, the scope of the Church's teaching has been widened beyond man's individual nature and destiny. Man's creation in the "image of God" is the core of his dignity and the source of his inviolable rights; he is also considered in his responsibility towards the world and society. Thus the doctrine about man leads to a theology of work, culture, history and society.

*   *   *

These then are the main doctrinal points contained in the following documents:

God created the whole world, spiritual and material: 5, 7, 12, 19, 22, 39/1, 328, 331, 403f, 408f, 411/2, 412, 414f, 418, 627/1.
The world is distinct from God: 402/5, 406/27, 411/1, 416f.
God created the world in freedom, and not from eternity: 19, 401/8, 406, 412, 418;
to manifest His goodness: 412;
for His glory: 418.
God guides the world through His providence: 402/9, 403, 411/2, 413, 627/1.
All created things are good: 19, 402/7.11.13, (404), 408.
The created world has its own 'autonomy': 423.
Man is created by God, in body and soul, as the crown of creation: 19, 39/1, 402/11-13, (404), 412, 421, 429;
as God's image: 425;
with a unique dignity: (421i), 421, 426;
and inviolable rights: 426.
He is created free: 430.
The human soul is created by God: 39/1, 402/5f, 406/27, 419.
It does not pre-exist before conception: 401/1, 402/6.

It is not begotten by the parents: 405, 407.
It is individual and immortal: 410, 421.
It is the 'form' of the body: 405, 410.
There is one human race: 420, 424.
Man is a person in society: 428.
Each man is related to Christ and the Church: 427.
Man is destined to master nature through his work: 422.

THE COUNCIL OF CONSTANTINOPLE
ANATHEMATISMS AGAINST THE ORIGENISTS (543)

*Under patriarch Menas this provincial Council of Constantinople edited
a series of canons against the Origenists which were later confirmed by
Pope Vigilius. The doctrine condemned is not directly that of Origen, but of
a group of monks of Jerusalem who exaggerated and proposed as firm
doctrine what Origen had advanced as a hypothesis for theological thinking. Their doctrine is influenced by Platonist philosophy. Two canons refer
to the doctrine of creation. Firstly, the theory according to which pre-
existing souls are inserted into bodies as a punishment for sin is condemned.
As proposed by the Origenists the theory made use of a peculiar etymology
of the word* psuchê. *This doctrine conceived the body as a degrading place
of exile; besides, the idea of a sin committed before the union with the body
dissolved the unity of the body and soul as constituents of one person. Here
lies the main anthropological argument against the concept of the transmigration of souls. Secondly, the Origenists conceived the origin of the world
as necessary; thus, they excluded the freedom of God's creative act. This
opinion too is condemned.*

401/1   If anyone says or thinks that human souls had a previous
403   existence, viz., that first they were spirits or blessed powers
            which, having become tired of the contemplation of God
and turned to evil, grew cold *(apopsugeisas)* in the love of God, and
for this reason came to be called souls *(psuchai)* and so were in
punishment sent down into bodies, *anathema sit.*

401/8   If anyone says or holds that God's power is finite, or that He
410   has created all that He could comprehend and think, or that
            creatures are co-eternal with God, *anathema sit.*

THE COUNCIL OF BRAGA
ANATHEMATISMS AGAINST THE PRISCILLIANISTS (561)

*Priscillian (ob. 385) was the founder of a Manichaean sect in Spain. He
taught that the devil was the evil principle and the creator of matter and of
the human body, whereas the soul is divine by nature and tied to the body in
punishment for previous sins. This teaching is borrowed from the Origenists. The canons of the Council of Braga, in Portugal, reject the radical
dualism of matter and spirit and the contempt of the human body which it
implies. All that exists is good because it is made by God.*

402/5   If anyone believes that the human souls or the angels come
455   from the substance of God as Manes and Priscillian have
            said, *anathema sit.*

402/6   If anyone says that the human souls first committed sin in

456 the heavenly abode and for this reason were thrown down on earth into human bodies, as Priscillian has said, *anathema sit.*

402/7 If anyone says that the devil was not first a good angel
457 created by God, or that his nature was not the work of God, but that he emerged from darkness, and had no creator but is himself the principle and substance of evil, as Manes and Priscillian have said, *anathema sit.*

402/8 If anyone says that the devil made some of the creatures in
458 the world, and that he is by his own power the author of thunder and lightning and storms and droughts, as Priscillian has said, *anathema sit.*

402/9 If anyone believes that the human souls and bodies are by
459 their fate bound to the stars, as pagans and Priscillian have said, *anathema sit.*

402/11 If anyone condemns human marriage and despises *(per-*
461 *horrescit)* the procreation of children, as Manes and Priscillian have said, *anathema sit.*

402/12 If anyone says that the formation of the human body is the
462 work of the devil and that the conception of children in their mothers' womb is brought about through the activity of the devil, and for this reason does not believe in the resurrection of the body, as Manes and Priscillian have said, *anathema sit.*

402/13 If anyone says that the creation of all flesh is not the work
463 of God but of bad angels, as Manes and Priscillian have said, *anathema sit.*

INNOCENT III

PROFESSION OF FAITH PRESCRIBED TO THE WALDENSIANS

(1208)

The medieval followers of Manichaeism were known in France, from 1180 onwards, under the name of Albigensians. They taught that matter was evil, that the Old Testament came under the influence not of God but of a demiurge or evil spirit. As to the dispensation of the New Testament, they denied the human body of Jesus Christ and rejected the sacraments as means of sanctification, while ascetical abstention from meat was consi- dered by them as of high moral value. A similar teaching was held by the Waldensians in France, and the Lombards in Italy. These movements had a strong anti-clerical character and were directed against the display of worldliness and power in the Church.

The Creed prescribed by Innocent III for those returning from these movements to the doctrine of the Church contains the rejection of dualism in its various aspects: it insists on the creation of all things by God, who is the author of the Old Testament as well as of the New.

403 We believe with our heart and confess with our tongue that
790 Father, Son, and Holy Spirit are one God... creator, maker, ruler and provider of all things, corporeal and spiritual, visible and invisible. We believe that one and the same God is author of the Old and the New Testaments.

THE FOURTH LATERAN GENERAL COUNCIL
SYMBOL OF LATERAN (1215)

(404) *This General Council held at the Lateran spoke the Church's final word against the Albigensian and Waldensian errors. Its teaching on creation was later adopted by the first Vatican Council (cf. nn. 412ff). The text is found in n. 19.*

THE GENERAL COUNCIL OF VIENNA (1311-1312)

This Council condemned the doctrine of John Olieu, O.F.M., who taught that the spiritual soul of man is not by itself the "form of the human body", i.e., the principle of organic life. Historically, this condemnation of Olieu, who in 1298 had died in peace with the Church, was an attempt to bring discredit on the so-called "Spirituals", namely on the radical Franciscans who had had Olieu as their leader. There is, however, a deeper meaning in the doctrine of the Council: the spiritualistic movements tended to separate the spirit from the realities of nature and history and so to split human nature into two heterogeneous spheres. The Council doctrine affirming that the spiritual soul is by itself also the principle of organic life is a strong assertion of the unity of man. It is in this sense that Olieu's teaching, which seems to be of merely philosophical interest, is said to go against the Catholic truth.

(The spiritual soul is the form of the body)

405 With the approval of the holy Council we reject as erroneous
902 and contrary to the truth of the Catholic faith any doctrine or opinion which rashly asserts that the substance of the rational and intellectual soul is not truly and of itself *(per se)* the form of the human body, or which calls this into doubt. In order that the truth of the pure faith may be known to all, and the path to error barred, we define that from now on whoever presumes to assert, defend, or obstinately hold that the rational and intellectual soul is not of itself and essentially the form of the human body, is to be censured as heretic.

JOHN XXII

ERRORS OF ECKHART ON THE RELATION BETWEEN GOD
AND WORLD AND MAN (1329)

Twenty-eight articles from Eckhart's sermons and writings were condemned after his death (1327). It is not clear whether he held these articles in the sense in which they are condemned by the Church. The condemnation, however, has doctrinal significance in so far as it brings out God's freedom in the work of creation.

The articles mentioned here, except 406/26, are condemned as "containing error or the blot of heresy, taken as they sound and according to the meaning of their words"; but article 406/26 is only condemned as "very offensive and rash and as suspect of heresy, even though with many supplementary explanations it can acquire or have a Catholic sense" (cf. DS 979).

[406/1] Asked why God did not create the world sooner, he
951   replied that God could not create the world sooner
           because nothing can act before it exists; therefore God
created the world as soon as He existed.

[406/2] Again, it can be granted that the world is from
952   eternity.

[406/3] Again, when God existed, and when He begot His Son,
953   God co-eternal with Himself and co-equal in all things,
           then at the same time and at once *(simul et semel)* He also
created the world.

[406/26] All creatures are one pure nothingness. I do not say that
976   they are little or that they are anything, but that they are
            pure nothingness.

Objection was also raised against Eckhart that he preached two other articles with these words:

[406/27] There is something in the soul that is uncreated and
977   cannot be created; this is the intellect. If the entire soul
            were such, it would be uncreated and could not be
created.

[406/28] God is not good, nor better, nor best; whenever I call
978   God good, I am equally wrong as if I were to call white
            black.

BENEDICT XII
LIBELLUS *CUM DUDUM* (1341)

Traducianism is the doctrine which teaches that not only the body but also the soul is generated by the parents. It affords an easy explanation for the inheritance of psychic qualities and defects, and, in theology, for the transmission of original sin, one which is not, however, in keeping with the Christian faith. Traducianism is unacceptable as it seems to exclude the spirituality of the human soul. It was condemned by Pope Anastasius II (498) (cf. DS 360). It is rejected again among various errors of the Armenians condemned by Pope Benedict XII.

(Condemnation of Traducianism)

407   A teacher among the Armenians... again introduced the
1007   teaching that the human soul of a son is propagated from the
soul of his father, as the body is from the body, and that angels are also propagated one from another. He gave as reason that, since the rational human soul and the intellectual nature of angels are like spiritual lights, they propagate from themselves other spiritual lights.

THE GENERAL COUNCIL OF FLORENCE
DECREE FOR THE JACOBITES (1442)

This decree (cf n. 322i) includes a statement on the Church's teaching on creation, and a condemnation of Manichaean dualism.

408   (The Holy Roman Church) most firmly believes, professes
1333   and proclaims that the one true God, Father, Son, and Holy
Spirit, is the creator of all things, visible and invisible, who, when He so willed, out of His bounty made all creatures, spiritual as well as corporeal. They are good since they were made by Him who is the highest good, but they are mutable because they were made out of nothing. She asserts that there is no such thing as a nature of evil, because all nature, as nature, is good.

409   Furthermore, the Church condemns the error of the Mani-
1336   cheans who asserted two first principles, one of visible, the
other of invisible things, and who said that the God of the New Testament is different from the God of the Old Testament.

THE FIFTH LATERAN GENERAL COUNCIL
BULL *APOSTOLICI REGIMINIS* (1513)

Once more the oneness and individuality of the human person had to be defended against Pietro Pomponazzi, Professor in Padua (1464-1525). Influ-

enced by Aristotelian philosophy, he taught that, because of its ability to grasp universal ideas, the spiritual soul of man is not an individual entity but is common to all men; in death it loses its individual identity and merges with the universal spirit. The principle of organic life, on the other hand, was understood by him to be bound up with matter and to perish in death. The Council proclaims the unity, individuality and immortality of the human soul, and thus re-asserts the oneness of the human nature, comprising the intellectual and organic life.

(The individuality and immortality of the soul)

410   The sower of cockle, the ancient enemy of the human race...,
1440   has dared to sow and make grow in the Lord's field some
pernicious errors which at all times were rejected by the faithful concerning in particular the nature of the rational soul: viz., that it is mortal and one and the same in all men. Some people, rash in their philosophising, assert that this is true at least philosophically speaking. We therefore wish to use the appropriate remedy against this error; and with the approval of the Council we condemn and reprove all those who assert that the intellectual soul is mortal or that it is one and the same in all men, or who raise doubts in this matter. The intellectual soul is not only truly, of itself and essentially, the form of the human body, as it is stated in the canon of Clement V, our predecessor of blessed memory, issued by the Council of Vienna *(cf. n. 405)*, but it is also immortal and, according to the number of bodies into which it is infused, it can be, has been and will be multiplied in individuals.

PIUS IX

SYLLABUS OF CONDEMNED ERRORS (1864)

On this syllabus, cf. n. 101i.

(Errors of Pantheism and Deism)

[411/1]   There does not exist any supreme, all-wise, all-provident
2901   divine being *(numen)* distinct from this universe of things;
God is identical with the nature of things, and therefore subject to change; God actually becomes Himself in man and in the world; all things are God and have the very substance of God; God is one and the same reality with the world, and so is spirit with matter, necessity with liberty, truth with falsehood, good with evil and justice with injustice.

[411/2]   Any action of God on man and the world must be
2902   denied.

THE FIRST VATICAN GENERAL COUNCIL
THIRD SECTION
DOGMATIC CONSTITUTION *DEI FILIUS* ON THE CATHOLIC
FAITH (1870)

The first Vatican Council expressed the Church's stand against the errors of the 19th century. Among these figured in particular materialism according to which only matter exists, and various forms of pantheism identifying in one way or another the world with God. The Council states the doctrine of creation and brings out its meaning. This first chapter on "God creator of all things" is largely based on the text of the Fourth Lateran General Council (cf. n. 19).

Chapter I: God Creator of All Things

(Creation)

412   This one and only true God, of His own goodness and
3002   almighty power, not for the increase of His own happiness,
          nor for the acquirement of His perfection, but in order to
manifest His perfection through the benefits which He bestows on
creatures, with absolute freedom of counsel, "from the beginning of
time made at once *(simul)* out of nothing both orders of creatures,
the spiritual and the corporeal, that is, the angelic and the earthly,
and then *(deinde)* the human creature, who as it were shares in both
orders, being composed of spirit and body" *(cf. n. 19).*

(Providence)

413   By His providence God protects and governs all things which
3003   He has made, "reaching mightily from one end of the earth to
          the other, and ordering all things well" *(Wis. 8.1).* For "all are
open and laid bare to His eyes" *(cf. Heb. 4.13),* also those things
which are yet to come to existence through the free action of
creatures.

Canons on Chapter I

414   1. If anyone denies the one true God, Creator and Lord of
3021   things visible and invisible, *anathema sit.*

415   2. If anyone is not ashamed to assert that nothing exists
3022   besides matter, *anathema sit.*

416   3. If anyone says that the substance and essence of God and
3023   of all things is one and the same, *anathema sit.*

417 4. If anyone says that finite beings, the corporeal as well as the
3024 spiritual, or at least the spiritual ones, have emanated from
the divine substance; or that the divine essence becomes all
things by self-manifestation or self-evolution; or lastly that God is the
universal or indefinite being which, by self-determination, constitutes
the universality of beings differentiated into genera, species and
individuals, *anathema sit.*

418 5. If anyone refuses to confess that the world and all things
3025 contained in it, the spiritual as well as the material, were in
their whole substance produced by God out of nothing; or
says that God created not by an act of will free from all necessity, but
with the same necessity by which He necessarily loves Himself; or
denies that the world was made for the glory of God, *anathema sit.*

PIUS XII

ENCYCLICAL LETTER *HUMANI GENERIS* (1950)

*In the context of other errors, Pius XII treats two questions regarding the
origin of man. Firstly, man's origin through evolution from other living
beings: while formerly evolution was rejected as irreconcilable with the
biblical account of man's creation (which was interpreted in too literal a
sense), and as implying a materialistic conception of man, the question is
now left open to scholarly investigation, supposing that the creation of the
soul by God is maintained. Secondly, monogenism or polygenism, i.e., the
question whether the human race must be conceived as descending from a
single couple or can be considered to originate from several couples:
polygenism is rejected because "it does not appear" to be reconcilable with
the doctrine of original sin inherited by all from Adam. Recent theology,
however, is seeking explanations of original sin under the supposition of
polygenism, and so tries to remove the reason for its rejection.*

(The origin of man through evolution)

419 The teaching of the Church does not forbid that the doctrine
3896 of evolutionism, in so far as it inquires into the origin of the
human body from already existing and living matter, be,
according to the present state of human disciplines and sacred
theology, treated in research and discussion by experts on both
sides; as to the souls, the Catholic faith demands us to hold that they
are immediately created by God....

(Polygenism)

420 As regards the other conjecture, viz., what is called

3897   polygenism, the sons of the Church do not at all have the same freedom. For the faithful cannot lend support to a theory which involves either the existence on this earth, after Adam, of true men who would not originate from him, as the ancestor of all, by natural generation, or that 'Adam' stands for a plurality of ancestors. For, it is not at all apparent how such a view can be reconciled with the data which the sources of revealed truth and the documents of the Church propose concerning original sin, namely, that it originates from a sin truly committed by one Adam, is transmitted to all through generation and is in each, proper to him *(cf. Rom. 5.12-19; nn. 508-511)*.

THE SECOND VATICAN GENERAL COUNCIL

The Council took place at a time when in the world "according to the almost unanimous opinion of believers and unbelievers alike all things should be related to man as their centre and crown" (GS 12). Among the Council documents the Pastoral Constitution Gaudium et Spes *on the Church in the modern world is the one most deeply centred on the question: "What is man?" (ibid.), but the other documents are also strongly influenced by the concern for man.*

In this broad anthropological outlook, the traditional doctrines about creation and human nature are taken for granted and re-asserted only in passing. The real concern of the Council is deeper. It consists in the Christian understanding of the human existence, of man's destiny and task in the world and beyond it.

The moral implications of the Conciliar doctrine of man are treated here in chapters XX to XXII. In this chapter the doctrinal principles are enumerated.

Man, made of body and soul, is the crown of creation (GS 10, 14). He is created in God's likeness (NA 5; AG 7; GS 12, 17, 29, 34), and, therefore, has a unique dignity (GS 12, 27, 40, 46, 63, 91; DH 1). This dignity is "known through the revealed word of God and by reason itself" (DH 2, 9). It is characteristic of modern man that he is deeply conscious of the human dignity (DH 1; GS 9, 27, 73).

All men are equal (GS 29; NA 5); man and woman are of equal dignity (GS 49). By his very nature man is social (GS 23, 24, 32); the human race has a common origin and shares in a common destiny (NA 1; AG 3).

Through work man extends his mastery over nature and betters his life-conditions (GS 33-35).

Man's personal and social life unfolds in the life of the family (GS 47-52), in culture (GS 53-62), in the socio-economic life (GS 25, 63-72), in the political life (GS 73-76), in the family of nations (GS 77-90).

PASTORAL CONSTITUTION *GAUDIUM ET SPES* (1965)

(Man's nature, body and soul)

421   14. Though made up of body and soul, man is one. Through his bodily condition he gathers into himself the elements of the material world: through him these reach their crown and raise their voice freely to praise the Creator. Man, therefore, may not despise his bodily life; rather, he is bound to regard his very body, which was created by God and is to be raised again on the last day, as good and honourable....

Man is not mistaken when he regards himself as superior to material things, and not a mere particle of nature or an anonymous element in the city of men. By his capacity for interior life, he outstrips the whole universe of things.... So, when he acknowledges in himself a spiritual and immortal soul, he is not the plaything of a deceptive fantasy resulting only from his physical and social conditions; rather he is getting at the very depth of reality.

(The value of human activity)

422 34. Considered in itself, human activity, individual and collective—all that tremedous effort which man has made throughout the centuries to better his living conditions—is in keeping with God's design. Man, created in God's image, was given the mandate to subject to himself the earth and all it contains, and to rule the world in justice and holiness; acknowledging God as the creator of all things, he was to refer to Him his own person and all creation; and thus, by the subjection of all things to man, the name of God would be wonderful in all the earth.

(The rightful autonomy of the temporal order)

423 36. ...If by the autonomy of earthly realities we understand that created things and societies have their own laws and values which man must gradually come to know, use and organise, then it is altogether right to demand that autonomy; it is not only requested by men of our day but is also in concordance with the will of the Creator. It is by virtue of their very creation that all things are provided with a stability, truth and goodness of their own, with their own laws and order. Man must respect all this, while acknowledging the methods proper to each science or art. Consequently, if methodical research in any branch of learning is carried out in a truly scientific manner, and in keeping with the norms of morality, it will never really conflict with the faith, because both secular things and the realities of faith derive from the same God....

But if by the phrase 'autonomy of temporal affairs' one means to say that created things do not depend on God, and that man can make use of them without any reference to the Creator, then anyone who believes in the existence of God will sense the falsehood of such opinions. For a creature without a creator vanishes into nothingness.... Indeed, forgetfulness of God makes the creature itself unintelligible.

DECLARATION *NOSTRA AETATE* (1965)

(The unity of the human race)

424 1. All peoples form a single community; their origin is one, for God made the whole human race to dwell over the entire face of the earth (*cf. Acts 17.26*). One also is their final goal, God. His providence, the manifestations of His goodness, His plan of salvation extend to all men (*cf. Wis. 8.1; Acts 14.17; Rom. 2.6f; 1 Tim. 2.4*), until the moment when the elect will be gathered in the Holy City whose light shall be the glory of God, when the nations will walk in His light (*cf. Rev. 21.23f*).

JOHN PAUL II

ADDRESS TO THE THIRD GENERAL ASSEMBLY OF LATIN AMERICAN BISHOPS

(Puebla, 28 January 1979)

Inaugurating the Third General Assembly of the Latin American Bishops on the theme "The Present and the Future of Evangelisation in Latin America", Pope John Paul II reminded the bishops of their pastoral mission. In this context he exposed the "truth concerning man". The text of the address is found in Osservatore Romano *(English Edition), 5 February, 1979, pp. 1-5.*

(Man in God's image)

425 1. (9) Thanks to the Gospel, the Church has the truth about man. This truth is found in an anthropology that the Church never ceases to fathom more thoroughly and to communicate to others. The primordial affirmation of this anthropology is that man is God's image and cannot be reduced to a mere portion of nature or a nameless element in the human city (*cf. n. 421 and GS 12*). This is the meaning of what St Irenaeus wrote: "Man's glory is God, but the recipient of God's every action, of his wisdom and of his power is man...."[1]

---

1. *Adv. Haer.*, III. 20.203.

(Basic rights)

426   3. (1) This dignity (of man) is infringed on the individual level
when due regard is not had for values such as freedom, the
right to profess one's religion, physical and mental integrity, the right
to essential goods, to life.... It is infringed on the social and political
level when man cannot exercise his right of participation, or when he
is subjected to unjust and unlawful coercion, or submitted to physical
or mental torture, etc....

3. (5) In the face of what has been said hitherto, the Church sees
with deep sorrow "the sometimes massive increase of human rights
violations in many parts of the world....Who can deny that today
individual persons and civil powers violate basic rights of the human
person with impunity: rights such as the right to be born, the right to
life, the right to reponsible procreation, to work, to peace, to freedom and social justice, the right to participate in the decisions that
affect people and nations? And what can be said when we face the
various forms of collective violence like discrimination against individuals and groups, the use of physical and psychological torture
perpetrated against prisoners or political dissenters? The list grows
when we turn to the instances of the abduction of persons for
political reasons and look at the acts of kidnapping for material gain
which attack so dramatically family life and the social fabric."[1] We
cry once more: Respect man! He is the image of God! Evangelise, so
that this may become a reality, so that the Lord may transform
hearts and humanise the political and economic systems with man's
responsible commitment as the starting point.

ENCYCLICAL LETTER *REDEMPTOR HOMINIS* (1979)

*The whole Encyclical Letter can be considered as a meditation on the
Biblical understanding of man as the object of God's love and redemption in
Jesus Christ, in the context of the present day world. The text is found in
AAS 71 (1979) 257ff.*

(Each concrete man is related to Christ and the Church)

427   13. What is in question here is man in all his truth, in his full
stature. We are not dealing with abstract man, but the real,
concrete, historical man. We are dealing with each man, for each one
is included in the mystery of the Redemption and with each one

---

1. Message of John Paul II to the Secretary General of the United Nations
Organization on 2 December 1978 (*AAS* 71 (1979) 122).

Christ has united himself for ever through this mystery. Every man comes into the world through being conceived in his mother's womb and being born of his mother, and precisely on account of the mystery of the Redemption is entrusted to the solicitude of the Church. Her solicitude is about the whole man and is focussed on him in an altogether special manner. The object of her care is man in his unique, unrepeatable, real existence, which keeps intact the image and likeness of God himself *(cf. Gen. 1.26)*. The Council points out this fact when, speaking of that likeness, it recalls that "man is the only creature on earth that God willed for itself" *(GS 24)*. Man as "willed" by God, as "chosen" by him from eternity and called, destined for grace and glory—this is each man, the most *concrete* man, the most *real*; this is man in all the fulness of the mystery in which he has become a sharer in Jesus Christ, the mystery in which each one of the four thousand million human beings living on our planet has become a sharer from the moment he is conceived beneath the heart of his mother.

(Personal and social aspects of man)

428   14. The Church cannot abandon man, for his "destiny", that is to say, his election, calling, birth and death, salvation or perdition, is so closely and unbreakably linked with Christ. We are speaking precisely of each man on this planet, this earth that the Creator gave to the first man, saying to man and woman: "Subdue it and have dominion" *(Gen. 1.28)*; of each man in all the unrepeatable reality of what he is and what he does, of his intellect and will, of his conscience and heart. Man in his singular reality, because he is a "person", has a history of his life that is his own, and, most important, a history of his soul. In keeping with the openness of his spirit and also with the many diverse needs of his body and his existence in time, he writes this personal history of his through numerous bonds, contacts, situations, and social structures that link him with other men, beginning to do so from the first moment of his existence on earth, from the moment of his conception and birth. Man in the full truth of his existence, of his personal being and also of his community and social being—in the sphere of his own family, in the sphere of society and very diverse contexts, in the sphere of his own nation or people (perhaps still only that of his clan or tribe), and in the sphere of the whole of mankind—this man is the primary route that the Church must travel in fulfilling her mission: he is the primary and fundamental way for the Church, the way traced out by Christ himself, the way that leads invariably through the mystery of the Incarnation and the Redemption.

It was precisely this man in the full truth of his life, with his conscience, his continual inclination to sin and at the same time his continual aspiration to truth, goodness, beauty, justice and love, that the Second Vatican Council had before its eyes, when, in outlining his situation in the modern world, it drew from the external elements and causes of this situation the immanent truth of humanity *(cf. GS 10)*.

(Man superior to his possessions)

429 16. The essential meaning of this "kingship" and "dominion" of man over the visible world, which the Creator himself gave man for his task, consists in the priority of ethics over technology, in the primacy of the person over things, and in the superiority of spirit over matter. This is why all phases of present day progress must be watched attentively. Each stage of that progress must, so to speak, be x-rayed from this point of view. What is in question is the advancement of persons, not just the multiplying of things that people can use. It is a matter—as a contemporary philosopher has said and as the Council has stated—not so much of "having more" as of "being more" *(cf. nn. 2059, 2145)*....Man cannot relinquish himself or the place in the visible world that belongs to him; he cannot become the slave of things, the slave of economic systems, the slave of his own products.

(Freedom)

430 21. Mature humanity means full use of the gift of freedom received from the Creator when he called to existence the man made "in his image, after his likeness"....Nowadays it is sometimes held, though wrongly, that freedom is an end in itself, that each human being is free when he makes use of freedom as he wishes, and that this must be our aim in the lives of individuals and societies. In reality, freedom is a great gift only when we know how to use it consciously for everything that is our true good. Christ teaches us that the best use of freedom is charity, which takes concrete form in self-giving and in service. For this "freedom Christ has set us free" *(Gal. 5.1; cf. 5.13)* and ever continues to set us free. The Church draws from this source the unceasing inspiration, the call and the drive for her mission and her service among all mankind. The full truth about human freedom is indelibly inscribed on the mystery of the Redemption.

CHAPTER V

ORIGINAL JUSTICE AND FALL

The Christian vocation leads man beyond his natural power to a destiny that is given to him by God's love. Hence the doctrine of creation does not by itself adequately describe the meaning of human life and work. It does say what man is in himself, but not what he is meant to be in God's plan; nor does it express the concrete sinful condition in which man finds himself and from which he is called to a new life. In the teaching of the Church man's supernatural destiny and his sinfulness are presented not merely by way of an analysis of his present condition but as the doctrine on man's origin, based on the biblical narration of paradise and the fall. It may be noted, however, that in the Bible, and consequently also in the doctrine of the Church, the origin of man is not primarily understood in a temporal sense, as though a precise account were intended of the early phase of events in human history, but in a theological sense in so far as these events constitute man's condition. What is said about original justice and sin is not something accidental that would affect only some individuals in a particular period of human history; it refers to facts which radically condition the life of all in all ages and from which is derived the concrete situation in which all must find and attain their salvation.

The doctrine of original justice and sin has been explicitated only from the fifth century onwards. The first occasion for an explicit reflection of the Church on the matter has been the challenge raised against it by Pelagius (cf. n. 1901). Pelagius saw primarily in man the subject of moral responsibility: essentially free, man must decide his own destiny. This moralistic system played down the role of grace. It also led Pelagius to reject the idea that in the present state man is weakened and does not enjoy the original condition of freedom in which he was constituted at first. The reality of original sin and its implications for man's life are clearly expressed by the Church against Pelagius.

The second occasion for a deeper reflection on man's original condition has been the rise of Protestantism. Luther's experience of our sinful state and of the apparently irresistible inclination to evil led him to exaggerations in his concept of the fall and to a minimising idea, if not to the denial, of the original state of righteousness. In this context, the Council of Trent enunciated the doctrine of original justice, of the fall of the first man and of the sinful state inherited by all. It stated explicitly what was lost by the fall: the life of grace, freedom from concupiscence and from liability to death; it also explained what is restored by baptism and what is not.

A third occasion offered itself for a renewed reflection on man's original condition; this was the rise of the modern theories of evolution. The new world vision of an evolving universe within which man makes his appearance at a certain point demanded a new assessment of the traditional doctrines: are the concepts of original justice and immortality, and of the subsequent fall into sin and death, compatible with an evolutionary idea of the world and of mankind? A new approach to these questions became all the more necessary as modern biblical research on the corresponding chapters of Genesis (cf. nn. 237 ff) and on the Pauline epistles progressed. The New approach to the question is reflected in recent papal pronouncements. Even today the Church remains engaged in a process of re-thinking and re-interpreting her doctrine on man's original state and fall in the double context of the evolutionary view of the world and of life and of the presence of evil structures in society.

*   *   *

The documents on original justice and sin contain the following doctrinal points:

The first man was endowed with the life of grace: 503,508f, (515).
He was free from death and concupiscence: 501, 508, 512.
These gifts were not due to man: 501, 514/26, 1984, 1998.
Adam lost the supernatural gifts through his sin: 39/9, 503f, 508, 516.
His sin and its fruits are transmitted to his offspring: 39/9, 420, 503, 505, 509–511, (515), 646, 1927.
Original sin differs from actual sin by the absence of personal consent: 506, 514.
It consists in the loss of grace: 503, 508f, 1925.
It brings death with it: 501, 508f.
It is the source of concupiscence which weakens man: 512, 1921, 1925, 1987, 1989.
It does not destroy freedom: 512, 1923/36, 1925, 1955f, 1987, 1989f, 1992.
Original sin is wiped out by baptism: 12, (502), 503, 506, 510–512, 1411, 1412, 1415, 1923–1927, 1932.

THE SIXTEENTH COUNCIL OF CARTHAGE (418)

The first doctrinal decrees on original justice and sin were occasioned by Pelagianism. In the context of the appeal which he made for moral renewal, Pelagius denied the necessity of grace (cf. n. 1901) and the reality of original sin. In 416 he was censured in a synod of Carthage for the following heresies: Adam was created mortal; his sin harmed himself only, not his offspring; newborn children are in the same condition as Adam before his fall; Christ's death and resurrection are not the cause of men's rising from death, since even before Christ's coming there were men without sin.

A number of decisions were made by the Church's teaching office in answer to these articles. First among these is the doctrine of the important provincial Council of Carthage attended by 200 bishops in 418; it is followed by the Indiculus *and the Council of Orange.*

501 1. This has been decided by all the bishops... gathered
222　together in the holy Synod of Carthage: Whoever says that
Adam, the first man, was made mortal in the sense that he was to die a bodily death whether he sinned or not, which means that to quit the body would not be a punishment for sin but a necessity of nature, *anathema sit.*

(502) 2. *(The second canon was later adopted with some minute addi-*
223　*tions by the Council of Trent: cf. n. 511).*

THE *INDICULUS* (between 435 and 442)

On this document, see n. 1907i.

503 1. In Adam's sin all men lost their natural power for good and
239　their innocence. No one can of his own free will rise out of the
depth of this fall if he is not lifted up by the grace of the merciful God. This is the pronouncement of Pope Innocent of blessed memory in his letter to the Council of Carthage: "He (Adam) acted of his own free will when he used his gifts thoughtlessly; he fell into the abyss of sin and sank and found no means to rise again. Betrayed by his freedom for ever, he would have remained weighed down by his fall had not later the advent of Christ raised him up by His grace when through the cleansing of a new regeneration he washed away all previous guilt in the bath of His baptism."[1]

---

1. *Epistola "In requirendis"*, 7.

THE SECOND COUNCIL OF ORANGE (529)

On this document, see n. 1915i.

504 1. If anyone says that through the offence of Adam's sin the
371 whole man, body and soul, was not changed for the worse, but
believes that only the body was subjected to corruption while
the freedom of the soul remained unharmed, he is misled by the error
of Pelagius and goes against Scripture which says: "the soul that sins
shall die" *(Ez. 18.20)*, and: "do you not know that if you yield
yourselves to anyone as obedient slaves you are slaves of the one
whom you obey?" *(Rom. 6.16)*; and again: "whatever overcomes a
man, to that he is enslaved" *(2 Pet. 2.19)*.

505 2. If anyone maintains that the fall harmed Adam alone and not
372 his descendants, or declares that only bodily death which is
the punishment of sin, but not sin itself which is the death of
the soul was passed on to the whole human race by one man, he
ascribes injustice to God and contradicts the words of the apostle:
"Sin came into the world through one man and death through sin and
so death spread to all men as all sinned in him" *(Rom. 5.12 Vulg.)*.

INNOCENT III

LETTER TO HUMBERT, ARCHBISHOP OF ARLES (1201)

*Pope Innocent defends infant baptism by which sin is forgiven without
personal conversion. This is explained by the different nature of personal
and original sin. Original sin is inherent in man by birth without implying a
personal offence against God; it consists in the condition of non-salvation in
which man needs God's saving grace; it can be cleansed through baptism
without a personal act of repentance. The punishment also differs: original
sin excludes from the beatific vision but does not lead to a positive punishment. See also n. 1409.*

(Original sin and actual sin)

506 We say that two kinds of sin must be distinguished, original
780 and actual: original which is contracted without consent and
actual which is committed with consent. Thus original sin,
which is contracted without consent, is remitted without consent by
the power of the sacrament (of baptism); but actual sin, which is
committed with consent, is by no means remitted without consent....

Further, the punishment for original sin is the loss of the beatific
vision, but the punishment of actual sin is the torture of eternal hell.

THE GENERAL COUNCIL OF TRENT
FIFTH SESSION
DECREE ON ORIGINAL SIN (1546)

Luther had taught that original sin consists in concupiscence which remains in man after baptism. Thus a baptised person remains a sinner but concupiscence is no longer laid to his charge because Christ's justice is imputed to the sinner.

The Council did not confine itself to the refutation of Luther's teaching but expounded the whole of Catholic teaching on the matter. The Pelagian errors were again refuted as well as those of the Manichaeans and Priscillianists who denied the existence of original sin in children born from a Christian marriage.

The doctrine is proposed in five canons: 1) Adam's sin and its effect on Adam himself; 2) the transmission of Adam's sin to his descendants: Rom. 5.12 is quoted against Erasmus who denied that it dealt with original sin; 3) the remission of original sin through the passion and death of Christ whose merits are applied to men in baptism; 4) the necessity of infant baptism: the Council quotes here, with slight modifications, canon 2 of the Council of Carthage (cf. n. 502); 5) the nature of original sin in opposition to the opinion of the Reformers. Two points of doctrine are here defined: original sin is wiped out by baptism; concupiscence remains after baptism, but is not sin.

The note on the Virgin Mary, as the only exception to the universality of original sin, is added to indicate the Council's intention not to cause prejudice to the doctrine of the Immaculate Conception.

507
1510
Our Catholic faith "without which it is impossible to please God" *(cf. Heb. 11.6)* must be kept free from errors, pure and unstained; Christian people should not be "carried about with every wind of doctrine" *(Eph. 4.14)* while the ancient serpent, the perpetual enemy of mankind, has stirred up among the many evils that beset the Church of God in this time of ours both new and old controversies about original sin and its remedy. For these reasons the holy ecumenical and general Council of Trent, duly assembled in the Holy Spirit, in order to call back the erring and to strengthen the wavering, following the witness of Holy Scripture, of the holy Fathers and of the approved Councils, and the judgment and consensus of the Church herself, states, professes and declares the following concerning original sin:

508
1511
1. If anyone does not profess that Adam, the first man, by transgressing God's commandment in paradise, at once lost the holiness and justice in which he had been constituted; and that, offending God by his sin, he drew upon himself the wrath and indignation of God and consequently death with which God had threatened him, and together with death captivity in the power of him

who henceforth "has the power of death" *(Heb. 2.14)* i.e., the devil; and that "the whole Adam, body and soul, was changed for the worse through the offence of his sin" *(cf. n. 504), anathema sit.*

509   2. If anyone asserts that Adam's sin harmed only him and not
1512   his descendants and that the holiness and justice received
from God which he lost was lost only for him and not for us also; or that, stained by the sin of disobedience, he transmitted to all mankind only death and the sufferings of the body but not sin as well which is the death of the soul, *anathema sit.* For, he contradicts the words of the apostle: "Sin came into the world through one man, and death through sin, and so death spread to all men as all sinned in him" *(Rom. 5.12 Vulg.; cf. n. 505)*

510   3. If anyone asserts that this sin of Adam, which is one in
1513   origin and is transmitted by propagation, not by imitation,
and which is in all men, proper to each, can be taken away by the powers of human nature or by any remedy other than the merits of the one mediator our Lord Jesus Christ who reconciled us with God by His blood, being "made our righteousness and sanctification and redemption" *(1 Cor. 1.30)*; or if anyone denies that the same merit of Christ Jesus is applied to adults and children alike through the sacrament of baptism duly administered in the form given by the Church, *anathema sit.* "For there is no other name under heaven given among men by which we must be saved" *(Acts 4.12).* Hence the words: "Behold the lamb of God who takes away the sins of the world" *(cf. Jn 1.29)*; and: "as many of you as were baptised in Christ have put on Christ" *(Gal. 3.27).*

511   4. If anyone denies that infants newly born from their
1514   mothers' womb are to be baptised, even when born from
baptised parents; or says that, though they are baptised for the remission of sins, yet they do not contract from Adam any trace of original sin which must be expiated by the bath of regeneration that leads to eternal life, so that in their case the formula of baptism 'for the forgiveness of sins' would no longer be true but would be false, *anathema sit.* For, what the apostle says: "Sin came into the world through one man and death through sin, and so death spread to all men as all sinned in him" *(Rom. 5.12 Vulg.),* should not be understood in another sense than that in which the Catholic Church spread over the whole world has understood it at all times. For, because of this rule of faith, in accordance with apostolic tradition,

even children who of themselves cannot have yet committed any sin are truly baptised for the remission of sins, so that by regeneration they may be cleansed from what they contracted through generation. For "unless one is born of water and the Spirit, he cannot enter the kingdom of God" *(Jn 3.5).*

512 5. If anyone denies that the guilt of original sin is remitted by
1515 the grace of our Lord Jesus Christ given in baptism, or
asserts that all that is sin in the true and proper sense is not taken away but only brushed over or not imputed, *anathema sit.* For, in those who are reborn God hates nothing, because there is no condemnation for those who were buried with Christ through baptism into death *(cf. Rom. 8.1 and 6.4),* "who do not walk according to the flesh" *(Rom. 8.4)* but who, putting off the old man and putting on the new man, created after the likeness of God *(cf. Eph. 4.22f; Col. 3.9f),* innocent, unstained, pure and guiltless, have become the beloved sons of God, "heirs of God and fellow heirs with Christ" *(Rom. 8.17),* so that nothing henceforth holds them back from entering into heaven.

The holy Council, however, professes and thinks that concupiscence or the inclination to sin remains in the baptised. Since it is left for us to wrestle with, it cannot harm those who do not consent but manfully resist it by the grace of Jesus Christ. Rather, "one who strives lawfully will be crowned" *(cf. 2 Tim. 2.5).* Of this concupiscence which the apostle occasionally calls "sin" *(cf. Rom. 6.12ff; 7.7, 14–20)* the holy Council declares: The Catholic Church has never understood that it is called sin because it would be sin in the true and proper sense in those who have been reborn, but because it comes from sin and inclines to sin. If anyone thinks the contrary, *anathema sit.*

513 This same holy Synod declares that it is not its intention to
1516 include in this decree dealing with original sin the Blessed and
Immaculate Virgin Mary, Mother of God, but that the Constitutions of Pope Sixtus IV of blessed memory are to be observed under the penalties contained in those Constitutions, which it renews *(cf. n. 704).*

PIUS V

BULL *EX OMNIBUS AFFLICTIONIBUS* (1567)
CONDEMNED PROPOSITIONS OF MICHAEL DE BAY

In his conception of grace, original justice and sin, de Bay was greatly influenced by the Reformers. He considered grace, immortality and freedom from concupiscence as due to man and given in creation; they were not gifts freely bestowed by God. Hence their loss through original sin was not merely the loss of a gratuitous privilege, but a wound of human nature itself. See on this document, n. 1984i. See also the other propositions of M. de Bay under n. 1984, the condemnation of Quesnel (DS 2384-2387) and of the Synod of Pistoia (DS 2616).

[514/26] The integrity at the beginning of creation was not a
1926   gratuitous exaltation of human nature but its natural
condition.

[514/46] Wilfulness does not belong to the essence and definition of
1946   sin; hence the question whether every sin must be
voluntary does not concern the definition of sin, but its
cause and origin.

[514/47] Therefore original sin has truly the nature of sin,
1948   irrespective and independently of the will from which it
took its origin.

[514/48] Original sin is wilful through the habitual will of a child. It
1948   habitually dominates the child because the child does not
make any contrary decision of his will.

[514/49] And through this habitually dominating will it happens that
1949   a child dying without the sacrament of regeneration, when
(after death) he reaches the use of reason, actually hates
God, blasphemes Him and resists the law of God.

THE SECOND VATICAN GENERAL COUNCIL

(515) *Vatican II does not deal ex professo with the doctrine of original
justice and sin. However, in the context of the history of salvation
and of man's actual condition and task in the world, these doctrines are
mentioned. They appear in their relevance for man today.*

*The Constitution on the Church describes in a comprehensive vision
the divine plan of our salvation: man's original dignity, his fall, and God's
continued care (LG 2).*

*The Constitution on the Church in the modern world unfolds man's
actual condition today: the evils of our world point to a deeper root, the
sinfulness of the human heart (GS 10) by which man is alienated from his
original destiny (GS 13).*

PAUL VI

ADDRESS TO THEOLOGIANS AT THE SYMPOSIUM ON ORIGINAL SIN (1966)

Paul VI had organised this symposium in order to take stock of the present state of exegetical studies and of the natural sciences, as anthropology and paleontology, with regard to the original condition of man. He demands an honest investigation of the existing problems, while at the same time stating the limits of this search. The text is found in AAS 58 (1966) 654.

516 It is evident that you will not consider as reconcilable with the authentic Catholic doctrine those explanations of original sin, given by some modern authors, which start from the presupposition of polygenism which is not proved, and deny more or less clearly that the sin which has been such an abundant source of evils for mankind has consisted above all in the disobedience which Adam, the first man and the figure of the future Adam, committed at the beginning of history. Consequently, these explanations do not agree either with the teachings of Holy Scripture, sacred Tradition and the Church's magisterium, which says that the sin of the first man is transmitted to all his descendants by way of propagation, not of imitation, that it is "proper to each", and is "the death of the soul", i.e., the privation and not merely the absence of holiness and justice, even in new-born infants *(cf. nn. 509, 510).*

As to the theory of evolutionism, you will not consider it acceptable if it is not clearly in agreement with the immediate creation of human souls by God and does not regard the disobedience of Adam, the first universal parent, as of decisive importance for the destiny of mankind *(cf. n. 509).* This disobedience should not be understood as though it had not caused in Adam the loss of the holiness and justice in which he was constituted *(cf. n. 508).*

JOHN PAUL II

ENCYCLICAL LETTER *REDEMPTOR HOMINIS* (1979)

In chapter II of the Encyclical, entitled "The Mystery of the Redemption", the Pope, alluding to the present state of the world, applies to it the Biblical doctrine of the fall: the present threat to ecology from industry and to the survival of mankind from the arms race witnesses today to the fall of man and to the world still in need of being saved in Jesus Christ. The text is found in AAS 71 (1979) 270–271.

(The present world in need of being recreated)

517   8. In Jesus Christ the visible world which God created for man
(*cf. Gen. 1.26-30*)—the world that, when sin entered, "was
subjected to futility" *(Rom. 8.20; cf. 8.19-22; GS 2 13)*—recovers
again its original link with the divine source of Wisdom and Love.
Indeed, "God so loved the world that he gave his only Son" *(Jn 3.16)*.
As this link was broken in the man Adam, so in the Man Christ it was
reforged *(cf. Rom. 5.11-21)*. Are we of the twentieth century not
convinced of the overpoweringly eloquent words of the Apostle of
the Gentiles concerning the "creation (that) has been groaning in
travail together until now" *(Rom. 8.22)* and "waits with eager longing
for the revelation of the sons of God" *(Rom. 8.19)*, the creation that
"was subjected to futility"? Does not the previously unknown
immense progress—which has taken place especially in the course
of this century—in the field of man's dominion over the world itself
reveal to a previously unknown degree that subjection "to futility"? It
is enough to recall certain phenomena, such as the threat of pollution
of the natural environment in areas of rapid industrialisation, or the
armed conflicts continually breaking out with growing intensity, or
the power, already present, of self-destruction through the use of
atomic, hydrogen, neutron and similar weapons, or the lack of
respect for the life of the unborn. The world of the new age, the world
of space flights, the world of the previously unattained conquests of
science and technology—is it not also the creation, "groaning in
travail", that "awaits with eager longing for the revelation of the sons
of God"?

CHAPTER VI

JESUS CHRIST THE SAVIOUR

The eternal Son of God, "one of the Trinity", became man in order to save men. Recapitulating all things in himself, He re-united the whole human race with God through the mystery of His death and resurrection, and reconciled all things among themselves. The mystery of the redemptive incarnation, together with that of the Trinity from which it is inseparable, constitutes the substance of the Christian message; it is at the centre of the Christian understanding of history and reveals to man his true vocation as a son of God in God's own Son.

The mysteries of Christ's person and of His work are also inseparable. If the man Jesus contains the fulness of God's revelation to the world, if His human actions have saving power for the entire human race, the reason is that in the Son incarnate God and man have been united in the unity of one person: the God-man is the mediator between God and men; His action flows from His being. This is why, in order to uphold and to proclaim the message of universal salvation in Christ, the Christian Tradition has had to preserve intact and to progressively explicitate the mystery of His person.

The mystery of the Word incarnate could be, and has in fact been approached since the earliest Christian Tradition, from two opposite directions with as their starting points the humanity of Christ and the divinity of the Son of God, respectively. These two avenues gave rise to two schools, equally legitimate though faced with opposite problems, the Antiochian and the Alexandrian. Both had the burden of showing that Christ is truly God and truly man and that He is one. They could and did in fact lead to opposite errors: Nestorianism denied the unity of person, Monophysitism the duality of natures after union. Against every danger of undermining either the divinity or the humanity of Christ, the Church had to affirm clearly the integrity of His two natures; the great Christological Councils of the fifth century were faced with the task of expressing in unequivocal terms the mysterious union of the two natures in one person.

Later, it also became necessary to explicitate the same mystery on the level of Christ's actions: against the Monothelitist tendency the Church explained that the two wills and actions, the divine and the human, remain distinct in the one person of the God-man. Except for the exclusion of the error of the Agnoetes who admitted the existence of ignorance in Christ, the Church's reflection on the mysterious union of the divine and the human knowledge was reserved for a much later period. Thus, the mystery of Christ, a mystery of unity in duality, has been through the centuries the object of a deep reflection; in recent years this reflection has taken a new dimension with the problem of the psychological unity of the God-man.

As compared with the mystery of Christ's person, that of His work has for many centuries been treated only cursorily in the Church documents. The Church has always believed in the salvific significance of the totality of the Christ-event. The early Creeds enumerated its various phases from the incarnation down to the Paschal mystery, including in this the death on the cross, the resurrection and the ascension. In the early Tradition, different schools, the Greek and the Latin, laid greater emphasis on the incarnation and on the Paschal mystery respectively. These various traditions were not, however, mutually exclusive: they rather complemented each other. It is only after the objective efficacy of Christ's redeeming death had been questioned in the Middle Ages that the doctrine of the merit and satisfaction of His expiatory sacrifice began to be explicitly stated. This doctrine needs even today to be harmoniously combined with the salvific meaning of the incarnation of the Word of God on the one hand and the saving power of His resurrection on the other. Nor must Christ's work be reduced to His redeeming function. Linking up with the earliest Christian Tradition, the Second Vatican Council has explained Christ's revelatory function in terms never found with such clarity in previous Church documents: the Word incarnate is through His deeds and words the fulness of God's revelation to the world. The same Council has also expressed better than previous official documents the central role of Christ in history and the significance of Christ for the Christian understanding of the mystery of man.

*   *   *

The main point of doctrine considered in this chapter fall under the following headings:

Christ is truly God, eternally begotten from the Father: 1–10, 12, 14, 17, 20, 23, 39/4, (601), 606/1, 606/5, 612, 617, 620/2, 627/4, 631, 632, 648, 650/27–30.

Christ is truly man, born in time from the Virgin Mary: 2-5, 7, 12, 15, 17, 20, 23, 39/4, (601), (602), 603/7, 610, 612, 617, 620/2, 620/6, 627/4, 628, 631, 632, 645, 648.

The two natures, the divine and the human, are united in the person of the Son of God: 17, 20, 23, 604, 606/2-4, 606/6-7, 607-608, 612, 613-616, 619/1-3, 620/4-5, 620/7-8, 621-623, 627/6-9, 629, 640, (641), (642), 644, 663, 670.

Christ has a double will and action, the divine and the human, both united in one person: 627/10-16, 635-637.

His human will is impeccable: 603/7, 614, 621, 627/5, 628, 634, 635.

Christ's pre-eminent human knowledge excludes ignorance and error: 619/4, 624-626, 650/32-34, 651/1-3, 661.

The divine Sonship of Christ excludes an adoptive sonship of God: 23, 603/6, 619/5, 638, 639, (642).

The Word incarnate must be adored by one worship which extends to His humanity: 606/8, 619/5, 620/9, 649.

Divine cult must be rendered to His Sacred Heart: 664-667.

Christ contains the fulness of God's revelation: 149, 151, 679.

Mediator between God and men, He has saved all men through the sacrifice of His cross: 6, 7, 10, 12, 15, 17, 20, 23, 39/5.10, 606/10, 606/12, 609, 611, 620/10, 627/2, 634, 645-646, 648, 650/38, 654-655, 712, 1546, 1989/5.

Christ saves and liberates: 672-673, 677-678.

He has satisfied and merited for all: 510, 643, 647, 712, 1631, 1926-1931, 1960.

By his resurrection He has become for all the source of a new life: 606/11, 650/36-37, 660.

Thus He has universal Lordship and Kingship: 9, 10, 12, 39/5, 652-653.

Christ is the goal of history: 669.

He is the new and perfect man who manifests man's true vocation: 668.

The truth about Jesus Christ may not be distorted: 670-671, 674-676.

THE FIRST GENERAL COUNCIL OF NICAEA
SYMBOL OF NICAEA (325)

(601)   *Arius conceived the "Word of God" as created by God in time and having in the fulness of time manifested Himself in human flesh for men's salvation. According to him, Christ was not God, for He did not share the divine nature; He was not man, for He did not have a complete human nature, made up of soul and body, but only human flesh. Thus, He was a composite intermediary being—the Word made flesh—neither true God nor true man. He was not the mediator who unites God and man in His own person. Against Arius, the Symbol of faith of the Council of Nicaea affirms the strict divinity of the Son of God, "one in being with the Father"; against the gnostic and docetist currents which undermined the realism of Christ's humanity and Arius who reduced it to human flesh the Council stresses the reality and completeness of Christ's humanity: He "became flesh, was made man." The mystery of Christ's full humanity combined with His true divinity will later raise many problems and call for more precise answers. But the foundation for this fundamental affirmation of faith is already found in Nicaea. Cf. introduction and text, n. 7.*

THE FIRST GENERAL COUNCIL OF CONSTANTINOPLE
SYMBOL OF CONSTANTINOPLE (381)

(602)   *Unlike Arius, Apollinaris of Laodicaea (310–390) strongly professed the divinity of the Son of God, "one in being" with the Father, as stated by the Council of Nicaea. In the process of trying to express how the eternal Word of God became man, he nevertheless unduly reduced the humanity of Christ as Arius had done before him. Apollinaris followed the Greek anthropology according to which man is made up of body and soul, the soul itself being composed of a lower and a higher part, the principles of life and of spiritual activity respectively. Apollinaris understood the mystery of the incarnation in the sense that the eternal Word of God substituted for and replaced the highest part of the human composite. Christ, the Son incarnate, was the eternal Word to whom were united the lower part of the human soul and a human body, but He had no spiritual human soul. To Apollinaris this seemed necessary to ensure the unity of Christ and His absolute freedom from sin. Pope Damasus I rejected this doctrine in several documents. Making use of the soteriological argument according to which it was necessary that Christ, in order to redeem man, should have a complete human nature, the Pope explained that Christ's humanity is made up of a body and a soul with its lower and higher faculties; a full humanity is united to the eternal Son of God. See the fragment of a letter written c. 374 (DS 146), and the letter Per Filium Meum (375) (DS 148). In another letter (c. 375) the same Pope condemned the doctrine of Apollinarism: cf. DS 149. In this context, it is clear that the double affirmation of the Council of Constantinople, "He became flesh...and was made man" intends, more directly than did the profession of faith of Nicaea, to affirm the integrity of Christ's humanity. Cf. introduction and text, n. 12.*

THE COUNCIL OF ROME
"TOME OF DAMASUS" (382)

Shortly after the general Council of Constantinople, Pope Damasus I (366-384) called a Council at Rome to renew the condemnation of various errors. Some of the canons of the "Tome of Damasus" condemn Trinitarian errors (cf. nn. 306/1ff); others Christological errors. Among these, the idea of a double sonship of Christ, one eternal, the other temporal (canon 6), was attributed to Diodorus of Tarsus (ob. 394); the error of Apollinaris is once again condemned (canon 7); so too is the error of "Patripassianism" according to which the Father Himself, not the Son incarnate, would have undergone the sufferings of the cross.

603/6
158
We condemn those who affirm two sons, one who is before the ages, the other after the assumption of the flesh from the Virgin.

603/7
159
We condemn those who say that the Word of God dwelling in human flesh took the place of the rational and spiritual soul, since the Son and the Word of God did not replace the rational and spiritual soul in His body but rather assumed our soul (i.e., a rational and spiritual one) without sin and saved it.

603/14
166
If anyone says that in the passion of the cross it is God Himself who felt the pain and not the flesh and the soul which Christ, the Son of God, had taken to Himself—the form of servant which He had accepted as Scripture says *(cf. Phil. 2.7)*—he is mistaken.

THE GENERAL COUNCIL OF EPHESUS (431)

Christ is God and man. The extremist representatives of the Antiochian school conceived the distinction of the two natures in Christ as one of two persons. Nestorius (ob. c. 450) belonged to this school. A priest in Antioch, he became patriarch of Constantinople in 428. There his doctrine met with strong opposition. The crisis broke out when Anastasius, a priest, publicly denied to Mary the title "Mother of God" (theotokos); according to him she was not the mother of God but only the mother of Christ (khristotokos) to whom the person of the Word of God had united Himself. This amounted to affirming in Christ two persons, one divine and one human.

Nestorianism is based on the idea that a complete human nature, as the faith forces us to affirm in Christ, necessarily implies a human person. Christ, therefore, was a human person to whom the divine person of the Word of God was united. Though this union was sublime and unique in the order of grace to the extent of constituting between the two a unique "figure" (prosôpon)—the Word of God dwelling in Christ "as in a temple"— it was nevertheless but an accidental union between persons. The divine and the human attributes which Scripture predicates of Christ belonged to either person respectively; accordingly Christ, not the Word of God, had died on the cross.

Nestorius' most ardent opponent was Cyril, bishop of Alexandria (c. 380-440). The final decision on the conflict which opposed Cyril to Nestorius fell to the General Council of Ephesus convened by emperor Theodosius II.

During the Council's first session (June 22), opened by Cyril before the arrival of the legates of Pope Celestine I, reading was done of the second of three letters addressed by Cyril to Nestorius. This letter, dated Jan.-Feb. 430, was officially approved by the Fathers as being in conformity with the Church's orthodox faith in the incarnation of the Word and consequently in Mary's divine motherhood (cf. nn. 604-605); this letter represents the official faith of the Council of Ephesus. Cyril's third letter to Nestorius, dated Nov. 430, to which were added the "twelve anathematisms" was also read before the Council Fathers but does not seem to have been officially approved by them; some of its formulations contain expressions which, though correctly meant by St Cyril, could and in fact would be misinterpreted later. The "Twelve Anathematisms" (cf. nn. 606/1-12) cannot be considered as definitions of faith. The first session ended with the formal condemnation and deposition of Nestorius. The Roman legates, soon after their arrival, gave their approval in the name of the Pope to the proceedings of the session. The second letter of St Cyril must be understood in its historical context; the terminology has not yet acquired the precision which it will have later.

Cf. P. T. CAMELOT, *Ephèse et Chalcédoine* (Paris 1961) 13-75.

SECOND LETTER OF CYRIL OF ALEXANDRIA TO NESTORIUS

604   For we do not say that the nature of the Word became flesh by
250   undergoing a change, nor that it was transformed into a complete man, made up of soul and body. Rather, we affirm that the Word, having united to Himself according to the hypostasis *(kath' hupostasin)* the flesh animated by a rational soul, became man in an ineffable and incomprehensible manner and was called Son of man. This union is not merely according to the will or to good pleasure; nor does it consist in the assumption of a *prosôpon* ("personality") only. And though the natures which are brought together into a true unity are distinct, from both there results one Christ and one Son; not as though the distinction of natures were suppressed by their union, but rather because the divinity and the humanity by their mysterious and ineffable coming together into unity have constituted for us the one Lord, Christ and Son....

605   It was not that an ordinary man was born first of the holy
251   Virgin, on whom afterwards the Word descended; what we say is that, being united with the flesh from the womb, (the Word) has undergone birth in the flesh, making the birth in the flesh

His own.... Thus (the holy Fathers) have unhesitatingly called the holy Virgin "Mother of God" *(theotokos)*. This does not mean that the nature of the Word or His divinity received the beginning of its existence from the holy Virgin, but that, since the holy body, animated by a rational soul, which the Word united to Himself according to the hypostasis *(kath' hupostasin)*, was born from her, the Word was born according to the flesh.

THE TWELVE ANATHEMATISMS OF CYRIL
AGAINST NESTORIUS

606/1 If anyone does not confess that the Emmanuel is truly God
252 and, therefore, that the holy Virgin is the Mother of God
(theotokos) (since she begot according to the flesh the
Word of God made flesh), *anathema sit.*

606/2 If anyone does not confess that the Word who is from God
253 the Father has been united to the flesh according to the
hypostasis *(kath' hupostasin)* and that Christ is one with His
own flesh, that is to say that the same is at once God and man,
anathema sit.

606/3 If in Christ who is one anyone divides the hypostases
254 after union, connecting them by a mere association in dignity
or authority or power, and not rather by a coming together
into "physical" *(phusikê)* union,[1] *anathema sit.*

606/4 If anyone ascribes separately to two persons or hypostases
255 the words which in the evangelical and apostolic writings are
either spoken of Christ by the saints or used by Christ about
Himself, and applies some to a man considered by himself, apart
from the Word, and others, because they befit God, solely to the
Word who is from God the Father, *anathema sit.*

606/5 If anyone dares to say that Christ is a man "bearing God"
256 *(theophoros)* and does not say that He is truly God, the one
Son by nature, since the Word became flesh and shares as
we do in the blood and the flesh, *anathema sit.*

---

1. This expression which in the still fluid terminology of St Cyril was designed to express the realism of the ineffable union of divinity and humanity was liable to be misinterpreted. At a later period it will in fact be made use of, against St Cyril's mind, in a Monophysite sense.

606/6   If anyone says that the Word who is from God the Father is
257   the God or Lord of Christ and does not rather confess that
         the same is at once God and man since, according to the
Scriptures, the Word became flesh, *anathema sit.*

606/7   If anyone says that Jesus is like a man acted upon by the
258   Word of God and that the glory of the only-begotten has
         been added to Him as belonging to another distinct from
Him, *anathema sit.*

606/8   If anyone dares to say that the man assumed ought to be
259   worshipped with God the Word and glorified with Him, and
         that He is to be called God conjointly with Him as one
person with another (for the continual addtion of "with" *(sun)* compels one to think in this way), and does not rather venerate the
Emmanuel with one worship and glorify Him with one praise because
the Word became flesh, *anathema sit.*

606/9   If anyone says that the one Lord Jesus Christ was glorified
260   by the Spirit, implying that through Him He had access to a
         power that was not His own, and that He received from the
Spirit the power to overcome unclean spirits and to work divine signs
among men, and does not rather say that He performed divine signs
by virtue of the Spirit which was His own, *anathema sit.*

606/10   Christ, divine Scripture says, has become "the High Priest
261   and Apostle of our confession" *(Heb. 3.1),* and He offered
         Himself for us as a fragrant sacrifice *(cf. Eph. 5.2)* to God
the Father. If anyone, therefore, says that it is not the Word of God
Himself who, when He became flesh and man like us, became High
Priest and our Apostle, but another, distinct from Him, who properly
speaking is a man born of a woman, or if anyone says that He offered
the sacrifice for Himself and not for us only—for He who knew no sin
had no need of sacrifice—, *anathema sit.*

606/11   If anyone does not confess that the flesh of the Lord is
262   life-giving and that it is the flesh of the Word of God
         Himself who is from the Father, but (regards it) as the flesh
of another than Him, united with Him in dignity or possessing only
divine indwelling, and if He does not confess that it is life-giving, as we
have said, because it has become the flesh of the Word Himself who
has the power to enliven all things, *anathema sit.*

606/12   If anyone does not confess that the Word of God suffered

263   in the flesh and was crucified in the flesh, and that He
tasted death in the flesh and became the first born from the
dead, being Life and giver of life as God, *anathema sit.*

THE FORMULA OF UNION BETWEEN CYRIL OF ALEXANDRIA
AND THE BISHOPS OF ANTIOCH (433)

The Council of Ephesus had not succeeded in dispelling all misunder-standings between Cyril of Alexandria on the one hand and the Orientals, mostly represented by the Antiochene bishops, on the other. These refused to adhere to some of the formulations used by St Cyril, notably in his Twelve Anathematisms against Nestorius. On the invitation of emperor Theodo-sius II, John of Antioch wrote a profession of faith to which Cyril was able to subscribe. It expressed better than Cyril had done the reality of Christ's distinct human nature, and the distinction between the two natures united in one person. Pope Sixtus III congratulated both parties on their mutual agreement, thus implicitly approving the formula which consecrated their union. It is chiefly through this formula that the Antiochian school made its contribution to the subsequent development of the Christological dogma at Chalcedon (cf. nn. 613-616).

607   We confess therefore our Lord Jesus Christ, the only-
272   begotten Son of God, perfect God and perfect man composed of rational soul and body, begotten before all ages from
the Father as to His divinity, and the same in the latter days born of
the Virgin Mary as to His humanity for us and for our salvation. The
same is one in being with the Father as to the divinity and one in being
with us as to the humanity, for a union of two natures has taken
place. Hence we confess one Christ, one Son, one Lord. In accordance with this union without confusion, we profess the holy Virgin
to be Mother of God *(theotokos)*, for God the Word became flesh
and was made man and from the moment of conception united to
Himself the temple He had taken from her.

608   As for the words of the gospels and of the apostles concerning
273   the Lord, we know that theologians have considered some as
common because they are said of the one person *(prosôpon)*,
while they have distinguished others as applying to the two natures
(phuseis), reserving those which befit God to Christ in His divinity
while assigning those which are lowly to Christ in His humanity.

LEO I

LETTER TO FLAVIAN OF CONSTANTINOPLE (13 June 449)

The formula of union notwithstanding, Dioscorus (ob. 454), St Cyril's successor in Alexandria, remained too literally dependent on some ambiguous formulations of Cyril. In his zeal against Nestorianism, he tended to conceive the union of divinity and humanity in Christ as realised not in the person but at the level of nature: distinct before their union, divinity and humanity merged on being united into one theandric nature. In Constantinople, the monk Eutyches (378-ob. after 454) carried this tendency to the extreme: according to him, on being united to the divine nature, the human nature became absorbed into it; there remained only one nature with the result that Christ's humanity was not consubstantial with ours. Condemned at a Synod held in Constantinople in 448, Eutyches appealed to other Synods in favour of his view. Dioscorus of Alexandria rehabilitated him in his communion.

But Leo the Great to whom Eutyches had also appealed took a definite stand against the new heresy of Monophysitism in a dogmatic letter addressed to Flavian, patriarch of Constantinople. The "Tome of Leo" contained the clearest expression to date of the doctrine of the incarnation. While distinguishing Christ's two natures clearly by use of antithetic expressions, it put in equal relief the unity of His person. The Tome of Leo I was immediately and universally accepted as rule of faith. It remained famous because of the influence it was to exercise later on the Council of Chalcedon (cf. nn. 613-616).

Cf. P. T. CAMELOT, *Ephèse et Chalcédoine* (Paris 1962) 79-114.

609   This eternal only-begotten Son of the eternal Father "was
291   born of the Holy Spirit and the Virgin Mary." This temporal
birth took nothing away from, and added nothing to, His divine and eternal birth. He spent Himself entirely to repair man who had been deceived, to conquer death and to destroy by His power the devil who held sway over death. For we could not overcome the author of sin and death unless He, whom sin could not defile nor death hold in bondage, took on our nature and made it His own.

He was conceived by the Holy Spirit in the womb of the Virgin Mother, who gave Him birth without losing her virginity as she conceived Him without losing her virginity....

610   But this unique and wonderful generation must not be under-
292   stood as if the newness of this creation had evacuated the
condition proper to our race. It is the Holy Spirit who made the Virgin fruitful, but a true body has been taken from her body. "Wisdom has built herself a house" *(Prov. 9.1)* and "the Word became flesh and dwelt among us" *(Jn 1.14)*, that is, in the flesh which He took from a human being and which was animated by the breath of rational life.

611   The character proper to each of the two natures which come
293   together in one person being therefore preserved, lowliness
was taken on by majesty, weakness by strength, mortality by

eternity. And, in order to pay the debt of our fallen state, the inviolable nature was united to one subject to suffering so that, as was fitting to heal our wounds, one and the same "mediator between God and men, the man Christ Jesus" (1 Tim. 2.5) could die in one nature and not in the other. The true God, therefore, was born with the complete and perfect nature of a true man; he is complete in His nature and complete in ours....

612   And so, the Son of God, descending from His heavenly
294   throne, yet not leaving the glory of the Father, enters into this
lowly world. (He comes) in a new order, generated by a new birth. In a new order, because, invisible in His nature, He became visible in ours; surpassing comprehension, He has wished to be comprehended; remaining prior to time, He began to exist in time. The Lord of all things hid His immeasurable majesty to take on the form of a servant. The impassible God has not disdained to be a man subject to suffering nor the Immortal to submit to the law of death. He is generated by a new birth, because an inviolate virginity, untouched by concupiscence, has provided the flesh of His body. From His mother, the Lord has assumed the nature of man, not his guilt. Yet, the miraculous manner of the birth of the Lord Jesus Christ, born from the womb of a virgin, does not make His nature different from ours. For He who is truly God is the same who is also truly man and there is no deception in this unity in which the lowliness of man and the divine majesty coincide. God suffers no change because of His condescension, nor is man consumed by such dignity. For each of the two natures performs the functions proper to it in communion with the other: the Word does what pertains to the Word and the flesh what pertains to the flesh. The one shines forth in miracles, the other is subjected to insults. And as the Word does not lose the glory which is His in equality with the Father, so the flesh does not abandon the nature of our race....

THE GENERAL COUNCIL OF CHALCEDON
SYMBOL OF CHALCEDON (451)

The strong rebuff given by Pope Leo I to the Monophysite heresy notwithstanding, Eutyches and Dioscorus, by making use of their influence at the imperial court, suceeded in having a Synod convened at Ephesus in August 449. The pressure exercised on the bishops at that Synod was so great as not to allow freedom of voting; as a result of which Eutyches was rehabilitated and his doctrine approved, while his main opponents, notably Theodoret of Cyrus (ob. 466) and Ibas of Edessa (ob. 457), were deposed

*from their sees. Pope Leo called this Synod of Ephesus a "robbery"(latroci-
nium) and it is known under the name of Latrocinium of Ephesus even
today. Its proceedings were condemned by a Synod of Rome on September
29, 449. This Synod requested emperor Theodosius II to convoke a general
Council in Italy. The emperor having refused to comply with the Roman
request, it is only under his successor Marcian that the fourth general
Council was convened in Chalcedon. It defined solemnly the doctrine of the
two natures of Christ united in the second person of the Trinity.*

*The Tome of Leo served as a preparation for the Council. When it was
read in assembly, the Council Fathers exclaimed: "Peter has spoken
through the mouth of Leo." The Symbol promulgated by the Council on
Oct. 22 borrows from Leo's firm terminology to repudiate the Nestorian
heresy on the one hand and the Eutychian on the other. It figures as a
synthesis of the Antiochian and the Alexandrian schools as regards the
mystery of the Word Incarnate.*

Cf. P. T. CAMELOT, *Ephèse et Chalcédoine* (Paris 1961) 95-150.

(Prologue)

613 (The Council) opposes those who attempt to divide the mys-
300   tery of the incarnation into two sons. It excludes from the
        sacred assembly those who dare to declare subject to suffering
the divinity of the only-begotten. It withstands those who imagine a
mixture or confusion of Christ's two natures *(phusis).* It rejects those
who fancy that the form of servant assumed by Him among us is of a
heavenly nature and foreign to ours in essence *(ousia).* It condemns
those who invent the myth of two natures of the Lord before the
union and of one nature after the union.

(Definition)

614 Following therefore the holy Fathers, we unanimously teach to
301   confess one and the same Son, our Lord Jesus Christ, the
        same perfect in divinity and perfect in humanity, the same truly
God and truly man composed of rational soul and body, the same
one in being *(homoousios)* with the Father as to the divinity and one
in being with us as to the humanity, like unto us in all things but sin
(cf. Heb. 4.15). The same was begotten from the Father before the
ages as to the divinity and in the latter days for us and our salvation
was born as to His humanity from Mary the Virgin Mother of God.

615 We confess that one and the same Lord Jesus Christ, the
302   only-begotten Son, must be acknowledged in two natures,
        without confusion or change, without division or separation.
The distinction between the natures was never abolished by their
union but rather the character proper to each of the two natures was

preserved as they came together in one person *(prosôpon)* and one hypostasis. He is not split or divided into two persons, but He is one and the same only-begotten, God the Word, the Lord Jesus Christ, as formerly the prophets and later Jesus Christ Himself have taught us about Him and as has been handed down to us by the Symbol of the Fathers.

(Sanction)

616   As these points have been determined by us with all possible
303   precision and care, the holy ecumenical Council has ordained
that no one may propose, put into writing, devise, hold or teach to others any other faith than this.

JOHN II

LETTER TO THE SENATE OF CONSTANTINOPLE (534)

Even after the important definitions on the person of Christ, the implications of the mystery of the incarnation remained obscure to many. Some bishops of Palestine and Egypt inclined to Monophysitism and thought that the doctrine of Chalcedon had contradicted that of Ephesus. In 519 some Scythian monks, also Monophysitists, sought from Pope Hormisdas the approbation of the fomula: "One of the three has suffered in the flesh"; they considered it as reflecting the 12th anathematism of St Cyril (n. 606/12) but interpreted it in a Monophysite way. They did not obtain satisfaction. Desirous to rally all Monophysitist tendencies to the common faith, emperor Justinian later enquired from Pope John II whether the formula, with its implications for God's passibility and Mary's divine motherhood, was acceptable. While answering positively, the Pope explains that "one" refers to "one person" of the Trinity who has suffered in the flesh, and draws the consequences as regards the "true and proper" divine motherhood of Mary.

617   (Emperor Justinian) has pointed out, as you have learned from
401   the contents of his letter, that disputes have arisen over the
following three questions: Can one say that Christ our God is "one of the Trinity", that is one holy person among the three persons of the Holy Trinity? Did Christ our God who in His divinity is impassible suffer in the flesh? Must Mary, the ever Virgin Mother of our Lord and God Jesus Christ, be called truly and properly Mother of God and Mother of God the Word incarnate from her?...

Christ is one of the Holy Trinity, that is one holy person or subsistence *(subsistentia)*—one hypostasis as the Greeks say—among the three persons of the Holy Trinity.

(There follow among other quotations: Gen. 3.22; 1 Cor. 8.6; the Nicene Symbol).

The fact that God did truly suffer in the flesh we confirm likewise by the following witnesses *(Deut. 28.66; Jn 14.6; Mal. 3.8; Acts 3.15; 20.28; 1 Cor. 2.8; Cyril of Alexandria, Anathematism 12; Leo I, Tome to Flavian, etc.).*

We teach that it is right for Catholics to confess that the glorious and holy Mary, ever Virgin, is truly and properly the Mother of God and Mother of God the Word incarnate from her. For it is He Himself who truly and properly became incarnate in these latter days and deigned to be born of the holy and glorious Virgin Mother. Hence, since the Son of God became incarnate and was born from her truly and properly, we confess her to be truly and properly the Mother of God incarnate and born from her. In proper terms, lest one should believe that the Lord Jesus Christ received the name of God as a title of honour or as a favour as Nestorius foolishly taught; truly, lest one should believe that from the Virgin He took on a mere appearance of flesh or in some other way a flesh which was not real, as Eutyches irreverently declared.

THE COUNCIL OF CONSTANTINOPLE

ANATHEMATISMS AGAINST THE ORIGENISTS (543)

Among the errors attributed to the disciples of Origen as regards the relation between soul and body (cf. n. 401i, 402), some touched on the doctrine of the incarnation of the Word.

618/2   If anyone says or holds that the soul of the Lord has existed
404   first and has been united to God the Word before the incarnation and the birth from the Virgin, *anathema sit.*

618/3   If anyone says or holds that the body of our Lord Jesus
405   Christ was first formed in the womb of the holy Virgin and that God the Word and the soul already in existence were later united with it, *anathema sit.*

VIGILIUS

CONSTITUTUM I (14 May 553)

The Monophysite danger persisted long after Chalcedon. In particular, there arose a "Neo-Chalcedonian" current which advocated a compromise between the Chalcedonian formula and Monophysitism. Its protagonists demanded the condemnation of the first opponents of Monophysitism, Theodoret of Cyrus (ob. 466) and Ibas of Edessa (ob. 457) as well as of Theodore of Mopsuestia (ob. 428), the teacher of Nestorius, all of whom they accused of Nestorian tendencies. The attention thus concentrated on the "three chapters", the name under which the three authors were grouped.

Emperor Justinian, anxious to re-unite the separated Churches, promulgated in 543 an edict favouring this condemnation. Pope Vigilius opposed it, the reason being the fact that the three authors incriminated had been recognised as orthodox by the Council of Chalcedon. Later, however, the Pope yielded to the pressure made on him, and, having been transferred by force to Constantinople, assented in 548 to the condemnation of the three chapters (in the falsified form in which their works were then known). This capitulation caused much unrest in the West and led the Pope to suggest to the emperor the convocation of a general Council which would settle the conflict. As relations between Vigilius and Justinian deteriorated to the point of rupture, Pope Vigilius wrote a profession of faith (552) against the Monophysite tendencies of the emperor (cf. DS 412-415); it is in rebellion against the Pope that the "Second Council of Constantinople" opened on May 5, 553.

The condemnations pronounced during the Council's first sessions led the Pope to dissociate himself from the assembly by publishing his first Constitutum. In this document he condemns some propositions attributed to Theodore of Mopsuestia but upholds the orthodoxy of the "three chapters". The document ends with five anathematisms directed against the Nestorian heresy and in which the formulations of Ephesus and Chalcedon are used to affirm the union of both natures in the one person of Christ.

619/1 If anyone, in maintaining the immutability of the divine
416 nature, does not confess that the Word became flesh and from the very conception in the womb of the Virgin united to Himself according to the hypostasis the human nature in its origin, but says that God the Word came to be with a man who had already been in existence with the result that the holy Virgin is not believed to be truly the Mother of God but is so called in words only, *anathema sit.*

619/2 If anyone denies that the unity of natures was effected in
417 Christ according to the hypostasis, but says that God the Word dwelt in a man having a separate existence as one among the just, and so does not confess the union of the natures according to the hypostasis which means that God the Word remained and still remains one hypostasis or person with the flesh which He assumed, *anathema sit.*

619/3 If anyone so divides in the one Christ the words of the
418 Gospels and of the apostles that he also introduces a division between the natures which are united in Him, *anathema sit.*

619/4   If anyone says that the one Jesus Christ who is both true
419   Son of God and true Son of man did not know the future or
            the day of the Last Judgment and that He could know only
as much as the divinity, dwelling in Him as in another, revealed to
Him, *anathema sit.*

619/5   If anyone, referring to the passage of the apostle in the
420   epistle to the Hebrews *(Heb. 5.8,7)* where it is said that
            Christ learned through experience what it means to obey
and that with loud cries and tears He offered up prayers and supplications to Him who was able to save Him from the dead, applies the
passage to Christ divested of His divinity and reaching perfection
through His virtuous efforts, with the result that he seems to introduce two Christs or two Sons and does not believe that we must
confess and worship one and the same Christ, Son of God and son of
man, of two natures and in two natures which are inseparable and
undivided, *anathema sit.*

THE SECOND GENERAL COUNCIL OF CONSTANTINOPLE
ANATHEMATISMS AGAINST THE THREE CHAPTERS (553)

*In the conflict which opposed emperor Justinian to Pope Vigilius the
Council sided with the emperor. It pursued its work, disregarding the first
Constitutum of Vigilius (nn. 619/1-5). In its last session it formulated 14
anathematisms. Among these the first ten (nn. 620/1-10) re-assert the
mystery of the incarnation mostly as expressed by St Cyril against Nestorius to whom they assimilate Theodore of Mopsuestia. Canon 8 (n. 620/8)
defends the orthodoxy of an expression used correctly by St Cyril but which
could and had been misused by the Monophysitists. Canon 11 is directed
against various heresies (DS 433); the last three canons, against the "three
chapters" and their writings, Theodore of Mopsuestia (n. 621), Theodoret of
Cyrus (n. 622), and Ibas of Edessa (n. 623), respectively.*

*In his second Constitutum of February 554, Pope Vigilius explicitly
approved the Council's condemnation of the "three chapters", thus conferring post factum the value of a general Council to part of the work of
Constantinople. This approval does not, however, seem to extend to all the
canons but only to the last three, directly concerned with the "three chapters". The Pope's approval of these canons implies the condemnation of the
propositions attributed in them to the "three chapters", without passing
judgment on the authors and their actual writings. The significance of the
second general Council of Constantinople consists in a reiterated condemnation of the Nestorian heresy.*

620/1   If anyone does not confess that Father, Son and Holy Spirit,
421   are one nature *(phusis)* or essence *(ousia)*, one might and
            power, a Trinity one in being *(homoousios)*, one Godhead to

be worshipped in three hypostases or persons *(prosôpon)*, *anathema sit.* For one is the God and Father from whom all things are, one is the Lord Jesus Christ through whom all things are and one the Holy Spirit in whom all things are.

620/2 If anyone does not confess two births of the Word of God,
422 one from the Father before the ages which is timeless and incorporeal, the other (which took place) in the latter days when the same (Word), descending from heaven, was made flesh from Mary, the holy and glorious Mother of God ever Virgin, and was born of her, *anathema sit.*

620/3 If anyone says that the Word of God who performed mira-
423 cles was someone other than the Christ who suffered, or that God the Word was with the Christ born of a woman *(cf. Gal. 4.4)* or was in Him as one in another, but (does) not (confess) one and the same our Lord Jesus Christ the Word of God incarnate and made man, to whom belong the miracles and the sufferings which He has voluntarily endured in the flesh, *anathema sit.*

620/4 If anyone says that the union of God the Word with the man
424 was no more than a union by grace or by operation *(ener-geia)*, or by equality of honour, or by authority or relation, affection or power; or if he says that it took place because of good-will, the Word of God being well pleased with the man for whom He had high esteem, as Theodore foolishly asserts; or if he speaks of a union by homonymy as the Nestorians who, by giving to God the Word the name of Jesus and of Christ and by calling the man separately considered Christ and Son, evidently speak of two persons while they pretend to speak of one person and one Christ because of the common appellation, honour, dignity and adoration; but does not confess that the union of God the Word with the flesh animated by a rational and intellectual soul took place by way of synthesis, that is according to the hypostasis, as the holy Fathers have taught, and consequently denies that He has only one hyposta-sis who is our Lord Jesus Christ, one of the Holy Trinity, *anathema sit.*

425 For, since union can be understood in various ways, some following the impiety of Apollinaris and Eutyches and uphold-ing the obliteration of the elements which come together, maintain a union by confusion. Others who think with Theodore and Nestorius, favouring division, introduce an accidental union. The Holy Church of God, rejecting these two impious heresies, confesses the union of God the Word with the flesh as being by synthesis, that is according to the hypostasis. For, in the mystery of Christ union by synthesis not only preserves from confusion what has come together but also tolerates no division.

620/5 If anyone understands the one hypostasis of our Lord Jesus
426   Christ as admitting the meaning of several hypostases, and
           so tries to introduce into the mystery of Christ two hypos-
tases or two persons, and, after having introduced two persons, speaks of one person as regards dignity, honour and adoration, as Theodore and Nestorius have written senselessly; and if he makes the slanderous assertion that the holy Council of Chalcedon has used the term "one hypostasis" in this impious way and does not confess that the Word of God has been united to the flesh according to the hypostasis and that, therefore, there is but one hypostasis or person, and that this is the sense in which the holy Council of Chalcedon confessed one hypostasis of our Lord Jesus Christ, *anathema sit.* For the Holy Trinity has had no person or hypostasis adjoined to it, even by the incarnation of God the Word, one of the Holy Trinity.

620/6 If anyone says that the glorious holy Mary, ever virgin, is not
427   Mother of God in the true sense but only by an abuse of
           language, or that she is so by relation, meaning that a mere
man was born from her and not God the Word made flesh in her, though, according to those who hold this, the birth of this man can be attributed to God the Word in so far as He was with the man at his birth; and if he makes the slanderous assertion that it was in this blasphemous sense thought out by Theodore that the holy Council of Chalcedon called the virgin "Mother of God"; or if anyone calls her mother of the man or mother of Christ as though Christ were not God, but does not confess that she is Mother of God in the true and proper sense since God the Word, begotten from the Father before the ages, became incarnate from her in the latter days, and this is the pious sense in which the holy Council of Chalcedon confessed her to be the Mother of God, *anathema sit.*

620/7 If anyone, while using the phrase "in two natures", does not
428   confess that the one Jesus Christ our Lord is acknowledged
           in divinity and humanity, signifying thereby the distinction of
the natures of which the ineffable union was made without any

confusion, without either the Word being transformed into the nature of the flesh or the flesh being translated into the nature of the Word—for each of the two remains what it is by nature, even after the union according to the hypostasis has taken place—, but if he applies the phrase to the mystery of Christ as meaning a division into parts, or if, while confessing the plurality of natures in one and the same Jesus, our Lord, the Word of God made flesh, he does not only accept in "theory" the distinction between the principles of which He is constituted, a distinction which is not suppressed by their union— for one is from both and both are by one—, but uses the number with the intention of separating the natures and of attributing to each its own hypostasis, *anathema sit.*

620/8 If anyone, while confessing that the union was made out of
429 two natures, the divinity and the humanity, or while speaking of "one incarnate nature *(phusis)* of God the Word",[1]
does not understand these expressions according to the teaching of the holy Fathers, that is as meaning that from the divine and the human natures, when the union according to the hypostasis was realised, there resulted one Christ; but if by these expressions he attempts to introduce one nature or essence *(ousia)* of the divinity and of the flesh of Christ, *anathema sit.*

430 For when we say that the only-begotten Word was united
according to the hypostasis, we do not say that there took place any confusion between natures; rather, we think that God the Word was united to the flesh, each of the two natures remaining what it is. This is why Christ is one, God and man; the same, one in being *(homoousios)* with the Father as to the divinity and one in being with us as to the humanity. For the Church of God repudiates and condemns equally those who introduce a separation or division and those who introduce a confusion into the mystery of the divine incarnation.

620/9 If anyone says that Christ is worshipped in two natures,
431 whereby he introduces two worships, one proper to God
the Word and the other proper to the man, or if anyone, in

---

1. This expression was first used by Apollinaris who denied the completeness of Christ's humanity. It was later attributed to St Athanasius and used by St Cyril who understood it correcly though its terminology remains deficient. Cf. also the third anathematism of Cyril (n. 606/3 and note).

order to suppress the flesh or to fuse the divinity and the humanity, speaks falsely of one nature *(phusis)* or essence *(ousia)* of the elements which have been united and worships Christ in this sense but does not venerate by one worship God the Word made flesh together with His own flesh, according to the Tradition received in the Church of God from the beginning, *anathema sit.*

620/10   If anyone does not confess that He who was crucified in
432   the flesh, our Lord Jesus Christ, is true God, Lord of glory
             and one of the Holy Trinity, *anathema sit.*

621   12. If anyone defends the impious Theodore of Mopsuestia
434   who said that God the Word is one while Christ is another
          who, disturbed by the passions of the soul and the desires of the flesh, freed himself gradually from inferior inclinations and, having improved through the progress of his works and having become irreproachable in his conduct, was baptised as a mere man in the name of the Father and of the Son and of the Holy Spirit; who received through baptism the grace of the Holy Spirit and was deemed worthy of (divine) adoption; who, much like an image of the emperor, is worshipped in the person of God the Word; who after the resurrection became perfectly steadfast in his thoughts and wholly impeccable.

Furthermore, the same impious Theodore has said that the union of God the Word with Christ is similar to that of man and wife, of which the apostle says: "the two shall be in one flesh" *(Eph. 5.31).* And, in addition to his other countless blasphemies, he dared to say that, when after the resurrection the Lord breathed on the disciples and said: "Receive the Holy Spirit" *(Jn 20.22),* He did not give them the Holy Spirit but only breathed on them figuratively. He also said, as regards the confession of Thomas after the resurrection, when having touched the hands and the side of Christ he said: "My Lord and my God" *(Jn 20.28),* that it was not addressed to Christ by Thomas, but that, struck by the miracle of the resurrection, Thomas praised God who had raised Christ.

435   Worse still, in the commentary which he wrote on the *Acts of
        the Apostles,* the same Theodore compares Christ with Plato, Manes, Epicurius and Marcion. As each one of these, he says, having devised his own doctrine, caused his disciples to be called Platonists, Manichaeans, Epicureans or Marcionites, similarly, Christ having devised a doctrine, it is after Him that Christians were named.

If anyone, therefore, defends the afore-mentioned most impious Theodore and his impious writings in which he spreads the blasphemies mentioned and countless others against our great God and Saviour Jesus Christ, and if he does not condemn him and his impious writings and those as well who accept him either by justifying him or by saying that his positions are orthodox, and those who have written in his favour and in favour of his impious writings, and those who hold similar opinions or once held them and remained to the end in such heresy, *anathema sit.*

622 13. If anyone defends the impious works of Theodoret against
436 the orthodox faith, against the first holy Council of Ephesus and against St Cyril and his twelve anathematisms, and if he defends all that he has written in favour of the impious Theodore and Nestorius ..., and, because of this, brands as impious those teachers of the Church who confess the union of God the Word according to the hypostasis and does not condemn the above mentioned impious writings and those who have held and hold like opinions together with all who have written against the orthodox faith and against St Cyril and his twelve anathematisms and have died in such impiety, *anathema sit.*

623 14. If anyone defends the letter said to have been written by
437 Ibas to Maris the Persian, which denies that God the Word, made flesh from Mary the holy Mother of God ever virgin, became man; but asserts (instead) that a mere man whom it terms Temple was born of her, as though God the Word was one and the man another; in which also St Cyril the herald of the orthodox faith of Christians is accused of being a heretic and of having written in the same vein as the impious Apollinaris; in which furthermore the first holy Council of Ephesus is blamed for having condemned Nestorius without investigation; the same impious letter moreover qualifies as impious and contrary to the orthodox faith the twelve anathematisms of St Cyril and justifies Theodore and Nestorius together with their impious doctrines and writings. If, therefore, anyone defends the above-mentioned letter and does not condemn it and its defenders who say that it is orthodox or that part of it is orthodox, together with those who have written or are writing in its favour or in favour of its impious contents, and those who dare to justify it and its impious contents in the name of the holy Fathers or of the holy Council of Chalcedon, and remain to the end in these errors, *anathema sit.*

GREGORY THE GREAT

LETTER TO EULOGIUS, PATRIARCH OF ALEXANDRIA (600)

In the sixth century, a sect originated from Monophysitism held what may be called an inverted monophysitism: the divine nature was rather reduced to the human than the human absorbed into the divine. Thus, as regards Christ's knowledge, its adherents, basing themselves on a passage of Mark's gospel, admitted lack of knowledge concerning the day of judgment. Against these "Agnoetes", Eulogius, patriarch of Alexandria (ob. 607) wrote an important treatise. Pope Gregory the Great approved it as conformable to the ideas of St Augustine. This document is not, however, a document of faith.

(On the knowledge of Christ against the Agnoetes)

624 Concerning the passage of Scripture according to which
474 "neither the Son nor the angels know the day and the hour"
(cf. Mk 13.32), your Holiness is entirely correct in judging that it is certainly not to be referred to the Son considered as the Head, but considered as the Body which we are. In a number of passages... Augustine understands it in this sense. He also says that it can be understood as referring to the Son Himself, because almighty God sometimes speaks in human fashion, as for instance when He says to Abraham: "Now I know that you fear God" *(cf. Gen. 22.12)*, which does not mean that God came then to know that He was feared but that He then made Abraham recognise that he feared God. Just as we speak of a joyful day not because the day is joyful but because it makes us joyful, so the almighty Son says that He does not know the day which He causes not to be known, not because He Himself does not know but because He does not in any way allow it to be known.

625 Thus, it is also said that only the Father knows, because the
475 Son who is one in being with Him *(consubstantialis)* has, from
the nature which He receives from Him and which is superior to that of the angels, a knowledge which angels do not have. This can also, therefore, be understood in a more subtle way by saying that the only-begotten Son incarnate, made perfect man for us, knew the day and the hour of judgment *in* His human nature but did not know it *from* His human nature. What He knew therefore *in* His humanity He did not know *from* it, because it is by the power of His divinity that God-made-man knew the day and the hour of judgment.... Thus it is that He denied having the knowledge which He did not have from the human nature by which He was a creature as the angels are, as He also denied it to the angels because they are creatures. The God-

man knows therefore the day and the hour of judgment, but precisely because God is man.

626 It is perfectly clear that whoever is not a Nestorian cannot in
476 any way be an Agnoete. For, how can one who professes that
the Wisdom of God Himself became incarnate ever maintain that there is anything which the Wisdom of God does not know? It is written: "In the beginning was the Word and the Word was with God and the Word was God.... All things were made through Him" *(Jn 1.1,3)*. If all things, then undoubtedly the day and the hour also. Who would then be so foolish as to say that the Word of the Father made something He did not know? Scripture again says: "Jesus knowing that the Father had given all things into His hands..." *(Jn 13.3)*. If all things, then certainly the day and the hour also. Who then is so foolish as to say that the Son received in His hands what He was ignorant of?...

THE COUNCIL OF LATERAN (649)

The first attempt to end the Monophysite schism by condemning the "three chapters" had not succeeded. Sergius, patriarch of Constantinople from 610 till 638, made a new effort to re-unite the separated Churches; he was sustained in this effort by emperor Heraclius desirous of strengthening his empire. The attempt of Sergius was not, however, without endangering the true faith. While acknowledging two natures in Christ after union, he transposed the Monophysite tendency to the level of Christ's actions and will: there would be in Him but one action (mono-energism) and one will (monothelitism).

Sergius had first recourse to Pope Honorius, suggesting that for the sake of maintaining peace among the Churches, the expression "two actions" which divided them be avoided; though holding the true faith, the Pope in a letter to Sergius (634) (DS 487–488) had for the sake of peace consented to the use of the expression "one will" and suggested that all controversial expressions be avoided. Emboldened by the Pope's failure to uphold the necessity of professing two wills and actions, Sergius exposed the doctrine of Monothelitism more definitely in his Ecthesis, promulgated by emperor Heraclius (638) after the death of Sergius and of Pope Honorius. This amounted to reviving Monophysitism by drawing the consequences naturally implied in it: if there is in Christ but one will and one action, the reason must be that there is only one nature, for action is derived from nature.

This is why Mono-energism and Monothelitism had to be condemned, notwithstanding the attempt made by emperor Constans II in his Typos (648) to end the controversy. It was condemned more than once, notably and with great solemnity by the Council of Lateran (649), convened by Pope Martin I, which gathered 105 bishops from Italy and Africa. This was not an ecumenical Council but the authority of its canons grew with their recognition by the Pope as rule of faith. The Greek text, more precise than the Latin, is followed here. Canons 5 (627/5) and 15 (627/15) give the official interpretation of expressions used by St Cyril (cf. n. 620/8, note) and Pseudo-Dionysius respectively. The final condemnation of Monothelitism will come later in the Third General Council of Constantinople (680-681) (cf. nn. 635-637).

627/1   If anyone does not, according to the holy Fathers, confess
501   truly and properly the Father and the Son and the Holy
Spirit, Trinity in unity and unity in Trinity, that is, one God in three consubstantial hypostases equal in glory; and for the three one and the same Godhead, nature, essence *(ousia),* power, Lordship, kingship, authority, will, action *(energeia)* and sovereignty; uncreated, without beginning, infinite, immutable, creator of all beings and holding them together in His providence, let him be condemned.

627/2   If anyone does not, according to the holy Fathers, confess
502   truly and properly that God the Word, one of the Holy,
consubstantial and adorable Trinity, descended from heaven, became incarnate from the Holy Spirit and from the most holy Mary, ever virgin, and was made man; that He was crucified and of His own free will suffered in the flesh for us and our salvation and was buried, that He rose again on the third day and ascended into heaven, that He is seated at the right hand of the Father and will come again with the glory of the Father, with the flesh assumed by Him and animated by an intellectual soul, to judge the living and the dead, let him be condemned.

(627/3)   *(See text in n. 703)*

627/4   If anyone does not, according to the holy Fathers, confess
504   truly and properly two births of the one our Lord Jesus
Christ Himself, one incorporeal and eternal from God the Father before all ages, the other, corporeal and in the last age, from holy Mary, ever virgin, Mother of God; and one and the same Jesus Christ our Lord and God, one in being with the Father as to His divinity, one in being with men and with His mother as to His humanity, subject to suffering in His flesh while He is impassible in His divinity, limited in His flesh while He is illimited in His spirit, at once created and uncreated, earthly and heavenly, perceptible by sense and by intellect, bound by space and beyond space, in order that the whole of man who had fallen a prey to sin be restored by one who is fully man and God at the same time, let him be condemned.

627/5   If anyone does not, according to the holy Fathers, confess

505   truly and properly "one incarnate nature of God the Word",
by which is meant that our substance is incarnate perfectly
and without restriction in Christ who is God, sin only being
excepted, let him be condemned.

627/6   If anyone does not, according to the holy Fathers, confess
506   truly and properly that one and the same Lord and God,
Jesus Christ, is out of two natures, the divinity and the
humanity, and in two natures, the divinity and the humanity united
according to the hypostasis without confusion or division, let him be
condemned.

627/7   If anyone does not, according to the holy Fathers, confess
507   truly and properly that, after their ineffable union by which
the one and only Christ exists, the essential distinction of
the natures is safeguarded in Him without confusion or division, let
him be condemned.

627/8   If anyone does not, according to the holy Fathers, confess
508   truly and properly that the union of the natures by synthesis, that is according to the hypostasis, by which the one and
only Christ exists, is verified in Him without confusion or division, let
him be condemned.

627/9   If anyone does not, according to the holy Fathers, confess
509   truly and properly that the natural properties of the divinity
of Christ and of His humanity are fully preserved in Him,
complete and undiminished, by which is truly confirmed the fact that
the same is perfect God and perfect man by nature, let him be
condemned.

627/10   If anyone does not, according to the holy Fathers, confess
510   truly and properly two wills, the divine and the human,
intimately united in one and the same Christ God, since it
is one and the same who by each of His two natures has willed our
salvation, let him be condemned.

627/11   If anyone does not, according to the holy Fathers, confess
511   truly and properly two actions *(energeia),* the divine and
the human, intimately united in one and the same Christ
God, since it is one and the same who by each of His two natures has
worked our salvation, let him be condemned.

627/12   If anyone, following the infamous heretics, confesses only

512   one nature or one will or one action of divinity and human-
            ity in the Christ God, destroying thereby what the holy
Fathers confess and denying the mystery of the incarnation of our
Saviour, let him be condemned.

627/13   If, in the Christ God in whom, as has been taught by our
513   holy Fathers, the two wills and the two actions, the divine
            and the human, are essentially preserved in their unity,
anyone, following the infamous heretics, confesses against the doctrine of the holy Fathers one will only and only one action, let him be
condemned.

627/14   If anyone, following the infamous heretics, confesses their
514   impious doctrine of one will and one action in the Christ
            God, and denies and rejects the two wills and two actions,
the divine and the human, "physically" *(phusikôs)* preserved in their
unity in the Christ God, as is professed about Him by the holy
Fathers according to orthodox doctrine, let him be condemned.

627/15   If anyone, following the infamous heretics, foolishly admits
515   the divine-human action which the Greeks call theandric
            (theandrikên) as being one action, but does not profess
according to the holy Fathers that it is two-fold, that is divine and
human, or if he professes that the new appellation "theandric" which
has been introduced designates one action only and does not rather
manifest the wonderful and glorious union of the two actions, let him
be condemned.

627/16   If, while in the Christ God, as piously taught by the holy
516   Fathers, the essential union of the two wills and of the two
            actions, the divine and the human, is preserved, anyone,
following the infamous heretics who seek to destroy, foolishly introduces oppositions and divisions in the mystery of His (incarnation)
and for this reason does not refer the evangelical and apostolic
sayings concerning the Saviour to the same Jesus Christ our Lord
and God according to the illustrious Cyril in order to confirm the fact
that one and the same is by nature truly God and truly man, let him
be condemned.

THE ELEVENTH COUNCIL OF TOLEDO
SYMBOL OF FAITH (675)

For this Symbol of faith, see n. 308i. The Symbol of faith borrows from

dogmatic statements already formulated in the professions of faith promulgated by previous Synods held in the same city, especially the fourth
Council of Toledo (633) (DS 485) and the sixth Council of Toledo (638) (DS
490-493). It also incorporates data from the Pseudo-Athanasian Symbol
Quicumque (nn. 16-17) and from the great Latin doctors, especially St
Augustine. It reflects the Latin approach to the basic mysteries of the faith
and contains its deepest insights and clearest formulations of the doctrine of
the Trinity and of the incarnation. Here the doctrine of the incarnation and
the redemption is quoted. For the doctrine on the Trinity, cf. nn. 308-316; for
the doctrine on the last things, cf. n. 2302.

(The Incarnation)

628 Of these three persons we believe that only the person of the
533   Son has assumed a true human nature, without sin, from the
holy and immaculate Virgin Mary, for the liberation of the
human race. He was begotten from her in a new order and by a new
birth: in a new order, because, invisible in His divinity, He is shown
visible in the flesh; by a new birth, because an inviolate virginity,
without knowing the contact of man, supplied the matter of His
body, being made fruitful by the Holy Spirit. This virgin-birth is
neither grasped by reason nor illustrated by example. Were it
grasped by reason , it would not be wonderful; were it illustrated by
example, it would not be unique. Yet, we must not believe that the
Holy Spirit is the Father of the Son because Mary conceived by the
overshadowing of the same Holy Spirit, lest we should seem to affirm
that the Son has two fathers—which it is certainly impious to say.

(One person and two natures)

629 In this wonderful conception, by which Wisdom built herself a
534   house, "the Word became flesh and dwelt among us" *(Jn 1.14).*
The Word Himself, however, was neither transformed nor
changed in the flesh in such a way that He who willed to be man
would have ceased to be God; but the Word became flesh in such a
way that in Him there is not only the Word of God and the flesh of
man, but also a rational human soul, and that this whole is called God
on account of God and man on account of man. In this Son of God
we believe that there are two natures, one the divine, the other the
human, which the one person of Christ has so united in Himself that
the divinity can never be separated from the humanity nor the
humanity from the divinity. Christ, therefore, is perfect God and
perfect man in the unity of one person. By asserting that there are
two natures in the Son, we do not, however, set up two persons in

Him, lest—which God forbid—the Trinity should seem to become a quaternity. For God the Word did not take the person of man but his nature; He took the temporal substance of the flesh into the eternal person of the divinity.

(Only the Son is incarnate)

630 Likewise, we believe that the Father and the Son and the Holy
535 Spirit are one substance; we do not, however, say that the Virgin Mary gave birth to the unity of this Trinity, but only to the Son who alone assumed our nature in the unity of His person. We must also believe that the entire Trinity brought about the incarnation of the Son of God, because the works of the Trinity are inseparable. However, only the Son took the form of a servant *(cf. Phil. 2.7)* in the singleness of person, not in the unity of the divine nature; He took it into what is proper to the Son, not into what is common to the Trinity. This form has been joined to Him in the unity of person, so that the Son of God and the Son of man are one Christ. Thus, the same Christ in His two natures is made of three substances: that of the Word which must be referred to the essence of God alone, that of the body and of the soul which belong to the true man.

(Two births of the Son of God)

631 He has therefore in Himself the double substance of His
536 divinity and of our humanity. By the fact that He has come forth from the Father without a beginning, He is said only to be born, not to be made or predestined; but by the fact that He was born from the Virgin Mary, we must believe that He was born and made and predestined. Yet, in Him both births are wonderful, because He was begotten from the Father without a mother before all ages, and in the end of the ages He was generated from a mother without a father. He who inasmuch as He is God created Mary, inasmuch as He is man was created from Mary. He is at once the Father and the Son of His Mother Mary. Similarly, by the fact that He is God, He is equal to the Father; by the fact that He is man, He is less than the Father. Likewise, we must believe that He is both greater and less than Himself: for in the form of God the Son Himself is greater than Himself because of the humanity which He has assumed and to which the divinity is superior; but in the form of the servant He is less than Himself, that is, in His humanity which is recognised as inferior to the divinity. For, while by the flesh which He has assumed He is

recognised not only as less than the Father but also as less than Himself, according to the divinity He is co-equal with the Father; both He and the Father are greater than man whose nature *(quem)* the person of the Son alone assumed.

(God and man)

632 Likewise, to the question whether the Son might be equal to,
537 and less than the Holy Spirit, as we believe Him to be now
equal to, now less than the Father, we answer: according to the form of God He is equal to the Father and to the Holy Spirit; according to the form of the servant, He is less than both the Father and the Holy Spirit. For neither the Holy Spirit nor the Father but only the person of the Son has assumed the flesh by virtue of which He is believed to be less than those two persons. Similarly, we believe that this Son is distinct though inseparable from God the Father and the Holy Spirit as a person, and distinct by nature from the humanity *(ab homine)* which He has assumed. Again, with His human nature *(cum homine)* He is one person; but with the Father and the Holy Spirit He is one in the nature or substance of the Godhead.

(Trinity and Incarnation)

633 Yet, we must believe that the Son was sent not only by the
538 Father but also by the Holy Spirit, for He Himself says through
the prophet: "And now the Lord God and His Spirit has sent me " *(Is. 48.16)*. He is also understood to be sent by Himself, because not only the will but also the action of the whole Trinity is believed to be inseparable. For He who before all ages was called the only-begotten became the first-born in time: He is the only-begotten on account of the substance of the Godhead, the first-born on account of the nature of flesh which He has assumed.

(The redemption)

634 In the form of man which He assumed, we believe, according
539 to the truth of the Gospel, that He was conceived without sin,
He who alone "was made sin" *(cf. 2 Cor. 5.21)* for our sake, that is who became sacrifice for four sins. And yet, He endured His passion for our offences without losing His divinity. Condemned to death, He has experienced on the cross a real death in the flesh and on the third day, restored to life by His own power, He rose from the grave.

THE THIRD GENERAL COUNCIL OF CONSTANTINOPLE
DEFINITION ON THE TWO WILLS AND ACTIONS IN CHRIST
(681)

Monothelitism and Mono-energism had been condemned by the Council of Lateran (nn. 627/10-14). The Third Council of Constantinople (680-681) gave to this condemnation the authority of an ecumenical Council. It was convoked by emperor Constantine IV with the full consent of Pope Agatho. In March 680 the Pope had written a letter to the emperor in which he explained the true doctrine as regards the two wills and actions in Christ and their union (cf. DS 544-545). This and a similar letter presented by a Synod of Rome (DS 547-548) were acclaimed by the Council in its fourth session in November 680. The Council meant to settle the matter definitively and to extirpate the Monothelistic tendency then mostly represented by Macarius, patriarch of Constantinople, who was condemned during the Council's 9th session. Pope Honorius too was taken to task in the 13th session for having failed to uphold the true doctrine against Sergius (DS 552) (cf. n. 627i). During its 18th and last session (16 Sept. 681), the Council approved a profession of faith, interspersed with anathematisms directed against the Monothelitists. It explicitates what was already implicitly contained in the doctrine of Leo the Great (n. 612) and in the dogma of Chalcedon (cf. nn. 614ff). One year later, Pope Leo II, successor of Agatho, approved the proceedings of the Council.

635 We likewise proclaim in Him, according to the teaching of the
556   holy Fathers, two natural volitions or wills and two natural
actions, without division, without change, without separation, without confusion. The two natural wills are not—by no means—opposed to each other as the impious heretics assert; but His human will is compliant, it does not resist or oppose but rather submits to His divine and almighty will. For, as the wise Athanasius says, it was necessary that the will of the flesh move itself *(kinêthênai)*, but also that it be submitted to the divine will;[1] because, just as His flesh is said to be and is the flesh of God the Word, so too the natural will of His flesh is said to be and is God the Word's very own, as He Himself declares: "I have come down from heaven, not to do my own will but the will of Him who sent me" *(Jn 6.38)*. He calls the will of His flesh His own will, because the flesh also has become His own. For just as His most Holy and immaculate flesh, animated by His soul, has not been destroyed by being divinised but remained in its own state and kind, so also His human will has not been destroyed by being divinised. It has rather been preserved, according to the words of Gregory the

---

1. ATHANASIUS OF ALEXANDRIA, *Tractatus in illud "Nunc anima mea turbata est"* *(Jn 12.27)* (this treatise has not been preserved).

theologian: "For His will—referring to that of the Saviour—, being fully divinised, is not opposed to God."[1]

636 In the same our Lord Jesus Christ, our true God, we glory
557 in proclaiming two natural actions, without division, without
change, without separation, without confusion, namely a divine action and a human action, as Leo, the master in matters related to God, asserts with utmost clarity: "For each of the two natures performs the function proper to it in communion with the other: the Word does what pertains to the Word and the flesh what pertains to the flesh" *(cf. n. 612).* For we do not in any way admit one natural action of God and the creature, so as neither to raise to the divine essence what is created nor lower the sublime divine nature to the level proper to creatures. For we know that both the miracles and the sufferings belong to one and the same, according to the different natures of *(ex)* which He consists and in which He has His being, as the admirable Cyril has said.[2]

637 Therefore, preserving entirely what is neither fused nor
558 divided, we proclaim the entire matter in this concise utter-
ance: believing that one of the Holy Trinity, who after the incarnation is our Lord Jesus Christ, is our true God, we say that His two natures shine forth in His one hypostasis. In it, throughout His entire human existence in the flesh, He made manifest His miracles and His sufferings, not in mere appearance but in reality. The difference of natures in that same and unique hypostasis is recognised by the fact that each of the two natures wills and performs what is proper to it in communion with the other. Thus, we glory in proclaiming two natural wills and actions concurring together for the salvation of the human race.

HADRIAN I

LETTER *SI TAMEN LICET* ADDRESSED TO THE SPANISH
BISHOPS (793)

Monothelitism represented an attempt to compromise with Monophys-itism ; it led back to it. Similarly, in the opposite direction, a new Adoption-ism arose in the eighth century which led back to Nestorianism by seeking a

---

1. GREGORY OF NAZIANZEN, *Oratio* 30, 12.

2. These words are not found *ad litteram* in any of the extant works of Cyril of Alexandria. They seem to sum up freely the doctrine exposed for instance in the *Epistolae Synodales ad Nestorium;* see also the anathematisms 4 and 9 of St Cyril *(cf. nn. 603/4.9)* and the Second Council of Constantinople *(cf. n. 620/3).*

compromise with it. The movement originated in Spain where it was headed by Elipandus, archbishop of Toledo. Wishing to stress the perfect consubstantiality of Christ with the rest of mankind, the Spanish Adoptionists came to affirm in Him a double sonship: His eternal, natural sonship due to His eternal generation from the Father and an adoptive sonship of God derived from His human birth from the Virgin Mary. This teaching overlooked the fact that the affirmation of a double sonship ultimately implied the affirmation of two persons and consequently was a return to Nestorianism. It met with opposition from Rome. Pope Hadrian I rejected it in a first letter to the Spanish bishops (cf. DS 595). The same Pope reiterated its condemnation in another letter, Si tamen licet, addressed to the same bishops in 793. The condemnation of the new Adoptionism would soon be taken up by local councils (cf. n. 639). It led to a further clarification of the mystery of the incarnation.

(Christ is not the Son of God by adoptive sonship but only by natural sonship)

638   The adoption of Jesus Christ the Son of God according to
610   the flesh...the Catholic Church has never believed, never
          taught, never accepted when it was asserted by a wrong
belief.... But with one voice with Peter she proclaims that Chrit is the
Son of God, because there is one Christ, Son of God and of man, not
by grace of adoption but by the dignity of natural sonship....

THE COUNCIL OF FRIULI

PROFESSION OF FAITH (796 or 797)

The new Adoptionism had spread to Gaul. Several Councils condemned it, among which figures the Council of Frankfurt (794) (DS 615) in which the Italian and French bishops played the leading role. Later, Paulinus, patriarch of Aquileia, who had drawn up the document submitted by the Italian bishops at Frankfurt, held his own Synod at Friuli. New precisions were added to the Symbol of Constantinople (cf. n. 12). Some of these are concerned with Trinitarian doctrine (cf. DS 616-618); others with the sonship of Christ: His unique natural divine sonship excludes all adoptive sonship, without preventing Him from being truly man by virtue of His human birth. The unity of person must be preserved. This is the clearest condemnation of the new Adoptionism which affirmed a double sonship in Christ. The same precisions will later be reflected in the profession of faith of Pope Leo IX (1053) (DS 681).

639   The human and temporal birth did not interfere with the
619   divine timeless birth, but in the one person of Jesus Christ are
          the true Son of God and the true son of man. There is not one
who is son of man and another who is Son of God, but one and the

same Son of God and son of man, in two natures, the divine and the human, true God and true man. He is not the putative Son of God, but the true Son; not the adoptive Son but the real Son, for He was never estranged from the Father because of the man (human nature) which He assumed.... And, therefore, we confess Him to be in each of the two natures the real, not the adoptive, Son of God, because, having assumed the human nature *(assumpto homine)*, one and the same is Son of God and son of man without confusion and without separation. He is naturally Son of the Father as to His divinity, naturally son of His Mother as to His humanity, but He is properly Son of the Father in both (natures).

INNOCENT III
PROFESSION OF FAITH PRESCRIBED TO THE WALDENSIANS
(1208)

The Waldensians held a sort of cosmological dualism, inherited from the Manichaeans, according to which matter is evil. This led them to several errors as regards creation (cf. n. 403). Applying the same principle to the mystery of Christ, they professed His human body to be but an appearance, not a real body. Thus, they returned to the early Christological heresy of Docetism. The profession of faith prescribed to them by Pope Innocent III lays stress on the reality of the human flesh of Christ from the incarnation down to His glorified state after the resurrection and to His return in glory. It also brings out the fact, already affirmed by the Council of Reims (DS 745i), that, since the three divine persons are one Godhead, in Christ the Godhead itself has become man, but only as subsisting in the person of the Son.

640 We heartily believe and we proclaim that the incarnation of
791 the Godhead has taken place, not in the Father or the Holy
Spirit, but only in the Son; so that He who in His divinity was the Son of God the Father, true God from the Father, became in His humanity son of man, true man from a mother, with a true flesh taken from the womb of His mother and a rational human soul. (Subsisting) at once in two natures, as God and as man, He is one person, one Son, one Christ; one God with the Father and the Holy Spirit and with them creator and ruler of all, He was born of the Virgin Mary by a true birth in the flesh. He ate and drank, slept and rested when He was tired from walking. He suffered a true passion in the flesh, died His own true bodily death, rose again by a true resurrection of His flesh and the true resumption of His body by His soul. He ate and drank in His risen flesh, and then ascended to heaven and is seated at the right hand of the Father. In the same flesh He will come to judge the living and the dead.

THE FOURTH LATERAN GENERAL COUNCIL
SYMBOL OF LATERAN (1215)

(641)   *This important profession of faith (cf. n. 19i) explicitates the tradi-*
tional doctrine of faith on the mystery of the incarnation. It is
fundamentally based on the doctrine of the Council of Ephesus (cf. nn. 604f)
and of Chalcedon (cf. nn. 613ff), but also includes further developments. It
points out that the incarnation of the Son is the common work of the whole
Trinity. See text in n. 20.

THE SECOND GENERAL COUNCIL OF LYONS
"PROFESSION OF FAITH OF MICHAEL PALAEOLOGUS" (1274)

(642)   *The "Profession of Faith of Michael Palaeologus" (cf. n. 22i) is, in its*
Christological article, basically inspired by the doctrine of the Coun-
cil of Chalcedon (cf. nn. 613ff), to which are added further well established
developments, as for instance the exclusion of an adoptive sonship of Christ
(cf. n. 639), and the reality of His human flesh (cf. n. 640). Its brief formula-
tion proposes the orthodox doctrine about Christ in a way which excludes
all the major Christological errors. See text in n. 23.

CLEMENT VI

JUBILEE BULL *UNIGENITUS DEI FILIUS* (1343)

The early documents of the Church were mostly concerned with the
mystery of the person of Christ and of the incarnation; in comparison with
this the doctrine of the redemption remained undeveloped. Christ's death
on the cross for men's salvation had, no doubt, been mentioned in the early
Symbols of the faith (cf. nn. 2ff) and again in later Symbols. But the
elaboration of the doctrine of the expiatory sacrifice and atoning death
came only later. Previous to the document under review may be mentioned
the following documents of the Middle Ages: the condemnation by the
Council of Sens (1141) of Abelard who tended to reduce the efficacy of
Christ's death to a purely subjective one (DS 723); the affirmation made by
the Council of Vienna (1312), against an opinion attributed to Peter John
Olivi, that Christ truly died on the cross for our salvation (DS 901)....

While proclaiming the Jubilee indulgences in 1343, Pope Clement VI
showed their foundation to lie in the sacrificial shedding of Christ's blood on
the cross. Union with the Word of God gave infinite value to the merits of the
Saviour's humanity; they are the main source of the treasure on which the
Church's indulgences are based. The doctrine of Christ's merit and satisfac-
tion will later be explicitated by the Council of Trent (cf. n. 647).

(The infinite merits of Christ)

643   The only-begotten Son of God..., "whom God made our
1025   Wisdom, our rightousness, and sanctification and redemption" *(cf. 1 Cor. 1.30)*, "entered once for all into the Holy
Place, taking not the blood of goats and calves but His own blood,

thus securing an eternal redemption" *(Heb. 9.12).* For "it is not with perishable things such as silver or gold, but with His own precious blood that He who is the Lamb without blemish or spot redeemed us" *(cf. 1 Pet. 1. 18f).* Immolated on the altar of the cross though He was innocent, He did not merely shed a drop of His blood—although this would have sufficed for the redemption of the whole human race because of the union with the Word—but a copious flood....

1027   To this mass of treasure the merits of the Blessed Mother of God and of all the elect, from the first just man to the last, also contribute, as we know; nor is it at all to be feared that it could be exhausted or diminished, first on account of the infinite merits of Christ, as already mentioned, and further because the more men are drawn to righteousness by having this treasure applied to them, so much the more does the store of those merits increase.

THE GENERAL COUNCIL OF FLORENCE
DECREE FOR THE JACOBITES (1442)

In its Bull Cantate Domino, *the Council of Florence (cf. n. 322i), after exposing the doctrine of the Trinity (cf. nn. 325f), treats of the mystery of Christ. A first section deals with the mystery of the incarnation and of the person of Christ in terms mostly borrowed from previous documents. A second section recalls the mystery of the redemption as contained in the early professions of faith, and, after condemning the main Christological heresies (cf. DS 1339-1346), goes on to explain that Christ's redemptive work is the source of salvation for all men.*

644   The Church firmly believes, professes and preaches that one
1337   person of the Trinity, true God, Son of God begotten from the Father, one in being with the Father and equally eternal with Him, has, in the fulness of time designed by the divine counsel in its inscrutable majesty, assumed from the immaculate womb of the Virgin Mary for the salvation of the human race a true and complete human nature and united it to Himself in the unity of person *(in unitatem personae).* This unity is so intimate that neither is anything which in Him belongs to God separated from the man, nor is anything belonging to the man divided from the divinity; one and the same is undivided, each of the two natures perduring with its own properties. He is God and man, Son of God and son of man, equal to the Father as to the divinity, inferior to the Father as to the humanity; immortal and eternal by His divine nature, subject to suffering and to time by the human conditon which He has assumed.

645 She firmly believes, professes and preaches that the Son of
1338 God was truly born of the Virgin in the humanity which He
assumed, that He truly suffered, truly died and was buried,
truly rose from the dead, ascended to heaven and is seated at the
right hand of the Father, and that He will come at the end of times to
judge the living and the dead.

646 She firmly believes, professes and preaches that no one ever
1347 conceived from man and woman has been freed from the
dominion of the devil, except through faith in Jesus Christ
our Lord, the mediator between God and men, who, conceived
without sin, having been born and having died, alone crushed the
enemy of the human race by His death which destroyed our sins, and
secured again entry into the kingdom of heaven which the first man
had lost by his sin and all his descendants with him....

THE GENERAL COUNCIL OF TRENT
SIXTH SESSION
DECREE ON JUSTIFICATION (1547)

*The Council of Trent was concerned with the doctrine of the redemption
only indirectly, in connection with the doctrine of justification which was the
fundamental issue raised by the Reformation. Nevertheless, the Decree on
Justification (cf. n. 1924i), when explaining the various causes of man's
justification, clearly states the traditional doctrine of the Middle Ages on
Christ's merit and satisfaction for all men. See the rest of the Decree on
Justification, especially nn. 1926-1932, and Canon 10 (n. 1960); see also the
Decree on Original Sin (n. 510).*

(Christ is the meritorious cause of man's justification)

647 The meritorious cause (of justification) is the beloved only-
1529 begotten Son of God, our Lord Jesus Christ who, "while we
were sinners" *(Rom. 5.10)*, "out of the great love with which
He loved us" *(Eph. 2.4)*, merited for us justification by His most holy
passion on the wood of the cross *(cf. n. 1960)* and made satisfaction
for us to God the Father.

PAUL IV

CONSTITUTION *CUM QUORUMDAM HOMINUM* (1555)

*Soon after the Reformation emerged, rationalism, which set reason
above Revelation, made its appearance in various sects issued from it.
These denied the fundamental mysteries of the Trinity, of the incarnation*

and redemption. They were condemned by Pope Paul IV in virtue of his "apostolic authority". The same Constitution also condemns errors concerning Marian doctrine (cf. n. 707). It may be regarded as the first condemnation of rationalism. The section concerned with the mystery of Christ and His work is given here.

648 In the name of almighty God, Father, Son and Holy Spirit, in
1880 virtue of our apostolic authority we enjoin and admonish all
those who up to this time have asserted, taught and believed... that our Lord is not true God, of the same substance in all things with the Father and the Holy Spirit, or that according to the flesh He was not conceived in the womb of the Blessed Mary ever Virgin from the Holy Spirit, but, as other men, from the seed of Joseph; or that the same Jesus Christ our Lord and God did not undergo the very violent death of the cross to redeem us from sins and from eternal death and to reconcile us with the Father unto life eternal.

PIUS VI

CONSTITUTION *AUCTOREM FIDEI* (1794)

This Constitution condemns several sets of propositions of a Synod which met at Pistoia in Toscany (1786) under the leadership of Scipio Ricci; many of its propositions reflect the basic tenets of Jansenism. One set deals with the divine worship due to the humanity of Christ. To deny, as the Synod of Pistoia did, that Christ must be adored in His humanity, while professing the divine worship due to His divinity, amounted to denying the unity of person and, therefore, was a subtle return to Nestorianism. The text of the condemned propositions, given below, indicates that, because of the assumption of Christ's humanity to union in the person of the Son of God, the divine worship due to Him extends to His humanity. Two other condemned propositions apply the same doctrine to the worship of the Sacred Heart: the cult of latria is due to it on account of the union of Christ's humanity with the person of the Word of God (cf. DS 2662-2663).

(On the adoration of the humanity of Christ)

649 The proposition which affirms that "to adore directly the
2661 humanity of Christ and all the more any part of His humanity
is always to render divine honour to a creature", where the use of the term "directly" is intended to bring condemnation on the cult of adoration which the faithful address to the humanity of Christ, as if such an adoration—by which the humanity and the living flesh of Christ is adored, not indeed for its own sake and merely as flesh *(tamquam nuda caro)* but as united to the divinity—were a divine honour paid to a creature, and not rather one and the same adora-

tion by which the Word incarnate together with His own flesh is adored, is false... and detracts from the pious and fitting cult rendered and rightly rendered by the faithful to the humanity of Christ....

PIUS X

DECREE *LAMENTABILI* OF THE HOLY OFFICE (1907)
ARTICLES OF MODERNISM CONDEMNED

Despite some genuine insights, the Modernist current of the early twentieth century thereatened the foundations of the faith (cf. n. 143i). The Modernists reduced the message of Christ to the proclamation of the eschatological Kingdom which Christ, they maintained, believed to be imminent. This led them to affirm in Christ not only ignorance but also error as regards the day of judgment, and to question His divinity and even His messianic character. In addition, they so stressed the role played by the early Christian community in the formation of the Gospels as to oppose by a sharp distinction the Christ of faith and the Jesus of history. Despite the dangers which it offered for the faith and which needed to be clearly pointed out, the Modernist current has had beneficial effects. It has prompted modern biblical scholarship to show the continuity between the Jesus of history and the Christ of faith, notwithstanding the fact that the New Testament writings contain primarily the proclamation of the faith of the early Christian community. The Decree Lamentabili enumerates the Christological errors of the Modernists. In his Encyclical Pascendi of the same year, Pope Pius X mostly expatiates on the alleged opposition between the Jesus of history and the Christ of faith (cf. DS 3479, 3485).

(Modernist errors about Christ condemned)

[650/27]   The divinity of Jesus Christ is not proved from the Gos-
3427   pels, but is a dogma which the Christian consciousness
                  has deduced from the notion of the Messiah.

[650/28]   When Jesus exercised His ministry, neither did He speak
3428   with the intention of teaching that He was the Messiah
                  nor were His miracles meant to prove it.

[650/29]   It may be granted that the Christ shown by history is
3429   much inferior to the Christ who is the object of faith.

[650/30]   In all the Gospel texts the term 'Son of God' merely
3430   means the same as Messiah and does not at all mean
                  that Christ is the true and natural Son of God.

[650/31]   The doctrine which Paul, John and the Councils of
3431   Nicaea, Ephesus and Chalcedon teach about Christ, is
                  not what Jesus taught but what the Christian conscious-
ness conceived about Jesus.

[650/32] The natural meaning of the Gospel texts cannot be rec-
3432 onciled with what our theologians teach about the consciousness and the infallible knowledge of Jesus Christ.

[650/33] It is evident to anyone with no preconceived opinions
3433 that either Jesus' teaching as regards the proximity of the
Messianic advent was erroneous or else the greater part
of His teaching contained in the Synoptic Gospels is unauthentic.

[650/34] A critic cannot assert that Christ's knowledge was unlim-
3434 ited, unless by making the hypothesis, which is historically inconceivable and morally repugnant, that Christ as
man had God's knowledge and yet was unwilling to communicate so
much knowledge to His disciples and posterity.

[650/35] Christ did not always have the consciousness of His
3435 messianic dignity.

[650/36] The resurrection of the Saviour is not properly a fact of
3436 the historical order but a fact of the purely supernatural
order, which is not and cannot be demonstrated, a fact
which the Christian consciousness derived gradually from other
sources.

[650/37] Faith in the resurrection of Christ has been from the
3437 beginning not so much faith in the fact of His resurrection
as in the immortal life of Christ with God.

[650/38] The teaching about the expiatory death of Christ is not
3438 evangelical but Pauline only.

BENEDICT XV

DECREE OF THE HOLY OFFICE (1918)

The great conciliar definitions had clearly exposed the main outlines of doctrine with regard to the person of Christ. They had opened the way for an attempt to penetrate more deeply into the mystery of the human psychology of the Son Incarnate. It is certain that by assuming human nature the Word took with him not only the heights but also the weaknesses of the human soul, having become similar to us in all things but sin. But it is no less certain that the hypostatic union postulated in His human soul unique privileges and that others were required for the exercise of His revelatory and redemptive functions. As regards Christ's knowledge, tradition had taught the absence of ignorance in Him (cf. nn. 624-626), but without always distinguishing clearly between the divine and the human knowledge. To penetrate more deeply into the mystery of the human knowledge of Christ was reserved to recent times; the questions raised by the Modernists invited such a study. Speculative attempts followed, some of which were not satisfactory in so far as they unduly undermined the privileges of the human soul of Christ. Having been consulted on definite questions by the S. Congregation for Seminaries and Universities, the Holy Office gave the following answers which were confirmed by Pope Benedict XV. The text must be carefully interpreted in its historical context; in particular, Christ's "beatific vision" remains open to different interpretations.

Question: Can the following propositions be taught safely:

651/1   It is not certain that the soul of Christ during His life among
3646   men had the knowledge which the blessed, that is those who
have achieved their goal *(comprehensores)*, have.

651/2   The opinion cannot be declared certain, which holds that
3446   the soul of Christ was ignorant of nothing but from the
beginning knew in the Word everything, past, present and future, that is to say everything which God knows with the "knowledge of vision".

651/3   The recent opinion of some about the limited knowledge of
3647   the soul of Christ is not to be less favoured in Catholic
schools than the ancient opinion about His universal knowledge.

Answer: No.

PIUS XI

ENCYCLICAL LETTER *QUAS PRIMAS* (1925)

In his encyclical letter on the Kingship of Christ, Pope Pius XI explains the double foundation of Christ's dominion over all things: it belongs to Him as the God-man and as Redeemer. The Pope goes on to explain the various powers which Christ's Kingship comprises, and that, though His Kingship is primarily spiritual, it also extends in a certain sense to civil matters (cf. DS 3677-3679). It must be noted that Kingship is not attributed to Christ and the earthly kings univocally. In our times, when earthly kings have lost much of their power and appeal little to the masses, the biblical roots and meaning of Christ's Lordship and Kingship need to be stressed.

(The Kingship of Christ as man)

652   If we ponder this matter more deeply, we cannot but see that
3675   the title and the power of King belong to Christ as man in
the strict and proper sense also. For it is only as man that He may be said to have received from the Father "dominion and glory and Kingdom" *(cf. Dan. 7. 13-14)*, since the Word of God, as consub-

stantial with the Father, has all things in common with Him, and therefore has necessarily supreme and absolute dominion over all things created.

(The twofold foundation of Christ's Kingship)

653 The foundation of this power and dignity of our Lord is
3676 rightly indicated by Cyril of Alexandria. He says: "Christ has dominion over all creatures, a dominion not seized by violence nor usurped, but His by essence and by nature."[1] His Kingship is founded upon the ineffable hypostatic union. From this it follows not only that Christ is to be adored by angels and men, but that to Him as man angels and men are subject, and must recognise His empire: by reason of the hypostatic union Christ has power over all creatures. But a thought that must give us even greater joy and consolation is this, that Christ is our King by acquired as well as by natural right, for He is our Redeemer....

ENCYCLICAL LETTER *MISERENTISSIMUS REDEMPTOR* (1928)

In his encyclical on the reparation due to the Sacred Heart of Jesus the same Pope explains that by the incarnation and redemption Christ has entered into an intimate communion with mankind: Head and members constitute one Body. Though Christ's redemptive work has been historically accomplished once for all, the application of its effects to all generations is a work which continues through the centuries and in which Christians must join. Thus mankind is drawn into the ever operative mysteries of the incarnation and the redemption. By reason of the mysterious bond between the Head and the members, Christians must carry on in their own life Christ's redemptive passion.

(Christ's redemptive sacrifice)

654 The plentiful redemption of Christ brought us abundant forgiveness of all our sins *(cf. Col. 2.13)*. Nevertheless, owing to the wonderful arrangement of divine Wisdom by which what is lacking in the sufferings of Christ is to be completed in our flesh for His Body which is the Church *(cf. Col. 1.24)*, we are able and, in fact, we ought to join our own acts of praise and satisfaction to those which Christ has presented to God in the name of sinners.

655 However, we must always remember that the entire expiatory value (of our acts) depends on the one bloody sacrifice of

---

1. CYRIL OF ALEXANDRIA, *Comment. in Joan.*, 12,18.

Christ, which is uninterruptedly renewed on our altars in an unbloody manner; for "the victim is one and the same: the same now offers through the ministry of priests, who then offered Himself on the cross; only the manner of offering is different" *(cf. n. 1548).*

(Community of atonement with Christ)

656   Therefore, an act of immolation on the part of both priests and the rest of the faithful must be joined with this most august eucharistic sacrifice so that they too may offer themselves as living victims, holy and pleasing to God *(cf. Rom. 12.1).* Indeed, St Cyprian unhesitatingly asserts that "the celebration of the Lord's sacrifice does not effect our proper sanctification, unless our sacrificial offering is in accord with His passion."[1] Accordingly, the apostle warns us that, "carrying in our body the death of Jesus" *(2 Cor. 4.10)* and being buried with Christ and united with Him in the likeness of His death *(cf. Rom. 6.4f),* we ought to crucify our flesh with its vices and lusts *(cf. Gal. 5.24),* "escaping from the corruption that is in the world because of passion" *(2 Pet. 1.4);* he exhorts us that "the life of Jesus may be manifested in our bodies" *(2 Cor. 4.10)* and that, as sharers in His eternal priesthood, we may offer "gifts and sacrifices for sins" *(Heb. 5.1).*

(The universal priesthood exercised in satisfaction and in the eucharistic sacrifice)

657   For participation in the mysterious priesthood and in the duty of offering satisfaction and sacrifice is not limited to those whom our High Priest Jesus Christ uses as His ministers to offer the clean oblation to the divine Majesty in every place from the rising of the sun to its setting *(cf. Mal. 1.11);* no, it is the duty of the entire Christian family, which the prince of the apostles rightly calls "a chosen race, a kingdom of priests" *(1 Pet. 2.9),* to offer expiatory sacrifice *(cf. Heb. 5.3)* not only for itself but also for the whole human race, in much the same way as every priest and "every high priest chosen from among men is appointed to act on behalf of men in relation to God" *(Heb. 5.1).*

658   We shall reap a more abundant harvest of mercy and forgiveness for ourselves and for others to the extent that our own offering and sacrifice correspond more perfectly to the sacrifice of

---

1. St Cyprian, *Epistola 63 ad Caecilium,* 9.

our Lord; in other words, to the extent that we immolate our self-love and our passions and crucify our flesh with that mystical crucifixion of which the apostle speaks. For there is a wonderfully close relationship between Christ and all the faithful—a relationship like that of the Head of a body to the rest of its members. Moreover, by the mysterious communion of saints, which we acknowledge by our Catholic faith, all men, as individuals and as nations, are joined not only in association with one another but also to Him "who is the Head, Christ, from whom the whole Body, joined and knit together by every joint with which it is supplied, when each part is working properly makes bodily growth and upbuilds itself in love" *(Eph. 4.15f)*. This indeed is what the Mediator between God and men, Christ Jesus, prayed for to His Father when He was approaching death: "I in them and You in Me, that they may become perfectly one" *(Jn 17.23)*.

659 A further consideration is the truth that Christ's expiatory suffering is renewed and in a way continued and completed in His mystical Body, which is the Church. For, to use St Augustine's words again: "Christ suffered all that He should have suffered; there is now nothing lacking in the measure of His sufferings. His sufferings as Head, then, were completed; yet, for Christ in His Body sufferings still remained."[1] The Lord Jesus Himself mercifully made this truth known when, speaking to Saul who was still breathing threats of slaughter against the disciples *(cf. Acts 9.1)*, He said: "I am Jesus whom you are persecuting" *(Acts 9.5)*. Obviously He means that, when persecutions are directed against the Church, it is the divine Head of the Church Himself who is attacked and afflicted. It is entirely proper, then, that Christ who is still suffering in His mystical Body should want to have us as His companions in the work of expiation. This is required of us also by our close union with Him, since we are "the Body of Christ and individually members of it" *(1 Cor. 12.27)*, and all the members ought to suffer with the Head anything that the Head suffers *(cf. 1 Cor. 12.26)*.

PIUS XII

ENCYCLICAL LETTER *MYSTICI CORPORIS* (1943)

Pope Pius XII's great Encyclical Letter on the mystery of the Church, the

---

1. St Augustine, *Enarrationes in Psalmos: in Ps. 86.5.*

mystical Body of Christ (cf. n. 847i), had naturally to be based on Christological doctrine. In particular, the Pope points out that Christ is the Head of His Body the Church; he affirms the fulness of grace of His humanity from which all men receive; touching on the question of the human knowledge of Christ, he reaffirms that Christ's human intellect possessed the "beatific vision" and explains that His human knowledge extended to all men.

(Christ, the Head of His mystical Body, has the fulness of grace)

660 A further reason why Christ is to be regarded as the Head of the Church lies in the surpassing plenitude and perfection of His supernatural gifts, in consequence of which His mystical Body draws upon that fulness. Many of the Fathers remark that just as the head of our mortal body is endowed with all the senses while the remainder has only the sense of touch, so all the virtues, gifts, and miraculous powers which are found in the Christian community exist in Christ its Head with the full perfection of their splendour. "For in Him all the fulness of God was pleased to dwell" *(Col. 1.19)*. He is adorned with all those supernatural gifts which accompany the hypostatic union; for in Him the Holy Spirit dwells with a fulness of grace than which no greater can be conceived. To Him has been given "power over all flesh" *(cf. Jn 17.2)* and "all the treasures of wisdom and knowledge" *(Col. 2.3)* abound in Him. He also enjoys the beatific vision in a degree, both as regards extent and clarity, surpassing that of all the saints in heaven. Indeed, so full of grace and truth is He that of His inexhaustible fulness we all receive *(cf. Jn 1.14-16)*.

(Christ's human knowledge)

661
3812 But the loving knowledge with which the divine Redeemer has pursued us from the first moment of His incarnation is such as completely to surpass all the searchings of the human mind; for by means of the beatific vision, which He enjoyed from the time when He was received into the womb of the Mother of God, He has for ever and continuously had present to Him all the members of His mystical Body, and embraced them with His saving love....

ENCYCLICAL LETTER *SEMPITERNUS REX* (1951)

This Encyclical celebrates the 15th centenary of the Council of Chalcedon. In the name of the Conciliar doctrine, the Pope rejects two errors. The first is that of the "kenotic theories" which have been prominent in Protestant theology, especially in Germany and England, during the 19th century. These theories held that the Word of God, by becoming incarnate, had really given up all or some of His divine attributes. The other is the tendency, among some recent Catholic theologians inspired by a Christology of the "assumptus homo", so to conceive the autonomy of Christ's humanity as to practically contradict its hypostatic union with the Word of God. But the Pope leaves open the question of a human psychological personality in Christ. Theologians can speak of a human 'ego' or psychological personality in Christ, provided the unique ontological personhood of the Son Incarnate is safeguarded. Theology is even today engaged in the study of the mysterious psychological unity of the God-man.

(Condemnation of the kenotic theory)

662 Likewise entirely opposed to Chalcedon's profession of faith is the erroneous opinion, rather widespread among non-Catholics, which imagines that in Christ the divinity of the Word is lost. Called the "kenotic theory", it finds a specious foundation in a rash misinterpretation of a text of the letter of the apostle Paul to the Philippians *(cf. Phil. 2.7)*. It is truly a blasphemous theory, and, like the doctrine of Docetism directly opposed to it, it makes the whole mystery of the incarnation and the redemption a lifeless and meaningless illusion. "The true God... was born with the complete and perfect nature of a true man; He is complete in His nature and complete in ours": this is the exalted doctrine of Leo the Great *(cf. n. 611)*.

(Christ's human nature is not an independent subject)

663
3905 Though it is legitimate to study the humanity of Christ from the psychological view-point, yet in this difficult matter there are some who too rashly set up novel constructions which they wrongly place under the patronage of the Council of Chalcedon. These theologians describe the state and condition of Christ's human nature in such terms that it seems to be taken for an independent subject *(subiectum sui iuris)*, as though it did not subsist in the person of the Word. Yet, the Council of Chalcedon, in complete agreement with that of Ephesus, clearly asserts that the two natures of our Redeemer were united in one person, and it does not allow us to put in Christ two individuals, so that some *homo assumptus*, endowed with complete autonomy, is placed by the side of the Word *(penes Verbum collocetur)*.

ENCYCLICAL LETTER *HAURIETIS AQUAS* (1956)

This Encyclical Letter on the cult of the Sacred Heart broadens the perspectives opened by previous papal encyclicals on the same subject. A certain disaffection towards the cult of the Sacred Heart was due to a lack

of perception of its true nature. It was necessary to give it a solid theological
foundation and to show its intimate relationship with the mystery of Christ.
The Pope shows that the cult of the Sacred Heart has deep roots in the
Scriptures themselves. As for its theological foundation, it is to be found in
the mystery of the incarnation and of the hypostatic union. Because the
Incarnate Word has united to Himself a complete human nature (cf. DS
3923), His human heart can rightly be recognised as the symbol and the
manifestation of His love for the Father and for men. It is therefore the
symbol of what is at the centre of the mystery of Christ. Theological
reflection serves here to show that the cult of the Sacred Heart deserves a
central place in the Christian life, and is not just an ordinary devotion among
others.

(The twofold reason for the cult of the Sacred Heart)

664   In order that all may more exactly grasp the import for this
3922   cult of the outstanding passages of the Old and of the New
          Testaments which contain a reference to it, we must keep
quite clearly in mind why the Church offers the worship of *latria* to
the divine Heart of the Redeemer.... This reason is twofold. The first,
which is applicable also to the other members of the Body of Jesus
Christ, rests on the principle according to which we acknowledge
that His Heart, the noblest part of human nature, is hypostatically
joined to the person of the divine Word; and therefore it must be
given the same worship of adoration as that with which the Church
honours the person of the Incarnate Son of God Himself.... The
other reason, which is proper to the Heart of the divine Redeemer,
and hence calls in a special way for the worship of *latria* to be offered
to it, is the fact that His Heart, more than all the other members of
His Body, is the natural sign and symbol of His boundless charity for
the human race....

(The Heart of the Incarnate Word is the symbol of a threefold love)

665   The Heart of the Incarnate Word is quite rightly considered
3924   the chief sign and symbol of the threefold love with which the
          divine Redeemer continually loves the eternal Father and all
men. It is a symbol first of that divine love which He has in common
with the Father and the Holy Spirit, but which only in Him, as the
Word Incarnate, is manifested to us through a weak and frail human
body.... It is a symbol secondly of that burning charity which, infused
into His soul, enriches the human will of Christ; the exercise of this
charity is illumined and guided by a twofold perfect knowledge,
namely, beatific knowledge and infused knowledge. And finally, in a
more direct and natural way, it is a symbol also of emotional affec-

tion, since the body of Jesus Christ, formed by the action of the Holy Spirit in the womb of the Virgin Mary, enjoys the most perfect powers of feeling and perception, to a greater degree in fact than the bodies of all other men.

(In Christ three loves are united)

666   This is why from the bodily organ of the Heart of Jesus Christ
3925   and from its natural meaning, we can and must, with the help
of Christian faith, ascend not only to the contemplation of His sensitive love, but, higher still, to the consideration and the adoration of His infused spiritual love; and finally to the meditation and adoration of the divine love of the incarnate Word.... This is legitimate since the faith according to which the two natures, the human and the divine, are united in the person of Christ, allows us to conceive the close relationships which exist between the sensitive love of the physical Heart of Jesus and His double spiritual love, the human and the divine. For these (three) loves not only exist simultaneously in the adorable person of the divine Redeemer, but also are united between themselves by a natural bond, since the human and sensitive love is subordinate to the divine love and analogically reflects its image....

(The natural symbolism of the physical Heart of Jesus is based on the hypostatic union)

667   It is therefore necessary...that each one hold ever in his
3925   mind that the natural symbolism by which the physical Heart
of Jesus is related to the person of the Word rests completely on the primary truth of the hypostatic union. If anyone were to deny this, he would renew errors which have already often been condemned by the Church, because they deny the unity of person in Christ in the distinction and integrity of the two natures.

THE SECOND VATICAN GENERAL COUNCIL

"The Council did not expressly deal with dogmas related to Christ as did the Councils of Nicaea, Ephesus and Chalcedon. Its central theme was the Church. But just because it endeavoured to understand the Church in her inmost reality, in the source of her vitality rather than in her historical and juridical aspects, the Council was happily obliged to refer everything to Christ Our Lord, not only as to the founder, but as to the Head, the principle of action and life of His Body which is the Church.... If then we wish to understand the central doctrine of the Council, we must understand the

Church; but to understand the Church, we must refer everything to Christ..."[1]

These words of Pope Paul VI indicate the place which the mystery of Christ occupies in the Second Vatican Council. While no Council document is explicitly devoted to the mystery of Christ, not even a chapter—as is the case for the mystery of the Virgin Mary in LG—the mystery of Christ is everywhere present as the standard of the Church's teaching and the practical rule of her concrete attitudes. The "Council of the Church" may be described as that of Christ's presence to the Church. Its Christ-centredness seems to have grown as the Council progressed; it found its clearest expression in GS 22 and 45.

In this perspective, what retained primarily the attention of the Council Fathers is the meaning of Christ in the divine plan and His place in the history of salvation. Without getting embarrassed with the scholastic disputes, the Council explains that the human race finds in Christ its centre, the whole cosmos its Head and history its goal (GS 45; cf. LG 13, 17, 48, etc.). The Church of Vatican II "believes that the key, centre and purpose of human history is to be found in her Lord and Master" (GS 10).

The Council does not fail to contemplate the sublime union of the divine and the human natures implied in the Christological doctrine; witness to this is the parallel which its draws—"in virtue of an analogy which is not far-fetched"—between Christ's two natures and the Church's twofold element, the divine and the human (LG 8). Beyond the ontological reality of the mysterious union of the two natures, it prefers, however, to dwell on the economy of the saving incarnation (LG 3, AG 3), on the mysterious human condition of the Word incarnate, on Christ's kenosis and glorification, on the depth of His identification with our human race in its concrete situation: "The Word Incarnate wished to enter fully into human fellowship" (GS 32; cf. 22). Christ's kenosis serves the pilgrim Church as a deep source of inspiration for her renewal and as guiding principle for her apostolic activity (LG 8; cf. AG 5). The same commands the Council's theology of the redemption. It is precisely in so far as by His incarnation the Son of God has united Himself in some way to every man that "as an innocent Lamb, freely shedding His blood, He merited life for us" (GS 22).

A special feature of the Council's Christology must be pointed out, for it will provide a frame to much of its Ecclesiology: the Council teaches insistently the existence in Christ of a threefold function: prophetic, sanctifying and pastoral (LG 21; cf. 13; OT 4). The same is found in the Church (LG 10–13), precisely in so far as she has been established by the risen Christ as the "universal sacrament of salvation" (LG 48). Christ's revelatory function is described in terms, inspired from Scripture, which had never before found in official documents the same deep echo: Christ is the mediator of God's revelation to the world; His person and His work contain the fulness of that revelation (DV 2, 4; cf. nn. 149, 151). His saving action culminates in His Paschal Mystery (SC 5). He is also the good Shepherd who gathers together the scattered people of God.

---

1. PAUL VI, Public audience, Nov. 23, 1966.

Thus, for Vatican II, the mystery of Christ is at every level the foundation of the mystery of the Church, whose task it is "faithfully (to) reveal in the world His mystery" (LG 8; cf. 15; GS 43) and so "to bring together all mankind with all its treasures under Christ the Head in the unity of the Holy Spirit" (LG 13). Christ is not merely the founder of the Church but the continuous source of her life (LG 8); her mission is the prolongation of His (LG 17); her action is destined to make His own action visibly present in the world (SC 7). Whether in doctrine or in action the Church lives by Him. The mystery of Christ is the vivifying centre of the Christian message and consequently of the priestly formation (OT 14).

It is so because Christ is the new man, who recapitulates all things in Himself (GS 22, 45), on whom the solidarity of all men is based (GS 32) and who leads them all to their eschatological fulfilment (GS 38). The problems that besiege modern man must find a solution in "the light and the principles that stem from Christ" (GS 46); above all, the mystery of man himself and his life is fully intelligible only in the light of the mystery of Christ (GS 22).

Thus, to put Christ at the centre of all things, both in practice and in doctrine, is one of the great preoccupations of Vatican II. The "Council of the Church" turns out to be a providential and inspired plea for her de-centring, so that she may appear to be what she is in reality, the sign of Christ raised among the nations.

PASTORAL CONSTITUTION *GAUDIUM ET SPES (1965)*

(Christ the new man)

668 22. In actual fact, it is only in the mystery of the Word incarnate that the mystery of man becomes clear. Adam the first man was a figure of Him who was to come, namely Christ the Lord. Christ, the new Adam, fully reveals man to himself in the very revelation of the Father and His love, and discloses to man His sublime calling....

He who is "the image of the invisible God" *(Col. 1.15)* is Himself the perfect man, who has restored to the sons of Adam the divine likeness deformed by the first sin. Since in Him human nature was assumed, not absorbed, it was, by that very fact, raised to a sublime dignity in us also. For by His incarnation the Son of God has united Himself in some way to every man. He worked with human hands, thought with a human mind, acted with a human will, and loved with a human heart. Born of the Virgin Mary, He truly became one of us, like unto us in all things except sin.

As an innocent Lamb, freely shedding His blood, He merited life for us. In Him God has reconciled us with Himself and among ourselves and delivered us from the bondage of the devil and of sin, so that now each one of us can say with the apostle: the Son of God "loved me and gave Himself for me" *(Gal. 2.20)*. By suffering for us he not only set an example for us to follow in His footsteps, but He also opened up a new path. If we follow it, life and death are made holy and take on a new meaning....

(Christ Alpha and Omega)

669 45. For the Word of God, through whom all things were made, was Himself made flesh so that, as the perfect man, He might save all men and recapitulate all things in Himself. The Lord is the goal of human history, the focal point to which converge the longings of history and civilisation, the centre of the human race, the joy of all hearts and the fulfilment of their aspirations. He it is whom the Father has raised from the dead, exalted and placed at His right hand, establishing Him as judge of the living and the dead. And we, quickened and united in His Spirit, we are on our pilgrimage towards the fulfilment of human history which perfectly coincides with the design of His love: "to unite all things in Him, things in heaven and things on earth" *(Eph. 1.10)*.

It is the Lord Himself who says: "Behold, I am coming soon, bringing my recompense, to repay everyone for what he has done. I am the Alpha and the Omega, the first and the last, the beginning and the end" *(Rev. 12.21f)*.

PAUL VI

DECLARATION *MYSTERIUM FILII DEI* OF THE
S. CONGREGATION FOR THE DOCTRINE OF THE FAITH
(21 February 1972)

In the Church's documents the mystery of Christ, the God-man, has traditionally been formulated with the terms: one person, two natures. These concepts, however, are for various reasons gradually becoming more difficult for modern man to understand. This is why several attempts have been made in recent years to re-formulate the mystery of Christ in terms more intelligible today. These attempts have not been altogether successful. It is not enough to believe that Christ is a man in whom God is fully present; the faith as formulated in the great Christological Councils implies that He is God's eternal Son who in time became man to reveal the Father fully. He is not a human person receiving the divine presence, but a divine person accepting human becoming. While encouraging theologians to expound the mystery of Christ in up-to-date terminology, the S. Congregation for the Doctrine of the Faith draws attention to the fundamental truth which must be preserved and to errors which would fall short of it. The text is found in AAS 64 (1972) 237ff.

(Recent errors with regard to the faith in the Son of God)

670 3. The opinions according to which it has not been revealed
and made known to us that the Son of God subsists from all
eternity in the mystery of the Godhead, distinct from the Father and
the Holy Spirit, are in open conflict with this belief (of the Councils);
likewise the opinions according to which we should abandon the
notion of the one person of Jesus Christ, begotten in His divinity of
the Father before all ages and, in time, begotten in His humanity of
the Virgin Mary; and lastly the assertion that the humanity of Christ
existed not as assumed into the eternal person of the Son of God, but
in itself as human person, and, therefore, that the mystery of Jesus
Christ consists only in the fact that God, in revealing Himself, was
present in the highest degree in the human person of Jesus.

This does not mean — Those who think in this way are far removed from the true faith in
Christ, even when they maintain that the special presence of God in
Jesus results in His being the supreme and final expression of divine
Revelation. Nor do they come back to the true belief in the divinity of
Christ by adding that Jesus can be called God by reason of the fact
that God is fully present in what they call His human person.

*(The mysteries of the Incarnation and of the Trinity are to be
faithfully preserved and expounded)*

671 6. What is expressed in the documents of the Councils
referred to above concerning the one and the same Christ, the
Son of God, begotten before the ages in His divine nature and in time
in His human nature, and also concerning the eternal person of the
Holy Spirit *(cf. n. 333),* belongs to the immutable truth of the Catholic
faith.

This does not mean that the Church should not consider it her
duty—taking also into account the progress of human thought—
never to stop in her effort to reach a better understanding of these
mysteries through contemplation and theological research, and to
have them more fully expounded in up-to-date terminology. But,
while this necessary task is being pursued, care must be taken that
these profound mysteries be not interpreted in a meaning different
from that in which the Church has understood and understands
them....

APOSTOLIC EXHORTATION *EVANGELII NUNTIANDI* (1975)

This Apostolic Exhortation was published by Pope Paul VI after the

*Synod of Bishops in Rome on Evangelisation (1974) and in continuation of
its work. Chapter I describes Jesus as the first evangeliser who preaches
the Kingdom of God. It goes on to explain the content of Jesus' Good News
as liberation-salvation. This Good News is now entrusted to the Church to
be proclaimed by her. Hence in Chapter III on the Content of Evangelisation
the Pope stresses that salvation in Jesus Christ is at the centre of the
Church's message. He defines this salvation as not merely immanent and
confined to temporal existence, but also transcendent and eschatological.
The text is found in AAS 68 (1976) 5ff.*

(Jesus proclaims liberating salvation)

672 9. At the kernel and centre of His Good News, Christ proclaims salvation, this great gift of God which is liberation from
everything that oppresses man but which is above all liberation from
sin and the Evil One, in the joy of knowing God and being known by
Him, of seeing Him, and of being given over to Him. All of this is
begun during the life of Christ and definitively accomplished by His
death and resurrection. But it must be patiently carried on during the
course of history, in order to be realised fully on the day of the final
coming of Christ, whose date is known to no one except the Father
(cf. Mt. 24.36; Acts 1.7; 1 Thess. 5.1–2).

(Salvation in Jesus Christ at the centre of the Church's message)

673 27. Evangelisation will always contain—as the foundation, centre and at the same time summit of its dynamism—a clear
proclamation that, in Jesus Christ, the Son of God made man, who
died and rose from the dead, salvation is offered to all men as a gift of
God's grace and mercy *(cf. Eph. 2.8; Rom. 1.16).* And not an immanent salvation, meeting material or even spiritual needs, restricted to
the framework of temporal existence and completely identified with
temporal desires, hopes, affairs and struggles, but a salvation which
exceeds all these limits in order to reach fulfilment in a communion
with the one and only divine Absolute: a transcendent and eschatological salvation, which indeed has its beginning in this life but which
is fulfilled in eternity.

JOHN PAUL II

ADDRESS TO THE THIRD GENERAL ASSEMBLY OF
LATIN AMERICAN BISHOPS
(Puebla, 28 January 1979)

The Third General Assembly of Latin American Bishops, held at Puebla,

Mexico, from January 27 to February 13, 1979, had for its theme "The Present and the Future of Evangelisation in Latin America". In his inaugural address Pope John Paul II warned against distortions of the revealed truth about Jesus Christ, the Church, and man (cf. nn. 425-426). In particular, he cautioned against "re-readings of the Gospel" which distort the person of Jesus and are at variance with the Church's faith in Him as the Son of God. The text is found in Osservatore Romano *(English Edition), 5 February, 1979, p.2.*

(Truth concerning Jesus Christ)

674 1.(2). From you, pastors, the faithful of your countries expect and demand above all a careful and zealous transmission of the truth concerning Jesus Christ. This truth is at the centre of evangelisation and constitutes its essential content: "There is no true evangelisation if the name, the teaching, the life, the promises, the kingdom and the mystery of Jesus of Nazareth, the Son of God, are not proclaimed" *(EN 22)*.

On the living knowledge of this truth will depend the vigour of the faith of millions of people. On it will also depend the strength of their support of the Church and of their active presence as Christians in the world. From this knowledge there will derive choices, values, attitudes and modes of behaviour capable of orienting and defining our Christian life and of creating new people and hence a new humanity for the conversion of the individual and social conscience *(EN 18)*.

It is from a solid Christology that there must come light on so many doctrinal and pastoral themes and questions that you intend to study in these coming days.

1.(3). And then we have to confess Christ before history and the world with a conviction that is profound, deeply felt and lived, just as Peter confessed him: "You are the Christ, the Son of the Living God" *(Mt. 16.16)*.

This is the Good News in a certain sense unique: the Church lives by it and for it, just as she draws from it everything that she has to offer to people, without any distinction of nation, culture, race, time, age or condition. For this reason "from that confession of faith (Peter's) the sacred history of salvation and of the People of God could not fail to take on a new dimension".[1]

---

1. Homily of Pope JOHN PAUL II at the solemn inauguration of his pontificate, 22 October 1978.

This is the one Gospel, and "even if we, or an angel from heaven, should preach to you a gospel contrary to that which we preached to you, let him be accursed" *(Gal. 1.8),* as the apostle wrote in very clear terms.

(Re-readings of the Gospel)

675 1.(4) In fact, today there occur in many places—the pheno-menon is not a new one—"re-readings" of the Gospel, the result of theoretical speculations rather than authentic meditation on the word of God and a true commitment to the Gospel. They cause confusion by diverging from the central criteria of the faith of the Church, and some people have the temerity to pass them on, under the guise of catechesis, to the Christian communities.

In some cases either Christ's divinity is passed over in silence, or some people in fact fall into forms of interpretation at variance with the Church's faith. Christ is said to be merely a "prophet", one who proclaimed God's kingdom and love but not the true Son of God, and therefore not the centre and object of the very gospel message.

In other cases people claim to show Jesus as politically commit-ted, as one who fought against Roman oppression and the authori-ties, and also as one involved in the class struggle. This idea of Christ as a political figure, a revolutionary, as the subversive man from Nazareth, does not tally with the Church's catechesis. By confusing the insidious pretexts of Jesus' accusers with the —very different— attitude of Jesus Himself, some people adduce as the cause of His death the outcome of a political conflict, and nothing is said of the Lord's will do deliver Himself and of His consciousness of His redemptive mission. The Gospels clearly show that for Jesus any-thing that would alter His mission as the servant of Yahweh was a temptation *(Mt. 4.8; Lk. 4.5).* He does not accept the position of those who mixed the things of God with merely political attitudes *(Mt. 22.21; Mk 12.17; Jn 18.36).* He unequivocally rejects recourse to violence. He opens His message of conversion to everybody, without excluding the very publicans. The perspective of His mission is much deeper. It consists in complete salvation through a transforming, peace-making, pardoning and reconciling love. There is no doubt, moreover, that all this is very demanding for the attitude of the Christian who wishes truly to serve his least brethren, the poor, the needy, the marginalised, in a word, all those who in their lives reflect the sorrowing face of the Lord *(LG 8).*

(Affirmation of the Church's faith)

676   1.(5) Against such "re-readings", therefore, and against the
perhaps brilliant but fragile and inconsistent hypotheses flowing from them, "evangelisation in the present and future of Latin
America" cannot cease to affirm the Church's faith: Jesus Christ, the
Word and the Son of God, become man in order to come close to
man and to offer him, through the power of His mystery, salvation,
the great gift of God *(EN 19 and 27).*

ENCYCLICAL LETTER *REDEMPTOR HOMINIS (1979)*

*The first Encyclical Letter of Pope John Paul II, published on 4 March,
1979, is devoted to "Jesus Christ, the Redeemer of Man". In Chapter II on
the "Mystery of the Redemption", the Pope explains that redemption in
Jesus Christ is a new creation brought about by God in His Son. He goes on
to expand the "divine" and the "human dimension of the mystery of the
redemption". Quoting the Pastoral Constitution Gaudium et Spes, 22 (cf. n.
668), the Pope concludes that in Jesus Christ not only is God fully revealed
to man, but also man's dignity is fully manifested. The text is found in AAS
71 (1979) 257ff.*

(The divine dimension of the mystery of redemption)

677   9. Jesus Christ, the Son of the living God, became our reconciliation with the Father *(Rom. 5.11; Col. 1.20).* He it was, and He
alone, who satisfied the Father's eternal love, that fatherhood that
from the beginning found expression in creating the world, giving
man all the riches of creation, and making him "little less than God"
(Ps. 8.6), in that he was created "in the image and after the likeness of
God" *(cf. Gen. 1.26).* He and He alone also satisfied that fatherhood
of God and that love which man in a way rejected by breaking the
first Covenant *(cf. Gen. 3.6-13)* and the later Covenants that God
"again and again offered to man" *(cf. Eucharistic Prayer IV).* The
redemption of the world—this tremendous mystery of love in which
creation is renewed *(GS 37)*—is, at its deepest root, the fulness of
justice in a human Heart—the Heart of the first-born Son—in order
that it may become justice in the hearts of many human beings,
predestined from eternity in the first -born Son to be children of God
(cf. Rom. 8.29-30; Eph. 1.8) and called to grace, called to love. The
Cross on Calvary, through which Jesus Christ—a Man, the Son of
the Virgin Mary, thought to be the son of Joseph of Nazareth—
"leaves" this world, is also a fresh manifestation of the eternal fatherhood of God, who in Him draws near again to humanity, to each

human being, giving him the thrice holy "Spirit of truth" *(cf. Jn 16.13).*

(The human dimension of the mystery of redemption)

678   10. Man cannot live without love. He remains a being that is
incomprehensible for himself, his life is senseless, if love is not
revealed to him, if he does not encounter love, if he does not
experience it and make it his own, if he does not participate intimately in it. This...is why Christ the Redeemer fully reveals man to
himself. If we may use the expression, this is the human dimension of
the mystery of the Redemption. In this dimension man finds again the
greatness, dignity and value that belong to his humanity. In the
mystery of the Redemption man becomes newly "expressed" and, in
a way, is newly created.... The man who wishes to understand
himself thoroughly—and not just in accordance with immediate,
partial, often superficial, and even illusory standards and measures
of his being—must with his unrest, uncertainty and even his weakness and sinfulness, with his life and death, draw near to Christ. He
must, so to speak, enter into Him with all his own self, he must
"appropriate" and assimilate the whole of the reality of the Incarnation and Redemption in order to find himself.

(Christ fully reveals God to man and man to himself)

679   11. The opening made by the Second Vatican Council has
enabled the Church and all Christians to reach a more complete awareness of the mystery of Christ, "the mystery hidden for
ages" *(Col. 1.26)* in God, to be revealed in time in the Man Jesus
Christ, and to be revealed continually in every time. In Christ and
through Christ God has revealed Himself fully to mankind and has
definitively drawn close to it; at the same time, in Christ and through
Christ man has acquired full awareness of his dignity, of the heights
to which he is raised, of the surpassing worth of his own humanity,
and of the meaning of his existence.

CHAPTER VII

THE MOTHER OF THE SAVIOUR

The significance of the Mother of God in the divine plan of salvation and in the order of grace cannot be brought out adequately in a collection of doctrinal documents directly concerned with her. Comparatively few official pronouncements deal exclusively with Mary. The doctrine on Mary is so closely linked with that about Jesus Christ and His work that the most fundamental affirmations regarding her are found in the Church's Christological documents.

There is, nevertheless, need for a special chapter on Mary, which is, as it were, a complement to Christology. It contains those documents on Mary which have not been mentioned in the Christological context. To gather these documents together in a separate chapter could create the impression that Mariology is dealt with as a special branch of theology. Indeed, the objection raised against Mariology in the past decades has been that it tended to remain isolated from the broader context of Christian doctrine, and was at times developed beyond proportion. Similar objections have been raised against the onesidedness and exaggerations of certain forms of Marian devotion. It surely is the merit of the Second Vatican Council to have re-integrated the doctrine on Mary into the comprehensive view of divine revelation and salvation. This integration is clearly manifested by the fact that the Marian doctrine of the Council forms part of the Constitution on the Church.

The documents mentioned here witness to three stages through which the mystery of Mary has been progressively unfolded in the consciousness of the Church. There are first the documents in which Mary's divine motherhood is taught: she is not merely the mother of the man Jesus, of a man united to the Son of God, but the Mother of God Himself; God truly became man through her. The doctrine of the 'theotokos' is central for the correct understanding of the person of Jesus Christ Himself.

The unique privilege of Mary's divine motherhood having been clearly stated, the way was open for a growing understanding of its implications for Mary herself. In the course of the centuries the doctrine on Mary's sinlessness, on her Immaculate Conception and on her bodily Assumption into heaven have been gradually expounded; this process has led to the two definitions of the Immaculate Conception and the Assumption.

Mariology would not, however, be complete were it to stop at the contemplation of Mary's personal vocation. Mary must be understood in the context of her role within the entire mystery of salvation; her place is in the midst of the people of God. This last phase in the unfolding of Marian doctrine has its roots in early patristic theology, but it has been developed extensively by modern Mariology. It is contained in recent papal documents, mainly since Leo XIII; it has been brought to a climax by the Second Vatican Council.

*   *   *

The main points of doctrine mentioned in this chapter may be grouped under the following headings:

Mary is Mother of God: 5, 10, 605, 606/1, 607, 614, 617, 620/6, (701), (702), 703;
through the overshadowing of the Holy Spirit: 3, 4, 5, 10, 12, 15, 23, 39/4, 609, 703, 707;
without loss of her virginity: 5, 10, 39/7, 609, 612, 620/2, 628, 703, 704, 707, 709.
She is free from original sin: 39/7, 704, 705, 708, 709;
and sinless: 706, 716, 1973.
She was assumed into heaven: 39/8, 713–715.
She played an active role in Christ's redemptive work: 710, 712, 716, 718.
She intercedes for all men: 39/8, 704, 710, 712, 717.
She is the type of the Church: 718.
Mary, the model of womanhood: 719.
Mary, sign of hope for modern man: 720.

THE GENERAL COUNCIL OF EPHESUS (431)

(701) *The basic Mariological dogma of the true divine motherhood of
Mary is in fact a Christological dogma asserted in the general
Council of Ephesus (431) against Nestorius. It is contained in the second
letter of Cyril of Alexandria to Nestorius which was solemnly approved by
the Council Fathers as representing the Catholic faith; it is also explicitly
affirmed in the first of the twelve anathematisms of St Cyril against
Nestorius. See the texts under nn. 605, 606/1.*

JOHN II

LETTER TO THE SENATE OF CONSTANTINOPLE (534)

(702) *The Christological dogma was formulated more precisely in the
Council of Chalcedon (451) than it had been at Ephesus; along with
it the doctrine of the divine motherhood of Mary was also repeated. Later
still, the import of the title 'Mother of God' (theotokos) was officially
declared by John II in a letter to the Senate of Constantinople. Among other
points under discussion, the Pope explains that this title must be strictly
understood against both the Nestorian and the Monophysite
interpretations. See text under n. 617.*

THE COUNCIL OF LATERAN (649)

*Martin I gathered a Council in the Lateran against the heresy of
Monothelitism (cf. n. 627i). In the context of the Christological doctrine this
Council also teaches in peremptory terms the perpetual virginity of Mary.*

(Mary, Mother of God and Virgin)

703 3. If anyone does not, according to the holy Fathers, confess
503   truly and properly that holy Mary, ever virgin and immaculate,
is Mother of God, since in this latter age she conceived in true
reality without human seed from the Holy Spirit, God the Word
Himself, who before the ages was born of God the Father, and gave
birth to Him without corruption, her virginity remaining equally
inviolate after the birth, let him be condemned.

SIXTUS IV

CONSTITUTION *CUM PRAEEXCELSA* (1477)

*Once Mary's divine motherhood and the unique place which it confers
upon her in God's plan of salvation had been clearly stated and understood,
the reflection of the Church turned to the implications of her role for Mary
herself. If she was to be at the service of God in the act by which God
brought about the salvation of mankind and the conquest of sin, she could
not be herself subject to sin. Thus the doctrine of Mary's Immaculate*

Conception, i.e., her freedom from sin from the very beginning of her existence, became more and more firmly established.

In fact, already the Council of Basel had decreed in its thirty-sixth session (1439): "The doctrine which asserts that the glorious Virgin Mary, Mother of God, through the working of a singular prevenient grace of the divine power was never subject to original sin and was always immune from original and actual sin, holy and immaculate, is a pious doctrine which accords with the liturgy of the Church, with the Catholic faith, with sound reasoning and Holy Scripture; we define that it is to be approved by all Catholics and that from now on no one should be allowed to preach or teach the contrary."[1]

This session of the Council of Basel, however, took place at a time when the Council was no longer in communion with the Pope and, therefore, its decrees were not held as binding. The controversy to which the doctrine of the Immaculate Conception had already previously been subjected went on. The Dominican school opposed it because it seemed to contradict the dogma of the universality of original sin; the Franciscans on the contrary defended it.

Pope Sixtus IV, himself a Franciscan, approved the feast of the Immaculate Conception in this Constitution; later, in Grave nimis (1483) he forbade anyone to censure those who celebrated the feast and held the Immaculate Conception as doctrine of faith (cf. DS 1425-1426).

(On the Immaculate Conception)

704   ...In His divine providence the almighty God looked from
1400   eternity on this humble virgin. Having prepared her by the
Holy Spirit, He made her the dwelling place of His only-begotten in order to reconcile to its author the human nature that had been subject to eternal death through the fall of the first man. From her He was to receive the flesh of our mortality for the redemption of His people, while she would remain an immaculate virgin also after His birth. All the faithful of Christ should give thanks and praise to almighty God for the wonderful conception of the immaculate virgin and should celebrate the Mass and the other divine offices instituted to this end in the Church of God and assist at them. With indulgences for the forgiveness of sins we invite them to do so in order that through the merits and the intercession of the same virgin they may become more capable of receiving divine grace.

THE GENERAL COUNCIL OF TRENT

The Council of Trent was concerned with re-asserting the Catholic faith

---

1. Cf. MANSI, 29, 183 BC.

against the challenge of the Reformers. It speaks of Mary only incidentally, with regard to the unique place which she holds in God's plan of salvation. The first reference is found in the Decree on Original Sin (1546). The Council states that it is not its intention to include Mary in the general condition of sinfulness of our race. The second reference is contained in the Decree on Justification (1547): while men in general are subject to sin in their daily life, Mary is free from it through a special grace.

FIFTH SESSION

DECREE ON ORIGINAL SIN (1546)

705 This same holy Synod declares that it is not its intention to
1516 include in this decree dealing with original sin the Blessed and
Immaculate Virgin Mary, Mother of God, but that the Constitutions of Pope Sixtus IV of blessed memory are to be observed under the penalties contained in those Constitutions, which it renews *(cf. n. 704).*

SIXTH SESSION

DECREE ON JUSTIFICATION (1547)

706 *Canon* 23: If anyone says...that a man once justified can avoid
1573 all sins, even venial ones, throughout his entire life, unless it
be by a special privilege of God as the Church holds of the Blessed Virgin, *anathema sit.*

PAUL IV

CONSTITUTION *CUM QUORUMDAM HOMINUM (1555)*

Soon after the emergence of the Reformation rationalist theology, which set reason above revelation, made its appearance within Protestantism. It denied all supernatural elements in revelation and attacked the doctrine of the Trinity, the incarnation and the redemption (cf. n. 648). The Constitution of Paul IV reflects the attacks of rationalism. The texts referring to Mary are quoted here.

(Mary's Virginity)

707 ...We question and admonish all those who...have asserted,
1880 taught and believed...that our Lord...was not conceived
from the Holy Spirit according to the flesh in the womb of the Blessed Mary ever Virgin but, as other men, from the seed of Joseph; ...or that the same Blessed Virgin Mary is not truly the mother of God and did not retain her virginity intact before the birth, in the birth, and perpetually after the birth.

PIUS V

BULL *EX OMNIBUS AFFLICTIONIBUS* (1567)
CONDEMNED PROPOSITIONS OF MICHAEL DE BAY

The teaching of de Bay and the Jansenists about Mary forms part of their rigorist views about the fundamental sinfulness of the human will (cf. n. 1984i), to which they did not admit any exception. See a similar Jansenist error about Mary in DS 2324.

[708] 73. Nobody but Christ is free from original sin; hence the
1973 Blessed Virgin died on account of the sin inherited from
Adam, and all her afflictions in this life were, like those of the
rest of the just, punishment for actual or original sin.

PIUS IX

BULL *INEFFABILIS DEUS* (8 Dec. 1854)

The doctrine of the Immaculate Conception had developed through many centuries (cf. n. 704). After the position taken by Trent (cf. nn. 705-706) and the condemnation of de Bay (cf. n. 708), Alexander VII in 1661 explained and defended the doctrine (cf. DS 2015-2017) in terms similar to those used in the definition of Pius IX. This Pope thus raised to a dogma of faith a doctrine which had behind it a long tradition.

709 To the glory of the holy and undivided Trinity, to the honour
2803 and renown of the Virgin Mother of God, the exaltation of the
Catholic faith and the increase of Christian religion; by the
authority of our Lord Jesus Christ, of the blessed apostles Peter and
Paul, and our own authority, we declare, pronounce and define: the
doctrine which holds that the most Blessed Virgin Mary was, from
the first moment of her conception, by the singular grace and privilege of almighty God and in view of the merits of Christ Jesus the
Saviour of the human race, preserved immune from all stain of
original sin, is revealed by God and, therefore, firmly and constantly
to be believed by all the faithful.

2804 If, therefore, any persons shall dare to think—which God
forbid—otherwise than has been defined by us, let them
clearly know that they stand condemned by their own judgment, that
they have made shipwreck of their faith and fallen from the unity of
the Church. Furthermore, they subject themselves *ipso facto* to the
penalties provided by law if by speech or writing or in any other
exterior way they shall dare to express their views.

LEO XIII

ENCYCLICAL LETTER *OCTOBRI MENSE* (1891)

Modern Mariology is centred round the problem of Mary's place in God's plan of salvation. Though a purely gratuitous and free gift on the part of God, salvation depends on man's free response to and acceptance of God's gift. Mary was the first to respond to the divine invitation made by God to men in Jesus Christ; this is why she plays a unique role in the work of salvation. She plays this role in two ways: first, through her share in the mystery of salvation itself, in her "fiat" to God at Nazareth which came to its full expression as she stood at the foot of the cross; secondly, in her heavenly role of intercession for all the faithful.

Until the Second Vatican Council this double role of Mary has been much debated. At times it has been exaggerated, as though her place were somewhat similar to that of her Son; at times, on the contrary, it has been unduly played down out of fear of obscuring the unique mediation of Christ. Since Vatican II strikes the correct balance most felicitously, only a few characteristic texts need to be quoted from among the many Mariological declarations of the last Popes before the Council. In this encyclical the Pope stresses the significance of Mary's consent to her divine motherhood.

(Mary's role in our salvation)

710   When the eternal Son of God willed to take the nature of
3274   man for the redemption and honour of man, and so wanted
in a certain sense to enter into a mystical marriage with the whole of the human race, He did not do so before His chosen mother had given her totally free consent. She impersonated in some way the human race, as Thomas Aquinas says beautifully and in full truth: "In the Annunciation the consent of the Virgin was awaited in place of that of the whole human nature."[1] Therefore, one may in truth and aptly say that nothing of the vast treasure of all grace which the Lord has brought—since "grace and truth came through Jesus Christ" *(Jn 1.17)*—is, according to God's will, given to us without Mary.

PIUS X

ENCYCLICAL LETTER *AD DIEM ILLUM* (1904)

This encyclical marks the fiftieth anniversary of the proclamation of the dogma of the Immaculate Conception. It develops mainly the theological foundations for Mary's mediation of grace.

---

1. *Summa Theologica*, III, 30, 1.

(The union of Mary with the sacrifice of her Son)

712   From the community of will and suffering between Christ
3370   and Mary she merited to become the restorer *(reparatrix)* of
the world that was lost, and the dispenser *(dispensatrix)* of all
the benefits which Jesus won for us by His death and at the price of
His blood. We do not deny indeed that the distribution of these gifts
belongs personally to Christ by a unique right. For they were won
through His death alone and He alone has the power to be mediator
between God and man. Nevertheless, on account of the union of
sorrow and pain between mother and Son, of which we have spoken,
it has been given to the august Virgin to be the most powerful
mediator *(mediatrix)* and advocate *(conciliatrix)* for the whole world
with her only-begotten Son.... Since she stands above all others in
sanctity and in union with Christ, and was drawn by Christ into the
work of man's salvation, she merits for us by equity *(de congruo)*, as
it is said, what Christ merited by right *(de condigno)*, and she is the
primary minister in the distribution of the divine graces.

PIUS XII

APOSTOLIC CONSTITUTION *MUNIFICENTISSIMUS DEUS* (1950)

*On November 1, 1950, Pius XII solemnly defined the Assumption of
Mary to the glory of heaven. The Constitution offers a survey of the belief in
Mary's Assumption, expressed in doctrine, popular piety and liturgy
through the ages. The final theological synthesis given by the Constitution,
and the definition itself are quoted here.*

(Mary's Assumption into heaven)

713   From all eternity and by one and the same decree of predesti-
3902   nation the august Mother of God is united in a sublime way
with Jesus Christ; immaculate in her conception, a spotless
virgin in her divine motherhood, the noble companion of the divine
Redeemer who won a complete triumph over sin and its consequences, she finally obtained as the crowning glory of her privileges to be
preserved from the corruption of the tomb and, like her Son before
her, to conquer death and to be raised body and soul to the glory of
heaven, to shine refulgent as Queen at the right hand of her Son, the
immortal King of ages *(cf. 1 Tim. 1.17)*.

714   The universal Church, in which the Spirit of truth actively
dwells, and which is infallibly guided by Him to an ever more

perfect knowledge of revealed truths, has down the centuries manifested her belief in many ways; the bishops from all over the world ask almost unanimously that the truth of the bodily Assumption of the Blessed Virgin Mary into heaven be defined as a dogma of divine and catholic faith; this truth is based on Sacred Scripture and deeply embedded in the minds of the faithful; it has received the approval of liturgical worship from the earliest times; it is perfectly in keeping with the rest of revealed truth, and has been lucidly developed and explained by the studies, the knowledge and wisdom of theologians. Considering all these reasons we deem that the moment pre-ordained in the plan of divine providence has now arrived for us to proclaim solemnly this extraordinary privilege of the Virgin Mary....

715 Therefore, having directed humble and repeated prayers to
3903 God, and having invoked the light of the Spirit of Truth; to the glory of almighty God who has bestowed His special bounty on the Virgin Mary, for the honour of His Son the immortal King of ages and victor over sin and death, for the greater glory of His august mother, and for the joy and exultation of the whole Church; by the authority of our Lord Jesus Christ, of the blessed apostles Peter and Paul, and by our own authority, we proclaim, declare and define as a dogma revealed by God: the Immaculate Mother of God, Mary ever Virgin, when the course of her earthly life was finished, was taken up body and soul into the glory of heaven.

Wherefore, if anyone—which God forbid—should wilfully dare to deny or call in doubt what has been defined by us, let him know that he certainly has abandoned the divine and Catholic faith.

THE SECOND VATICAN GENERAL COUNCIL

The references of the Council texts to the Blessed Virgin are many. She has her place in the documents concerning liturgy, the ministry and life of priests, religious and lay-people, the formation of seminarians; she is mentioned in the description of the Eastern Churches (UR 15 and OE 30) and also in the outline of the faith of Muslims (NA 3).

However, the Council could not limit itself to such occasional references. It had to fulfil a difficult and urgent task with regard to the doctrine on the Blessed Virgin and her place in the life of the Church. Different, even contrasting tendencies existed within the Church, often described as maximalist and minimalist trends (however inadequate such terms may be). The impression was created that there existed two different Mariologies which tended to drift apart. It was a matter of grave concern for the Council to propose a coherent synthesis of the Catholic teaching about Mary which would meet with the approval of the various tendencies. It had to fulfil the following demands: 1) not to formulate a new dogma (some were apprehensive that Mary's mediation of all graces might by defined); 2) to dispel the impression that Mariology is a separate and isolated domain of theological research and reflection, by integrating it into a comprehensive view of the mystery of salvation; 3) to show in particular its connection with, and relevance for, the life of the Church, and the Christian life in general; 4) to avoid unnecessary tensions on the ecumenical plane, and present the Catholic position in a way which could be intelligible for Protestants.

Thus the document of the Council on Mary became a comprehensive and constructive document, reconciling different tendencies through "studied ambiguities", yet sufficiently articulated and founded on Scripture, Tradition and modern theological reflection. To emphasise its intimate connection with the whole mystery of salvation, the Council Fathers, after a heated discussion and a close vote, decided to join this document to the Constitution Lumen Gentium on the Church, of which it constitutes the eighth and last chapter.

DOGMATIC CONSTITUTION LUMEN GENTIUM (1964)

The introduction to chapter eight outlines the intention of the Council to describe Mary's place in the mystery of salvation: on the one hand, she plays a unique role; on the other hand, she fully belongs to our race, being "redeemed in an eminent manner" (52–54).

Part I describes Mary's role in the work of salvation: it is foreshadowed in the Old Testament (55); she enters into her role through the free assent to her vocation to be mother of the Saviour; thus she is not a passive instrument of God's design, but through her obedience plays an irreplaceable part in the salvation of mankind. Her response, asked for by God and freely offered by her, is the core of the Marian mystery, and the starting point of Mariology (56). Her role is unfolded in the mysteries of the infancy of Jesus (57) and in His public life (58). It is fulfilled in her presence in the midst of the Church on Pentecost, and finally in the Assumption (59).

Part II unfolds the continuation of Mary's role in the life of the Church. First, the exclusive role of Jesus Christ as the only mediator between God and man is stressed; Mary's role does not rival that of her Son but rather enhances it (60). It flows from her co-operation in our salvation (61), and consists in her maternal solicitude and intercession for all, until the end of time (62). Her virginal motherhood is the 'type' (63) which is fulfilled in the Church (64); while she has already reached the final glory, the Church is still on her pilgrimage, following her (65).

Part III treats of the veneration of Mary. From the beginning Mary held a unique place in the cult of the Church (66). Her cult must be fostered, though in the right direction and measure; it must also be conceived in an ecumenical spirit (67).

The conclusion considers Mary in her glory as a sign of hope for all the faithful (68). All Christians should join in venerating her and imploring her intercession (69).

The following three texts are characteristic of this Mariological document, the most important to date.

(Mary's free consent to the divine motherhood)

716   56. ...Adorned from the first moment of her conception with the radiance of a unique holiness, the virgin of Nazareth is greeted, in the name of God, by an angel as "full of grace" *(cf. Lk. 1.28)*; and she replies to the heavenly messenger: "Behold I am the handmaid of the Lord; let it be to me according to your word" *(Lk. 1.38)*. Thus it came to pass that Mary, a daughter of Adam, became mother of Jesus through her consent to the divine word. With her whole heart, unhindered by sin, she embraced the salvific will of God and consecrated herself totally as a handmaid of the Lord to the person and work of her Son, under whom and with whom, by the grace of the Almighty, she served in the mystery of the redemption. Justly, therefore, do the holy Fathers consider Mary not merely as a passive instrument in the hands of God, but as freely co-operating in the salvation of mankind by her faith and obedience. As St Irenaeus says: "Through her obedience she became cause of salvation both for herself and for the whole human race."[1]

(Mary's intercession)

717   62. Mary's motherhood in the economy of grace continues without interruption, from the moment of her consent—which she gave at the annunciation and maintained unwaveringly under the cross—until the eternal consumption of all the elect. Her assumption into heaven does not mean that she has laid aside her salvific role; she continues to obtain by her constant intercession the graces we need for eternal salvation. In her maternal love, she takes care of her Son's brothers, still journeying on earth and surrounded by dangers and difficulties, until they reach their blissful home. That is why the Blessed Virgin is invoked in the Church under the titles of Advocate, Auxiliatrix, Adjutrix, Mediatrix. All of which, however, have to be so understood that they in no way diminish or add to the dignity and efficacy of Christ the one Mediator.

(Mary, type of the Church)

718   63. ... The Blessed Virgin is also intimately united with the Church. Already St Ambrose called her the type of the Church, or exemplar, in the order of faith, charity and perfect union

---

1. St Irenaeus, *Adversus Haereses*, III, 22, 4.

with Christ.[1] Indeed, in the mystery of the Church, who herself is rightly called mother and virgin, the Blessed Virgin Mary came first, standing out as an eminent and unequalled exemplar of both motherhood and virginity. For, by her faith and obedience she brought forth on earth the Father's own Son, without loss of her virginity but overshadowed by the Holy Spirit, not listening to the serpent as Eve of old, but as the new Eve believing God's messenger with unhesitating faith....

PAUL VI

APOSTOLIC EXHORTATION *MARIALIS CULTUS* (1974)

This lengthy document bears the date of 2 February, 1974, but was published on 21 March. Its intention is to give guidelines for the "right ordering and development of the devotion to the Blessed Virgin Mary". It shows the place of the Marian devotion in the context of the liturgical reform of Vatican II and indicates its theological and pastoral significance for our time. Its theology is widely based on Chapter VIII of Lumen Gentium. The document also shows the significance of Marian devotion in the context of modern movements for the liberation of women. Thus it describes Mary as presenting an ideal of womanhood widely different from that of traditional Marian piety. The Gospel shows Mary in the essential situations of womanhood, responding to God's will; it is for each generation to articulate this ideal within the context of its own culture. In the last section the document points to Mary's significance in the crisis of modern man. The text is found in AAS 66 (1974) 113ff.

(Mary, the model of womanhood)

719 34. The picture of the Blessed Virgin presented in a certain type of devotional literature cannot easily be reconciled with today's life-style, especially the way women live today.

(Women strive for co-responsibility in the home and for their legitimate role in the social, political, cultural spheres of society).

In consequence of these phenomena some people are becoming estranged from the devotion to the Blessed Virgin and find it difficult to take as an example Mary of Nazareth because the horizons of her life, so they say, seem rather restricted in comparison with the vast spheres of activity open to mankind today....

35. First, the Virgin Mary has always been proposed to the faithful by the Church as an example to be imitated, not precisely in

---

1. St Ambrose, *Expos. Lc.*, II, 7.

the type of life she led, and much less for the socio-cultural background in which she lived and which today scarcely exists anywhere. She is held as an example to the faithful rather for the way in which, in her own particular life, she fully and responsibly accepted the will of God (cf. Lk. 1.38); because she received the word of God and acted on it; because charity and a spirit of service were the driving force of her actions; because she was the first and the most perfect of Christ's disciples. All of this has a permanent and universal exemplary value.

36. Secondly... the difficulties alluded to above are not connected with the true Gospel image of Mary nor with the doctrinal data.... It is not surprising that Christians who lived in different social and cultural conditions... saw in Jesus' mother the outstanding type of womanhood and the prominent example of a life lived according to the Gospel, and expressed their sentiments with the mentality and images corresponding to their age. They looked at Mary and her mission as the New Woman and the perfect Christian who united in herself the characteristic situations of a woman's life as Virgin, Spouse and Mother. When the Church considers the long history of Marian devotion she rejoices at the continuity of her veneration, but she does not bind herself to any particular expression of an individual cultural epoch or to the particular anthropological ideas underlying such expressions.

(Mary in the crisis of modern man)

720 57. Mary, the New Woman, stands at the side of Christ, the New Man, within whose mystery the mystery of man alone finds true light (cf. n. 668); she is given to us as a pledge and guarantee that God's plan in Christ for the salvation of the whole man has already achieved realisation in a creature: in her. Contemplated in the vicissitudes of her earthly life and in the heavenly bliss which she already possesses in the City of God, the Blessed Virgin Mary offers a calm vision and a reassuring word to modern man, torn as he often is between anguish and hope, defeated by the sense of his own limitations and assailed by limitless aspirations, troubled in his mind and divided in his heart, uncertain before the riddle of death, oppressed by loneliness while yearning for fellowship, a prey to boredom and disgust. She shows forth the victory of hope over anguish, of fellowship over solitude, of peace over anxiety, of joy and beauty over boredom and disgust, of eternal visions over earthly ones, of life over death.

CHAPTER VIII

THE CHURCH

Salvation in Christ is offered to all men. However, as the Second Vatican Council teaches, "it has pleased God to call men to share His life not merely as individuals without relation to each other"— irrespective of their social nature and the continuity of human history—"but to make of them a people in which His sons who were scattered far and wide may be brought together into one" (AG 2). Thus the word of God and the saving grace of Jesus Christ are enshrined in the Church.

The Church is not primarily an object of theology, but its subject. The revealed word of God is entrusted to her; she must teach it, interpret it and defend it. The Church has exercised her function long before she enunciated it explicitly. This is why her reflection on her own nature belongs to a late period. In fact, this reflection has developed in relation to the situations and problems with which the Church found herself confronted in the fulfilment of her mission.

In the early Church two questions required explicit considera-tion. First was the unity of the Church, expressed in the hierarchical authority with its centre in the bishop of Rome, successor of the apostle Peter. In the second place came a question more directly related to the Church's inner life: the necessity of belonging to the Church in order to find salvation. These questions remained alive throughout the centuries and are of central importance in modern ecclesiology.

In the Middle Ages new factors have influenced the reflection on the Church. The rivalry between the secular and the ecclesiastical powers led to acute canonical controversies about the nature of Church authority. The defence of the rights of the hierarchy, and mainly of the papacy, often resulted in presenting a one-sided view of the Church, mostly garbed in juridical language. The great Schism gave rise to an acute crisis of ecclesiastical authority, viz., the idea of conciliarism, or the theory of the superiority of the Council over the Pope. This could be resolved only in the General Council of Constance. The increasing worldliness of the hierarchy and the frequent misuse of ecclesiastical power for political and other earthly interests disfigured the Church and made it difficult to recognise in her the mystery of Jesus Christ. To this current must be traced the attacks launched against, and the rejection of, the ecclesiastical authority by the various anti-clerical movements of the Middle Ages. The crisis came to a climax with the Reformation. The historical context thus explains why ecclesiastical documents up to recent times are mostly concerned with the rejection of errors and the answer to problems related to authority.

The first large scale attempt to frame an official document on the nature of the Church was made in preparation for the first Vatican general Council. Political circumstances, however, prevented this Council from completing its work. The comprehensive schema had to be abandoned and only the papal primacy and infallibility were in fact defined. This unhappy situation contributed to the one-sided stress laid on central authority in the Church and to a defensive attitude against disruptive forces. This attitude is reflected even in relatively recent documents, as in the rejection of Modernism and in the encyclical Humani Generis of Pope Pius XII.

These facts notwithstanding, it is also certain that a new understanding of the inner reality of the Church has developed during the last decades. It found expression in the great encyclical letter Mystici Corporis of Pope Pius XII. It is fully expounded by the doctrine of the Second Vatican Council. Among the conciliar documents two have a special significance for the Council's ecclesiology: the dogmatic Constitution Lumen Gentium unfolds the various aspects of the Church's life; the pastoral Constitution Gaudium et Spes on the Church in the modern world explains her place and mission in human society. In these documents two extremes are avoided: a one-sided juridical conception of the Church, on the one hand, and, on the other, an unearthly spiritualisation which would separate the mystery of Christ from society and history. The Church is presented as the universal sign and sacrament of salvation, for she is at once a "visible assembly and a spiritual community,... one complex reality composed of a divine and of a human element" (LG 8).

* * *

Thus the documents mentioned here contain the following points:

Jesus Christ founded one Church: 21, 25, 39/12, 143/3, 804, 818, 846/52, 848, 854, (860), (866f), (869), (871).

The Church is a visible community: (802), 808, (812), 847, (860), (866-869).

The Church is inseparable from Christ: 884.

She is Christ's Mystical Body: 847-849, 852, (862);

animated by His Spirit: 3, 851, (860), (867), (881).

The Church continues Christ's saving mission: 818, (860), (862), (864f), (867-870).

The charismatic and the hierarchical aspects of the Church must not be separated: 848, 853, (860), (869), 1710, 1719.

The Church is a pilgrim community with an eschatological destiny: (862), (865), (868), (882).

The Church, universal and particular: 885.

The word of revelation is entrusted to the Church who interpretes the Scriptures authoritatively: 31, 39/13, 121, 123, 134, 139f, 143/3.9.11, 208, 210, 215, 217, 220, 221, 228/1.4, 238, 248, 836f, 858f, (863), (877).

The Church is infallible in her teaching; in particular the Roman Pontiff is infallible when speaking 'ex cathedra': 831-840, 841, (862f), 883.

The Church exerises a legitimate authority to which submission is due: 805, 807f, (811f), 815, 818, 846, 848, 858f, (863), (874f), (879).

The college of the bishops, united with the Pope, and the general Councils constitute the highest authority in the Church: 806, 863, 875.

Peter and his successors, the Roman Pontiffs, are given authority over the whole Church: 29, 36, 143/3, 801, 803-805, 807-809, (811f) 815f, 818-830, 841, 846/55f, (860), (863).

Bishops have ordinary jurisdiction over the local Churches of their dioceses: 827, 841, 850, (863), (874), (876), (878f), 1711, 1720f.

The members of the Church are those who, being baptised, confess their faith and acknowledge her authority: 847, 849, 854, (862), (864), (871), 1412, 1427, 1439-1440, 1441.

Membership of the Church is necessary for salvation: 21, 38, 39/16, (802), 804, 810, 813f, 847, 849, 854f, (862), (871).

At least the desire of the Church, accompanied with faith and charity, is required for salvation: 813f, 847, 855-857, (862), (871-873).

The Church is for man: 886.

INNOCENT I

LETTER *IN REQUIRENDIS* TO THE AFRICAN BISHOPS (417)

In the fifth and sixth centuries, the doctrine of the primacy of authority of the See of Rome was very much developed and affirmed by the reigning Pontiffs. Two important documents from this period were later embodied in the decree of the First Vatican Council. They are: 1) the declaration made by the Papal Legate to the Council of Ephesus (431) about the primacy of the Bishop of Rome (cf. n. 822); 2) the "Formula of Pope Hormisdas" whose signature by some two hundred and fifty Oriental bishops put an end to the Acacian schism (484-519) and which was later adopted by the fourth General Council of Constantinople (869) (cf. n. 832). In these texts the authority of the Roman Pontiffs is based on the authority given by Christ to Peter (Mt. 16.18-19) who lives on in his successor. In the following letter praising the bishops of Africa for their condemnation of the Pelagians, Innocent I takes up the idea, first found in Africa and adopted by St Cyprian, that the episcopate had its birth or origin in Peter. The Pope closely associates the See of Rome and the apostle Peter. And where Cyprian thought of the unity of the episcopate manifested in the oneness of its origin, Innocent proposes the Roman See as the source and norm of the life and teaching of the Church. This position was very much developed in later centuries.

801   In your pursuit of the things of God, ... following the examples
217   of ancient tradition, ... you have made manifest by your
proper course of action the vitality of our religion... when you agreed to have recourse to our judgment, knowing what is due to the apostolic See, since all of us placed in this position wish to follow the apostle (Peter), from whom have come this episcopate and all the authority belonging to this dignity. By following him we know how to condemn what is wrong, and approve what is praiseworthy. Moreover, in safeguarding the ordinances of the Fathers with your priestly zeal, you certainly believe that they must not be trodden underfoot. They decreed, not with human but with divine judgment, that no decision (even though it concerned the most remote provinces) was to be considered final unless this See were to hear of it, so that all the authority of this See might confirm whatever just decision was reached. From this See the other Churches receive the confirmation of what they ought to ordain, just as all waters proceed from their source and through diverse regions of the world remain pure liquids of an uncorrupted source.

THE FOURTH LATERAN GENERAL COUNCIL
SYMBOL OF LATERAN (1215)

(802) *The spiritualist and anti-ecclesial movements of the 12th century were in great part a protest against a worldly Church whose ecclesiology (following on the Gregorian Reform) was often dominated by the category of power and favoured a clerical, sacerdotal, and even curialist conception of the Church. They advocated a lay fraternity with emphasis on personal evangelism. Their critique contained a part of truth and was nourished by profound religious perceptions, but in conceiving of the Church uniquely as the "congregatio fidelium" they denied its incarnational and mediatory nature, and consequently its visible sacramental structure. Thus in the definition against the Albigensians and Cathars the Fourth Council of the Lateran included a profession of faith in the visible sacramental and eucharistic community, "outside which no one at all is saved" See text in n. 21.*

THE SECOND GENERAL COUNCIL OF LYONS

"PROFESSION OF FAITH OF MICHAEL PALAEOLOGUS" (1274)

(803) *The formula on the role and authority of the Roman Pontiff, proposed by Clement IV in 1267 to the emperor in the East, Michael VIII Palaeologus, was finally accepted by him through his ambassadors at the Second Council of Lyons, which sought to bring about reunion with the Greek Church. This fomula (the first enuntiated on the level of the solemn magisterium, and explicitly quoted by the First Vatican Council: cf. DS 3066) sums up the entire development, theological and canonical, that had taken place during the 13th century: the universal pre-eminence of the Roman Church in the sense of an ecclesial monarchy; the function of the superme magisterium; the supreme and universal judging function of Rome in matters of faith; the "fulness of power" understood in the sense that Rome is the source of power for the other Churches, including the patriarchal 'privileges'. The document lacked appreciation for, and openness to a tradition other than that of the Latin Church, and was severely criticised in the East. The reunion itself was short-lived. See text in n. 29.*

BONIFACE VIII
BULL *UNAM SANCTAM* (1302)

During the reign of Boniface VIII and the Avignon Popes, the question of the two powers, spiritual and temporal, and of their inter-relationship, dominated ecclesiastical thought. This Bull, which issued from the acrimonious dispute between Boniface and Philip the Fair of France over the rights of the King in temporal matters, admits that there are two swords (the temporal and the spiritual powers), but, dominated as it is by the idea and ideal of unity, affirms that the temporal is under the control of the spiritual; concretely, of the Pope. Boniface, therefore, seems to propose the hierocratic theory in an extreme form. In any case, it is necessary to distinguish the conclusion of the Bull, which is a doctrinal declaration (submission to the Roman Pontiff is necessary for salvation), and the body of the document which develops an ideology bound to the concepts of the time. Positively, the Bull affirms clearly the unity of the Church, its necessity for salvation, its divine origin, and the foundation of the authority of the Roman Pontiff. But Boniface goes on to assert that Christ and the Pope form one head; the Pope is therefore head of the mystical Body, which in the process is identified with the juridical reality, the body of men submitting itself to the jurisdiction of the Pope.

(The one Church, necessary for salvation)

804 That there is only one, holy, catholic and apostolic Church
870 we are compelled by faith to believe and hold, and we firmly believe in her and sincerely confess her, outside of whom there is neither salvation nor remission of sins.... She represents one mystical Body; the head of this body is Christ, but the head of Christ is God. In her there is "one Lord, one faith, one baptism" (Eph. 4.5)....

872 This one and unique Church, therefore, has not two heads, like a monster, but one body and one head, viz., Christ and His vicar, Peter's successor, for the Lord said to Peter personally: "Feed my sheep" (Jn 21.17). 'My' He said in general, not individually, meaning these or those; whereby it is understood that He confided all His sheep to him. If therefore Greeks or others say that they were not confided to Peter and his successors, they must necessarily confess that they are not among Christ's sheep, for the Lord said in John: "there shall be one fold and one shepherd" (Jn 10.16).

875 Furthermore we declare, state and define that it is absolutely necessary for the salvation of all men that they submit to the Roman Pontiff.

JOHN XXII

CONDEMNATION OF ERRORS OF MARSILIUS OF PADUA
ON THE CONSTITUTION OF THE CHURCH (1327)

The book Defensor Pacis written by Marsilius of Padua (1280–1343) (it is not certain whether his pupil, John of Jandun collaborated in writing it) was one of the most famous of the 14th century, and influenced conciliarist thought and the theologians of the Reformation, especially Luther. Marsilius attributed a normative value to Scripture alone, and rigorously applied the political philosophy of Aristotle to the Church. Pope John XXII in the Bull Licet Juxta Doctrinam condemned especially the following points:

denial of the divine institution of the hierarchy, of the papal primacy, of all ecclesial coercive power; and the subordination of the Pope to the emperor.

[805/2] That the apostle St Peter had no more authority than the
942   other apostles had;... similarly, that Christ did not provide any head for His Church, nor appoint anyone His vicar.

[805/3] That it is the emperor's duty to correct the Pope, to
943   appoint and depose him, and to punish him.

[805/4] That according to the institution of Christ, every priest,
944   whether he be Pope, archbishop or simple priest, has equal authority and jurisdiction.

THE GENERAL COUNCIL OF CONSTANCE
DECREE *HAEC SANCTA* (1415)

The Council of Constance is of crucial importance in the history of the Church, for it succeeded in bringing to an end the 40 year old "Western Schism" when the allegiance of the Church was divided between 2 (later 3) rival popes. Gregory XII of the Roman obedience resigned spontaneously (July 4, 1415); Benedict XIII of the Avignon obedience and John XXIII of the Pisan obedience were deposed (May 29, 1415, and July 26, 1417). In their place Martin V was elected on November 11, 1417. Besides the condemnation of the errors of Wyclif and Hus, the Council is important for ecclesiology because of its famous decree Haec Sancta *adopted at the fifth session of the Council, April 6, 1415. While many historians today would agree that* Haec Sancta *has to be counted as a valid decree of an ecumenical Council, disagreement remains with regard to the interpretation of its content.* Haec Sancta *affirms two things: 1) the general Council receives its power not from the Pope but immediately from Christ; 2) every Catholic, including the Pope, owes obedience to the Council in matters of faith, for the extinction of actual heresy and for the reform of the Church in its head and members. The wording is ambivalent, and was later interpreted in a conciliarist sense (permanent superiority of a Council over the Pope); yet it seems to be in keeping with the traditional heresy clause of the canonists, who, to the principle of the immunity of the "first See"* (Prima sedes a nemine iudicatur), *added the words: "unless he is found to deviate from the faith"* (nisi deprehendatur a fide devius).

806 This holy Synod of Constance holding a general Council in order to uproot the present schism, and to unite and reform the Church in its head and members,... orders, defines, fixes, decrees and declares the following in order to achieve more easily, securely, fully and freely the union and reform of the Church of God.

And first of all it declares that, having assembled legitimately in the Holy Spirit, and being a general Council and representing the

Catholic Church militant, it has its power immediately from Christ, which every state and dignity, even if it be the papal dignity, must obey in what concerns faith, the eradication of the mentioned schism and the reformation of the said Church in head and members.

CONDEMNATION OF THE ERRORS OF WYCLIF AND HUS (1415)

John Wyclif (1324–1384) was the forerunner of the Reformation in England. A reformer, his main attack was directed against the riches and temporal pretensions of the clergy. He refused to define the Church by profession of the true faith or as a sacramental institution, because he desired a spiritual Church, defined by a purely divine element. This element for him was predestination: that which constitutes the Church and its unity is the predestining love of Christ. The Church, therefore, is the congregation of all the predestined; the reprobate (the "foreknown") are not members of it and cannot hold office in it. John Hus (1369-1415), patriot and reformer in Bohemia, was Wyclif's spiritual heir. In his De Ecclesia *(1412–1413) he reproduced entire passages from Wyclif's writings. Summoned to the Council of Constance, he was tried and condemned, and then turned over to the secular authorities to be burnt at the stake (July 6, 1415). The errors of Wyclif and Hus were collated and condemned by the Council.*

(Wyclif's errors condemned)

[807/8]   If the Pope be a reprobate and an evil man and, conse-
1158   quently, a member of the devil, he has no power over the
               faithful given him by anyone, except perhaps by the state.

[807/37]   The Roman Church is the synagogue of Satan, and the
1187   Pope is not the proximate and immediate vicar of Christ
               and of the apostles.

(Hus' errors condemned)

[808/1]   The only and holy universal Church is the aggregate of the
1201   predestined. And it follows: the holy universal Church is
               one only, just as the number of all the predestined is one.

[808/3]   The reprobates are not parts of the Church, since no part
1203   of the Church will ultimately fall away from it for the
               charity of predestination, which keeps it together, will not
fail.

[808/5]   Even if sometimes a reprobate is in grace according to his
1205   actual state of justice, he is, nevertheless, never a part of
               the holy Church; and a predestined always remains a
member of the Church, even though sometimes he may fall from

temporary grace, but not from the grace of predestination.

[808/6] The Church is an article of faith only if by the Church is
1206   meant the gathering of the predestined, whether they are
            in grace according to their actual state of justice or not.

[808/10] It would be unreasonable for anyone without a revelation
1210   to make the claim for himself or for anyone that he is the
            head of a particular Church; and not even the Roman
Pontiff is the head of the particular Roman Church.

[808/13] The Pope is not the true and manifest successor of
1213   Peter, the first of the apostles, if he lives in a manner
            contrary to Peter; and if he be avaricious, then he is the
vicar of Judas Iscariot....

[808/15] Ecclesiastical obedience is obedience according to the
1215   invention of the priests of the Church without the express
            authority of the Scriptures.

THE GENERAL COUNCIL OF FLORENCE

*Florence, under the leadership of Pope Eugene IV, was yet another
attempt to bring about reunion between the Eastern Churches and Rome.
This sinuous and eventful "Council of union" held its sessions from 1431 till
1445. It started its career at Basel, was transferred to Ferrara in 1438 and to
Florence the following year where the decrees of union with the Armenian,
Greek and Coptic ("Jacobite") Churches were approved. In 1443 it was
finally transferred to Rome where other decrees of union with the Syrians of
Mesopotamia, with the Chaldeans and with the Maronites of Cyprus were
passed. The decrees of Ferrara, Florence and Rome are in the form of Bulls,
as these sessions were presided over by the Roman Pontiff himself. The
Council endorsed the Roman texts presented to it for approval.*

*The Decree for the "Jacobites" or Copts from Egypt was partly inspired
by the* Treatise on Faith *of Fulgentius of Ruspa (647-533), an African bishop,
disciple of St Augustine. This decree deals less with specific points of dissent
than does the one for the Greeks; it rather offers a summary of the Christian
belief.*

*The question at issue with the Greeks was that of the Papal primacy.
The act of union with the Greeks uncompromisingly delineates the dogma
of the privileges of the apostolic See and the Roman Pontiff while at the
same time recognising the traditional privileges of the ancient patriarchates.*

*In the Decree for the Jacobites, the necessity of the Church for salvation
is expressed in a rigid formula taken* verbatim *from Fulgentius. It exposes
the order of salvation as follows: Jesus Christ is the final revelation of God;
His mission is entrusted to the Church; thus, separation from this Church
means separation from Christ and hence loss of salvation. This is the first
official Church document in which mention is made of the "pagans" in*

connection with the axiom Extra Ecclesiam nulla salus. *Previous documents had made use of the axiom in relation to Christian schism and heresy (cf. nn. 802i, 804; cf. also DS 792, 1051). In view of the historical context, this remains even in this Decree the first intention of the Council. See also n. 1003i.*

DECREE FOR THE GREEKS (1439)

(The Primacy of the Roman Pontiff)

809 Likewise, we define that the holy apostolic See and the
1307 Roman Pontiff have the primacy over the whole world, and
that the same Roman Pontiff is the successor of St Peter, the prince of the apostles, and the true vicar of Christ, the head of the whole Church, the father and teacher of all Christians; and that to him, in the person of St Peter, was given by our Lord Jesus Christ the full power of feeding, ruling, and governing the whole Church as is also contained in the acts of the ecumenical Councils and in the sacred canons.

(The order of patriarchates)

1308 Besides, we declare anew the order of the other venerable
patriarchates, as transmitted in the canons: the patriarch of Constantinople is second after the most holy Roman Pontiff; third is that of Alexandria, fourth that of Antioch, fifth that of Jerusalem; all of whose privileges and rights evidently remain intact.

DECREE FOR THE JACOBITES (1442)

(The unity of the Catholic Church and its necessity for salvation)

810 (The holy Roman Church)... firmly believes, professes and
1351 preaches that "no one remaining outside the Catholic
Church, not only pagans", but also Jews, heretics or schismatics, can become partakers of eternal life; but they will go to the "eternal fire prepared for the devil and his angels" *(Mt. 25.41),* unless before the end of their life they are received into it. For union with the body of the Church is of so great importance that the sacraments of the Church are helpful to salvation only for those remaining in it; and fasts, almsgiving, other works of piety, and the exercises of a militant Christian life bear eternal rewards for them alone. "And no one can be saved, no matter how much alms he has given, even if he sheds his

blood for the name of Christ, unless he remains in the bosom and unity of the Catholic Church."[1]

LEO X

BULL *EXSURGE DOMINE* (1520)

ERRORS OF LUTHER CONDEMNED

(811)   *The protest against the misuse of ecclesiastical authority and the worldly patterns of the hierarchical regime came to a climax with the Reformation. Luther and the other Reformers took up the ideas of Wyclif and Hus, based on the conceptions of Marsilius of Padua (cf. n. 805). Among the propositions of Luther condemned by Pope Leo X there is the denial of the papal authority and of ecclestastical authority in general (cf. DS 1475-1479). Since they contain no new elements, they need not be quoted here. Many of the ecclesiological problems raised by the Reformers were in fact treated by the Council of Trent in the context of the sacraments, especially of the sacrament of Order (cf. nn. 1706ff). It was, however, only in Vatican I and mainly Vatican II that the most basic ecclesiological issues raised by the Reformation were explicitly dealt with.*

PIUS VI

CONSTITUTION *AUCTOREM FIDEI* (1794)

(812)   *The two most powerful movements that affected the life of the Church in the post-Reformation period were Jansenism (cf. n. 1989i) and Febronianism with its tendency to subordinate the life of the Church to political interests, and therefore to play down the ecclesiastical authority. These trends found expression in the synod of the Italian province of Toscany in Pistoia (1786). A series of 85 propositions taken from the acts of this synod were condemned by Pius VI in the Constitution* Auctorem Fidei *(1794). Among the propositions condemned, 1-15 belong to the doctrine on the Church (DS 2601-2615). They concern the origin of ecclesiastical authority, and mainly of the authority of the Pope, which is attributed to the Christian community, not to an institution by Christ (2,3); the denial of the Church's disciplinary authority over the faithful (4,5); the independence of bishops from the papal authority (6-8); the democratic conception of ecclesiastical authority according to which the entire Christian people is established as judge of the faith (9-11); the Jansenistic conception of a Church constituted only by saints (15). All these issues, however, are dealt with more explicitly in the documents of the 19th and 20th centuries.*

PIUS IX

ALLOCUTION *SINGULARI QUADAM* (1854)

Denial of supernatural revelation entails denying the Church as the

---

1. FULGENTIUS OF RUSPA, *De fide liber ad Petrum,* 38, 79 and 39, 80.

unique God-given community necessary for salvation. Rationalism and indifferentism (according equal value to all forms of religion) are closely connected. Again and again they were condemned alongside one another in Church documents of the nineteenth century. The present document is of importance because it makes a clear distinction between the objective necessity of the Church for salvation as willed by God, and the subjective guilt or innocence of people outside the Church.

(Salvation in the Church)

813   It must, of course, be held as a matter of faith that outside the
2865i   apostolic Roman Church no one can be saved, that the
        Church is the only ark of salvation, and that whoever does
not enter it will perish in the flood. On the other hand, it must likewise
be held as certain that those who live in ignorance of the true religion,
if such ignorance be invincible, are not subject to any guilt in this
matter before the eyes of the Lord. But then, who would dare to set
limits to this ignorance, taking into consideration the natural differences of people, lands, native talents, and so many other factors?

ENCYCLICAL LETTER *QUANTO CONFICIAMUR MOERORE* (1863)

This encyclical addressed to the bishops of Italy warns again against a liberal indifferentism that would deny the necessity of the Church for salvation, but also states in a more positive way the possibility of salvation for those living in ignorance of the Christian revelation.

(Salvation in the Church)

814   And here, beloved Sons and venerable Brethren, it is neces-
2865   sary once more to mention and censure the serious error into
        which some Catholics have unfortunately fallen. For they are
of the opinion that men who live in errors, estranged from the true
faith and Catholic unity, can attain eternal life. This is in direct
opposition to Catholic teaching.

2866   We all know that those who suffer from invincible ignorance
        with regard to our holy religion, if they carefully keep the
precepts of the natural law which have been written by God in the
hearts of all men, if they are prepared to obey God, and if they lead a
virtuous and dutiful life, can, by the power of divine light and grace,
attain eternal life. For God, who knows completely the minds and
souls, the thoughts and habits of all men, will not permit, in accord
with His infinite goodness and mercy, anyone who is not guilty of a
voluntary fault fo suffer eternal punishment.

2867 However, also well known is the Catholic dogma that no one can be saved outside the Catholic Church, and that those who obstinately oppose the authority of the definitions of the Church, and who stubbornly remain separated from the unity of the Church and from the successor of Peter, the Roman Pontiff, to whom the Saviour has entrusted the care of His vineyard, cannot obtain salvation.

ENCYCLICAL LETTER *QUANTA CURA* (1864)

In this doctrinal letter, issued on the same day as the Syllabus *of condemned errors, Pius IX reviews some of the errors of his time on the relationship between Church and State. He stresses the Church's full independence from temporal power and the divine origin of its authority. See also the* Syllabus: *DS 2919-2938.*

(Ecclesiastical authority)

815 Others have revived the evil and often condemned errors of
2893 the Reformers. Acting with extraordinary boldness they dare
to submit to the judgment of civil authority the supreme authority of the Church and of this apostolic See—an authority which was received from Christ our Lord. And they deny the Church and this See any rights in matters belonging to the external order.

816 They do not hesitate to profess openly and publicly an hereti-
2895 cal principle that has led to very many perverse opinions
and errors. For they say: "It is not of divine law that the power of the Church be distinct and independent from the civil power. Indeed it is impossible to keep such independence and distinction without having the Church infringe upon and usurp essential rights of the civil power." Nor can we be silent about the arrogant claim of those who... maintain: "It is possible, without sinning and without at all departing from the profession of the Catholic faith, to refuse assent and obedience to those decisions and decrees of the apostolic See whose declared object is the general good of the Church and its rights and discipline, provided only that such decisions do not touch upon dogmas of faith or morals." No one can fail to see that this doctrine directly opposes Catholic dogma according to which Christ our Lord with His divine authority gave to the Roman Pontiff the supreme power of shepherding, ruling, and governing the Church.

THE FIRST VATICAN GENERAL COUNCIL

THIRD SESSION

DOGMATIC CONSTITUTION *DEI FILIUS* ON THE CATHOLIC FAITH (1870)

(817) *In its Dogmatic Constitution on the Catholic Faith (nn. 113ff), Vatican I dealt with the role of the Church as guardian and teacher of the revealed word. This Constitution contains important affirmations about the ordinary universal magisterium and the "irreformability" of dogmas, as well as the affirmation that the Church as a sign raised among the nations manifests in its life and structures the victorious grace of Christ, and so is in itself a perpetual motive of credibility of its divine mission. See text in nn. 121, 122, 123, 136, 139.*

FOURTH SESSION

DOGMATIC CONSTITUTION *PASTOR AETERNUS* ON THE CHURCH OF CHRIST (1870)

Vatican I's solemn definition of the primacy of jurisdiction of the Roman Pontiff and his infallible teaching function was the culmination of a long development in the ecclesiology of the Western Church that had in great part been centred on the theme of the unity of the universal Church and on the role of the Petrine office as the centre and support of that unity. Against all attempts to limit juridically the scope and extent of the primatial authority, it affirms in precise juridical terminology the universal authority of the Roman Pontiff as the centre and guardian of the Church's unity in faith and communion. The Council's definition of the universal and infallible (under precise conditions) teaching office of the Popes flows from its teaching regarding the nature and role of the primatial See in the Church. The Council had prepared and intended to debate and promulgate a Constitution on the Church as a whole. Unfortunately, the untimely termination of the Council prevented it from carrying out this project. As a result the definitions regarding the primacy tend to give a one-sided view of the Church's life and structure. The Second Vatican Council in its Constitution on the Church, while re-affirming the teaching of Vatican I, will seek to integrate that teaching in a much more complete exposition of the mystery of the Church and its hierarchical structure.

Introduction: The Institution and Foundation of the Church

818 The eternal Shepherd and Guardian of our souls *(cf. 1 Pet.*
3050 *2.25),* in order to continue for all time the saving work of redemption, determined to build His holy Church so that in it, as in the house of the living God, all who believe might be united together in the bond of one faith and one love. For this reason, before

he was glorified, He prayed to the Father not for the apostles only but for those also who would believe in Him on their testimony, that all might be one as He, the Son, and the Father are one *(cf. Jn 17.20ff)*. Therefore, just as He sent the apostles, whom He had chosen for Himself out of the world, as He Himself was sent by the Father *(cf. Jn 20.21)*, so also He wished shepherds and teachers to be in His Church until the consummation of the world *(cf. Mt. 28.20)*.

3051 In order that the episcopate itself might be one and undivided, and that the whole multitude of believers might be preserved in unity of faith and communion by means of a closely united priesthood, He placed St Peter at the head of the other apostles, and established in him a perpetual principle and visible foundation of this twofold unity, in order that on his strength an everlasting temple might be erected and on the firmness of his faith a Church might arise whose pinnacle was to reach into heaven.

3052 But the gates of hell, with a hatred that grows greater every day, are rising up everywhere against the Church's divinely established foundation with the intention of overthrowing the Church, if this were possible. We, therefore, with the approval of the sacred Council, judge it necessary, for the protection, the safety and the increase of the Catholic flock, to propose to all the faithful what is to be believed and held, according to the ancient and constant belief of the universal Church, with regard to the establishment, the perpetuity and the nature of this sacred apostolic primacy, in which is found the strength and solidity of the entire Church. Likewise we judge it necessary to proscribe with sentence of condemnation the contrary erroneous opinions so detrimental to the Lord's flock.

Chapter I: The Establishment of the Apostolic Primacy in St Peter

819 We, therefore, teach and declare, according to the testimony
3053 of the Gospel, that the primacy of juridiction over the whole Church was immediately and directly promised to and conferred upon the blessed apostle Peter by Christ the Lord. To Simon alone He had first said: "You shall be called Cephas" *(Jn 1.42)*; to him alone, after he had acknowledged Christ with the confession: "You are the Christ, the Son of the living God" *(Mt. 16.16)*, these solemn words were also spoken: "Blessed are you, Simon Bar-Jona! For

flesh and blood have not revealed this to you, but my Father who is in heaven. And I tell you: you are Peter, and on this rock I will build my Church, and the powers of death shall not prevail against it. I will give you the keys of the Kingdom of heaven, and whatever you bind on earth shall be bound in heaven, and whatever you loose on earth shall be loosed in heaven" *(Mt. 16.17-19)*. And after His resurrection, Jesus conferred upon Simon Peter alone the jurisdiction of supreme shepherd and ruler over His whole flock with the words: "Feed my lambs....Feed my sheep" *(Jn 21.15,17)*.

820   In clear opposition to this very clear teaching of the Holy
3054   Scripture, as it has always been understood by the Catholic
Church, are the perverse opinions of those who wrongly explain the form of government established by Christ in His Church; either by denying that Peter alone in preference to the other apostles, either singly or as a group, was endowed by Christ with the true and proper primacy of jurisdiction; or by claiming that this primacy was not given immediately and directly to blessed Peter, but to the Church and through the Church to Peter as a minister of the Church.

Canon

821   Therefore, if anyone says that the blessed apostle Peter was
3055   not constituted by Christ the Lord as the Prince of all the
apostles and the visible head of the whole Church militant, or that he received immediately and directly from Jesus Christ our Lord only a primacy of honour and not a true and proper primacy of jurisdiction, *anathema sit*.

Chapter II: The Perpetuity of
St Peter's Primacy in the Roman Pontiffs

822   Now, what Christ, the Lord, the Prince of Shepherds and the
3056   great Shepherd of the flock, established in the person of the
blessed apostle Peter for the perpetual safety and everlasting good of the Church must, by the will of the same, endure without interruption in the Church, which was founded on the rock and which will remain firm until the end of the world. Indeed, "no one doubts, in fact it is obvious to all ages, that the holy and most blessed

Peter, Prince and head of all the apostles, the pillar of faith and the foundation of the Catholic Church, received the keys of the Kingdom from our Lord Jesus Christ, the saviour and redeemer of the human race; and even to this time and forever he lives", and governs, "and exercises judgment in his successors", the bishops of the holy Roman See, which he established and consecrated with his blood.[1]

823 Therefore, whoever succeeds Peter in this Chair, according
3057 to the institution of Christ Himself, holds Peter's primacy over the whole Church. "Therefore, the dispositions made by truth perdure, and St Peter still has the rock-like strength that has been given to him, and he has not surrendered the helm of the Church with which he has been entrusted."[2] For this reason, "because of its more powerful principality", it was always "necessary for every Church, that is, the faithful who are everywhere, to be in agreement" with the Roman Church;[3] thus in that See, from which "the bonds of sacred communion"[4] are imparted to all, the members will be joined as members under one head and coalesce into one compact body.

Canon

824 Therefore, if anyone says that it is not according to the
3058 institution of Christ our Lord Himself, that is, by divine law, that St Peter should have perpetual sucessors in the primacy over the whole Church; or if anyone says that the Roman Pontiff is not the successor of St Peter in the same primacy, *anathema sit*.

Chapter III: The Power and Nature of the Primacy of the Roman Pontiff

(Declaration of the Primacy)

825 Wherefore, relying on the clear testimony of the Holy Scrip-
3059 tures and following the express and definite decrees of our predecessors, the Roman Pontiffs, and of the general Coun-

---

1. PHILIP, legate of the Pope, *Oratio* at the Council of Ephesus (11 July, 431).

2. LEO THE GREAT, *Sermo 3 de natali ipsius*, 3.

3. IRENAEUS, *Adversus Haereses*, III, 3, 2.

4. AMBROSE, *Epistola* 11, 4.

cils, We reaffirm the definition of the ecumenical Council of Florence. According to this definition all the faithful must believe "that the holy apostolic See and the Roman Pontiff have the primacy over the whole world; and that the same Roman Pontiff is the successor of St Peter, the Prince of the apostles, and the true vicar of Christ, the head of the whole Church, the father and teacher of all Christians; and that to him, in the person of St Peter, was given by our Lord Jesus Christ the full power of feeding, ruling and governing the whole Church, as is also contained in the proceedings of the ecumenical Councils and in the sacred canons" *(cf. DS 1307).*

(Consequences that the Reformers denied)

826   And so We teach and declare that, in the disposition of God,
3060   the Roman Church holds the pre-eminence of ordinary
power over all the other Churches; and that this power of jurisdiction of the Roman Pontiff, which is truly episcopal, is immediate. Regarding this jurisdiction, the shepherds of whatever rite or jurisdiction and the faithful, individually and collectively, are bound by a duty of hierarchical subjection and of sincere obedience; and this not only in matters that pertain to faith and morals, but also in matters that pertain to the discipline and government of the Church throughout the whole world. The result is that, when this bond of unity, both of communion and of profession of the same faith, is guarded, then the Church of Christ is one flock under one supreme shepherd. This is the doctrine of Catholic truth; and no one can deviate from it without loss of faith and salvation.

(The jurisdiction of the Roman Pontiff and the Bishops)

827   This power of the Supreme Pontiff is far from standing in the
3061   way of the power of ordinary and immediate episcopal juris-
diction by which the bishops who, under appointment of the Holy Spirit *(cf. Acts 20.28),* succeeded in the place of the apostles, feed and rule individually, as true shepherds, the particular flock assigned to them. Rather this latter power is asserted, confirmed and vindicated by this same supreme and universal shepherd, as in the words of St Gregory the Great: "My honour is the honour of the whole Church. My honour is the firm strength of my brothers. I am truly honoured when due honour is paid to each and every one."[1]

---

1. GREGORY THE GREAT, *Epistola ad Eulogium Alexandrinum.*

(Thr right to deal freely with all the faithful)

828   Furthermore, from his supreme power of governing the
3062   whole Church, the Roman Pontiff has the right of freely
communicating with the shepherds and flocks of the whole
Church in the exercise of his office so that they can be instructed and
guided by him in the way of salvation. Hence, we condemn and reject
the opinions of those who say that it can be licit to hinder the
communication of the supreme head with the shepherds and the
flocks; or those who make this communication subject to the secular
power in such a way that they claim that whatever is decreed for the
goverment of the Church by the apostolic See or by its authority has
no binding force unless it is confirmed by the placet of the secular
power.

(The right of recourse to the Roman Pontiff as supreme judgè)

829   And because, by the divine right of apostolic primacy, the
3063   Roman Pontiff is at the head of the whole Church, we also
teach and declare that he is the supreme judge of the faithful;
and that one can have recourse to his judgment in all cases pertaining
to ecclesiastical jurisdiction. We declare that the judgment of the
apostolic See, whose authority is unsurpassed, is not subject to
review by anyone; nor is anyone allowed to pass judgment on its
decision. Therefore, those who say that it is permitted to appeal to an
ecumenical Council from the decisions of the Roman Pontiff, as to an
authority superior to the Roman Pontiff, are far from the straight
path of truth.

Canon

830   And so, if anyone says that the Roman Pontiff has only the
3064   office of inspection and direction, but not the full and
supreme power of jurisdiction over the whole Church, not
only in matters that pertain to faith and morals, but also in matters
that pertain to the discipline and government of the Church throughout the whole world; or if anyone says that he has only a more
important part and not the complete fulness of this supreme power;
or if anyone says that this power is not ordinary and immediate either
over each and every Church or over each and every shepherd and
faithful, *anathema sit.*

Chapter IV: The Infallible Magisterium of the Roman Pontiff

(Arguments based on doctrinal documents)

831 Moreover, this holy See has always held, the perpetual prac-
3065 tice of the Church confirms, and the ecumenical Councils,
especially those in which the Western and Eastern Churches
were united in faith and love, have declared that the surpeme power
of teaching is also included in this apostolic primacy which the
Roman Pontiff, as the successor of St Peter, the Prince of the
apostles, holds over the whole Church.

832 For the Fathers of the Fourth Council of Constantinople,
3066 following closely in the footsteps of their predecessors, made
this solemn profession: "The first condition of salvation is to
keep the norm of the true faith.... And because it is impossible that
those words of our Lord Jesus Christ: "You are Peter and upon this
rock I will build my Church" *(Mt. 16.18),* should not be verified, their
truth has been proved by the course of history, for in the apostolic
See the Catholic religion has always been kept unsullied, and its
teaching kept holy. Desiring in no way to be separated from this faith
and doctrine..., we hope that we may deserve to be associated with
you in the one communion which the apostolic See proclaims, in
which the whole truth and perfect security of the Christian religion
resides" *(cf. DS 363f).*

833 Furthermore, with the approval of the Second Council of
3067 Lyons, the Greeks professed that "the holy Roman Church
possesses the supreme and full primacy and authority over
the universal Catholic Church, which she recognises in truth and
humility to have received with fulness of power from the Lord
Himself in the person of Blessed Peter, the Prince or head of the
apostles, of whom the Roman Pontiff is the successor. And, as she is
bound above all to defend the truth of faith, so too, if any questions
should arise regarding the faith, they must be decided by her judgment" *(cf. n. 29).*

834 Finally, the Council of Florence defined "that the Roman
3068 Pontiff is the true vicar of Christ, the head of the whole
Church, the father and teacher of all Christians; and that to

him, in the person of St Peter, was given by our Lord Jesus Christ the full power of feeding, ruling, and governing the whole Church" *(cf. n. 809)*.

(Argument based on the agreement of the Church)

835 To satisfy this pastoral care, our predecessors have always
3069 expended untiring effort to propagate Christ's doctrine of salvation among all the peoples of the world, and with similar care they were watchful that the doctrine might be preserved genuine and pure wherever it was received. Therefore, the bishops of the whole world, sometimes singly, sometimes assembled in Councils, following the long-standing custom of the Churches and the form of the ancient rule, reported to this apostolic See those dangers especially which arose in matters of faith, so that here where the faith can suffer no diminution, the harm suffered by the faith might be repaired. For their part, the Roman Pontiffs, according as the conditions of the times and the circumstances dictated, sometimes by calling together ecumenical Councils or sounding out the mind of the Church throughout the world, sometimes through regional Councils, or sometimes by using other helps which divine Providence supplied, have defined as having to be held those matters which, with the help of God, they had found consonant with the Holy Scripture and with the apostolic Tradition.

836 For the Holy Spirit was not promised to the successors of
3070 Peter that they might disclose a new doctrine by His revelation, but rather, that, with His assistance, they might jealously guard and faithfully explain the revelation or deposit of faith that was handed down through the apostles. Indeed it was this apostolic doctrine that all the Fathers held, and the holy orthodox Doctors reverenced and followed, fully realising that this See of Saint Peter always remains untainted by any error, according to the divine promise of our Lord and Saviour made to the Prince of His disciples: "But I have prayed for you that your faith may not fail; and when you have turned again, strengthen your brethren" *(Lk. 22.32)*.

837 Now this charism of truth and of never-failing faith was
3071 conferred upon Peter and his successors in this Chair, in order that they might perform their supreme office for the salvation of all; that by them the whole flock of Christ might be kept away from the poison of error and be nourished by the food of

heavenly doctrine; that, the occasion of schism being removed, the whole Church might be preserved as one, and, resting on its foundation, might stand firm against the gates of hell.

(The definition of infallibility)

838 But since in this present age, which especially requires the
3072 salutary efficacy of the apostolic office, not a few are found
who minimise its authority, We think it extremely necessary to assert solemnly the prerogative which the only-begotten Son of God deigned to join to the highest pastoral office.

839 And so, faithfully keeping to the tradition received from the
3073 beginning of the Christian faith, for the glory of God our
Saviour, for the exaltation of the Catholic religion, and for the salvation of Christian peoples, We, with the approval of the sacred Council, teach and define:

3074 It is a divinely revealed dogma that the Roman Pontiff, when
he speaks *ex cathedra,* that is, when, acting in the office of shepherd and teacher of all Christians, he defines, by virtue of his supreme apostolic authority, a doctrine concerning faith or morals to be held by the universal Church, possesses through the divine assistance promised to him in the person of Blessed Peter, the infallibility with which the divine Redeemer willed His Church to be endowed in defining the doctrine concerning faith or morals; and that such definitions of the Roman Pontiff are therefore irreformable of themselves, not because of the consent of the Church *(ex sese, non autem ex consensu ecclesiae).*

Canon

840 But if anyone presumes to contradict this our definition—
3075 which God forbid—,*anathema sit.*

COLLECTIVE DECLARATION BY THE GERMAN HIERARCHY (1875)

On May 14, 1872, Bismark, the German Chancellor, issued a circular in which he maintained that the teaching of Vatican I about the direct and universal jurisdiction of the Pope made bishops into mere executive organs of the Pope, and that they were thus degraded to the status of mere officials. Against this view the collective declaration of the German hierarchy was issued (January-February 1875). In an apostolic brief of March 6, 1875, Pius IX gave approval to this declaration in an unusually solemn form. He wrote:

"Your declaration gives the genuine Catholic doctrine, which is also that of the holy Council and of this holy See; it defends it with illuminating and irrefutable reasoning, and sets it out so clearly that it is plain to any honest man that there is no innovation in the definitions attacked..." (cf. DS 3117). The document is important because of the clarification which it gives regarding the relationship between the papal and episcopal authority as understood in the era immediately following upon the definition of papal primacy at Vatican I. This is brought out clearly in the passage given below.

841 It is in virtue of the same divine institution upon which the
3115 papacy rests that the episcopate also exists. It, too, has its rights and duties, because of the ordinance of God Himself, and the Pope has neither the right nor the power to change them. Thus it is a complete misunderstanding of the Vatican decrees to believe that because of them "episcopal jurisdiction has been absorbed into the papal", that the Pope has "in principle taken the place of each individual bishop", that the bishops are now "no more than tools of the Pope, his officials, without responsibility of their own". According to the constant teaching of the Catholic Church, expressly declared at the Vatican Council itself, the bishops are not mere tools of the Pope, nor papal officials without responsibility of their own, but, "under appointment of the Holy Spirit, they succeeded in the place of the apostles, and feed and rule individually, as true shepherds, the particular flock assigned to them" *(cf. n. 827).*

PIUS X

DECREE *LAMENTABILI* OF THE HOLY OFFICE (1907) ARTICLES OF MODERNISM CONDEMNED

In the decree Lamentabili, *published by the Holy Office, several errors connected with the doctrine of the Church which were bound up with the Modernist position (cf. n. 143i) were explicitly condemned. They flow from the Modernist ideas either with regard to the understanding of revelation and dogma, or with regard to exegetical and historical conclusions about the founding of the Church by Christ and its essential structures.*

[846/6] The learning Church and the teaching Church so work
3406 together in defining truths, that the only function of the teaching Church is to ratify the generally held opinions of the learning Church.

[846/7] In proscribing errors the Church cannot exact from the
3407 faithful any internal assent by which the judgments that it has decreed are accepted.

[846/52] It was far from the mind of Christ to establish the Church
3452 as a society that would last on earth for a long succession
of centuries; in fact, in the mind of Christ the kingdom of
heaven together with the end of the world was imminent.

[846/53] The organic constitution of the Church is not unchange-
3453 able; rather, the Christian society is just as subject to
perpetual evolution as human society is.

[846/54] Dogmas, sacraments, hierarchy—both in their notion
3454 and their reality—are nothing but evolutions and interpretations of Christian thought which caused the tiny
seed, hidden in the Gospel, to grow through external accretions and
to be brought to fruition.

[846/55] Simon Peter never even suspected that the primacy in
3455 the Church was entrusted to him by Christ.

[846/56] The Roman Church became the head of all Churches
3456 not because of any determination on the part of divine
providence but because of political conditions.

PIUS XII

ENCYCLICAL LETTER *MYSTICI CORPORIS* (1943)

Between the two world wars there was a renewed interest in and development of the theology of the Church as the mystical Body of Christ (cf. especially the works of Emile Mersch and Sebastian Tromp). Along with the positive developments, there also appeared a trend toward a sort of pan-Christism. In his great encyclical, Pius XII, while warning against such excesses, gave official recognition and expression to the riches of this theology. While taking as his point of departure the Counter-Reformation theology of the Church as a visible hierarchical society, which he identified with the mystical Body of Christ, the Pope sought to incorporate into this theology the stress laid by patristic and scholastic thought on the interior reality of grace and the role of the Holy Spirit. According to the teaching of the encyclical the Church is a body because it is one visible, hierarchically structured, society. It is the Body of Christ, because He is its founder, head, sustainer and saviour. It is called mystical Body in order to distinguish it clearly both from the physical body of Christ as well as from any other body, whether physical or moral. The passages given here bring out the most important teachings of the encyclical: the identification of the Roman Catholic Church with the mystical Body of Christ (reaffirmed in the encycli-cal Humani Generis); the requirements for membership (distinguishing between those who are 'really' members, and those who are members only 'in voto'); the demonstration that without prejudice to the Church's juridical structure and official 'offices', the charismatic element also pertains to the

Church; the unity of the Church of law and the Church of love in the true Church of Christ; the nature and significance of the episcopal office (with the statement that the bishops' power of ordinary jurisdiction is received directly from the Pope); the theology of the Holy Spirit as the 'soul' of the Church, a doctrine which is important in combating a naturalistic concep- tion of the Church with undue emphasis on its sociological and juridical aspects.

(The Catholic Church is the Mystical Body)

847   If we would define and describe this true Church of Jesus Christ—which is the holy, catholic, apostolic, Roman Church—we shall find no expression more noble, more sublime or more divine than the phrase which calls it "the mystical Body of Jesus Christ". This title is derived from and is, as it were, the fair flower of the repeated teaching of Sacred Scripture and the holy Fathers.

That the Church is a body is frequently asserted in Sacred Scripture. "Christ", says the apostle, "is the head of His body, the Church" *(Col. 1.18)*. If the Church is a body, it must be an unbroken unity according to those words of Paul: "So we, though many, are one body in Christ" *(Rom. 12.5)*. But it is not enough that the Body of Christ be an unbroken unity: it must be also something definite and perceptible to the senses, as our predecessor of happy memory, Leo XIII, in his encyclical *Satis Cognitum* asserts: "The Church is visible because she is a body." It is an error in the matter of divine truth to imagine that the Church is invisible, intangible, something merely spiritual *(pneumaticum)*, as they say, by which many Christian com- munities, though they differ from each other in their profession of faith, are united by a bond that is invisible to the senses.

(Church, hierarchical and charismatic)

848   One must not think, however, that this ordered or 'organic'
3801   structure of the body of the Church contains only hierarchi- cal elements and with them is complete; or as an opposite opinion holds, that it is composed only of those who enjoy charis- matic gifts—though members gifted with miraculous powers will never be lacking in the Church. It is certainly true that those who hold sacred power in this body are its first and chief members. It is through them, in accordance with the plan of the divine Redeemer Himself, that Christ's functions as Teacher, King and Priest endure forever. However, when the Fathers of the Church mention the

ministries of this body, its grades, professions, states, orders and offices, they rightly have in mind not only persons in sacred orders, but also all those who have embraced the evangelical counsels and lead either an active life among men or a hidden life in the cloister, or else contrive to combine the two, according to the institution to which they belong; those also who, though living in the world, actively devote themselves to spiritual or corporal works of mercy; and also those who are joined in chaste wedlock.

(Members of the Mystical Body)

849   Only those are to be accounted as members of the Church in
3802   reality *(reapse)* who have been baptised and profess the true
faith and who have not had the misfortune of withdrawing from the body or for grave faults been cut off by legitimate authority. For, as the apostle says: "For by one Spirit we were all baptised into one body—Jews or Greeks, slaves or free" *(1 Cor. 12.13)*. As, therefore, in the true Christian community there is only one Body, one Spirit, one Lord, one baptism, so there can be only one faith *(cf. Eph. 4.5)*. And so, if a man refuses to listen to the Church, he should be considered, so the Lord commands, as a heathen and publican *(cf. Mt. 18.17)*. It follows that those who are divided in faith and government cannot be living in one body such as this, and cannot be living the life of its one divine Spirit.

(Bishops in the Church)

850   What we have thus far said of the universal Church must be
3804   understood also of the individual Christian communities,
whether Eastern or Latin, which go to make up the one Catholic Church. For they, too, are ruled by Christ Jesus through the authoritative voice of their own respective bishops. Bishops, then, must be considered as the nobler members of the universal Church, for they are linked in an altogether special way to the divine Head of the whole Body and so are rightly called "first among the members of the Lord";[1] what is more, as far as each one's own diocese is concerned, they each and all as true shepherds feed the flocks entrusted to them and rule them in the name of Christ. Yet in exercising this office they are not altogether independent, but are duly subordinate to the authority of the Roman Pontiff; and although

---

1. GREGORY THE GREAT, *Moralium*, XIV, 35, 43.

their jurisdiction is inherent in their office, yet they receive it directly from the same supreme Pontiff. Hence, they should be revered by the faithful as divinely appointed successors of the apostles....

(The Holy Spirit in the Church)

851 If we examine closely this divine principle of life and power
3807 given by Christ, in so far as it constitutes the very source of every gift and created grace, we easily see that it is nothing else than the Holy Spirit, the Paraclete who proceeds from the Father and the Son, and who is called in a special way the "Spirit of Christ" or the "Spirit of the Son" *(cf. Rom. 8.9; 2 Cor. 3.17; Gal. 4.6).* For it was by His breath of grace and truth that the Son of God adorned His own soul in the immaculate womb of the Blessed Virgin; this Spirit delights to dwell in the dear soul of our Redeemer as in His most cherished shrine; this Spirit Christ merited for us on the cross by shedding His own blood; this Spirit He bestowed on the Church for the remission of sins, when He breathed on the apostles *(cf. Jn 20.22);* and while Christ alone received this Spirit without measure *(cf. Jn 3.34),* to the members of the mystical Body He is imparted only according to the measure of the giving of Christ, from Christ's own fulness *(cf. Eph. 1.8; 4.7).* But after Christ's glorification on the cross, His Spirit is communicated to the Church in an abundant outpouring, so that the Church and each of its members may become daily more and more like to our Saviour. It is the Spirit of Christ that has made us adopted sons of God *(cf. Gal. 4.6-7; Rom. 8.14-17)* in order that one day all of us with faces unveiled, reflecting as in a mirror the glory of the Lord, may be transformed into His very image from glory to glory *(cf. 2 Cor. 3.18).*

852 To this Spirit of Christ, too, as an invisible principle, is to be
3808 ascribed the fact that all the parts of the Body are joined one with the other and with their exalted Head; for the whole Spirit of Christ is in the Head, the whole Spirit is in the Body, and the whole Spirit is in each of the members. He is present in the members and assists them in proportion to their various tasks and offices and to the degree of spiritual health which they enjoy. It is He who through His heavenly grace is the principle of every truly supernatural act in all parts of the Body. It is He who, while He is personally present and divinely active in all the members, also acts in the inferior members through the ministry of the higher members. Finally, while with His grace He provides for the constant growth of the Church,

He yet refuses to dwell with sanctifying grace in members that are wholly severed from the Body. This presence and activity of the Spirit of Jesus Christ are tersely and vigorously described by our predecessor of immortal memory Leo XIII in his Encyclical Letter *Divinum Illud* in these words: "Let it suffice to say that, as Christ is the head of the Church, so is the Holy Spirit its soul."[1]

(The juridical Church and the Church of love)

853 We, therefore, deplore and condemn the pernicious error of those who conjure up from their fancies an imaginary Church, a kind of Society that finds its origin and growth in charity, to which they somewhat contemptuously oppose another which they call juridical. To draw such a distinction is utterly futile. For they fail to understand that the divine Redeemer had one single purpose in view when He wanted the community of men of which He was the founder to be established as a society perfect in its own order and possessing all juridical and social elements—the purpose, namely, of perpetuating the salutary work of the redemption here on earth. And it was for the very same purpose that He wanted that society to be enriched with the heavenly gifts of the consoling Spirit. The eternal Father, indeed, wished it to be the "Kingdom of His beloved Son" *(Col. 1.13)*, but it was to be a real kingdom, in which all believers would make the obeisance of their intellect and will, and humbly and obediently model themselves on Him, who for our sake "became obedient unto death" *(Phil. 2.8)*. There can, then, be no real opposition or conflict between the invisible mission of the Holy Spirit and the juridical commission of ruler and teacher received from Christ. Like body and soul in us, they complement and perfect one another, and have their source in our one Redeemer, who not only said, as He breathed on the apostles: "Receive the Holy Spirit" *(Jn 20.22)*, but also clearly commanded: "As the Father has sent me, even so I send you" *(Jn 20.21)*, and again: "He who hears you, hears me" *(Lk. 10.16)*.

LETTER OF THE HOLY OFFICE TO THE ARCHBISHOP OF BOSTON (1949)

An unfortunate controversy in the United States (the Leonard Feeney case) over the meaning of the axiom Extra Ecclesiam nulla salus was the occasion of the following letter, dated August 8, 1949. It is important because, while emphasising once more the ancient doctrine of the necessity

---

1. *ASS* 29 (1896-97) 650.

of the Church for salvation, it clarifies what this must mean for each and every individual. All, in order to be saved, must be in some way related to the Church, but actual membership is not absolutely required. Provided that one is related to the Church in desire or longing, even implicitly, and this desire is informed by supernatural faith and love, he can be saved.

854
3866 The infallible dictum which teaches us that outside the Church there is no salvation, is among the truths that the Church has always taught and will always teach. But this dogma is to be understood as the Church itself understands it. For the Saviour did not leave it to private judgment to explain what is contained in the deposit of faith, but to the doctrinal authority of the Church.

3867 The Church teaches, first of all, that there is question here of a very strict command of Jesus Christ. In unmistakable words He gave His apostles the command to teach all nations to keep whatever He had commanded *(cf. Mt. 28.19f)*. Not least among Christ's commands is the one which orders us to be incorporated by baptism into the mystical Body of Christ, which is the Church, and to be united to Christ and to His vicar, through whom He Himself governs the Church on earth in a visible way. Therefore, no one who knows that the Church has been divinely established by Christ and, nevertheless, refuses to be a subject of the Church or refuses to obey the Roman Pontiff, the vicar of Christ on earth, will be saved.

3868 The Saviour did not make it merely a necessity of precept for all nations to enter the Church. He also established the Church as a means of salvation without which no one can enter the kingdom of heavenly glory.

855
3869 As regards the helps to salvation which are ordered to the last end only by divine decree, not by intrinsic necessity, God, in His infinite mercy, willed that their effects which are necessary to salvation can, in certain circumstances, be obtained when the helps are used only in desire or longing. We see this clearly stated in the Council of Trent about the sacrament of regeneration and about the sacrament of penance *(cf. nn. 1928, 1944)*.

3870 The same, in due proportion, should be said of the Church in so far as it is a general help to salvation. To gain eternal salvation it is not always required that a person be incorporated in reality *(reapse)* as a member of the Church, but it is required that he belong to it at least in desire and longing *(voto et desiderio)*. It is not always necessary that this desire be explicit, as it is with catechumens. When a man is invincibly ignorant, God also accepts an implicit desire, so called because it is contained in the good disposition of soul by which a man wants his will to be conformed to God's will.

856 This is clearly taught by the Sovereign Pontiff Pope Pius XII
3871 in his doctrinal letter on the mystical Body of Christ.... In this letter the Sovereign Pontiff clearly distinguishes between those who are actually *(re)* incorporated into the Church as members and those who belong to the Church only in desire *(voto tantummodo)*. In treating of members who make up the mystical Body on earth, the Sovereign Pontiff says: "Only those are to be accounted as members of the Church in reality *(reapse)* who have been baptised and profess the true faith and who have not had the misfortune of withdrawing from the Body or for grave faults been cut off by legitimate authority" *(cf. n. 849)*. Towards the end of the same encyclical, when with all his heart he invites to union those who do not pertain to the body of the Catholic Church, the Pope mentions those "who are ordained to the mystical Body of the Redeemer by some kind of unconscious desire or longing". He by no means excludes these men from eternal salvation; but, on the other hand, he does point out that they are in a condition "in which they cannot be secure about their salvation... since they lack many great gifts and helps from God which they can enjoy only in the Catholic Church" *(cf. DS 3821)*.

3872 With these prudent words the Pope censures those who exclude from eternal salvation all men who adhere to the Church only with an implicit desire; and he also censures those who falsely maintain that men can be saved equally well in any religion.

857 It must not be imagined that any desire whatsoever of entering the Church is sufficient for a man to be saved. It is necessary that the desire by which a man is related to the Church be informed with perfect charity. And an implicit desire cannot have its effect unless a man has supernatural faith. "Without faith it is impossible to please Him. For whoever would draw near to God must believe that He exists and that He rewards those who seek Him" *(Heb. 11.6)*. And the Council of Trent says: "Faith is the beginning of man's salvation, the foundation and source of all justification, without which it is impossible to please God and to be counted as His sons" *(cf. n. 1935)*.

ENCYCLICAL LETTER *HUMANI GENERIS* (1950)

The following extract from the encyclical Humani Generis *(cf. n. 144i) is an important statement about the relationship between theologians and the official teaching authority in the Church. It brings out the fact that the theologian, as a member of the believing community, cannot pursue his scientific investigations independently of the magisterium, to whose teaching, even when not definitive, due submission is due. Though the Pope stresses the role of the theologian to illuminate and defend the Church's official teaching by recourse to Scripture and Tradition, he also recognises that the theologian must not stop there, but probe ever deeper into the inexhaustible riches of the divine revelation.*

(The ordinary teaching authority)

858
3885
It is not to be supposed that a position advanced in an encyclical does not, *ipso facto,* claim assent. In writing them, it is true, the Popes do not exercise their teaching authority to the full. But such statements come under the day-to-day teaching of the Church, which is covered by the promise: "He that hears you, hears me" *(Lk. 10.16).* For the most part the positions advanced and the duties inculcated by these encyclical letters are already bound up, under some other title, with the general body of Catholic teaching. And when the Roman Pontiffs carefully pronounce on some subject which has hitherto been controverted, it must be clear to everybody that, in the mind and intention of the Pontiffs concerned, this subject can no longer be regarded as a matter of free debate among theologians.

859
3886
It is true, again, that a theologian must constantly have recourse to the fountains of divine revelation. It is for him to show how the doctrine of the teaching authority of the Church is contained in Scripture and in the sacred Tradition, whether explicitly or implicitly. This twofold spring of doctrine divinely made known to us contains, in any case, treasures so varied and so rich that it must ever prove inexhaustible. That is why the study of these hallowed sources, gives the sacred sciences a kind of perpetual youth, while, on the contrary, if the labour of probing deeper and deeper into the sacred deposit is neglected, speculation—as experience shows—grows barren. Theology, however, even what is called positive theology, cannot for that reason be put on a level with the merely historical sciences. For, side by side with these hallowed sources God has given His Church a living teaching authority to make clear for us and to unravel what in the

deposit of faith is contained only in an obscure manner and implicitly. The task of interpreting the deposit authentically was entrusted by our divine Redeemer not to the individual Christian, nor even to the theologians, but only to the Church's teaching authority.

THE SECOND VATICAN GENERAL COUNCIL

The teaching of the Second Vatican Council on the Church is found primarily in the Dogmatic Constitution Lumen Gentium. *This Constitution must, however, be studied along with the other conciliar documents, for it can be said that the Church, in all the manifold aspects of its mystery and structure, of its life and mission, constitutes the central and unifying object of the Council's teaching.*

Since it is impossible, within the limits of this chapter, to do justice to the richness of the entire Council doctrine, some introductory guide-lines to the Constitution on the Church only are given here; a reading list is added which refers to some of the most significant passages of the Constitution.

DOGMATIC CONSTITUTION *LUMEN GENTIUM* (1964)

(The nature and mission of the Church)

(860) *The nature and mission of the Church are first situated in the only context in which they can be adequately understood, that of the mystery of salvation: God's gracious will and purpose, hidden from all eternity, but now revealed and realised in Christ through the Church, to share with men the riches of His own divine life in an ineffable communion of love through Christ in the sanctification of the Holy Spirit (2–4). This is the mystery of the Kingdom of God which Christ proclaimed and manifested in His person and work; it will be fully realised only at the end of time when Christ comes in His glory, but the Church on earth both announces this mystery of God's saving love revealed in Christ, and already experiences it as a present reality (5). This inner nature of the Church is made known to us in the Scriptures by various images, above all by the Pauline doctrine of the Body of Christ (6–7). As both the manifestation and the present realisation of the mystery of our salvation through Christ in the Spirit, it is at once and inseparably a visible hierarchically structured community and the spiritual communion of those who have been incorporated into Christ through the Spririt: "one complex reality composed of a divine and of a human element" (8). This one Church of Christ, "constituted and organised in this world as a society, subsists in the Catholic Church, which is governed by the successor of Peter and the bishops in communion with him, although many elements of sanctification and truth can be found outside of her visible structure" (8). This important affirmation, more nuanced than that of Pope Pius XII in his encyclical Mystici Corporis (cf. n. 847), both re-affirms the traditional teaching about the unique ecclesial status of the Catholic communion, and opens the way for a positive evaluation of the ecclesial reality of the other Christian communions (15) (cf. nn. 909, 913).*

(The pilgrim Church)

(861) *The first chapter concludes with some important reflections on the present status of the Church on earth, situated as she is between the definitive revelation of God's saving will in Christ and the final and perfect restoration of all things at the time of His second coming. She must follow Christ's path toward glory in poverty, humility and suffering; she is upheld by the victorious grace of Christ and hence is essentially indefectible in her faith and structures, but at the same time is always called to renewal and repentance. This pilgrim situation of the Church in the context of her eschatological nature and goal, and the consequences that flow from this for our understanding of her structures, life and mission, are emphasised throughout the Constitution: see mostly 48; but also 9, 12, 13, 17, 39, etc.*

(The people of God)

(862) *Reflection on the pilgrim status of the Church leads naturally to the theme of the Church as the People of God of the new and eternal Covenant, which is developed in chapter II. The mystery of the Church finds its concrete expression and realisation in an historical people (9),the sacramentally structured community of believers in Jesus Christ, which He uses as His instrument for the redemption of mankind (10–11). Throughout this chapter the emphasis is on the common dignity and vocation of all the members of the Church, and it is significant that it has been deliberately placed before the consideration of the Church's hierarchical structure in chapter III. Of special doctrinal importance is the teaching about the* 'sensus fidelium' *and the specifically charismatic element as a perduring reality in the life of the Church (12).*

Chapter II, 13–17, forms a whole. In the context of the Church's true Catholicity, which is both an essential property and a dynamic exigency of the Church's life (13), the Constitution exposes the different ways by which men belong or are related to the Catholic unity of the people of God: Catholics (14), other Christians (15), non-Christians (16); and this exposition leads naturally to the essentially missionary nature of the Church (17). In its teaching (14–16), the Constitution avoids the terminology of membership, because of the continuing theological debate about its precise meaning. While not conflicting with the teaching of Pope Pius XII in Mystici Corporis *(cf. n. 849), the Council's doctrine is more descriptive and flexible and takes more adequately into account the ecclesial status of non-Catholic Christians. Number 15 should be studied in the context of the Decree* Unitatis Redintegratio *on Ecumenism (cf. n. 909i); number 16 in that of the Declaration* Nostra Aetate *on non-Christian religions (cf. n. 1019i); number 17 in that of the Decree* Ad Gentes *on the Church's missionary activity (cf. n. 1136i).*

(The hierarchical structure of the Church)

(863) *The teaching of chapter III on the hierarchical structure of the Church and in particular the episcopate both complements and qualifies the teaching of Vatican I on the primatial office of the bishop of Rome (cf. nn. 818ff). The teachings on the sacramentality of the episcopate (21), and on the nature, meaning and implications of the collegiality of the* bishops (22–23) are doctrinally the most important of this chapter, and perhaps of the entire Constitution. This teaching may be briefly summarised. The bishops, who succeed to the apostles as shepherds of the flock (19–20), form a college or stable group (22), which, united with its head, is also the subject of full and supreme authority over the universal Church (23). As members of the episcopal college, the bishops must live in communion with one another, be solicitous for the unity in faith and love of the entire Church (23), and promote the preaching of the Gospel, a task which pertains to all of them in common (23). One is constituted a member of the college by the sacramental consecration and hierarchical communion with the head and the other members of the college (22). Episcopal consecration confers the fulness of the sacrament of Order. it confers, together with the function of sanctifying, the function also of teaching and governing, though these latter of their nature can only be exercised in hierarchical communion with the head and other members of the college (21). This teaching should be read in conjunction with the Nota explicativa, which, though not an integral part of the Constitution, is an authoritative declaration of its meaning and import.

Chapter III contains a number of other points that are doctrinally important for understanding the nature and exercise of the episcopal office in the Church. A few are noted here: 1) all ecclesiastical authority is seen as essentially a service or diakonia within the context of the Spirit-filled community and ordained toward the building up of the Body in truth and love (18, 24, 27); 2) number 27 further clarifies the teaching of Vatican I (cf. n. 827) on the ordinary pastoral function of each bishop in his own diocese, and its relationship with the ordinary and universal authority of the Pope; 3) number 25 on the magisterial authority of the hierarchy explains more adequately the 'ex sese, non autem ex consensu Ecclesiae' of Vatican I (cf. n. 839); cf. also its nuanced statement on the object of the infallible magisterium.

This chapter also contains important statements on the collegial nature of the Church herself, which, though one and universal, is made present and realised in each fully constituted local community. Hence the Church is seen as a communion of local Churches united in the bonds of faith, love and mutual service (cf. especially 26 and 23; cf. also 13).

(The laity)

(864) *Chapter IV on the laity summarises recent developments in the theology of the laity. In this descriptive definition of the laity, special emphasis is placed on their secular character (31). While making special reference to the laity as distinguished from the hierarchy, this chapter further develops the teaching of chapter II on the common dignity of all the members of the Church (32): all share in her mission (33), and in her priestly (34), prophetic (35) and kingly (36) nature and function, each according to his specific state in the Church and his own gifts. Number 37 states the general principle that should govern the relationship between the laity and the hierarchy.*

(Universal call to holiness and religious life; eschatological nature of the Church)

(865) *Chapter V and VI on the universal call to holiness and the religious life respectively express, as it were, the end of all the Church's activity, viz., the building up of the Body of Christ in holiness. With regard to chapter VII, reference has already been made to the important number 48 on the eschatological character of the pilgrim Church (cf. n. 2311). As is clear from the Constitution as a whole, this eschatological perspective is vital for our understanding of the entire structure and life of the Church. The rest of chapter VII contains important teaching on the communion of the Church on earth with the glorified Church of heaven, and on the meaning and veneration of the saints (cf. nn. 2312–2314; 1258i). For chapter VIII on the Blessed Virgin Mary in the mystery of Christ and the Church, cf. n. 716i.*

READING LIST OF IMPORTANT TEXTS

(866) 1. *(The sacramentality of the Church)*
(867) 2–4. *(The Church in the divine plan of salvation)*
(868) 5. *(The Church and the Kingdom of God)*
(869) 8. *(The Church : one complex reality, divine and human; the Church subsists in the Catholic Church; the Church in constant need of reform)*
(870) 12. *(The prophetic office of the faithful; sense of faith and charisms)*
(871) 14. *(The necessity of the Church)*
(872) 15. *(Ties between the Church and other Christians)*
(873) 16. *(The non-Christians and the people of God)*
(874) 21. *(The episcopate as sacrament)*
(875) 22. *(The college of bishops and its head)*
(876) 23. *(Relations of bishops in the çollege; the Church as communion of Churches)*
(877) 25. *(The magisterium of the Church)*
(878) 26. *(The function of bishops as sanctifiers and the local Churches)*
(879) 27. *(The pastoral function of bishops)*
(880) 31. *(The meaning of the laity)*
(881) 39. *(The indefectible holiness of the Church)*
(882) 48. *(The eschatological nature of the Church)*

PAUL VI

DECLARATION *MYSTERIUM ECCLESIAE* OF THE S. CONGREGATION FOR THE DOCTRINE OF THE FAITH
(11 May 1973)

The mystery of the Church has been the object of much theological rethinking in recent years. Among the attempts made at presenting the

mystery in more understandable language, not all have been equally suc-
cessful. This Declaration issued by the S. Congregation for the Doctrine of
the Faith, "intends to gather together and explain a number of truths
concerning the mystery of the Church which at the present time are being
either denied or endangered". It is mostly concerned with the question of
infallibility, intended by God in order that "what He has revealed for the
salvation of all nations would abide perpetually in its full integrity" (DV 7).
The Declaration first speaks of the charism of "shared infallibility" granted
by God to the whole Church: "The Body of the faithful as a whole...cannot
err in matters of belief." However, "the Holy Spirit enlightens and assists the
People of God inasmuch as it is the Body of Christ united in a hierarchical
community." Thus there must be recognized a special charism of infallibility
of the Church's teaching authority, for "by divine institution it is the exclu-
sive task of the pastors, the successors of Peter and the other apostles, to
teach the faithful authentically, that is with the authority of Christ shared in
different ways." The infallibility of the Magisterium has its source in Christ.
Explaining its object, the Document repeats the doctrine of the First and
Second Vatican Councils: it "extends not only to the deposit of faith but also
to those matters without which that deposit cannot be rightly preserved and
expounded"; but, while its application to the deposit of faith itself is a matter
of revealed truth, the extension to its secondary object merely belongs to
"Catholic doctrine" (cf. LG 25). Thus, "the matter of Catholic faith" is
limited to things "to be believed as having been divinely revealed" (cf. n.
121). The Declaration proceeds to reject three ways in which the Church's
gift of infallibility would be unduly diminished. The text is found in AAS 65
(1973) 396–408.

(The Church's gift of infallibility is not to be diminished)

883   From what has been said about the extent of the conditions
governing the infallibility of the People of God and of the
Church's Magisterium, it follows that the faithful are in no way
permitted to see in the Church merely a fundamental permanence in
truth which, as some assert, could be reconciled with errors contained here and there in the propositions that the Church's Magisterium teaches to be held irrevocably, as also in the unhesitating assent
of the People of God concerning matters of faith and morals.

It is of course true that through the faith that leads to salvation
men are converted to God, who reveals Himself in His Son Jesus
Christ; but it would be wrong to deduce from this that the Church's
dogmas can be belittled or even denied. Indeed, the conversion to
God which we should undergo through faith is a form of obedience
(cf. Rom. 16.26), which should correspond to the nature of divine
Revelation and its demands. Now this Revelation, in the whole plan
of salvation, reveals the mystery of God who sent His Son into the

world *(cf. 1 Jn 4. 14)* and teaches its application to Christian conduct. Moreover it demands that, in full obedience of the intellect and will to God who reveals, we accept the proclamation of the good news of salvation as it is infallibly taught by the pastors of the Church. The faithful, therefore, through faith are converted as they should to God, who reveals Himself in Christ, when they adhere to Him in the integral doctrine of the Catholic faith.

It is true that there exists an order and as it were a hierarchy of the Church's dogmas, as a result of their varying relationship to the foundation of the faith *(cf. n. 912)*. This hierarchy means that some dogmas are founded on other dogmas which are the principal ones, and are illuminated by these latter. But all dogmas, since they are revealed, must be believed with the same divine faith.

APOSTOLIC EXHORTATION *EVANGELII NUNTIANDI* (1975)

As a result of the Synod of bishops on Evangelisation in 1974, on the 10th anniversary of the conclusion of the Council, Paul VI published this Apostolic Exhortation which is an important document on the Church's mission (cf. Chapter XI). Two paragraphs are of special significance for the understanding of the mystery of the Church: the Pope explains the inseparable link between Christ and the Church, and the relation of the particular Church to the universal Church. The text is found in AAS 68(1976) 5ff.

(The Church is inseparable from Christ)

884 16. There is a profound link between Christ, the Church and evangelisation. In this era of the Church, the mandate to evangelise is entrusted to her. It is not right to carry out this mandate without her, much less against her. It is certainly fitting to recall this fact at the present moment when, not without sorrow, we can hear people—whom we wish to believe are well intentioned, but who are certainly misguided from the right path—continually claiming that they want to love Christ but not the Church. The absurdity of this dichotomy is clearly evident from this phrase of the Gospel: "He who rejects you rejects me" *(Lk. 10.16)*. And how can we wish to love Christ without loving the Church, if the finest witness to Christ is that of Saint Paul: "Christ loved the Church and gave Himself up for her" *(Eph. 5.25)?*

(The universal and the particular Church)

885 62. The universal Church is in reality incarnate in the particular Churches that are made of this or that part of humanity, use such or such a language, are heirs of a cultural patrimony, of a vision of the world, of an historical past, of a particular human substratum, and remain closely linked to it. Receptivity to the wealth of the particular Church corresponds to a special sensitivity of modern man.

Let us, however, be very careful not to conceive of the universal Church as the sum or, if one can say so, the more or less heterogeneous federation of essentially different particular Churches. In the mind of the Lord the Church is universal by vocation and mission, but when she puts down her roots in a variety of cultural, social and human terrains, she takes on different external expressions and appearances in each part of the world.

Thus each particular Church that would voluntarily cut itself off from the universal Church would lose its relationship to God's plan and would be empoverished in its ecclesial dimension. But at the same time a Church which is spread all over the world would become an abstraction if she did not take body and life precisely through the particular Churches. Only continuous attention to these two poles of the Church will enable us to perceive the richness of this relationship between the universal Church and the particular Churches.

JOHN PAUL II

ENCYCLICAL LETTER *REDEMPTOR HOMINIS* (1979)

In his first encyclical John Paul II sees his ministry for the Church linked with the incarnation in which God's concern and love for man find their full expression. God's saving presence to man must be embodied in His Church. Thus the Pope sees the very essence of the Church in her service to man to help him realise and fulfil his full human destiny in Christ. This vision contains the guidelines for his pontificate. The text is found in AAS 71(1979) 257ff.

(The Church is for men)

886 18. If Christ united Himself with each man *(cf. n. 668)*, the Church lives more profoundly her own nature and mission by penetrating into the depth of this mystery and into its rich universal meaning. It was not without reason that the Apostle spoke about Christ's Body, the Church. If this Mystical Body of Christ is God's people,... this means that each man who belongs to it is filled with that breath of life that comes from Christ. This means that the Church herself, who is a body, an organism, a social unit, when she turns to man with his real problems, his hopes and sufferings, his achievements and falls, receives the same divine influances, the light and strength of the Spirit that comes from the crucified and risen Christ. It is for this very reason that she lives her life. The Church has no other life but that which is given her by her Spouse and Lord. Indeed, precisely because Christ united her to Himself in the mystery of Redemption, the Church must be firmly united with each man.

CHAPTER IX

THE CHURCH AND THE CHURCHES

In view of the perfect Kingdom of the future, the Church is sent into the world to be the efficacious sign and instrument of the reconciling grace of Christ, drawing men into a unity of faith, hope and love, across all the barriers of sin and human division. It is, therefore, and is called to be the sacrament of unity (cf. LG 1), a unity that is at once visible and invisible, human and divine. Yet from the very beginning of the life and mission of the Church there were rifts, and in the course of the centuries large bodies of Christians were separated from one another, and continue to this day to live in isolation and opposition. This is the scandal of Christian disunity, and the problem and challenge of ecumensim, which seeks the restoration of unity among Christians in one visible communion, in the one Church of Christ.

In the first millenium of the Church's history movements toward disunity were blunted and checked by the great Councils of the times, especially the first four. Arianism, Donatism, Novatiansim, Priscillianism, Montanism and Nestorianism—all movements that could have torn the Church apart—were rejected by the Councils and gradually disappeared, not without the help of the secular power. Yet the efforts to preserve the unity of the Church were not completely successful: the Monophysite Churches, which rejected the Council of Chalcedon (431), still exist today, mainly in Egypt and Ethiopia.

The first great and lasting division between Christians was that between the Churches of the East and the Church of the West. The gradual estrangement between West and East took a decisive turning point in 1054 with the severing of relations between the Patriarch of Constantinople and the Pope. Even then the break was not complete, and two attempts were made on the conciliar level to heal the wounds of disunity. The first was that of the Council of Lyons (1274), when the emperor Michael Palaeologus accepted the Roman terms of reunion. Politically motivated, and manifesting little understanding of the theological and ecclesial position of the East, the settlement was doomed to failure from the beginning. The second was that of the Council of Florence (1439-1445), in which

East and West took part as equal partners, and real agreement was reached in the disputed question of the Filioque. However, agreement was only apparent with regard to the understanding of the primacy of the Pope, especially in its relationship to the rights and privileges of the patriarchs of the East. Officially rejected in 1483, the union actually came to an end as early as 1453 when Constantinople was captured by the Turks. Both before and after these attempts to reunite East and West, individual Eastern Churches or sections of these Churches again entered into communion with Rome, e.g., the Maronites already in the 13th century, the Byzantine Ukranians at the union of Brest-Litovsk in 1595, the Malankara Catholics in India in the 20th century. Despite a considerable degree of latinisation, these "Uniate Churches" have preserved their own spirituality, liturgy, and, to a lesser extent, their own ecclesiastical structures within the Catholic communion.

As a result of the upheaval of the Protestant Reformation in the 16th century, the Church in the West was split into numerous Churches and Ecclesial Communities. In the early part of the 16th century, before positions hardened, attempts were made to stem the tide of division. But the leaders of the Catholic Church did not at first realise the seriousness of the situation; the Protestants too were unwilling to compromise and, in drawing up their own confessional statements, they settled down into their own separate communities. Desire for reconciliation gave way to polemics and mutual antagonism, and from the 17th century to almost the present day little serious effort was made to bring about union with the Protestants. In fact the ecclesiology of the counter-Reformation with its understanding of the Church as one visible hierarchical society left little or no room for dialogue with the Protestant communities as such. It is against the historical background and in relation to the ecclesiology of the times that the documents issued by the Magisterium in the 19th century and at the beginning of the 20th century must be read and understood.

The renewed ecclesiology which found its official expression in the Second Vatican Council offers possibilities to approach the ecumenical problems in a new light. Its vision is no longer limited to the firmly established Catholic Church to which all must return; it starts from the divine plan for the human race and the common Christian calling. It is God's will that the Christian life be lived in a visible community which is one and comprehensive; a community which prefigures the final communion to which all nations are called at the end of time. This mystery of unity is sacramentally present in the Catholic Church, but is also expressed, in various degrees, in other Christian communities; they too contain ecclesial elements by virtue of which they may be called Churches. Vatican II no longer views these communities in their deficiencies only; it sees the positive values of their life and traditions. Thus the solution to the problem of Christian unity is no longer sought by merely inviting other Christians to join the Catholic Church, but by integrating into the one Church willed by Christ whatever Christian values are found also in non-Catholic Christian communities. The aim must be the fulness of the Christian life, comprising all traditions, for "whatever is truly Christian is never opposed to the genuine values of the faith; indeed it can always help to a better realisation of the mystery of Christ and the Church" (UR 4).

All the documents given here belong to the 19th and 20th centuries; they are a rapid survey of the evolution in the attitude of the Catholic Church towards the ecumenical movement characteristic of modern times. Earlier pertinent documents are found in other chapters, especially in the chapter on the Church. Besides, the doctrinal differences that separate Christians cover almost the entire spectrum of Christian doctrine; these are dealt with directly under their specific headings.

*   *   *

The main points of doctrine covered in this chapter may be grouped under the following headings:

The Church is the sacrament of unity: (866).

Its mystery subsists in the Catholic Church in which is found the fulness of the means of salvation: (869), 909;

but it is also present, though imperfectly and in various degrees, in Churches which do not have full communion with Rome: 39/15, (872), 909.

In particular, the Eastern Churches separated from Rome share with it the same faith and sacramental life: 904, 914.

The Church's reform is an essential requirement for Church unity: 910, 911.

The status and privileges of the Eastern patriarchates must be respected: 809, 906.

The ancient traditions and customs of these Churches must also be preserved: 914, 1206, 1207, 1235-1236.

All Christians must strive after Christian unity: 39/15, 902, 903, 905, 907, 908, 914.

The hierarchy of truths must be kept in mind: 913.

Principles for common worship: 912.

Principles for admission of other Christians to the Eucharist: 915.

Dialogue with the Orthodox Churches: 916-921.

Dialogue with the Evangelical Churches: 922-927.

PIUS IX

LETTER *IAM VOS OMNES* TO PROTESTANTS AND OTHER
NON-CATHOLICS (1868)

*After announcing to them his intention to convoke a general Council,
the Pope invites the dissidents to examine whether or not they are walking
in the way of salvation, and to seize upon the occasion of the Council to
return to the unity of the Catholic Church.*

(Dissident religious societies do not constitute the true Church)

901   Now anyone who wishes to examine with care and to medi-
2998   tate on the condition of the different religious societies
          divided among themselves and separated from the Catholic
Church, who, since the time of our Lord Jesus Christ and His
apostles has always exercised by her legitimate pastors and still
exercises today the divine power which was given to her by the same
Lord, will easily be convinced that no one of these societies nor all of
them together in any way constitute or are that one Catholic Church
which our Lord founded and established and which He willed to
create. Nor is it possible, either, to say that these societies are either
a member or a part of this same Church, since they are visibly
separated from Catholic unity....

(Exhortation to return to the Church)

902   Let all those, therefore, who do not possess the unity and
2999   truth of the Catholic Church seize upon this occasion of the
          Council, where the Catholic Church to which their ancestors
belonged is going to give again a striking proof of her unity and her
invincible life-force, to strive conformably to the needs of their hearts
to disengage themselves from a state where they cannot be assured
of their own salvation. And let them not cease to offer the most
fervent prayers to the God of mercies so that He will break down the
wall of division, dissipate the clouds of error, and bring them back to
holy Mother Church, in the bosom of which their fathers found the
saving food of life, in which alone is kept and tansmitted in its entirety
the doctrine of Jesus Christ, and where alone are dispensed the
mysteries of heavenly grace....

ENCYCLICAL LETTER *QUARTUS SUPRA* TO THE ARMENIANS
(1873)

This Encyclical Letter was addressed by Pope Pius IX to the Armenians in the context of a recent schism among them. The Pope strongly urges the indispensable need of recognition of and communion with the apostolic See of Rome in order for a local Church to be truly part of the Church of Christ. The text is found in The Church, Papal Teachings, *pp. 235-236.*

903   If, therefore, the sovereign Pontiff is called a stranger by any one of the Churches, that Church will be, in consequence, a stranger to the apostolic See, that is, to the Catholic Church which is one, and which alone was founded on Peter by the Lord's word. Whoever separates the Church from this foundation no longer preserves the divine and Catholic Church, but is striving to make a human church. Now a church like that, united solely by human bonds, bonds that are called national, would not be united by the bond of priests firmly attached to the Chair of Peter; it would not be made firm by the solidity of that same Chair, and would not belong to the universal and perfect unity of the Catholic Church.

LEO XIII

ENCYCLICAL LETTER *PRAECLARA GRATULATIONIS* (1894)

Written on the occasion of the fiftieth anniversary of his episcopal consecration, this letter by Pope Leo XIII expresses a sincere and ardent desire for Christian unity. In its appeal to first the Eastern Churches, and then the Protestant 'nations', it brings out clearly the consistent recognition by the Roman Pontiffs of the ecclesial status of the Eastern Churches separated from Rome. They are always referred to as 'Churches'; the appeal made to them is for the re-establishment of full communion with the See of Rome. The often repeated assurance is given that in any reunion with Rome, the special status and privileges of the Patriarchates (cf. n. 809), as well as the ancient traditions and customs of these Churches (cf. n. 1206) will be fully respected and safeguarded. Though in practice the latinisation of the uniate Churches did occur—as was, perhaps, inevitable in the ecclesial situation of the time—the affirmation of the principle of legitimate diversity was in itself significant. It is all the more important today in the context of a broader ecclesiology. The text is found in Rome and Reunion: A Collection of Papal Pronouncements, *pp. 5-8.*

904   First of all, then, we cast an affectionate look upon the East. from where in the beginning came forth salvation to the whole world. Yes, and the yearning desire of our heart bids us to conceive the hope that the day is not far distant when the Eastern Churches, so illustrious in their ancient faith and glorious past, will return to the fold they have abandoned. We hope it, all the more, because that which divides them from us is not so great: nay, with few exceptions, we agree so entirely on other topics that, in defence of the Catholic faith, we often have recourse to arguments and testimonies borrowed from the teaching, the rites, and customs of the East....

905 Weigh carefully in your minds and before God the nature of our request. It is not for any human motive, but impelled by divine charity and a desire for the salvation of all, that we urge your reconciliation and union with the Church of Rome; and we mean a perfect and complete union, such as could not subsist in any way if nothing else were brought about but a certain degree of agreement in the tenets of belief and an exchange of fraternal love. The true union between Christians, and that which Jesus Christ, the Author of the Church, instituted and desired, consists in oneness of faith and of government.

906 Nor is there any reason for you to fear that we or any of our successors will ever diminish your rights, the privileges of the patriarchs, or the established rite of any of your Churches. It has been and always will be the intent and discipline of the apostolic See, to allow a just and good place to the primitive traditions and special customs of every nation. Indeed, if you return to communion with us, you will see how much, by God's bounty, the glory and dignity of your Churches will be increased....

PIUS XI

ENCYCLICAL LETTER *MORTALIUM ANIMOS* (1928)

This letter, which was occasioned by the Faith and Order Conference held at Lausanne in 1927, took a very negative attitude towards the modern ecumenical movement. The Pope condemned wholesale the various conferences, congresses and assemblies of the time, which sought to bring about unity among Christians. The reason for this stern attitude was the persuasion that the movement among "pan-Christians", as he called them, was based on a false religious indifferentism which "holds any religion whatever to be more or less good and praise-worthly, although not all in the same way, because they all reveal and explain the significance of the native, inborn instinct which turns us towards God and makes us acknowledge His sovereignty". While forbidding Catholics to have anything to do with this movement, the Pope laid down the principles which should guide Catholics at all times. There can be no true religion other than that revealed by God. That revelation, which reached its perfection in Jesus Christ, has been entrusted by Him to the one and only Church which He founded on Peter. This Church, which is a perfect society, remains always identical to itself and visibly one. It is the guardian of the immutable deposit of revelation, and, within it, it belongs to the Roman Pontiff and the Bishops in communion with

him to teach authoritatively and infallibly the deposit of faith. This docu-
ment, which must be read in the context of the narrow ecclesiology of its
time, concludes as follows. The text of the encyclical is found in AAS 20
(1928) 13ff.

907   It is clear, therefore, Venerable Brothers, why this apostolic
See has never permitted its subjects to take part in the congresses of non-Catholics. The union of Christians cannot be fostered
otherwise than by promoting the return of the dissidents to the one
true Church of Christ, which in the past they so unfortunately
abandoned; return, we say, to the one true Church of Christ which is
plainly visible to all and which by the will of her Founder forever
remains what He Himself destined her to be for the common salvation of men. For the mystical Spouse of Christ has never been
contaminated in the course of centuries, nor will she ever be contaminated.... No one is in the Church of Christ, and no one remains in it,
unless he acknowledges and accepts with obedience the authority
and power of Peter and his legitimate successors.... Therefore, to
this apostolic See, founded in the City which Peter and Paul, the
Princes of the apostles, consecrated with their blood, to this See
which is the 'root and matrix of the Catholic Church', may our
dissident sons return; let them do so, not with the thought and hope
that 'the Church of the living God, the pillar and ground of the truth',
will sacrifice the integrity of the faith, but, on the contrary, with the
intention of submitting to her authority and government....

PIUS XII

INSTRUCTION *ECCLESIA CATHOLICA* OF THE HOLY OFFICE
(1949)

This instruction is important because it marks a turning point in the
official approach of the Catholic Church to the modern ecumenical move-
ment. Within clearly defined limits, it encourages the ecumenical dialogue
between Catholics and other Christians, though stopping short of any
official Catholic participation in ecumenical conferences. More signifi-
cantly, it takes a cautiously positive approach toward the ecumenical
movement, and in this contrasts sharply with Pius XI's encyclical Mortalium
animos. *Due to more recent developments in doctrine and in attitudes, the*
practical directives of the instruction have since been superseded. The text
is found in Documents on Christian Unity, *4th series (1948-1957), p. 22.*

908   The Catholic Church takes no part in 'Ecumenical' conferences or meetings. But, as may be seen from many papal
documents, she has never ceased, nor ever will, from following with

deepest interest and furthering with fervent prayer every attempt to attain that end which Christ our Lord had so much at heart, namely, that all who believe in Him "may become perfectly one" *(Jn 17.23)....* The present time has witnessed in different parts of the world a growing desire amongst many persons outside the Church for the reunion of all who believe in Christ. This may be attributed, under the inspiration of the Holy Spirit, to external factors and the changing attitude of men's minds, but above all to the united prayers of the faithful. To all children of the true Church this is a cause for holy joy in the Lord; it urges them to extend a helping hand to all those sincerely seeking after the truth by praying fervently that God may enlighten them and give them strength....

THE SECOND VATICAN GENERAL COUNCIL

It was Pope John XXIII's explicit intention that the Second Vatican Council should have an ecumenical orientation. The creation of the Secretariat for Promoting Christian Unity in 1960 and the presence at the Council of observers from the other Churches helped to ensure this. The Council made its own the new perspectives in Catholic ecclesiology which had developed in the years preceding it, and whose renewed outlook also commanded new attitudes.

Symptomatic of the ecumenical approach of the Council is the fact that references to ecumenism, in its theory and practice, pervade the various conciliar documents. The theological foundation for the new Catholic ecumenism is explained in the Dogmatic Constitution Lumen Gentium *(15): this fundamental text enumerates the ties that bind the Church in various ways to the members of other Churches or ecclesial communities (cf. n. 872). The Decree* Ad Gentes *on the Church's missionary activity recommends the right ecummenical orientation in newly founded Churches; it does not merely advocate practical collaboration between Christian communities, but also calls for a common witness of faith as far as the already existing unity in faith permits (15; cf. 12, 41). Ecumenical formation and orientation is expected to be given in seminaries (OT 16), especially in mission countries (AG 16), and among religious (PC 2). Special attention is given by the Council to the Oriental Churches. The Decree* Orientalium Ecclesiarum, *after paying due respect to the rich patrimony of the Oriental tradition and to the Oriental patriarchates, explains at length the Church's present attitude towards the Eastern Churches separated from it (24-30).*

DECREE *UNITATIS REDINTEGRATIO* (1964)

Passing references to ecumenism could not, however, suffice. It was necessary that a special Decree be devoted to ecumenism, in which the fundamental principles and basic attitudes would be explicitly stated. The Decree Unitatis Redintegratio *was promulgated in November 1964 after prolonged debate. The openness of this decree and its positive evaluation of* the other Christian Churches have no real precedent in official Church teaching. It proposes a clear and coherent theological foundation for the full and unequivocal participation of the·Catholic Church in the modern ecumenical movement.

The document is divided into an Introduction and three Chapters. The introduction states the purpose of the decree, namely, to set before all Catholics the ways and means by which they can respond to the grace and divine call so obviously present in the concerted efforts of Christians everywhere to overcome the scandal of Christian disunity.

Chapter I is doctrinally the most important, for it lays down the Catholic principles of ecumenism. It exposes the mystery of the Church's unity as that of a dynamic communion in faith and sacramental life, at once visible and invisible, and it affirms that this communion is realised, acording to the will of Christ, in the Catholic Church governed by the Pope and the bishops in communion with him. The ecclesial reality and the salvific efficaciousness of the other Christian Communities, however, are also affirmed. They are said to be in real, though imperfect, communion with the Catholic Church, and the establishment of full and perfect communion which is hoped for is seen as enriching and perfecting not only the other Churches, but also the Catholic Church itself.

Chapter II is concerned with the practice of ecumenism. Of special significance is the affirmation of the need for inner renewal and reform in the Church and for a conversion of heart, without which the Church cannot contribute to Church unity. Also of ecumenical importance is the statement regarding the manner of exposing the faith: although the doctrine of the Church should be clearly presented in its entirety, it must be remembered that there is a "hierarchy" of truths, since not all the truths of Catholic doctrine are equally connected with the fundamental Christian faith (n. 912).

Chapter III turns the attention to a concrete exposition of the Churches and Ecclesial Communities separated from the See of Rome. The special position of the Eastern Churches is clearly underlined: their origin; their situation as fully constituted Churches; their rich heritage of spirituality and liturgy, of law and theology, which belong to the full catholic and apostolic character of the Church, and which must be fully respected in any reunion. The Decree is more guarded in its exposition of the ecclesial reality, faith, in and structures of the separated Churches and Ecclesial Communities in the West, which have arisen as a result of the Reformation in the 16th century. Yet here also the exposition is positive. Emphasis is placed upon their essential faith in Christ and the Trinity, their zeal for and devotion to the word of God in Scripture, their sacramental life founded on Baptism, and the richness of their Christian life.

The Decree must be read and studied in its entirety, together with the Council's Dogmatic Constitution on the Church. Here only those passages are quoted which are of special doctrinal importance.

(The ecclesial reality of the other Christian Churches and their relationship to the Catholic Church)

909   3. Moreover, from among the elements and endowments which together go to build up and give life to the Church itself, some and indeed very many and significant ones can exist outside the visible boundaries of the Catholic Church: the written word of God, the life of grace, faith, hope and charity with the other interior gifts of the Holy Spirit, and visible elements too. All of these, which come from Christ and lead back to Christ, belong by right to the one Church of Christ.

The brethren divided from us also use many liturgical actions of the Christian religion. These most certainly can truly engender a life of grace in ways that vary according to the condition of each Church or Community; they must be regarded as capable of giving access to the community of salvation.

It follows that the separated Churches and Communities as such, though we believe them to be deficient in some respects, are by no means deprived of significance and importance in the mystery of salvation. For the Spirit does not decline to use them as means of salvation—means which derive their efficacy from the very fulness of grace and truth entrusted to the Catholic Church.

Nevertheless, our separated brethren, whether considered as individuals or as Communities and Churches, are not blessed with that unity which Jesus Christ wished to bestow on all those who through Him were born again into one body and with Him quickened to newness of life—that unity which the Holy Scriptures and the ancient Tradition of the Church proclaim. For it is only through Christ's Catholic Church, which is the all-embracing means of salvation, that the fulness of the means of salvation can be enjoyed. We believe that our Lord entrusted all the treasures of the new Covenant to the apostolic college alone, of which Peter is the head, in order to build up the one Body of Christ on earth into which all should be fully incorporated who already belong in any way to the people of God....

(Renewal of the Church)

910   6. Since every renewal of the Church essentially consists in a greater fidelity to her vocation, this unquestionably is also the basis of the movement towards unity. The pilgrim Church is summoned by Christ to continual reformation—of which, as an institution made up of men here on earth, she stands ever in need. If then, in various times and circumstances, there have been deficiencies in moral conduct or in Church discipline, or even in the formulation of Church teaching—to be clearly distinguished from the deposit of faith itself—these should be set right at the opportune moment.

(Conversion of heart)

911   7. There can be no ecumenism worthy of the name without a
change of heart. For it is from renewal of our minds, from
self-denial and generous love that desires of unity arise and come to
maturity.... The words of St John hold good also about faults against
unity: "If we say we have not sinned, we make Him a liar, and His
word is not in us" *(1 Jn 1.10).* So we humbly beg pardon of God and of
our separated brethren, just as we forgive them that trespass against
us.

(Communicatio in sacris)

912   8. Worship in common may not be considered as a means to
be used indiscriminately for the restoration of Christian unity.
There are two main principles governing the practice of such common worship: first the bearing witness to the unity of the Church,
and second, the sharing in the means of grace. Witness to the unity of
the Church generally forbids common worship; the grace to be
obtained from it sometimes commends it.

(The manner of exposing the faith)

913   11. In ecumenical dialogue, when Catholic theologians, while
standing fast by the teaching of the Church, join with separated brethren in common study of the divine mysteries, they should
pursue the work with love for the truth, with charity and with
humility. When comparing doctrines with one another, they should
remember that among the truths of Catholic doctrine there exists a
'hierarchy', since not all these truths are equally connected with the
fundamental Christian faith. Thus, by this kind of 'fraternal rivalry' all
will be spurred on to a deeper knowledge and a clearer expression of
the unfathomable riches of Christ.

(Special position of the Eastern Churches)

914   14. For many centuries the Church of the East and that of the
West each followed its own ways, though linked in a brotherly
union of faith and sacramental life; the Roman See by common
consent acted as guide when disagreements arose between them
over matters of faith or discipline. Among other matters of moment,
it is a pleasure for this Council to remind everyone that there exist in
the East many particular or local Churches, among which the patriarchal Churches hold first place, many of which trace their origins

back to the apostles themselves. Hence a matter of primary concern and care among the Easterns has been, and still is, to preserve the bonds of common faith and charity which ought to exist between local Churches as between sisters.

It must not be forgotten that from the beginning the Churches of the East have had a treasury from which the Western Church has drawn extensively—in liturgical practice, spiritual tradition and law. Nor must we undervalue the fact that it was the ecumenical Councils held in the East that defined the basic dogmas of the Christian faith, on the Trinity and the Word of God who took flesh of the Virgin Mary. To preserve this faith these Churches have suffered and still suffer much.

However, the inheritance handed down by the apostles was received with differences of form and manner, so that from the earliest times of the Church it was explained variously in different places, owing to diversities of genius and conditions of life. All this, besides external causes, and combined with a lack of charity and mutual understanding, prepared the way for divisions.

For this reason the Council urges all, but especially those who intend to devote themselves to the restoration of the desired full communion between the Churches of the East and the Catholic Church, to give due consideration to this special feature of the origin and growth of the Eastern Churches, and to the character of the relations which obtained between them and the Roman See before separation. A right appreciation of these elements will greatly contribute to the dialogue in view.

POST-CONCILIAR DOCUMENTS ON ECUMENISM

The Vatican II Council Decree on Ecumenism laid down the goal and principles of ecumenism and gave general norms for its practice. These new attitudes and the practical ways of proceeding had to be spelled out in subsequent documents. As these are easily accessible in A. FLANNERY (ed.), Vatican Council II, The Conciliar and Post-Conciliar Documents, *Dominican Publications, Dublin 1975, only their nature is indicated here.*

There are first the joint declarations of the Pope with heads of other ecclesial communities:

—The common Declaration of Paul VI and Patriarch Athenagoras I at the conclusion of the Council, 7 December, 1965, withdrawing the mutual excommunication of the Churches of Rome and Constantinople in a spirit of forgiveness, and pledging mutual trust and dialogue towards complete communion.

—*The Joint Declaration of Paul VI and Archbishop Ramsey of Canterbury on cooperation and dialogue (22 March 1966).*

—*The Joint Declaration of Paul VI and Vasken I, Catholicos, Supreme Patriarch of the Armenians pledging to work for more profound unity on the basis of reciprocal acknowledgment of the common Christian faith and sacramental life (12 May 1970).*

— *The Joint Declaration of Paul VI and Archbishop Coggan of Canterbury, encouraging continued dialogue (29 April 1977). Text in AAS 69 (1977) 286-289.*

—*The Joint Declaration of John Paul II and Patriarch Dimitrios I pledging to work towards full communion (30 November 1979). Text in AAS 71 (1979) 1603ff.*

— *The Joint Declaration of John Paul II and Archbishop Runcie of Canterbury, pledging to pursue the theological dialogue in view of the restoration of full communion (29 May 1982). Text in* Osservatore Romano *(English Edition), 7 June 1982, p. 2.*

The Apostolic Letter Motu Proprio of Paul VI, Matrimonia Mixta *(7 January 1970), finalises earlier norms given by the Secretariat for Promoting Christian Unity on Marriages of Catholics with non-Catholics, Christian and non-Christian.*

There are, besides, the various documents of the Secretariat for Promoting Christian Unity. Most important among them is the Directory Concerning Ecumenical Matters, *published in two parts:*
Part I: Ad Totam Ecclesiam *(14 May 1967);*
Part II: Spiritus Domini, *on Ecumenism in Higher Education (16 April 1970).*

Other documents concern specific problems:

—*Instruction on Mixed Marriages,* Matrimonii Sacramentum *(18 March 1966).*
—*On Marriages between Roman Catholics and Orthodox,* Crescens Matrimoniorum *(22 February 1967).*
—*Declaration on the Common Eucharistic Celebration by Christians of Different Confessions,* "Dans ces derniers temps" *(7 January 1970).*
—*Reflections and Suggestions Concerning Ecumenical Dialogue (15 August 1970) (a semi-official document for practical guidance).*
—*On admitting other Christians to Eucharistic Communion in the Catholic Church,* In quibus rerum circumstantiis *(1 June 1972).*
—*Note interpreting the preceding instruction (17 October 1973).*
—*Ecumenical Collaboration at the Regional, National and Local Levels (22 February 1975). Text in* Osservatore Romano *(English Edition), 17 July 1975, pp. 6-11.*

PAUL VI

SECRETARIAT FOR PROMOTING CHRISTIAN UNITY
IN QUIBUS RERUM CIRCUMSTANTIIS
(1 June 1972)

Two problems of ecumenism have special theological relevance: the question of baptism and its validity, and, if necessary, of re-baptising in the Catholic Church (cf. Chapter XIV); and the question of admitting Christians of other Churches to the Eucharist in the Catholic Church. In this matter the Directory had already restated the guidelines of the Council Decree (n. 912), and given detailed norms with regard to admission of Christians of Eastern Churches and of members of other Christian communities to the Eucharist. In the statement of 1 June, 1972, the Secretariat explains the theological rationale which underlies these norms. The text has relevance for this burning question also in the future. It is found in AAS 64(1972) 522-523.

(Norms for admission of other Christians to Catholic eucharistic communion)

915 The ecumenical directory has already shown how we must safeguard simultaneously the integrity of ecclesial communion and the good of souls. Behind the directory lie two main governing ideas:

1. The strict relationship between the mystery of the Church and the mystery of the Eucharist can never be altered, whatever pastoral measures we may be led to take in given cases. Of its very nature, the celebration of the Eucharist signifies the fulness of profession of faith and the fulness of ecclesial communion. This principle must not be obscured and must remain our guide in this field.

2. The principle will not be obscured if admission to Catholic eucharistic communion is confined to particular cases of those Christians who have a faith in the sacrament in conformity with that of the Church, who experience a serious spiritual need for the eucharistic sustenance, who for a prolonged period are unable to have recourse to a minister of their own community, and who ask for the sacrament of their own accord; all this provided that they have proper dispositions and lead lives worthy of a Christian. This spiritual need should be understood in the sense defined above: a need for the increase in spiritual life and a need for a deeper involvement in the mystery of the Church and of its unity.

(Disturbance of Catholics should be avoided; the assessment of the actual situation belongs to the bishop, and, in cases of similar conditions in a wider region, to episcopal conferences).

JOHN PAUL II

DISCOURSE AT THE LITURGY IN ST GEORGE'S AT PHANAR

(30 November 1979)

*Following the example of John XXIII and Paul VI in their cordial rela-
tions with Patriarch Athenagoras, John Paul II visited Patriarch Dimitrios I
in Istanbul for the celebration of the feast of St Andrew in November 1979.
On this occasion the Pope and the Patriarch signed a Joint Declaration in
which they announced the inauguration of the theological dialogue between
the Catholic and the Orthodox Churches. This theological dialogue aims
"not only at progressing towards the re-establishment of full communion
between the Catholic and Orthodox Sister-Churches, but also at contributing to the multiple dialogues that are developing in the Christian world in
search of its unity" (Osservatore Romano, English Edition, 10 December
1979, p.4). The Pope also attended the Byzantine Liturgy celebrated by
Patriarch Dimitrios in the Greek Orthodox Cathedral of St George at the
Phanar, and at the end of the Liturgy delivered a discourse which gives fresh
impetus to the re-union movement between the two Churches. In particular, the Pope placed the emphasis on the communion of the Churches; he
presented the Petrine office as one in the service of unity, without mentioning papal jurisdiction. The text of this address, from which the quotations
below are taken, is found in* Osservatore Romano *(English Edition), 10
December 1979, p.5.*

(Rome and Constantinople are Sister-Churches)

916   The Apostle Andrew, patron saint of the illustrious Church of
Constantinople, is Peter's brother.... Today's celebration
reminds us that special bonds of brotherhood and intimacy exist
between the Church of Rome and the Church of Constantinople,
and that a closer collaboration is natural between these two
Churches.

(Peter's ministry of unity)

917   Peter, Andrew's brother, is the leader *(choryphée)* of the
Apostles. Thanks to the inspiration given him by the Father,
he fully recognized in Jesus Christ the Son of the living God *(cf. Mt.
16.16)*. For this act of faith he received the name 'Peter' in order that
the Church might be founded on this rock. He was commissioned
with the task of ensuring unity in the apostolic preaching. As a
brother among brothers he received the mission of strengthening
them in faith *(cf. Lk. 22.32)*; he is the first to have the responsibility of
watching over the union of all, of ensuring the symphony of the holy
Churches of God, in faithfulness to "the faith which was once for all
delivered to the saints" *(Jude 3)*. It is in this spirit, animated by these
sentiments, that the successor of Peter has wished on this day to visit
the Church whose patron is St Andrew....

(Union with the Orthodox Churches is basic for ecumenism)

918　This visit to the primatial See of the Orthodox Church shows clearly the will of the entire Catholic Church to go forward in the march towards the unity of all, and also its conviction that the restoration of full communion with the Orthodox Church is a fundamental stage of the decisive progress of the entire ecumenical movement. Our division may not, perhaps, have been without an influence on the other divisions that followed it.

(Revising canonical rules)

919　We must not be afraid to reconsider, on both sides, and in consultation with one another, canonical rules established at a time when awareness of our communion—now close even if still incomplete—was still obscured. These rules are perhaps no longer consistent with the results achieved in our dialogue of love and with the possibilities opened up for us by these results.

(The theological dialogue)

920　The theological dialogue which is about to begin will have the task of overcoming the misunderstandings and disagreements which still exist between us, if not at the level of faith, at least at the level of theological formulation. It should be carried on not only in the atmosphere already created by the dialogue of love, which must be developed and intensified, but also in an atmosphere of worship and availability.

(Duty to be united)

921　It is only in worship, with a keen sense of the transcendence of the ineffable mystery "which surpasses knowledge" *(Eph. 3.19)* that we will be able to situate our differences and "lay on... no greater burden than the things necessary" *(Acts 15.28)* to re-establish communion. It seems to me, in fact, that the question we must ask ourselves is not so much whether we can re-establish full communion, as whether we still have the right to remain separated. We must ask ourselves this question in the very name of our faithfulness to Christ's will for His Church....

HOMILY TO THE DIASPORA-CATHOLICS AT OSNABRUCK
(16 November 1980)

The visit of the Pope to Germany in November 1980 had great ecumenical significance. Germany had been the cradle of the Reformation and continues to be a centre of Protestant life and theology. 1980 was the 450th anniversary of the Confessio Augustana, compiled by Melanchton, with Luther's approval, in an attempt to demonstrate the doctrinal orthodoxy of the Protestant movement before the Emperor and the diet of the empire. It was later accepted as an official document of the evangelical Churches. It contains the common basis of faith of Catholics and Protestants but remains ambiguous mostly in the understanding of the Church, grace and the sacraments. The possibility of accepting it as a basis for reunion was discussed again in the last years.

At various occasions during his visit to Germany the Pope spoke about different aspects of ecumenism. In the homily he pronounced during the eucharistic celebration at Osnabrück, he insisted on what Catholics and evangelical Christians already have in common and hoped that this unity may grow. The text is found in Osservatore Romano *(English Edition), 1 December 1980. p.5.*

(The growing union with other ecclesial communities)

922 5. The ecumenical movement in the last few decades has clearly shown you how much evangelical Christians are united with you in their concerns and joys, and how much you have in common with them when you live your faith in Our Lord Jesus Christ together, sincerely and consistently. So let us thank God from the bottom of our hearts that the various ecclesial communities in your regions are no longer divided by misunderstanding or even barricaded against one another in fear. You rather have already had the happy experience that mutual understanding and acceptance were particularly easy when both sides knew their own faith well, professed it joyfully, and encouraged concrete communion with their own brothers in faith. I would like to encourage you to continue along this way.

Live your faith as Catholics with gratitude to God and to your ecclesial community. Bear a credible witness, in all humility and without any complacency, to the deep values of your faith, and encourage, discreetly and amiably, also your evangelical brothers to strengthen and deepen in Christ their own convictions and forms of religious life. If all Churches and communities really grow in the fulness of the Lord, His Spirit will certainly indicate to us the way to reach the full internal and external unity of the Church.

ADDRESS TO THE EVANGELICAL CHURCH

COUNCIL OF GERMANY
(Mainz, 17 November 1980)

On the third day of his visit to Germany (cf. n. 922i), Pope John Paul II addressed the Council of the German Evangelical Church in Mainz. He stressed the urgency for a common confession of faith and the need of conversion on the part of all in order that full unity may be obtained. Remarkable here is the positive way in which the Pope referred to Luther. The text is found in Osservatore Romano *(English Edition), 9 December 1980, p.3.*

(The need of conversion of all)

923 There is no Christian life without repentance. "There can be no ecumenism worthy of the name without a change of heart" *(n. 911).* "Let us no more pass judgment on one another" *(Rom. 14.13).* Let us rather recognise our guilt. "All have sinned" *(Rom. 3.23),* applies also with regard to the grace of unity.

(The urgency of the common confession of faith)

924 All the gratitude for what remains common to us and unites us (the common faith in Jesus Christ) cannot make us blind to what still divides us. We must examine it together as far as possible, not to widen the gaps, but to bridge them. We cannot stop at the acknowledgment: "we are and remain divided for ever and against each other." We are called to strive together, in a dialogue of truth and love, towards full unity in faith. Only full unity gives us the possibility of gathering with the same sentiments and the same faith at the Lord's one table.

(We are divided through the doctrine of the Church)

925 (In) the lectures given by Luther on the Letter to the Romans in the year 1516-1517,... he teaches that "faith in Christ through which we are justified, is not just belief in Christ, or more exactly in the person of Christ, but belief in what is Christ's".... "We must believe in Him and what is His." For the question: "What is this then?", Luther refers to the Church and to her authentic teaching. If the difficulties that exist between us were only a question of "ecclesiastical structures set up by men",[1] we could and should eliminate

---

1. Cf. *Confessio Augustana,* VIII.

them immediately. According to the conviction of Catholics, disagreement revolves around "what is Christ's", around "what is His": His Church and her mission, her message, her sacraments, and the ministries placed in the service of the Word and the Sacrament. The dialogue established since the Council has brought us a good way further in this respect.

(The efforts for unity must continue)

926   We must remain in dialogue and in contact.... I hope that we will find together the way to continue our dialogue.... We must leave no stone unturned. We must do what unites. we owe it to God and to the world. "Let us then pursue what makes for peace and for mutual upbuilding" *(Rom. 14.19)*....Christ's message requires us to bear witness together. Allow me to repeat what I said on 25 June of this year on the occasion of the jubilee of the *Confessio Augustana:* "The will of Christ and the signs of the times urge us to common witness in growing fulness of truth and love".

ADDRESS TO THE GERMAN EPISCOPAL CONFERENCE
(Munich, 17 November 1980)

Also during his visit to Germany (cf. n. 922i), Pope John Paul II addressed the German Episcopal Conference in Munich. He again returned to the theme of ecumenism, this time stressing that the way to unity must pass through the Cross. The text is found in Osservatore Romano *(English Edition), 22 December 1980, p. 9.*

(Unity in truth through the cross)

927   We often hear it said today that the ecumenical movement of the Churches is at a standstill....I cannot agree with this judgment. Unity, which comes from God, is given to us at the Cross. We must not want to avoid the Cross, passing to rapid attempts at harmonising differences, excluding the question of truth. But neither must we abandon one another, and go on our separate ways, because drawing closer calls for the patient and suffering love of Christ crucified. Let us not be diverted from the laborious way in order to remain where we are, or to choose ways that are apparently shorter and lead astray.

CHAPTER X

THE CHURCH AND THE WORLD RELIGIONS

The problem of the significance of the many religions of mankind in God's plan of salvation has struck the modern Christian with full force especially after World War II. The collapse of the colonial system, the revolution in world communications, the emergence of a truly pluralistic international society, have forced him to consider more seriously, indeed often with anguish, the meaning of the religions which he encounters constantly and comes to know better and better. Moreover, the new discoveries in the human sciences and a better knowledge of population statistics make him realise that in the enormous span of human history the Judaeo-Christian event fills only a tiny fraction, and that those who profess Jesus as the Lord are a diminishing minority of the world population. This naturally leads to a more intense theological reflection on the "other" religions. This is why, "in our time" especially, the Church "examines with great attention what is her relation to non-Christian religions" (NA 1).

In her proclamation of the Gospel of Christ she had, of course, always encountered peoples professing various forms of religious beliefs, more or less at variance with the contents of her own preaching; but in the earliest centuries the teaching Church did not find it necessary to make any statement about these religions. The Christian attitude towards them was in fact for the main part a negative one; it was taken for granted that the other religions cannot lead to salvation. This, however, was a negative way of expressing an important aspect of the Christian faith, viz., the uniqueness of Jesus Christ as the only Mediator between God and men (cf. 1 Tim. 2.5). Little positive thinking was done about the possible role of those religions in God's plan.

The first official pronouncements bearing on other religions appeared in the social and political context of the Middle Ages, and were occasioned by the continued presence of distinct Jewish communities in the Western world and by the Muslim threat. The sociological background of these conciliar or papal statements is that of a Christian commonwealth threatened by the economic power of the Jews and the military advances of Islam. In this context sociological discrimination based on religious principles was often practised. This negative attitude notwithstanding, the need was also recognised of sending to various peoples preachers full of sympathy and understanding (see chapter XI). And, though pressure could be exerted on the Jews to listen to the Gospel message, nobody was to be forced to conversion. Of this early period only three documents are given here which keep some relevance today.

A second group of documents deals mostly with the danger of indifferentism which contact with non-Christian religions can bring about. These documents are written against the background of nineteenth century Liberalism. They contain harsh statements, much influenced by the current theology; at the same time they keep an element of permanent value. For, they witness to the Church's awareness of an objective order of salvation to which man is called to submit, and to a consciousness of the fact that the salvific grace of God comes to all men through Christ. Therefore, the Church, because of her unique relation to Christ, cannot be reduced to the level of other religious communities; her function is unique. This does not prevent the fact, already acknowledged in the documents of this period, that the grace of Christ reaches beyond the visible boundaries of the Catholic Church. The Jansenist proposition, "no grace is granted outside the Church", had already been condemned by Clement XI in 1713 (cf. DS 2429). As regards the danger of indifferentism, the documents quoted here show that the Church's stern attitude has gradually softened down. More and more recognition is given to the principle of religious liberty; the previous attitude will be completely superseded by the new theological climate of Vatican II.

The third group of documents concerning the religions of the world reflects mostly the new and much more open theological outlook characteristic of the Second Vatican Council. The Council recognises the moral and spiritual values of these religions and urges the Church not only to enter into fraternal dialogue with their adherents but also to learn from contact with their traditions.

*   *   *

The Church's doctrine on the religions of the world covers the following points:

Religions in relation to the Gospel

Though abrogated by the Gospel, practices of Judaism were allowable in early Christianity: 1003, 1004.

Religions are related to the Christian economy of salvation: 39/16, 1003, 1018, 1034.

Outside this relationship they have no salvific power: 810, 1003, 1005, 1008, 1009, 1013/16f.

Yet their votaries can find salvation: 39/16, 814, 854-857, 1010, 1018.

They are not on an equal footing with the Christian faith; hence indifferentism is condemned: 1006f, 1008, 1013/15, 1013/21.77.78.79, 1016.

The Gospel must be announced to them: 1036, 1039.

Religions considered in themselves

They contain many spiritual, moral and human values, though often mixed with error, and hence need to be purified: 1017, 1018, 1025, 1026, 1030, 1035.

They even contain elements of the supreme Truth, seeds of the Word; divine grace is at work in them: 1021, 1023, 1025, 1036, 1037, 1038, 1040.

They deal with the one God and with the ultimate questions of man: 1002, 1019f, 1031, 1033, 1038.

The Christian attitude to world religions

There must be true religious freedom, tolerance and respect: 1001, 1014f, 1027, 2048-2050.

There should reign an attitude of acceptance, collaboration and dialogue: 1022, 1024, 1027, 1028, 1029, 1032, 1037, 1039, 1040.

The Christian attitude is charity towards all: 1011, 1012.

Christians should learn from the values of other religious traditions: 1025, 1037.

THE SECOND GENERAL COUNCIL OF NICAEA (787)

The Council was convoked in the midst of the iconoclast controversy by Irene and her son emperor Constantine IV, at the request of Paul IV, patriarch of Constantinople, and Tarasius, his successor. The Council was presided over, at least nominally, by the legate of Pope Hadrian I. Besides settling the doctrinal matters on the veneration of images (cf. nn. 1251f), it passed several disciplinary canons, among which is found the following one. The canon states the obligation laid on all those who claim to be Christians of professing the Christian faith without ambiguity. An open allegiance to Judaism is preferable to a Christian profession which is not sincere. The text is found in COD, *pp. 121–122.*

(Jews must not be received, unless sincerely converted)

1001   Canon 8: Since those who live in the error of the Hebrew religion seem to make a mockery of Christ, our God, pretending to be Christians while in fact they deny Him and secretly keep the Sabbath and other customs of the Jews, we determine that such people must not be received into the communion, nor in prayer, nor in the Church; but let them be Hebrews openly, according to their own religion. Nor should their children be baptised or their slaves bought or acquired. But if any one among them should with a sincere heart and true faith be converted and profess (the faith) with his whole heart, showing that he has triumphed over their customs and practices by striving that others be convinced and corrected, such a one should be received and baptised, and his children too. And we determine that it must be made sure that they have turned away from the Jewish practices; and if this is not the case, they should by no means be received.

GREGORY VII

LETTER TO ANZIR, KING OF MAURITANIA (1076)

In a letter to the Muslim King of Mauritania, referred to in the Council Vatican II (NA 3), the Pope thanks Anzir for gifts he has received from him as well as for freeing some prisoners and for his promise to free others. He also sends him a delegation as a token of Christian friendship and love and as a proof of his desire to be of service to him "in all things agreeable to our Fathers". The most significant part of the letter is the following extract in which the Pope explains that Christians and Muslims worship the same God. See Epistola 21, PL 48, 450–452.

(Christians and Muslims adore the same God)

1002   God, the Creator of all, without whom we cannot do or even think anything that is good, has inspired to your heart this act of kindness. He who enlightens all men coming into this world *(Jn 1.9)* has enlightened your mind for this purpose. Almighty God, who desires all men to be saved *(1 Tim. 2.4)* and none to perish, is well pleased to approve in us most of all that besides loving God men love other men, and do not do to others anything they do not want to be done unto themselves *(cf. Mt.7.14)*. We and you must show in a special way to the other nations an example of this charity, for we believe and confess one God, although in different ways, and praise and worship Him daily as the creator of all ages and the ruler of this world. For as the apostle says: "He is our peace who has made us both one" *(Eph. 2.14)*. Many among the Roman nobility, informed by us of this grace granted to you by God, greatly admire and praise your goodness and virtues....God knows that we love you purely for His honour and that we desire your salvation and glory, both in the present and the future life. And we pray in our hearts and with our lips that God may lead you to the abode of happiness, to the bosom of the holy patriarch Abraham, after long years of life here on earth.

THE GENERAL COUNCIL OF FLORENCE
DECREE FOR THE JACOBITES (1442)

On this document, see n. 809i. This is the first official document in which reference is explicitly made to the "pagans" in connection with the axiom Extra Ecclesiam nulla salus; previous official pronouncements had applied the principle to situations of schism and heresy within the Christian fold. The formulation of the axiom is borrowed from Fulgentius of Ruspa (467-533). As it stands, the document takes a negative attitude as regards the role of "pagan" religions in the objective economy of salvation. It does not, however, deny what it was beyond its scope to consider, viz., the presence of grace beyond the boundaries of the Church and the limitations of subjective human knowledge and responsibility. As regards the place of the Jewish religion in the Christian economy of salvation, the attitude is also rather negative: though tolerated at the beginning of the Church's existence, it must eventually disappear. As far as Christians are concerned, it states clearly that, though Jewish religious practices could licitly be kept by them in the earliest period of the Church's existence, this is no longer true in the present. At the same time, it insists that Christian freedom makes all human customs lawful, provided that the faith is intact and edification attended to.

(Jewish religious practices are abrogated with the promulgation of the Gospel)

1003   (The Holy Roman Church) firmly believes, professes and
1348   teaches that the legal (statutes) of the Old Testament or
          Mosaic Law, divided into ceremonies, holy sacrifices and

sacraments, were instituted to signify something to come, and therefore, although in that age they were fitting for divine worship, they have ceased with the advent of our Lord Jesus Christ, whom they signified. (With Him) the sacraments of the New Testament have begun. Whoever puts his hope in these legal (statutes) even after the passion (of Christ) and submits himself to them as though faith in Christ was unable to save without them, sins mortally. Yet (the Church) does not deny that between the passion of Christ and the promulgation of the Gospel they could be observed, provided one in no way believed that they were necessary for salvation. But she asserts that after the promulgation of the Gospel they cannot be observed without the loss of eternal salvation. Therefore, she denounces as foreign to the faith of Christ all those who after that time observe circumcision, the Sabbath and other laws, and she asserts that they can in no way be sharers of eternal salvation, unless they sometime turn away from their errors. She therefore commands to all who glory themselves in the Christian name that they must, sometime or other, give up circumcision fully, either before or after baptism, because, whether one puts one's hope in it or not, it cannot in any way be observed without the loss of eternal salvation.

(All things are lawful but not all things are helpful)

1004 (The Holy Roman Church) firmly believes, professes and
1350 preaches that "everything created by God is good and
nothing is to be rejected if it is received with thanksgiving" *(1 Tim. 4.4);* because, according to the word of the Lord, it is "not what goes into the mouth that defiles a man" *(Mt. 15.11).* She asserts that the distinction of clean and unclean food in the Mosaic Law belongs to the religious observances which have passed away with the rise of the Gospel and have ceased to be efficacious. It also asserts that the command of the apostles to "abstain from what has been sacrificed to idols and from blood and from what is strangled" *(Acts 15.29)* was fitting in those times when the one Church was emerging from the Jews and the Gentiles, who previously had observed different religious customs and moral habits. For, in this way the Gentiles would share some observances in common with the Jews, and, the causes of dissent being removed, it would be possible to come to a common worship and profession of faith. For, to the Jews, because of their ancient traditions, blood and what is strangled is abhorrent; thus, if they saw the Gentiles eat what was sacrificed to idols, they could

suspect them of returning to idolatry. But, once the Christian religion has been so well spread that no Jew according to the flesh is found in it but all who enter the Church agree on the same rites of the Gospel and modes of worship, believing that "to the pure all things are pure" (Tit. 1.15), the reason for the apostolic prohibiton has ceased to exist and, therefore, the prohibition itself has also ceased. The Church declares, therefore, that none among the kinds of food which human civilisation admits must be condemned; and that no distinction must be made between animals, whoever be the person, man or woman by whom they are killed, and whatever be the way in which they are killed. However, for the sake of bodily health, for the exercise of virtue, for the observance of monastic and ecclesiastical discipline, a man may and must refrain from many things which are not condemned. For, as the apostle says: "All things are lawful but not all things are helpful" (1 Cor. 6.12; 10.22).

(The necessity of the Church for salvation)

1005   (The Holy Roman Church)...firmly believes, professes and
1351   preaches that "no one remaining outside the Catholic
        Church, not only pagans", but also Jews, heretics or schismatics, can become partakers of eternal life; but they will go to the "eternal fire prepared for the devil and his angels" (Mt. 25.41), unless before the end of their life they are received into it. For union with the body of the Church is of so great importance that the sacraments of the Church are helpful to salvation only for those remaining in it; and fasts, almsgiving, other works of piety, and the exercises of a militant Christian life bear eternal rewards for them alone. "And no one can be saved, no matter how much alms he has given, even if he sheds his blood for the name of Christ, unless he remains in the bosom and unity of the Catholic Church."[1]

LEO XII

ENCYCLICAL LETTER *UBI PRIMUM* (1824)

The intellectual climate of Europe in the nineteenth century was largely derived from Descartes. It was a strange combination of rationalism and fideism. The rationalistic tenets led to the doctrine of religious indifferentism which ascribed equal value to all religions. The philosophical roots of this movement were clearly incompatible with the Christian faith; they tended

---

1. Cf. FULGENTIUS OF RUSPA, *De fide liber ad Petrum*, 38, 79 and 39, 80.

to deny all divine revelation or at least to refuse any finality to God's revelation in Christ. No word of God was recognised as demanding from man a religious assent. The doctrine was vigorously opposed by the official teaching of the Church, especially by Pope Pius IX. Pope Leo XII, in his first Encyclical Letter, Ubi Primum, defined what the Church understood by indifferentism.

(Condemnation of religious indifferentism)

1006 (A certain sect), putting on airs of piety and liberality, pro-
2720 fesses what they call 'tolerantism' or indifferentism, and extols it not only in matters of politics, about which We are not speaking, but also in matters of religion. It teaches that God has given to every man a great freedom, so that man can embrace and adopt without any danger to his salvation any sect that attracts him according to his own private judgment and opinion.

(Against this, Rom. 16.17f is quoted.)

GREGORY XVI

ENCYCLICAL LETTER *MIRARI NOS ARBITRAMUR* (1832)

In this letter the Pope condemns the liberal doctrines spread by the French writer, F. de Lamennais (1782-1854), who after having first submitted, later reiterated the same teaching. He was again condemned by the same Pope in the Encyclical Singulari Nos (1834) (D 1617).

(Condemnation of religious indifferentism)

1007 We now come to another important cause of the evils with
2730 which we regret to see the Church afflicted, namely indiffer-
entism, or that wrong opinion according to which... man can attain the eternal salvation of his soul by any profession of faith, provided his moral conduct conforms to the norms of right and good.... From this foulest source of indifferentism there flows the absurd and wrong view, or rather insanity, according to which freedom of conscience must be asserted and vindicated for everybody.

PIUS IX

ENCYCLICAL LETTER *QUI PLURIBUS* (1846)

In this first encyclical Pius IX already condemns the doctrine of indifferentism, which he was to reject repeatedly later: in the allocution Singulari Quaedam (1854), in the encyclical Quanto Conficiamur Moerore (1863) (cf. DS 2865-2867), and again in the Syllabus of Condemned Errors (1864). His teaching, which today sounds very harsh, must, in order to be correctly interpreted, be placed in its historical context. The presupposition of indifferentism was the negation of revelation upon which there followed the equality of all religions. This context did not favour the recognition of what is good in religions outside Christianity. What remains valid in this teaching found a more careful theological expression in the Dogmatic Constitution on the Catholic Faith of the First Vatican Council (cf. nn. 113ff).

(Condemnation of religious indifferentism)

1008   (Among errors against the Catholic Faith) must be included
2785   the horrible system, repugnant even to the natural light of
          reason, according to which there is no difference between
religions (indifferentism). These crafty men, doing away with all
distinction between virtue and vice, truth and error, honesty and
dishonesty, feign that men can attain to eternal salvation by the
practice of any religion whatever.

ALLOCUTION *SINGULARI QUADAM* (1854)

In this allocution, delivered one day after the definition of the dogma of the Immaculate Conception, the Pope exposed to the Cardinals the dangers that beset the right doctrine of the Church, i.e., Rationalism and Indifferentism. For the first time an official document on the necessity of the Church for salvation speaks of the "invincible ignorance" by which men are subjectively excused from embracing Christianity. This admission, completing the previous doctrine (cf. n. 1003i), considerably tempers its harshness. The same doctrine was repeated nine years later in the encyclical Quanto Conficiamur Moerore *(cf. DS 2865–2867).*

(There is no salvation outside the Church)

1009   We have learnt not without sorrow that another error, no
          less destructive than the previous one, has invaded some
parts of the Catholic world and affects the minds of many Catholics.
They think that there is good hope for the eternal salvation of all
those who do not in any way belong to the Church of Christ.
Therefore they are in the habit of frequently inquiring about the
future lot and condition after death of those who in no way have given
their adherence to the Catholic faith. Advancing the flimsiest arguments, they expect a reply that will support their erroneous opinion.
Far from Us, Venerable Brethren, be the idea of daring to set limits to
the divine mercy, which is infinite; far also from Us to want to
penetrate the secret plans and judgments of God which are "like the
great deep" *(cf. Ps. 36 (35) 6),* impenetrable to human thought. But,
in accordance with our apostolic office, We want you to be on the
alert, with episcopal care and vigilance, so as to keep away from

men's minds, by all possible efforts, that opinion which is as unholy as it is deadly, namely that the way of eternal salvation can be found in any religion whatever. With all the learning and ingenuity that is yours, teach the people entrusted to your care that the dogmas of the Catholic faith are not in the slightest manner opposed to the divine mercy and justice.

(Invincible ignorance excuses from belonging to the Church)

1010　It must, of course, be held as of faith that no one can be saved outside the apostolic Roman Church, that the Church is the only ark of salvation, and that whoever does not enter it will perish in the flood. Yet, on the other hand, it must likewise be held as certain that those who are in ignorance of the true religion, if this ignorance is invincible, are not subject to any guilt in this matter before the eyes of the Lord. Now, who could presume for himself the ability to set the boundaries of such ignorance, taking into consideration the natural differences of peoples, lands, talents and so many other factors? Only when we have been released from the bonds of this body and "shall see God as He is" *(1 Jn 3.2)* shall we understand how closely and wonderfully the divine mercy and justice are linked. But, as long as we dwell on earth, encumbered by this mortal body that dulls our soul, let us tenaciously hold the Catholic doctrine that there is "one God, one faith, one baptism" *(cf. Eph. 4.5)*. To push our inquiry further is not right.

(Condemnation of religious indifferentism)

1011　For the rest, as charity demands, let us pray continually for the conversion to Christ of all nations everywhere. Let us devote ourselves to the salvation of all men as far as we can, for "the Lord's hand is not shortened" *(Is. 59.1)*. The gifts of heavenly grace will assuredly not be denied to those who sincerely wish and pray to be renewed by the divine light. These truths need to be deeply fixed in the minds of the faithful, so that they may not be infected with doctrines tending to foster the religious indifferentism which We see spreading widely, with growing strength, and with destructive effect upon souls.

ENCYCLICAL LETTER *QUANTO CONFICIAMUR MOERORE* (1863)

In this letter addressed to the Bishops of Italy, Pius IX repeats the teaching he had given nine years earlier (cf. nn. 1009-1011), but he further stresses the duty of brotherly relations with men of all religions.

1012   But let it never happen that the children of the Catholic Church be in any way at enmity with those who are not joined to them by the bonds of the same faith and love. On the contrary, if they are poor or sick or afflicted by any other evils, let the children of the Church endeavour to succour and help them with all the services of Christian love. First and foremost, let them try to lead them from the shadows of error in which they lie to the Catholic truth and to the most loving mother the Church. She never ceases to extend lovingly her maternal arms towards them and to call them to her bosom, so that, grounded in faith, hope and love, and "bearing fruit in every good work" *(Col. 1.10),* they may find eternal salvation.

SALLABUS OF CONDEMNED ERRORS (1864)

The full title of this document is: "A Syllabus containing the most important errors of our time which have been condemned by our holy Father Pius IX in allocutions, at consistories, in encyclicals and other apostolic letters." It is the final outcome of the Pope's protracted effort to comply with the request made to him by the Council of Spoleto in 1851 that he should list and condemn the principal errors of the times. The final list of 80 errors, divided into ten sections, draws from previous statements of the Pope, and, although not signed by him, was sent together with his Encyclical Quanta Cura, *accompanied by a letter of the Cardinal Secretary of State. The Syllabus is very harsh in some respects, but its propositions must be interpreted in the light of the original documents to which they refer. These documents generally belonged to European ideological movements which were much more in conflict with Christian revelation than the ambiguous and vague wording used in the Syllabus would suggest. The errors listed here are taken from the third section of the Syllabus dealing with indifferentism (15-17), from the fourth section on various errors (21), and from the last or tenth section on modern liberalism (77-79). Cf. also other propositions in n. 112.*

(Errors of indifferentism condemned)

[1013/15]   Every one is free to embrace and profess the religion
2915   which by the light of reason he judges to be true.

[1013/16]   Men can find the way of eternal salvation and attain
2916   eternal salvation by the practice of any religion
                  whatever.

[1013/17]   We should at least have good hopes for the eternal
2917   salvation of all those who are in no way in the true
                  Church of Christ.

(Error against the Church condemned)

[1013/21] The Church has no power to define dogmatically that
2921 the religion of the Catholic Church is the only true
religion.

(Errors of liberalism condemned)

[1013/77] In our age it is no longer advisible that the Catholic
2977 religion be the only State religion, excluding all the
other cults.

[1013/78] Therefore it is praiseworthy that in some Catholic
2978 regions the law has allowed people immigrating there to
exercise publicly their own cult.

[1013/79] It is false to assert that civil freedom of cult and the full
2979 right granted to all to express openly and publicly any
opinions and views leads to an easier corruption of
morality and of the minds of people and helps to propagate the pest
of indifferentism.

LEO XIII

ENCYCLICAL LETTER *IMMORTALE DEI* (1885)

*From their opposition to indifferentism earlier Popes had drawn the
conclusion that the secularism of the State was also wrong, since it seemed
to be intimately linked with religious indifferentism. Thus Pius IX had
condemned it in the Encyclical* Quanta Cura *(1864) (cf. D. 1039). Leo XIII
softens this unnecessary conclusion. The condemnation of the secularism
of the State will be completely superseded by the doctrine of the Second
Vatican Council in its declaration* Dignitatis Humanae *on religious freedom
(cf. nn. 2048-2050).*

(On the secularism of the State)

1014 Although the Church does not consider it licit that various
3176 forms of worship of God should have the same rights as the
true religion, yet she does not thereby condemn the authorities of the nations who, for the sake of attaining a great good or of
avoiding to cause evil, tolerate in practice and by custom that they all
have the same place in the city.

(There must be no forced conversion)

1015 The Church is also always very careful that nobody be

3177   forced to join the Catholic faith against his will, for, as
Augustine wisely admonishes: "only he who wills so can
believe."[1]

THE FIRST PLENARY COUNCIL OF INDIA (1950)

*This Council, demanded by the bishops of India and convoked in Banga-
lore by the papal legate Cardinal Gilroy, is the ony fully official statement of
doctrine and practice made by the Magisterium of the Church in India. Its
decrees, approved by Pope Pius XII in 1951, contain a doctrinal part and a
much larger disciplinary and pastoral part. While it rejects the indifferentist
attitude, the Council is the first official Church document offering a clearly
positive approach to the spiritual values of the world religions. It represents
a first step in the Church's new understanding of these religions, which will
find its full expression in the Second Vatican Council. The texts quoted here
belong to the doctrinal section, dealing with the true religion. See Acta et
Decreta primi Concilii plenarii Indiae, 2nd ed. (Ranchi 1959) , pp. 24,25.*

(Against indifferentism and syncretism)

1016   11. We therefore reject the view so widely spread in our
regions which holds that all religions are equal among themselves, and that, provided they are adhered to with sincerity, all are
various ways to one and the same end, namely God and eternal
salvation. We equally reject the syncretism according to which the
ideal religion or the religion of the future is conceived as a sort of
synthesis to be worked out by men from various religions that exist.

(Positive values and limitations of non-Christian religions)

1017   We acknowledge indeed that there is truth and goodness
outside the Christian religion, for God has not left the nations
without a witness to Himself, and the human soul is naturally drawn
towards the one true God. But with the passage of the centuries
serious errors have almost everywhere been mixed with these
truths, and this is why the various religions contradict each other
even on essential points. But the inadequacy of all non-Christian
religions is principally derived from this, that, Christ being constituted the one Mediator between God and men, there is no salvation
by any other name.

THE SECOND VATICAN GENERAL COUNCIL

While maintaining unshaken the belief in the uniqueness of Christ and of

---

1. *In evang. Ioan: tract.,* 26, 2.

His revelation, the Second Vatican Council took a clearly positive approach to the religions of the world. It devoted a special declaration, Nostra Aetate, to the relation of the Church to these religions. This is the first Conciliar document to deal with this important subject. Besides the Declaration, other documents of Vatican II, especially LG and AG, also contain important references to the place of these religions in God's plan of salvation.

The Council does not intend to provide on this point an elaborate theology; but it clearly adopts a new attitude by stressing what Christians share with other men, and thereby fosters unity (NA 1). It mentions with respect the great world religions (AG 10); more specifically, it refers to the primitive religions (NA 2), Hinduism (ibid.), Buddhism (ibid.), Islam (NA 3 and LG 16) and Judaism (NA 4; LG 16 and passim). It recognises in them not ony human answers to the fundamental problems of life (NA 2), but also precious religious values (GS 12). They represent a wealth of goodness embedded in the hearts of men, which finds expression in rites and symbols, and is a true preparation for the Gospel (LG 16; AG 9). They contain treasures of ascetical and contemplative life whose seeds have been planted in men by God before the preaching of the Gospel (AG 15, 18); hence in them are found "Seeds of the Word" (LG 17; AG 11).

The Council thus acknowledges in the faith of the adherents of these religions a response to the voice and self-manifestation of God (GS 16 and 22). It mentions that the Holy Spirit was already at work in the world before Christ was glorified (AG 4), referring to St Leo who said: "When on Pentecost day the Holy Spirit filled the disciples of the Lord, He did not bring His first gift, but came with new graces; for the patriarchs and prophets and priests and all the saints of former times were enlivened and sanctified by the same Spirit...though they did not receive the same measure of His gifts."[1] Hence the Council recognises that the religious traditions have their place in God's universal design of salvation (AG 3), although it does not explain theologically the exact nature of the role they play in it. The Church of Vatican II looks at the religious traditions of mankind not as rivals, nor as historical movements wholly foreign to her, but as values intimately related to the divine mystery of which she is the depositary (LG 16; NA 2).

It is not surprising therefore that the Council makes a strong appeal to Christians for a new attitude towards the religions of the world (cf. especially NA 1-5). The Church rejects nothing of the truth and holiness found in them (NA 2); it considers with respect even those doctrines of theirs which differ from her teaching but often contain a ray of the eternal Truth (NA 2; GS 57). Hence Christians must not only discover what is true and good in other religions (OT 16) and feel at home in the national and religious traditions of various peoples (AG 11); they must also learn to acknowledge, preserve and foster their spiritual, moral and socio-cultural values (NA 2). Thus they will appreciate the riches of the gifts which God in His generosity has dispensed to the peoples of the world (AG 11, 18).

Moreover, in Vatican II the Church asserts vigorously the right to religious freedom (cf. nn. 2048ff). Christians must oppose every form of discrimination among men, based on status, race or creed (NA 5). They

---

1. LEO THE GREAT, Sermo 76.

must be open to all forms of dialogue, imbued with the spirit of justice and love (GS 92; AG 11, 16, 34; NA 2, 3). Dialogue must be practised not only at the level of co-operation in humanitarian tasks (AA 27; AG 12; GS 92); it is also a common search for socio-cultural, moral and spiritual enrichment (NA 5; AG 18). This requires discernment, for sin and evil have not been absent in human, even religious, endeavours (LG 16, 17; AG 9); but it is part of the Church's task and can be done without detriment to her duty of witnessing to the fulness of revelation addressed by God to all men in Jesus Christ (NA 2, 5; GS 28, etc.).

DOGMATIC CONSTITUTION *LUMEN GENTIUM* (1964)

(The non-Christians and the People of God)

1018   16. There are finally those who have not yet received the Gospel; they too are ordained in various ways to the People of God. In the first place there stands that people to which the covenants and promises were given and from which Christ was born according to the flesh *(cf. Rom. 9.4-5),* a people of election most dear to God because of their Fathers; for the gifts and the call of God are irrevocable *(cf. Rom. 11.28-29).* The plan of salvation includes those also who acknowledge the Creator; foremost among these are the Muslims: they profess fidelity to the faith of Abraham and, with us, adore the one and merciful God who will judge mankind on the last day. Nor is God far from those who in shadows and images seek the unknown God; for He gives to all men life and breath and all things *(cf. Acts 17.25-28),* and as Saviour desires all men to be saved *(cf. 1 Tim. 2.4).* For those also can attain eternal salvation who without fault on their part do not know the Gospel of Christ and His Church, but seek God with a sincere heart, and under the influence of grace endeavour to do His will as recognised through the promptings of their conscience *(cf. nn. 855-857).* Nor does divine Providence deny the help necessary for salvation to those who, without fault on their part, have not yet reached an explicit knowledge of God, and yet endeavour, not without divine grace, to live a good life, for whatever goodness or truth is found among them is considered by the Church as a preparation for the Gospel,[1] a gift from Him who enlightens every man that he may finally have life. But, often enough, deceived by the evil one, men have become futile in their thinking and have exchanged the truth about God for a lie, serving a creature rather than the Creator *(cf. Rom. 1.21, 25):* there are some who, living and

---

1. Cf. EUSEBIUS OF CAESAREA, *Praeparatio Evangelica*, 1, 1.

dying without God in this world, are a prey to utter despair. That is why the Church, in order to promote God's glory and the salvation of all these men, fosters the missions with great solicitude, mindful as she is of the Lord's command: "Preach the Gospel to the whole creation" *(Mk 16.15)*.

DECLARATION *NOSTRA AETATE* (1965)

This is the first conciliar document dealing directly and explicitly with non-Christian religions. Its title, "Declaration on the relationship (habitudo) *of the Church to the non-Christian religions", is already in itself a theological statement. The history of this document is long and complex. It began with the wish expressed by Pope John XXIII that the Council should issue a statement on the Jews, to clarify the Church's stand with regard to the Jews. Various drafts for such a statement met with difficulties, caused by political (anti-Zionism of the Arabs) and theological (Jews and Christ's death) tensions. After an abortive attempt to push the declaration on to other documents, its scope was finally enlarged so as to include the attitude of the Church not only to Judaism, but also to Islam and other religions; the final draft was approved and voted on October 28, 1965. The whole document breathes an atmosphere of respect and sympathy for the religions of the world, whose authentic values it expounds while, at the same time, showing the finality of Christ's revelation which the Church is commissioned to proclaim.*

Number 1 places the meeting of the Church with the world religions in the broad context of the common origin and destiny of all men and their search for an answer to the ultimate questions that beset them. Number 2 gives a positive description of the so-called "primitive religions", of Hinduism and of Buddhism; it explains the Church's attitude to these religions as one not merely of acceptance, but of respect and appreciation; it calls for dialogue and collaboration, whereby, while proclaiming Christ, Christians will share in the authentic values possessed by others. Number 3 describes appreciatively the Muslim beliefs; referring to the historical frictions between Christians and Muslims, it exhorts all to mutual understanding and to collaboration in common tasks. Number 4 deals with the mystery of Judaism and the Church's close relationship to it; it calls for mutual support, especially in biblical studies, and condemns all forms of anti-Semitism. Number 5 condemns in general all forms of discrimination between men.

(The unity of the human race)

1019   1. For all peoples form a single community; their origin is one for God made the whole human race to dwell over the entire face of the earth *(cf. Acts 17.26)*. One also is their final goal, God. His providence, the manifestations of His goodness, His plan of salvation extend to all men *(cf. Wis. 8.1; Acts 14.17; Rom. 2.6f; 1 Tim. 2.4)*, until the moment when the elect will be gathered in the Holy City whose light shall be the glory of God, when the nations will walk in His light *(cf. Rev. 21.23f)*.

(The place of religion in men's life)

1020   Men expect from the various religions answers to those unsolved riddles of the human condition—riddles which today as in olden times deeply stir the hearts of men: What is man? What is the meaning and the goal of our life? What is moral good and what is sin? What is the origin of suffering and what purpose does it serve? What is the way to true happiness? What are death, judgment, retribution after death? What, finally, is that ultimate and ineffable mystery which enfolds our existence, from which we come and to which we are going?

(The Church's stand towards other religions)

1021   2. The Catholic Church rejects nothing of what is true and holy in these religions. With sincere respect she looks on those ways of conduct and life, those precepts and teachings which, though differing on many points from what she herself holds and teaches, yet not rarely reflect a ray of the Truth which enlightens all men. But she proclaims and must ever proclaim Christ, "the way, the truth and the life" *(Jn 14.6)*, in whom men find the fulness of religious life, and in whom God has reconciled all things to Himself *(cf. 2 Cor. 5.18f)*.

(The Church's concrete attitude)

1022   And so the Church has this exhortation for her sons: prudently and lovingly, through dialogue and collaboration with the followers of other religions, and in witness to the Christian faith and life, acknowledge, preserve and promote the spiritual and moral good, as well as the socio-cultural values found among them.

DECREE *AD GENTES* (1965)

(Religions are a preparation for the Gospel)

1023   3. This universal design of God to save the human race is not achieved only in secret, as it were, in the hearts of men; nor merely through the undertakings *(incepta)*, including religious ones, by which they seek God in many ways, in the hope that they may feel after Him and find Him, though indeed He is not far from each one of us *(cf. Acts 17.27).* For these undertakings need to be enlightened and healed, even though, in the merciful design of the provident God, they may sometimes be taken as leading the way *(paedagogia)* to the true God and as a preparation for the Gospel *(cf. n. 1018).*

(Christ heals and perfects all religious values)

1024   9. But whatever truth and grace is already found among the nations as a sort of secret presence of God (the missionary activity) frees from evil influences and restores to Christ, their author, who overthrows the reign of the devil and wards off the manifold malice of sin. So whatever good is found sown in the hearts and minds of men, or in the rites and cultures proper to various peoples, is not only saved from destruction but is also healed, ennobled and brought to perfection, for the glory of God, the confusion of the devil and the happiness of man *(cf. n. 1136).* Thus missionary activity tends towards the eschatological fulfilment. For through it the People of God grows to the measure and time which the Father has fixed by His own authority *(cf. Acts 1.7).*

(The seeds of the Word must be illumined by the Gospel)

1025   11. In order to be able to witness to Christ fruitfully, Christians must be united to those (other) men in esteem and love. They must regard themselves as real members of the groups in which they live. They must take part in the cultural and social life through the various dealings and occupations of human life. They must be familiar with their national and religious traditions; with joy and reverence they must discover the seeds of the Word hidden in these traditions.... Just as Christ searched the hearts of men and led them to the divine by truly human contacts, so His disciples, deeply imbued with the Spirit of Christ, should know the men among whom they live and associate with them. In this way, through sincere and patient dialogue they will learn what treasures the bountiful God has distributed among the nations. At the same time they should strive to illumine those riches with the light of the Gospel, to liberate them and bring them under the dominion of God the Saviour.

(The Christian religious life must assume the religious traditions of the nations)

1026   18. The religious institutes which are working for the planting of the Church and are deeply imbued with the treasures of mysticism for which the religious tradition of the Church is so remarkable, should strive to express and hand on these treasures in a way suitable to the natural gifts and character of each people. There are ascetical and contemplative traditions in some ancient cultures the seeds of which were implanted by God before the Gospel was ever preached there. The religious institutes should carefully study how best these ascetical and contemplative traditions may be assimilated into Christian religious life.

PASTORAL CONSTITUTION *GAUDIUM ET SPES* (1965)

The Pastoral Constitution on the Church in the Modern World complements the Dogmatic Constitution on the Church (LG) and the Decree on the Church's Missionary Activity (AG). It presents a Church open to and in dialogue with the world and all its values, including religious ones.

After a preliminary description of the cultural and spiritual situation of the world today the Constitution in its first part speaks of the Church in relation to man's vocation. Chapter I of this first part, dealing with the mystery of the human person, recognises that the grace of the risen Lord acts invisibly in the heart of all men of good will (22). Chapter II on human society stresses the need for love, mutual understanding and dialogue, whereby, while error is rejected, persons will always find acceptance (28). Chapter III is dedicated to human activity and Chapter IV to the Church's role in the modern world. This world is ever stirred by the Holy Spirit (41); this is why for the unique contribution which she must make the Church receives help from all forms of human culture which open new ways towards truth (44) (cf. n. 1145).

This point is taken up especially in the second part which deals with particular problems, especially in the important Chapter II on promoting cultural values, a task which above all requires openness (57). The conclusion of the Constitution finds the roots for the Christian attitude of dialogue with all men, specifically of inter-religious dialogue, in the missionary call of the Church (92).

(Respect and love of adversaries)

1027 28. Respect and love ought to be extended also to those who think and act differently from us in social, political and even religious matters. In fact, the more deeply we come to understand their ways of thinking through sympathy and love, the more easily shall we be able to enter into dialogue with them.

Of course, this love and kindness must never make us in any way indifferent to what is true and good. Rather, love itself impels the disciples of Christ to announce the saving truth to all men. But we must distinguish between the error, which is always to be repudiated, and the man in error who always keeps the dignity of being a person, even when he is flawed by false or less accurate religious ideas *(cf. n. 2140)*. God alone is the judge and searcher of hearts; hence He forbids us to make judgment about the interior guilt of any one *(cf. Lk. 6.37f; Mt. 7.1f; Rom. 2.1-11; 14.10-12)*.

(Dialogue among all men)

1028 92. By virtue of her mission to shed on the whole world the light of the Gospel message and to gather together in the one Spirit all men of every nation, race and culture, the Church stands forth as a sign of that brotherliness which makes possible, indeed stimulates, a sincere dialogue.

But this requires that first of all within the Church itself we foster esteem, respect and concord, with full recognition of legitimate differences....

We also turn our thoughts to all those who acknowledge God and preserve in their traditions precious elements of religion and humanity. We wish that a frank dialogue may lead us all to welcome faithfully the impulses of the Spirit and to carry them out courageously.

For our part, the desire for such dialogue—which should be guided by the sole love of truth though with due prudence—does not exclude any one: neither those who cultivate noble human values without as yet recognising their Author, nor those who oppose the Church and persecute her in various ways. Since God the Father is the beginning and the end of all men, we are all called to be brothers. And thus, sharing the same vocation, both human and divine, we can and must work together, without violence or deceit, to build up the world in true peace.

PAUL VI

ENCYCLICAL LETTER *ECCLESIAM SUAM* (1964)

While presenting the programme of his pontificate in his first Encyclical Letter, Pope Paul VI spoke of the attitudes which the Church must develop in our times. He stressed the need for fraternal dialogue with all men. This fundamental openness to others gives to the Letter a tone which is in sharp contrast with the polemic attitude of many earlier documents. Dialogue is not merely a matter of policy; it is based on God's free initiative in revealing Himself to man from whom He expects a free response. God's revelation discloses His own intimate life. The same notion of dialogue is found in the later documents of Vatican II (cf. especially NA 2-3; AG 16, 34, 41; cf. also n. 1027). In the encyclical the Pope distinguishes by way of concentric circles four classes of men with whom the Church must be in dialogue. The first

and the widest circle comprises all men, for there is scope for dialogue with
all on the fundamental problems of human life (cf. nn. 155-159). In the
second circle, the Church reaches out to all believers, in the third to all
Christians; the fourth or inner circle concerns dialogue within the Church.
The extract quoted here belongs to the second circle, that of dialogue with
all believers. The text is found in AAS 56 (1964) 654-655. The Pope came
back on the same topic in his Djakarta address (December 3, 1970) (cf.
AAS 63 (1971) 74).

(Dialogue with all believers)

1029 Then we see another circle around us. This too is vast in
extent; yet it is not so far away from us. It is made first and
foremost of those men who adore the one, supreme God, whom we
also worship. We refer here to the children of the Hebrew race,
worthy of our respect and love. They are faithful to the tradition
proper to what we call the Old Testament. We refer also to those
who adore God according to the conception of monotheism, especially that of the Muslims, whom we rightly admire for the truth and
goodness found in their religion. Finally we refer to the followers of
the great religions of Africa and Asia. It is obvious that we cannot
agree with various aspects of these religions, and that we cannot
overlook differences or be unconcerned with them, as if all religions
had, each in its own way, the same value, which would dispense
those who follow them from the need of inquiring whether God has
revealed a way free from all error and certain, by which He desires to
make Himself known, loved and served. Indeed, honesty compels us
to declare openly what we believe, namely that there is one true
religion, the Christian religion, and that we hope that all who seek
God and adore Him, will come to acknowledge this.

1030 Yet we do, nevertheless, acknowledge with respect the spiritual and moral values of various non-Christian religions, for
we desire to join with them in promoting and defending common
ideals in the spheres of religious liberty, human brotherhood, teaching and education, social welfare and civil order. On these great
ideals that we share with them we can have dialogue, and we shall
not fail to offer opportunities for it whenever, in genuine mutual
respect, our offer would be received with good will.

ADDRESS TO REPRESENTATIVES OF VARIOUS RELIGIONS
(1964)

During the 38th International Eucharistic Congress held in Bombay, the
Pope, in an address to representatives of various religions, stressed the

need of mutual respect and acceptance. In this and in other Bombay speeches he quoted approvingly from the sacred books of Hinduism. The text quoted below is found in AAS 57 (1965) 132-133.

(The Indian religious heritage)

1031 This visit to India is the fulfilment of a long cherished desire.

Yours is a land of ancient culture, the cradle of great religions, the home of a nation that has sought God with a relentless desire, in deep meditation and silence, and in hymns of fervent prayer. Rarely has this longing for God been expressed with words so full of the spirit of Advent as in the words written in your sacred books many centuries before Christ: "From the unreal lead me to the real; from darkness lead me to light; from death lead me to immortality."[1] This is a prayer which belongs also to our time. Today more than ever it should rise from every human heart.

(Towards a universal communion based on love)

1032 Therefore we must come closer together, not only through the modern means of communication, through press and radio, through steamships and jet planes; we must come together with our hearts, in mutual understanding, esteem and love. We must meet not merely as tourists, but as pilgrims who set out to find God, not in buildings of stone but in human hearts. Man must meet man, nation meet nation, as brothers and sisters, as children of God. In this mutual understanding and friendship, in this sacred communion, we must also begin to work together to build the common future of the human race. We must find the concrete and practical ways of organisation and cooperation, so that all resources be pooled and all efforts united towards achieving a true communion among all nations. Such a union cannot be built on universal terror or the fear of mutual destruction; it must be built on a common love that embraces all and has its roots in God who is Love.

LETTER *AFRICARUM TERRARUM* TO THE HIERARCHY AND THE PEOPLES OF AFRICA (1967)

In this important letter the Pope dwells at length on man's basic religious experience which is sometimes unduly restricted to the so-called primitive peoples. A similar but less elaborate description is found in Vatican II (NA 2), where it is followed by the religious experience proper to Hinduism and

---

1. *Bṛhādaraṇyaka Upaniṣad*, 1, 3, 28.

Buddhism. The Pope shows the value of this fundamental religious expe-
rience of man. The text is found in AAS 59 (1967) 1077-1078, 1080.

(Man's basic religious experience)

1033 7. ...We think it opportune to dwell on some general concepts, characteristic of the ancient cultures of Africa, as their
moral and religious value demands, we think, a careful consideration.

8. As firm foundation there is in all the traditions of Africa a
sense of the spiritual realities. This sense must not be understood
merely as what scholars of the history of religion at the end of the last
century used to call animism. It is something different, something
deeper, vaster and more universal. It is the realisation that all
created realities, and in particular visible nature itself, is united with
the world of invisible and spiritual realities. As for man, he is not
considered as mere matter or limited to this earthly life, but is
recognised as having a spiritual active element, so that his mortal life
is seen as connected at every moment with life after death.

A very important and common factor of this sense of spiritual
realities is the notion of God as the first and ultimate cause of things.
Such a notion is more experienced than described, more realised in
life than apprehended by thought. It is expressed in many different
ways according to the variety of cultural forms. In reality, a living
sense of God as the supreme, personal and mystical Being, pervades the whole of African culture.

People have recourse to God in all the more important moments
of life, when recourse to another intercessor is thought to be useless. Generally He is invoked as Father, without any fear of the
divine power. The prayers addressed to Him either individually or
collectively are very genuine and often touch deeply the hearts of
those who hear them. Among the ritual actions peformed by people
one of the purest and most significant is the sacrifice of the first
fruits....

(Christianity assumes all that is good)

1034 14. The Catholic Church holds in great regard the moral and
religious values proper to the African traditions, not only
because of their own significance but also because she sees them as a
providential and most fruitful foundation on which the preaching of
the Gospel can be based and a new society centred on Christ can be
built....

In fact the doctrine and redemption of Christ fulfils, renews and perfects whatever good is found in all human traditions. Therefore, the African who is consecrated as a Christian is not forced to renounce his own self, but assumes the ancient values of his people "in spirit and in truth" *(Jn 6.24)*.

RADIO-MESSAGE TO THE GOVERNMENTS
AND PEOPLES OF ASIA (1970)

This message was transmitted from Manila over Radio Veritas during the visit of the Pope to East Asia and Oceania, on November 1, 1970. In it the Pope salutes an immense land, "the source of great civilisations, the birth-place of world religions, the treasure-house of ancient wisdom." The whole speech is imbued with the concern to show how the values of material progress can be combined with those of the spirit. The text is found in AAS 63 (1971) 37-38.

(Spiritual values and human progress)

1035　　In fact, brethren, while we contemplate the past history of your nations, we are impressed most of all by the sense of spiritual values dominating the thoughts of your sages and the lives of your vast multitudes. The discipline of your ascetics, the deep religious spirit of your peoples, your filial piety and attachment to the family, your veneration of ancestors:—all point to the primacy of the spirit; all reveal your unceasing quest for God, your hunger for the supernatural.

These characteristics are not only of value for your spiritual life. For, taken together, they not only constitute no obstacle for the attainment of the technical, economic and social progress to which your immense peoples rightly aspire; but, indeed, they offer a foundation of immeasurable might for full development which does not sacrifice the deepest and most precious values, those namely which make of man a being directed by spiritual influences, the master, at least potentially, of the cosmos and of its forces, and likewise master of himself.

PAUL VI

APOSTOLIC EXHORTATION *EVANGELII NUNTIANDI*
(8 December 1975)

In his Apostolic Exhortation on Evangelization in which he resumes the work of the Synod of Bishops in Rome on the same topic (1974), Pope Paul VI speaks of non-Christian religions in the context of the Church's evangel-

izing mission. While recognising after Vatican II that authentic values are found in those religions, he notes that their relation to Christianity raises many questions which need to be further studied, and stresses what distinguishes the religion of Jesus which the Church proclaims through evangelization. The text is found in AAS 68 (1976) 41-42.

(Non-Christian religions and the Church's evangelizing mission)

1036   53. This first proclamation (of the Gospel) is also addressed to the immense sections of mankind that practise non-Christian religions. The Church respects and esteems highly these non-Christian religions, the living expression of the soul of vast groups of people. They carry within them the echo of thousands of years of searching for God, a quest incomplete indeed but often made with great sincerity and righteousness of heart. They possess an impressive patrimony of deeply religious texts and have taught generations of people how to pray. They are impregnated with innumerable "Seeds of the Word" and therefore constitute an authentic "preparation for the Gospel", to quote felicitous expressions used by the Second Vatican Council *(nn. 1025, 1136; LG 16)* and borrowed from Eusebius of Caesarea.

As we reflect on this there certainly arise many complex questions that require a great deal of prudence. These questions, which are neither light nor easy, have still to be studied by theologians, with due regard for the Christian tradition and the Church's Magisterium, so as to open to missionaries of today and of tomorrow new ways in their contacts with non-Christian religions.

But neither respect and high esteem for these religions nor the complexity of the theological questions raised is an invitation to the Church to withhold from these non-Christians the proclamation of Jesus Christ. On the contrary, the Church holds that these multitudes have the right to know the riches of the mystery of Christ *(cf. Eph. 3.8)*—riches in which, we believe, the whole humanity can find in unsuspected fulness everything that it is gropingly searching for concerning God, man and his destiny, life and death, and truth.

Therefore, even in the face of the highest forms of natural religions, the Church thinks that she has a unique function: the religion of Jesus which she proclaims through evangelization truly puts man in contact with the plan of God, with his living presence and his action. It thus enables him to meet the mystery of the Fatherhood of God that bends over towards humanity. In other words, through our religion an authentic and living relationship with God is truly established, such as other religions cannot bring about even though they have, as it were, their arms stretched out towards heaven.

JOHN PAUL II

ENCYCLICAL LETTER *REDEMPTOR HOMINIS* (1979)

At the beginning of his first Encyclical Letter on "Jesus Christ Redeemer of Man" Pope John Paul II expresses appreciation for the progress of inter-religious dialogue between Christians and non-Christians, showing what benefit Christians can derive from such dialogue. In chapter II, entitled "The Mystery of Redemption", he describes the values contained in those religions and exhorts Christians of various denominations to share in the same mission towards them in an open spirit. The text is found in AAS 71 (1979) 257ff.

(Fostering inter-religious dialogue)

1037   6. It is obvious that this new stage in the Church's life demands of us a faith that is particularly enlightened, profound and responsible. True ecumenical activity means openness, drawing closer, availability for dialogue, and a shared investigation of the truth in the full evangelical and Christian sense; but in no way does it or can it mean giving up or in any way underestimating the treasures of divine truth that the Church has constantly confessed and taught....

What we have just said (about ecumenical action) must also be applied—although in another way and with the due differences—to activity for coming closer together with representatives of the non-Christian religions, an activity expressed through dialogue, contacts, prayer in common, investigation of the treasures of human spirituality, in which, as we well know, the members of these religions are indeed not lacking. Does it not sometimes happen that the firm belief of the followers of the non-Christian religions—a belief that is also an effect of the Spirit of truth operating outside the visible confines of the Mystical Body—can make Christians ashamed at often being themselves so disposed to doubt concerning the truths revealed by God and proclaimed by the Church and so prone to relax moral principles and open the way to ethical permissiveness? It is a noble thing to have a predisposition for understanding every person, analysing every system and recognizing what is right; this does not at all mean losing certitude about one's faith *(cf. n. 130)* or weakening the principles of morality....

(Union with God and full humanity, goal of all religions)

1038   11. The Council document on non-Christian religions... is filled with deep esteem for the great spiritual values, indeed for the primacy of the spiritual, which in the life of mankind finds expression in religion and then in morality, with direct effects on the whole of culture. The Fathers of the Church rightly saw in the various religions as it were so many reflections of the one truth, "seeds of the Word" *(cf. nn. 1025, 1136)*, attesting that, though the routes taken may be different, there is but one single goal to which is directed the deepest aspiration of the human spirit as expressed in its quest for God, and also in its quest, through its tending towards God, for the full dimension of its humanity, or, in other words, for the full meaning of human life.

(Missionary attitude towards non-Christians)

1039   12. Thanks to this unity (of all Christians in mission) we can together come close to the magnificent heritage of the human spirit that has been manifested in all religions, as the Second Vatican Council's Declaration *Nostra Aetate* says *(cf. nn. 1019-1022)*. It also enables us to approach all cultures, all ideological concepts, all people of good will. We come to them with the esteem, respect and discernment that since the time of the Apostles has marked the missionary policy and the attitude of the missionary. Suffice it to mention St Paul and, for instance, his address in the Areopagus at Athens *(Acts 17.22-31)*. The missionary attitude always begins with a feeling of deep esteem for "what is in man" *(Jn 2.26)*, for what man has himself worked out in the depths of his spirit concerning the most profound and important problems. It is a question of respecting everything that has been brought about in him by the Spirit, which "blows where it wills" *(Jn 3.8)*. The mission is never destruction, but instead is a taking up and fresh building, even if in practice there has not always been full correspondence with this high ideal. And we know well that the conversion that is begun by the mission is a work of grace, in which man must fully find himself again.

MESSAGE TO THE PEOPLE OF ASIA

(Manila, 21 February 1981)

During his journey to several Asian Churches in 1981 Pope John Paul II delivered a message to the people of Asia from the Auditorium of Radio Veritas in Manila. After summarising the teaching of the Declaration Nostra

Aetate *of Vatican II (cf. nn. 1019-1023), the Pope expressed the desire that inter-religious dialogue may grow, especially in Asia which is the cradle of ancient religions, in common concern for spiritual values and for the dignity of man. The text is found in AAS 73 (1981) 391-398.*

(Fostering inter-religious dialogue)

1040 4. In this age the Church of Jesus Christ experiences a profound need to enter into contact and dialogue with all these religions. She pays homage to the many moral values contained in these religions, as well as to the potential for spiritual living which so deeply marks the traditions and the cultures of whole societies. What seems to bring together and unite, in a particular way, Christians and believers of other religions is an acknowledgment of the need for prayer as an expression of man's spirituality directed towards the Absolute. Even when, for some, He is the Great Unknown, He nevertheless remains always in reality the same living God. We trust that wherever the human spirit opens itself in prayer to this Unknown God, an echo will be heard of the same Spirit who, knowing the limits and weakness of the human person, Himself prays in us and on our behalf, "expressing our plea in a way that could never be put into words" *(Rom. 8.26).* The intercession of the Spirit of God who prays in us and for us is the fruit of the mystery of the Redemption of Christ, in which the all-embracing love of the Father has been shown to the world.

5. All Christians must therefore be committed to dialogue with the believers of all religions, so that mutual understanding and collaboration may grow; so that moral values may be strengthened; so that God may be praised in all creation. Ways must be developed to make this dialogue become a reality everywhere, but especially in Asia, the continent that is the cradle of ancient cultures and religions.... Christians will, moreover, join hands with all men and women of good will who share a belief in the inestimable dignity of each human person. They will work together in order to bring about a more just and peaceful society in which the poor will be the first to be served. Asia is the continent where the spiritual is held in high esteem and where the religious sense is deep and innate: the preservation of this precious heritage must be the common task of all.

CHAPTER XI

THE CHURCH AND THE MISSIONS

"Go and make disciples of all nations" (Mt. 28.19): such was the command of the risen Christ to His apostles; "and they went forth and preached everywhere" (Mk 16.20). The Acts of the Apostles testify to the missionary activity of the apostolic Church. Ever since, the Church, obeying Christ's mandate, has continued to proclaim His message to new peoples. This effort sustained through the centuries witnesses to the Church's sure instinct as regards her missionary vocation.

To be missionary is not for the Church a merely accidental function; it belongs to her very nature. The reason is that in God's plan of salvation for the world her mission prolongs the mission of the Incarnate Son. What God has once for all accomplished in Jesus Christ for the salvation of men is, as it were, actuated in space and time through the Church: His saving word remains audible in her proclamation of the Gospel; His redeeming work becomes tangible in her actions. Established by Christ as the "universal sacrament of salvation" (AG 1), the Church must fulfil her function at all times and in every place. Through her God's design must be realised that all may come to the full knowledge of the Truth. Hence the Church's urge to communicate the Good News to all men.

In the early centuries few official documents spoke of the Church's missionary activity. Here as in other areas of the Church's life, practice has preceded theory; the conversion of the ancient Christian world witnesses, however, to the vitality of the Church's mission during that period. The conditions created by the Middle Ages, while offering to the Church new opportunities to meet the outside world, did not favour a profound reflection on the mission. A few texts belonging to this period are mentioned here; they witness to the positive and negative elements in the Church's discharge of her mandate. The modern times have brought with them a great missionary movement. It is a well known fact that the vast extension of the boundaries of the Church to remote lands during this period has sometimes been unduly linked to worldly interests and has suffered from this association. Yet, not to mention the boundless zeal of missionaries, this period is also marked with deep missionary insights and with a great foresight on the part of the Church in the exercise of her missionary action. Texts testify to both. The elaboration of an explicit theology of the missions remains, nevertheless, a later development, characteristic of this century. Its progress can be followed through the missionary encyclicals of the Popes. The fundamental principles of missionary theology emerge more and more definitely in these documents. An adequate definition of the purpose of missionary activity evolves gradually; the role of the local clergy and hierarchy stands out more and more clearly; progressive recognition is given to the principle of missionary adaptation.

This impressive elaboration notwithstanding, the missions have in recent years met with new questioning. A first reason for this is the Church's renewed awareness of the fact that God can save men by ways known to Him alone; prolonged and sincere contact with other religions and their adherents has, moreover, convinced the Church that they too already live by God's grace which reaches them in the concrete circumstances of their religious life. Another reason is that to the outsider the Christian mission appears as imposing a narrow institutional set-up with its inherent limitations and its own cultural heritage; the Church herself has become more conscious of the constant danger that threatens her of sacrificing the mystery to the institution. All this has led to a new reflection on the true nature of the Church and of her missionary activity which it is the merit of the Second Vatican Council to have brought to fruition. The Council has shown that the institution of the Church is rooted in the mystery of Christ. She is not an end in herself, but has for her only purpose to make Christ and His work visibly present in the world. This renewed understanding of the Church, implying a radical de-centring, brings with it a new theological perception of her missionary activity and a new approach to her missionary practice. Based essentially on presence and witnessing, it overcomes all the antinomies and embraces all the various forms of Christian action. It is the shared responsibility of the whole Church, especially of all the members of the local Churches where Christ remains unknown to many. It is in order to be as perfect a sign of Christ as possible that the local Churches must be endowed with all the elements that constitute the mystery of the Church.

*   *   *

The doctrinal points dealt with in this chapter may be grouped under the following headings:

The Church is essentially missionary: (1136i), 1136, 1137, 1141.

Her missionary activity takes a special form in the missions: 1136, 1138, 1143.

The purpose of the missions is to evangelise and to establish the Church: 1116, 1123, 1126, 1138, 1149.

Missionary motivation is to bring others to Christ and the Church: 1115, 1139, 1140.

The local Churches must develop to maturity: 1142, 1143.

They must make their contribution to the universality of the Church: 1119, 1120, 1124, 1125, 1131, 1144, 1145.

They must have their local hierarchy: 1107, 1112, 1116, 1142;

their local priests: 1107, 1112, 1116, 1142;

their local religious and an active laity: 1117, 1128, 1133, 1135, 1142.

All share in the missionary activity of the local Church: 1118, (1136i).

Priests of local Churches must be well trained: 1112, 1132, (1136i).

The laity must be well trained: 1101, 1133, 1134, (1136i).

The local Church must be rooted in the culture of the land and assume all its values: 1102, 1109, 1120, 1121, 1122, 1125, 1129, 1136, 1144.

Adaptation to local customs is the law of the mission: 1102, 1108, 1109, 1120, 1121, 1129, 1144, 1145, 1233.

Theological reflection must seek ways of presenting the message adapted to the country: 1132, 1144, 1145.

The law of adaptation applies especially to foreign missionaries: 1104, 1105, 1106, 1109, 1113, 1114, 1122.

They are destined to become auxiliaries to the local clergy: 1127.

Evangelisation means the renewal of humanity and of culture: 1150-1152.

Witnessing, dialogue and evangelisation, all belong to missionary activity: 1111, (1136i).

Evangelisation and development complement each other: 1146-1148, (1155).

Evangelisation includes liberation: (1153)-(1154).

Two dimensions of liberation proclaimed by the Church: (1156), 1158.

Evangelisation includes the promotion of justice: 1159, 2159.

THE FIRST GENERAL COUNCIL OF NICAEA (325)

Besides its Symbol of faith (cf. n. 7), the first Council of Nicaea promulgated a series of canons. Among these one recommends a long catechesis for new converts to the faith and forbids that neophytes be promoted to the episcopate or presbyterate without adequate probation. The text is found in COD, *pp. 5-6.*

(On neophytes)

1101 Canon 2: Many things have been done against the ecclesiastical rule, either out of necessity or under pressure from men. Thus men acceding to the faith from the life of the gentiles are soon led to the spiritual cleansing, and at once after baptism are promoted to the episcopate or the presbyterate. It has seemed best that nothing of the sort be done hereafter. For catechesis requires time and after baptism a long probation is needed. The text of the apostle is indeed clear where it says: "he must not be a recent convert, or he may be puffed up with conceit and fall into condemnation and the snare of the devil" *(cf. 1 Tim. 3.6-7)....*

GREGORY THE GREAT (590-604)

LETTER TO ABBOT MELLITUS

This letter was addressed by Pope Gregory the Great to Mellitus, abbot in France, who was about to join St Augustine of Canterbury as a fellow missionary. The Pope instructs his correspondent to show his letter to Augustine, as it is concerned with the missionary methods to be used for an easier conversion of England. This instruction is a practical combination of sound psychology, tolerance and firmness. Rather than destroy the temples of the people they evangelise, missionaries should aim at converting them into churches. Thus there will be continuity and newness between the people's ancient religion and their new faith; being allowed to retain their places of worship, they will more readily accept the mystery of Christ celebrated in them. Nor is it to be expected that new Christians will grasp at once the full meaning of the Christian faith; this requires time. If allowed to continue some of their time-honoured customs, they will gradually discover the new meaning they take on in Christianity. See Epistola *76,* PL *77, 1215-1216.*

(The temples must not be destroyed but converted into Christian Churches)

1102 Tell Augustine that he should by no means destroy the temples of the gods but rather the idols within those temples. Let him, after he has purified them with holy water, place altars and relics of the saints in them. For, if those temples are well built, they should be converted from the worship of demons to the service of the true God. Thus, seeing that their places of worship are not destroyed, the people will banish error from their hearts and come to places familiar and dear to them in acknowledgment and worship of the true God.

Further, since it has been their custom to slaughter oxen in sacrifice to the demons, they should receive some solemnity in exchange. Let them, therefore, on the day of the dedication of their churches, or on the feast of the martyrs whose relics are preserved in them, build themselves huts around their one-time temples and celebrate the occasion with religious feasting. They will sacrifice and eat the animals not any more as an offering to the devil, but for the glory of God to whom, as to the giver of all things, they will give thanks for having been satiated. Thus, it they are not deprived of all the exterior joys, they will more easily taste the interior ones. For surely it is impossible to efface all at once everything from their strong minds, just as, when one wishes to reach the top of a mountain, he must climb by stages and step by step, not by leaps and bounds....

Mention this then to our brother the bishop, that he may dispose of the matter as he sees fit according to the conditions of time and place....

THE FOURTH LATERAN GENERAL COUNCIL (1215)

Besides its doctrinal pronouncements on the Catholic faith (cf. nn. 19-21) and on the mystery of the Trinity (cf. nn. 317-320), the Council also promulgated other "Constitutions" mostly concerned with practical matters, for instance liturgical (cf. nn. 1201-1202). Among these is found a chapter forbidding converts from Judaism to retain their Jewish practices. The text must be understood in the historical context of the times when the Church was engaged in her effort to free the Holy Land from the Saracens. This context was not conducive to a friendly attitude towards Judaism. Christianity appeared as a complete break with Judaism and little attention was given to the religious patrimony which it inherited from the Jewish tradition. In fact, as the Council testifies (68, 69), social discrimination against the Jews, including distinction in dress and exclusion from public offices, was part of the policy enforced by the Church. Neither were converts from Judaism allowed to identify themselves with their people of origin; sincere conversion seemed to demand a complete break. The text is found in COD, p. 243.

Chapter LXX: Jewish Converts to the Faith May Not Retain their Ancient Practices

1103 There are some, as has been reported to us, who after having freely approached the sacred bath of baptism do not put off the old man fully in order the better to put on the new one *(cf. Col. 3.9)*; they retain elements of their former rites and thus by a sort of mixture introduce confusion in the splendour of the Christian religion. Since it is written: Woe to the man who walks along two ways *(cf. Sir. 2.12)*, and that one must not wear mingled dress, wool and linen together *(cf. Deut. 22.11)*, we decide that such converts must be forced by those who preside over the Churches to abandon altogether the observance of their ancient rites so that, after having given to the Christian religion the assent of their free will, they may be preserved in its observance by the pressure of salutary compulsion. For it is a lesser evil not to recognise the way of the Lord than to step back after having recognised it.

THE GENERAL COUNCIL OF VIENNA (1311-1312)

This Council also met in the context of the long drawn-out crusade for the liberation of the Holy Land from the Saracens. Besides its doctrinal decrees (cf. n. 405), it contains others on practical matters. One of these (25) legislates that the cult rendered to Mohammed by the Saracens must be forbidden in Christian lands. This stricture notwithstanding, the Council recognises the demands which the work of evangelisation makes on the preachers of the Gospel in foreign lands: they must be thoroughly conversant with the languages required for convincingly presenting the message of Christ. In the historical context mention is made of the languages needed for the evangelisation of the Muslims. The text of this decree 24 is found in COD, pp. 355-356.

(On the knowledge of languages required for the work of evangelisation)

1104   24. ...Therefore, unworthy as we are of the commission which Christ has entrusted to us in this world, following His own example when He wished that the apostles who were to go to evangelise the whole world should be well versed in all languages *(cf. Acts 2.4; 1 Cor. 12.30)*, we desire that the holy Church should have an abundant number of Catholics well versed in the languages, especially in those of the infidels, so as to be able to instruct them in the sacred doctrine and to join them to the Christian community by the acceptance of the Christian faith and the reception of holy baptism.... Once they have learned and are sufficiently proficient in those languages (Hebrew, Arabic, Chaldaean), they will be able by

God's grace to bear the fruit which is hoped for and to present the faith adequately to the infidel peoples....

THE GENERAL COUNCIL OF BASEL
DECREE ON JEWS AND NEOPHYTES (1434)

This decree belongs to the Basel period of the 17th general Council, celebrated from 1431 to 1445, which held its sessions at Basel, Ferrara, Florence and Rome, successively. The decrees of sessions I to XXI of Basel, though passed almost in their entirety while the Council was under censure from Pope Eugene IV, were subsequently approved by him and form an integral part of the work of the general Council. The decree quoted here (session XIX) again witnesses to the Church's stern attitude towards the Jews during this entire period; various strictures were imposed on them, including the prohibition of mixed marriages. At the same time it was recognised that missionaries ought to be not only learned but also full of sympathy in order to bring the Jews to the faith; and though pressure could be exercised on them to hear the Christian message, yet conversions had to be free and sincere. The text of the decree is found in COD, pp. 459-460.

A similar decree of the same session, "on those who wish to be converted to the faith" (ibid., 460-461), strongly forbids Jews who have become Christians to return to Jewish practices; but it also expects all Christians to show the greatest charity towards those who have been converted to the faith and to help them materially when in need. Nor should pastors be satisfied with exhorting their flock in this respect; they themselves should set an example for them to emulate.

(The qualities required from missionaries to the Jews)

1105 ...Following in the steps of Jesus Christ our Saviour *(cf. 1 Pet. 2.21)*, this holy Synod desires with the most intense love that all may come to recognise the truth of the Gospel and, after they have accepted it, that they may perservere in it faithfully. It wishes, therefore, to take salutary measures in order that the Jews and other infidels may be converted to the orthodox faith and that converts may persevere in it steadfastly. First of all it decrees that all bishops must sometimes each year send some men well grounded in the divine word to those parts where Jews and other infidels live, to preach and explain the truth of the Catholic faith in such a way that the infidels who hear them may come to recognise their errors. Let them compel them to hear their preaching...; but let also the bishops and preachers show themselves so full of sympathy and charity towards their hearers as to win them to Christ not only by declaring the truth to them but also through other human good offices....

ALEXANDER VII

S. CONGREGATION *DE PROPAGANDA FIDE*
INSTRUCTION TO THE VICARS APOSTOLIC OF TONKIN
AND COCHINCHINA (1659)

In May 1658 the S. Congregation de Propaganda Fide presented to Pope Alexander VII the first two candidates for the episcopate in Indochina. Bishop Francis Pallu was appointed Vicar apostolic of Tonkin and put in charge of all missions in Western China, while bishop Lambert de la Motte was appointed Vicar apostolic of Cochinchina, responsible for all the missions in Southern China. Before their departure for the missions the new Vicars apostolic received specific instructions from the S. Congregation. Conditions were not favourable to Catholic missionaries in those countries at that particular time and Propaganda wished to ensure in missionaries the necessary qualities. More important, however, was the need to promote a local clergy. It was recognised as imperative to establish the local Church with its own clergy and, eventually, its own hierarchy. The S. Congregation was also anxious to respect the traditions and customs of those countries, thus carrying on the early tradition of the Church to assume into Christianity whatever was good in the ways of the people and gradually to eradicate what was not compatible with it. The text is found in Collectanea Sacrae Congregationis de Propaganda Fide *(Rome, 1907) 1, 42-43.*

(Qualities required of missionaries)

1106   Your first care must be to seek out and select with great diligence, from among many, men whose age and health will enable them to cope with sustained work, and—what is more important—who are distinguished for their charity and prudence. These qualities must be ascertained, not through the opinion or conjectures of others, but through the candidates' sustained behaviour and successful accomplishment of diverse responsible tasks. They must be men who can keep secrets and guard them tenaciously; men who, by the integrity of their conduct, by their courtesy, meekness, patience, humility and the example of all their virtues, bear witness in their lives to the Christian faith which their lips profess. Finally, by conforming to the norms of evangelical charity, they must be ready to adapt themselves to the mentality and customs of others so as not to be a burden to the companions with whom they live, nor earn the disfavour or even the dislike of outsiders, but rather become, like the apostle, all things to all men.

(On preparing a local clergy)

1107   The chief reason which has induced the S. Congregation to send you as bishops to these regions is that, by every means and method possible, you so take in hand the education of young people that they may become capable of attaining to the priesthood. You will then ordain them and assign them in those vast territories, each to his own region, with the mission to serve Christianity there with the utmost diligence, under your direction. Therefore, you must always have this end in view: to lead to holy orders as many and as suitable candidates as possible, to form them and to promote them in due time.

If, among those whom you have promoted, there are some worthy of the episcopate,... inform the S. Congregation of their names, age, qualities and whatever else it may be useful to know about them such as where they could be consecrated, in charge of which dioceses they could be appointed....

(The directives of Propaganda must not be imposed forcibly)

1108 If, in carrying out the orders of the S. Congregation, you meet or foresee difficulties to the extent that these orders will not be accepted without revolt, avoid at all cost imposing them on the persons concerned against their will. Do not urge them by force or the fear of censures and avoid sowing the seed of division which would result from the disobedience of some, for you would thus alienate them and arouse strong passions. On the contrary, it will be better to take into account the recent conversion and consequent weakness of the neophytes and therefore not to apply the decree immediately. Take time to write and explain fully and sincerely the whole question to the S. Congregation and await its instructions on what you must do.

(Western customs must not be introduced but local ones adopted)

1109 Do not in any way attempt, and do not on any pretext persuade these people to change their rites, habits and customs, unless they are openly opposed to religion and good morals. For what could be more absurd than to bring France, Spain, Italy or any other European country over to China? It is not your country but the faith you must bring, that faith which does not reject or belittle the rites or customs of any nation as long as these rites are not evil, but rather desires that they be preserved in their integrity and fostered. It is, as it were, written in the nature of all men that the customs of their country and especially their country itself should be esteemed, loved and respected above anything else in the world.

There is no greater cause of alienation and hatred than to change the customs of a nation, especially when they go back as far as the memory of ancestors can reach. What then if, having abrogated them, you attempt to replace them with the customs of your country imported from abroad? Never make comparisons between the customs of these peoples and those of Europe; on the contrary show your anxiety to become used to them. Admire and praise whatever merits praise. As regards what is not praiseworthy, while it must not be extolled as is done by flatterers, you will be prudent enough not to pass judgment on it, or, in any case, not to condemn it rashly or exaggeratedly. As for what is evil, it should be dismissed by a nod of the head or by silence rather than by words, without losing the occasions, when souls have become disposed to receive the truth, to uproot it imperceptibly.

(The witness of evangelical poverty)

1110   You would not wish to incur hatred as a result of material interests. Remember the poverty of the apostles who earned with their own hands what was needed for themselves and their companions. All the more reason why you who emulate and imitate them, being content with your food and clothing, should abstain from any base profit. Do not beg alms or collect money, gifts or riches. If some of the faithful force you to accept offerings in spite of your protests, distribute them to the poor under their own eyes, knowing well that nothing is more astounding to the people and nothing attracts their attention more than to witness contempt for temporal goods. This is the evangelical poverty which prepares for itself a treasure in heaven by raising itself above all things human and earthly.

BENEDICT XV

APOSTOLIC LETTER *MAXIMUM ILLUD* (1919)

This Apostolic Letter by Pope Benedict XV, the first in a series of great encyclicals explicitly concerned with the full organisation of mission work in this century, represents an important break-through for the modern concept of the Church's missionary activity. Written at a time when the mission lands had been considerably depleted of foreign personnel as a consequence of the first world war, it does not only plead for the recruitment of more foreign missionaries and for help in alms and prayers from Catholics in Christian countries; it exposes in a forceful manner some of the basic principles which must guide the authentic growth of the Church in mission lands. *Insistence is laid on the Church's responsibility to all the inhabitants of mission countries, on the primary importance of training a local clergy which will be able to take into their hands the destiny of the Church in their country, on the disinterestedness required from foreign missionaries and their full adaptation to the country of their adoption. The text is found in AAS 11 (1919) 440ff.*

(Missionary zeal must extend to all the inhabitants of the land)

1111   The superior of a mission should make it one of his primary concerns to expand and fully develop his mission. The entire region within the boundaries of his mission has been committed to his care. Consequently, he must work for the eternal salvation of all its inhabitants. If, out of an immense population, he has converted a few thousand people, he has no reason to fall into complacency. He must become a guide and a protector for these children he has brought forth in Jesus Christ; he must see to their spiritual nourishment and he must not let a single one of them slip away and perish. But he must do more than this. He must not consider that he is properly discharging the duties of his office unless he is working constantly and with all the vigour he can muster to bring the other, far more numerous, inhabitants of the area to partake of the Christian truth and the Christian life.

(The primary concern is the formation of the local clergy)

1112   Anyone who has charge of a mission must make it his special concern to secure and train local candidates for the sacred ministry. In this policy lies the greatest hope of the new Churches. For the local priest, one with his people by birth, by nature, by his sympathies and his aspirations, is remarkably effective in appealing to their mentality and thus attracting them to the faith. Far better than anyone else he knows the kind of argument they will listen to, and, as a result, he often has easy access to places where a foreign priest would not be tolerated.

If, however, the local clergy is to achieve the results we hope for, it is absolutely necessary that they be well trained and well prepared. We do not mean a rudimentary preparation, the bare minimum for ordination. No, their education should be complete and finished, excellent in all its phases.... For the local clergy is not to be trained merely to perform the humbler duties of the ministry, acting as the assistants of foreign priests. On the contrary, they must take up God's work as equals, so that some day they will be able to enter upon the spiritual leadership of their people. The Church of God is

Catholic, and cannot be a stranger to any nation nor alien to any people. It is only right, then, that she chooses in every nation ministers of the Lord to instruct their countrymen in the faith and to lead them on the way to salvation. Wherever the local clergy exist in sufficient numbers and are suitably trained and worthy of their holy vocation, there you can justly assume that the work of the missionaries has been successful and that the Church has laid her foundations well....

(Foreign missionaries must forget their country of origin)

1113   ...Remember that your duty is not the extension of a human realm, but of Christ's; and remember too that your goal is the acquisition of citizens for a heavenly fatherland, and not for an earthly one. It would be tragic indeed if any of our missionaries forgot the dignity of their office so completely as to busy themselves with the interests of their terrestrial homeland instead of with those of their homeland in heaven. It would be a tragedy indeed if an apostolic man were to spend himself in attempts to increase and exalt the prestige of the native land he once left behind him. Such behaviour would infect his apostolate like a plague. It would destroy in him, the representative of the Gospel, the sinews of his love for souls and it would destroy his reputation with the people.... For they will subject him in their own way to a very searching investigation, and if he has any object in view other than their spiritual good, they will find out about it. If it becomes clear that he is involved in worldly schemes of some kind, and that, instead of devoting himself exclusively to the work of the apostolate, he is serving the interests of his homeland as well, the people will immediately suspect everything he does. And, in addition, such a situation could easily give rise to the conviction that the Christian religion is the national religion of some foreign people and that anyone converted to it is abandoning his loyalty to his own people and submitting to the pretensions and domination of a foreign power.

(The command of the local language is needed)

1114   Among the attainments necessary for the life of a missionary, a place of paramount importance must obviously be given to the language of the people to whose salvation he will devote himself. He should not be content with a smattering of the language, but should be able to speak it readily and competently. For in this respect he is under an obligation to all those he deals with, the learned and the ignorant alike, and he will soon realise the advantage a command of their language gives him in the task of winning the confidence and sympathy of the people.... There will be occasions when, in his position as representative and interpreter of our holy faith, he will have to associate with the dignitaries of the place, or he may be invited to appear at scholarly gatherings. How will he maintain his dignity under these circumstances if he cannot make himself understood because he does not know the language?

PIUS XI

ENCYCLICAL LETTER *RERUM ECCLESIAE* (1926)

Following in the footsteps of his predecessor Benedict XV, Pope Pius XI made it one of the main preoccupations of his pontificate to foster the growth of the Church in mission countries. In this encyclical the "Pope of the missions" wrote: "As long as divine Providence shall grant us life, we shall ardently busy ourselves with this duty of our apostolic office." The Pope appeals to all the bishops, who share in his own solicitude, for more missionaries. He defines the purpose of the missions, stresses the role of the local clergy and the need to prepare them adequately for their task; he insists on the creation in mission lands of new religious congregations better adapted than foreign ones to local conditions; he recommends the creation of the religious contemplative life in the missions and the cooperation of all, diocesan clergy and religious institutes, at the service of the local Church. The text of this encyclical is found in AAS 18 (1926) 65ff.

(Missionary motivation)

1115 ...Our obligation of charity towards God demands that we labour to the utmost not only to increase the number of those who know and adore Him "in spirit and in truth" *(Jn 4.24)*, but also to bring as many as possible under our Saviour's sweet yoke. Thus will "the profit in His blood" *(cf. Ps. 30 (29) 10 Vulg.)* become daily more fruitful. Thus also will we ourselves become more acceptable to Him to whom, indeed, there is nothing more agreeable than that men be saved and come to the knowledge of the truth *(cf. 1 Tim. 2.4)*. Since Christ Himself proclaimed as characteristic of His disciples their sincere love for one another *(cf. Jn 13.35; 15.12)*, can we possibly render our neighbours a greater or more signal charity than by trying to lead them out of the darkness of fear and to communicate to them the true faith in Christ?

(The purpose of the missions and the role of the local clergy)

1116 ...Unless you provide to the very best of your ability for priests from the land, your apostolate will remain crippled and the establishment of a fully organised Church in your territories will encounter still further delay....

What, we may ask, is the purpose of the missions, if not that the Church of Christ be established and solidly rooted in those immense regions? And how will this be realised today among the nations, if not through all the forces which brought it about among us in olden times, namely the faithful, the clergy, the religious men and women of each nation?

...You must supply your territories with enough local priests to extend the frontiers of Christianity and to govern the faithful by themselves alone, without the help of any outside clergy....

(The role of local religious congregations and the contemplative life)

1117   Since you should make use of all the means offered by divine Providence for the organisation of Christ's Church in your territory, you ought to consider as one of the principal duties of your office the establishment of indigenous religious communities both of men and women. For if these new followers of Christ feel called by God to a more perfect life, what is to prevent their pronouncing the vows of religion? ... However, you should seriously and impartially consider whether it might not be more useful to establish new congregations more in keeping with the local character and temperament, and therefore better suited to the particular needs of your region....

...We have earnestly exhorted the superiors of.... contemplative orders to establish monasteries in missionary regions, so that their austere mode of life may there flourish and grow more widespread. You should second our efforts... by extending to them repeated invitations, for these solitary monks will win for you and your labours an abundance of heavenly graces. One cannot doubt, moreover, that these foundations will find in your missions a very favourable soil, for their people—especially in some countries where precisely the non-Christians are a vast majority—have a natural bent for solitude and contemplative prayer.

(Collaboration of all)

1118   ...Since the territories which the Holy See has entrusted to your devoted labour in order that you may win them to Christ Our Lord are in most instances very extensive, it may easily happen that your own particular institute is unable to supply as many missionaries as are needed. In such cases, even in well established dioceses, it is customary for religious congregations of men and women, both clerical and lay, to assist the bishop in his work. Therefore, do not hesitate to seek help from other institutes in order to promote the Christian faith. Welcome these missionaries to your territory, to help you in preaching the faith, teaching the youth, and directing other useful projects. The various religious orders and congregations can justly be proud of their conquests for Christ among the people entrusted to their care, but they should remember that they possess no exclusive or permanent title to their mission areas....

PIUS XII

ENCYCLICAL LETTER *SUMMI PONTIFICATUS* (1939)

In his first Encyclical Letter Pope Pius XII outlines the programme of his pontificate. A section is devoted to the missions; it states clearly the principle of adaptation which must pervade the entire activity of the Church in mission countries. The doctrine is based on the unity of the human race and the equality of all men. Hence the right for all nations to preserve and develop their cultural patrimony, and the duty for the Church to assume it into the life of the new Churches. So will the Church show her true catholicity; her ideal is not exterior uniformity, but a healthy pluralism in the unity of faith. The Pope sees this spirit exemplified in the recent decrees of Propaganda, promulgated by his predecessor and by himself (1935 to 1939), which recognise the liceity in China and Japan of certain rites and ceremonies connected with the veneration of Confucius and of ancestors, and with patriotic festivities. These decrees abrogate the censures imposed by Benedict XIV in the apostolic Constitutions Ex quo Singulari (1742) and Omnium Sollicitudinem (1744), thus bringing to an end the long drawn-out controversy on the Chinese rites. The Pope also declares his intention of fostering the formation of the local clergy in mission lands and of "gradually increasing the number of native bishops". The text of the encyclical is found in AAS 31 (1939) 413 ff.

(The unity of the human race and diversity of nations)

1119 The nations, despite a difference of development due to diverse conditions of life and culture, are not destined to break the unity of the human race but rather to enrich and embellish it by the sharing of their own peculiar gifts and by that reciprocal interchange of goods which can be possible and efficacious only when a mutual love and a lively sense of charity unite all the sons of the same Father and all those redeemed by the same divine blood.

(The aim of the Church is supernatural unity in the diversity of gifts)

1120   The Church of Christ, the faithful depositary of the teaching
of divine Wisdom, cannot and does not think of depreciating
or disdaining the peculiar characteristics which each people, with
jealous and understandable pride, cherishes and retains as a precious heritage. Her aim is supernatural union in all-embracing love,
deeply felt and practised, and not a uniformity which can only be
external and superficial and by that very fact weak. The Church hails
with joy and follows with her maternal blessing every method of
guidance and care which aims at a wise and orderly evolution of
peculiar forces and tendencies having their origin in the individual
character of each race, provided that they are not opposed to the
duties incumbent on men from their unity of origin and common
destiny.

*(The spiritual values of the nations must be assumed into the
Church's mission)*

1121   She has repeatedly shown in her missionary enterprises that
such a principle of action is the guiding star of her universal
apostolate. Pioneer research and investigation, involving sacrifice,
devotedness and love on the part of her missionaries of every age,
have been undertaken in order to gain a deeper appreciative insight
into the civilisation and customs of diverse people so as to put their
intellectual and spiritual endowments to account for a living and vital
preaching of the Gospel of Christ. All that in such usages and
customs is not inseparably bound up with religious errors will always
be the object of sympathetic consideration and, whenever possible,
will be preserved and developed....Those who enter the Church,
whatever be their origin or their speech, must know that they have
equal rights as children in the house of the Lord, where the law of
Christ and the peace of Christ prevail.

ADDRESS TO THE DIRECTORS OF PONTIFICAL MISSION WORKS
(1944)

In this address the Pope spoke of the future of the Church in mission
countries. Having taken stock of the fact that the modern view of the
mission leans more and more towards the principle of adaptation, he
re-expresses his faith in this principle which in Summi Pontificatus he had
already considered as the "guiding star" of the Church's apostolate (cf. n.
1121). Referring to the universality of the Church "which is above all

national frontiers", he defines the aim of the missions as the exercise of the
catholicity of the Church. The text is found in AAS 36 (1944) 210.

(The principle of missionary adaptation)

1122 ...The specific character, the traditions, the customs of each
nation must be preserved intact, so long as they are not in
contradiction with the divine law. The missionary is an apostle of
Jesus Christ. His task is not to propagate European civilisation in
mission lands, like a tree which is transposed to foreign soil. Rather it
is his function so to train and guide other peoples, some of whom
glory in their ancient and refined civilisation, as to prepare and
dispose them for the willing and hearty acceptance of the principles
of Christian life and behaviour. These principles, moreover, are
compatible with any wholesome and healthy civilisation whatever
and can imbue it with a keener zest for the protection of human
dignity and the attainment of happiness. Granted that Catholic
inhabitants of a country are primarily members of God's noble family
and citizens of His Kingdom, they do not on that account cease to be
citizens of their earthly fatherland also.

(The purpose of missionary activity)

1123 ...It is this universality (of the Church) which spurs you on
towards the goal you want to reach, namely, to make the
frontiers of the Kingdom of God coincide with those of the world....It
is the great aim of the missions to establish the Church in new
regions and to make her take root there, so that one day she may be
able to live and develop without the assistance of Mission Works.
The Mission Work is not an end in itself; it ardently tends to the
realisation of that lofty goal, but retires when it has reached its aim.

CHRISTMAS MESSAGE (1945)

In this allocution the Pope insists on the Catholic and supra-national
character of the Church which is the foundation of its missionary activity;
he explains that this universal character does not make the Church less
sensitive to human realities for it is founded on the mystery of the incarna-
tion. The text is found in AAS 38 (1946) 18, 20.

(The supra-national character of the Church)

1124 The Catholic Church of which Rome is the centre is supra-
national by her very nature.... The Church is a Mother,
Sancta Mater Ecclesia, a true mother, mother of all nations and all

peoples no less than of all men individually. And because she is a Mother, she does not and cannot belong exclusively to this or that people, not more to one than to others, but must belong equally to all. Since she is a Mother, she is not and cannot be a stranger anywhere; she dwells, or at least should, because of her nature, dwell among all peoples. Nay more, while a mother with her spouse and children forms one family, the Church in virtue of a union incomparatively more intimate, constitutes more and better than a family, the mystical Body of Christ. The Church is thus supra-national because she is an indivisible and universal whole.

(The Church's catholicity is based on the mystery of the incarnation)

1125   The Church is not, because of her supra-natural character, a remote reality, as though suspended in an inaccessible and intangible isolation above the nations.... As the Son of God assumed a real human nature, so too the Church takes to herself the fulness of all that is genuinely human, wherever and under whichever form she finds it, and transforms it into a source of supernatural energy. She lives and develops her life in all the countries of the world, and all the countries of the world contribute to her life and development.

ENCYCLICAL LETTER *EVANGELII PRAECONES* (1951)

Pope Pius XII wrote this encyclical at the occasion of the 25th anniversary of Rerum Ecclesiae *of Pius XI. The great themes of the previous encyclicals are taken up anew, but the Pope also turns his attention to other problems as, for instance, the Church's responsibility for promoting social justice in mission lands. Especially noteworthy are the purpose assigned to the Church's missionary activity and the insistence on the role to be played by the laity in the work of evangelisation. In view of the recent growth of the local clergy, the Pope explains how to conceive the function which foreign missionaries still retain. He recommends that they should "look upon the country where they come to shed the Gospel light as a second fatherland and love it with due charity". Again he stresses the need of preserving and promoting the local culture and explains the principle of Christian acculturation. The text of this encyclical in found in AAS 43 (1951) 497ff.*

(The purpose of the missions)

1126   The primary object of the missions, as everyone knows, is to bring the shining light of Christian truth to new peoples and to suscitate new Christians. But, in view of this, the ultimate goal to which they must tend—and which one must always keep before his eyes—is that the Church be established on firm and definitive foundations among new peoples and that it be endowed with its own hierarchy, chosen from among the people of the place.

(The subordinate role of the foreign missionaries)

1127 It is not expected that a religious society whose members have laboured to plough a field for the Lord should forsake it entirely when the vineyard, now prospering and filled with ripe fruit, is handed over to other husbandmen.... Such a society will perform a useful and gratifying service if it offers to assist the new bishop born in the land. Just as religious usually tender their help to local ordinaries in all the rest of the Catholic dioceses in the world, so too, in missionary regions they, though of a different country of origin, will not cease to fight the holy fight as auxiliary troops....

(The role of the laity)

1128 It is altogether imperative... that magnanimous lay-people should contribute their diligent and self-sacrificing cooperation to the hierarchical apostolate of the clergy. This they can do by forming solid ranks of Catholic Action.... Although... Catholic Action should employ its energies specifically to further the activities of the Christian apostolate, nothing prevents its members from joining associations intended to bring social and political affairs into conformity with the principles and methods of the Church. This is a right which they enjoy not only as citizens but also as Catholics. It is, moreover, a duty to which they are obligated.

(The local culture must be preserved and fostered)

1129 When the Gospel is accepted by diverse nations, it does not crush or repress anything good and honourable and beautiful which they have achieved by their inborn genius and natural endowments. When the Church calls and guides a people to a higher refinement and a better way of life under the inspiration of the Christian religion, she does not act like a woodsman who recklessly cuts down and devastates a luxuriant forest. Rather she acts like an orchardist who grafts an excellent scion upon the wild stock so that later on fruits of a more tasty and richer quality may issue forth and mature.

Although human nature by Adam's unhappy sin has been tainted with an hereditary blemish, it still keeps in itself something that is 'naturally Christian'. If this is illumined by divine light and nurtured by God's grace, it can in time rise to genuine virtue and supernatural life.

Accordingly, the Catholic Church has neither scorned nor rejected the learning of the nations, but rather has freed it from all error and alloy, and then sealed and perfected it by Christian wisdom. The same holds true for the fine arts and culture, which in some countries have reached a high degree of perfection. The Church received them in sympathy, encouraged them assiduously, and lifted them up to a peak of beauty never, perhaps, previously excelled. So too, with regard to particular customs and traditional institutions of peoples. The Church did not simply suppress them but in some way sanctified them. Even in the matter of local feasts, she merely altered their meaning by transforming them into commemorations of the martyrs or into occasions for celebrating the mysteries of the faith.

ENCYCLICAL LETTER *FIDEI DONUM* (1957)

From this other letter of Pope Pius XII, dedicated to the development of missionary activity especially in Africa, only two passages are quoted here, in which the Pope stresses the Church's mission in the social field and explains the Catholic spirit which must inspire its whole action. The text is found in AAS *49 (1957) 231, 237.*

(The Church's social responsibility in mission lands)

1130 At a moment when new structures are being sought, ... it is the Church's sacred duty to make all people share as fully as possible in the outstanding advantages of her way of life and culture, so that a new social order may arise, based on Christian principles.

(The missionary spirit is based on the catholicity of the Church)

1131 The missionary spirit and the Catholic spirit...are one and the same thing. To be Catholic is the Church's principal distinguishing mark. Hence the individual can scarcely be called a Christian and a member of the Church if he is not at the same time a devoted fellow-member of the whole body of the faithful, desiring the Church to strike her roots and flourish everywhere on earth.

JOHN XXIII

ENCYCLICAL LETTER *PRINCEPS PASTORUM* (1959)

This Encyclical Letter on the missions was written by Pope John XXIII at the occasion of the 40th anniversary of Maximum Illud. *It prolongs the thought of Pope Benedict XV and his successors and applies it to new circumstances obtaining in mission lands. There is a new insistance on the thorough training of the local clergy. A special characteristic of this letter is the stress it lays on the cooperation of the laity in the Church's mission, to which Pope Pius XII had already given impetus. The laity, as the clergy themselves, must be adequately prepared to assume fully their responsibility, especially in the field of public life. The organisation of lay missionary activity must be adapted to local circumstances. The text of the encyclical is found in* AAS 51 (1959) 833ff.

(The study of missiology in seminaries)

1132 Local seminaries in mission lands will not fail to provide study courses in the various branches of Missiology and in such special skills and techniques as are likely to be of particular value to the clergy of those regions in their future ministry....This instruction... should... be aimed at sharpening the students' minds, so as to enable them to form a true estimate of the cultural traditions of their own homelands, especially in matters of philosophy and theology, and to discern the special points of contact which exist between these systems and the Christian religion.

(The responsibility of the laity and its training)

1133 There is need for organising the Church in all those lands where she has led her armies of peace, and this organic structure of hers consists not merely in the hierarchy and its various orders, but in the laity as well. In pursuing her work of salvation the Church must act through the medium of the clergy and the laity alike.

...It is necessary... to give the people a Christian education suited to their age and environment, an education which will fit them to make their own contribution to the present and future welfare of the Church and to its spread throughout the world.... The profession of the Christian faith is no mere question of statistics. It is the creation of a new man. It is a supernatural vitality that takes possession of the whole man, inspiring, directing, and governing all his actions.... It is a primary and fundamental duty of every Christian to witness to the truth he believes in, and to the grace that has transformed him....

(The lay apostolate must be adapted to local conditions)

1134 We must insist... upon the need to adapt this form of the apostolate to local needs and conditions. What has proved successful in one country cannot without more ado be transferred to another....What may appear suitable in one area may be less advantageous in another where needs and circumstances differ materially.

(The responsibility of the laity in public life)

1135   It is in the sphere of public life that the laity of mission lands have their most direct and influential part to play. It is, therefore, a matter of utmost urgency that the Christian communities be able to offer men to take up public life in their own homelands for the common good; men who will be a credit to their various professions and the public offices they hold, and will also, by reason of their truly Christian lives, reflect honour on the Church that has regenerated them through grace....

THE SECOND VATICAN GENERAL COUNCIL

The Dogmatic Constitution Lumen Gentium *had stressed the full Catholicity of the Church in which "each individual part contributes by its special gifts to the gifts of the other parts and of the whole Church" (13). It had devoted its number 17 to the missionary character of the Church, conceived as derived from the Son's own mission, and prompting her to send heralds of the Gospel to foreign lands "until the infant Churches are fully established and are able themselves to carry on the task of evangelising." It was, however, necessary to issue a special conciliar document on the missions.*

The Decree Ad Gentes *on the Church's Missionary Activity reflects the Church's new understanding of her mystery, her new openness to all that is good and her new attitude towards the religions of the world. It provides a deep theological concept of the missions which, while owing much to the teaching of the great missionary encyclicals of this century, also completes them and leads to a further stage of development.*

The Decree is divided into six chapters, dealing respectively with the doctrinal principles, missionary work, particular Churches, missionaries, the organisation of missionary activity, and cooperation.

Chapter I on doctrinal principles (2–9) offers a synthesis of missiological doctrine in line with the Council's ecclesiology. "The pilgrim Church is missionary by her very nature, since she draws her origin from the mission of the Son and the mission of the Holy Spirit according to the design of the Father" (2). A Trinitarian preamble traces the origin of her missionary activity to the Father's calling of all men (2) through the Son Incarnate (3) in the Holy Spirit (4). The Church, born of the Spirit at Pentecost to continue Christ's mission, is essentially missionary (5). Her role as "universal sacrament of salvation" (1) is to unfold in the course of history the mission of Christ Himself (5). Her function is fundamentally the same in all parts of the world and is realised by her presence and action(5); but the exercise of the mission takes different forms according to circumstances (6). One special form is found in those countries where the Church still remains to be fully planted; these are the 'missions' commonly so-called (6).

The necessity of the missions flows from Christ's explicit command (5) as well as from the Church's intimate nature (6). She must become present to all nations in order to make Christ known to them and to gather them into one people of God according to the divine plan of salvation and for God's glory (7). Thus she must be missionary, irrespective of what God can do and does for the salvation of those whom the Gospel does not reach (7). To make Christ known to them is to bring them to the full knowledge of their dignity and vocation, for Christ is the principle of a new humanity (8). Missionary activity, which is the manifestation of God's plan of salvation, extends from the first coming of the Lord to the second and tends to its eschatological fulfilment when the Church will be gathered into the kingdom of God (9).

The purpose of the missions finds here a theological structure, and missionary motivation a theological foundation, which integrate the recent theology on salvation 'outside the Church' and on the significance of the religions of the world in God's plan, as well as the new awareness regarding the meaning and implications of the Church's catholicity.

Chapter II deals with missionary work (10–18). It proposes to synthetise Christian witness through dialogue (11) and the presence of charity (12) on the one hand, and, on the other hand, evangelisation which gathers the people of God through the preaching of the Gospel (13–14). The first, which is already missionary activity, will normally lead to the second. Christians, by the witness of their lives and by promoting spiritual and moral values, already contribute to the salvation of other men and "gradually open the way to a fuller access to God" (12); but, when the way is open for the Gospel, the full mystery of Christ must be announced (13). Conversion is a personal and free response to God's calling "to enter into a personal relationship with Him in Christ" (13). For the building up of a Christian community a solid training of its members (15), and especially of its local clergy (16), is necessary, as well as the training of catechists to whose role the Council gives full recognition (17), and the advancement of the religious life, particularly in forms deeply rooted in the religious tradition of the nation (18).

Chapter III on particular Churches (19–22) is symptomatic of the renewed awareness regarding the significance of the local Church in the Church universal. The local Church must grow to full maturity (19); to the end of representing the mystery of the Church as perfectly as possible in a particular place, it must be endowed with all its constitutive elements (20), which include a mature Christian laity (21), fully equipped to co-operate with the local hierarchy in the Church's mission (22); following the economy of the incarnation, it must also be fully at home in the traditions of the land, in view of which a clear plan of adaptation is necessary (22).

Chapter IV is concerned with missionaries (23–27). It draws considerably from the missionary encyclicals of recent Popes as regards the formation, spiritual, doctrinal and apostolic, of missionaries, whether local or from abroad (24–26); it stresses the special role to be played by missionary institutes (27). Chapter V is devoted to the organisation of missionary activity (28–34). Co-ordination is needed at all levels: between the local Church and the centre in Rome (29), and in the field between bishops and missionaries (30) as well as among bishops (31) and missionary institutes (32). Chapter VI on co-operation explains that the entire People of God

must co-operate in the Church's missionary activity (36). It analyses the
missionary duty of Christian communities (37), of bishops (38), priests (39),
religious (40), and laity (41).

Thus the Decree offers a synthetic structure of the Church's missionary
activity which is remarkably coherent and new. That activity is the imme-
diate task of all those who in a given territory constitute the Church's
presence. The whole local Church and each one of her groups and
members are missionary; in communion with one another and with the
Church universal, they are in a particular country the sign of Christ's
salvation for all men.

DOGMATIC CONSTITUTION *LUMEN GENTIUM* (1964)

(The Church's missionary character)

1136   17. ...It is the Holy Spirit who impels the Church to do her part
in bringing about the full realisation of the plan of God who
has established Christ as the source of salvation for the whole world.
By proclaiming the Gospel she moves her hearers to receive and to
profess the faith, she prepares them for baptism, she sets them free
from the slavery of error and incorporates them into Christ, so that
they may grow up through charity into full maturity in Christ. By her
activity whatever good is found sown in the hearts and minds of men,
or in the rites and cultures proper to various peoples, is not only
saved from destruction, but is also healed, ennobled and brought to
perfection, for the glory of God, the confusion of the devil and the
happiness of man....

DECREE *AD GENTES* (1965)

(The Church's mission)

1137   5. ...The Church fulfils her mission by that activity by which,
in obedience to the command of Christ and under the
impulse of the grace and love of the Holy Spirit, she becomes fully
and actively present among all men or nations so as to lead them, by
living example, by preaching, by the sacraments and other channels
of grace, to the faith, the liberty and the peace of Christ. Thus a free
and safe path is opened for men to fully participate in the mystery of
Christ.

(Missionary activity)

1138   6. This duty must be fulfilled by the order of bishops with the
successor of Peter as their head and with the prayers and

co-operation of the whole Church. It remains one and the same everywhere and in every situation, even though it is not exercised in the same way in all circumstances. It follows that the differences which must be recognised in the activity of the Church do not derive from the intimate nature of the mission itself but from the conditions in which the mission is carried out.

... The special undertakings by which the heralds of the Gospel, sent by the Church into the whole world, discharge their task of preaching the Gospel and planting the Church among the peoples and groups which do not as yet believe in Christ, are commonly called "missions". These are carried out by missionary activity and are usually exercised in certain territories recognised by the Holy See. The specific aim of this missionary activity is evangelisation and the planting of the Church among the peoples and groups in which she has not yet taken root. Thus from the seed of the word of God there should increase everywhere enough autochtonous local Churches, endowed with their own resources and maturity. These must have their own hierarchy united with the faithful, and be provided with sufficient and apt means to live a fully Christian life, and so to contribute their share to the good of the whole Church. The chief means for this planting of the Church is the preaching of the Gospel of Jesus Christ. It was to announce the Gospel that the Lord sent His disciples into the whole world, so that men, reborn by the word of God *(cf. 1 Pet. 1.23),* might by baptism be joined to the Church which, as the Body of the Word Incarnate, is nourished and lives by the word of God and the eucharistic bread *(cf. Acts 2.43).*

(Motives for and necessity of missionary activity)

1139 7. Though God can, by ways known to Himself, lead men who through no fault of their own are ignorant of the Gospel, to the faith without which it is impossible to please Him *(cf. Heb. 11.6),* yet there is incumbent upon the Church both the necessity *(cf. 1 Cor. 9.16)* and the sacred right to evangelise; consequently, the missionary activity retains its full force and necessity today as ever.

... Through it God's design is fulfilled...that the entire human race should form one People of God, should coalesce into one Body of Christ, should be built together into one temple of the Holy Spirit....

(Missionary activity in the life and history of men)

1140 8. ...By the very fact of manifesting Christ, the Church reveals to men the real truth about their condition and their complete vocation. For Christ is the principle and exemplar of that new humanity, animated by fraternal love, sincerity and a spirit of peace, which all men long for. Christ, and the Church which by the preaching of the Gospel bears testimony to Him, transcend all peculiarity of race and nation; therefore, they cannot be considered foreign anywhere or to anybody. Christ Himself is the truth and the way which the evangelical preaching lays open to all men.... All are in need of Christ as their exemplar, their master, their liberator, their Saviour and life-giver....

(Eschatological aspect of missionary action)

1141 9. ...Missionary activity is nothing else and nothing less than the manifestation or the epiphany of God's plan and its fulfilment in the world and its history, in which God through the mission visibly accomplishes the history of salvation. By the preaching of the word and the celebration of the sacraments whose centre and culminating point is the Holy Eucharist, it makes present Christ, the author of salvation....Thus missionary activity tends towards the eschatological fulfilment....

(The growth of the local Church)

1142 19. The work of planting the Church in a particular society of men reaches a definite turning point when the community of the faithful, firmly established in the social life and to some extent adapted to the culture of the place, possesses a certain stability and firmness: equipped with its own supply, insufficient though it be, of local priests, religious and laity, it is endowed with those ministries and institutions which are necessary for leading the life of the People of God and expanding it, under the direction of its own bishop.

(Missionary activity in local Churches)

1143 20. Since the particular Church must represent the universal Church as perfectly as possible, it must realise that it is sent also to those in the same territory who do not believe in Christ, in order that, by the witness of the life of each individual faithful and of the whole community, it may be a sign showing Christ to them.

(Diversity in unity)

1144 22. ...Following the economy of the incarnation, the new Churches, rooted in Christ and built upon the foundation of the apostles, take to themselves in a wonderful intercourse all the riches of the nations which have been given to Christ as His inheritance *(cf. Ps. 2.8)*. They borrow from the customs, traditions, wisdom, learning, arts and sciences of their own people everything which can serve to confess the glory of the Creator, to illustrate the grace of the Saviour and rightly order the Christian life *(cf. LG 13)*.

To achieve this purpose, it is necessary that theological reflection should be stimulated in every large socio-cultural area. The deeds and words revealed by God, as contained in Holy Scripture and explained by the Fathers and magisterium of the Church, should be subjected to a new investigation in the light of the Tradition of the universal Church. Thus it will become clearer in what ways the faith can seek understanding by taking into account the philosophy and wisdom of the peoples concerned; how the customs, outlook on life and social order may be harmonised with the norms indicated in divine revelation. This will open the way for a more profound adaptation covering the whole compass of the Christian life. By proceeding in this way every appearance of syncretism and false particularism will be avoided; the Christian life will be accommodated to the mentality and characteristics of each culture, and particular traditions together with the endowments of each family of peoples will be illuminated by the light of the Gospel and taken up into Catholic unity. The new local Churches, adorned with their own traditions, will take their place in the ecclesial communion, without prejudice to the primacy of Peter's chair, which presides over the universal assembly of charity *(cf. LG 13)*....

PASTORAL CONSTITUTION *GAUDIUM ET SPES* (1965)

(Adaptation of the message is the law of evangelisation)

1145   44. ...The experience of the past centuries, the progress of sciences, the treasures hidden in the various forms of human culture which manifest more fully man's own nature and lay open new ways towards the truth—all these profit also the Church. For from the beginning of her history, she has endeavoured to express the message of Christ by means of the concepts and the languages of various peoples, and has, besides, tried to clarify it with the help of the wisdom of the philosophers. She has done so for the purpose of adapting the Gospel, as far as is proper, to both the understanding of all and the demands of the learned. Indeed, this adaptation of the preaching of the revealed word must remain the law of all evangelisation. For thus every nation develops the ability to express the message of Christ in its own way, and at the same time a living exchange is fostered between the Church and the diverse cultures of peoples (cf. LG 13).

PAUL VI

MISSION SUNDAY MESSAGE (1970)

In this message, Pope Paul VI notes that in the last years "a new era has dawned for the missions". This is due partly to the fast developing means of communication among men, in the growth of which he recognises a 'sign of the times'. "This means...that a new approach is needed in the underlying principles, in publicity, recruitment, training...". The Pope examines especially the relationship between evangelisation and human development. After defining clearly the two concepts, he goes on to show that, though distinct, the two realities complement each other. There is between them no dilemma. If in the order of ends and intentions priority must be given to evangelisation, pastoral priority may be given to development according to circumstances. The mission of the Church must be seen in its totality. The text is found in AAS 62(1970)534ff.

(Definition of evangelisation and development)

1146   In the rethinking of the Church's missionary vocation there is one question that stands out in particular, opposing two concepts of what the general direction of missionary activity should be—concepts which may be summed up in two words: evangelisation and development. By evangelisation is meant the strictly religious activity, aimed at the preaching of God's kingdom, of the Gospel as a revelation of the plan of salvation in Christ, through the action of the Holy Spirit. This activity has the ministry of the Church as its instrument, the building up of the Church itself as its aim, and God's glory as its final end. This is the traditional doctrine and to it the Council has given its authoritative support. By development is meant the human, civil, temporal promotion of those peoples who, by contact with modern civilisation and with the help that it provides, are becoming more conscious of themselves and are stepping out on the road to higher levels of culture and prosperity. The missionary cannot excuse himself from taking an interest in this promotion (cf. AG 11).

(Evangelisation and development complement each other)

1147 The confrontation between these two concepts is a serious one and entails two dangers: that we may consider them as mutually exclusive, and that we may fail to establish a correct relationship between them. We hope that the confrontation will not be looked upon as a dilemma that precludes a synthesis between evangelisation and development in which the one complements the other. For us believers it would be unthinkable that missionary activity should make of earthly realities its only or principal end and lose sight of its essential end, namely, to bring all men to the light of faith, to give them a new birth in baptism, to incorporate them into the mystical Body of Christ that is the Church, to teach them what is the life beyond. It is equally inadmissible that the Church's missionary activity should be indifferent to the needs and aspirations of developing countries and, because of its religious orientation, neglect the basic duties of human charity....We ourselves, in our encyclical *Populorum Progressio,* have stressed the duty of resolutely and intelligently fostering the growth of economic, cultural, social and spiritual well-being among peoples, especially those of the so-called Third World where missionary activity finds its main scope for the carrying out of its programme *(cf. AG 12).*

There should be no dilemma. It is a question of priority of ends, of intentions, of duties; and there is no doubt that missionary activity is concerned primarily with evangelisation and that it must maintain this priority both in the concept that inspires it and in the way in which it is organised and exercised. Missionary activity would be failing in its *raison d'etre* if it turned aside from its religious axis: the Kingdom of God before everything else; the Kingdom of God understood in its vertical, theological, religious sense, freeing man from sin and presenting him with the love of God as his ultimate destiny; that is to say, the "Kerygma", the word of Christ, the Gospel, faith, grace, prayer, the Cross, Christian living....

(A question of method)

1148 The debate between evangelisation and development is rather, then, a question of method: must evangelisation precede or come after development? The answer cannot be the same for all cases, but must depend on particular circumstances.... We could distinguish three phases: before, during and after evangelisation—evangelisation always retaining its essential and

intentional priority, while development, with its use of temporal
means, may be given pastoral priority. There is first what some refer
to as pre-evangelisation, that is, making contact with future Christians by living among them, helping them and giving the example of a
good Christian life. Then there is service: when the Gospel comes to
a place, charity comes with it, bearing witness to the human validity
of Christ's message, and taking the form of schools, hospitals, social
assistance and technical training. In the third phase, there comes the
result of this activity, in a new way of life.

PAUL VI

APOSTOLIC EXHORTATION *EVANGELII NUNTIANDI* (1975)

*In his Apostolic Exhortation on Evangelisation which resumes and
prolongs the work of the 1974 Synod of Bishops in Rome devoted to the
same topic, Pope Paul VI dwells on the Church's mission in the world and
clarifies theologically the nature of her evangelising activity. Showing the
link between Jesus the evangeliser (cf. n. 672) and the Church, the Pope
affirms that evangelisation is the Church's essential mission. But evangelisation is a complex activity. The Pope develops a comprehensive view of
evangelisation, centred on the renewal of humanity and the transformation
of culture. He further shows that human liberation—not only
development—is part of the Church's evangelising mission. The text is
found in AAS 68 (1976) 5ff.*

(Evangelisation, vocation proper to the Church)

1149   14. The Church... has a vivid awareness of the fact that the
Saviour's words, "I must proclaim the Good News of the
kingdom of God" *(Lk. 4.43)*, apply in all truth to herself. She willingly
adds with Saint Paul: "Not that I boast of preaching the Gospel, since
it is a duty that has been laid on me; I should be punished if I did not
preach it!" *(1 Cor. 9.16)*. It is with joy and consolation that at the end
of the great Assembly of 1974 we heard these illuminating words:
"We wish to confirm once more that the task of evangelizing all
people constitutes the essential mission of the Church."[1] It is a task
and mission which the vast and profound changes of present-day
society make all the more urgent. Evangelizing is in fact the grace and
vocation proper to the Church, her deepest identity. She exists in
order to evangelize, that is to say in order to preach and teach, to be

---

1. Declaration of the Synod Fathers, 4. See *Osservatore Romano*, English Edition,
27 October 1974, p. 6.

the channel of the gift of grace, to reconcile sinners with God, and to perpetuate Christ's sacrifice in the Mass, which is the memorial of his death and glorious Resurrection.

(Evangelization means the renewal of humanity...)

1150   18. For the Church, evangelizing means bringing the Good News into all the strata of humanity, and through its influence transforming humanity from within and making it new: "Now I am making the whole of creation new" *(Rev. 21.5; cf. 2 Cor. 5.17; Gal. 6.15).* But there is no new humanity if there are not first of all new persons renewed by Baptism *(cf. Rom. 6.4)* and by lives lived according to the Gospel *(cf. Eph. 4.23-24; Col. 3.9-10).* The purpose of evangelization is therefore precisely this interior change, and, if it had to be expressed in one sentence, the best way of stating it would be to say that the Church evangelizes when she seeks to convert *(cf. Rom. 1.16; 1 Cor. 1.18, 2.4),* solely through the divine power of the Message she proclaims, both the personal and collective consciences of people, the activities in which they engage, and the lives and concrete milieux which are theirs.

(...and of the strata of humanity)

1151   19. We spoke of the strata of humanity which are transformed: indeed, for the Church it is a question not only of preaching the Gospel in ever wider geographic areas or to ever greater numbers of people, but also of affecting and as it were upsetting, through the power of the Gospel, mankind's criteria of judgment, scales of values, points of interest, ways of thinking, sources of inspiration and models of life, which are in conflict with the Word of God and the plan of salvation.

(Evangelization of cultures)

1152   20. All this could be expressed in the following words: What matters is to evangelize man's culture and cultures (not in a purely decorative way as it were by applying a thin veneer, but in a vital way, in depth and right to their very roots), in the wide and rich sense which these terms have in *Gaudium et Spes* (53), always taking the person as one's starting-point and always coming back to the relationships of people among themselves and with God.

The Gospel, and therefore evangelization, are certainly not identical with culture, and they are independent in regard to all cultures. Nevertheless, the Kingdom which the Gospel proclaims is lived by men who are profoundly linked to a culture, and the building up of the Kingdom cannot avoid borrowing the elements of human culture or cultures. Though independent of cultures, the Gospel and evangelization are not necessarily incompatible with them; rather they are capable of permeating them all without becoming subject to any one of them.

The split between the Gospel and culture is without a doubt the drama of our time, just as it was of other times. Therefore every effort must be made to ensure a full evangelization of culture, or, more correctly, of cultures. They have to be regenerated by an encounter with the Gospel. But this encounter will not take place if the Gospel is not proclaimed.

(Evangelization includes liberation)

(1153) *See text in n. 2167.*

(The Church's task in people's liberation)

(1154) *See text in n. 2168.*

(Evangelization necessarily linked with human advancement)

(1155) *See text in n. 2169.*

(The Church's mission not to be reduced to a temporal project)

(1156) *See text in n. 2170.*

(True liberation involves a necessary conversion)

(1157) *See text in n. 2171.*

JOHN PAUL II

ADDRESS TO WORKMEN IN SÃO-PAULO
(3 July 1980)

During his journey to Brazil, Pope John Paul II addressed a large gathering of workers at São-Paulo. The Pope affirmed that the world willed by God is a just world. He went on to show that the promotion of justice is part of the Church's evangelizing mission, whose message of salvation has both a historical and an eschatological dimension. The text is found in Osservatore Romano *(English Edition), 21 July, 1980, pp. 4-5.*

(The Church's message of salvation has two dimensions)

1158   3. It is Christ who sends his Church to all men and to all societies with a message of salvation. This mission of the Church is carried out in two perspectives at the same time: the eschatological perspective which considers man as a being whose definitive destiny is God; and the historical perspective which regards this same man in his concrete situation, incarnate in the world of today.

(The promotion of justice is part of the Church's mission)

1159   This message of salvation which the Church, by virtue of her mission, brings to every man and also to the family, to the different social environments, to the nations and to the whole of mankind, is a message of love and brotherhood, a message of justice and solidarity, in the first place for the neediest. In a word, it is a message of peace and of a just social order.

...The world willed by God is a world of justice. The order that must govern relations between men is based on justice. This order must be continually realized in this world, and it must even always be realized anew, as situations and social systems grow and develop, in proportion to new conditions and economic possibilities, new possibilities of technology and production, and at the same time new possibilities and necessities of distributing goods.

The Church, when she proclaims the Gospel, also tries to ensure,without, however, forgetting her specific task of evangelization, that all aspects of social life in which injustice is manifested undergo a change towards justice.

CHAPTER XII

CHRISTIAN WORSHIP

The liturgy is at the centre of the Church's life. Founded by Christ as the sign of the salvation which He gained for men, enlivened by the Spirit of Christ to signify this mystery effectively, the Church finds the deepest raison d'être *of her entire activity in her union with Christ. But nowhere does the Church signify the mystery of Christ as deeply as in her liturgical life. In her liturgy the Church is mysteriously united with her Head, the Lord of glory, from whose glorified humanity there proceed at once men's santification and the perfect worship of God. This is why, in different ways and at different levels, the Church in her various liturgical actions prolongs on earth the dispensation of God's grace to men and renders to God a worthy cult of adoration. The liturgy, then, is the exercise of Christ's mediatory and priestly function through His Body, the Church. It is Jesus Christ calling men to salvation through the signs of the Church and calling them through the same signs to worship in spirit and in truth. In the liturgy, heaven and earth are united; in it the Christian discovers his true vocation to serve God and men; from it he draws the Christian spirit at its deepest source.*

From the apostolic age down the centuries the Church has always lived her liturgical life. She did so with great spontaneity and creativeness during the first centuries. At various intervals of her history the Church has also experienced the need for liturgical reform; for, in an institution which is at once divine and human, the human forms must constantly evolve in order adequately to convey the mystery which they contain. But never before had the Church experienced such a deep current of liturgical renewal as she has known this century; this renewal has been officially sanctioned by the Second Vatican Council. The Council of Trent had previously initiated a liturgical reform, which was realised by Pope Pius V. At that time it was found necessary, in the context of a universal reform of Church traditions, to unify the existing liturgical trends. Unification and stabilisation, however, resulted in uniformity and formalism. The progressive clericalisation of the liturgy and an individualistic approach obscured the traditional doctrine that con-

scious and active participation by the people of God is required if they are to derive profit from the Church's liturgical life. The rediscovery of this basic principle was bound to lead and has in fact led in recent years to far-reaching changes. For participation, as is today fully recognised, requires intelligibility, meaningfulness and adaptation.

The documents mentioned in this chapter mostly outline the new awareness which has developed in this century as regards the nature and laws of the Church's liturgy and the constant need of renewal it imposes on the Church in order that through it the people may be able to enter more deeply, as persons and as members of a community, into the mystery of Christ.

*   *   *

The main points of doctrine considered in this chapter fall under the following headings:

The liturgy is an exercise of Christ's priestly function through the Church: 1218.

It is the work of the entire Body of Christ, Head and members: 1216, 1228, 1229, 1231.

Christ is present in the Church's liturgy: (1217), 1331, 1334.

His mysteries are present in the Church's liturgical cycle: (1226), 1234, 1333.

Liturgical prayer can be addressed to Christ: 1215.

The liturgy of the Word must be fostered: 1202, 1203–1205.

Lex orandi, lex credendi: 1211, 1212, 1223.

There are various degrees of efficacy in the Church's liturgical actions: 1221.

Active participation is required on the part of the people: 1208, 1219–1220, 1230.

Subjective dispositions are needed to derive profit from the liturgy: 1209/1–4, 1232.

Liturgy implies interior and exterior cult: 1219–1220, 1230.

Liturgical and personal piety must be combined: 1214, 1222.

The liturgy must be adapted to the people, especially in mission countries: 1129, 1213, 1214, 1224, 1227, 1233, 1237–1239.

The different liturgical rites of the Church must be fostered: 39/14, 1201, 1206, 1207, 1210, 1235–1236.

THE FOURTH LATERAN GENERAL COUNCIL (1215)

The fourth Lateran Council, convened by Pope Innocent III, is one of the greatest Western Councils. Its profession of faith (cf. nn. 19–20) and its Trinitarian doctrine (cf. nn. 317–320) are important documents. But the Council also dealt with practical matters which had a bearing on Church union. It required from the Greeks re-uniting with the Church that they show respect for Roman liturgical customs as Rome respected their own rites (cf. DS 810). Basing its legislation on the equality of all liturgical traditions in the unity of faith, it prescribed that worship according to their own traditions be made available to the people in all ecclesiastical provinces where the case arose. Regarding Church reform, the Council gave much importance to the preaching of the word of God and called on bishops unable to perform this duty by themselves to see to it that it be adequately fulfilled by others. The text is found in COD, p.215.

Chapter IX: On the Diversity of Rites in the Unity of Faith

1201   Because in many regions people of different languages live in the same city or diocese, keeping different rites and customs in the unity of faith, we clearly prescribe that the bishops of such cities or dioceses must provide men capable of celebrating for them the divine liturgy and of administering to them the sacraments of the Church as the variety of rites and languages will require, and who will instruct them by word and example. But we altogether forbid one and the same city or diocese to have several bishops, like one body having several heads, which is a monstrous thing. If for the reasons mentioned above, it is found urgent and necessary, let the bishop of the place after due consideration appoint a Catholic prelate*(praesul)* from those nations to be his vicar in these matters; he will be subject and obedient to the bishop in all things....

Chapter X: On Providing Preachers

1202   Among other things pertaining to the salvation of the Christian people, it is known that the food of the word of God is of the utmost necessity, since, as the body is nourished by material food, so the soul is by spiritual food, for "man shall not live by bread alone, but by every word that proceeds from the mouth of God" *(Mt. 4.4)*. Hence, since it often happens that bishops because of many occupations or ill-health or hostilities or other reasons...cannot by themselves suffice to administer the word of God to their people, especially in vastly spread-out dioceses, in order that the sacred duty of preaching be duly fulfilled, we ordain by this general Constitution that bishops must enrol for it capable men, mighty in deed and in word *(cf. Lk. 24.19)*. When the bishops are not able to do so themselves, these men will visit the people entrusted to the bishops, in their name and with due solicitude, and will edify them by word and example. When the preachers are in need, the bishops will provide them with what is reasonable and necessary, lest because of want they be compelled to give up the ministry they have undertaken....

THE GENERAL COUNCIL OF TRENT
FIFTH SESSION
DECREE ON TEACHING AND PREACHING THE WORD OF GOD
(1546)

In its 7th session the Council of Trent stressed the efficacy of the sacraments against the denial of the Reformers (cf. nn. 1310ff); in its 22nd session, however, while exposing the doctrine of the sacrifice of the Mass, it ordered that, during the celebration of the Mass, pastors frequently explain to the people some of its readings (cf. n. 1554). Previous to this, the primary obligation to preach had been the object of detailed legislation in a Decree of Reformation promulgated by the Council's 5th session. This decree shows the importance which the Council attributed to the ministry of teaching and preaching the word of God. The Council refers to the legislation previously made by the fourth Lateran Council (cf. n. 1202). The full text is found in COD, pp. 643-646; only three paragraphs of the Decree's second chapter, dealing with preaching, are quoted here (COD, p. 645).

(On preaching the word)

1203   In view of the fact that the preaching of the Gospel meets as important a need of the Christian people as does lecturing about it—and indeed preaching is the main *(praecipuum)* office of the bishops—the Holy Synod has ordained and decreed that all bishops, archbishops, primates and all other prelates of the Church are bound to preach the Holy Gospel of Jesus Christ by themselves, unless a legitimate reason prevents them.

1204   If it should happen that bishops or the other persons mentioned here above are prevented by a legitimate reason, they are bound to follow the decision taken by the general Council *(cf. n. 1202)* to enrol capable men who will duly fulfil this duty of preaching....

1205   Let archbishops, parish-priests, priests in rural areas *(plebani)* and whoever has the care of souls in any Church, either by themselves or, if they are prevented by a legitimate reason, through other capable persons, provide the people entrusted to their care, at least on Sundays and feast-days, with salutary preaching, according to their own ability and in keeping with the level of their people....

PIUS IX

ENCYCLICAL LETTER *AMANTISSIMUS* (1862)

In this Encyclical Letter, Pius IX, after explaining that the Holy See is the foundation of unity and faith in the Church, remarks that the plurality of liturgical rites in no way obscures but rather enhances this unity. The pluralism of liturgical forms is legitimate and must be preserved. The text is found in Acta, Vol. 3, 424.

(Unity of the Church and diversity of rites)

1206   The rich variety of legitimate rites is not in any way opposed to the unity of the Catholic Church; rather, it is most conducive to the Church's dignity, majesty, ornament and splendour.... Our predecessors...have repeatedly affirmed their express will that the rites of the Oriental Churches, provided they contain no error on the Catholic faith..., be preserved intact....

LEO XIII

CONSTITUTION *ORIENTALIUM DIGNITAS* (1894)

In this Constitution, the Pope shows, better than previous documents had done, the rich contribution which the Oriental rites make to the catholicity of the Church. The text is found in ASS 1894, pp. 257ff.

(On preserving the Oriental rites)

1207   The most important thing, it seems to us, is to give our attention and care to the preservation of the particular discipline of the East; and this we have always done....

The noble and glorious antiquity of those various rites is the ornament of the whole Church; it enhances the divine unity of the Catholic faith. (Those rites) clearly manifest to the main Eastern Churches their apostolic origin, while illustrating at the same time their intimate union with the Roman Church from the origin of Christianity. For nothing, perhaps, manifests better the catholicity of the Church of God than does the singular homage of ceremonies of various forms, celebrated in languages of venerable antiquity, and ennobled even more by the use which the apostles and the Fathers made of them. It imitates as it were the exquisite worship which Christ, the divine founder of the Church, received at His birth when the Magi came from various regions of the East.

Here it is worth noting that, though holy ceremonies have not been directly instituted to prove the truth of Catholic doctrine, they nevertheless show forth its vitality in a wonderful manner. Thus, while the Church of Christ jealously preserves in their integrity the dogmas she has received, which their divine character makes immutable, she allows and makes provision for some innovations in exterior forms, mostly when they are in conformity with the ancient past. Thus is made manifest the vigour of the Church's eternal youth, and she shines with ever renewed brightness. This is the Church of which the Fathers found a type in the words of David: "The princess is decked in her chamber with gold-woven robes...in many-coloured robes" *(cf. Ps. 45(44)13-14).*

PIUS X

MOTU PROPRIO *TRA LE SOLLECITUDINI* (1903)

In this Motu Proprio *Pope Pius X lays down the rules to be followed in order that sacred music be truly worthy of the liturgical worship of God. The introduction contains a passage, often quoted later, in which the Pope considers active participation in the Church's liturgy as the principal source of renewal for the Christian life. The text is found in ASS 1903, pp. 329ff.*

(Active participation in the liturgy is the source of Christian renewal)

1208   ...Since we have very much at heart that the true Christian spirit be revived in all possible ways and that it be maintained among all the faithful, it is above all necessary to provide for the holiness and dignity of the sacred places where precisely the faithful gather to draw this spirit at its primary and indispensable source, that is, active participation in the sacred mysteries and in the public and solemn prayer of the Church....

DECREE *SACRA TRIDENTINA* (1905)

By this Decree Pope Pius X allowed the practice of daily communion which he considered to be "the desire of Christ and of the Church". After a brief survey of the history of frequent communion and of the discussions regarding the necessary dispositions, the Pope lays down definite rules on the observance of which the fruit of the practice depends. Though partly conditioned by the theology of the time, this is a clear statement of the personal appropriation required from the recipient of the sacrament for its fruitful reception. The first four rules, theologically more important, are quoted here.

(Decree on daily communion)

1209/1 Frequent and daily communion, because ardently desired
3379 by Christ and the Church, must be open to all the faithful of whatever class or condition, so that none who is in the state of grace and approaches the holy table with a right intention may be turned away from it.

1209/2 The right intention consists in this, that a person approach
3380 the holy table, not from routine, vanity or human motives, but because he wishes to please God, to be more closely united with Him in charity, and to overcome his infirmities and defects by means of this divine remedy.

1209/3 Though it is extremely desirable that those who practise
3381 frequent and daily communion be free from venial sins, or at least from fully deliberate ones, and from all attachment to them, yet it is enough that they be free from mortal sins and resolved never to sin again; with this sincere proposal, it is impossible that they should not gradually correct themselves from venial sin and from attachment thereto.

1209/4 Though the sacraments of the New Law obtain their effect
3382 *ex opere operato,* yet their fruit increases with the dispositions of the recipient; hence care must be taken that holy Communion be preceded by a solid preparation and followed by a proper thanksgiving, according to each one's strength, condition and duties.

APOSTOLIC CONSTITUTION *TRADITA AB ANTIQUIS* (1912)

As a result of the practice of daily Communion, the desire was expressed in regions with Catholics belonging to different rites, that the faithful be allowed to receive the sacrament in any rite in which it was available to them. In his Apostolic Constitution Tradita ab antiquis, *Pope Pius X recalls that in the ancient tradition the faithful, when travelling, were allowed to participate in the celebration of the mysteries in the local rite. The Schism and the controversy on the validity of consecration with unleavened bread interrupted this practice. But the Council of Florence recognised the validity of the discipline of both the Roman and the Oriental rites as regards the matter of the Eucharist (cf. n. 1508), and allowed the faithful to partake of it in either form. If the practice of inter-ritualism was short-lived after the Council of Florence, the reason is that the union attempted by the*

Council was itself short-lived. Later, the Holy See again permitted the practice in various circumstances. The Pope recalls that, in his Constitution Orientalium dignitas, *his predecessor Leo XIII gave permissions in that direction, while, for the sake of respecting the equal rights of the Oriental rites (cf. n. 1207), he also recommended that Oriental priests be provided in order that the Orientals living in Rome be able to partake of the Eucharist in their own rite. Now, in view of the fact that such priests are not always easily available, and considering especially the new needs that have arisen from the pratice of daily Communion, the Pope grants without any restriction to all Catholics the permission to share in the Eucharist celebrated in any Catholic rite. The text is found in* AAS 4 (1912) 609ff.

(All restriction about rites is abrogated with regard to the reception of the Eucharist)

1210   Therefore, considering the unanimity of the Catholic faith as regards the validity of consecration done with either unleavened or leavened bread; convinced, moreover, that for many Latins as well as Orientals the prohibition to share in each other's rite is a source of annoyance and a matter of scandal; having consulted the S. Congregation of Propaganda for the affairs of the Oriental rites, and having closely examined the question, we have deemed it opportune to abrogate all the decrees forbidding or restricting the mutual sharing of rites in the reception of the Holy Eucharist, and to allow all, Latins and Orientals, to be fed with the august sacrament of the Body of the Lord consecrated by Catholic priests either with unleavened or leavened bread, in Catholic churches of either rite according to the ancient custom of the Church, in order that "all Christians may be joined together and united in this symbol of unity and charity" *(cf. n. 1512).*

PIUS XI

ENCYCLICAL LETTER *QUAS PRIMAS* (1925)

In this Encyclical Letter, Pope Pius XI, after explaining the theology of the Kingship of Christ (cf. nn. 652–653), prescribes the celebration of the feast of Christ the King for the universal Church. On this occasion, he explains the educative value of the liturgy in the life of Christians. The text is found in AAS 17 (1925)593ff.

(On the didactic role of the liturgy)

1211   That these blessings may be abundant and lasting in Christian society, it is necessary that the Kingship of our Saviour should be as widely as possible recognised and understood, and to this end nothing would serve better than the institution of a special feast in honour of the Kingship of Christ. For people are instructed in the truths of the faith and brought to appreciate the inner joys of religion far more effectively by the annual celebration of our sacred mysteries than by any pronouncement, however weighty, made by the teaching of the Church. Such pronouncements usually reach only a few and the more learned among the faithful; feasts reach them all. The former speak but once; the latter speak every year—in fact, for ever. The Church's teaching affects primarily the mind; her feasts affect both mind and heart, and have a salutary effect upon the whole of man's nature. Man is composed of body and soul, and he needs these external festivities so that the sacred rites, in all their beauty and variety, may stimulate him to drink more deeply of the fountain of God's teaching, to make it a part of himself, and to use it with profit for his spiritual life.

APOSTOLIC CONSTITUTION *DIVINI CULTUS* (1928)

In this Apostolic Constitution, Pope Pius XI recalls the Motu proprio *of Pius X on sacred music (1903) and gives further directives on the same subject. The document shows the important place which music occupies in the sacred action of the liturgy. It situates the liturgy in the life of the Church by showing, according to the ancient axiom* Lex orandi, lex credendi, *that it is a privileged expression of the Church's faith and therefore a source of theological knowledge. The text is found in* AAS 21 (1929) 33ff.

(Lex orandi, lex credendi)

1212 The liturgy is indeed sacred. Through it we lift ourselves to God and we are united with Him, we profess our faith and fulfil our grave duty of giving thanks to God for the benefits and the help which He bestows on us and which we constantly need. There exists, therefore, a close relationship between dogma and the sacred liturgy, as also between the Christian cult and the sanctification of the people. This is why Pope Celestine I thought that the rule of faith is expressed in the ancient liturgical formulations; he said that "the norm of prayer establishes the norm of belief". "For, when the leaders of the holy assemblies exercise the office entrusted to them, they plead the cause of the human race before the divine mercy and they offer prayers and supplications while the whole Church joins in their entreaty" *(cf. n. 1913).*

LETTER *MISSIONALIUM RERUM* (1937)

In a letter addressed to Cardinal Fumasoni-Biondi on the occasion of an exhibition devoted to sacred art in mission lands, the Pope explains the

*function of sacred art in the liturgy and states the principle of missionary
adaptation in its application to sacred art. The text is found in AAS 29 (1937)
413ff.*

(On sacred art in the missions)

1213   Art ranks among the highest manifestations of the genius
and culture of all peoples; it also offers to the Church the
most worthy and the most important elements which the exterior
celebration of the divine cult must assume....The exhibition will show
the truly Catholic spirit and action of the Church of Christ, for the
holy Church respects the artistic and cultural patrimony, the laws
and customs of each people, provided that they are not contrary to
the holy law of God. Since its origin the Church repeats with St Paul
that it seeks souls only *(cf. 2 Cor. 12.14-15)* and that it wishes to be all
things to all men *(cf. 1 Cor. 9.22)*. The exhibition will also show to all
the inexhaustible fecundity of Christian doctrine even in the field of
art; it will show that, overcoming many painful divisions, Christian
doctrine is capable of gathering in the house of the common Father
under the same wonderful spiritual unity the artistic productions by
which various peoples seek to glorify God through the homage of
beauty.

PIUS XII

ENCYCLICAL LETTER *MYSTICI CORPORIS* (1943)

*In his great Encyclical Letter on the mystery of the Church, Pius XII
shows the place which the sacraments occupy in the Church's life (cf. nn.
1328-1330); the doctrine of the Eucharist, the visible sign of the Church's
unity, receives special treatment (cf. nn. 1564-1565). Broadening the perspective, the encyclical touches on several themes pertaining to the liturgy in
general. The Pope considers how liturgical and private prayer must be
combined in the life of Christians. He also explains why liturgical prayer can
be addressed to Christ Himself and need not always be directed to God
through Him: Christ is not only mediator between God and men, but God
Himself. The early centuries had made it a rule to address liturgical prayer
to the Father, as the Council of Hippo (393) for instance testifies: "At the
altar, let prayer always be addressed to the Father" (cf. Mansi, 3. 922). This
rule is not, however, exclusive as more recent liturgical developments show.
The text is found in AAS 35 (1943) 193ff.*

(Liturgical and private prayer)

1214   There are some...who deny to our prayers of petition any
3819   real efficacy, or who suggest that private prayers to God are
to be accounted of little value, inasmuch as it is rather the

public prayers offered in the name of the Church which have real worth, since they proceed from the mystical Body of Jesus Christ. This suggestion is quite untrue. For the divine Redeemer holds in close union with Himself not only His Church, as His beloved Bride, but in her also the souls of each one of the faithful, with whom He ardently desires to have intimate converse, especially after they have received holy communion. And although public prayer, as proceeding from Mother Church herself, excels beyond any other by reason of the dignity of the Bride of Christ, nevertheless all prayers, even those said most privately, have their dignity and their efficacy, and are also of great benefit to the whole mystical Body; for in that Body there can be no good and virtuous deed performed by individual members which does not, through the communion of saints, redound also to the welfare of all....

(Liturgical prayer can be addressed to Christ)

1215 Finally, there are those who say that our prayers ought not to
3820 be addressed to the person of Jesus Christ Himself, but rather to God, or through Christ to the eternal Father, on the ground that our Saviour in His capacity as Head of His mystical Body is to be regarded only as the "mediator between God and men" *(cf. 1 Tim. 2.5)*. But this is not only contrary to the mind of the Church and to Christian practice; it is also untrue. For Christ, strictly speaking, is Head of the whole Church according to both natures together; moreover He Himself has solemnly declared: "whatever you ask in my name, I will do it" *(Jn 14.14)*. Thus, although it is true that prayers are usually addressed to the eternal Father through His only-begotten Son, especially in the eucharistic sacrifice where Christ, being both Priest and Victim, discharges in a special manner His office of Mediator, nevertheless, on not a few occasions, even during the holy Sacrifice, prayers are directed also to the divine Redeemer; because it is necessary for all Christians to know and to understand clearly that the man Christ Jesus is truly the Son of God, and Himself truly God....

ENCYCLICAL LETTER *MEDIATOR DEI* (1947)

This encyclical is the "magna charta" of the liturgical renewal of this century. It is the result of several decades of scientific research directed to giving new vigour to the Church's liturgy; it marks also a new point of departure for a more pastorally oriented liturgical life. It is divided into four parts: 1) the nature, origin and development of the liturgy; 2) eucharistic worship; 3) the divine office and the liturgical year; 4) pastoral instruction. Here are mentioned mostly passages dealing with the general principles of the liturgy, exposed in the first part of the encyclical. For the doctrine of the Eucharist, cf. nn. 1566–1570 and nn. 1735–1736; for the sacramental doctrine in general, cf. nn. 1331–1333. Are found there the passages of the encyclical dealing with the various modalities of Christ's presence and action in the Church's liturgy and the presence in it of His mysteries; this doctrine extends beyond the Church's sacramental actions to other liturgical celebrations and applies to the entire liturgical cycle. The text is found in AAS 39 (1947) 521ff.

(Christ's priestly function is continued in the Church's liturgy)

1216   ... The Church at the bidding of her founder continues the priestly office of Jesus Christ, especially in the liturgy. This she does first and chiefly at the altar, where the sacrifice of the cross is perpetually represented *(cf. n. 1546)* and, with a difference only in the manner of offering, for ever renewed *(cf. n. 1548)*. She does it secondly by means of the sacraments, those special means for communicating supernatural life to men. She does it thirdly by the tribute of praise which is daily offered to almighty God....

(The presence of Christ in the Church's liturgy)

(1217)   *(See text in n. 1331)*

(Definition of the sacred liturgy)

1218   The sacred liturgy, then, is the public worship which our
3841   Redeemer, the Head of the Church, offers to the heavenly
Father, and which the community of Christ's faithful pays to its Founder, and through Him to the eternal Father; briefly, it is the whole public worship of the mystical Body of Jesus Christ, Head and members.

(External and internal worship: the external element is necessary)

1219   The whole of the Church's divine worship must be both
3842   external and internal. It must be external; for this is required
by the nature of man, composed of soul and body, and it is also required by the divine plan according to which, "while recognising God in visible form, we may through Him be rapt to the love of things invisible."[1] Moreover, it is natural that the outpourings of the

---

1. Cf. *Roman Missal*, Preface for Christmas.

soul should be expressed by the senses. Furthermore, divine worship is a duty for human society as such and not only for individuals; and how can religion be social unless it too has its external bonds and signs? Finally, the external element in divine worship is an important manifestation of the unity of the mystical Body; it also fosters its holy endeavours, invigorates its powers and intensifies its activity....

(External and internal worship: internal worship is the chief element)

1220 But most important in divine worship is the internal element. 3842 If it is with Christ and through Him that due glory is to be given to our heavenly Father, then we must always live in Christ and devote ourselves entirely to Him. The sacred liturgy itself requires these two elements to be closely combined and repeatedly insists on this whenever it enjoins some external act of divine worship—as when it exhorts us that our acts of fasting "may inwardly effect what they outwardly proclaim."[1] Otherwise, religion becomes nothing but an empty ceremony and pure formalism.... Consequently, it is a total misunderstanding of the true meaning of the liturgy to regard it as the merely external and visible element in divine worship, or as the outward splendour of ceremonial; it is equally wrong to see in it a mere catalogue of rules and regulations issued by the hierarchy of the Church for the conduct of the sacred rites.

(Efficacy ex opere operato and ex opere operantis Ecclesiae)

1221 ...God cannot be worthily honoured unless the mind and will 3844 are intent upon spiritual perfection; and for the achievement of holiness the worship which the Church, united with her divine Head, offers to God is the most efficacious possible means.

This efficacy, so far as the eucharistic sacrifice and the sacraments are concerned, is primarily *ex opere operato.* In the case of the prayers and sacred ceremonies which Christ's immaculate Bride the Church uses to adorn the sacrifice and the sacraments, and also in the case of the sacramentals and other rites instituted by the hierarchy of the Church, the efficacy is rather *ex opere operantis Ecclesiae,* inasmuch as the Church is holy and acts in the closest union with her Head.

---

1. Cf. *Roman Missal,* Prayer over the gifts for Thursday after the second Sunday of Lent.

(Complementarity of various elements)

1222   ...In the spiritual life there can be no discrepancy bet-
3846   ween the divine action which, perpetuating the work of
           our redemption, pours out grace into our souls, and the
active co-operation of man which must ensure that the gift of God is
not in vain; no opposition between the *ex opere operato* efficacy of
the external sacrament and the meritorious or *ex opere operantis*
action of its minister or recipient; no opposition between public and
private prayer, between the active and the contemplative life,
between the ascetical life and liturgical piety....

(Lex orandi, lex credendi: a double interaction)

1223   ...In the liturgy we make explicit profession of our Catholic
           faith; not only by celebrating the various mysteries, not only
by offering the sacrifice and administering the sacraments, but also
by reciting or singing the Creed (the Christian watchword), by
reading other documents as well as the divinely inspired Scriptures.
Thus the whole liturgy contains the Catholic faith, inasmuch as it is a
public profession of the faith of the Church.... This is the origin of the
well-known and time-honoured principle: "the norm of prayer establishes the norm of belief" *(cf. n. 1913)*.

   Thus the sacred liturgy does not absolutely or of itself designate
or constitute the Catholic faith. The fact is that the liturgy, besides
being divine worship, is also a profession of heavenly truth subject to
the Church's supreme teaching authority, and therefore it can provide important indications to decide some particular point of Catholic
doctrine. Indeed, if we wanted to state quite clearly and absolutely
the relation existing between the faith and the sacred liturgy, we
could rightly say that "the norm of our faith must establish the norm
of our prayer"....

(Divine and human elements in the liturgy)

1224   ...In the liturgy there are human elements as well as divine
           ones. The latter, obviously, having been established by the
divine Redeemer, cannot under any circumstances be changed by
men; but the human elements may be modified in various ways
approved by the hierarchy under the guidance of the Holy Spirit,
according as time, circumstances, and the needs of the souls may
demand. This explains the admirable variety of rites in East and
West; it explains the progressive development whereby particular

religious customs and pious practices gradually come into existence though earlier times show very little trace of them, while others which in course of time had fallen into disuse are revived. It is a proof that the immaculate Bride of Jesus Christ is vigorously alive, that in the coure of ages there has been development in the language which she uses to express to her divine Bridegroom her own faith and inexhaustible love and that of her people. It is a proof of her skill as a teacher, always inculcating and increasing in the faithful the 'sense of Christ'.

(The divine office is the prayer of the mystical Body of Christ)

1225   The divine Office is the prayer of the mystical Body of Jesus Christ, offered to God in the name of all Christians and for their benefit, since it is recited by priests, by other ministers of the Church and by religious, who are officially appointed by the Church to that function....

The Word of God, when He assumed a human nature, introduced into this land of exile the hymn that in heaven is sung throughout all ages. He unites the whole community of mankind with Himself and associates it with Him in singing this divine canticle of praise....

(The presence of the mysteries of Christ in the Church's liturgical cycle)

(1226)   *(See text in n. 1333)*

ENCYCLICAL LETTER *MUSICAE SACRAE DISCIPLINA* (1955)

In his Encyclical Letter on Sacred Music, Pope Pius XII stresses the need to create in mission countries a genuine sacred music by which the people will be able to celebrate the mysteries of the faith in a manner congenial to their culture. The text is found in AAS 48 (1956) 5ff.

(On sacred music in mission lands)

1227   It is remarkable how, among the peoples entrusted to the ministry of missionaries, many delight in musical chants and adorn the ceremonies dedicated to the worship of images with sacred singing. The heralds of Christ the true God cannot afford to overlook or to neglect this effective help of apostolate. Therefore, in the discharge of their apostolic duty, let the messengers of Christ in mission lands gladly promote the love for religious music characteristic of the peoples entrusted to their care. Thus, beside the religious songs of those peoples which often arouse the admiration of the most cultured nations there will flourish a Christian sacred music, similar to it, by means of which the truths of the faith, the life of Christ the Lord and of the Blessed Virgin Mary and the praise of the saints will be celebrated in the language and with melodies congenial to those peoples.

DISCOURSE AT THE INTERNATIONAL CONGRESS
ON PASTORAL LITURGY (Assisi 1956)

In his address at the International Congress on Pastoral Liturgy held at Assisi in 1956, Pope Pius XII recalled the teaching of the encyclical Mediator Dei, according to which the liturgy is the work of the whole Church (cf. n. 1218). He showed, even better than in the encyclical, that in the liturgy the hierarchy and the faithful are united in a common action, though exercising distinct functions. The text is found in AAS 48(1956)711ff.

(The liturgy is the work of the whole Church)

1228   The contributions which the hierarchy and the faithful make to the liturgy are not added to each other as separate entities; they rather represent the co-operation of members of one and the same organism acting as one living being. Pastors and flock, teaching Church and the Church which is taught, constitute only one Body of Christ.... Thus, it is in this unity that the Church prays, offers, is sanctified; and it can truly be said that the liturgy is the work of the whole Church.

INSTRUCTION OF THE S. CONGREGATION OF RITES
ON SACRED MUSIC AND THE SACRED LITURGY (1958)

This instruction prolongs Pope Pius XII's two encyclicals on the liturgy (Mediator Dei) and sacred music (Musicae sacrae disciplina); it gives practical norms for the application of their doctrine. It contains a clear definition of the liturgical action which it distinguishes from exercises of piety. In connection with the liturgy of the Mass it explains what is meant by interior and exterior participation and what is the relationship between both. The text is found in AAS 50(1958) 630-663.

(Definition of liturgical action)

1229   Liturgical actions are those sacred actions which are instituted by Jesus Christ or the Church and are performed in their name by legitimately deputed persons, in accordance with the prescriptions of the liturgical books approved by the Holy See, in order to render to God, the saints and the blessed the cult due to them. The other sacred actions, performed either in Church or outside, even if presided over or conducted by the priest, are called 'pious exercises'.

(Active participation, interior and exterior)

1230   The Mass by its very nature requires that all present participate in it according to the mode proper to them. This participation must first of all be interior; this consists in the pious attention of the mind and intimate sentiments of the heart. By this participation the faithful "are intimately united with the sovereign Priest... and, together with Him and through Him, offer the sacrifice and dedicate themselves with Him" *(cf. n. 1734)*.

The participation of those present becomes more effective if to interior participation is joined exterior participation, that, namely, which is expressed in external actions like postures..., gestures, and especially responses to prayers and singing.

THE SECOND VATICAN GENERAL COUNCIL
CONSTITUTION *SACROSANCTUM CONCILIUM* (1963)

The Council of Trent had been concerned with liturgical reform, but in the historical context of the times its scope for liturgical renewal remained very limited: besides stressing the priest's duty to preach (cf. n. 1203ff), it mostly decreed a reform of liturgical books, which did not, however, animate the liturgy with a new spirit and a new life. The context of Vatican II is entirely different. The deep renewal to which it was to give official sanction had been prepared by the liturgical movement of the last half century, marked, as the years went by, with a more and more definite pastoral orientation. The Council itself, being essentially pastoral in purpose, turned to the liturgy as one of the important areas in which renewal would contribute to the aim it had in view (SC 1). In fact, Vatican II is the first general Council to have set in motion a liturgical renewal of such large proportions, based, moreover, on a thorough statement of doctrine on the liturgy: the Constitution Sacrosanctum Concilium *has no precedent in the history of the Councils.*

This Constitution represents the first fruits of the Council, and in a true sense made a break-through for the entire conciliar work. In particular, much of the doctrinal statements made by the Constitution Lumen Gentium *on the mystery of the Church is already implied and virtually contained in the theological concept of the liturgy proposed here. Thus, for instance, the idea of the liturgical action as the action of the whole Church in which all play their respective part led to that of the Church as the People of God with distinct and complementary functions. The mystery of the Church as a hierarchical communion finds a privileged field of application in the liturgy, which is "the summit towards which the activity of the Church*

is directed and at the same time the fount from which all her power flows"
(SC 10).

The Constitution is divided into seven chapters. The first is devoted to
general principles for the restoration and promotion of the sacred liturgy;
the second treats of the Eucharist, the centre of the Church's liturgical life;
the third deals with the other sacraments and with sacramentals. One
chapter lays down the principles for a reform of the liturgy of the hours.
There follow three chapters on the liturgical year, sacred music and sacred
art, respectively.

The first chapter on general principles is the most elaborate and important; the following chapters represent various applications of those principles. To explain the nature of the sacred liturgy and its place in the
Church's life, the Constitution goes back to Christ Himself in whom "our
perfect reconciliation (with God) has been achieved and the fulness of
divine worship has been inserted among us" (SC 5). The Church continues
on earth the priestly mediation of Christ, especially in the liturgy; Christ
associates her with Himself and is present in her action (SC 7); hence, the
twofold end of the Church's liturgical action "wherein God is perfectly
glorified and men are sanctified" (SC 7). Hence also, the liturgy is an
exercise of the priestly office of Jesus Christ by His entire Body, Head and
members (SC 7). Though it does not exhaust the Church's entire activity, it
represents nevertheless its summit (SC 9-10).

In order that the liturgy may attain its twofold end, it is necessary that
the members of the Church take part in it "consciously, actively and
fruitfully" (SC 11). A constant preoccupation to promote in all the conscious
and active participation "which is demanded by the very nature of the
liturgy" (SC 14) underlies all the guide-lines laid down by the Constitution in
view of the liturgical reform (SC 14). This participation supposes that all are
effectively involved in the liturgical action (SC 20) and that each person does
all that belongs to his role and only that (SC 28); it requires that the rites be
meaningful (SC 21), which in turn implies intelligibility and a noble simplicity
(SC 34). All the rest flows naturally from these premises, from the adoption
of the local language (SC 36) down to the principle of liturgical adaptation,
especially in mission countries. This principle often stated by papal documents as regards the Church's missionary activity in general (cf. chapter
XI), had never before been as directly applied as it is here to all that belongs
to the liturgical life of the Church (SC 37-40); particular applications are also
made to sacred art (123) and music (119). In order that the aim which the
Council has in view be attained, it is not enough that liturgical books be
revised and, where the need arises, adapted; a whole programme for
promoting the liturgical life of dioceses and parishes (SC 41f) and for
pastoral liturgical action (SC 43ff) is necessary.

Among the most significant reforms made by the Constitution the new
emphasis given to the liturgy of the word deserves special mention (SC 35).
The Council strikes a new balance between Word and Sacrament, as
appears most clearly in its doctrine on the eucharistic celebration: the
liturgy of the word and the eucharistic liturgy proper "form but one single
act of worship" (SC 56). In order to restore the liturgy of the word to its due
place in the liturgy of the Mass, the Council directs that "the treasures of the
Bible are to be opened up more lavishly, so that a richer fare may be
provided for the faithful at the table of God's word" (SC 51).

The Constitution Sacrosanctum Concilium *provides a plan of action for a far-reaching liturgical renewal, which has not finished to produce its fruits. Symptomatic of the potential for change contained in the spirit of the Constitution is the fact that, when in post-conciliar years the Church entered on the way opened by the Council, some of the norms explicitly set by it soon appeared too restrictive and needed to be broadened. Examples of this are: the use of the local language (SC 36) and the practice of concelebration (SC 57).*

(The liturgy is the work of the whole Church, Head and members)

1231   7. Christ indeed always associates the Church with Himself in this great work wherein God is perfectly glorified and men are sanctified. The Church is His beloved Bride who calls to her Lord, and through Him offers worship to the eternal Father.

Rightly, then, the liturgy is considered as an exercise of the priestly office of Jesus Christ. In the liturgy the sanctification of man is signified by signs perceptible to the senses and is effected in a way which corresponds with each of these signs; in the liturgy the whole public worship is performed by the mystical Body of Jesus Christ, that is, by the Head and His members.

From this it follows that every liturgical celebration, because it is an action of Christ the Priest and of His Body which is the Church, is a sacred action surpassing all others: no other action of the Church can equal its efficacy by the same title and to the same degree.

(Place of the liturgy in the life of the Church: the two ends of the liturgical action)

1232   10. ...The liturgy is the summit towards which the activity of the Church is directed; at the same time it is the fount from which all her power flows. For the aim of apostolic works is that all, after being made sons of God by faith and baptism, should come together to praise God in the midst of His Church, to take part in the sacrifice, and to eat the Lord's Supper.

The liturgy in its turn moves the faithful, filled with "the paschal sacraments", to be "united in God's love";[1] it prays that "they may hold fast in their lives to what they have received in faith";[2] the renewal in the Eucharist of the Covenant between the Lord and men draws the faithful into the compelling love of Christ and sets them on

---

1. Cf. *Roman Missal,* Prayer after communion in the Mass of Easter Vigil and Easter Sunday.

2. Cf. *Roman Missal,* Prayer of the Mass of Tuesday in the octave of Easter.

fire. From the liturgy, therefore, and especially from the Eucharist, as from a fount, grace is poured forth upon us; and the sanctification of men in Christ and the glorification of God, to which all other activities of the Church are directed as towards their end, is achieved in the most efficacious way.

(On liturgical adaptation, especially in mission lands)

1233   37. Even in the liturgy, the Church has no wish to impose a rigid uniformity in matters which do not involve the faith or the good of the whole community; rather does she respect and foster the genius and talents of the various races and peoples. Anything in these peoples' way of life which is not indissolubly bound up with superstition and error she studies with sympathy and, if possible, preserves intact, and cultivates. Sometimes in fact she admits such things into the liturgy itself, so long as they harmonise with the principles of the true and authentic liturgical spirit.

Provision shall also be made, when revising the liturgical books, for legitimate variations and adaptations to different groups, regions and peoples, especially in mission lands, provided that the substantial unity of the Roman rite is preserved....

(The mystery and the mysteries of Christ in the liturgical year)

1234   102. Holy Mother Church is conscious that she must celebrate the saving work of her divine Spouse by devoutly recalling it on certain days throughout the course of the year. Every week, on the day which she has called the Lord's day, she keeps the memory of the Lord's resurrection, which she also celebrates once in the year, together with His blessed passion, in the most solemn festival of Easter. Within the cycle of the year, moreover, she unfolds the whole mystery of Christ, from the incarnation and birth until the ascension, the day of Pentecost, and the expectation of blessed hope and of the coming of the Lord.

Recalling thus the mysteries of redemption, the Church opens to the faithful the riches of her Lord's powers and merits, so that these mysteries are in some way present for all time, and the faithful are enabled to lay hold upon them and become filled with saving grace.

DECREE *ORIENTALIUM ECCLESIARUM* (1964)

This Decree on the Oriental Catholic Churches states in all clarity the equal rights of the various traditions, liturgical and spiritual, proper to the

Eastern and Western Churches. All must be fostered and allowed to develop their own genius, for all contribute to the Catholicity of the Church universal. The doctrine is based on a clear theology of the mystery of the Church as a communion of particular Churches in the bond of unity which is effectively symbolised by the Roman See.

(The particular Churches or Rites)

1235 2. The holy Catholic Church, which is the mystical Body of Christ, consists of believers who are organically united in the Holy Spirit by the same faith, the same sacraments and the same government. Grouped in different communities around their hierarchies, the faithful constitute particular Churches or Rites. Between these Churches there exists a wonderful communion, so that diversity, far from harming the Church's unity, rather manifests it. The Catholic Church, indeed, means to keep intact the traditions of each particular Church or Rite and she wants to adapt her mode of life to the various needs of times and places.

1236 3. These particular Churches of both East and West, though partially differing from one another by their 'rites'—i.e., their liturgy, ecclesiastical discipline and spiritual patrimony—are all equally entrusted to the pastoral direction of the Roman Pontiff, who by divine institution succeeds St Peter in the primacy over th universal Church. All have the same dignity, none is higher than the others by reason of its rite; all have the same rights and the same obligations, also as regards the preaching of the Gospel in the whole world (*cf. Mk 16.15*), under the guidance of the Roman Pontiff.

POST-CONCILIAR DOCUMENTS ON SACRED WORSHIP

The Constitution Sacrosanctum Concilium *of the Second Vatican Council had laid down the principles of liturgical renewal. After the Council several Roman documents applied those principles to various aspects of the Church's liturgical life. New rites were promulgated for the celebration of the sacraments; the documents promulgating these new rites are mentioned here in the various chapters on the sacraments. Other documents applied the principles of the Council to the Church's liturgy in general. Among these may be mentioned :*

— The Motu Proprio of Pope Paul VI on the Sacred Liturgy, Sacram Liturgiam *(25 January 1964);*

— The First Instruction on the Proper Implementation of the Constitution on the Sacred Liturgy by the Sacred Congregation of Rites, Inter Oecumenici *(26 September 1964);*

— The Instruction on Music in the Liturgy by the Sacred Congregation of Rites, Musicam Sacram *(5 March 1967) ;*

— *The Second Instruction on the Proper Implementation of the Constitution on the Sacred Liturgy by the Sacred Congregation of Rites*, Tres Abhinc Annos *(4 May 1967) ;*

— *The Third Instruction on the Correct Implementation of the Constitution on the Sacred Liturgy by the Sacred Congregation for Divine Worship*, Liturgiae Instaurationes *(5 September 1970).*

As these documents are easily accessible in A. FLANNERY *(ed.),* Vatican Council II, The Conciliar and Post-Conciliar Documents, *Dominican Publications, Dublin 1975, they need not be included here.*

JOHN PAUL II
ADDRESS TO THE BISHOPS OF ZAÏRE
(3 May 1980)

The Constitution Sacrosanctum Concilium *of the Second Vatican Council foresaw the need for a profound adaptation of the liturgy to different regions and peoples, especially in mission lands (cf. n. 1233). After the Council, efforts began to me made to adopt the Roman liturgy, especially the celebration of the sacraments, to the culture of the people in mission lands. This process of inculturation of the liturgy has unhappily been to a large extent hindered by a cumbersome procedure and the continued dependence on the central authority for liturgical adaptations. During his visit to Africa in 1980, Pope John Paul II, addressing the bishops of Zaïre, clearly stated the principle of inculturation of the Gospel. He went on to stress the responsibility of the local bishops in this matter, and applied the principle of inculturation to various fields, in particular to theology and to liturgy. The text is found in* Osservatore Romano (English Edition). 12 May 1980, pp. 6-7.

(The inculturation of the Gospel)

1237 4. One of the aspects of evangelisation is the *inculturation* of the Gospel. the *Africanisation* of the Church.... That is part of the indispensable efforts to incarnate the message of Christ. The Gospel, certainly, is not identified with cultures, and transcends them all. But the Kingdom that the Gospel proclaims is lived by men deeply tied to a culture; the building up of the Kingdom cannot dispense with borrowing elements of human culture *(cf. n. 1152).* Indeed, evangelisation must help the latter to bring forth out of their own tradition original expressions of Christian faith, celebration and thought.[1]

---

1. Apostolic Exhortation *Catechesi Tradendae*, 53.

(The responsibility of the local hierarchy)

1238 It is up to you, bishops, to promote and harmonize the advance in this field, after mature reflection, in concerted action among yourselves, in union also with the universal Church and with the Holy See. Inculturation, for the people as a whole, cannot be, moreover, but the fruit of gradual maturity in faith. For you are convinced as I am that this work...requires a great deal of theological lucidity, spiritual discernment, wisdom and prudence, and also time.

(Liturgical inculturation)

1239 5. In the field of sacred actions and the liturgy, a whole enrichment is possible *(cf. n. 1233)*, provided the meaning of the Christian rite is always preserved and the universal, Catholic element of the Church is clearly seen ("the substantial unity of the Roman rite"), in union with other local Churches and in agreement with the Holy See.

APPENDIX

ON THE CULT OF SAINTS AND SACRED IMAGES

In appendix to this chapter are mentioned the Church's most important documents on the cult of saints, of relics and of sacred images. Though she submits it to some laws, the Church has always defended as legitimate the veneration of sacred images ; the reason is that their veneration goes to the person whom they represent. As for the veneration of saints, it arises naturally from the lively awareness of the deep communion which binds together in Christ all those redeemed by Him. While venerating the saints, the Church celebrates in them the triumph of the mystery of Christ; she draws inspiration from their example and pleads for God's favour through their intercession. It is an historical fact that protests against the veneration of saints have always resulted from a loss of ecclesial consciouness, prompted by a tendency towards a purely interior and individualistic religion. While speaking out against abuses, the Church has upheld such veneration as being based on the mystery of the communion of saints.

* * *

The Church recommends the cult of saints : 35, 39/22-23, 1255, 1258, 2311f, (2313f).

It also recommends the cult of relics and of sacred images : 35, 1251-1252, 1253, 1254, 1256, 1257.

It also recommends popular piety, provided this is purified of possible distortions : 1259.

THE SECOND GENERAL COUNCIL OF NICAEA

DEFINITION ON SACRED IMAGES (787)

The 8th century of Christianity has known the outburst of a heated controversy over sacred images; opposition to the veneration of sacred images representing Christ can be considered as remotely inspired by a Monophysite tendency. It is true that the cult of images in the East sometimes led to reprehensible abuses ; some Fathers of the Church, rigorist in tendency, even feared the danger of idolatry. Iconoclasm first made its appearance in Constantinople under Manichaean influence. The crisis broke out when in 730 emperor Leo III ordered the destruction of icons, a special object of piety in the Byzantine tradition. This action met with much opposition and was condemned by Rome. But it is only after the accession to the throne of empress Irene, who favoured the cult of images, that the case could be submitted to the judgment of a general Council which met at Nicaea.

In its 7th session the Second Council of Nicaea solemnly defined that the cult of images is legitimate and explained that the veneration of images is addressed to the persons whom they represent. In order to distinguish the adoration due to God alone from the veneration which is given to the cross and to images of Christ and the saints, the Council reserved the Augustinian term latria (latreia) *to the cult or worship addressed to God Himself while it applied the ancient term of adoration* (proskunesis) *to the veneration of sacred images. This verbal distinction will not, however, impose itself later. Nor did the Council distinguish, as later tradition will, the relative cult of divine worship due to the images of Christ from the veneration addressed to those of the saints.*

1251 We define that...the representations of the precious
600 and life-giving cross, and the venerable and holy images as well,...must be kept in the holy Church of God..., in houses and on the roads, whether they be images of God our Lord and Saviour Jesus Christ or of our immaculate Lady the Mother of God, or of the holy angels and of all the saints and just.

1252 For, the more frequently one contemplates these pictorial
601 representations, the more gladly will he be led to remember the original subject whom they represent, the more too will he be drawn to it and inclined to give it...a respectful veneration *(proskunesis. adoratio)*, which, however, is not the true adoration *(latria, latreia)* which, according to our faith, is due to God alone. But, as is done for the image of the revered and life-giving cross and the holy Gospels and other sacred objects and monuments, let an oblation of incense and light be made to give honour to those images according to the pious custom of the ancients. For "the honour given

to an image goes to the original model";[1] and he who venerates an image, venerates in it the person represented by it.

THE FOURTH GENERAL COUNCIL OF CONSTANTINOPLE
(869-870)

The iconoclast crisis which seemed to have been settled by the Second Council of Nicaea was revived two decades after the Council. Three Asiatic emperors convened iconoclast Councils and persecuted the patriarchs and monks who favoured the veneration of images. The persecution was once again brought to an end by an empress, Theodora by name, who had come to power in 842. The conflict nevertheless went on and had to be dealt with by the Fourth Council of Constantinople. The Council treated the question of images in its 10th session held in 870. Canon 3 develops the definition of the Second Council of Nicaea and explains that colours play in images the role which words play in writing. Thus images constitute a language accessible to the illiterate.

(On the veneration of sacred images)

1253 *Canon* 3 : We decree that the sacred image of our Lord Jesus
653 Christ, the liberator and Saviour of all men, must be
venerated with the same honour as is given to the book of the holy Gospels.

654 For, as through the language of the words contained in
this book all can reach salvation, so, due to the action which these images exercise by their colours, all, wise and simple alike, can derive profit from them. For, what speech conveys in words, pictures announce and bring out in colours. It is fitting, in accordance with sane reason and with the most ancient tradition, since the honour is referred to the principal subject, that the images derived from it be honoured and venerated, as is done for the sacred book of the holy Gospels and for the image of the precious cross....

MARTIN V
BULL *INTER CUNCTAS* (1418)

The list of questions proposed to the followers of Wyclif and Hus which are contained in this Bull mostly pertains to the doctrine of the sacraments (cf. n. 1304 ; nn. 1507/16-17 ; 1611/20ff). One deals with the cult of saints. Some exaggerations and deviations of medieval piety had provoked legitimate reactions. But, with the forerunners of the Reformation, Wyclif and

---

1. ST BASIL, *De Spiritu Sancto*, 18, 45.

Hus and their followers, the reaction against abuses took the form of a contestation of the cult itself.

(Question proposed to the followers of Wyclif and Hus)

1254 Does he believe and does he affirm that it is legitimate
1269 for the faithful of Christ to venerate relics and images of saints?

THE GENERAL COUNCIL OF TRENT

TWENTY-FIFTH SESSION

DECREE ON THE INVOCATION, THE VENERATION AND

THE RELICS OF SAINTS AND ON SACRED IMAGES (1563)

After Wyclif and Hus, the Reformers took an even more hostile attitude towards the cult of saints which they soon came to view as opposed to the spirit of Christianity. Luther, while admitting the legitimacy of the veneration and the imitation of saints, rejected their invocation and denied their intercession. Zwingli advocated suppressing all cult of saints because God alone must be invoked; Calvin considered the cult of saints as the devil's invention and the veneration of images as idolatry.

The Council of Trent meant to condemn the new iconoclasm of the Reformation, while at the same time suppressing the abuses to which an ill-inspired piety had often given rise on the Catholic side (cf. DS 1825). This Decree, promulgated during the Council's 25th session, provides a clearer statement on the subject of the veneration of saints and of sacred images than was found in previous documents.

(Veneration of saints)

1255 The holy Council, in accordance with the practice of the
1821 Catholic and apostolic Church from the early years of the Christian religion, and in accordance with the common teaching of the holy Fathers and the decrees of the sacred Councils, orders all bishops and others who have the official charge of teaching to instruct the faithful diligently, in particular as regards the intercession and the invocation of the saints, the honour due to their relics, and the lawful use of images. Let them teach the faithful that the saints, reigning together with Christ, pray to God for men; that it is good and useful to invoke them humbly and to have recourse to their prayers, to their help and assistance, in order to obtain favours from God through His Son, our Lord Jesus Christ, who alone is our Redeemer and Saviour. Those who deny that the saints enjoying eternal happiness in heaven are to be invoked; or who claim that saints do not pray for men or that calling upon them to pray for each of us is idolatry or is opposed to the word of God and is prejudicial to

the honour of Jesus Christ, the one Mediator between God and men *(cf. 1 Tim. 2.5);* or who say that it is foolish to make supplication orally or mentally to those who are reigning in heaven; all those entertain impious toughts.

(Veneration of relics)

1256 The sacred bodies of the holy martyrs and of the other saints
1822 living with Christ, which have been living members of Christ
and the temple of the Holy Spirit *(cf. 1 Cor. 3.16; 6.19; 2 Cor. 6.16),* and which are destined to be raised and glorified by Him unto life eternal, should also be venerated by the faithful. Through them many benefits are granted to men by God. For this reason, those who say that veneration and honour is not due to the relics of the saints, or that these relics and other sacred memorials are honoured in vain by the faithful, and that it is futile to visit the places where the martyrs have died to implore their assistance, are to be condemned absolutely, just as the Church has already condemned them and even now condemns them.

(Veneration of images)

1257 Further, the images of Christ, of the Virgin Mother of God
1823 and of other saints are to be kept and preserved, in places of
worship especially; and to them due honour and veneration is to be given, not because it is believed that there is in them anything divine or any power for which they are revered, nor in the sense that something is sought from them or that a blind trust is put in images as once was done by the gentiles who placed their hope in idols *(cf. Ps. 135 (134) 15ff);* but because the honour which is shown to them is referred to the original subjects which they represent. Thus, through these images which we kiss and before which we kneel and uncover our heads, we are adoring Christ and venerating the saints whose likeness these images bear. That is what was defined by the decrees of the Councils, especially the Second Council of Nicaea, against the opponents of images *(cf. nn. 1251f.)*

THE SECOND VATICAN GENERAL COUNCIL

The Council of Trent had stated clearly that the veneration of saints is legitimate and in accordance with the Church's Tradition. Reigning with Christ, they intercede for us and can be invoked for help. The Second Vatican Council has further deepened the theological foundation for the *cult of saints. It is treated in the Constitution Lumen Gentium in the context of the eschatological nature of the pilgrim Church and her union with the Church of heaven (49-50). The Constitution explains the full significance of the mystery of the communion of saints. If the saints intercede for us, it is in virtue of the mysterious communion between the pilgrim Church and the Church triumphant. Nor does the intercession of saints exhaust the meaning of the cult rendered to them by the Church. The saints are for the pilgrim Church on earth striking examples of conformity to the mystery of Christ and a powerful incentive to holiness. What the Church primarily celebrates in their cult is the triumph of the mystery of Christ in their lives. See nn. 2311-(2314). Here is mentioned a short passage of the Constitution Sacrosantum**Concilium** to which the Constitution **Lumen Gentium gave a more ample development.***

CONSTITUTION *SACROSANCTUM CONCILIUM* (1963)

(The memory of saints in the liturgical cycle)

1258 104. The Church has also included in the annual cycle days devoted to the memory of the martyrs and of the other saints. Raised up to perfection by the manifold grace of God, and already in possession of eternal salvation, they sing God's perfect praise in heaven and offer prayers for us. By celebrating the passage of these saints from earth to heaven the Church proclaims the paschal mystery achieved in the saints who have suffered and been glorified with Christ; she proposes them to the faithful as examples drawing all to the Father through Christ, and through their merits she pleads for God's favours.

PAUL VI

APOSTOLIC EXHORTATION *EVANGELII NUNTIANDI* (1975)

During the 1974 Synod of Bishops in Rome on Evangelization, Bishops, especially from Latin America stressed the value of popular religiosity for evangelization. Though popular piety needs to be purified of possible distortions, if well oriented it can bring people to a true encounter with God in Jesus Christ. The Apostolic Exhortation published by Pope Paul VI after the Synod echoes the bishops' positive appraisal of popular piety. The text is found in AAS 68 (1976) 37-38.

(Popular piety)

1259 48. One finds among the people particular expressions of the search for God and for faith, both in the regions where the Church has been established for centuries and where she is in the course of becoming established. These expressions were for a long time regarded as less pure and were sometimes despised, but today they are almost everywhere being rediscovered. During the last Synod the Bishops studied their significance with remarkable pastoral realism and zeal.

Popular religiosity, of course, certainly has its limits. It is often subject to many distortions of religion and even superstitions. It frequently remains at the level of forms of worship not involving a true acceptance by faith. It can even lead to the creation of sects and endanger the true ecclesial community.

But if it is well oriented, above all by a pedagogy of evangelization, it is rich in values. It manifests a thirst for God which only the simple and poor can know. It makes people capable of generosity and sacrifice even to the point of heroism, when it is a question of manifesting belief. It involves an acute awareness of profound attributes of God : his fatherhood, providence, his loving and constant presence. It engenders interior attitudes rarely observed to the same degree elsewhere : patience, the sense of the Cross in daily life, detachment, openness to others, devotion. By reason of these aspects, we readily call it "popular piety", that is, religion of the people, rather than religiosity.

Pastoral charity must dictate to all those whom the Lord has placed as leaders of the ecclesial communities the proper attitude in regard to this reality, which is at the same time so rich and so vulnerable. Above all one must be sensitive to it, know how to perceive its interior dimensions and undeniable values, be ready to help it to overcome its risks of deviation. When it is well oriented, this popular religiosity can be more and more for multitudes of our people a true encounter with God in Jesus Christ.

CHAPTER XIII

THE SACRAMENTS OF THE CHURCH

Salvation history is the history of God's personal dealings with men and the unfolding in history of His saving design. This personal encounter of God with men, the initiative for which comes from God and can only come from Him, has been accomplished once for all in Jesus Christ: in the one Mediator the infinite distance which separates men from God has been bridged; through Christ's Paschal Mystery all mankind has been saved and united with God. Yet, the mystery accomplished once for all must remain present and operative at all times and in all places, and its saving effects must be applied to all men. The sacraments are privileged means instituted by Christ and entrusted by Him to the Church, by which the mystery of salvation becomes, for every age till the end of the world, a living and tangible reality. Through them the mystery of Christ is ever actual and effective. Christ who has died and is risen is present in them and exercises through them His saving power. In them men come in personal contact with the risen Lord and His saving action. Humble human signs which of themselves could never have any supernatural efficacy have become the channels of God's grace because Christ has made their dispensation by the Church the visible expression of His sanctifying will.

Thus, two fundamental affirmations belong to the Church's teaching on the sacraments. First, the Church is the depositary of the signs instituted by Christ, which He entrusted to her to be faithfully preserved and administered. Second, these signs, because they are the signs of the action of the glorified Christ, are efficacious signs of grace. Designed by Him to communicate His salvation and assumed by Him as His own actions, they are not hindered in their efficacy by the human deficiencies of those who administer them so long as they mean to communicate what Christ has entrusted to the Church.

Through the centuries the Church has progressed in the explicit awareness of her sacramental deposit. Her sacramental doctrine has grown out of the exercise of her sacramental life ; in particular, the doctrine on the number of seven sacraments has been explicitly stated at a relatively late period. After having long been tranquilly possessed, the Church's sacramental doctrine was seriously chal-

lenged for the first time by the Reformation. The Church defended her sacred deposit and affirmed clearly the objective efficacy attached to the sacraments by Christ's institution. But, in the process of stressing the ex opere operato efficacy of the sacramental signs, post-Tridentine theology has, to an extent, lost sight of their personal aspect. This has once again been stressed in recent years : the sacraments are personal encounters of Christ with men in the signs of the Church. Their significance in the life of the Church has also received new emphasis: as the visible expression and continued actuality of the mystery of Christ, they are an essential element of the mystery of the Church.

*   *   *

The main points of doctrine found in the official documents can be summarised as follows :

The sacraments are instituted by Christ : 32, 1311, 1326/39-40, 1327.
Their administration is entrusted by Christ to the Church : 32, 1323, 1324.
There are seven sacraments : 28, 32, (1302), 1305, 1311, 1328.
They differ from the sacraments of the Old Law : 1003, 1305, 1312.
The sacraments confer the grace which they signify : 1305, 1309, 1316, 1317, 1318, 1327, 1335.
They sanctify men and give worship to God : 1334, 1335.
They are the actions of Christ : 1329, 1330, 1334.
Christ is present and active in them : 1331, 1332, 1334.
Christ's mysteries are present in the sacraments : 1234, 1333.
Three sacraments imprint an indelible character : 1308. 1319, 1710.
The sacraments are necessary, but not all equally, for salvation: 32, 810, 1313, 1314.
The sacraments are validly administered by carrying out the sign with the proper intention : 1304, 1307, 1321, 1325.
The validity of the sacraments is independent of the worthiness of the minister : 1301, 1303, 1304, 1322, 1504, 1627, 1650.
Not all are equally qualified to administer all the sacraments : 1320, 1627.
The fruitful reception of the sacraments depends on the disposition of the recipient : 1209/1-4, 1309, 1316, 1332, 1335.
Word, faith and sacrament are linked together : 1336.

INNOCENT III

PROFESSION OF FAITH PRESCRIBED TO THE WALDENSIANS
(1208)

The thirteenth century was marked by a spirit of reform which found its expression in the orders founded by St Francis of Assisi and St Dominic. No less zealous for reform were the followers of Peter Waldo. Nevertheless, they inherited some of the errors of the Albigensians (cf. n. 403i). In their zeal to counteract the worldliness and unworthiness of the clergy which they held responsible for the decay of the religious life, they regarded only those who embraced religious poverty in its most extreme form as worthy ministers of the sacraments. Accordingly, the hierarchy of orders was to yield to a hierarchy of saints. In the process they made the validity of the sacraments dependent on the worthiness of the minister, thus failing to distinguish between the person and the office. The profession of faith prescribed by Innocent III shows that the validity of a sacrament does not depend on the worthiness of the minister.

1301 Furthermore, we do not reject the sacraments which are
793 conferred in the Church, in co-operation with the inestimable and invisible power of the Holy Spirit, even though these sacraments be administered by a sinful priest, as long as he is recognised by the Church. And we do not disparage ecclesiastical duties and blessings performed by such a one; but we accept them with benevolence, as we would those performed by the most just man. For the evil life of a bishop or a priest has no harmful effect on either the baptism of an infant or the consecration of the Eucharist or other ecclesiastical duties performed for the faithful.

THE SECOND GENERAL COUNCIL OF LYONS
"PROFESSION OF FAITH OF MICHAEL PALAEOLOGUS" (1274)

(1302) *Despite divergences of opinions among theologians as regards their significance and divine efficacy, the number of seven major rites or sacraments in the strict sense came to be explicitly recognised in the West towards the middle of the twelfth century. Though less precise, the faith of the Eastern Church was fundamentally the same. The profession of faith of Michael Palaeologus (cf. n. 22i) affirms that there are seven sacraments and enumerates them. Previous to this document the catalogue of seven sacraments is found with less clarify in the profession of faith prescribed to the Waldensians (cf. DS 794). See text in n. 28.*

THE GENERAL COUNCIL OF CONSTANCE
CONDEMNATION OF ERROS OF WYCLIF AND HUS (1415)

Wyclif's errors on the sacraments were not without relation to his ideas about the Church to which only the predestined belonged (cf. n. 807/8i). The same ideas were taken over by John Hus and spread by him in Bohemia. After healing the schism, Church reform and the campaign against the errors of Wyclif and Hus were for the Council of Constance the most urgent tasks. It conaemmed those errors in its 8th session (May 4, 1415). According to Wyclif, a sinful man loses all power in both the civil and the religious spheres. Sacraments administered by a sinner, priest or bishop, are not true sacraments.

(Error of Wyclif condemmed)

[1303]   If a bishop or priest is in mortal sin, he does not ordain,
1154   he does not consecrate, he does not perform (the Eucharist,
             he does not baptise.

MARTIN V

BULL *INTER CUNCTAS* (1418)

Soon after his election as Pope, Martin V meant to sanction the decisions taken by the Council of Constance. In this Bull he comes back to the errors of Wyclif and Hus already condemmed by the Council; he adds a series of 39 questions addressed to their followers. One of these is again concerned with the problem of the validity of a sacrament administered by an unworthy minister

(Question proposed to the followers of Wyclif and Hus)

1304   Likewise, whether he believes that a bad priest who uses the
1262   correct matter and form and has the intention of doing what
           the Church does, truly performs (the Eucharist), truly
absolves, truly baptises, truly confers the other sacraments.

THE GENERAL COUNCIL OF FLORENCE

DECREE FOR THE ARMENIANS (1439)

Soon after the Bull Laetentur Coeli *destined to bring about the union of the Greeks which in fact did not materialise (cf. n. 322i), the Council issued a decree for the union of the Armenians; this document too was published as a Bull of Pope Eugene IV, entitled* Exsultate Domino. *The Decree for the Armenians was accepted by the delegates of their Church. The Bull mentions the doctrine of the early Councils on the Trinity (including the* Filioque *in the profession of faith of the Council of Constantinople: cf. n. 12), and on the two natures and two wills of Christ; it insists on the authority of Chalcedon and of St Leo. It then comes to its main purpose, the sacraments.*

It recalls that there are seven sacraments and determines their effects; it explains that the sacraments are made up of matter and form, and the minister, all three elements constituting together the sacramental action; it further declares that baptism, confirmation and Order confer an "indelible character". *A development on each of the sacraments follows, in which their constitutive elements are respectively determined (cf. nn. 1412-1418, 1509-1511, 1612-1613, 1705, 1803). This entire sacramental doctrine follows very closely St Thomas Aquinas' short treatise* "On the articles of faith and the sacraments of the Church". *The document is neither an infallible definition, nor a document of faith. It is a clear exposition of the sacramental theology commonly held at that time in the Latin Church. The limits of its authority must be borne in mind, especially with regard to the question of the essential rite of the sacrament of Order (cf. n. 1705).*

The Bull ends by repeating the Pseudo-Athanasian Symbol of faith (cf. nn. 16-17), by recalling the Council's Decree for the Greeks, and by making prescriptions regarding dates for the celebration of feasts by the Armenians.

1305 ...We here set out the true doctrine of the sacraments of the
1310 Church in a brief formula which will facilitate the instruction of the Armenians, both now and in the future. There are seven sacraments of the New Law, namely, baptism, confirmation, the Eucharist, penance, extreme unction, Order and matrimony; and they differ greatly from the sacraments of the Old Law. For these did not cause grace but were only a figure of the grace that was to be given through the passion of Christ; but our sacraments both contain grace and confer it on those who receive them worthily.

1306 The first five of these are ordained to the interior spiritual
1311 perfection of the person himself; the last two are ordained to the government and the increase of the whole Church. For by baptism we are spiritually reborn and by confirmation we grow in grace and are strengthened in the faith; being reborn and strengthened, we are nourished with the divine food of the Eucharist. If by sin we become sick in soul, we are healed spiritually by penance; we are also healed in spirit, and in body in so far as it is good for the soul, by extreme unction. Through Order the Church is governed and receives spiritual growth; through matrimony she receives bodily growth.

1307 All these sacraments are constituted by three elements: by
1312 things as the matter, by words as the form, and by the person of the minister conferring the sacrament with the intention of doing what the Church does. And if any one of these three is lacking, the sacrament is not effected.

1308 Among these sacraments there are three, baptism, confirma-
1313 tion and Order, which imprint on the soul an indelible character, that is a certain spiritual sign distinguishing (the recipient)

from others. Hence, these are not repeated for the same person. The other four, however, do not imprint a character and may be repeated.

LEO X

BULL *EXSURGE DOMINE* (1520)

The Bull Exsurge Domine *condemns 41 propositions extracted from Luther's writings. Based on his doctrine of salvation through faith alone, they mostly refer to his teaching on the Church (cf. n. 811), on grace (cf. n. 1923/2i), on the sacrament of penance (cf. n. 1614/5i), on indulgences (cf. n. 1685/17i) and purgatory. One proposition denied the efficacy of the sacraments; it is quoted here. The condemnation by Leo X did not stop Luther from spreading his ideas; it rather prompted him to write the major works which will give to the Reformation its definitive orientation.*

(Error of Luther condemned)

[1309] It is a heretical, though wide-spread, opinion that the sacra-
1451 ments of the New Law give justifying grace to those who do
not place an obstacle in the way.

THE GENERAL COUNCIL OF TRENT

SEVENTH SESSION

DECREE ON THE SACRAMENTS (1547)

After having exposed the doctrine on justification in its 6th session (cf. nn. 1924ff), the Council of Trent devoted its 7th session to the doctrine of the sacraments, and in particular to baptism and confirmation (cf. nn. 1420ff). The Decree on the Sacraments comprises no chapters but only canons preceded by a brief foreword. The canons are mostly directed against the errors of Luther, of the Augsburg confession (1530) and of Melanchton. Canon 1 maintains that there are seven sacraments, against Luther who reduced their number to three and later to two (baptism and Eucharist). It affirms that the seven sacraments are instituted by Christ, but without excluding the possibility of the "mediate institution" of some as held then by some Catholic theologians. Canon 4 is directed against Luther's opinion according to which, salvation being through faith alone, the sacraments are superfluous; canon 5 against an article of the Augsburg confession which reduced their efficacy to the arousing of faith. Canons 6-8 determine the efficacy of grace proper to the sacraments and its necessary conditions. Canon 9 affirms the existence in three sacraments of a sacramental character, which it describes in terms of the theology of St Thomas Aquinas (cf. n. 1308). Canons 10 to 12 are directed against Luther who taught that, since the sacraments are effective only through the faith of the recipient, their efficacy in no way depends on the person and intention of the minister.

Foreword

1310 In order to bring to completion to salutary doctrine of justifi-
1600 cation promulgated with the unanimous consent of the
Fathers in the session immediately preceding, it seemed
fitting to deal with the holy sacraments of the Church. For all true
justification either begins through the sacraments, or, once begun,
increases through them, or when lost is regained through them.
Therefore, in order to do away with errors and to root out heresies
which in this our age are directed against the holy sacraments—
partly inspired by heresies already condemned in the past by our
Fathers and partly newly devised—and which are doing great harm
to the purity of the Catholic Church and to the salvation of souls, the
most holy, ecumenical and general Council of Trent, lawfully
assembled in the Holy Spirit under the presidency of the same
legates of the apostolic See, adhering to the teaching of the Holy
Scriptures, to the apostolic traditions and to the consensus of the
Fathers and of the other Councils, has thought that the present
canons should be drawn up and decreed. The canons which remain
for the completion of the work begun, the Council will, with the help
of the Holy Spirit, publish hereafter.

Canons on the Sacraments in General

1311 1. If anyone says that the sacraments of the New Law
1601 were not all instituted by Jesus Christ our Lord; or that
there are more or fewer than seven, that is: baptism, confirmation, the Eucharist, penance, extreme unction, Order and
matrimony; or that any one of these is not truly and properly a
sacrament, *anathema sit.*

1312 2. If anyone says that these same sacraments of the New
1602 Law do not differ from the sacraments of the Old Law, except
that the ceremonies and external rites are different,
anathema sit.

1313 3. If anyone says that these sacraments are so equal to one
1603 another that one is not in any way of greater worth than
another, *anathema sit.*

1314 4. If anyone says that the sacraments of the New Law are not
1604 necessary for salvation, but that they are superfluous; and
that without the sacraments or the desire of them men obtain

from God the grace of justification through faith alone, although it is true that not all the sacraments are necessary for each person, *anathema sit.*

1315 5. If anyone says that these sacraments are instituted only
1605 for the sake of nourishing the faith, *anathema sit.*

1316 6. If anyone says that the sacraments of the New Law do not
1606 contain the grace which they signify or that they do not
confer that grace on those who do not place an obstacle in the way, as if they were only external signs of the grace or justice received through faith and a kind of marks of the Christian profession by which among men the faithful are distinguished from the unbelievers, *anathema sit.*

1317 7. If anyone says that, as far as God's part is concerned,
1607 grace is not given through these sacraments always and to
all, even if they receive them rightly, but only sometimes and to some, *anathema sit.*

1318 8. If anyone says that through the sacraments of the New
1608 Law grace is not conferred by the performance of the rite
itself (*ex opere operato*) but that faith alone in the divine promise is sufficient to obtain grace, *anathema sit.*

1319 9. If anyone says that in three sacraments, namely, baptism,
1609 confirmation and Order, a character is not imprinted on the
soul, that is, a kind of indelible spiritual sign by reason of which these sacraments cannot be repeated, *anathema sit.*

1320 10. If anyone says that all Christians have the power (to
1610 preach) the word and to administer all the sacraments,
anathema sit.

1321 11. If anyone says that the intention, at least of doing what
1611 the Church does, is not required in the ministers when they
are performing and conferring the sacraments, *anathema sit.*

1322 12. If anyone says that a minister in the state of mortal sin,
1612 though he observes all the essentials that belong to the
performing and conferring of the sacrament, does not perform or confer the sacrament, *anathema sit.*

1323 13. If anyone says that the accepted and approved rites of
1613 the Catholic Church which are customarily used in the
solemn adminstration of the sacraments may be despised or

omitted without sin by the ministers as they please, or that they may be changed to other new rites by any pastor in the Church, *anathema sit.*

TWENTY-FIRST SESSION

DOCTRINE ON COMMUNION UNDER BOTH SPECIES AND ON COMMUNION OF LITTLE CHILDREN (1562)

In its 21st session the Council of Trent dealt with the much disputed question of the admission of lay people to communion with the chalice (cf. nn. 1537ff). The legitimacy of communion under one kind only which had become the received practice is based on the principle that, the substance of the sacraments instituted by Christ being preserved, the Church has power to determine the modality of their dispensation. Much later (1947), Pope Pius XII will refer to the same principle in order to determine the essential rite of the sacrament of Order (cf. n. 1737i). He will further define the "substance" of the sacraments over which the Church has no power, as consisting of "those things which, on the testimony of the sources of divine revelation, Christ the Lord Himself has determined as having to be preserved in the sacramental sign" (DS 3857).

Chapter II: The Power of the Church concerning the Dispensation of the Eucharist

1324 (The Holy Council) furthermore declares that in the dispen-
1728 sation of the sacraments, provided their substance is preserved, the Church has always had the power to determine or change, according to circumstances, times and places, what she judges more expedient for the benefit of those receiving them or for the veneration of the sacraments. It seems that the apostle referred to this power rather clearly when he said: "This is how one should regard us, as servants of Christ and stewards of the mysteries of God" (*1 Cor. 4.1*). It is sufficiently clear that he himself used this power not only in many other instances but also with regard to this very sacrament, when he laid down certain regulations for its use and said: "About the other things I will give directions when I come" (*1 Cor. 11.34*). Therefore, ... holy Mother Church, conscious of her authority in the administration of the sacraments ....

(There follows the approval of Communion under one kind.)

ALEXANDER VIII

DECREE OF THE HOLY OFFICE (1690)

The Council of Trent had purposely left indeterminate the "intention of doing what the Church does" which is required in the administration of the sacraments. Among the errors of the Jansenists condemned by this decree of the Holy Office is found a proposition attributed to Farvacques according to which a sacrament is validly conferred by a minister who duly performs the rite even though he interiorly resolves not to do what the Church does. From this condemnation (which is not a document of faith), it results that the so-called "external intention" (shown in the performance of the rite itself) is not sufficient, but that a certain "interior intention" is required on the part of the minister for a valid administration of the sacraments.

(Jansenist error condemned)

[1325] Baptism is valid, when coferred by a minister who observes
2328   all the external rites and the form of baptising, but interiorly
       within his heart resolves: I do not intend what the Church
does.

PIUS X

DECREE *LAMENTABILI* OF THE HOLY OFFICE (1907)

ARTICLES OF MODERNISM CONDEMNED

The Church's doctrine on the institution of the sacraments by Christ and their efficacy ex opere operato were regarded by the Modernists, in accordance with their basic tenets (cf. n. 143i), as typical examples of the way in which religious forms established in the first centuries of Christianity were progressively fixed and presented in the Church's teaching as immutable dogmas. According to them, the sacraments are an interpretation, in no way absolute, of the mind of Christ by early Christianity. The Decree Lamentabili *condemns three fundamental errors of the Modernists on the sacraments in general (cf. also nn. 1437/42ff; 1660/46ff; 1729/49).*

[1326/39] The opinions on the origin of the sacraments with which
3439   the Tridentine Fathers were imbued and which undoubt-
       edly influenced their dogmatic canons are far removed
from those which are now rightly held by research historians of
Christianity.

[1326/40] The sacraments owe their origin to the fact that the
3440   apostles and their successors interpreted some idea
       and intention of Christ under the influence and pressure
of circumstances and events.

[1326/41] The purpose of the sacraments is only to recall to the
3441   mind of man the ever beneficent presence of the
       Creator.

ENCYCLICAL LETTER *PASCENDI* (1907)

Completing the Decree Lamentabili, *the encyclical* Pascendi *of Pius X*

exposes at length and attempts to synthetise in their diversity the ideas of
the Modernists (cf. n. 143i). One passage refers to the Modernist opinion
according to which the sacraments, as all that belongs to the cult, have only
a symbolic value.

1327   On the question of worship, little would have to be said were
3489   it not for the fact that the sacraments come under this
heading; and here the Modernists fall into the gravest errors.
They attempt to show that worship results from a twofold impulse or
necessity; for, as we have seen, everything in their system is
explained by inner impulses or necessities. The first impulse is to
attribute some sensible element to religion; the second impulse is to
make it known, and this could not be done without some sensible
form and sanctifying actions which we call sacraments. For the
Modernists, the sacraments are mere symbols or signs, though not
altogether without power. To explain the nature of this power, they
compare it to the power of certain phrases which in common par-
lance "have caught on", inasmuch as they have acquired the power
of propagating mighty ideas capable of deeply striking men's minds.
What these phrases are to ideas, the sacraments are to the religious
sense—that, and nothing more. Now, surely, the Modernists would
speak more plainly, were they to affirm that the sacraments were
instituted solely to foster faith. But this the Council of Trent has condemned: "If anyone says that these sacraments were instituted only
for the sake of nourishing the faith, *anathema sit" (cf. n. 1315).*

PIUS XII

ENCYCLICAL LETTER *MYSTICI CORPORIS* (1943)

In his great Encyclical Letter on the mystery of the Church (cf. nn. 847 ff),
Pope Pius XII shows the meaning of the various sacraments for the spiritual
life of individual Christians and in relation to the mystery of the Church.
Linking up with the persuasion of the early Tradition, he re-states the
theological principle that the sacraments are the actions of Christ through
the Church.

(The Church, Mystical Body of Christ, and the sacraments)

1328   The human body... has its own means for fostering the life,
health and growth of itself and each of its members. And the
Saviour of the human race in His infinite goodness has in like manner
admirably equipped His mystical Body by endowing it with the
sacraments, making available for its members a progressive series of
graces to sustain them from the cradle to their last breath, and

abundantly providing also for the social needs of the whole Body. By baptism those who have been born to this mortal life are regenerated from the death of sin and made members of the Church, and also invested with a spiritual character which makes them able and fit to receive the other sacraments. The chrism of confirmation gives believers new strength so that they may strenuously guard and defend Mother Church and the faith which they have received from her. The sacrament of penance offers a saving remedy to members of the Church who have fallen into sin, and this not only for the sake of their own salvation but also in order that their fellow-members may be saved from the danger of contagion, and receive instead an example and incentive to virtue. Nor is this all : in the Holy Eucharist the faithful are nourished and fortified at a common banquet, and by an ineffable and divine bond united with one another and with the divine Head of the whole Body. And when at last they are mortally ill, loving Mother Church is at their side with the sacrament of extreme unction, and although, God so willing, she may not always thereby restore health of the body, she nevertheless applies a supernatural balm to the wounded soul, thus providing new citizens for heaven and new heavenly intercessors for herself, who will enjoy the divine goodness for all eternity.

For the social needs of the Church Christ has also provided in a particular way by two other sacraments which He instituted. The sacrament of matrimony, in which the partners become the minis-ters of grace to each other, ensures the regular numerical increase of the Christian community, and, what is more important, the proper and religious education of the offspring, the lack of which would constitute a grave menace to the mystical Body. And holy Order, finally, consecrates to the perpetual service of God those who are destined to offer the eucharistic victim, to nourish the flock of the faithful with the bread of angels and with the food of doctrine, to guide them by the divine commandments and counsels, and to fortify them by their other supernatural functions.

(The sacraments are the actions of Christ through the Church)

1329 Christ is the author and efficient cause of holiness ; for there can be no salutary act which does not proceed from Him as from its supernatural source: "Apart from Me you can do nothing", He said (*Jn 15.5*)....His inexhaustible fulness is the fount of grace and glory....And when the Church administers the sacraments with external rites, it is He who produces their effect in the soul. He it is, too, who feeds the redeemed with His own flesh and blood....

1330 ...In the first place, in virtue of the juridical mission by which the divine Redeemer sent forth His apostles into the world as He Himself had been sent by the Father (*cf. Jn 17.18; 20.21*), it is indeed He who baptises through the Church, He who teaches, governs, absolves, binds, offers and makes sacrifice.

ENCYCLICAL LETTER *MEDIATOR DEI* (1947)

This Encyclical Letter prolongs Mystici Corporis *and further develops its doctrine with regard to the Church's liturgical life. Regarding the sacraments, it lays stress on Christ's presence and action; it explains that Christ's action does not dispense the recipient from personally appropriating to himself the gift of grace. It also touches on the difficult question of the presence of the historical mysteries of Christ in the sacraments and in the entire liturgical life of the Church. The theological discussion on this point had received impetus mostly from the works of Dom Odo Casel (1886-1948), a Benedictine monk of Maria Laach, and the theory of the "mysteric presence" proposed by him. The encyclical does not favour explanations which would seem too obscure, but neither does it propose one which would answer all the questions. It leaves open a discussion in which theologians and liturgists are engaged even today.*

(Christ's presence in the sacraments)

1331
3840 ...In the whole conduct of the liturgy the Church has her divine founder present with her. Christ is present in the august sacrifice of the altar, both in the person of His minister and especially under the eucharistic species; He is present in the sacraments by His power which He infuses into them as instruments of sanctification; He is present, finally, in the prayer and praise which are offered to God, in accordance with His promise : "Where two or three are gathered in my name, there am I in the midst of them" (*Mt. 18.20*)

(Christ's action must be personally appropriated)

1332 It is certainly true that the sacraments and the Mass possess an intrinsic efficacy, because they are actions of Christ Himself transmitting and distributing the grace of the divine Head to the members of the mystical Body. But to have their proper effect they require our souls also to be in the right dispositions. This is why St Paul warns us in regard to the Eucharist : "Let a man examine himself, and so eat of the bread and drink of the cup" (*1 Cor.*

11.28)....For it must be borne in mind that the members of this Body are living members, endowed with intellect and will ; therefore they must deliberately set their lips to this source of grace, absorb and assimilate this food of life, and uproot from themselves anything that may obscure its efficacy. So the work of our redemption, though in itself something independent of our will, really calls for an interior effort from our souls if we are to attain eternal salvation.

(The presence of the mysteries of Christ)

1333   ...The liturgical year, animated throughout by the devotion of
3855   the Church, is no cold and lifeless representation of past
events, no mere historical record. It is Christ Himself, living on in His Church, and still pursuing that path of boundless mercy which, going about doing good (*cf. Acts 10.38*), He began to tread during His life on earth. This He did in order that the souls of men might come into contact with His mysteries and, so to speak, live by them. And these mysteries are still now constantly present and active, not in the vague and nebulous way which recent authors describe, but as Catholic doctrine teaches us. The Doctors of the Church tell us that the mysteries of Christ's life are at the same time most excellent models of virtue for us to imitate and also sources of divine grace for us by reason of the merits and intercession of the Redeemer. They live on in their effect in us, since each of them is, according to its nature and in its own way, the cause of our salvation.

THE SECOND VATICAN GENERAL COUNCIL

Though the Council of Trent in its Decree on Justification referred to Christ's continuous vital action on His members (cf. n. 1947), its canons on the sacraments made no reference to Christ beyond stating that they have been instituted by Him. Partly prepared by the encyclicals Mystici Corporis *and* Mediator Dei, *the* **sacramental** *doctrine of Vatican II is more comprehensive than that of the Council of Trent. It is deeply Christocentric, while at the same time stressing the ecclesial dimension of the sacraments. It combines harmoniously two complementary aspects of the sacraments, at once efficacious signs of Christ's sanctifying power and concrete expressions of the faith of the Church; for God's gratuitous initiative does not dispense man from responding to it in faith. Again, without toning down the idea of efficacy, the Council makes a strong plea for the meaningfulness of the signs (SC 59). Its doctrine is found in the two Constitutions on the Sacred Liturgy (SC) and on the Church (LG).*

The perfect achievement of our reconciliation and the fulness of divine worship are found in Christ the Word Incarnate (SC 5); His earthly work consisted in "redeeming mankind and giving perfect glory to God" (SC 5).

The Church as "universal sacrament of salvation" (LG 48; cf. 1, 9; SC 5, 26; GS 45 ...) prolongs Christ's action; for Christ associates her with Himself in the work by which God is perfectly glorified and men sanctified (SC 7). This is true especially of the liturgy (SC 10); hence the twofold end which the Council assigns to it (SC 10) (cf. n. 1232). In the liturgical life of the Church, however, the sacraments obtain a privileged place: "around the sacrifice and the sacraments the entire liturgical life revolves" (SC 6; cf. 2, 7, etc.). The sacraments draw their power from the Paschal Mystery (SC 61). Like the Paschal Mystery itself, they are directed to a double end, the sanctification of men and the praise of God (SC 61); thus, they build up the Body of Christ (SC 59).

While referring to the mystery of salvation contained in the sacraments, the Council purposely avoids the controversial phrase ex opere operato. It is replaced by the concept of Christ's presence and action. Christ's presence in the Church's sacraments is stressed in SC 7. This text, partly prepared by Mediator Dei (cf. n. 1731), is among the most profound and far-reaching theological statements of Vatican II. By affirming Christ's presence in the liturgy of the word (not mentioned in Mediator Dei), it opens the way for a theology which will combine harmoniously the efficacy of the word of God and of the sacraments. Not only is Christ present in the sacramental actions of the Church, but His mysteries too are present there in a mysterious manner: by baptism men are inserted into the Paschal mystery of Christ (SC 6; cf. 61); this indicates that Christ's Paschal Mystery is present and operative in the sacraments. SC 102 extends the presence of the mysteries of Christ to the Church's liturgical year (cf. n. 1234).

The sacraments are also a mystery of divine worship on the part of the Church: they not only presuppose faith, but also nourish, strengthen and express it; this is why they are called "sacraments of faith" (SC 59). Thus, correlative to the stress put on Christ's presence and action in the sacraments, Vatican II insists on the role of faith. It rejuvenates the phrase of an old tradition: the sacraments are sacramenta fidei. On the part of the Church, they are communal acts of worship, in so far as here, even more than in other liturgical actions, Christ associates her with Himself in the work of God's glorification (SC 7). As to the recipient of the sacrament, what the Council says explicitly of the faithful participating in the liturgy applies to him in a special manner: "It is necessary that the faithful come to it with proper dispositions, that their minds should be attuned to their voices, and that they should co-operate with divine grace lest they receive it in vain" (SC 11).

CONSTITUTION *SACROSANCTUM CONCILIUM* (1963)

(Christ's manifold presence and action in the Church's liturgy)

1334 7. To accomplish so great a work, Christ is always present to His Church, especially in her liturgical celebrations. He is present in the sacrifice of the Mass, not only in the person of His minister, "the same now offering through the ministry of priests, who then offered Himself on the cross" *(cf. n. 1548)*, but especially under the eucharistic species. By His power He is present in the sacraments, so that when a man baptises it is really Christ Himself who baptises. He is present in His word, since it is He Himself who speaks when the Holy Scriptures are read in the Church. He is present, lastly, when the Church prays and sings, for He promised: "Where two or three are gathered in my name, there am I in the midst of them" (Mt. 18.20).

Christ indeed always associates the Church with Himself in this great work wherein God is perfectly glorified and men are sanctified. The Church is His beloved Bride who calls to her Lord and through Him offers worship to the eternal Father.

Rightly, then, the liturgy is considered as an exercise of the priestly office of Jesus Christ. In the liturgy the sanctification of man is signified by signs perceptible to the senses, and is effected in a way which corresponds with each of these signs; in the liturgy the whole public worship is performed by the mystical Body of Jesus Christ, that is, by the Head and His members....

(Sanctification of men and worship of God in the sacraments)

1335   59. The purpose of the sacraments is to sanctify men, to build up the Body of Christ, and, finally, to give worship to God; because they are signs, they also instruct. They not only presuppose faith, but by words and objects they also nourish, strengthen and express it; that is why they are called "sacraments of faith". They do indeed impart grace, but, in addition, the very act of celebrating them most effectively disposes the faithful to receive this grace in a fruitful manner, to worship God duly, and to practise charity.

It is therefore of the highest importance that the faithful should easily understand the sacramental signs, and should frequent with great eagerness those sacraments which were instituted to nourish the Christian life.

PAUL VI

APOSTOLIC EXHORTATION *EVANGELII NUNTIANDI* (1975)

Chapter III of the Apostolic Exhortation on Evangelization of Pope Paul VI is devoted to the "Methods of Evangelization". It affirms the need for preaching and verbal proclamation and in this context stresses the role of the liturgy of the word. It goes on to show the link between word, faith and sacrament and concludes that sacramentalization cannot be opposed to evangelization. The text is found in AAS 68 (1976) 36-37.

(Word, faith and sacrament)

1336 47. Evangelization exercises its full capacity when it achieves the most intimate relationship, or better still a permanent and unbroken inter-communication, between the Word and the Sacraments. In a certain sense it is a mistake to build a contrast between evangelization and sacramentalization, as is sometimes done. It is indeed true that a certain way of administering the Sacraments, without the solid support of catechesis regarding these same Sacraments and a global catechesis, could end up by depriving them of their effectiveness to a great extent. The role of evangelization is precisely to educate people in the faith in such a way as to lead each individual Christian to live the Sacraments as true Sacraments of faith—and not to receive them passively or to undergo them.

CHAPTER XIV

BAPTISM AND CONFIRMATION

To be a Christian is to be conformed to the mystery of Christ's death and resurrection in order to live a new life in Christ and to continue His mission in the world as a member of His Church. Baptism, confirmation and the Eucharist are the three sacraments that initiate the members of the Church into this new life; but, while the Eucharist is meant to strengthen day by day the Christian life, baptism and confirmation mark a person once for all as a member of Christ in His Church. This is why these two sacraments are closely connected; together they confer full Church membership.

Through baptism "as through a door" (cf. AG 7) men enter the Church. Plunged into the mystery of Christ's death and resurrection, they are once for all sacramentally conformed to this mystery, become members of Christ's mystical Body and receive a spiritual rebirth. But, though already destined through baptism to share in the life of the Church and her mission, they are even more directly ordained to witness to Christ in word and deed through confirmation.

The sacrament of baptism has from the earliest Tradition been present to the explicit consciousness of the Church. In it all who bear the name of Christian are united; no heresy claiming that name ever could or did question it seriously. Doubts were raised only as regards the manner of conferring it, its effects and its mode of efficacy. The Church clarified these issues as they arose. For the most part, her official documents answer concrete questions and refute errors; they do not exhaust the riches of the 'sacrament of faith' upon which the patristic catechesis had dwelt with predilection.

The Church has grown through the centuries in her explicit awareness of confirmation as a distinct sacrament. Its intimate connection with baptism and the early practice of conferring the Christian initiation in one liturgical celebration caused this distinction to remain latent. Yet, the early documents witness to the fact that the Christian initiation conferred by the priest is completed by the bishop. This element has played a decisive role in the explicitation of the faith about confirmation. As sacramental doctrine developed in the 12th century, confirmation found its proper place in the sacramental system. Its specific significance, however, was not *always equally well understood; linking with Scripture and a strong current of Tradition, the recent documents show more and more clearly that confirmation strengthens the Christian with the gift of the Spirit to enable him to bear witness to Christ.*

Summing up the data of the Christian Tradition, the Second Vatican Council has brought out the distinction and complementarity of the two sacraments that make the Christian. Both together constitute the foundation of the common priesthood of the People of God and are the basis for the lay apostolate. Baptised in Christ and confirmed with the Spirit, all Christians are called upon to take an active part in the Church's life and mission.

*   *   *

The main points of doctrine contained in this chapter may be summed up under the following headings:

Baptism

Baptism is a true sacrament instituted by Christ: 25, 28, 32, 39/11, 1305f, 1311, 1412, 1420.

It introduces into the Church and incorporates into Christ: 849, 1412, 1439, 1440, 1441, 1618.

It confers a sacramental character by which Christians share in the priesthood of Christ: 32, 1308, 1319, 1410, 1439, 1441, 1710.

It confers all the rights and enjoins all the duties of the Christian life: 1425-1429, 1433.

It cannot be repeated: 32, 1401, 1404, 1430, 1432, 1440a-1440b.

It remits sins, original and personal, and confers the life of grace: 9, 10, 12, 39/11, 503, 510-512, 1306, (1407), 1409, 1411, 1412, 1415, 1439, 1441, 1615, 1619, 1923/2, 1932, 1944, 2302.

It is administered with water and the Trinitarian formula: 21, 1413, 1421.

Baptism at least of desire is necessary for salvation: 510, 1405, 1408, 1419, 1424, 1437/42, 1928.

Infants can and should be baptised: 21, 39/11, 511, 1405, (1407), 1409, 1411, 1419, 1431f, 1437/43, 1443-1446.

Adults must be free in receiving baptism: 1410.

Every man can baptise validly: 1401, 1402, 1403, 1404, 1414, 1423.

Confirmation

Confirmation is a true sacrament, instituted by Christ: 28, 32, 1305, 1311, 1416, 1434, 1435.

It completes baptism but is distinct from it: 1402, 1404, 1437/44, 1439, 1440, 1441.

It confers a sacramental character which binds Christians more deeply to the Church: 32, 1319, 1439, 1440, 1441, 1710.

It confers the gift of the Spirit for strength in the Christian witness: 1306, 1404, 1406, 1416, 1418, 1439, 1440, 1441.

It is administered by an anointing with chrism accompanied with the words: 28, 1308, 1404, 1406, 1416, 1442.

The chrism must be blessed by the bishop: 1417.

The bishop is the oridinary minister of confirmation, the priest the extraordinary minister: 28, 1404, 1406, 1417, 1436, (1438).

Baptism and confirmation are the foundation of the common priesthood of all Christians and of the lay apostolate: 1439, 1440, 1441.

STEPHEN I

LETTER TO CYPRIAN, BISHOP OF CARTHAGE (256)

In Rome as in Alexandria and Palestine, the custom when receiving heretics who had been baptised was to lay hands on them as a sign of reconciliation. In Carthage, the persuasion was that persons baptised in heresy had to be re-baptised. Pope Stephen I who had received notification of this practice objects to it and claims his right to impose the Roman practice. The same doctrine on the validity of baptism received in heresy will later be repeated by Pope Innocent I (cf. DS 211) and Pope Gregory II (cf. DS 580).

(On baptism of heretics)

1401 If, therefore, some come to you from any heresy whatsoever
110 let no innovation be made except according to what has been handed down, namely, let an imposition of hands be made on them by way of penance; for the heretics themselves are right in not baptising other heretics who come over to them but simply receiving them into their communion.

THE COUNCIL OF ELVIRA (c. 300-303)

This local Council held in Spain shows the distinction and connection between baptism and its "perfection" through an imposition of hand by the bishop. See also canon 77 of the same Council (DS 121).

(On baptism and its completion by the bishop)

1402 *Canon 38:* ...A faithful who has been fully baptised and is
120 not bigamous may in case of need arising from sickness baptise a catechumen, so that, if he survives, he will bring him to the bishop that he may be perfected by the imposition of hand.

THE FIRST GENERAL COUNCIL OF NICAEA (325)

The decision of Pope Stephen notwithstanding (cf. n. 1401), conditions could arise in which heretics had to be rebaptised. Such was the case with the Paulianists (followers of Paul of Samosata, bishop of Antioch, c. 260) who denied the divinity of the Son and therefore were not baptised in the name of the Blessed Trinity. The Council of Nicaea orders that they be re-baptised. See similar decisions by the Council of Arles (314) (DS 123) and later by Pope Innocent I (DS 214) and Pope Gregory I (DS 478).

(Some baptisms of heretics are not valid)

1403 *Canon 19:* As for the Paulianists who seek refuge in the
128 Catholic Church, the decision has been taken that they be re-baptised by all means.

SIRICIUS

LETTER TO HIMERIUS, BISHOP OF TARRAGONA (385)

In this letter the Pope distinguishes baptism from the gift of the Spirit through the bishop's imposition of hand: the first is not repeated in the case of heretics, while the other is conferred on them (see also Leo I: DS 320). After having insisted on the observance of the liturgical time (Easter and Pentecost) for the conferring of baptism, he goes on to explain the necessity of baptism for salvation (see also Innocent I: DS 219) which may require that other provisions be made.

(Baptism and its completion by the bishop)

1404   These (Arians) as well as the Novatians and other heretics we
183   join to the Catholic assembly merely by the invocation of the
            septiform Spirit through the bishop's imposition of hand, as
has been decided by the Synod. The same is observed everywhere in
East and West....

(Necessity of baptism for salvation)

1405   As we maintain that the observance of the holy Paschal time
184   should in no way be relaxed, in the same way we desire that
            infants who, on account of their age, cannot yet speak, or
those who, in any necessity, are in want of the water of holy baptism,
be succoured with all possible speed, for fear that, if anyone who
leaves this world should be deprived of the life of the Kingdom for
having been refused the source of salvation which he desired, this
may lead to the ruin of our souls. If anyone threatened with shipwreck, or the attack of enemies, or the uncertainties of a siege, or
anyone put in a hopeless condition due to some bodily sickness, asks
for what in his faith is his only help, let him receive at the very
moment of his request the reward of the regeneration he begs for.
Enough of the past mistakes! From now on, let all the priests observe
the aforesaid rule if they do not want to be separated from the solid
apostolic rock on which Christ has built His universal Church.

INNOCENT I

LETTER TO DECENTIUS, BISHOP OF GUBBIO (416)

In this letter the Pope distinguishes clearly baptism (comprising an anointing with chrism) which is conferred by the presbyter from the signing (consignatio) with chrism reserved to the bishop.

(Signing with chrism is reserved to the bishop)

1406   As for the signing of infants (with chrism) (*de consignandis*
215   *infantibus*), it is clear that it may only be done by the bishop.
For, though the presbyters are priests of the second order,
yet they do not have the fulness of the pontificate. That this pontifical
authority of confirming (*ut consignent*) or of conferring the Spirit the
Paraclete is proper only to the bishops is clearly shown, not only by
the Church's custom, but by that passage of the Acts of the Apostles
which affirms that Peter and John were directed to confer the Holy
Spirit to those who were already baptised (*cf. Acts 8.14-17*). For it is
allowed to presbyters when they baptise either in the absence of the
bishop or in his presence to anoint with chrism those who are being
baptised, though only with chrism consecrated by the bishop; but
not to sign their forehead with the same oil, which is reserved to the
bishops when they confer the Spirit the Paraclete....

THE SIXTEENTH COUNCIL OF CARTHAGE (418)

(1407)   *In its canon 2 on original sin this local Council clearly states*
223   *that baptism truly remits original sin in infants and that, therefore,*
baptism for the remission of sins is properly verified in them. For
the historical context of this document, see n. 501i. The text of the Council
of Carthage was adopted with minute additions by the Council of Trent in
its Decree on Original Sin; the text of Trent is quoted in n. 511.

INNOCENT II (1130-1143)

LETTER TO THE BISHOP OF CREMONIA (time unknown)

In this letter Pope Innocent II explains that "baptism of desire" can remit
original sin and lead to salvation. The same doctrine is taught by Pope
Innocent III in a letter to Bertolius, bishop of Metz (1206) (cf. DS 788).

(On baptism of desire)

1408   We affirm without hesitation that the old man who, according
741   to the information received from you, died without having
received the baptism of water, has been relieved of original
sin and granted the joy of the heavenly home, because he has
persevered in the faith of holy Mother the Church and in the confession of Christ's name. Read on this the eighth book of Augustine's
"The City of God"[1] where among other things we read the following:
"Baptism is invisibly administered which has been impeded, not by

---

1. The correct reference is to ST AUGUSTINE'S *De baptismo contra Donatistas*, IV,
22, 29.

contempt for religion, but by unavoidable death." And read over again the book of St Ambrose *"On the Death of Valentianus"*[1] which affirms the same doctrine....

INNOCENT III

LETTER TO HUMBERT, ARCHBISHOP OF ARLES (1201)

Some heretics, perhaps the Waldensians, considered infant baptism profitless. In this letter, the Pope explains the effect of baptism of children and compares it with the effect of circumcision: circumcision made men belong to the chosen people, remission of original sin included, but only baptism opens the Kingdom of heaven. Thus it is eminently fruitful. A second passage of the same letter (quoted under n. 506) explains why original sin can in baptism be remitted without consent; this is due to the nature of original sin as distinct from personal sin (cf. n. 506i). A third passage, while treating of the freedom required for the baptism of adults, alludes to the character produced by the sacrament.

(The effect of baptism)

1409 Even though original sin was remitted by the mystery of
780 circumcision and the danger of damnation avoided, man could not reach the Kingdom of heaven, which remained closed for all till the death of Christ. But through the sacrament of baptism...the guilt is remitted and one also reaches the Kingdom of heaven, whose gate the blood of Christ mercifully opened to His faithful. Far from us the thought that all the small children, of whom such a great multitude dies every day, should perish without the merciful God, who wishes no one to perish, having provided for them also some means of salvation....

(Freedom required for baptism; its character)

1410 It is contrary to the Christian religion to force someone into
781 accepting and practising Christianity if he is always unwilling and totally opposed. Wherefore, some, not without reason, distinguish between unwilling and unwilling, forced and forced. For whoever is violently drawn by fear of punishments and receives the sacrament of baptism to avoid harm to himself, such a one, just like the one who comes to baptism in bad faith, receives the imprint of the Christian character; and, since he gave his consent conditionally though not absolutely, he is to be held to the observance of the Christian faith....But one who never consents and is absolutely unwilling receives neither the reality nor the character of the sacra-

---

1. St Ambrose, *De obitu Valentiani*, 51.

ment because express dissent is something more than the absence of any consent....

PROFESSION OF FAITH PRESCRIBED TO THE WALDENSIANS
(1208)

For this document, see n. 403i. One arrticle treats infant baptism and explains the effect of baptism in general.

1411   We therefore approve the baptism of infants. We profess and
794   believe that they are saved if they die after baptism before
having committed any sins. And we believe that all sins are remitted in baptism, the original sin which has been contracted as well as those committed voluntarily.

THE GENERAL COUNCIL OF FLORENCE
DECREE FOR THE ARMENIANS (1439)

For the doctrinal value of this document see n. 1306i. After treating the sacraments in general, the Decree turns to each in particular, explaining its matter, form, minister and effect, successively. It begins with baptism and confirmation. For confirmation see, previous to this document, the questions which, in 1351, Pope Clement VI put to Catholicos Mekhitar to ascertain the correct faith of the Armenians at a time (1198 to 1375) when they were united with Rome (DS 1068-1071); the various elements mentioned there are included in this Decree. As regards the matter of confirmation, the Decree merely says that it is the chrism with which the candidate is signed. It does not mention that this signing with chrism implies in itself an imposition of hand, as had been explained by some earlier documents. Thus, for instance, in 1204 Innocent III had written: "By the chrismation of the forehead is signified the imposition of hand which is also called confirmation..." (DS 785); see also Innocent IV (DS 831).

1412   Among all the sacraments holy baptism holds the first place
1314   because it is the gateway to the spiritual life; by it we are
made members of Christ and belong to His body, the Church. And since through the first man death has entered into all (*cf. Rom. 5.12*), unless we are born again of water and the Spirit, we cannot, as the Truth said, enter into the Kingdom of heaven (*cf. Jn 3.5*).

1413   The matter of this sacrament is true natural water; it does not
1314   matter whether it is cold or warm. The form is: "I baptise you
in the name of the Father and of the Son and of the Holy Spirit." We do not deny, however, that true baptism is also effected by these words: "May the servant of Christ, N., be baptised in the

name of the Father and of the Son and of the Holy Spirit", or: "By my hands N. is baptised in the name of the Father and of the Son and of the Holy Spirit." For as the principal cause from which baptism derives its virtue is the Holy Trinity, while the instrumental cause is the minister who confers the sacrament externally, the sacrament is performed whenever the act carried out by the minister is expressed along with the invocation of the Holy Trinity.

1414 The minister of this sacrament is the priest, to whom by
1315 reason of his office it belongs to baptise. But in case of necessity not only a priest or deacon, but also a layman, or a woman, or even a pagan and a heretic may baptise, provided he observes the Church's form and intends to do what the Church does.

1415 The effect of this sacrament is the remission of all guilt,
1316 original and actual, and also of all punishment due to the guilt itself. For this reason, no satisfaction is to be enjoined on the baptised for their past sins; and if they die before committing any fault, they immediately gain access to the Kingdom of heaven and the beatific vision.

1416 The second sacrament is confirmation. Its matter is chrism
1317 made from oil, signifying the purity of conscience, and balsam, signifying the fragrance of a good reputation; it is blessed by the bishop. The form is: "I sign you with the sign of the cross and I confirm you with the chrism of salvation, in the name of the Father and of the Son and of the Holy Spirit."

1417 The ordinary minister is the bishop. Whereas other anoint-
1318 ings may be performed by a simple priest, this one must only be conferred by the bishop. For we read that only the apostles, whose place the bishops hold, imparted the Holy Spirit by the laying on of hand. Reading the *Acts of the Apostles* makes this clear, for it is said: "Now when the apostles at Jerusalem heard that Samaria had received the word of God, they sent to them Peter and John, who came down and prayed for them that they might receive the Holy Spirit; for it had not yet fallen on any of them, but they had only been baptised in the name of the Lord Jesus. Then they laid their hands on them and they received the Holy Spirit" (*Acts 8.14-17*). Confirmation given by the Church takes the place of that imposition of hand. Nevertheless, we read that sometimes through a dispensation of the apostolic See for a reasonable and very urgent

cause a simple priest has administered the sacrament of confirmation with chrism prepared by the bishop.

1418   The effect of this sacrament is that in it the Holy Spirit is given
1319   for strength, as He was given to the apostles on the day of
Pentecost, in order that the Christian may courageously
confess the name of Christ. And, therefore, the one to be confirmed
is anointed on the forehead which is the seat of shame, so that he
may not be ashamed to confess the name of Christ, and chiefly His
cross, which, according to the apostle, is a stumbling block for the
Jews and foolishness for the Gentiles (*cf. 1 Cor. 1.23*). This is why he
is signed with the sign of the cross.

DECREE FOR THE JACOBITES (1442)

*For this document see nn. 809i and 1003i. The scope of the Decree is
limited. It states the objective order of salvation through the Church without
considering how those outside can subjectively be saved. A fortiori where
infants are concerned, it does not consider any other means of salvation
than the objective means of sacramental baptism. Only later theology will
consider the possibility of a baptism of desire in infants. For adults this
possibility had already been recognised in documents previous to this (cf. n.
1408); its application to children who have not reached the age of reason is a
more recent development and remains even today the object of theological
reflection.*

(The necessity of baptism of children)

1419   With regard to children, on account of the danger of death
1349   which can often occur, since no other remedy can help them
than the sacrament of baptism by which they are snatched
away from the devil's dominion and made the adopted sons of God,
(the Church) warns that holy baptism should not be delayed for forty
or eighty days, or for some other length of time according to the
custom observed by some; but it must be conferred as soon as can
suitably be done, with the provision that, if the peril of death is
imminent, the children be baptised at once without any delay, even, if
no priest is available, by a layman or a woman, in the form of the
Church, as is more fully explained in the decree for the Armenians
(*cf. n. 1414*).

THE GENERAL COUNCIL OF TRENT
SEVENTH SESSION
CANONS ON THE SACRAMENT OF BAPTISM (1547)

Trent contains no doctrinal chapter on the sacrament of baptism, as it merely intended to condemn the heresies that had become widespread. Nevertheless, these canons are of decisive importance for the Catholic doctrine of baptism.

Canon 1 affirms the difference between the baptism of John and that of Christ against an error of Melanchton. Canon 2 deals with the matter of baptism. Canon 3 affirms the truth of the Catholic doctrine of baptism against the Anabaptists and Luther. Canon 4 on the minister and form of baptism contains the final definition of a doctrine which had been firmly held for centuries. The validity of baptism conferred by heretics had been affirmed from the earliest times (cf. n. 1401); it was considered as proving that the efficacy of the sacrament does not depend on the faith or worthiness of the minister, but on the proper carrying out of Christ's command. Canon 5 affirms the necessity of baptism against the Manichaeans and Messalians. Canons 6 to 10 reject conclusions wrongly derived by the Reformers from the doctrine of baptism, which had been partly dealt with in the decree and canons on justification (cf. nn. 1934, 1968-1970). Canon 6 is directed against Luther's opinion that the only sin whereby man loses justification is unbelief (cf. nn. 1945, 1977), Canons 11 to 13 are directed against the Anabaptists. Canon 14 opposes the "liberal" opinions of Erasmus and Bucer.

1420 1. If anyone says that the baptism of John had the same force
1614 as the baptism of Christ, *anathema sit.*

1421 2. If anyone says that true and natural water is not necessary
1615 for baptism and therefore reduces to some sort of metaphor
the words of our Lord Jesus Christ: "Unless one is born of
water and the Spirit" (*Jn 3.5), anathema sit.*

1422 3. If anyone says that the Roman Church (the mother and
1616 teacher of all Churches) does not have the true doctrine
concerning the sacrament of baptism, *anathema sit.*

1423 4. If anyone says that baptism, even that given by heretics
1617 in the name of the Father and of the Son and of the Holy
Spirit, with the intention of doing what the Church does, is
not true baptism, *anathema sit.*

1424 5. If anyone says that baptism is optional, that is, not neces-
1618 sary for salvation, *anathema sit (cf. n. 1928).*

1425 6. If anyone says that one baptised cannot lose grace, even if
1619 he wishes to, no matter how much he sins, unless he is
unwilling to believe, *anathema sit (cf. n. 1945).*

1426 7. If anyone says that those baptised are by the fact of their
1620 baptism obliged merely to faith alone, but not to the observance of the whole law of Christ, *anathema sit.*

1427 8. If anyone says that those baptised are free from all the
1621 percepts of holy Church, whether written or handed down,
so that they are not bound to observe them unless, of their
own accord, they wish to submit to them, *anathema sit.*

1428 9. If anyone says that the remembrance of the baptism which
1622 they have received ought to be so impressed on men that
they be brought to understand that all vows taken after
baptism are void in virtue of the promise already made in baptism
itself, as if those vows detracted from the faith which they have
professed and from baptism itself, *anathema sit.*

1429 10. If anyone says that all sins committed after baptism are
1623 either remitted or made venial by the mere remembrance
of, and faith in, the baptism once received, *anathema sit.*

1430 11. If anyone says that for one who has denied the faith of
1624 Christ before infidels, baptism truly and rightly conferred
must be repeated when he is converted to repentance,
anathema sit.

1431 12. If anyone says that no one is to be baptised except at
1625 the age at which Christ was baptised, or on the point of
death, *anathema sit.*

1432 13. If anyone says that because little children do not have
1626 actual faith, they are not to be numbered among the faithful
after receiving baptism, and that, for this reason, they are to
be re-baptised when they have reached the age of discretion; or that
it is better to omit their baptism rather than to baptise them solely in
the faith of the Church while they do not believe by an act of their
own, *anathema sit.*

1433 14. If anyone says that when the little children thus baptised
1627 have grown up, they are to be asked whether they wish to
ratify what their sponsors promised in their name when they
were baptised; and if they answer that they are unwilling, they are to
be left to their own judgment; and if he says that they are not
meanwhile to be forced to a Christian life by any penalty other than
the exclusion from receiving the Eucharist and the other sacraments
until they repent, *anathema sit.*

CANONS ON THE SACRAMENT OF CONFIRMATION (1547)

The specific teaching of the Council of Trent on the sacrament of confirmation is limited to the following three canons which, mainly in opposition to Luther, Melanchton and Calvin, affirm that confirmation is a true sacrament. Its institution by Christ and the sacramental character it confers had already been taught in the general doctrine on the sacraments (cf. nn. 1311, 1319). The Augsburg Confession considered confirmation as instituted by the apostles. As regards its meaning, Melanchton in particular reduced it to a solemn confession of belief ; Canon 1 is directed against this opinion. Canon 3 lays down that the ordinary minister of confirmation is the bishop, but does not disavow the practice of the Greeks among whom the sacrament is usually administered by priests.

1434 1. If anyone says that the confirmation of those baptised is a
1628 useless ceremony and not a true and proper sacrament ; or
that of old it was nothing more than a sort of catechesis in which those nearing adolescence gave an account of their faith before the Church, *anathema sit.*

1435 2. If anyone says that those who ascribe any power to the
1629 sacred chrism of confirmation are offending the Holy Spirit, *anathema sit.*

1436 3. If anyone says that the ordinary minister of holy
1630 confirmation is not the bishop but any simple priest, *anathema sit.*

PIUS X

DECREE *LAMENTABILI* OF THE HOLY OFFICE (1907)

ARTICLES OF MODERNISM CONDEMNED

On this document see n. 143i. The articles of Modernism mentioned here were part of their attempt to explain the contents of the Catholic faith and, in particular, the origin and development of the doctrine of the sacraments (cf. n. 1327) as a natural development of the religious life of the Christian community. To this evolution were assigned the idea of the necessity of baptism, the distinction between baptism and penance on the one hand, and baptism and confirmation on the other.

[1437/42] The Christian community introduced the necessity of
3442 baptism by adopting it as a necessary rite and attach-
ing to it the obligation of Christian profession.

[1437/43] The custom of conferring baptism on infants was a
3443 disciplinary evolution which was one of the reasons
why the sacrament became divided into two, baptism
and penance.

[1437/44]   There is no proof that the rite of the sacrament of
3444   confirmation was used by the apostles; the formal
                 distinction of the two sacraments, baptism and confir-
mation, has nothing to do with the history of primitive Christiantiy.

PIUS XII

DECREE *SPIRITUS SANCTI MUNERA* ON THE

MINISTER OF CONFIRMATION (1946)

(1438) *By this decree, dated 14 September, 1946, the Pope grants to
some categories of priests a general indult empowering them to
confer as extraordinary ministers the sacrament of confirmation to the
faithful in their territories who, due to serious illness, are in danger of death,
provided that no bishop is available. The list of priests to whom the indult is
given includes parish priests to whom is entrusted the stable care of souls in
territories not yet erected as parishes. The text is found in AAS 38 (1946)
349-358. This is the first step, followed by others, in the extension of the
faculty to confirm to priests of the Latin Church. The latest legislation on the
subject is found in the Apostolic Constitution* Divinae Consortium Naturae
*of Pope Paul VI, dated August 15, 1971 (cf. AAS 63 (1971) 657 ff). While the
bishop remains the ordinary minister* (minister originarius), *priests who in
virtue of their office (parish priests,...) baptise adults or children of "catechetical age", or receive baptised persons into the Church, may confirm
them; thus the connection between baptism and confirmation becomes
more apparent. In case of danger of death any priest may confirm if neither
bishop nor priest in charge is available.*

THE SECOND VATICAN GENERAL COUNCIL

*The Council mentions several times the intimate connection between
baptism, confirmation and the Eucharist, as constituting together the full
initiation into the Christian life (cf. LG 11; AA 3) which is a share in the
Paschal mystery (AG 14). The renewal of the baptismal promises just
before confirmation and the celebration of confirmation within the Mass,
are destined to make this connection apparent (cf. SC 71). The link between
baptism and confirmation is particularly evident from the fact that both
assign the Christian to the apostolate (LG 33; AA 3; cf. AG 11); yet, the two
sacraments remain distinct.*

*Through baptism, man enters the Church (LG 14), Christ's mystical
Body (SC 6 ; AA 3) ; being plunged into Christ's Paschal mystery (SC 6), he
is conformed to Christ (LG 7) and receives the spirit of adoption (SC 6; AG
14) which makes him a son of God (LG 40 ; SC 6, 10) and of the Church (LG
64). Freed from the power of darkness (AG 14 ; SC 6), he is reborn to a new
life (LG 64; UR 22; AG 15, 21); consecrated as a member of the kingdom of
priests (cf. 1. Pet. 2.9), he is enabled by his baptismal character (LG 11) to
offer spiritual sacrifices (AA 3) and to participate in the Church's liturgical
life (SC 14 ; cf. LG 10, 11). Finally his membership of the People of God
through baptism already requires from him that he bears witness to his faith
and participates in the Church's salvific mission (LG 33 ; AA 3 ; cf. AG 11,*

36) . As to the profession of the evangelical counsels in the religious life, it is deeply rooted in baptism ; its special consecration expresses the baptismal consecration in its fulness (PC 5; cf. LG 44).

The Council rejoices at the "sacramental bond of unity" which baptism establishes among all Christians (UR 22), even though communion with the Catholic Church remains imperfect for those belonging to other Churches (UR 3). Through baptism as through a door men enter the Church (AG 7) which, as the "universal sacrament of salvation" (LG 48) making Christ present to them, is necessary for salvation (LG 14); this is why missionary activity seeks to incorporate into Christ through baptism those who have come to recognise Him as their Saviour (AG 7).

The Council's description of the effect of confirmation lays stress on a special gift of the Holy Spirit ordained to the Christian witness in word and deed (AA 3 ; LG 10, 11). The participation of the laity in the Church's mission was one of the Council's important themes (cf. LG 30ff ; AA). It is based on the two sacraments of baptism and confirmation, which together constitute the foundation of the common priesthood of the people of God (LG 11).

The Council reaffirms that the bishop is the ordinary minister of confirmation (LG 26). But it also decrees that in Catholic Eastern Churches the ancient discipline allowing priests to confer the sacrament with holy chrism blessed by the patriarch or bishop will be fully restored (OE 13).

DOGMATIC CONSTITUTION LUMEN GENTIUM (1964)

(The common priesthood founded on baptism and confirmtion)

1439 11. The sacred and organic nature of the priestly community enters into operation through the sacraments and the practice of virtues. Through baptism, the faithful are incorporated into the Church and receive a character that destines them to the worship of the Christian religion ; they are reborn as sons of God and, as such, they are in duty bound to profess before men the faith they have received from God through the Church. Through the sacrament of confirmation, they are bound more perfectly to the Church ; they are endowed with special strength of the Holy Spirit, and are thus more strictly obliged, as true witnesses of Christ, to spread and defend the faith by word and by deed....

DECREE APOSTOLICAM ACTUOSITATEM (1965)

(Foundations of the apostolate of the laity)

1440 3. The laity derive the duty and the right to the apostolate from their very union with Christ the Head. Incorporated into the mystical Body of Christ by baptism, and strengthened by the power of the Holy Spirit in confirmation, they are assigned to the apostolate by the Lord Himself. They are consecrated to form a kingdom of priests and a holy people *(cf. 1 Pet. 2.4-10),* so that by all their actions they may offer spiritual sacrifices and bear witness to Christ throughout the world....

PAUL VI

DIRECTORY CONCERNING ECUMENICAL MATTERS,

PART I, *AD TOTAM ECCLESIAM*
(14 May 1967)

The Secretariat for Promoting Christian Unity, created by John XXIII in 1960, issued a set of norms for the implementation of the Vatican II decisions regarding ecumenism. The document was published with the approval and authority of Paul VI (cf. AAS 59 (1967) 574-592 and 62 (1970) 705-724). The following doctrinal and pastoral teachings regarding the sacrament of baptism are found in the first part of the document.

(Validity of all Christians baptism)

1440a 11. Baptism is...the sacramental bond of unity, indeed the foundation of communion among all Christians. Hence its dignity and the manner of administering it are matters of great importance to all Christ's disciples. Yet a just evaluation of the sacrament and the mutual recognition of each other's baptisms by different Communities is sometimes hindered because of a reasonable doubt about the baptism conferred in some particular case. To avoid difficulties which may arise when some Christian separated from us, led by the grace of the Holy Spirit and by his conscience, seeks full communion with the Catholic Church, the following guiding principles are put forward:

12. There can be no doubt cast upon the validity of baptism as conferred among separated Eastern Christians. It is enough therefore to establish the fact that baptism was administered....

13. In respect of other Christians a doubt can sometimes arise:

(a) Concerning *matter and form.* Baptism by immersion, pouring or sprinkling, together with the Trinitarian formula, is of itself valid. Therefore if the rituals and liturgical books or established customs of a Church or Community prescribe one of these ways of baptising, doubt can only arise if it happens that the minister does not observe the regulations of his own Community or Church. What is necessary and sufficient, therefore, is evidence that the minister of baptism was faithful to the norms of his own Community or Church. For this purpose generally one should obtain a written baptismal certificate with the name of the minister. It will normally be possible to request the other community to cooperate in establishing whether or not, in generasl or in a particular case, a minister is to be considered as having baptised according to the approved ritual.

(b) Concerning *faith and intention*. Because some consider that insufficiency of faith or intention in a minister can create a doubt about baptism, these points should be noted:

— The minister's insufficient faith never of itself makes baptism invalid.

— Sufficient intention in a baptising minister is to be presumed unless there is serious ground for doubting that he intends to do what Christians do.

(c) Concerning *the application of matter*. Where doubt arises about the application of matter, both reverence for the sacrament and respect for the ecclesial nature of the other Communities demand that a serious investigation of the Community's practice and of the circumstances of the particular baptism be made before any judgment is passed on the validity of a baptism by reason of its manner of administration.

(Baptism is not to be repeated)

1440 b 14. Indiscriminate conditional baptism of all who desire full communion with the Catholic Church cannot be approved. The sacrament of baptism cannot be repeated, and therefore to baptize again conditionally is not allowed unless there is prudent doubt of the fact, or of the validity, of a baptism already administered (*cf. n. 1423*).

APOSTOLIC CONSTITUTION *DIVINAE CONSORTIUM*

NATURAE (1971)

In this Apostolic Constitution the Pope determines the essential rite of the sacrament of confirmation and approves the revised rite of confirmation prepared by the S. Congregation for Divine Worship. The sacrament is conferred by the anointing with chrism (which implies a laying on of hand) and the accompanying words. The traditional 'form' is replaced by the Byzantine formula, more expressive of the meaning of the sacrament. More important than the determination of the rite is the statment of the meaning of the sacrament which no previous document had ever expressed with the same clarity. Christ Himself in His baptism at the Jordan was anointed with the Holy Spirit for the exercise of His public ministry (cf. Mk 1.10); this was a prophetic anointing (cf. Lk. 4.17-21). Similarly, Christ promised to the apostles that the Spirit would come upon them in order that they might be His witnesses (cf. Jn 15.26-27; Acts 1.8). This promise was realised at Pentecost (Acts 2). The pentecostal gift of the Spirit is ordained to the mission, common to all Christians, to be witnesses to Christ. As in the apostolic Church the gift of the Spirit was communicated to the neophytes by a laying on of hand, so it is now through the sacrament of confirmation "which in a certain way perpetuates in the Church the grace of Pentecost". On these premises the Pope explains what he calls "the specific significance of confirmation". The text is found in AAS 63 (1971) 657 ff.

(The specific significance of confirmation)

1441   ...In baptism, neophytes receive forgiveness of sins and adoption as sons of God as well as the character of Christ whereby they are made members of the Church and given a first sharing in the priesthood of their Saviour *(cf. 1 Pet. 2.2-9)*. Through the sacrament of confirmation, those who have been born anew in baptism receive the ineffable gift, the Holy Spirit Himself, by which "they are endowed with special strength" and by the character of this sacrament "are bound more perfectly to the Church" *(cf. n. 1439)*, and "are more strictly obliged, as true witnesses of Christ, to spread and defend the faith by word and by deed" *(cf. n. 1439)*....

(The essential rite)

1442   The sacrament of confirmation is conferred through the anointing with chrism on the forehead, which is done by the laying on of hand, and through the words: "Receive the seal of the gift of the Holy Spirit" *(Accipe signaculum doni Spiritus Sancti)*.

JOHN PAUL II

INSTRUCTION ON INFANT BAPTISM *PASTORALIS ACTIO*

OF THE S. CONGREGATION FOR THE DOCTRINE OF THE FAITH

(20 October 1980)

With the approval of Pope John Paul II, the S. Congregation for the Doctrine of the Faith issued an Instruction on Infant Baptism. The practice of infant baptism appears more problematic in the present pluralistic society. The Instruction first reviews the practice of baptising infants in the data of early tradition, stating that "both in the East and in the West the practice of baptising infants is considered a rule of immemorial tradition" (4). It goes on to reaffirm the validity and normativeness of the traditional practice, bringing out its theological meaning. But it also gives important pastoral guidelines to protect the practice from possible abuses. The text is found in AAS *72 (1980) 1137-1156.*

(Theological meaning of infant baptism)

1443   9. Baptism is a manifestation of the Father's prevenient love, a sharing in the Son's Paschal Mystery, and a communication of new life in the Spirit; it brings people into the inheritance of God and joins them to the Body of Christ, the Church.

   10. In view of this, Christ's warning in St John's Gospel, "Unless one is born of water and the Spirit, he cannot enter the kingdom of God" *(Jn 3.5)*, must be taken as an invitation of universal and limitless love, the words of a Father calling all his children and wishing them to have the greatest of blessings. This pressing and irrevocable call cannot leave us indifferent or neutral, since its acceptance is a condition for achieving our destiny....

   12. This is how the Church has understood her mission from the beginning, and not only with regard to adults. She has always understood the words of Jesus to Nicodemus to mean that children should not be deprived of baptism. Jesus' words are so universal and absolute in form that the Fathers employed them to establish the necessity of baptism, and the Magisterium applied them expressly to infants: the sacrament is for them too entry into the people of God and th gateway to personal salvation.

(Infants baptised in the faith of the Church)

1444   14. The fact that infants cannot yet profess personal faith does not prevent the Church from conferring this sacrament on them, since in reality it is in her own faith that she baptizes them. This point of doctrine was clearly defined by St Augustine: "When children are presented to be given spiritual grace", he wrote, "it is not so much those holding them in their arms who present them— although, if they are good Christians, they also present the children—as the whole company of saints and faithful Christians.... It is done by the whole of Mother Church which is in the saints, since it is as a whole that she gives birth to each and every one of them. "[1] This teaching is repeated by Saint Thomas Aquinas and all the theologians after him: the child who is baptized believes not on its own account, by a personel act, but through others, "through the Church's faith communicated to it".[2] This same teaching is also

1. *Epist.* 98,5: *PL* 33, 362; cf. *Sermo* 176, 2,2: *PL* 38, 950.

2. *Summa Theologica*, III, q. 69, a.6, ad 3; cf. q. 68, a.9, ad 3.

expressed in the new Rite of Baptism, when the celebrant asks the parents and godparents to profess the faith of the Church, the faith in which the children are baptised.[1]

(Limits to infant baptism)

1445 15. Although the Church is truly aware of the efficacy of her faith operating in the baptism of children, and aware of the validity of the sacrament that she confers on them, she recongnises limits to her practice, since, apart from cases of danger of death, she does not admit a child to baptism without its parents' consent and serious assurance that after baptism it will be given a Catholic upbringing. This is because she is concerned both for the natural rights of the parents and for the requirements of the development of faith in the child.

(Practical guidelines for infant baptism)

1446 28. It is important to recall that the baptism of infants must be considered a serious duty. The questions which it poses to pastors can be settled only by faithful attention to the teaching and the constant practice of the Church. Concretely, pastoral practice regarding infant baptism must be governed by two great principles, the second of which is subordinate to the first:

1) Baptism, which is necessary for salvation, is the sign and the means of God's prevenient love, which frees us from original sin and communicates to us a share in divine life. Considered in itself, the gift of these blessings to infants must not be delayed.

2) Assurances must be given that the gift thus granted can grow by an authentic education in the faith and Christian life, in order to fulfil the true meaning of the sacrament. As a rule, these assurances are to be given by the parents or close relatives, although various substitutions are possible within the Christian community. But if these assurances are not really serious there can be grounds for delaying the sacrament; and if they are certainly non-existent the sacrament should be refused.

---

1. *Ordo baptismi parvulorum*, Praenotanda, 2; cf. 56.

CHAPTER XV

THE EUCHARIST

The new Covenant between God and men has been sealed by the mystery of Christ's death and glorification. Summing up in Himself the entire human race, Christ has once for all offered to the Father the sacrifice of atonement; in Him mankind has been reunited to God. Accomplished once for all in time, the Paschal mystery remains sacramentally present to every generation of men in the mystery of the Eucharist. For, at the last Supper, Christ instituted the memorial of His death and resurrection and gave it to the Church to celebrate. The Eucharist is the Church's greatest treasure. It is the summit of her liturgy, the centre of her life, the source of her power, the visible sign on which her unity is built.

The Eucharist is at once sacrifice and meal : it perpetuates the sacrifice of Christ in the Church and makes her members share in the sacred banquet of His body and blood. For it contains Christ Himself, who in it is present to the Church not merely by the power of His grace but in the reality of His glorified humanity. In this it surpasses all the other sacraments given by Christ to the Church.

Sacrifice, presence, meal : all three aspects of the eucharistic mystery are united by an indissoluble bond. But the truth of the sacrifice and of the banquet stands or falls with the reality of the presence ; this is why the Church has always maintained its realism. During the first millennium of Christianity this faith remained tranquilly possessed. It is not suprising, however, that this aspect of the mystery, which the human mind can hardly conceive and words hardly express, gave rise to questions. Doubts called for a clear affirmation of the Church's faith by official documents. Besides the eucharistic presence, the Reformers also challenged the sacrificial value of the Eucharist, which they feared would detract from the uniqueness of Christ's sacrifice. The Church explained that the eucharistic sacrifice takes nothing away from the sacrifice accomplished once for all in history, for the one is entirely related to the other. The sacrifice of the Mass rather enhances the uniqueness of Christ's sacrifice than it detracts from it, for it perpetuates its memory and applies its power.

The eucharistic mystery is so rich in meaning as to defy comprehension. Historically conditioned as they often were, the Church's *documents have at different times emphasised different aspects; these, however, must always be perceived within the totality of the mystery. In particular, the stress often laid on the eucharistic presence must not be allowed to obscure in the Christian consciousness its essential relation to that totality; there is no eucharistic presence which is not ordained to the eucharistic meal: "Take, eat; this is my body" (Mt. 26.26). Similarly, the eucharistic meal is prepared only by the eucharistic sacrifice: "This is my body which is given up for you; do this as a memorial of me" (Lk. 22.19).*

In our own day the Church is seeking through her renewed eucharistic life to establish the balance between the various facets of the mystery. The Second Vatican Council has contributed to such a balance. Better than previous documents it has also shown the intimate relationship which exists between the mystery of the Eucharist and the mystery of the Church.

*   *   *

The main points of doctrine on the Eucharist can be grouped under the following headings :

The eucharistic mystery is at the centre of the Church's life: (1574i), 1574, 1576, 1582.

Various aspects of the eucharistic celebration : 1575, 1581,1588-1589.

All, priests and laity together, play an active, though distinct, part in the whole celebration : 1576, 1583.

The Eucharistic Sacrifice

The Mass is a true sacrifice instituted by Christ at the Last Supper: 34, 1546, 1555.

It perpetuates the memory of the sacrifice of the cross: 39/17, 655, 1546, 1558, 1566, (1574i), 1575, 1581, 1588.

Christ is the priest and the victim of the sacrifice: 21, 1546, 1548.

He offers Himself in an unbloody manner through the priest acting in His name: 39/17, 655, 1546, 1548, 1556, 1566, (1567), 1570, 1572, 1734, 1740.

The faithful offer the sacrifice through the priest and with him: 1564, (1568), 1572, (1574i), 1576, 1735-1736, 1738, 1740.

The sacrifice of the Mass is offerd to God in praise and thanksgiving, petition and propitiation: 34, 1546, 1548, 1549, 1555, 1557.

It is offered for the living and the dead: 34, 1548, 1557.

Every Mass, even celebrated privately, is the Mass of the Church: 1569.

Concelebration is the eminent manner of celebrating the Eucharist: 1584.

It requires that concelebrants say the words of consecration: 1573.

The determination of the rites of the Mass belongs to the Church's authority: 1550, (1551), (1553), 1554, 1560, 1561, (1574i).

The Eucharistic Presence

Among the various modes of Christ's presence it is His presence par excellence: (1574i), 1578, 1585, 1588.

Christ Himself, whole and entire, is substantially present under each species: 21, 34, 39/17, 1501, 1502, 1504, (1505), 1506, 1507/16f, 1510, 1513, 1516-1518, 1526, 1528, 1579.

This presence is realised by a complete change of the substance of bread and wine into the body and blood of Christ: 21, 28, 34, 39/17-18, 1501, (1505), 1510, 1519, 1527, 1571, 1577, 1580.

This change is aptly called transubstantiation: 21, 28, 34, 39/18, 1502, (1505), 1519, 1527, 1571, 1577, 1580.

Of bread and wine only the appearances remain: 39/19, 1502.

Christ is present under the species even outside communion: 39/19, 1516, 1529.

Hence the sacred species deserve honour and adoration: 39/19, 1520, 1521, 1531, 1532.

The consecration is done by the ministerial priest: 21, 1504, (1505), 1510, 1546, 1556, 1572, 1703, 1707, 1714.

The Eucharistic Meal

The Eucharist is a true sacrament instituted by Christ at the Last Supper: 28, 32, 1305, 1311, 1514, 1515.

Christ is received in the eucharistic banquet: 1533, 1575, 1581.

The whole Christ is received under one species: 34, 1506, (1537-1539), 1541-1543.

Communion under both kinds shows forth better the sacramental sign: (1574i), 1581i.

Only the communion of the priest is required: 1552, 1563.

Communion perfects the participation of the faithful in the Mass: 1552, 1570, (1574i), 1576, 1583.

The Eucharist is the sacrament of unity and love: 21, 1511, 1515, 1524, 1565, (1574i), 1575, 1576.

Social implications of the eucharistic meal: 1590-1591.

It is also the sacrament of life, by which the life of grace is nourished: 1306, 1511, 1515, 1524, 1530.

The sacred banquet must be received worthily, which supposes the state of grace: 1209/1-3, 1511, 1522, 1523, 1536.

Little children are not bound to communion: (1540), 1544.

Eucharistic Worship

The worship due to the eucharist: 1520, 1524, 1531.

The reservation of the Blessed Sacrament: 1521, 1532.

Prayer before the Blessed Sacrament: 1586.

Eucharistic devotions: 1587.

THE COUNCIL OF ROME

OATH OF BERENGAR OF TOURS (1079)

In the 11th century the "ontological symbolism" by which some of the Church Fathers had expressed their faith in the reality of the sacramental presence of Christ's body and blood in the Eucharist was no longer understood. The Church had recourse to other categories to express the same reality. Berengar (1005-1088), head of the school of St Martin at Tours, was the first to deny the change of substance; he seemed to reduce the eucharistic presence to a dynamic presence of Christ, sign of our spiritual union with Him. Repeatedly condemned, he also retracted more than once. A Council of Rome (1059) prescribed to him a profession of faith some formulations of which St Thomas Aquinas himself (cf. S.T. III, 71, 7, ad 3m) will later consider as ultra-realistic (cf. DS 690). Another Council of Rome (1079), more sober in its wording, asked Berengar to subscribe to the following oath. The oath states that the eucharistic signs are no mere signs but Christ is present by a change of substance.

(On the eucharistic presence of Christ)

1501 I, Berengar, believe in my heart and confess with my lips that
700   the bread and wine which are placed on the altar are, by the
mystery of the sacred prayer and the words of the Redeemer, substantially changed into the true and proper and life-giving body and blood of Jesus Christ our Lord; and that, after consecration, they are Christ's true body, which was born of the virgin and hung on the cross, being offered for the salvation of the world, and which sits at the right hand of the Father; and Christ's true blood, which was poured forth from His side; not only by way of sign and by the power of the sacrament, but in their true nature and in the reality of their substance *(in proprietate naturae et veritate substantiae)....*

INNOCENT III

LETTER *CUM MARTHAE CIRCA* TO JOHN, FORMER ARCHBISHOP OF LYONS (1202)

Pope Innocent III had been consulted on the words of Christ at the Last Supper, and especially on the meaning and origin of the words "Mystery of faith" (mysterium fidei) which are found inserted in the institution narrative for the first time in the Gelasian sacramentary. Some had recourse to these words to support the interpretation according to which the eucharistic presence is a purely figurative one. The Pope, answering as a private theologian, seems wrongly to attribute these words to Christ Himself. He nevertheless distinguishes well the faith of the Church in the change of substance from minimalist spiritualistic interpretations of Christ's presence in the Eucharist. The letter also reflects the clear terminology and the elaborate distinctions which contemporary scholasticism used in its theology of the eucharistic presence.

(On the sacramental form of the Eucharist)

1502   You have asked who has added to the words of the formula
782   used by Christ Himself when He transubstantiated (*transub-*
        stantiavit) the bread and wine into His body and blood, the words which are found in the Canon of the Mass generally used by the Church, but which none of the evangelists has recorded ....Namely, in the Canon of the Mass, we find the words "Mystery of faith" inserted into the words of Christ....Surely there are many words and deeds of the Lord which have been omitted in the gospels; of these we read that the apostles have supplemented them by their words and expressed them in their actions.... But, in the words which are the object of our inquiry, Brother, namely the words "Mystery of faith", some have thought to find support for their error; they say that in the sacrament of the altar it is not the reality of the body and blood of Christ which is (there) but only an image, an appearance, a symbol (*figura*), since Scripture sometimes mentions that what is received at the altar is sacrament, mystery, figure (*exemplum*). These people fall into such error because they neither understand correctly the testimony of the Scriptures nor receive respectfully the divine sacraments, ignorant of both the Scriptures and the power of God (*cf. Mt. 22.29*).... Yet, the expression "Mystery of faith" is used, because here what is believed differs from what is seen, and what is seen differs from what is believed. For what is seen is the appearance of bread and wine and what is believed is the reality of the flesh and blood of Christ and the power of unity and love....

(On the elements of the Eucharist)

1503   We must, however, distinguish accurately between three
783   (elements) which in this sacrament are distinct; namely: the
        visible form, the reality of the body, and the spiritual power. The form is of bread and wine; the reality is the flesh and blood; the power is for unity and charity. The first is 'sacrament and not reality'; the second is 'sacrament and reality'; the third is 'reality and not sacrament'. But, the first is the sacrament of a twofold reality; the second is the sacrament of one (element) and the reality of the other; the third is the reality of a twofold sacrament. Therefore, we believe that the apostles have received from Christ the words of the formula found in the Canon, and their successors have received them from the apostles....

PROFESSION OF FAITH PRESCRIBED TO THE WALDENSIANS
(1208)

After affirming in general the validity of sacraments administered by unworthy ministers (cf. n. 1301), the profession of faith prescribed by Pope Innocent III to the Waldensians treats the various sacraments successively. The sacraments of the Eucharist and of Order are considered together. The Waldensians are urged to profess the reality of the presence of Christ's body and blood in the Eucharist which only the ordained priest can consecrate.

(The Eucharist contains the true body and blood of Christ)

1504   ...With sincere hearts, we firmly and unhesitatingly believe
794   and loyally affirm that after consecration the Sacrifice, that is,
the bread and the wine are the true body and the true blood of our Lord Jesus Christ. And we believe that in the Sacrifice a good priest effects nothing more than a bad priest; because it is not by the merit of the one consecrating that the sacrifice is accomplished, but by the word of the Creator and by the power of the Holy Spirit.

(There follows the text mentioned under n. 1703.)

THE FOURTH LATERAN GENERAL COUNCIL
SYMBOL OF LATERAN (1215)

(1505) *In its ecclesiology which is centred on the sacraments of the Church the fourth Lateran Council mentions in the first place the Eucharist, considered as effecting the mystery of unity between God and men. This document also reflects a long theological elaboration. The term 'transubstantiation', previously used by Pope Innocent III (cf. n. 1502), is found here for the first time in an official document. The term will be used again soon after by the Second General Council of Lyons (1274) (cf. n. 28). The text of this profession of faith is found under n. 21.*

THE GENERAL COUNCIL OF CONSTANCE
DECREE ON COMMUNION UNDER THE SPECIES OF BREAD ALONE (1415)

First to claim communion from the chalice for the laity were the disciples of John Hus in Bohemia. Their claim was based on the precept given by the Lord at the Last Supper and the practice of the early centuries. For reasons of expediency the Council thought it appropriate to maintain the practice of communion under one kind. What remains of value in this document is the doctrinal reason advanced to justify, against those who denied it, the validity of the practice: both the body and blood of Christ are present under each kind. The Council of Trent will further explain the same doctrine (cf. nn. 1537ff).

1506 The present custom has been introduced for good reasons
1199 to avoid some dangers and scandals and thus it has been
legitimate to maintain and observe it for similar or even
greater reasons. It is true that in the early Church this sacrament was
received by the faithful under both kinds, but later it came to be
received under both kinds by those who consecrate it and under the
species of bread alone by the laity. (This custom is legitimate) for it
must be firmly believed and can in no way be doubted that the body
and the blood of Christ are truly and integrally contained under the
species of bread as well as under that of wine.

MARTIN V

BULL *INTER CUNCTAS* (1418)

Among the errors of the followers of Wyclif and Hus condemned by
Martin V several are related to the Eucharist. First the opinion is con-
demned according to which the reality of bread and wine continue to exist
after the consecration. The second error is more directly concerned with
the modality of the presence of Christ's body and blood. This is a delicate
point of doctrine which requires a well-balanced exposition: while the
realism of the eucharistic presence must be maintained, its sacramental
modality must also be kept in mind. Too materialistic a concept of the
presence of Christ's body and blood and a purely symbolical conception of
the same are equally erroneous. The Church rejected the ultra-realism
stigmatised as Capharnaitic eating which led to false problems (cf. DS
1101-1103). In this text, the Pope upholds the realism of the eucharistic
presence against the tendency of the followers of Wyclif and Hus to reduce
it to a mere symbol. The errors of Wyclif on this point had already been
condemned by the Council of Constance (DS 1151-1153), of which the Bull
of Martin V is a confirmation.

(Questions proposed to the followers of Wyclif and Hus)

1507/16 Likewise, whether he believes that in the sacrament of the
1256 altar, after the consecration by the priest, there is under
the veil of bread and wine no material bread and wine, but
the very same Christ who suffered on the cross and sits at the right
hand of the Father.

1507/17 Likewise, whether he believes and affirms that after the
1257 priest has consecrated, the true flesh and blood of Christ,
His soul and divinity, the whole Christ, are present under
the species of bread alone, even apart of the species of wine,
and that the same body is present absolutely and under each of these
species taken separately.

THE GENERAL COUNCIL OF FLORENCE
DECREE FOR THE GREEKS (1439)

The Decree of the Council of Florence for the Greeks, which attempted to bring about their union with Rome, recognised that the Eucharist can be consecrated with either unleavened or leavened bread according to the different practice of the Western and the Eastern traditions.

1508 Likewise, we define that the body of Christ is truly effected
1303 with either unleavened or leavened wheaten bread; and that priests must consecrate the body of the Lord in one way or the other, namely each following the custom of their Church, either the Western or the Oriental Church.

DECREE FOR THE ARMENIANS (1439)

For the Eucharist as for the other sacraments (cf. n. 1305i), the Decree for the Armenians is an elaborate exposition of current Latin theology which follows very closely St Thomas Aquinas; it cannot be considered as a document of faith but rather as a clear statement, for the benefit of the Armenians, of what was then the sacramental theology commonly received in the Western Church. The sacramental form of the Eucharist is said to consist in the words of institution; no mention is made of the epiclesis to which the Eastern tradition attributed sacramental value. Following the decree, later documents will go on exposing the Latin view without consideration for the Eastern one. Examples of this are a brief of Pope Pius VII (1822) (cf. DS 2718) and a letter of Pius X (1910) (cf. DS 3556). It is important to note that none of these documents is a document of faith. In recent years, a broader approach to sacramental efficacy has sought to reconcile the Western and the Eastern traditions by attributing complementary sacramental value to the words of institution and to the epiclesis.

(The matter of the Eucharist)

1509 The third sacrament is the Eucharist. The matter of this
1320 sacrament is wheat-bread and grape-wine with a small amount of water to be mixed in before the consecration. Water is mixed in because, according to the testimony of the holy Fathers and Doctors of the Church mentioned in the preceding discussions, it is believed that our Lord Himself instituted this sacrament with wine mixed with water. Furthermore, this is a fitting representation of our Lord's passion. For, as Blessed Alexander, the fifth Pope after St Peter, says: "In the oblation of the mysteries which are offered to the Lord during the solemnities of the Mass, let only bread and wine mixed with water be offered in sacrifice. Not wine only nor water only should be offered in the chalice of the Lord, but a mixture of both. For we read that both, that is, blood and water,

flowed from the side of Christ" *(cf. Jn 19.34)*.[1] Finally, this is a fitting way to signify the effect of this sacrament, that is, the union of the Christian people with Christ. For, water represents the people as the Apocalypse says: "many waters....many peoples" *(cf. Rev. 17.15)*. And Julius, the second Pope after Blessed Sylvester, says: "According to the prescription of the canons, the Lord's chalice should be offered with wine mixed with water. For we see that the water represents the people and the wine manifests the blood of Christ. Thus, when wine and water are mixed in the chalice, the people are united with Christ, and the faithful people are closely joined to Him in whom they believe."[2] Therefore, since the holy Roman Church which was instructed by the Blessed apostles Peter and Paul, and all the other Churches of Latins and Greeks, in which have shone luminaries of sanctity and learning, have followed this custom from the beginning of the early Church and still follow it, it seems entirely improper for any region whatsoever not to follow this reasonable and universal practice. We therefore decree that the Armenians must conform to the whole Christian world and that their priests must mix a small amount of water with the wine, as has been said, in the offering of the chalice.

(The form of the Eucharist)

1510 The form of this sacrament is the words of the Saviour with
1321 which He effected this sacrament; for the priest effects the
sacrament by speaking in the person of Christ. It is by the power of these words that the substance of bread is changed into the body of Christ, and the substance of wine into His blood; in such a way, however, that the whole Christ is contained under the species of bread and the whole Christ under the species of wine. Further, the whole Christ is present under any part of the consecrated host or the consecrated wine when separated from the rest.

(The effect of the Eucharist)

1511 The effect which this sacrament produces in the soul of a
1322 person who receives it worthily, is to unite him with Christ.
For, since it is by grace that a man is incorporated into Christ and united to His members, it follows that those who receive this sacrament worthily receive an increase of grace. And all the effects

---

1. Pseudo-Alexander I, *Epistola ad omnes orthodoxos*, 9.
2. Pseudo- Iulius I, *Epistola ad episcopos Aegypti.*

which material food and drink have on the life of the body—maintaining and increasing life, restoring health and giving joy—all these effects this sacrament produces for the spiritual life. As Pope Urban says (cf. DS 846), in this sacrament we celebrate in thanksgiving the memory of our Saviour, we are drawn away from evil, we are strengthened in what is good, and we advance and increase in virtue and in grace.

THE GENERAL COUNCIL OF TRENT
THIRTEENTH SESSION
DECREE ON THE MOST HOLY EUCHARIST (1551)

The doctrine of the Eucharist is among those on which the Council of Trent had to pronounce clearly in the face of the violent attacks it met with on the part of the Reformers. For this as for other matters the Council did not mean to propose a complete doctrine but to affirm clearly the important points which were being denied. In the historical circumstances, the Council found it necessary first to state the doctrine related to the presence of Christ's body and blood in the Eucharist; this would be complemented by another decree on the sacrifice of the Mass, which, because of the unfortunate interruption of the Council, was only promulgated 11 years later.

The discussion on the Eucharist began as early as 1547, though the decree on the eucharistic presence could only be published by the Council's 13th session in 1551. The decree contains 8 chapters and 11 canons. It deals with the following points.

1) The fact and the meaning of the presence of Christ's body and blood in the Eucharist, based on scriptural evidence. This is not directed against Luther who never denied the "real presence", but against Zwingli (1484-1531) who opposed Luther on this point; according to Zwingli Christ is present in the Eucharist "in sign" only. Also opposed to the Church's doctrine was the theory of Christ's dynamic presence "by his power" as proposed by Calvin (nn. 1513-1515, 1526).

2) The presence of Christ is complete under each species. This point already affirmed in previous documents against the fore-runners of the Reformation (cf. nn. 1506, 1507/17) is further elaborated because of the new denials (n. 1516).

3) Though it is ordained to sacramental communion, the eucharistic presence exists prior to it and continues in the sacred species which have not been consumed. Luther himself was hesitant on this point; Melanchthon clearly denied it (nn. 1516, 1529).

4) The eucharistic presence is effected by transubstantiation. Following Wyclif (cf. n. 1507/16), Luther thought that bread and wine subsist together with Christ's body and blood. Against this, the Council affirms a complete change of substance with the result that of the bread and wine only the outward appearances remain; it declares appropriate the term of "transubstantiation" which since the fourth Lateran Council (cf. n. 1505) was officially used to express this change of substance (nn. 1519, 1527).

5) *From this exposition of doctrine, the Council derives concrete conclu-sions as regards mostly the reception and use ·of the sacrament (nn. 1521-1524, 1532-1536) and the cult of the Eucharist (nn. 1520, 1531).*

This decree requires careful interpretation. In particular, the doctrine of faith proposed by the Council must be distinguished from the theological concept of "transubstantiation" which is only recognised as an appropriate enunciation of its content.

For a detailed analysis of the text, cf. K. RAHNER, Theological Investigations, *vol.4, pp. 291ff.*

Foreword

1512 The holy, ecumenical and general Council of Trent, lawfully
1635 assembled in the Holy Spirit, and presided over by the afore-
mentioned legates and nuncios of the holy, apostolic See, under the special guidance and direction of the Holy Spirit, has assembled to set forth the true and ancient doctrine on the faith and on the sacraments and to supply a remedy for all the heresies and the other serious evils which now deeply trouble God's Church and divide it into so many different parts. But, from the beginning it has always been the Council's special desire to uproot completely the cockle of the damnable errors and schisms which in these fateful times of ours the enemy has sown (*cf. Mt. 13.25*) in the doctrine of faith, and in the use and worship of the most holy Eucharist; that very Eucharist which our Saviour has left in His Church precisely as a symbol of the unity and charity with which He desired all Christians to be joined together and united. And so this holy Council teaches the true and genuine doctrine about this venerable and divine sacra-ment of the Eucharist—the doctrine which the Catholic Church has always held and which she will hold until the end of the world, as she learned it from Jesus Christ our Lord Himself, from His apostles, and from the Holy Spirit, who continually reminds her of all truth (*cf. Jn 14.26*). The Council forbids all the faithful of Christ henceforth to believe, teach, or preach anything about the most holy Eucharist that is different from what is explained and defined in this present decree.

Chapter I: The real presence of our Lord Jesus Christ in the most holy sacrament of the Eucharist

1513 To begin with, the holy Council teaches and openly and
1636 straightforwardly professes that in the blessed sacrament of
the holy Eucharist, after the consecration of the bread and

wine, our Lord Jesus Christ, true God and man, is truly, really and
substantially contained under the appearances of those perceptible
realities (*cf. n. 1526*). For, there is no contradiction in the fact that our
Saviour always sits at the right hand of the Father in heaven according to His natural way of existing and that, nevertheless, in His
substance He is sacramentally present to us in many other places.
We can hardly find words to express this way of existing; but our
reason, enlightened through faith, can nevertheless recognise it as
possible for God, and we must always believe it unhesitatingly.

1514   For all our predecessors in the true Church of Christ who
1637   treated of this most holy sacrament very clearly professed
          that our Redeemer instituted this wonderful sacrament at the
Last Supper, when, after He had blessed bread and wine, He
declared in plain, unmistakable words, that He was giving to them
His own body and His own blood. These words, recorded by the
evangelists (*cf. Mt. 26. 26ff; Mk 14.22ff; Lk. 22.19f*) and afterwards
repeated by St Paul (*1 Cor. 11.23ff*), have this proper and obvious
meaning and were so understood by the Fathers. Consequently, it is
indeed the greatest infamy that some contentious, evil men, distort
these words into fanciful, imaginary figures of speech where the truth
about the body and blood of Christ is denied, contrary to the
universal understanding of the Church. The Church, which is "the
pillar and bulwark of the truth" (*cf. 1 Tim. 3.15*), has detested as
satanical these interpretations invented by impious men, and it
acknowledges in a spirit of unfailing gratitude this most precious gift
of Christ.

*Chapter II: The reason for the institution of
this most holy sacrament*

1515   Our Saviour, therefore, instituted this sacrament before leav-
1638   ing this world to go to the Father. He poured out, as it were, in
          this sacrament the riches of His divine love for men, "causing
His wonderful works to be remembered" (*cf. Ps. 111 (110) 4*), and He
wanted us when receiving it to celebrate His memory (*cf. 1 Cor.
11.24*) and to proclaim His death until He comes to judge the world
(*cf. 1 Cor. 11.26*). His will was that this sacrament be received as the
soul's spiritual food (*cf. Mt. 26.26*) which would nourish and strengthen (*cf. n. 1530*) those who live by the life of Him who said: "He who
eats Me will live because of Me" (*Jn 6.57*); and that it be also a remedy

to free us from our daily faults and to preserve us from mortal sin. Christ willed, moreover, that this sacrament be a pledge of our future glory and our everlasting happiness and, likewise, a symbol of that one "Body" of which He Himself is "the Head" (cf. 1 Cor. 11.3; Eph. 5.23), and to which He willed that we, as members, should be linked by the closest bonds of faith, hope and love, so that we might all say the same thing, and that there might be no dissensions among us (cf. 1 Cor. 1.10).

Chapter III: The pre-eminence of the most holy Eucharist over the other sacraments

1516 In common with the other sacraments, the most holy Eucha-
1639 rist is "a symbol of a sacred thing and a visible form of invisi-
ble grace".[1] But the Eucharist also has this unique mark of distinction that, whereas the other sacraments have the power of sanctifying only when someone makes use of them, in the Eucharist the Author of Sanctity Himself is present before the sacrament is used (cf. n. 1529).

1517 For the apostles had not yet received the Eucharist from the
1640 hands of the Lord (cf. Mt. 26.26; Mk 14.22) when He Himself
told them that it was truly His body that He was giving them. This has always been the belief of the Church of God that immediately after the conscration the true body and blood of our Lord, together with His soul and divinity, exist under the species of bread and wine. The body exists under the species of bread and the blood under the species of wine by virtue of the words. But the body too exists under the species of wine, the blood under the species of bread, and the soul under both species in virtue of the natural connection and concomitance by which the parts of Christ the Lord, who has already risen from the dead to die no more (cf. Rom. 6.9), are united together. Moreover, the divinity is present because of its admirable hypostatic union with the body and the soul (cf. nn. 1526, 1528).

1518 It is, therefore, perfectly true that just as much is present
1641 under either of the two species as is present under both. For
Christ, whole and entire, exists under the species of bread

---

1. Cf. ST AUGUSTINE, *Quaestionum in Heptateuchum*, 3, 84.

and under any part of that species, and similarly the whole Christ exists under the species of wine and under its parts (*cf. n. 1528*).

Chapter IV: Transubstantiation

1519 Because Christ our Redeemer said that it was truly His body
1642 that He was offering under the species of bread (*cf. Mt. 26.26ff; Mk 14.22ff; Lk. 22.19f; 1 Cor. 11.24ff*), it has always been the conviction of the Chuch of God, and this holy Council now again declares that, by the consecration of the bread and wine there takes place a change of the whole substance of bread into the substance of the body of Christ our Lord and of the whole substance of wine into the substance of His blood. This change the holy Catholic Church has fittingly and properly named transubstantiation (*cf. n. 1527*).

Chapter V: The worship and veneration to be shown to this most holy sacrament

1520 There remains, therefore, no room for doubting that all the
1643 faithful of Christ, in accordance with the perpetual custom of the Catholic Church, must venerate this most holy sacrament with the worship of *latria* which is due to the true God (*cf. n. 1531*). Nor is it to be less adored because it was instituted by Christ the Lord to be received (*ut sumatur*) (*cf. Mt. 26.26ff*). For in it we believe that the same God is present whom the eternal Father brought into the world, saying: "Let all God's angels worship Him" (*Heb. 1.6; cf. Ps. 97 (96)7*), whom the Magi fell down to worship (*cf. Mt. 2.11*) and whom, finally, the apostles adored in Galilee as Scripture testifies (*cf. Mt. 28.17*)....

Chapter VI : The reservation of the sacrament of the holy Eucharist and taking it to the sick

1521 The custom of reserving the holy Eucharist in a sacred place
1645 is so ancient that it was recognised already in the century of the Council of Nicaea. That the holy Eucharist should be taken to the sick and that it should be carefully kept in the churches for this purpose is right and very reasonable. Moreover, this is prescribed by many Councils and goes back to the most

ancient custom in the Catholic Church. Consequently, this holy Council has decreed that this most salutary and necessary custom be retained (cf. n. 1532).

Chapter VII : The preparation to be made to receive the holy Eucharist worthily

1522 It is not right that anyone should participate in any sacred
1646 functions except in a holy manner. Certainly, then, the more
a Christian is aware of the holiness and the divinity of this heavenly sacrament, the more careful he should be not to receive it without great reverence and sanctity (cf. n. 1536), especially since we read in the apostle the fearful words : "Anyone who eats and drinks unworthily, without discerning the body of the Lord, eats and drinks judgment upon himself" (1 Cor. 11.29 Vulg.). Therefore, whoever desires to communicate must be reminded of the precept : "Let a man examine himself" (1 Cor. 11.28)....

Chapter VIII : The use of this wonderful sacrament

1523 As regards the use, our Fathers have correctly and
1648 appropriately distinguished three ways of receiving this holy
sacrament. They teach that some receive it only sacramentally because they are sinners. Others receive it only spiritually; they are the ones who, receiving in desire the heavenly bread put before them, with a living faith "working through love" (cf. Gal. 5.6), experience its fruit and benefit from it. The third group receive it both sacramentally and spiritually (cf. n. 1533); they are the ones who examine and prepare themselves beforehand to approach this divine table, clothed in the wedding garment (cf. Mt. 22.11ff)....

1524 Finally, with fatherly affection the holy Council warns,
1649 exhorts, asks and pleads, "through the tender mercy of our
God" (Lk. 1.78), that each and all who bear the name of Christians meet at last in this "sign of unity", in this "bond of charity",[1] in this symbol of concord, to be finally of one heart. Keeping in mind the great majesty and the most excellent love of our Lord Jesus Christ, who laid down His precious life as the price of our salvation, and who gave us His flesh to eat (cf. Jn 6.48ff), may all

---

1. Cf. ST AUGUSTINE, In evang. Iohan. tract., 26, 13.

Christians have so firm and strong a faith in the sacred mystery of His body and blood, may they worship it with such devotion and pious veneration, that they will be able to receive frequently their "supersubstantial bread" (cf. Mt. 6.11 Vulg.). May it truly be the life of their souls and continual health for their minds; strengthened by its power (cf. 1 Kings 19.8), may they, after journeying through this sorrowful pilgrimage, reach their home in heaven, where they will eat without any veil the same "bread of angels " (cf. Ps. 78 (77) 25) which they eat now under sacred veils.

1525 But, since it is not enough to state the truth without
1650 pointing out and refuting errors, it has pleased the
holy Council to add the following canons so that all, already knowing the Catholic doctrine, may also realise what are the heresies that they must beware of and avoid.

Canons on the most holy sacrament
of the Eucharist

1526 1. If anyone denies that in the sacrament of the most holy
1651 Eucharist the body and blood, together with the soul and
divinity, of our Lord Jesus Christ and, therefore, the whole Christ is truly, really and substantially contained, but says that He is in it only as in a sign or figure or by His power, *anathema sit (cf. nn. 1513, 1517).*

1527 2. If anyone says that in the holy sacrament of the Eucharist
1652 the substance of bread and wine remains together with the
body and blood of our Lord Jesus Christ, and denies that wonderful and unique change of the whole substance of the bread into His body and of the whole substance of the wine into His blood while only the species of bread and wine remain, a change which the Catholic Church very fittingly calls transubstantiation, *anathema sit (cf. n. 1519).*

1528 3. If anyone denies that in the venerable sacrament of the
1653 Eucharist the whole Christ is contained under each species
and under each part of either species when separated, *anathema sit (cf. n. 1518).*

1529 4. If anyone says that after the consecration the body and
1654 blood of our Lord Jesus Christ are not in the marvellous
sacrament of the Eucharist but that they are there only in the

use of the sacrament (in usu), while it is being received, and not before or after, and that in the consecrated hosts or particles which are preserved or are left over after communion the true body of the Lord does not remain, anathema sit (cf. n. 1516f).

1530 5. If anyone says that the principal fruit of the most holy
1655 Eucharist is the forgiveness of sins, or that no other effects come from it, anathema sit (cf. n. 1515).

1531 6. If anyone says that Christ, the only-begotten Son of God,
1656 is not to be adored in the holy sacrament of the Eucharist with the worship of *latria*, including external worship, and that the sacrament therefore is not to be honoured with special festive celebrations nor solemnly carried in processions according to the praise-worthy universal rite and custom of the holy Church; or that it is not to be publicly exposed for the people's adoration, and that those who adore it are idolaters, anathema sit (cf. n. 1520).

1532 7. If anyone says that it is not lawful to keep the sacred
1657 Eucharist in a sacred place, but that it must necessarily be distributed immediately after the consecration to those who are present; or that it is not lawful to carry it with honour to the sick, anathema sit (cf. n. 1521).

1533 8. If anyone says that Christ presented in the Eucharist is
1658 only spiritually eaten and not sacramentally and really as well, anathema sit (cf. n. 1523).

1534 9. If anyone denies that each and all of Christ's faithful of
1659 both sexes are bound, when they reach the age of reason, to receive communion every year, at least during the Paschal season, according to the precept of Holy Mother Church, anathema sit (cf. DS 812).

1535 10. If anyone says that it is not lawful for the celebrating
1660 priest to communicate himself, anathema sit (cf. DS 1648).

1536 11. If anyone says that faith alone is a sufficient preparation
1661 for receiving the sacrament of the most holy Eucharist, anathema sit. And, lest so great a sacrament be received unworthily and hence unto death and condemnation, this holy Council determines and decrees that those whose conscience is burdened with mortal sin, no matter how contrite they may think they are, must necessarily make first a sacramental confession if a confessor is

available. If anyone presumes to teach, or preach, or obstinately maintain, or defend in public disputation the opposite of this, he shall by the very fact be excommunicated *(cf. DS 1647).*

TWENTY-FIRST SESSION

DOCTRINE ON COMMUNION UNDER BOTH SPECIES AND ON

COMMUNION OF LITTLE CHILDREN (1562)

After having been interrupted since 1552, the Council resumed its deliberations in 1562 under Pope Pius IV. In its 21st session it turned to the controversial questions of communion from the chalice for the laity and communion of little children. Adopting the position of Hus and his followers (cf. n. 1506i), the Reformers were also claiming the chalice for the laity. In this decree, made up of 4 chapters and 4 canons, the Council affirms the following:

1) No divine precept requires the faithful to communicate under both kinds (cf. nn. 1537, 1541).
2) Cosequently, the Church has the power to determine the modality of the administration of the sacrament (cf. nn. 1538, 1542).
3) Communion under one kind only causes no substantial spiritual loss (cf. nn. 1539, 1543). The Council, however, deliberately left undecided the question whether or not communion under both kinds gives grace more abundantly; the reason is that different schools held different opinions on this point.
4) As for little children, there is no need to admit them to communion (cf. nn. 1540, 1544).

While maintaining the principles laid down by the Council of Trent, and in no way contradicting its doctrine, the Second Vatican Council in its Constitution on the Sacred Liturgy will decree that "communion under both kinds may be granted when the bishops think fit, not only to clerics and religious, but also to the laity..." (SC 55). This new attitude does not necessarily imply the persuasion that grace is more abundantly given when communion is received under both kinds; it is inspired by a new appreciation of the sign-value of the Church's sacramental actions, especially in the Eucharist.

Chapter I: Lay people and clerics who do not celebrate are not bound by divine law to communion under both kinds

(1537) *(The reception of the one species of bread is sufficient for salva-*
1726 *tion. Those who advocate the chalice for the laity cannot claim it*
1727 *to be a binding precept of the Lord, for Christ Himself in St John's*
Gospel sometimes speaks of His body and blood (cf. Jn 6.54, 55, 57), and sometimes mentions only His body (cf. Jn 6.52, 59).)

Chapter II: The power of the Church concerning the dispensation of the sacrament of the Eucharist

(1538) *(The substance of the sacarments being preserved, the Church*
1728   *has the power to determine the modality of their dispensation.*
St Paul taught this and took steps in this direction. It is by making use of this power that the Church has for serious reasons decreed communion under one kind).
(The principle laid down here is an important principle of sacramental theology; the text is found under n. 1324.)

Chapter III: The whole and entire Christ and the true sacrament are received under either species

(1539) *(Those who receive the sacrament under one species only are not*
1729   *deprived of any grace necessary for salvation, for the whole Christ is received under one species.)*

Chapter IV: Little children are not obliged to receive sacramental communion

(1540) *(They are incorporated into Christ by baptism and cannot at their*
1730   *age lose grace. Nevertheless, the practice of the early centuries when small children occasionally received communion is not to be condemned. But communion is not necessary for salvation before the age of reason.)*

Canons on communion under both species and on communion of little children

1541   1. If anyone says that each and all of Christ's faithful ought to
1731   receive both species of the most holy sacrament of the
Eucharist, because of a command from God or because it is
necessary for salvation, *anathema sit (cf. n. 1537).*

1542   2. If anyone says that the holy Catholic Church was not led
1732   by lawful and good reasons to have the laity and the clerics
who are not celebrating communicate under the species of
bread alone, or that the Church erred in so doing, *anathema sit (cf.
n. 1538).*

1543   3. If anyone denies that the whole and entire Christ, the
1733   source and author of all graces, is received under the species
of bread alone, because, as some falsely affirm, He is not
received under both species in accordance with the institution of
Christ Himself, *anathema sit (cf. n. 1737).*

1544 4. If anyone says that eucharistic communion is necessary
1734 for little children before they reach the age of reason,
anathema sit (cf. n. 1540).

TWENTY-SECOND SESSION

DOCTRINE ON THE MOST HOLY SACRIFICE
OF THE MASS (1562)

In its 13th session the Council had re-affirmed the Church's faith in the reality of the presence of Christ's body and blood in the Eucharist. There remained to state, against the denial of the Reformers, the sacrificial value of the Mass. This decree brings the eucharistic doctrine of the Council to completion. Its first chapters contain a remarkable synthesis, deeply rooted in Scripture, on the Mass as sacrifice and its relationship to the sacrifice of the cross. The Council does not, however, decide what is the essence of sacrifice, a point on which various opinions were held by theologians. The document is made up of 9 chapters and 9 canons, of vastly different doctrinal import:

1) The salvation of mankind has been effected by the sacrifice of the cross. Holy Mass is not a sacrifice independent of the cross. It is the sacrifice of the cross now offered by the Church, whenever, following Christ's command, she celebrates the ritual of the Last Supper in which Christ offered Himself. This doctrine is directed against Luther, Melanchton, Calvin, who, restricting Christ's sacrifice to the cross and denying all relationship of the Last Supper to His sacrificial death, reduced the Lord's Supper celebrated by the Church to a sacred meal without sacrificial value (cf. nn. 1546, 1556).
2) The sacrifice of the Mass is a true propitiatory sacrifice as was the sacrifice of the cross. Its propitiatory value takes nothing away from the uniqueness of the sacrifice of the cross, since it is essentially related to it. All share in the fruits of the sacrifice of the Mass (cf. nn. 1548, 1557-1558).
3) Against the objections advanced by the Reformers, the Council explains in what sense Masses are legitimately offered in honour of the saints (cf. nn. 1549, 1559).
4) Explanations are given regarding some special rites in the celebration of the Mass. The chapters and canons dealing with these are of secondary importance and must be read in the historical context. Some of their disciplinary prescriptions have, for liturgical and pastoral reasons, been changed by and after the Second Vatican Council (cf. nn. 1550-1554, 1560-1563).

Primarily intent on defending the Church's doctrine on the sacrificial aspect of the Mass which was denied by the Reformers, the Council did not attempt a complete exposition of doctrine on the significance of the Eucharist. The historical circumstances explain why the meal-aspect receives less emphasis than the sacrificial aspect; it had been partly dealt with in the Decree on the most holy Eucharist. In a climate with no controversial issues involved, the Second Vatican Council will establish the balance between the two inseparable aspects of the Eucharist, sacrifice and meal.

Foreword

1545   In order to retain in the holy Catholic Church and to preserve
1738   in its purity the ancient, absolute and completely perfect faith
        and doctrine about the great mystery of the Eucharist and to
avert heresies and errors, the holy, ecumenical and general Council
of Trent, lawfully assembled in the Holy Spirit, presided over by the
same apostolic legates, teaches and lays down, under the guidance
and light of the Holy Spirit, the following doctrine about the Eucharist
as true and unique sacrifice and declares that this doctrine is to be
preached to the faithful.

Chapter I: The institution of the most holy
sacrifice of the Mass

1546   As the Apostle testifies, there was no perfection under the
1739   former Covenant because of the insufficiency of the levitical
        priesthood. It was, therefore, necessary (according to the
merciful ordination of God the Father) that another priest arise after
the order of Melchizedek (*cf. Gen. 14.18; Ps. 110 (109) 4; Heb. 7.11*),
our Lord Jesus Christ who could make perfect all who were to be
sanctified (*cf. Heb. 10.14*) and bring them to fulfilment.

1740   He, then, our Lord and God, was once and for all to offer
        Himself to God the Father by His death on the altar of the
cross, to accomplish for them an everlasting redemption. But,
because His priesthood was not to end with His death (*cf. Heb. 7.24,
27*), at the Last Supper, "on the night when he was betrayed" (*1 Cor.
11.23*), in order to leave to His beloved Spouse the Church a visible
sacrifice (as the nature of man demands) (*cf. n. 1555*)—by which the
bloody sacrifice which He was once for all to accomplish on the cross
would be represented, its memory perpetuated until the end of the
world and its salutary power applied for the forgiveness of the sins
which we daily commit—; declaring Himself constituted "a priest for
ever after the order of Melchizedek" (*Ps. 110 (109)4*), He offered His
body and blood under the species of bread and wine to God the
Father, and, under the same signs (*sub earundem rerum symbolis*)
gave them to partake of to the diciples (whom He then established as
priests of the New Convenant), and ordered them and their successors in the priesthood to offer, saying: "Do this as a memorial of Me",
etc. (*Lk. 22.19; 1 Cor. 11.24*), as the Catholic Church has always
understood and taught (*cf. n. 1556*).

1741 For, after He celebrated the old Pasch, which the multitude
of the children of Israel offered *(immolabat)* to celeberate the
memory of the departure from Egypt *(cf. Ex. 12.1ff),* Christ instituted
a new Pasch, namely Himself to be offered by the Church through
her priests under visible signs in order to celebrate the memory of
His passage from this world to the Father when by the shedding of
His blood He redeemed us, "delivered us from the dominion of
darkness and transferred us to His Kindom" *(cf. Col. 1.13).*

1547 This is the clean oblation which cannot be defiled by any
1742 unworthiness or malice on the part of those who offer it, and
which the Lord foretold through Malachi would be offered in
all places as a clean oblation to His name *(cf. Mal. 1.11).* The apostle
Paul also refers clearly to it when, writing to the Corinthians, he says
that those who have been defiled by partaking of the table of devils
cannot be partakers of the table of the Lord. By 'table' he understands 'altar' in both cases *(cf. 1 Cor. 10.21).* Finally, this is the
oblation which was prefigured by various types of sacrifices under
the regime of nature and of the Law *(cf. Gen. 4.4; 8.20; 12.8; 22; Ex.
passim).* For it includes all the good that was signified by those
former sacrifices; it is their fulfilment and perfection....

*Chapter II: The visible sacrifice is propitiatory
for the living and the dead*

1548 In this divine sacrifice which is celebrated in the Mass, the
1743 same Christ who offered Himself once in a bloody manner
(cf. Heb. 9.14, 27) on the altar of the cross is contained and is
offered in an unbloody manner. Therefore, the holy Council teaches
that this sacrifice is truly propitiatory *(cf. n. 1557),* so that, if we draw
near to God with an upright heart and true faith, with fear and
reverence, with sorrow and repentance, through it "we may receive
mercy and find grace to help in time of need" *(cf. Heb. 4.16).* For the
Lord, appeased by this oblation, grants grace and the gift of repentance, and He pardons wrong-doings and sins, even grave ones. For,
the victim is one and the same: the same now offers through the
ministry of priests, who then offered Himself on the cross; only the
manner of offering is different. The fruits of this oblation (the bloody
one, that is) are received in abundance through this unbloody oblation. By no means, then, does the latter detract from the former *(cf.
n. 1558).* Therefore, it is rightly offered according to apostolic tradi-

tion, not only for the sins, punishments, satisfaction and other necessities of the faithful who are alive, but also for those who have died in Christ but are not yet wholly purified (*cf. n. 1557*).

Chapter III: Masses in honour of the saints

1549 And, although it is the custom of the Church occasionally to
1744 celebrate some Masses in honour and in remembrance of the
saints, the Church teaches that sacrifice is offered not to the
saints, but to God alone who has given them their crown (*cf. n. 1559*).
Therefore, "the priest does not say: 'I offer the sacrifice to you, Peter
and Paul' ";[1] but, giving thanks to God for the victory of the saints, he
implores their protection "in order that those whose remembrance
we celebrate on earth may intercede for us in heaven".[2]

Chapter IV: The canon of the Mass

1550 Holy things must be treated in a holy way and this sacrifice is
1745 the most holy of all things. And so, that this sacrifice might be
worthily and reverently offered and received, the Catholic
Church many centuries ago instituted the sacred Canon. It is so free
from all error (*cf. n. 1560*) that it contains nothing which does not
savour strongly of holiness and piety and nothing which does not
raise to God the minds of those who offer. For it is made up of the
words of our Lord Himself, of apostolic tradtions, and of devout
instructions of the holy pontiffs.

Chapter V: The solemn ceremonies of the
sacrifice of the Mass

(1551) *(The Council upholds the legitimacy of some prescriptions*
1746 *made by the Church for the celebration of the Mass (cf. n. 1563)*
and of some ceremonies to be observed (cf. n. 1561).)

Chapter VI: The Mass in which the priest
alone communicates

1552 The holy Council would wish that in every Mass the faithful
1747 who are present communicate not only in spiritual desire, but
by a sacramental reception of the Eucharist, so that they may

---

1. Cf. ST AUGUSTINE, *Contra Faustum Manichaeum,* XX, 21.

2. *Roman Missal,* Order of the Mass.

derive more abundant fruits from this most holy sacrifice. Nevertheless, if such is not always the case, the Council does not on that
account condemn the Masses in which the priest alone communicates sacramentally as private and illicit (cf. n. 1562). Rather, it
approves them and endorses them since such Masses too are to be
considered as truly public, partly because the people communicate
at them spiritually and partly because they are celebrated by a public
minister of the Church, not for himself alone, but for all the faithful
who belong to the Body of Christ.

Chapter VII: Water must be mixed with the wine to be offered in the chalice

(1553) *(The Council reminds priests of the precept of the Church. It*
1748 *attributes to the rite the same symbolism as was already pro-*
posed by the Council of Florence in the decree for the
Armenians *(cf. n. 1509). See also n. 1563.)*

Chapter VIII: Mass should not be celebrated in the vernacular indiscriminately; the mysteries of the Mass are to be explained to the people

1554 Although the Mass contains much instruction for the faithful,
1749 the Fathers did not think that it should be celebrated in the
vernacular indiscriminately (c.f. n. 1563). Therefore, the
ancient rite of each Church, approved by the holy Roman Church,
the mother and teacher of all the Churches, being everywhere
maintained, the holy Council, in order that the sheep of Christ may
not go unfed, lest "the children beg for food but no one gives to them"
(*Lam. 4.4*), orders that pastors and all who have the care of souls
must frequently, either by themselves or through others, explain
during the celebration of Masses some of the readings of the Mass,
and among other things give some instruction about the mystery of
this most holy sacrfice, especially on Sundays and feastdays.

Canons on the most holy sacrifice of the Mass

1555 1. If anyone says that in the Mass a true and proper sacrifice
1751 is not offered to God or that the offering consists merely in
the fact that Christ is given to us to eat, *anathema sit.*

1556 2. If anyone says that by the words "Do this as a memorial of
1752 Me" (*Lk. 22.19; 1 Cor. 11.24*) Christ did not establish the
apostles as priests or that He did not order that they and

other priests should offer His body and blood, *anathema sit (cf. n. 1546)*.

1557 3. If anyone says that the sacrifice of the Mass is merely an
1753   offering of praise and thanksgiving, or that it is a simple
         commemoration of the sacrifice accomplished on the cross,
but not a propitiatory sacrifice, or that it benefits only those who
communicate; and that it should not be offered for the living and the
dead, for sins, punishments, satisfaction and other necessities,
anathema sit (cf. n. 1548).

1558 4. If anyone says that the sacrifice of the Mass constitutes a
1754   blasphemy against the most holy sacrifice which Christ
         accomplished on the cross, or that it detracts from that
sacrifice, *anathema sit (cf. n. 1548)*.

1559 5. If anyone says that it is an imposture to celebrate Masses
1755   in honour of the saints and in order to obtain their inter-
         cession with God as the Church intends, *anathema sit (cf. n.
1549)*.

1560 6. If anyone says that the Canon of the Mass contains errors
1756   and therefore should be abolished, *anathema sit (cf. n. 1550)*.

1561 7. If anyone says that the ceremonies, vestments and exter-
1757   nal signs which the Catholic Church uses in the celebration
         of Masses are incentives to impiety rather than works of
piety, *anathema sit (cf. n. 1551)*.

1562 8. If anyone says that Masses in which the priest alone
1758   communicates sacramentally, are illicit and therefore should
         be abolished, *anathema sit (cf. n. 1552)*.

1563 9. If anyone says that the rite of the Roman Church prescrib-
1759   ing that part of the Canon and the words of consecration
         be recited in a low voice, must be condemned; or that Mass
should be celebrated only in the vernacular; or that water should not
be mixed with the wine to be offered in the chalice because this would
be contrary to Christ's institution, *anathema sit (cf. nn. 1551, 1553f)*.

PIUS XII

ENCYCLICAL LETTER *MYSTICI CORPORIS* (1943)

*The more recent documents of the Church have brought to light, in
accordance with the tradition of the early centuries, the close relationship*

between the mystery of the Eucharist and the mystery of the Church. Previous to this document may be mentioned the Encyclical Letter Mirae Caritatis *(1902) of Pope Leo XIII (cf. DS 3360-3364) in which the Eucharist is said to be "as it were the soul of the Church" (DS 3364). The great Encyclical Letter of Pope Pius XII rightly considers (after a previous encyclical of Leo XIII) the Holy Spirit to be the soul of the Church (cf. n. 852); the Eucharist has, nevertheless, a unique significance for the mystery of the Church, for it is the visible sign of the mysterious union which binds together the members of Christ's mystical Body with their Head and among themselves. In the Eucharist Christ unites the Church to His sacrifice: the priests, representing at once Christ and His mystical Body, offer the sacrificial victim while the faithful offer through the priests; in the sacramental banquet of Christ's body and blood, all receive the life of Christ which binds together the members of His Body. The text is found in AAS 35 (1943) 193ff.*

(The eucharistic sacrifice and the Church)

1564 ...Christ our Lord willed that in the eucharistic sacrifice this wonderful and inestimable union, binding us with one another and with our divine Head, should find a special manifestation before the eyes of the faithful. Herein the sacred ministers represent not only our Saviour but also the whole mystical Body and each one of its members; in that sacrifice the faithful are associated in the common prayer and supplication and, through the hands of the priest, whose voice alone renders the immaculate Lamb present on the altar, they themselves offer to the eternal Father this most pleasing Victim of praise and propitiation for the needs of the whole Church. And as the divine Redeemer, when He was dying on the cross, offered Himself as the Head of the whole human race to the eternal Father, so in this "clean oblation" (*cf. Mal. 1.11*) He offers to the heavenly Father not only Himself as the Head of the Church, but in Himself also His mystical members, for He embraces them all, even the weak and the frail among them, most lovingly in His heart.

(The sacrament of the Eucharist and the Church)

1565 Moreover, the sacrament of the Eucharist, while also presenting a vivid and marvellous picture of the unity of the Church—since the bread to be consecrated results from the kneading together of many grains of wheat [1]—gives to us the very author of supernatural grace, from whom we are enabled to draw that Spirit of charity which bids us live not our own life, but the life of Christ, and whereby we love the Redeemer Himself in all the members of His social Body.

---

1. Cf. *Didachê* IX, 4.

ENCYCLICAL LETTER *MEDIATOR DEI* (1947)

Pope Pius XII's great encyclical on the liturgy continues Mystici Corpo-
ris, but contains a much more elaborate treatment of the Eucharist. The
Pope shows the central place which the Eucharist occupies in the Church's
liturgical life; the Eucharist is "the summit of the Christian religion". The
doctrine is to a great extent based on the Council of Trent but it also reflects
recent theological advances. It explains that Christ is offered in the state of
victim in which He is made present on the altar and which is symbolised by
the double consecration (cf. n. 1566). It goes beyond Mystici Corporis, when
it states that the faithful, though exercising no ministerial priestly power as
does the priest representing Christ at the altar (cf. n. 1567), nevertheless do
not merely offer through the priest (cf. n. 1564), but also together with him
(n. 1568). It shows that every Mass, even celebrated privately, has a public
and social character and is the Mass of the Church (n. 1569). In line with,
but more precise than the Council of Trent (cf. n. 1562), it explains that
communion, though a participation in the sacrifice, belongs to its integrity,
not to its essence; this is why only the communion of the priest is required
though the comunion of the faithful is highly recommended (n. 1570). The
text is found in AAS 39(1947) 521ff.

(Christ is offered in the Mass under signs symbolic of His death)

1566 ...On the cross Christ offered to God the whole of Himself
3848 and His sufferings, and the victim was immolated by a bloody
death voluntarily accepted. But on the altar, by reason of the
glorious condition of His humanity "death no longer has dominion
over Him" (*Rom. 6.9*), and therefore the shedding of His blood is not
possible. Nevertheless, the divine wisdom has devised a way in which
our Redeemer's sacrifice is marvellously shown forth by external
signs symbolic of death. By the transubstantiation of bread into the
body of Christ and of wine into His blood both His body and blood
are rendered really present; but the eucharistic species under which
He is present symbolise the violent separation of His body and blood,
and so a commemorative showing forth of the death which took
place in reality on Calvary is repeated in each Mass, because by
distinct representations Christ Jesus is signified and shown forth in
the state of victim.

(At the altar the priest represents Christ)

(1567) *(See text under n. 1734)*

(The faithful offer through the priest and with him)

(1568) *(See text under nn. 1735-1736)*

(Every Mass, even celebrated privately, is the Mass of the whole Church)

1569 ...Every time the priest re-enacts what the divine Redeemer
3853 did at the Last Supper, the sacrifice is really accomplished;
and this sacrifice, always and everywhere, necessarily and of its nature, has a public and social character. For he who offers it acts in the name both of Christ and of the faithful, of whom the divine Redeemer is the Head, and he offers it to God for the holy Catholic Church, and for the living and the dead. And this happens whether the faithful are present—and we would indeed have them assisting in great numbers and with great devotion—or whether they are absent, because it is in no way necessary that the people should ratify what has been done by the sacred minister....

(Communion belongs to the integrity, not to the essence of the Mass)

1570 ...The eucharistic sacrifice is essentially the unbloody immo-
3854 lation of the divine Victim, an immolation mystically mani-
fested in the separation of the sacred species and the offering made of them to the eternal Father. The communion belongs to the integrity of the sacrifice; it is a participation of the sacrifice by the reception of the blessed sacrament. And, while it is quite necessary for the sacrificing minister, to the faithful it is only to be highly recommended.

ENCYCLICAL LETTER *HUMANI GENERIS* (1950)

Modern scientific research, probing the secret of the composition of matter, has led to a physical concept of substance which is considerably new, ad consequently to a re-consideration of the meaning of transubstanti-ation. Some assumed that the doctrine of transubstantiation is based on the philosophical concept of substance which is no longer tenable; on the other hand, they perceived the difficulty of applying to the eucharistic presence of Christ's body and blood the new physical concept of substance. Hence they could be tempted to reduce that presence to a symbolic one. Pope Pius XII rejects a solution which would tend to destroy the Church's doctrine.

1571 There are some who pretend that the doctrine of transub-
3891 stantiation, based, as they say, on a philosophical notion of
substance which is now out of date, must be corrected in such a way that the presence of Christ in the most holy Eucharist is reduced to some sort of sybolism; the consecrated species would be merely efficacious signs of Christ's spiritual presence and of His intimate union with His faithful members in the mystical Body.

DISCOURSE AT THE INTERNATIONAL CONGRESS ON
PASTORAL LITURGY (Assisi 1956)

Recent years have witnessed a growing awareness of the communita-
rian meaning of the Eucharist; consequently, the desire has also been felt
that this aspect be expressed in the way in which the Eucharist is cele-
brated. The ancient practice of sacramental concelebration which, though
always retained in the Oriental Churches, had almost entirely disappeared
in the West, brought out this aspect in striking manner. At a time when it
could not be foreseen that the practice of concelebration would soon be
re-introduced in the Latin rite by the Second Vatican Council, some theolo-
gians advocated the attendance by priests and people at a Mass celebrated
by one priest. Pope Pius XII draws the attention to the action which only the
celebrating priest performs, as acting in the person of Christ. Not only the
personal fruit derived from the Mass but the nature of the action must be
considered in the participation by priests in the celebration of the Eucharist.
The Discourse delivered at the Assisi congress repeats on this point and
further elaborates a previous allocution (2 Nov. 1954), the text of which is
found in AAS 46 (1954) pp. 668-670. The Pope also states that for sacramen-
tal concelebration it is required that concelebrants recite the words of
institution together with the main celebrant; he does not, however, attribute
this requirement to the "institution of Christ" as does a decree of the Holy
Office issued the following year (1957) (cf. DS 3928). The text is found in
AAS 48(1956) 711ff.

(Only the celebrating priest performs the act of Christ offering
Himself, as representing His person)

1572   The priest-celebrant, putting on the person of Christ, alone
offers sacrifice, and not the people, nor the clerics, nor even
the priests who reverently assist. All, however, can and should take
an active part in the sacrifice....With regard to the offering of the
eucharistic sacrifice, the actions of Christ, the High Priest, are as
many as are the priests celebrating, not as many as are the priests
reverently hearing the Mass of a bishop or a priest; for those present
at the Mass in no sense sustain, or act in, the person of Christ
sacrificing, but are to be compared to the faithful lay people who are
present at the Mass....The central element of the eucharistic sacrifice is that in which Christ intervenes as "offering Himself"—to adopt
the words of the Council of Trent (*cf. n. 1548*). That happens at the
consecration when, in the very act of transubstantiation worked by
the Lord, the priest-celebrant is "acting in the person of Christ"
(*personam Christi gerens*).... After the consecration is performed,
the "offering of the victim placed on the altar" (*oblatio hostiae super*
altare positae) can be accomplished and is accomplished by the
priest-celebrant, by the Church, by the other priests, by each of the
faithful. But this action is not the action of Christ Himself through the

priest representing Him *(actio ipsius Christi per sacerdotem ipsius personam sustinentem et gerentem).*

(Sacramental concelebration requires that the concelebrants say the words of consecration)

1573 In reality, the action of the consecrating priest is the very action of Christ who acts through His minister. In the case of a concelebration in the proper sense of the word, Christ, instead of acting through one minister, acts through several. On the other hand, in a merely ceremonial concelebration, which could also be the act of a lay person, there is no question of simultaneous consecration, and this fact raises the important question: What intention and what exterior action are required to have a true concelebration and simultaneous consecration ?... It is not sufficient to have and to indicate the will to make one's own the words and the actions of the celebrant. The concelebrants must, themselves, say over the bread and the wine: "This is my body", "This is my blood". Otherwise, their concelebration is purely ceremonial.

THE SECOND VATICAN GENERAL COUNCIL

The Council of Trent devoted separate sessions to the "sacrament of the Eucharist" (cf. nn. 1512ff) and the "sacrifice of the Mass" (cf. nn. 1545ff). The doctrine of the sacrifice of the Mass is among the most beautiful documents issued by it. Yet, the twofold division between sacrament and sacrifice, imposed by the context of the Reformation as well as the lapse of 11 years that—due to historical circumstances—separated the two sessions, was little conducive to a fully integrated doctrine. Vatican II is less doctrinal in purpose than Trent had been; its outlook is primarily pastoral. Nevertheless, its eucharistic doctrine, if less technically elaborated, is more complete and provides a more balanced view of the mystery than that of the Tridentine Council. The main documents are the constitutions on the Sacred Liturgy (SC) and on the Church (LG), as well as the decrees on ecumenism (UR) and on the priestly ministry (PO)

Three main features characterise the eucharistic doctrine of Vatican II: its comprehensiveness; the stress it lays on the intimate relationship between the eucharistic mystery and the mystery of the Church; its keen sense of the value of signs in the eucharistic celebration.

SC 47 enumerates the various aspects of the eucharistic mystery: it perpetuatès the sacrifice of the cross through the centuries; it is a Paschal banquet in which Christ is eaten; it is the memorial of Christ's death and resurrection, the sacrament of love, sign of unity and bond of charity. In the Mass, therefore, the sacrifice and sacred meal belong to the same mystery (cf. LG 11). Sacrifice and meal, the eucharistic mystery is the sacramental celebration of Christ's Paschal mystery (SC 6); this is why it is especially from it "as from a fount" that are derived "the sancification of men in Christ and the glorification of God" (SC 10; cf. LG 3).

As a sacrifice, the eucharistic mystery makes Christ's sacrifice present to the Church. Christ instituted it in order to perpetuate the sacrifice of the cross through the centuries and to entrust to the Church a memorial of His death and resurrection (SC 47; cf. LG 3, 7, 26, 28; SC 2, 6, 7; PO 2, 5, 13; CD 15, etc.). Thus, in the Mass the sacrifice which Christ made of Himself once for all is represented and the offerings of the faithful are joined to the sacrifice of their Head (LG 28). The faithful do not merely offer through the priest; for even though the priest alone, acting in the name of Christ the Head, consecrates and makes the sacrifice of Christ present on the altar, they too offer "not only through the hands of the priest, but also together with him" (SC 48 after Mediator Dei; cf. n. 1568). This is why every Mass, even celebrated privately, is "an act of Christ and of the Church" (PO 13; cf. LG 26; SC 26). As to the assembled congregation, it is urged to enter into the Mass effectively through active participation (SC 48).

The eucharistic presence of Christ is viewed in its relationship to the mysteric action by which the Paschal mystery is represented. SC 7 distinguishes various modalities of Christ's presence in the liturgical celebration. The liturgy of the word and the eucharistic liturgy proper constitute one single act of worship (SC 56). However, Christ is present "especially" under the eucharistic species (SC 7).

The eucharistic mystery is also the sacred banquet in which the sacrificial victim is shared. Through sacramental communion the faithful achieve a more perfect participation in the Mass (SC 55). This is why communion is strongly recommended to them. Heavy emphasis is laid on the Eucharist as the sacrament of unity: the unity of God's people is "aptly signified and admirably realised by this most august sacrament" (LG 11; cf. LG 26; UR 2). In fact, "no Christian community can be built up unless it be rooted and centred in the celebration of the Holy Eucharist: all education in community spirit must start there" (PO 6). The unity signified and effected by the eucharistic banquet has a double aspect, ecclesial and Christological: the Eucharist unites the members among themselves and through Christ with God. "By really partaking of the Lord's body in the breaking of the eucharistic bread, we are taken up into communion with Him and with one another" (LG 7); we are day by day drawn "into ever more perfect a union with God and with each other" (SC 48). Through the eucharistic celebration, the Covenant of God with men, ratified once for all in the blood of Christ, is renewed (SC 10). While looking back to the Christ-event, the eucharistic reality also looks towards eschatological salvation: it is a pledge of resurrection. Hence, the threefold dimension of the eucharistic banquet: it is at once a memorial of the Paschal mystery, an event of grace, and a pledge of future glory (SC 47).

The 'Council of the Church' was bound to throw new light on the theme: Eucharist and Church. In fact, the emphasis laid on the close relationship between the two mysteries is one of the remarkable achievements of Vatican II. From the outset, SC notes that the Eucharist, which occupies the central place among the Church's sacraments (PO 5) and in her entire liturgical life (SC 10), is quite particularly "the outstanding means whereby the faithful can express in their lives and manifest to others the mystery of Christ and the real nature of the true Church" (SC 2). The sacramental representation of the mystery of Christ is also the celebration of the mystery of the Church. The social character of the Eucharist is inscribed in its very nature: as sacrifice it is the one sacrifice of Christ represented in the Church

(LG 28); as meal, it is "a meal of fraternal communion" (GS 38). However, the Church is a hierarchical communion; hence the hierarchical character of the eucharistic assembly. From the bishop, the high priest of his flock, "the life of Christ in his faithful is in some way derived and dependent" (SC 41). The bishop exercises his function as steward of grace mostly in the Eucharist (LG 26). Thus, the Eucharist at which he presides, surrounded by his college of priests, is the eucharistic celebration par excellence (SC 41; cf. LG 26). Every other celebration is related to him (SC 42). At the same time, each eucharistic assembly is a sign of the unity of the mystical body (SC 26; LG 26). On the relationship between Church and Eucharist, cf. also LG 3, 7, 11, 15, 26, 28, 50; UR 2, 3, 15; PO 5, 7, etc.

A last important feature of the eucharistic doctrine of Vatican II is its sense of the value of sacramental sybolism. The reforms introduced by the Constitution SC for the celebration of the Eucharist as for other liturgical actions are directed to a greater intelligibility of the sacramental signs (cf. SC 59, 33). This is the reason for the restoration of the communion under both kinds (SC 55). Of sacramental concelebration SC 57 affirms that by it "the unity of the priesthood is appropriately manifested".

CONSTITUTION *SACROSANCTUM CONCILIUM* (1963)

(The Liturgy, especially the Eucharist, in the life of the Church)

1574   2. The Liturgy, "through which the work of our redemption is accomplished", most of all in the divine sacrifice of the Eucharist, is the outstanding means whereby the faithful can express in their lives and manifest to others, the mystery of Christ and the real nature of the true Church. It is of the essence of the Church that she be both human and divine, visible and yet invisibly endowed, eager to act and yet intent on contemplation, present in this world and yet a pilgrim; and she is all these things in such a wise that in her the human is directed and subordinated to the divine, the visible likewise to the invisible, action to contemplation, and this present world to that city yet to come, which we seek (*cf. Heb. 13.14*). Hence, while the liturgy daily builds up those who are within into a holy temple in the Lord,into a dwelling place for God in the Spirit (*cf. Heb. 2.21-22*) to the mature measure of the fulness of Christ (*cf. Eph. 4.13*), at the same time it marvellously strengthens their power to preach Christ, and thus shows forth the Church to those who are outside as a sign lifted up among the nations (*cf. Is. 11.12*) under which the scattered children of God may be gathered together (*cf. Jn 11.52*) until there is one sheepfold and one shepherd (*cf. Jn 10.16*).

The various aspects of the Eucharist)

1575   47. At the Last Supper, on the night when He was betrayed, our Saviour instituted the eucharistic sacrifice of His body and blood. He did this in order to perpetuate the sacrifice of the cross throughout the centuries until He should come again, and so to entrust to His beloved Spouse, the Church, a memorial of His death and resurrection: a sacrament of love, a sign of unity, a bond of charity, a paschal banquet "in which Christ is eaten, the mind is filled with grace, and a pledge of future glory is given to us."[1]

DOGMATIC CONSTITUTION *LUMEN GENTIUM* (1964)

(Participation by all)

1576 11. Whenever they take part in the eucharistic sacrifice, fount and summit of the entire Christian life, (the faithful) offer to God the divine victim and themselves along with it; and thus, both for the offering and in holy communion, all act their own part in the liturgical action, not indeed indiscriminately but in various ways. Strenghtened at the holy table by the body of Christ, they manifest in a concrete manner the unity of God's people, aptly signified and admirably realised by this most august sacrament.

PAUL VI

ENCYCLICAL LETTER *MYSTERIUM FIDEI* (1965)

The Constitution of the Second Vatican Council on the Sacred Liturgy had shown the various modalities of the presence of Christ in the liturgy (cf. n. 1334). The encyclical Mysterium Fidei states that all these different modalities of Christ's presence must be called "real". Yet, the presence of Christ under the eucharistic species surpasses them all and is "presence in the fullest sense". Alluding to attempts made by recent theologians to express the eucharistic presence in terms of 'transignification' and 'transfinalisation', the Pope remarks that these terms do convey a real aspect of the mystery; they do not, however, by themselves suffice to express it adequately. The term of transubstantiation must continue to be used, for it is the change of substance which gives to the eucharistic species their new meaning and their new finality. The text is found in AAS 57 (1965) 753ff.

(The change of substance must be preserved)

1577 It is not allowable...to exaggerate the element of sacramental sign as if the symbolism, which all certainly admit in the Eucharist, expressed fully and exhausted the mode of Christ's presence in this sacrament. Nor is it allowable to discuss the mystery of transubstantiation without mentioning what the Council of Trent stated about the marvellous change of the whole substance of bread into the body and of the whole substance of wine into the blood of

---

[1]. *Roman Breviary,* Feast of Corpus Christi.

Christ (*cf. n. 1519*), speaking rather only of what is called "transignification" and "transfinalisation"....

(The presence of Christ under the eucharistic species is His presence in the fullest sense)

1578 But there is yet another manner in which Christ is present to His Church, a manner which surpasses all the others; it is His presence in the sacrament of the Eucharist, which is for this reason "a more consoling source of devotion, a more lively object of contemplation, a more effective means of sanctification than all the other scraments."[1] The reason is clear: it contains Christ Himself....

This presence is called "real" not in an exclusive sense, as if the other kinds of presence were not real, but 'par excellence', because it is a substantial presence by which Christ, the God-man, whole and entire, becomes present *(cf. nn. 1516f)*. It would therefore be wrong to explain this presence by imagining a "spiritual" nature, as it is called, of the glorified body of Christ, which would be present everywhere, or by reducing it to a kind of symbolism, as if this most august sacrament consisted of nothing else than an efficacious sign "of Christ's spiritual presence and of His intimate union with His faithful members in the mystical Body" *(cf. n. 1571)*.

(Eucharistic symbolism is no adequate expression of this presence)

1579 While the eucharistic symbolism brings us to an understanding of the effect proper to this sacrament which is the unity of the mystical Body, it does not indicate or explain the nature of this sacrament which makes it different from all others. The constant teaching which the Catholic Church passes on to her catechumens, the understanding of the Christian people, the doctrine defined by the Council of Trent, the very words used by Christ when He instituted the most holy Eucharist, compel us to acknowledge that "the Eucharist is the flesh of our Saviour Jesus Christ, which suffered for our sins and which the Father in His loving kindness raised again."[2]

(The change of substance gives to the eucharistic species their new signification and finality)

1580 The way Christ is made present in this sacrament is none other than by the change of the whole substance of the bread

---

1. ST THOMAS AQUINAS, *S.T.,* III, 73, 3c.

2. ST IGNATIUS OF ANTIOCH, *Epistola ad Smyrnas,* 7, 1.

into His body and of the whole substance of the wine into His blood, and this unique and truly wonderful change the Catholic Church rightly and properly calls transubstantiation (*cf. nn. 1519, 1527*). As a result of transubstantiation, the species of bread and wine undoubtedly take on a new meaning and a new finality, for they no longer remain ordinary bread and ordinary wine, but become the sign of something sacred, the sign of a spiritual food. However, the reason why they take on this new significance and this new finality is because they contain a new "reality" which we may justly term ontological. For there no longer lies under those species what was there before, but something quite different; and that, not only because of the faith of the Church, but in objective reality, since after the change of the substance or nature of the bread and wine into the body and blood of Christ, nothing remains of the bread and wine but the appearances, under which Christ, whole and entire, in His physical "reality" is bodily present, although not in the same way as bodies are present in a given place.

INSTRUCTION *EUCHARISTICUM MYSTERIUM* OF THE S. CONGREGATION OF RITES (1967)

This instruction, published by the Sacred Congregtion of Rites to put into effect the renewal desired by the Second Vatican Council in the celebration of the eucharistic mystery, is essentially practical and pastoral in scope. Nevertheless, it is based on doctrine and on more than one point expresses the doctrine of Vatican II even better than the conciliar documents. It enumerates the various aspects of the eucharistic mystery and stresses the close bond which exists between sacrifice and meal (cf. n. 1581). It shows the relationship between the Eucharist and the mystery of the Church (cf. n. 1582). It brings out the full import of the people's active participation in the eucharistic celebration (cf. n. 1583). It shows how in the unfolding of the eucharistic celebration the various modes of Christ's presence in the liturgical assembly are progressively revealed (cf. n. 1585). It insists that the social aspect inscribed in the very nature of the Eucharist be brought out in the manner of celebration; in this regard it points to concelebration as the "eminent manner" of celebrating, and brings out its full significance not merely in the order of signification but also of efficacy.

A remarkable feature of this document is its insistence on the full orchestration of sacramental symbolism in the celebration of the Eucharist. On the foundation of what the Second Vatican Council has stated concerning the need for intelligibility of the sacramental signs (cf. SC 59, 33), the instruction concludes that "the more intelligible the signs by which (the Eucharist) is celebrated and worshipped, the more firmly and effectively will it enter into the lives and minds of the faithful" (4). All the norms and directives given in view of a renewal of the Church's eucharistic life are based on this fundamental principle (20). Hence the expression "ratione signi" recurs everywhere in the instruction: "even through signs" commun-

ion ought to be perceived as a participation in the sacrifice (31); the sign of the eucharistic banquet is more complete in communion under both kinds (32); "by reason of the sign" it is fitting that priests participate in the common Eucharist by actually exercising their priestly order (43). Similarly, all eucharistic devotions must by signs be perceived as essentially related to the celebration of the mystery (cf. nn. 60, 55, etc.). The text is found in AAS 59 (1967) 539ff.

(The various aspects of the eucharistic celebration)

1581   3. The Mass, the Lord's Supper, is at the same time and inseparably: a sacrifice in which the sacrifice of the cross is perpetuated; a memorial of the death and resurrection of the Lord, who said: "Do this as a memorial of Me" *(Lk. 22.19);* a sacred banquet in which, through the communion of the body and blood of the Lord, the people of God share the benefits of the Paschal sacrifice, renew the new Covenant which God has made with men once for all through the blood of Christ, and in faith and hope foreshadow and anticipate the eschatological banquet in the Kingdom of the Father, proclaiming the Lord's death "until He comes" *(1 Cor. 11.26).*

In the Mass, therefore, the sacrifice and sacred meal belong to the same mystery—so much so that they are linked by the closest bond.

(The Eucharist is the centre of the Church's life)

1582   6. The catechesis of the eucharistic mystery should aim to help the faithful to realise that the celebration of the Eucharist is the true centre of the whole Christian life both for the universal Church and for the local congregations of that Church. For "the other sacraments as well as every ecclesiastical ministry or work of the apostolate are connected with the Holy Eucharist and directed towards it. For the Holy Eucharist contains the whole of the Church's spiritual treasure, namely Christ Himself, our Pasch and the living bread who gives life to men by His flesh made living and vivifying by the Holy Spirit. Thus, men are invited and led to offer themselves and their labours and all things created together with Christ" *(PO 5).*

(The fulness of the people's active participation in the eucharistic celebration)

1583   12. It should be made clear that all who gather together for the Eucharist constitute the holy people which, together with the minister, plays its part in the sacred action. It is indeed the priest alone, who, acting in the person of Christ, consecrates the bread and wine, but the role of the faithful in the Eucharist is to recall the passion, resurrection and glorification of the Lord, to give thanks to God, and to offer the immaculate victim not only through the hands of the priest, but also together with him, and finally, by receiving the body of the Lord, to perfect their communion with God and among themselves which should be the effect of participation in the sacrifice of the Mass. For the faithful achieve a more perfect participation in the Mass, when, with proper dispositions, they receive the body of the Lord sacramentally in the Mass itself, in obedience to His words: "Take and eat."

(The meaning of concelebration)

1584   47. Concelebration in the Eucharist aptly demonstrates the unity of the sacrifice and of the priesthood. Moreover, whenever the faithful take an active part, the unity of the people of God is strikingly manifested, particularly if the bishop presides.

Again, concelebration both symbolises and strengthens the brotherly bond between priests, because "by virtue of the sacred ordination and mission which they have in common, all priests are bound together in an intimate brotherhood" *(cf. LG 28)*.

Therefore, unless it conflicts with the needs of the faithful, which must always be attended to with the deepest pastoral concern, and although every priest retains the right to celebrate alone, it is desirable that priests should celebrate in this eminent manner....

(The various modes of Christ's presence are progressively revealed in the eucharistic celebration)

1585   55. In the celebration of the Mass, the principal modes of Christ's presence to His Church are gradually revealed. First of all, Christ is seen to be present in the assembly of the faithful gathered in His name; then in His word, as the scriptures are read and explained; in the person of the minister; finally and in a unique way *(modo singulari)* under the species of the Eucharist....

(Prayer before the Blessed Sacrament)

1586   50. When the faithful adore Christ present in the sacrament, they should remember that this presence derives from the Sacrifice and is directed towards both sacramental and spiritual communion.

In consequence, the devotion which leads the faithful to visit the Blessed Sacrament draws them into an ever deeper participation in the Paschal Mystery. It leads them to respond gratefully to the gift of Him who through His humanity constantly pours divine life into the members of His Body *(PO 5)*. Dwelling with Christ Our Lord, they enjoy His intimate friendship and pour out their hearts before Him for themselves and their dear ones, and pray for the peace and salvation of the world. They offer their entire lives with Christ to the Father in the Holy Spirit, and receive in this wonderful exchange an increase of faith, hope and charity. Thus they nourish those right dispositions which enable them with all devotion to celebrate the memorial of the Lord and receive frequently the bread given us by the Father.

The faithful should therefore strive to worship Christ Our Lord in the Blessed Sacrament, in harmony with their way of life.

(Eucharistic devotion)

1587 58. Devotion, both private and public, towards the Sacrament of the Altar even outside Mass, provided it observes the norms laid down by the legitimate authority and those of the present Instruction, is highly recommended by the Church, since the Eucharistic Sacrifice is the source and summit of the whole Christian life *(n. 1576)*.

In determining the form of such devotions, account should be taken of the regulation of the Second Vatican Council concerning the relationship to be maintained between the liturgy and other non-liturgical celebrations. Especially important is the rule which states: "the liturgical seasons must be taken into account, and those devotions must harmonize with the liturgy, be in some way derived from it and lead the people towards the liturgy as to something which, of its nature, is far superior to these devotions" *(SC 13)*.

GENERAL INSTRUCTION ON THE ROMAN MISSAL
OF THE SACRED CONGREGATION FOR DIVINE WORSHIP
(26 March 1970)

On 3 April, 1969, Pope Paul VI, by the Apostolic Constitution Missale Romanum, *approved the new Roman Missal prepared by the Sacred Congregation for Divine Worship in accordance with the Constitution on Liturgy of the Second Vatican Council. On 26 March, 1970, the Sacred Congregation, at the mandate of the Pope, promulgated and declared typical the new edition of the* Roman Missal. *The new Missal is preceded by a General Instruction. The passages quoted here explain the nature of the eucharistic celebration and its basic structure.*

(Nature of the eucharistic celebration)

1588 7. The Lord's Supper or Mass gathers together the people of God, with a priest presiding in the person of Christ, to celebrate the memorial of the Lord or eucharistic sacrifice *(cf. PO 5; SC 33).* For this reason the promise of Christ is particularly true of such a local congregation of the Church: "Where two or three are gathered in my name, there am I in their midst" *(Mat. 18.20).* In the celebration of Mass, which perpetuates the sacrifice of the cross *(n. 1740),* Christ is really present in the assembly itself, which is gathered in His name, in the person of the minister, in His word, and indeed substantially and unceasingly under the eucharistic species *(SC 7).*

(General structure of the Mass)

1589 8. Although the Mass is made up of the liturgy of the word and the liturgy of the eucharist, the two parts are so closely connected as to form one act of worship *(SC 56).* The table of God's word and of Christ's body is prepared and from it the faithful are instructed and nourished *(SC 48, 51).* In addition, the Mass has introductory and concluding rites.

JOHN PAUL II

LETTER TO THE BISHOPS OF THE CHURCH, *DOMINICAE CENAE*
(24 February 1980)

On the occasion of Maundy Thursday, 1980, Pope John Paul II addressed to all the Bishops of the Church, and through them to all priests, a letter on the mystery and the cult of the Eucharist. One section of the letter develops the traditional doctrine on the Eucharist as sacrament of unity and love. The Pope prolongs this traditional doctrine by showing the social implications of the sacrament. The text is found in AAS 72 (1980) 123-124.

(Eucharist and neighbour)

1590 6. The authentic sense of the Eucharist becomes of itself the school of active love for neighbour. We know that this is the true and full order of love that the Lord has taught us : "By this all men will know that you are my disciples, if you have love for one another" *(Jn 13, 35).* The Eucharist educates us to this love in a deeper way; it shows us, in fact, what value each person, our brother or sister, has in God's eyes, if Christ offers himself equally to each one, under the species of bread and wine. If our eucharistic worship is authentic, it must make us grow in awareness of the dignity of each person. The awareness of that dignity becomes the deepest motive of our relationship with our neighbour.

We must also become particularly sensitive to all human suffering and misery, to all injustice and wrong, and seek the way to redress them effectively. Let us learn to discover with respect the truth about the inner self that becomes the dwelling-place of God present in the Eucharist. Christ comes into the hearts of our brothers and sisters and visits their consciences. How the image of each and every one changes, when we become aware of this reality, when we make it the subject of our reflections ! The sense of the Eucharistic Mystery leads us to love for our neighbour, to love for every human being.

HOMILY AT THE INAUGURAL MASS OF THE NATIONAL EUCHARISTIC CONGRESS AT FORTALEZA

(8 July 1980)

During his visit to Brazil, Pope John Paul II inaugurated the X National Eucharistic Congress at Fortaleza. During the inaugural Mass he delivered a homily in which he stressed the social implications of the Eucharist. One passage of the homily is quoted here. The text is found in Osservatore Romano *(English Edition), 11 August 1980, p. 7.*

(Social implications of the Eucharist)

1591 4. Eucharistic communion is the sign of the meeting of all the faithful. A truly inspiring sign, because at the holy table all the differences of race or social class disappear, leaving only the participation of all in the same holy food. This participation, identical in all, signifies and realizes the suppression of all that divides men, and brings about the meeting of all at a higher level, when all opposition is eliminated. Thus the Eucharist becomes the great instrument of bringing men closer to one another. Whenever the faithful take part in it with a sincere heart, they receive a new impetus to establish a better relationship among themselves, leading to recognition of one another's rights and corresponding duties as well. In this way the satisfaction of the requirements of justice is facilitated, precisely because of the particular climate of interpersonal relations that brotherly charity creates within the same community.

CHAPTER XVI

RECONCILIATION AND THE ANOINTING OF THE SICK

The beginning of the Christian vocation is marked by a call to repentance, linked with the promise of forgiveness, and leading to God's kingdom. Thus, penance has its place in the initiation to the Christian life; but it is not limited to it. It is called for even after baptism and it always includes the assurance of God's mercy.

There is, however, a difference between the first turning to God and the reconciliation of those who have fallen into sin after baptism. The first forgiveness is given in the birth to a new existence; it coincides with a person's entrance into the Church, the communion of those who believe and have life in Jesus Christ through the Holy Spirit. The Christian's new situation after baptism gives to sin and repentance a new dimension: both affect man's relation not only to God but also to the Church. Sin remains, no doubt, an offence against the Creator and Saviour; but it also implies an inner dissociation from the spiritual communion with God's people. Similarly, repentance requires, together with a return to God, the desire to share once again in the life of the community. Forgiveness comes from God's mercy but includes the readmission into the Church's life. From the earliest times this has been concretely apparent in the fact that a grave offence was sanctioned by the exclusion from the Eucharist, and forgiveness signified by the re-admission to the sacrificial banquet.

Hence the doctrine of sacramental penance must take into account two distinct yet closely interwoven realities: firstly, the inner renewal of the sinner whose relation to God, severed by sin, is restored in conversion and repentance; secondly, the ecclesiastical discipline by which the reconciliation of the sinner takes place within the Christian community.

No other sphere of the Church's life has, perhaps, undergone through the centuries such radical changes as has the penitential discipline. The patristic period was characterised by the practice of public penance. Having been excluded from the community, the sinner was reconciled after a period of penance; the reconciliation was granted only once in a life-time and therefore was frequently postponed to the time of death. Some rigoristic groups, however, denied altogether the power of the Church to remit sins; others made the demands for reconciliation too exacting. Hence the early ecclesiastical documents had to be concerned with the Church's right to forgive; they stressed the obligation to grant forgiveness at least at the time of death.

The documents of the early Middle Ages reflect the transition to a new penitential system, which gradually led to the present practice. With the fourth Lateran Council the general frame of the penitential discipline, including confession at least once a year, was settled.

Most documents reflect the theology of sacramental penance progressively developed by scholastic theology. It took its specific orientation at the time of the pre-Reformation controversies, and with greater precision during the Reformation period. Thus, in the Council of Trent, emphasis was laid on the acts of the penitent and on the Church's sacramental action; but the relation of sin and forgiveness to the community of the faithful was not stressed. In recent years, however, the renewed ecclesiology which the Second Vatican Coucil made its own once again brought to the fore the relation of sin and reconciliation to the life of the Christian community.

The anointing of the sick is closely related to penance. Classical theology conceived it as the Christian's final preparation and purification for the heavenly glory, according to the prevalent interpretation given to this sacrament during the Middle Ages. The biblical text on which it is based (James 5.14f), however, already testified to the fact that it is ordained to the healing of both soul and body. A certain ambiguity has long prevailed in the ecclesiastical documents concerning this sacrament. Early texts witness to its practice in the early Church; the documents of the Middle Ages and the Council of Trent conceive it as "extreme unction", i.e., as the sacrament of the dying. Once again it is the merit of the Second Vatican Council to have harmonised the two aspects of the anointing of the sick, healing and disposing for final glory.

*   *   *

Thus the main points of doctrine in the Church documents on sacramental reconciliation and the anointing of the sick are the following:

Reconciliation

The Church has the power to forgive sins: 21, 25, 1601, 1615, 1616, 1617, 1643, 1660/46.47, 1943. 1979.

Penance is a sacrament instituted by Jesus Christ: 28, 32, 1305, 1311, 1612, 1615, 1617, 1641, 1943.

It is distinct from baptism as a judicial act: 1618, 1619, 1642, 1944.

Sacramental penance is necessary: 1429, 1610, 1611/20, 1623, 1626, 1646, 1944, 1979.

The Church must offer reconciliation at least at the time of death: 1602, 1604.

On the part of the penitent are required contrition, confession and satisfaction: 1612, 1614/5.14, 1620, 1644, 1944.

Contrition, its nature and necessity: 1612, 1614/6.7.11.12.14, 1622, 1645, 1944.

Through perfect contrition sins are forgiven: 1623.

Imperfect contrition, i.e., attrition, is a sufficient disposition for confession and is salutary: 1614/6.7, 1624, 1645.

Confession of all mortal sins committed after baptism is required: 1610, 1611/20, 1612, 1614/8.9, 1625, 1626, 1646-1648, 1670,1944.

It must be practised at least once a year: 1608. 1670.

Confession should be private: 1606, 1608, 1609, 1672.

Norms for general absolution: 1670.

Satisfaction, its need and meaning: 1611/21, 1612, 1630-1634, 1652-1655, 1944 .

On the part of the Church sacramental absolution is required: 1612, 1614/10, 1620.

It is a judicial act: 1628, 1649.

Formula of absolution: 1671.

Cases can be reserved: 1611/25, 1614/13, 1629, 1651.

The minister of the sacrament of penance is the priest, authorised by the bishop: 1605, 1611/20.21, 1612, 1614/12.13, 1627, 1629, 1650, 1707, 1714, 1740.

The fruit of sacramental penance is the reconciliation with God: 1306, 1612, 1614/10, 1621, 1943f, 1980;

and with the Church: 1662, 1667, 1669.

Not all temporal punishment is remitted: 1630, 1652, 1944, 1980.

Anointing of the Sick

It is a true sacrament: 28, 32, 1305, 1311, 1635, 1636, 1656, 1660/48;

instituted by Christ: 1311, 1636, 1637, 1656;

promulgated by St James: 1636, 1656.

It is administered by an anointing with oil accompanied by a prayer: 1603, 1613, 1636, 1658, 1668.

The minister of the sacrament is the priest: 1603, 1613, 1659.

It is to be received by the faithful who are dangerously ill: 1603, 1613, 1635, 1638, 1661, 1664.

The fruit of the sacrament is the strength of the soul: 1306, 1613, 1637, 1657;

and, at times, health of the body: 1306, 1613, 1637, 1664. 1665, 1667.

It can also remit sins: 1637, 1657.

THE FIRST GENERAL COUNCIL OF NICAEA (325)

Many local Councils of the early centuries dealt with the reconciliation of sinners, e.g., Carthage (251 and 252) at the time of the Decian persecution, Elvira in Spain (c. 300-303) during the persecution of Diocletian, the general Council of the Western Church in Arles (314), the Synod of Ancyra (314). Great differences as regards practical norms of the reconciliation of apostates and other public sinners are found in these Councils. Yet in the general Council of Nicaea a consensus on the basic attitudes was reached. This gathering of 318 bishops took a definite stand against Novatianism, which denied the power of the Church to forgive sins; against rigoristic practices it also decided that reconciliation must not be denied at the time of death, though with the proviso that in case of recovery such persons would be ranked among the penitents

(The reconciliation of Novatians)

1601 *Canon 8:* As to those who call themselves Cathars, i.e., the
127 "pure" (the Novatians), if they come to the Catholic and apostolic Church, this holy and great Synod has decided that after receiving the imposition of hands they remain in the ranks of the clergy. They must, however, above all promise in writing to accept and follow the doctrines of the Catholic and apostolic Church, to have communion with 'digamists' (people living in a second marriage) and with those who have lapsed in persecution, for whose reconciliation provision has been made and a time has been fixed.

(Reconciliation of the dying)

1602 *Canon 13:* As to those who are departing from this life, the
129 old canonical law is now to be kept. If anyone is about to die he should not be deprived of the ultimate and most necessary viaticum. If, after having been reconciled and received again into the fellowship, he should recover his health, he should be placed in the ranks of those who share only in the communion of prayer. In general, to anyone who is departing from this life and asks to partake of the Eucharist the bishop after investigation should grant it.

INNOCENT I

LETTER TO DECENTIUS, BISHOP OF GUBBIO (416)

This letter intends merely to clarify practical points regarding the administration of the anointing of the sick, viz., who is to administer it; but in reality it sums up the contemporary teaching. It links the anointing with the text of James; the oil is blessed by the bishop; it is used, apart from the sacramental rite, also for other purposes; the anointing is done by bishop or priests; it is called a 'sacrament' which, however, must not be understood in the later technical sense as one of the seven sacraments. Still, the fact that those who undergo penance and hence are excluded from the Eucharist cannot receive it, indicates that it is considered as something more than a pious custom.

(On the anointing of the sick)

1603 (Your next question) concerns the text from the epistle of
216 the blessed apostle James: "Is any among you sick ? Let him call for the elders of the Church, and let them pray over him, anointing him with oil in the name of the Lord; and the prayer of faith will save the sick man, and the Lord will raise him up; and if he has committed sins, he will be forgiven *(James 5.14f)*.   This must undoubtedly be accepted and understood as referring to the oil of Chrism, prepared by the bishop, which can be used for anointing not only by priests but also by all Christians whenever they themselves or their people are in need of it. The question whether the bishop can do what undoubtedly can be done by priests seems superfluous, for priests are mentioned simply because bishops are prevented by other occupations and cannot visit all the sick. But if a bishop is in a position to do so and thinks it proper, he, to whom it belongs to prepare the Chrism, can himself without hesitation visit the sick to bless them and anoint them with Chrism. But it may not be used on those undergoing penance for it is of the nature of a sacrament. How could one think that one kind of sacrament should be allowed to those to whom the rest is denied ?

CELESTINE I

LETTER TO THE BISHOPS OF VIENNA AND NARBONNE (428)

Reconciliation at the time of death remained controversial on various grounds: 1) suspicions concerning the sincerity of those in danger of death, as they seemed to seek absolution only out of fear; 2) the need for works of satisfaction which seemed indispensable for reconciliation. In this official letter Pope Celestine insists on offering reconciliation to all the dying who ask for it. His letter reflects a great pastoral concern for the faithful in the decisive hour of their death, and an absolute trust in God's mercy.

(Reconciliation at the time of death)

1604 It came to our notice that penance is denied to the dying, and
236 that the desire of those who in the hour of death wish to be helped by this remedy for their souls is not fulfilled. We confess to be horrified that anyone should be so impious as to despair of God's mercy, as if He could not succour a man who takes

refuge in Him at any time and liberate him who is oppressed by the weight of sins, from the burden of which he wishes to be freed. What else is this but to inflict death on the dying, and by one's cruelty to kill his soul that it may not be absolved? Because God is most ready with His assistance, He adds this promise to the invitation to penance: "On whatever day the sinner will turn to me, his sins will not be remembered against him" (cf. Ez. 33.12 and 16 Vulg).... Since God is the knower of the heart, at no time must penance be denied to him who asks for it.

LEO I

LETTER TO THEODORE, BISHOP OF FREJUS (452)

This great Pope also takes up the doctrinal and pastoral problems of the penitential discipline, mainly the need to offer reconciliation to the dying. In this letter, he explains the role of the priest in reconciliation. His role is indispensable. It is described by Leo as 'supplication', which reflects the consciousness of the early Church that in forgiving sins the priest does not act in his own right but carries out the mediating mission of Christ. Yet this supplication is not merely a personal prayer of the priest, but the official intercession of the Church who has the mandate to lead sinners through penance to reconciliation with God.

(The priest's role in reconciliation)

1605 God's manifold mercy comes to the aid of men who have 308 fallen so that the hope of eternal life may be restored not only through the grace of baptism but also through the remedy of penance. Thus, those who have violated the gifts of their new birth can come to the forgiveness of their crimes by a judgment in which they condemn themselves. These remedies of the divine goodness have been so ordained that God's forgiveness cannot be obtained except through the supplication of the priests. For "the mediator between God and men, the man Jesus Christ" (1 Tim. 2.5) gave to those who hold authority in the Church the power to grant the discipline of penance to those who confess and, after they have been purified through salutary satisfaction, to admit them to the communion of the sacraments through the door of reconciliation.

LETTER TO THE BISHOPS OF ROMAN RURAL DISTRICTS (459)

In this letter, the same Pope deals with the secrecy required in confession to safeguard the reputation of the penitent; the practice is presented as apostolic tradition.

(Private confession)

1606 I order that all measures be taken to eradicate the presump-
323 tuous deviation from the apostolic rule through an illicit
abuse of which I have learned of late. In the procedure of
penance, for which the faithful ask, there should be no public confession of sins in kind and number read from a written list, since it is
enough that the guilt of conscience be revealed to the priests alone in
secret confession. Though such fulness of faith seems praiseworthy
which out of the fear of God is not afraid of shame before men, yet
not all sins are such that those who ask for penance would not fear
them to become publicly known. Hence this objectionable practice
must be removed lest many be kept away from the remedies of
penance, either out of shame or for fear that their enemies may come
to know of facts which could bring harm to them through legal
procedures. For that confession is sufficient which is first offered to
God, then also to the priest whose role is that of an intercessor for
the sins of the penitents. Finally a greater number will be induced to
penance only if the conscience of the penitent is not made public for
all to hear.

THE THIRD COUNCIL OF TOLEDO (589)

*The 11th canon of this regional Council is of particular interest as it
belongs to a period of transition. It sternly reasserts the old penitential order
with its basic structure of exclusion from the community, satisfaction
through a protracted period of time, and finally reconciliation. Ever since
Hermas, this way of penance was granted only once in a life-time. The
Council reflects the new practice of granting reconciliation to penitents as
often as they ask for it, according to a new code of canons. The new
practice had come from Ireland and England to France, and from there had
spread also to Spain. The text is found in* Mansi, IX, 995.

(The old penitential system against the new procedure)

1607 It came to our knowledge that in some Churches in Spain
people go through the discipline of penance for their sins, not
according to the canons but in a most shameful manner, viz., as often
as they happen to fall into sin they ask for reconciliation from the
priest. To eradicate this execrable presumption this holy Council
commands that penance be granted according to the old canons,
which means that (the priest) first suspends from the communion the
man who repents of his deed, that he lets him come frequently to the
imposition of hands along with the other penitents, that after he has
completed the time of satisfaction with the approval of the priest, the
priest restores him to communion. But those who fall back into their

former vices, either during the time of penance or after reconciliation, should be condemned in accordance with the severity of the
earlier canons.

THE FOURTH LATERAN GENERAL COUNCIL (1215)

*This Council is a landmark in the history of ecclesiastical penance. In its
Symbol it re-asserts the power of the Church to forgive sins, against the
anti-clerical sects of the Albigensians and the Waldensians (cf. n. 21).
Concerning the discipline of penance it prescribes as a minimum the annual
reception of the Eucharist. Such a legislation was called for, once the
possibility of repeated absolution was generally accepted (cf. n. 1607i). The
rule of annual confession puts an end to the many fluctuations of the
previous centuries. The Council also exhorts the priests to fulfil their spiritual and pastoral office in the administration of sacramental penance (cf. DS
813); finally it puts strict sanctions on the breach of the seal of sacramental
confession.*

(The rule of annual confession)

1608   Every faithful of either sex who has reached the age of
812   discretion should at least once a year faithfully confess all his
sins in secret to his own priest. He should strive as far as
possible to fulfil the penance imposed on him, and with reverence
receive at least during Easter time the sacrament of the Eucharist....
But if anyone wishes for good reasons to confess his sins to another
priest, he must first ask and obtain permission from his own priest
because otherwise that priest has no power to bind or loose him

(The seal of confession)

1609   Let (the confessor) take absolute care not to betray the sinner
814   through word or sign, or in any other way whatsoever. In
case he needs expert advice he may seek it without, however, in any way indicating the person. For we decree that he who
presumes to reveal a sin which has been manifested to him in the
tribunal of penance is not only to be deposed from the priestly office,
but also to be consigned to a closed monastery for perpetual
penance.

THE GENERAL COUNCIL OF CONSTANCE

CONDEMNATION OF ERRORS OF WYCLIF AND HUS (1415)

*Wyclif in England (ob. 1384) and Hus in Bohemia (ob. 1415, burned at
the stake) were the forerunners of the Reformtion. In accordance with their
doctrine of the Church (cf. n. 807/8i) and the sacraments (cf. n. 1303i), they*

maintained that the forgiveness of sins is obtained not through the ecclesiastical authority but simply by the contrition of the heart.

(Error of Wyclif condemned)

[1610] 7. If a man is duly contrite, any exterior confession is
1157   superfluous and useless.

MARTIN V
BULL *INTER CUNCTAS* (1418)

On this document, see n. 1304i.

(Questions proposed to the followers of Wyclif and Hus)

1611/20 Whether he believes that, apart from heartfelt contrition,
1260   if a qualified priest is available, a Christian is bound by a
          necessity of salvation to confess only to him, and not to
one or more laymen, however good and devout they may be.

1611/21 Whether he believes that a priest, in the cases permitted
1261   to him, can absolve from sin a sinner who has confessed
          and is contrite, and impose a penance on him.

1611/25 Whether he believes that the jurisdictional authority of
1265   the Pope, of an archbishop and bishop, in loosing
          and binding is greater than the authority of a simple
priest, even if he has the care of souls.

THE GENERAL COUNCIL OF FLORENCE
DECREE FOR THE ARMENIANS (1439)

On this document see n. 1305i. The decree proposes an interpretation of sacramental penance along the lines of Thomas Aquinas' theology. Thus, it keeps the balance between the pre-Thomist conception which placed the essence of sacramental penance on the side of the penitent, his works of satisfaction, his confession and his contrition, and the later Scotist view for which the essence of the sacrament consists only in the absolution, while the acts of the penitent are considered merely as preparatory disposition. With St Thomas the Decree considers the acts of the penitent as the 'quasi-matter', therefore as a constitutive element of the sacrament, and the absolution as the 'form'.

The text on "extreme unction" is also based on St Thomas. It includes the positive aspect of healing for mind and body; thus the sacrament is presented not as that of the dying only, but of the sick.

(The Sacrament of Penance)

1612 The fourth sacrament is penance. Its quasi-matter

1623   consists in the actions of the penitent which are divided into three parts. The first of these is contrition of the heart, which requires that he be sorry for the sin committed with the resolve not to sin in the future. The second is oral confession which requires that the sinner confess to his priest in their integrity all the sins he remembers. The third is satisfaction for the sins according to the judgment of the priest, which is mainly achieved by prayer, fasting and almsgiving. The form of this sacrament is the words of absolution spoken by the priest who has authority to absolve, either ordinary or by commision from his superior. The effect of this sacrament is absolution from sins.

(The sacrament of "extreme unction")

1613   The fifth sacrament is extreme unction. Its matter is olive oil
1324   blessed by the bishop. This sacrament may not be given except to a sick person whose life if feared for. He is to be anointed on these parts: on the eyes on account of sight, on the ears on account of hearing, on the nostrils on account of smelling, on the mouth on account of taste and speech, on the hands on account of touch, on the feet on account of movement, on the loins on account of the lust seated there.

1325   The minister of this sacrament is the priest. The effect is the healing of the mind and, as far as it is good for the soul, of the body as well. Of this sacrament blessed James the apostle says: "Is any among you sick ?..." *(James 5.14f).*

LEO X

BULL *EXSURGE DOMINE* (1520)

Luther's theology of penance is part and parcel of his doctrine on justification: grace is exclusively God's gift; it is ours not on account of any work or merit on our part, but only through faith. As regards penance, Luther considered it a sacrament, and he encouraged confession as a means of awakening faith in God's forgiveness; but confession had to be entirely free from any coercion. In the words of absolution the sinner found the assurance of God's promise. Luther polemised against the practice of the Church in which, he thought, the works of the penitent were considered more important than the faith in God's mercy, so that man relied on himself more than on God. He further objected to the reservation of the power of forgiveness to priests because of which, in his view, the sacrament of penance became a means of clerical domination.

The Bull Exsurge Domine is the first official rejection of Luther's doctrine. The propositions which are condemned are selected from his works,

*mostly in his own words. To understand Luther's position and the signifi-
cance of the conflict, the propositions must, however, be read in the wider
context of his theology.*

(Errors of Luther condemned)

[1614/5] That there are three parts of penance: contrition, con-
1455   fession and satisfaction, is not founded on Holy Scripture
          nor on the holy ancient Christian Doctors.

[1614/6] Contrition which arises from examination, consideration
1456   and detestation of sins, whereby one recounts his years
          in the bitterness of his soul, pondering over the grievous-
ness, number and ugliness of his sins, over the loss of eternal
happiness and the fall into eternal damnation, such a contrition
makes him a hypocrite and a greater sinner than before.

[1614/7] Very true, and better than all the previous teaching on
1457   the kinds of contrition is the maxim: not to do it again is
          the height of penance; the best penance is a new life.

[1614/8] Do not on any account presume to confess venial sins,
1458   nor even all mortal sins, for it is impossible for you to
          recall all mortal sins. This is why only public mortal sins
were confessed in the early Church.

[1614/9] If we wish to confess everthing clearly, we desire in reality
1459   to leave nothing to the mercy of God to forgive.

[1614/10] Sins are not remitted to anyone unless, when the priest
1460   remits them, he believes that they are remitted; rather
          the sin would remain if he did not believe that it is
remitted. For, the remission of sin and the giving of grace are not
sufficient; it is also necessary to believe that sin is remitted.

[1614/11] Do not believe that you are absolved on account of your
1461   contrition, but on account of Christ's word: "Whatever
          you loose...", etc. *(Mt. 16.19).* Hence I say: If you have
received the absolution of a priest, have confidence and firmly
believe that you are absolved; and absolved you will truly be, whatever your contrition.

[1614/12] In the impossible supposition that one who confesses
1462   would not be sorry, or that the priest would give absolu-
          tion not seriously but in jest, yet, if he believes that he is
absolved, the penitent is in very truth absolved.

[1614/13]   In the sacrament of penance and the remission of guilt,
1463   the Pope or the bishop does no more than the lowliest
               priest; in fact, where there is no priest, any Christian can
do as much, even a woman or a child.

[1614/14]   No one needs to answer a priest that he is sorry; nor
1664   should the priest inquire.

THE GENERAL COUNCIL OF TRENT
FOURTEENTH SESSION
DOCTRINE ON THE SACRAMENT OF PENANCE (1551)

The Council of Trent not only answers the attacks of the Reformers against sacramental penance, but at the same time gives a coherent and complete exposition of the nature and structure of this sacrament. It insists primarily on the fact that penance is a sacrament instituted by Christ (Chapter 1), distinct from baptism since it consists, on the part of the minister, in a judicial act exercised on the members of the Christian community (Chapter 2). Thus the basis of the Catholic doctrine is proposed against the Protestant position. In the following chapter the parts of sacramental penance are described in general terms: the three acts of the penitent are contrition, confession and satisfaction (Chapter 3). Then these parts are described in detail: first, contrition, with special reference to imperfect contrition, i.e., attrition, which is vindicated against Luther's attacks (Chapter 4); then confession of all mortal sins (Chapter 5); the absolution by the minister, who is the priest only (Chapter 6); the need for the priest to have jurisdiction, and the possibility of reserving cases to the bishops (Chapter 7); finally the need of imposing a penance, along with the meaning of satisfaction (Chapters 8 and 9).

Chapter I: The necessity and the institution of the sacrament of penance

1615   If in all those who are regenerated there were such gratitude
1668   towards God that through His bounty and grace they con-
           stantly preserved the justice which they have received in
baptism, there would have been no need to institute another sacrament for the forgiveness of sins besides baptism itself. But since God, who is "rich in mercy" (*Eph. 2.4*), "knows our frame" (*Ps. 103 (102)14*), He has given a remedy of life also to those who after baptism have delivered themselves up to the bondage of sin and the devil's power, namely the sacrament of penance whereby the benefit of Christ's death is applied to those who have fallen after baptism.

1616   Penance was indeed at all times necessary for all men who
1669   had stained themselves by any mortal sin in order to obtain
           grace and justice—not excepting those who desired to be

cleansed by the sacrament of baptism—so that they might turn from their preversion, make amendment, and detest so great an offence of God with hatred of sin and a sincere and heartfelt sorrow. Therefore the Prophet says: "Be converted and do penance for all your iniquities, and iniquity shall not be your ruin" (Ez. 18.30 Vulg.). The Lord also said: "Unless you repent, you will all likewise perish" (Lk. 13.5). And Peter, prince of the apostles, recommended penance to sinners who were about to receive baptism with the words: "Repent and be baptised everyone of you" (Acts 2.38).

1617 Yet before the coming of Christ penance was not a sacra-
1670 ment; nor is it one after His coming for anyone who has not been baptised. But the Lord instituted the sacrament of penance, principally when after His resurrection He breathed upon His disciples and said: "Receive the Holy Spirit. If you forgive the sins of any, they are forgiven; if you retain the sins of any, they are retained" (Jn 20.22f). The universal consensus of the Fathers has always acknowledged that by so sublime an action and such clear words the power of forgiving and retaining sins was given to the apostles and their lawful successors for reconciling the faithful who have fallen after baptism; and with good reason the Catholic Church denounced and condemned as heretics the Novatians who in the past stubbornly denied the power of forgiveness. Therefore this holy Council approves and accepts the words of the Lord in their full and true meaning and condemns the fictitious interpretations of those who, in contradiction with the institution of this sacrament, distort these words to make them refer to the power of preaching the word of God and of proclaiming the Gospel of Christ.

*Chapter II: The difference between the
sacraments of penance and baptism*

1618 Besides, it is clear that this sacrament differs in many ways
1671 from baptism. Apart from the fact that it differs very widely in matter and form, which constitute the essence of a sacrament, it is beyond question that the minister of baptism need not be a judge since the Church does not exercise judgment on anyone who has not first entered it through the gate of baptism. "For what have I to do", the apostle asks, "with judging outsiders ?" (1 Cor. 5.12). It is otherwise with those who are of the household of the faith, whom Christ the Lord has once made members of His Body by the bath of

baptism (*1 Cor. 12.12*). For, it was His will that, if afterwards they should defile themselves by some crime, they would not be cleansed by receiving baptism again—this is not allowed under any condition in the Catholic Church—but that they would present themselves before this tribunal in order that they might be set free through the sentence of the priest; and this not once only, but as often as, repentant of the sins committed, they turn to that tribunal.

1619 Moreover, the effect of baptism is different from that of
1672   penance. For by baptism we "put on Christ" (*Gal. 3.27*) and
          are made an entirely new creature in Him, receiving full and integral remission of all sins. To this newness and integrity, however, we are by no means able to arrive by the sacrament of penance without many tears and labours on our part, as divine justice demands. Hence penance has rightly been called by the holy Fathers "a laborious kind of baptism".[1] This sacrament of penance is necessary for salvation for those who have fallen after baptism, just as baptism itself is for those who have not yet been regenerated.

Chapter III: The parts of penance and its effect

1620 The holy Council teaches moreover that the form of the
1673   sacrament of penance, in which its power principally resides,
          consists in these words of the minister: I absolve you, etc. In accordance with a custom of the holy Church certain prayers are laudably added to these words; they do not, however, in any way belong to the essence of the form, nor are they necessary for the administration of the sacrament. The "quasi-matter" (*quasi materia*) of this sacrament is the acts of the penitent himself, viz., contrition, confession and satisfaction. Inasmuch as these acts are by divine institution required in the penitent for the integrity of the sacrament and for the full and complete forgiveness of sins, they are called parts of penance.

1621 As to the reality (*res*) and the effect of this sacrament, so far
1674   as concerns its power and efficacy, it consists in reconcilia-
          tion with God. In persons who are pious and receive this sacrament with devotion, it is likely to be followed at times by peace and serenity of conscience with an overwhelming consolation of spirit.

---

1. Cf. v.g. GREGORY OF NAZIANZEN, *Oratio* 39, 17.

1675   In declaring this doctrine on the parts and the effect of this
        sacrament, the holy Council at the same time condemns the
view of those who maintain that the parts of penance consist in the
terrors of a striken conscience and in faith.

Chapter IV: Contrition

1622   Contrition holds the first place among the acts of the peni-
1676   tent mentioned above. It consists in the sorrow of the soul
        and the detestation of the sin committed, together with the
resolve not to sin any more. This disposition (*motus*) of contrition
was necessary at all times for the attainment of the remission of sins.
In a person who has fallen after baptism it prepares for the forgiveness of sins if it is joined with trust in the divine mercy and the
intention to fulfil whatever else is required for the right reception of
this sacrament. Therefore the holy Council declares that this contrition implies not only cessation from sin and the resolve and beginning
of a new life, but also the hatred of the old according to the word:
"Cast away from you all the transgressions which you have committed against me, and get yourselves a new heart and a new spirit" (*Ez.
18.31*)....

1623   Moreover, the Council teaches that, although it sometimes
1677   happens that this contrition is perfect through charity and
        reconciles man to God before this sacrament is actually
received, this reconciliation, nevertheless, is not to be ascribed to
cotrition itself without the desire of the sacrament, a desire which is
included in it.

1624   As to imperfect contrition, which is called attrition, since it
1678   commonly arises either from the consideration of the hei-
        nousness of sin or from the fear of hell and of punishment, the
Council declares: If it excludes the will to sin and implies the hope for
pardon, it not only does not make one a hypocrite and a greater
sinner, but is a gift of God and a prompting of the Holy Spirit, not
indeed as already dwelling in the penitent but only moving him—an
impulse by which the penitent is helped to prepare for himself a way
unto justice. Though without the sacrament of penance it cannot of
itself lead the sinner to justification, it nevertheless disposes him to
obtain the grace of God in the sacrament of penance. For, it is thanks
to this salutary fear that the Ninivites, after the terrifying preaching of
Jonas, did penance and obtained mercy from the Lord (*cf. Jonas 3*).

Falsely, therefore, do some accuse Catholic writers as if they maintained that the sacrament of penance confers grace without any good disposition *(motu)* on the part of those receiving it; this is something which the Church of God never taught or accepted. Falsely also do they assert that contrition is extorted or forced, not free and voluntary.

Chapter V: Confession

1625 From the institution of the sacrament of penance as already
1679 explained the whole Church has always understood that the
complete confession of sins was also instituted by the Lord
(cf. James 5.16; 1 Jn 1.9), and is by divine Law necessary for all who have fallen after baptism. For, when He was about to ascend from earth to heaven, our Lord Jesus Christ left priests to represent Him *(cf. Mt. 16.19; 18.18; Jn 20.23)* as presiding judges to whom all mortal sins into which the faithful of Christ would have fallen should be brought that they, in virtue of the power of the keys, might pronounce the sentence of remission or retention of sins. For it is clear that without knowledge of the case priests could not exercise this judgment, nor could they observe equity in the imposition of penances if the penitents declared their sins only in general and not specifically and in particular.

1626 Thus it follows that all mortal sins of which penitents
1680 after a diligent self-examination are conscious must be
recounted by them in confession, though they may be most secret and may have been committed only against the last two precepts of the decalogue *(cf. Ex. 20.17; Mt. 5.28);* for these sins sometimes wound the souls more grievously and are more dangerous than those which are committed openly. As regards venial sins by which we are not excluded from the grace of God and into which we fall more frequently, it is right and profitable, and implies no presumption whatever, to declare them in confession, as can be seen from the practice of devout people; yet, they may be omitted without guilt and can be expiated by many other remedies. But since all mortal sins, also those of thought, make of men "children of wrath" *(Eph. 2.3)* and enemies of God, there is need to seek God's pardon equally for them all through an open and humble confession. Hence when Christ's faithful strive to confess all sins that occur to their memory, they undoubtedly place all of them before the divine mercy for pardon. But those who fail to do so and knowingly withhold some,

place nothing before the divine goodness for remission, "for if the sick is ashamed to lay open his wound before the physician, the medicine does not heal what it does not know."[1]

(Also those circumstances which change the species of the sin must be confessed (DS 1681). Confession is not a torture since only confession of those sins is required which after diligent examination come to mind; sins which are not remembered are included in the confession and forgiven (DS 1682). The practice of secret confession is based on old traditions; public confession is never obligatory. The obligation to confess was not introduced by the fourth Lateran Council; this Council only determined that the existing precept of confession should be fulfilled at least once a year (DS 1682).)

Chapter VI: The minister of the sacrament and absolution

1627 With regard to the minister of this sacrament the holy Coun-
1684 cil declares: False and totally foreign to the truth of the Gospel are all doctrines which in a very destructive manner extend the ministry of the keys to all other men besides bishops and priests. They do so in the belief that the words of the Lord: "Whatever you bind on earth shall be bound in heaven, and whatever you loose on earch shall be loosed in heaven" *(Mt. 18.18),* and: "If you forgive the sins of any, they are forgiven; if you retain the sins of any, they are retained" *(Jn 20.23),* were, in contradiction with the institution of this sacrament, addressed to all the faithful of Christ without difference or distinction, with the result that everyone has the power to forgive sins, public ones by public correction, if the sinner complies, and secret ones by spontaneous confession to anyone. The Council likewise teaches that even priests who are in mortal sin exercise the office of forgiving sins as ministers of Christ through the power of the Holy Spirit conferred in ordination, and that the opinion of those who maintain that bad priests do not possess this power is wrong.

1628 It is true that priestly absolution is the dispensation of
1685 another's bounty; yet, it does not consist in the mere ministry of proclaiming the Gospel or of declaring that the sins have been forgiven, but it has the pattern of a judicial act in which the priest pronounces sentence as judge. Hence the penitent should not be so complacent about his faith as to consider himself truly absolved before God on account of his faith alone, even if he has no

---

1. St Jerome, *Comment. in Ecclesiasten,* 10, 11.

contrition, or if the priest has no mind to act seriously and to absolve truly. For faith without penance would effect no remission of sins, and one would be most negligent about his salvation if, knowing that a priest absolved him jokingly, he would not diligently seek another who would act seriously.

Chapter VII: Jurisdiction and reservation of cases

1629 It is in the nature and meaning of a judgment that the
1686 sentence be pronounced only over one's subjects. Hence the
Church of God has always been convinced, and this Synod confirms as fully true, that absolution is of no value if it is pronounced by a priest on one over whom he has neither ordinary nor delegated jurisdiction.

(For pastoral reasons the absolution of special sins may be reserved to the bishop; but on the point of death all reservations are cancelled (DS 1687f).)

Chapter VIII: The necessity and fruit of satisfaction

1630 Finally, as regards satisfaction: it is among the parts of
1689 penance the one which, though at all times recommended to
the Christian people by our Fathers, yet in our age has become the main target of attack under the pretext of piety by those "who hold the form of religion but deny the power of it" *(2 Tim. 3.5)*. The holy Synod declares: It is utterly false and contray to the word of God that the guilt is never remitted by the Lord, without the entire punishment also being condoned. For, apart from the divine Tradition, clear and striking examples are found in Holy Scripture by which this error is refuted in the plainest possible manner *(cf. Gen. 3.16ff; Num. 12.14f; 20.11f; 2 Sam. 12.13f, etc.)*.

1631 Indeed, the nature of divine justice seems to demand that
1690 those who have sinned through ignorance before baptism be
received in grace in one manner, and in another manner those who have already once been liberated from the slavery of sin and the devil, who have received the gift of the Holy Spirit, and yet have not feared knowlingly to "violate the temple of God" *(1 Cor. 3.17)* and to grieve the Holy Spirit *(Eph. 4.30)*. It is also in keeping with the divine clemency that sins should not be pardoned to us without any satisfaction, with the consequence that we would consider sin as trivial and, when the occassion arises, would fall into

more grievous sins, insulting as it were and outraging the Holy Spirit (cf. Heb. 10.29), storing up wrath for ourselves on the day of wrath (cf. Rom. 2.5; James 5.3). For without doubt these satisfactory penances greatly detach penitents from sin; they act like a bridle to keep them in check, and make them more cautious and vigilant in the future. They also heal the after-effects of sin and destroy evil habits, acquired through a bad life, by acts of virtues opposed to them. And no way of averting the punishments which threaten us from the Lord was ever held in the Church of God more secure than the practice of the works of penance done with a sorrowful heart (Mt. 3.2, 8; 4.17; 11.21, etc.). Besides, when we suffer in satisfaction for our sins we conform ourselves to Christ Jesus who made satisfaction for our sins (cf. Rom 5.10; 1 Jn 2.1f), from whom comes all our sufficiency (cf. 2 Cor. 3.5); this gives us the surest pledge that, while suffering with him, we shall also be glorified with him (cf. Rom. 8.17).

1632 However, this satisfaction which we make for our sins is not
1691 ours in such a way that it be not through Christ Jesus. For, while we can do nothing of ourselves as of ourselves, we can do everything with the cooperaton of Him who strengthens us (cf. Phil. 4.13). Thus man has nothing wherein to glory, but all our glorying is in Christ (cf. 1 Cor. 1.31; 2 Cor. 10.17; Gal. 6.14), in whom we live (cf. Acts 17.28), in whom we merit, in whom we make satisfaction, bringing forth worthy fruits of penance (cf. Lk. 3.8); these fruits have their efficacy from Him, by Him they are offered to the Father, and through Him they are accepted by the Father.

1633 Hence the priests of the Lord have the duty to impose
1692 salutary and proportionate satisfactions as suggested by spiritual prudence, in accordance with the nature of the crime and the ability of the penitents, lest they become partakers of the sins of others (cf. 1 Tim. 5.22) if they connive at their sins and deal too leniently with them by imposing only some sort of slight penance for very grave delicts. Let them keep in mind that the satisfaction imposed by them is meant not merely as a safeguard for the new life and as a remedy to weakness, but also as a vindicatory punishment for former sins. For the early Fathers also believe and teach that the keys of the priests are given not only to loose but also to bind (cf. Mt. 16.19; 18.18; Jn 20.23). They did not for that reason consider the sacrament of penance as a tribunal of wrath and punishment; similarly no Catholic ever thought that through these satisfactions of ours the value of the merit and satisfaction of our Lord Jesus Christ

is obscured or to some extent diminished. This is the interpretation of the innovators when they teach that a new life is the best penance, with the result that they do away with all efficacy and practice of penance.

Chapter IX: The works of satisfaction

1634 Moreover, (this Council) teaches that the generosity of *1693* the divine bounty is so great that we are able to make satisfaction before God the Father through Christ Jesus, not only by the penances which we voluntarily undertake for the expiation of sin, or which are imposed on us by the priest's judgment according to the measure of the sin, but also—and this is the most forceful proof of love—by the temporal affliction imposed on us by God, if we bear them with patience.

DOCTRINE ON THE SACRAMENT OF EXTREME UNCTION (1551)

The Council of Trent enunciated the doctrine on the anointing of the sick in the same session as, and in continuation to, the doctrine on the sacrament of penance, of which it is the complement. The document offers a complete treatment of the subject.

The introduction places the sacrament in the context of the Christian life. Chapter 1 deals with the controversial question of its institution. Some theologians had taught that it was instituted by St James. Luther had vigorously denied that an apostle could institute a sacrament. The Council teaches the institution of the sacrament by Christ, and its promulgation by the apostle James. Chapter 2 treats the effect of the sacrament; chapter 3 its minister and recipient. Luther had objected to the practice of anointing only the dying, a restriction not found in James' text. The Council still continues the Scholastic tradition which had made the anointing the "extreme" unction, but mitigates the scholastic stand by extending the sacrament to those "dangerously ill" and by including among its effects the psychological and physical relief.

Foreword

1635 It seemed good to the holy Council to add to the preceding *1694* doctrine on penance the following concerning the sacrament of extreme unction, which was considered by the Fathers as the complement not only of penance but also of the whole Christian life, which ought to be a continual penance. First, therefore, with regard to its institution, it declares and teaches the following: our most merciful Redeemer wished His servants to be provided at all times with salutary remedies against all weapons of all enemies; as in the other sacraments He prepared the greatest aids for Christians to keep themselves, during their lifetime, free from every grave spiritual evil, so did He protect the end of life with the sacrament of extreme unction as with a very strong safeguard. For, though throughout our whole life, our adversary seeks and seizes upon occasions to devour our souls in any possible way (*cf. 1 Pet. 5.8*), yet there is no time when he strains more vehemently all the powers of his cunning to ruin us utterly, and, if possible, to make us lose even faith in the divine mercy, than when he perceives that the end of our life is near.

Chapter I: The institution of the sacrament of extreme unction

1636 This sacred anointing of the sick was instituted by Christ our
1695 Lord as a true and proper sacrament of the New Testament.
It is alluded to indeed by Mark (*6.13*), but is recommended to the faithful and promulgated by James the apostle and brother of the Lord: "Is any among you sick ?", he says, "let him call for the elders of the Church, and let them pray over him, anointing him with oil in the name of the Lord; and the prayer of faith will save the sick man, and the Lord will raise him up; and if he has committed sins, he will be forgiven" (*James 5.14f*). By these words, as the Church has learned from the apostolic Tradition handed down and received by her, he teaches the matter, the form, the proper minister and the effect of this salutary sacrament. For the Church has understood that the matter is oil blessed by the bishop, because the anointing very aptly represents the grace of the Holy Spirit with which the soul of the sick is invisibly anointed. And the form consists of these words: "By this unction", etc.

Chapter II: The effect of this sacrament

1637 Further, the reality (*res*) and effect of this sacrament are
1696 explained in the words: "and the prayer of faith will save the
sick man, and the Lord will raise him up; and if he has committed sins, he will be forgiven" (*James 5.15*). For the reality is the grace of the Holy Spirit, whose anointing takes away the sins if there be any still to be expiated, and also the remains of sin; it comforts and strengthens the soul of the sick person by awakening in him great confidence in the divine mercy; supported by this, the sick bears more lightly the inconveniences and trials of his illness and

resists more easily the temptations of the devil who lies in wait for his heel (*cf. Gen. 3.15*); at times it also restores bodily health when it is expedient for the salvation of the soul.

Chapter III: The minister of this sacrament, and the time of its administration

1638 The directives as to who must receive and administer this
1697 sacrament are also clearly transmitted in the words already quoted. They indicate that the proper ministers of this sacrament are the presbyters of the Church. In this text this word does not refer to those who are senior in age or more influential among the people, but either to bishops or to priests duly ordained by them through the laying on of hands of the presbyterium (*cf. 1 Tim. 4.14*).

1698 It is also declared that this anointing is to be administered to the sick, especially to those who are so dangerously ill that they seem near to death; hence it is also called the sacrament of the dying. If, however, the sick recover after receiving this anointing, they can again receive the help and assistance of this sacrament if they fall into another similar critical condition.

1639 On no account, then, should any attention be paid to those
1699 who, contradicting this plain and lucid doctrine of the apostle James, teach that this anointing is a human invention or a rite received from the Fathers, which has no mandate from God and no promise of grace; nor to those who assert that this anointing has already ceased, as if it referred only to the gift of healing in the primitive Church; nor to those who maintain that the rite and usage observed in the holy Roman Church in the administration of this sacrament is contrary to the doctrine of the apostle James and, therefore, must be changed; nor finally to those who say that this extreme unction can, without sin, be held in contempt by the faithful. For all this is very plainly contrary to the clear words of this great apostle. Indeed, in the administration of this anointing, as far as what constitutes the substance of this sacrament is concerned, the Roman Church, the mother and teacher of all other Churches, observes nothing different from what blessed James has prescribed. No contempt of so great a sacrament is then possible without a great sin and without offence to the Holy Spirit Himself.

1640 These are the points concerning the sacraments of penance
1700 and extreme unction which this holy, ecumenical Synod professes and teaches, and proposes to all the faithful to be

believed and held. Besides, it submits the following canons to be observed without violation; those who affirm the contrary it condemns and anathematises for ever.

Canons on the sacrament of penance

1641   1. If anyone says that in the Catholic Church penance is not
1701   truly and properly a sacrament, instituted by Christ our Lord
to reconcile the faithful with God Himself as they fall into sin after baptism, *anathema sit (cf. nn. 1615ff).*

1642   2. If anyone confuses the sacraments and says that baptism
1702   itself is the sacrament of penance, as though these two
sacraments were not distinct, and that, therefore, penance is not correctly called "the second plank after shipwreck", *anathema sit (cf. nn. 1618f, 1943).*

1643   3. If anyone says that these words of the Lord Saviour:
1703   "Receive the Holy Spirit. If you forgive the sins of any, they
are forgiven; if you retain the sins of any, they are retained" *(Jn 20.22f),* are not to be understood as referring to the power of forgiving and retaining sins in the sacrament of penance, as the Catholic Church has always understood them from the beginning; but if he distorts them, in contradiction with the institution of this sacrament, to make them refer to the authority of preaching the Gospel, *anathema sit (cf. n. 1617).*

1644   4. If anyone denies that for the full and perfect remission of
1704   sins three acts are required of the penitent, constituting as it
were the matter of the sacrament of penance, namely, contrition, confession and satisfaction, which are called the three parts of penance; or says that there are only two parts of penance, namely, the terrors of a conscience stricken by the realisation of sin, and the faith derived from the Gospel or from absolution, by which one believes that his sins are forgiven him through Christ, *anathema sit (cf. nn. 1620, 1621).*

1645   5. If anyone says that the contrition which is evoked by
1705   examination, consideration and hatred of sins, whereby one
recounts his years in the bitterness of his soul *(cf. Is. 38.15),* reflecting on the grievousness, the multitude and baseness of his sins, the loss of eternal happiness and the incurring of eternal damnation, along with the resolve of amendment, is not a true and beneficial sorrow and does not prepare for grace, but makes a man a hypocrite

and a greater sinner; or finally that this sorrow is forced and not free and voluntary, *anathema sit (cf. nn. 1622, 1614/6).*

1646 6. If anyone denies that sacramental confession was insti-
1706 tuted, and is necessary for salvation, by divine Law; or says
that the manner of confessing secretly to a priest alone, which the Catholic Church has always observed from the beginning and still observes, is at variance with the institution and command of Christ and is a human invention, *anathema sit (cf. nn. 1625ff).*

1647 7. If anyone says that for the remission of sins in the sacra-
1707 ment of penance it is not necessary by divine Law to confess
each and all mortal sins which one remembers after a due and diligent examination, also secret ones, and those against the last two precepts of the decalogue, as also the circumstances that change the species of a sin; but says that such a confession is useful only to instruct and console the penitent, and that in olden times it was observed only in order to impose a canonical penance; or says that those who endeavour to confess all sins want to leave nothing to the divine mercy to pardon; or finally that it is not allowed to confess venial sins, *anathema sit (cf. nn. 1625ff).*

1648 8. If anyone says that confession of all sins as it is observed in
1708 the Church is impossible and is a human tradition which
pious people must abolish; or that it is not binding on each and all of the faithful of Christ of either sex once a year in accordance with the Constitution of the great Lateran Council, and that for this reason the faithful of Christ are to be persuaded not to confess during Lent, *anathema sit.*

1649 9. If anyone says that the sacramental absolution of the
1709 priest is not a judicial act but a mere ministry of pronouncing
and declaring to him who cofesses that his sins are forgiven, provided only he believes himself absolved, even if the priest does not absolve seriously but in jest; or says that the confession of the penitent is not required in order that the priest be able to absolve him, *anathema sit (cf. nn. 1628, 1614/12).*

1650 10. If anyone says that priests who are in mortal sin do not
1710 have the power of binding and loosing, or that priests are not
the only ministers of absolution, but that to each and all of the faithful it was said: "Whatever you bind on earth shall be bound in

heaven, and whatever you loose on earth shall be loosed in heaven"
(*Mt. 18.18*), and "If you forgive the sins of any, they are forgiven; if
you retain the sins of any, they are retained" *(Jn 20.23)*, so that by
virtue of these words everyone could absolve from sins, from public
ones merely by correction, if the sinner complies, and from secret
ones by voluntary confession, *anathema sit (cf. n. 1627)*.

1651 11. If anyone says that bishops do not have the right to
1711 reserve cases to themselves, except such as pertain to external goverhment, and that, therefore, the reservation of cases
does not prevent a priest from truly absolving from such reserved
sins, *anathema sit*.

1652 12. If anyone says that the whole punishment is always remit-
1712 ted by God together with the guilt and that the satisfaction of penitents is nothing else but the faith by which they
realise that Christ has satisfied for them, *anathema sit (cf. n. 1630)*.

1653 13. If anyone says, concerning temporal punishments, that
1713 no satisfaction is made to God through the merits of Christ
by means of the punishments inflicted by Him and patiently
borne, or of those imposed by the priest, or finally of those voluntarily undertaken, as fasts, prayers, alms-giving or other works of piety;
and that, therefore, the best penance is merely a new life, *anathema
sit (cf. nn. 1631ff)*.

1654 14. If anyone says that the satisfactions by which penitents
1714 atone for their sins through Christ Jesus are not worship of
God but traditions of men which obscure th doctrine of
grace, the true worship of God and the benefit of Christ's death itself,
anathema sit (cf. n. 1633).

1655 15. If anyone says that the keys have been given to the
1715 Church only to loose and not also to bind and that, therefore,
the priests, when imposing penances on those who confess,
act contrary to the purpose of the keys, and to the institution of
Christ; and that it is a fiction that, after the eternal punishment has
been removed by virtue of the keys, there often remains a temporal
punishment to be expiated, *anathema sit (cf. n. 1633)*.

Canons concerning extreme unction

*Canon 1 teaches, against Luther, Calvin and Melanchton, that the
anointing of the sick is a true sacrament. Canon 2 teaches its spiritual effect.
The text of James is not to be intrepreted, as Calvin did, as referring merely*

to the charism of healing. Canon 4 affirms that the priest is the only minister of the sacrament, and rejects the interpretation given by the Reformers to the text of James, namely that 'presbyters' has a purely secular meaning, referring to seniority or social influence on the community.

1656   1. If anyone says that extreme unction is not truly and
1716   properly a sacrament instituted by Christ our Lord (*cf. Mt.*
    6.13) and promulgated by the blessed apostle James (*James 5.14*), but only a rite received from the Fathers or a human invention, *anathema sit* (*cf. nn. 1636, 1639*).

1657   2. If anyone says that the sacred anointing of the sick neither
1717   confers grace, nor remits sins, nor comforts the sick; but
    that it does no longer exist as if it consisted only in the grace of healing of olden days, *anathema sit* (*cf. nn. 1639, 1637*).

1658   3. If anyone says that the rite and usage of extreme unction
1718   which the holy Roman Church observes is contrary to the
    doctrine of the blessed apostle James and, therefore, must be changed; and that it can without sin be held in contempt by Christians, *anathema sit* (*cf. n. 1639*).

1659   4. If anyone says that the presbyters of the Church who, as
1719   blessed Jame exhorts, should be brought to anoint the sick
    are not priests ordained by a bishop but the senior members of each community, and that, for this reason, the proper minister of extreme unction is not only the priest, *anathema sit* (*cf. n. 1638*).

PIUS X

DECREE *LAMENTABILI* OF THE HOLY OFFICE (1907)

ARTICLES OF MODERNISM CONDEMNED

Though the practice of penance and reconciliation underwent profound changes in the Church, its substance as an authoritative action of the Church, expressed already in the biblical texts, always remained intact. But the way in which Modernists used biblical criticism and historical research, led them to unduly undermine the foundation of the doctrinal tenets on sacramental penance. Hence some of the Modernist articles condemned by Pius X refer to penance. As regards the anointing of the sick, the Modernists understood the text of James as alluding merely to a pious custom. The text affirms more, though obviously it does not imply a definition of sacrament which came much later in history. For this document, cf. n. 143i.

(Modernist errors about penance and anointing condemned)

[1660/46]   In the primitive Church the concept of a Christian
3446   sinner reconciled through the authority of the Church
    did not exist; only very slowly did the Church become

accustomed to such an idea. Furthermore, even after penance was acknowledged as an institution of the Church it was not called a sacrament, because it would have been taken for a shameful sacrament.

[1660/47]   The words of the Lord: "Receive the Holy Spirit. If you
3447   forgive the sins of any, they are forgiven; if you retain
                 the sins of any, they are retained" *(Jn 20.22f)*, refer in no way to the sacrament of penance, in spite of what the Fathers of Trent were pleased to affirm.

[1660/48]   In his epistle *(5.14f)* James does not intend to promul-
3448   gate a sacrament of Christ, but he recommends some
                 pious custom; if perhaps he sees in this custom a certain means of grace, he does not accept it in the rigorous sense in which it is understood by theologians who determined the notion and the number of sacraments.

BENEDICT XV

APOSTOLIC LETTER *SODALITATEM NOSTRAE DOMINAE* (1921)

Canon Law (1917) followed the old scholastic tradition which required that those receiving the anointing of the sick be "in danger of death on account of illness or old age" (canon 940). However, in a letter addressed to the sodality of 'Bona Mors', dedicated to the care of the dying, the Pope interpreted the law in a liberal sense. Shortly later Pius XI took the same attitude (cf. AAS 15 (1923) 105). The text of this letter is found in AAS 13 (1921) 345.

(The time for the anointing of the sick)

1661   The members join this sodality in order to exercise the
            apostolate of 'good health' according to the rules of the sodality. They should make every effort in order that those who are in their last crisis may not delay the reception of the viaticum and the extreme unction till they are about to lose their consciousness. On the contrary, according to the teaching and the precepts of the Church, they should be strengthened by these sacraments as soon as their condition worsens and one may prudently judge that there is danger of death.

PIUS XII

ENCYCLICAL LETTER *MYSTICI CORPORIS* (1943)

In keeping with its general theme, this encyclical views sin and reconcili- ation in their ecclesial context. The sinner is not separated from the Church, but he defiles Christ's Body; he must be restored to full life with the help of the Body. Text in AAS 35 (1943) 203. The same encyclical contains an exhortation to frequent devotional confession (ibid., 235).

1662 The fact that the Body of the Church bears the august name of Christ must not lead anyone to suppose that, also during this time of its earthly pilgrimage, its membership is restricted to those who are eminent in sanctity, or that it is composed only of those whom God has predestined to eternal beatitude. For it is in keeping with the infinite mercy of our Saviour that He does not here refuse a place in His mystical Body to those whom He formerly admitted to His table *(cf. Mt. 9.11; Mk 2.16; Lk. 15.2)*. Schism, heresy, or apostasy are such of their very nature that they sever a man from the Body of the Church; but not every sin, even the most grievous,is of such a kind. Nor does all life depart from those, who, though by sin they have lost charity and divine grace and are consequently no longer capable of a supernatural reward, nevertheless retain Christian faith and hope, and, illuminated by heavenly light, are moved by the inner promptings and stirrings of the Holy Spirit to conceive a salutary fear and divinely urged to prayer and repentance of their sin.

Let all men, therefore, abhor sin, which defiles the mystical members of the Redeemer; but should anyone have unhappily fallen, if he has not by his obstinacy rendered himself unworthy of the fellowship of the faithful, then let him be welcomed most lovingly, and let a practical charity see in him a frail member of Jesus Christ. For it is better, as St Augustine says, "to be healed within the organism of the Church than to be cut off from its body as an incurable member."[1] "So long as a member still adheres to the body its cure is not beyond all hope; but if it has been cut off it cannot be cured or made whole."[2]

THE SECOND VATICAN GENERAL COUNCIL

With regard to sacramental penance, the Council mostly makes its own the general pastoral tradition of the Church: priests must be aware of the importance of the sacrament; they must instruct the faithful, and be available for hearing confessions (CD 30; PO 5, 13). They too should frequently avail themselves of this sacrament (PO 18).

Two texts, however, open new perspectives: the very brief description of sacramental penance in the Constitution on the Church presents the

---

1. Cf. ST AUGUSTINE, *Epistola* 157, 3, 22.

2. Cf. ST AUGUSTINE, *Sermo* 137, 1.

sacrament in its ecclesiological context; the Constitution on the liturgy decrees that a new rite, more expressive of the meaning of the sacrament, must be prepared to overcome the dangers of routine and individualism inherent in the present practice.

The Constitution on the Church gives to the anointing of the sick a rich meaning in the life of the Church. It clearly repudiates the trend which connected this sacrament too exclusively with the time of death. While accepting the scholastic conception according to which the sacrament is the ultimate purification and the preparation for final glory, it connects it with the other tradition which included healing among its effects. Most of all, it integrates the sufferings of the sick into the mystery of Christ's saving passion and death; conformation to the mystery of Christ makes human sufferings fruitful for the entire people of God.

The change in outlook had been prepared by the Constitution on the liturgy where the term 'anointing of the sick' is used in preference to the traditional term 'extreme unction'. The Constitution states that the sacrament should be administered early, when illness becomes serious. It further requests that the ritual be revised; a continuous ceremony must be prepared, which will integrate the various rites for the sick in a new sequence: confession, anointing and viaticum, as against the traditional sequence of confession, viaticum and anointing.

CONSTITUTION SACROSANCTUM CONCILIUM (1963)

(The sacrament of penance)

1663   72. The rite and formulas for the sacrament of penance are to be revised so that they more clearly express both the nature and the effect of the sacrament.

(The anointing of the sick)

1664   73. "Extreme unction", which may also and more fittingly be called "anointing of the sick", is not a sacrament for those only who are at the point of death. Hence, as soon as one of the faithful begins to be in danger of death from sickness or old age, the fitting time for him to receive this sacrament has certainly already arrived.

1665   74. In addition to the separate rites for anointing of the sick and for viaticum, a continuous rite shall be prepared according to which the sick person is anointed after he has made his confession and before he receives viaticum.

1666   75. The number of anointings is to be adapted to the situation, and the prayers which belong to the rite of anointing are to be revised so as to correspond with the varying conditions of the sick who receive the sacrament.

DOGMATIC CONSTITUTION *LUMEN GENTIUM* (1964)

(On penance and the anointing of the sick)

1667   11. Those who approach the sacrament of penance obtain pardon from the mercy of God for their offences committed against Him. They are, at the same time, reconciled with the Church whom they have wounded by their sin, and who, by her charity, her example and her prayer, collaborates in their conversion. Through the sacred anointing of the sick and the prayer of her priests, the entire Church commends the sick to the suffering and glorified Lord, imploring for them relief and salvation (*cf. James 5.14-16*). She exhorts them, moreover, to associate themselves freely with the passion and death of Christ (*cf. Rom. 8.17; Col. 1.24; 2 Tim. 2.11f; 1 Pet. 4.13*) for the welfare of the people of God.

PAUL VI

APOSTOLIC CONSTITUTION *SACRAM UNCTIONEM INFIRMORUM*
(30 November 1972)

By this Apostolic Constitution, Pope Paul VI promulgates the new rite for the sacrament of the anointing of the sick, prepared by the S. Congregation for Divine Worship in 1971. The rite is called "Rite for Anointing a Sick Person at the Beginning of the Danger of Death". In promulgating it, the Pope uses his apostolic authority, as the sacramental rite itself has been modified "in such a way that, in view of the words of St James, the effects of the sacrament might be better expressed". The Pope quotes the doctrine of the Second Vatican Council with regard to the dangerous illness required for receiving the sacrament (cf. n. 1664); he adds that the sacrament "can be repeated if the sick person, having once received the anointing, recovers and then again falls sick, or if, in the course of the same illness, the danger becomes more acute". The text is found in AAS 65 (1973) 5ff.

(The rite of the anointing of the sick)

1668   Since this revision in certain points touches upon the sacramental rite itself, by our apostolic authority we lay down that the following is to be observed for the future in the Latin Rite:

The sacrament of the anointing of the sick is administered to those who are dangerously ill, by anointing them on the forehead and hands with properly blessed olive oil, or, if opportune, with another vegetable oil, and saying once only the following words: *Per istam sanctam unctionem et suam piissimam misericordiam adiuvet te Dominus gratia Spiritus Sancti, ut a peccatis liberatum te salvet atque propitius allevet* (Through this holy anointing may the Lord in

His love and mercy help you with the grace of the Holy Spirit. Amen.
May the Lord who frees you from sin save you and raise you up.
Amen).

THE NEW *ORDO PAENITENTIAE*
(2 December 1973)

The Decree Reconciliationem inter Deum et homines *of the S. Congregation for Divine Worship, dated December 2, 1973, promulgates with the
approval of Pope Paul VI the new order for the administration of the
sacrament of penance. The Second Vatican Council had requested that the
rite for this sacrament be revised (cf. n. 1663). The old ritual was found too
jejune: no place was given in it to the word of God, nor did it express the
ecclesial dimension of sin and reconciliation. The deficiencies often led to a
routine performance of the rite. The text of the Decree of promulgation of
the new rite is found in* AAS 66 (1974) 172-173

The new Ordo Paenitentiae, *published shortly after, begins with an
extensive doctrinal exposition of the sacrament of penance. It then outlines
the various forms in which the sacrament can be celebrated: reconciliation
of individual penitents; of several penitents with individual confession and
absolution. Non-sacramental penitential services are also foreseen. Norms
are given for the adaptation of the new rites to varying circumstances; the
rites are marked by considerable flexibility. Insistence is laid on the use of
the Bible for the preparation of the penitent and on a greater personal
commitment on the part of both priest and penitent.*

*The first part of the Document places the sacrament of reconciliation in
the context of God's saving action through Jesus Christ in the Church.
Thus its doctrinal presentation becomes more biblical, spiritual and pastoral than has been customary in former documents. The nature of the
sacrament is described as reconciliation with God (in a Trinitarian perspective), as reconciliation among men, and as the expression of a common
striving for peace and justice in the world. Thus the ecclesial dimension of
the sacrament is made to stand out clearly.*

*In the same document the norms for reconciliation of several penitents
without individual confession are repeated in a condensed form. These
norms had been given earlier in the* Normae Pastorales *of June 16, 1972; cf.
AAS 64 (1972) 510-514. The obligation of confessing mortal sins individually,
affirmed by the Council of Trent, is maintained; it cannot be replaced by
general confession and absolution. Where grievous sins are absolved in a
general absolution, they must be confessed individually afterwards. These
norms, repeated in both documents, while meeting urgent pastoral needs,
reflect the anxiety lest the practice of individual confession be undermined.*

(Reconciliation with God and with the Church)

1669   5. Since sin is an offence against God and breaks our friendship with Him, penance "has for its ultimate objective that we
should love God and commit ourselves wholly to him."[1] When the

---

1. P AUL VI, Apostolic Constitution *Paenitemini* (17 February 1966); *AAS* 58 (1966)
179.

sinner, therefore, by God's mercy takes the road of penance, he returns to the Father who "first loved us" *(1 Jn 4.19),* to Christ who gave Himself up for us *(cf. Gal. 2.20; Eph. 5.25),* and to the Holy Spirit who is poured out on us abundantly *(cf. Tit. 3.6).*

But, "because of a secret and loving mystery of dispensation, men are joined together by a supernatural bond in such wise that the sin of one injures the others, and the holiness of one benefits the others."[1] In the same way, penance always brings with it reconciliation with the brothers whom sin likewise injures.

Further, men often act together in perpetrating injustice. In the same way they help one another when doing penance so that, freed from sin by the grace of Christ, they might, with all men of good will, make peace and achieve justice in the world.

(Norms for general absolution)

1670 31. Particular, occasional circumstances may render it lawful and even necessary to give general absolution to a number of penitents without their previous individual confession.

In addition to cases involving danger of death, it is lawful to give sacramental absolution to several faithful at the same time, after they have made only a generic confession but have been suitably called to repentance, if there is grave need, namely when, in view of the number of penitents, sufficient confessors are not available to hear individual confessions within a suitable period of time so that the penitents would, through no fault of their own, have to go without sacramental grace or holy communion for a long time. This may happen especially in mission territories but in other places as well and also in groups of persons when the need is established.

General absolution is not lawful, when confessors are available, for the sole reason of the large number of penitents, as may be on the occasion of some major feast or pilgrimage.

32. The judgment about the presence of the above conditions and the decision concerning the lawfulness of giving general sacramental absolution are reserved to the bishop of the diocese who is to consult with the other members of the episcopal conference.

Over and above the cases determined by the diocesan bishop, if any other serious need arises for giving sacramental absolution to several persons together, the priest must have recourse to the local Ordinary beforehand, when this is possible, if he is to give absolution

---

1. PAUL VI, Apostolic Constitution *Indulgentiarum Doctrina* (1 January 1967); *AAS* 59 (1967) 9.

lawfully. Otherwise he should inform the Ordinary as soon as possible of the need and of the absolution which he gave.

(N. 33 stresses the need of proper disposition on the part of the penitents in case of general absolution. N. 34 demands that those who have received absolution from a grave sin in general absolution, confess this sin within one year; besides, the obligation to confess all grave sins at least once a year remains in force).

(The formula of absolution)

1671 46. The priest, with his hands extended over the penitent's head (or at least with his right hand extended), says : *Deus, Pater misericordiarum, qui per mortem et resurrectionem Filii sui mundum sibi reconciliavit et Spiritum Sanctum effudit in remissionem peccatorum, per ministerium Ecclesiae indulgentiam tibi tribuat et pacem. Et ego te absolvo a peccatis tuis in nomine Patris, et Filii, + et Spiritus Sancti.* (God, the Father of mercy, reconciled the world to Himself through the death and resurrection of His Son and poured out the Holy Spirit for the forgiveness of sins. May He grant you pardon and peace through the ministry of the Church. And I absolve you from your sins in the name of the Father, and of the Son, + and of the Holy Spirit).

JOHN PAUL II

ENCYCLICAL LETTER *REDEMPTOR HOMINIS* (1979)

In the concluding section of the encyclical the Pope speaks about the Church's role in realising the redemptive mission of Jesus Christ. In particular, a fuller realisation of the central place of the Eucharist is needed and a deeper understanding of sacramental penance. He develops the reasons why individual confession remains important in the Christian life. The text is found in AAS 71 (1979) 314-315.

(The significance of individual confession)

1672 20. In the last years much has been done to highlight in the Church's practice—in conformity with the most ancient tradition of the Church—the community aspect of penance and especially of the sacrament of penance itself. Such efforts are certainly very useful and are bound to contribute much to the enrichment of the penitential practice in the Church today. However, we cannot forget that conversion is a particularly profound inward act in which the individual cannot be replaced by others, where the community cannot become a substitute in place of the single members. Although participation by the fraternal community of the faithful in a common penitential celebration is a great help for the act of personal conversion, nevertheless, in the final analysis, it is necessary that in this act there should be a pronouncement of the individual himself from the depth of his conscience with his full sense of guilt and of trust in God, placing himself like the Psalmist before Him to confess : "Against thee, thee only have I sinned" *(Ps. 51 (50) 4)*. Thus, in faithfully observing the century-old practice of the Sacrament of Penance— i.e., the practice of individual confession with a personal act of sorrow and the intention to amend and make satisfaction—the Church defends the human soul's individual right to a more personal encounter of each man with the crucified forgiving Christ, with Christ who says through the minister of the Sacrament of Reconciliation : "Your sins are forgiven" *(Mk 2.5)*, "go, and do not sin again" *(Jn 8.11)*. As is evident, this is also a right on Christ's part with regard to every human being redeemed by Him : His right to meet each one of us in that key moment in the soul's life, in the moment of conversion and forgiveness. By guarding the Sacrament of Penance, the Church expressly affirms her faith in the mystery of the Redemption as a living and life-giving reality that fits in with man's inward truth, with human guilt and also with the desires of the human conscience.

APPENDIX

INDULGENCES

Not all the temporal punishment for sins is forgiven through sacramental absolution. The penances imposed on the penitent are meant to reduce this punishment. In the Middle Ages penances were protracted and burdensome. They could be reduced or remitted by the ecclesiastical authority on certain conditions ; good works, prayers, and contributions to pious causes played an important role in this discipline. This remission of penances, and with them of the temporal punishment of sins, either partially or totally, is called indulgences. These are to be clearly distinguished from the forgiveness of the sins themselves which must first be obtained in the sacrament of penance. The foundation of the Church's power to forgive temporal punishment is the treasury of the merits of Jesus Christ Himself, and with Him of all the Saints, whose life is pleasing to God.

Indulgences have, in the course of history, given rise to many problems. During the Middle Ages there was, on the part of those who grantd them, the danger of misusing their power for the sake of material gains; on the part of those who made use of them, there was the danger of a mechanical, superstitious conception of good works and supernatural merits. In fact, abuses in the practice of indulgences and misunderstandings as regards their meaning were among the primary causes that brought about the Reformation.

At a deeper level, indulgences raise important theological problems. What does the Church's power to grant the remission of temporal punishment consist in ? What is meant by the "treasury" of the Church which can be applied to all the faithful, living and dead ? This theology developed only gradually, and found its mature expression in the Apostolic Constitution of Pope Paul VI (1967).

Thus, the ecclesiastical documents concerned with indulgences treat mainly two aspects : the practical problems of abuses to be remedied ; the progressive theological understanding of indulgences.

*   *   *

The main doctrinal points covered by these documents are the following :

Indulgences are granted from the "treasury" of the merits of Christ and the Saints : 1681, 1683, 1685/17, 1687, 1688.

The Church has the authority to grant the faithful the remission of temporal punishments : 35, 1682, 1684/26.27, 1685/17-19, 1686, 1690/1-5.

Indulgences may be applied to the dead : 1685/22, 1689, 1690/3.

The use of indulgences is salutary : 35, 1685/20-22, 1686.

Abuses must be avoided: 1686.

CLEMENT VI

JUBILEE BULL *UNIGENITUS DEI FILIUS* (1343)

The Bull of Clement VI is the most important document in the early history of indulgences. In 1300 Boniface VIII had proclaimed a Jubilee year which was to be celebrated every hundred years, with a plenary indulgence for all who made a pilgrimage to Rome and fulfilled certain conditions. In 1343 Clement VI decided that the Jubilee should be held every fiftieth year, beginning with 1350. He took this occassion to set out the doctrinal foundation of indulgences as it had been developed by scholastic theology. The doctrine comprises three points : Christ's merits are superabundant ; to the treasure of Christ's merits, the merits of the Saints are added ; this treasury is entrusted to the Church. A more complete understanding of this 'treasury' will only be worked out by later theology.

1681 The only-begotten Son of God..."whom God made our Wis-
1025 dom, our righteousness, and sanctification and redemption"
(*1 Cor. 1.30*), "entered once for all into the Holy place, taking not the blood of goats and calves but His own blood, thus securing an eternal redemption" (*Heb. 9.12*). For "it is not with perishable things such as silver or gold, but with His own precious blood that He who is the Lamb without blemish or spot redeemed us" (*1 Pet. 1.18f*). Immolated on the altar of the cross though He was innocent, He did not merely shed a drop of His blood—although this would have sufficed for the redemption of the whole human race because of the union with the Word—but a copious flood, like a stream, so that "from the sole of the foot even to the head there was no soundness in Him" (*cf. Is. 1.6*). What a great treasure, then, has the good Father acquired for the Church militant, if the merciful shedding of blood is not to be empty, meaningless and superfluous. He wanted to lay up for His sons, so that there might be "an unfailing treasure for men"; those who draw from it "obtain friendship with God" (*cf. Wis. 7.14*).

1682 This treasure...(Christ) has committed to the care of St Peter,
1026 who holds the keys of heaven, and to his successors, His own
vicars on earth, who are to distribute it to the faithful for their salvation. And they are to apply it with compassion, for pious and good reasons, in order that it may benefit those who are truly contrite and who have confessed, at times for the complete remission of the temporal punishment due to sin, at times for the partial remission, either by general or particular disposition, as before God they judge more expedient.

1683 To this mass of treasure the merits of the Blessed Mother of
1027 God and of all the elect, from the first just man to the last, also

contribute, as we know ; nor is it at all to be feared that it could be exhausted or diminished, first on account of the infinite merits of Christ, as already mentioned, and further because the more men are drawn to righteousness by having this treasure applied to them, so much the more does the store of those merits increase.

MARTIN V

BULL *INTER CUNCTAS* (1418)

On this document, see n. 1304i.

(Questions proposed to the followers of Wyclif and Hus)

1684/26 Whether he believes that for a pious and just cause the
1266 Pope can grant indulgences for the remission of sins to all
Christians who are truly contrite and have confessed,
especially to the pilgrims to the holy places and those who offer them
a helping hand.

1684/27 Whether he believes that through this grant those who
1267 visit the churches and those who offer them a
helping hand can obtain such indulgences.

LEO X

BULL *EXSURGE DOMINE* (1520)

The abuses in granting and popularising indulgences had already led to the attacks made against the Church by Wyclif and Hus (cf. n. 1684). The indulgence offered by Pope Julian II to all those who contributed in the sumptuous restoration of the Basilica of St Peter (1510), and its popular promulgation through Tetzel in Germany became the occassion for Luther's revolt againt the Church. The condemnation of Luther by Leo X contains six propositions concerning indulgences.

(Errors of Luther condemned)

[1685/17] The treasures of the Church from which the Pope gives
1467 indulgences are not the merits of Christ and of the
Saints.

[1685/18] Indulgences are a pious fraud on the faithful dispensing
1468 them from doing good works; they are among those
things that are allowed, not among those that are
expedient.

[1685/19] Indulgences, for those who really gain them, do not
1469 have the value of remitting the punishment incurred
before the divine justice by actual sins.

[**1685/20**] They are led astray who believe that indulgences are
1470   salutary and spiritually fruitful.

[**1685/21**] Indulgences are necessary only for public crimes ; they
1471   are rightly granted only to the hardened and impatient.

[**1685/22**] There are six kinds of people for whom indulgences are
1472   neither necessary nor useful, viz., the dead or the dying,
    the infirm, those who are legitimately prevented, those
who have committed no crimes, those who have committed crimes
but not public ones, those who perform better works.

THE GENERAL COUNCIL OF TRENT
TWENTY-FIFTH SESSION
DECREE ON INDULGENCES (1563)

*The Council of Trent first took up the pending question of indulgences at
the disciplinary level. In its 21st Session (1562) it decided that no fees should
be collected on granting indulgences. In this way one of the rampant
malpractices was stopped. However, deep doctrinal problems had been
raised by the controversy with the Reformers. These questions were postponed to the end of the Council which had to be precipitated, partly on
account of the illness of Pope Pius IV. Hence only a short decree was issued
in the 25th Session (1563). In this Decree the deeper theological issues about
the meaning of temporal punishment, the authority of the Church to remit
them, and the concept of the treasury of the Church were bypassed ; only
the basic truths about indulgences were re-stated : the Church's power to
grant them and the need of discernment in the use of this power.*

1686 Since the power of granting indulgences was conferred on
1835   the Church by Christ, and as she made use of this power
    divinely given to her *(cf. Mt. 16.19 ; 18.18)* even in the early
times, the holy Council teaches and commands that the use of indulgences, most salutary to the Christian people and approved by the
authority of the holy Councils, is to be retained in the Church ; and it
condemns with anathema those who assert that they are useless or
who deny that the Church has the power to grant them.

In granting them, however, it desires that moderation be observed
in accordance with the ancient custom approved in the Church, lest
too much relaxation should weaken the ecclesiastical discipline....

*(Abuses must be suppressed and all evil traffic in indulgences, which is a
source of scandal, must be abolished. The people must get proper instruction so that superstition, ignorance and irreverence be avoided. Synods
should study the problems that arise and report their findings to the Holy
See).*

PAUL VI

APOSTOLIC CONSTITUTION *INDULGENTIARUM DOCTRINA*
(1967)

During the Second Vatican Council the Bishops' Conferences were asked to submit their opinion on a reform of the system of indulgences. Though the question referred only to the canonical and pastoral aspects of indulgences, the doctrinal problems, shelved ever since the Council of Trent, could not be ignored. The Apostolic Constitution of Jan. 1, 1967, provides an answer to these problems.

Most important in this document is the explanation of the 'treasury' of the Church, which is presented not in terms of a quantitative storing up of treasures, but in a personalistic way as being identical with Jesus Christ Himself. Significant is, further, the new definition of indulgences and the way in which the role of the Church in granting them is conceived. New norms are then laid down for gaining plenary and partial indulgences. The text is found in AAS 59 (1967) 5-24.

1687 Christ, who comitted no sin, suffered for us *(cf. 1 Pet. 2.21f)*; He was wounded for our transgressions, bruised for our iniquities, and with His stripes we are healed *(cf. Is. 53.4f)*.

Following in Christ's footsteps, the faithful have always endeavoured to help one another on their pilgrimage to the heavenly Father by prayer, the performance of good works and by penitential expiation. The more fervently they were inspired by charity, the more closely they followed the suffering Christ carrying each one his own cross in expiation of their sins and of the sins of others, convinced that they could assist their brothers to obtain salvation from God the Father of mercy. This is the ancient dogma of the communion of Saints, according to which the life of each of the sons of God is joined, in Christ and through Christ, to the lives of all his brother Christians by a wonderful link in the supernatural oneness of the mystical Body of Christ, in one mystical person as it were.

1688 It is thus that one should understand the term 'treasury of the Church'. It is not to be regarded as something akin to a hoard of material wealth accumulated over the centuries. Rather it is the infinite and inexhaustible value which the expiation and merits of Christ have in the sight of God, offered to the end that the whole of humanity might be freed from sin and arrive at fellowship with the Father. It is Christ the Redeemer Himself in whom the satisfaction and merits of His redemption still exist and retain their efficacy. Further, this treasury also includes the truly immense value, immeasurable and constantly renewed, which the prayers and good works of the Blessed Virgin Mary and all the Saints possess in the sight of God; they followed in the footsteps of Christ the Lord with the help of His grace, sanctified themselves and completed the work which the Father had given them to do, so that, effecting their own salvation, they also contributed to the salvation of their brothers in the unity of the mystical Body.

1689 "For all who belong to Christ and have His Spirit are brought together into one Church and cleave together in Him *(cf. Eph. 4.16)*. Therefore the union of the wayfarers with the brethren who have gone to sleep in the peace of Christ is in no way interrupted; on the contrary, according to the perennial faith of the Church it is strengthened through the exchange of spiritual goods. For, because those in heaven are more closely united with Christ, they establish the whole Church more firmly in holiness... and in many ways contribute to its further upbuilding *(cf. 1 Cor. 12.12-27)*. This is because, from the moment they have been received into the heavenly home and enjoy the presence of the Lord *(cf. 2 Cor. 5.8),* through Him and with Him and in Him they unceasingly intercede with the Father for us, laying before Him the merits which, through Christ Jesus, the one Mediator between God and men *(cf. 1 Tim. 2.5)*, they have won on earth while they were serving God in all things and completing in their flesh what is lacking in the sufferings of Christ on behalf of His Body, the Church *(cf. Col. 1.24)*. In this way, their brotherly interest is of great help for our weakness" *(LG 49)*.

Thus there is indeed a perennial bond of charity and an abundant exchange of all goods among the faithful, whether they have already taken possession of the heavenly home, or expiate their failings in purgatory, or are still on their pilgrimage on earth ; thereby all the sins of the entire mystical Body are expiated and the divine justice is placated ; and the divine mercy is moved to forgiveness so that the contrite sinners be brought sooner to the full fruition of the goods of God's family.

(Norms for indulgences)

1690/1 An indulgence is the remission in the sight of God of the temporal punishment due to sins which have already been blotted out as far as guilt is concerned ; the Christian believer who is properly disposed gains it on certain conditions with the help of the Church which, as the minister of redemption, authoritatively dispenses and applies the treasury of the satisfactions of Christ and the Saints.

1690/2 An indulgence is either plenary or partial, according to whether it involves total or partial remission of the temporal punishment due to sins.

1690/3 Indulgences, either plenary or partial, can always be applied to the dead by way of intercession (*suffragium*).

1690/4 Henceforth a partial indulgence will be described merely by the term 'partial indulgence', with no additional determination of days or years.

1690/5 The Christian faithful who is contrite at least interiorly and fulfils a work to which a partial indulgence is attached, obtains through the help of the Church a remission of temporal punishment equal to that which he has already obtained through his own action.

CHAPTER XVII

ORDER

Christ, the only mediator between God and men (cf. 1 Tim. 2.5), possesses a unique and absolute priesthood which, while fulfilling the Old Testament priesthood, surpassed it and abolished it (cf. Heb.). He exercised His priesthood as Prophet by revealing the Father and as Shepherd by gathering God's scattered people; He crowned it in His Paschal Mystery by the offering of the sacrifice of the Cross. He communicated His priesthood to the Church in order that through her it might be present in the world to men of all ages; the Church is established by Him as a "kingdom of priests" (1 Pet. 2.9). Consecrated and sent on a mission through baptism and confirmation, every Christian is made to share in Christ's priestood; as a member of the priestly people he shares in the Church's mission of representing Christ's unique mediatory function. The Church, however, as the Body of Christ, is a living organism with various functions exercised by various members. Christ entrusted a special function to the apostles whom He chose to be His authentic witnesses, the dispensers of His mysteries and the shepherds of His flock. They passed on their ministry to their successors, who in turn shared it with others in various degrees through the sacrament of Order. Through the ministerial priesthood Christ's function as Head is represented in the hierarchical communion which is the Church. The common priesthood of the Christians and the ministerial priesthood entrusted to the hierarchy are two inseparable and essentially related elements of her mystery.

For many centuries the Church lived in the quiet possession of this doctrine. The only serious crisis it encountered is that of the Reformation. Reacting excessively against a one-sided stress on the ministerial priesthood which did not do full justice to the common priesthood of all, the Reformers were led to deny the existence of a sacrament of Order instituted by Christ, and considered the ministry as a function delegated by the Christian community to some of its members. The denial of a sacramental ministry deprived the Church of one of the constitutive elements willed for her by Christ. This is why the Church upheld strongly against the Reformers the existence of the sacrament of Order. Due to the historical circumstances of the times, she did so with special stress on the ministerial power to offer the eucharistic sacrifice and to remit sins. This emphasis on the cultic aspect of the ministry led, in post-Tridentine times, to a certain empoverishment of its theology. Recent times, however, have been marked by a return to the biblical and patristic sources of the ministerial priesthood; the ministry is once again understood in its full dimension, as a service, at once prophetic, sanctifying and pastoral, to the communtiy of the faithful. At the same time, the essential relatedness between the common priesthood and the ministerial priesthood in the mystery of the Church is once again brought to the fore. The Second Vatican Council has made this rich and well poised doctrine its own; by clearly declaring that the episcopate confers the fulness of the ministerial priesthood, it has further high-lighted the three sacramental degrees of the sacrament of Order.

* * *

The main points of doctrine on the sacrament of Order fall under the following headings:

Order is a true sacrament: 28, 32, 1305, 1311, 1709, 1714, 1716.
It is instituted by Christ: 32, 1305, 1311, 1707, 1716, 1731, 1749.
It is conferred through the imposition of hands and the key-phrases of the ordination preface: 1705, 1722-1726, 1737, (1744).
The minister of the sacrament of Order is the bishop: 1704, 1720, 1730.
The sacrament of Order confers the Holy Spirit: 1717.
It imprints a sacramental character which conforms to Christ the Priest: 32, 1308, 1319, 1710, 1717, 1733, 1750.
The ordained minister can never become a layman again: 1710.
The sacrament also confers grace for the exercise of the ministry: 1709, 1733.
Ordination is not subject to civil authority: 1712, 1720.
Bishops are superior to priests: 1711, 1719, 1720.
The episcopate confers the fulness of the ministerial priesthood: 1739.
The presbyterate is required to preside over the Eucharist and to remit sins: 21, 39/17, 1546, 1556, 1627, 1650, 1703, 1707, 1714, 1729/1, 1734, 1738, 1740.
The priesthood has a threefold function, prophetic, sanctifying and pastoral: 1740.

Only men can be ordained to the priestly ministry: 1752.

The law of priestly celibacy in the Latin Church: 1743, 1753.

The diaconate confers a ministry of service: 1741, 1741a, (1742), (1748).

The ministerial priesthood differs in essence from the common priesthood: 1710, 1732, 1734, 1735, 1738, 1746, 1751, 1754.

Some ministries can be conferred on lay people by 'installation': 1747, 1751, 1754.

These may not obscure the distinct role of ordained priests: 1754.

CEMENT I

LETTER TO THE CORINTHIANS (c. 96)

Some seditious members of the Christian community of Corinth had unjustly taken upon themselves to depose several "episkopoi" from their office. The report had reached Rome and Pope Clement intervenes to restore order.

(The Church's hierarchy)

1701 40. Exploring the depths of the divine knowledge, we must
101 methodically carry out all that the Lord has commanded
us to perform at stated times: namely, He has enjoined the offerings and the services to be performed, not at random or without order, but at fixed times and seasons. He Himself, by His sovereign will, has determined where and by whom He wants them to be performed. Then, everything being religiously accomplished with His approval, will be acceptable to His will.... To the high priest special functions have been attributed; to the priest a special place has been assigned, and special services fall to the levite. The layman is bound by the precepts laid down for the laity.

42. The apostles received the Gospel for us from the Lord Jesus Christ; Jesus Christ was God's ambassador. Thus Christ (is sent) from God and the apostles from Christ; both these dispositions originated in an orderly way from God's will. Having thus received their mandate and fully convinced by the resurrection of (our) Lord Jesus Christ, and committed to the Word of God, they went forth with the full assurance of the Holy Spirit, announcing the good news that the Kingdom of God was close at hand. Preaching from country to country and from city to city, they established some of their first followers as *"episkopoi"* and *"diakonoi"* of the future believers, after having tested them by the Spirit.

44. Our apostles were also given to know by Jesus Christ our Lord that the name (office) *"episkopos"* would give rise to rivalries. This is why, endowed as they were with a perfect knowledge, they established the men mentioned above and for the future laid down the rule that, after their death, other approved men should succeed them in their office. Therefore, those who are established by them or later by other eminent men with the consent of the whole Church, and have served Christ's flock faultlessly, humbly...we judge it an injustice to deprive them of their office.... For it will be no small sin if we eject from the episcopacy those who have offered the gifts (sacrifice) piously and without reproach.

GREGORY I

LETTER TO THE BISHOPS OF GEORGIA (c. 601)

(Orders of heretics)

1702 Without any doubt let your Holiness receive them (the con-
478   verts from Nestorianism) into your assembly, preserving
their own Orders, so that...you will snatch them away from
the mouth of the ancient enemy, while by your gentleness you do not
raise any opposition or difficulty as regards their own Orders.

INNOCENT III

PROFESSION OF FAITH PRESCRIBED TO THE WALDENSIANS
(1208)

On this profession of faith, cf. n. 1301i and n. 1504.

(Priestly ordination is necessary to celebrate Mass)

1703 ...Hence we firmly believe and confess that nobody, however
794   honest, religious, holy and prudent he may be, either can or
should consecrate the Eucharist and perform the Sacrifice of
the altar, if he is not a priest regularly ordained by a bishop, visible
and tangible. According to our faith, three things are necessary for
this office, namely: a definte person, i.e., a priest who, as we have said
above, has been properly constituted in that office by a bishop; those
solemn words which have been expressed in the canon by the holy
Fathers; the faithful intention of the one who pronounces them. And,
therefore, we firmly believe and confess that anyone who believes
and contends that he can perform the Sacrifice of the Eucharist
without having first been ordained by a bishop as mentioned above,
is a heretic.

BONIFACE IX

BULL *SACRAE RELIGIONIS* (1400)

The Bull Sacrae Religionis *concedes to the Abbot of St Osith in Essex,
who was not a bishop, and to his successors, the privilege of conferring
minor and major Orders, including the priesthood, on the members of their
community. This privilege was revoked three years later by the Bull* Apostolicae Sedis *of the same Pope (1403) (cf. DS 1146). The reason for the
revocation was not doctrinal; it was meant, at the instance of the bishop of
London himself, to safeguard the jurisdiction of the local bishop. By the Bull*
Gerentes ad vos *(1427), Pope Martin V granted, for a period of five years, a
similar privilege to the Abbot of the Cistercian Monastery of Altzelle in*

Saxony; it included the permission to confer on his monks "all, even the sacred Orders" (cf. DS 1290). Pope Innocent VIII's Bull (Exposcit tuae devotionis) *(1489) granted to the Cistercian Abbots of the Monastery of Citeaux (France) and its four main sub-foundations, and to their successors, the privilege of conferring the Subdiaconate and the Diaconate on their own monks (cf. DS 1435). This privilege has been used by the Cistercians till the end of the 18th century.*

The authenticity of these three documents cannot reasonably be questioned. In view of the definition of Trent (cf. nn. 1711, 1720) regarding the bishop as minister of the sacrament of Order, they can be understood either as "untying" a radical power conferred by priestly ordination which needs to be untied for its valid exercise, or as an exceptional power granted to priests as extraordinary ministers of the sacrament, in virtue of the Pope's own "eminent power" (potestas excellentiae) *over the sacramental rites and their ministers.*

(Extraordinary minister of ordination)

1704 ... In compliance with the request made by the abbot and
1145 community (of the Monastery of St Osith in the diocese
of London), we concede to the same abbot, and to his successors in perpetuity as abbots of the same Monastery, the power to confer freely and licitly on each and all professed Canons of the same Monastery, now and in future, all the minor orders as well as the orders of the subdiaconate, diaconate and presbyterate at the time fixed by law; and we decree that the aforesaid Canons who have thus been promoted by the afore-mentioned abbots may freely and licitly exercise their ministry in the Orders thus received, no apostolic Constitution whatsoever withstanding....

THE GENERAL COUNCIL OF FLORENCE
DECREE FOR THE ARMENIANS (1439)

For the doctrinal value of this document, cf. n. 1305i. As regards the matter and form of the sacrament of Order, the Decree follows the teaching of St Thomas which departs from the earlier persuasion expressed for instance in the Ancient Statutes of the Church *(DS 326-328) or by Pope Gregory IX (DS 826). St Thomas' teaching on this point has later been almost universally abandoned, even before Pope Pius XII promulgated the Apostolic Constitution* Sacramentum Ordinis *on the matter and form of Order (cf. n. 1737).*

1705 The sixth sacrament is that of Order. Its matter is that by the
1326 handing over *(traditio)* of which the Order is conferred: thus
the presbyterate is conferred by handing over *(porrectio)* the chalice with wine and the paten with the bread; the diaconate by giving the book of the gospels; the subdiaconate by handing over the

empty chalice covered with an empty paten; and similary the other orders by assigning the things pertaining to their office. The form of the presbyterate is this: "Receive the power of offering the Sacrifice in the Church for the living and the dead, in the name of the Father and of the Son and of the Holy Spirit." And similarly for the forms of the other Orders, as is contained in detail in the Roman Pontifical. The ordinary minister of this sacrament is the bishop. The effect is an increase of grace so that one may be a suitable minister of Christ.

THE GENERAL COUNCIL OF TRENT
TWENTY-THIRD SESSION
DOCTRINE ON THE SACRAMENT OF ORDER (1563)

According to the doctrine of the Reformers, there exists in the Church no ministerial power received through the sacrament of Order. The unicity of the priesthood of Christ, the only Mediator, and of His redemptive act leaves room only for the universal priesthood of all Christians. To preside over the Christian communities, ministers do not require any special sacramental power. This doctrine is closely linked with the basic tenet of the Reformation, according to which justification by faith, being a personal commitment to God in Christ, allows no human mediation. Consequently, the Reformers considered the ministry as a power delegated by the community and denied its sacramental character. Faith was not communicated by a visible teaching body; grace was not conferred through outward signs entrusted to a special sacramental ministry; the Church was not governed by an authority instituted by Christ. In particular, the denial of the sacrificial value of the Eucharist made the ministerial power of Order superfluous.

The Council had rejected the foundation of the Reformers' doctrine in its Decree on Justification (cf. nn. 1924ff). In subsequent sessions, it reaffirmed against them the Church's doctrine of the sacraments. Thus it was led to reassert the existence in the Church of a ministerial priesthood based on the sacrament of Order. The XXIIIrd session devoted to this sacrament is that which together with the session on justification required the most thorough preparatory work.

1706 This is the true and Catholic doctrine on the sacrament
1763 of Order. It is decreed and published by the holy Tridentine Council in its seventh session (under Pius IV), to condemn the errors of our time.

Chapter I: The institution of the priesthood of the new law

1707 Sacrifice and priesthood are by the ordinance of God so
1764 united that both have existed under every law. Since, therefore, in the New Testament the Catholic Church has

received from the institution of Christ the holy, visible sacrifice of the Eucharist, it must also be acknowledged that there exists in the Church a new, visible and external priesthood (*cf. n. 1714*) into which the old one was changed (*cf. Heb. 7.12ff*). Moreover, the Sacred Scriptures make it clear and the Tradition of the Catholic Church has always taught that this priesthood was instituted by the same Lord our Saviour (*cf. n. 1716*), and that the power of consecrating, offering and administering His body and blood, and likewise of remitting and retaining sins, was given to the apostles and to their successors in the priesthod (*cf. n. 1714*).

Chapter II: The seven orders

1708 But since the ministry of so holy a priesthood is something
1765 divine, in order that it might be exercised in a more worthy
manner and with greater veneration, it was fitting that in the perfectly ordered disposition of the Church there should be several distinct Orders of ministers (*cf. Mt. 16.19; Lk. 22.19; 20.22f*), serving in the priesthood by virtue of their office, and that they be so distributed that those already having the clerical tonsure should ascend through the minor to the major Orders (*cf. n. 1715*). For the Sacred Scriptures mention unmistakably not only the priests but also the deacons (*Acts 6.5; 1 Tim. 3.8ff; Phil. 1.1*), and teach in the most authoritative words what is chiefly to be observed in their ordination. And from the very beginning of the Church the names of the following Orders and the ministries proper to each one, namely, those of subdeacon, acolyte, exorcist, lector and porter, are known to have been in use, though they were not of equal rank. For the subdiaconate is counted among the major orders by the Fathers and the Holy Councils, in which very frequently we also read about the other, lower Orders.

Chapter III: Order is truly a sacrament

1709 Since from the testimony of Scripture, apostolic Tradition and
1766 the unanimous agreement of the Fathers it is clear that grace
is conferred by sacred Ordination, which is performed by words and outward signs, no one ought to doubt that Order is truly and properly one of the seven sacraments of Holy Church (*cf. n. 1716*). For the Apostle says: "I remind you to rekindle the gift of God that is within you through the laying on of my hands; for God did not give us a spirit of timidity but a spirit of power and love and self-control" (*2 Tim. 1.6f; cf. 1 Tim. 4.14*).

*Chapter IV: The ecclesiastical hierarchy
and ordination*

1710 But since in the sacrament of Order, as also in baptism and
1767 confirmation, a character is imprinted (*cf. n. 1717)* which can
neither be erased nor taken away, the Holy Council justly
condemns the opinion of those who say that priests of the New
Testament have ony a temporary power, and that those who have
once been rightly ordained can again become laymen if they do not
exercise the ministry of the word of God (*cf. n. 1714).* And if anyone
should assert that all Christians are without distinction priests of the
New Testament, or that all are equally endowed with the same
spiritual power, he seems to be doing nothing else than upset the
Church's hierarchy which is "like an army with banners" (*cf. Song
6.3) (cf. n. 1719),* as if, contrary to the teaching of St Paul, all were
apostles, all prophets, all evangelists, all pastors, all doctors (*cf. 1
Cor. 12.39; Eph. 4.11).*

1711 Therefore the holy Council declares that, besides the other
1768 ecclesiastical grades, the bishops, who have succeeded the
apostles, principally belong to this hierarchial Order and
have been, as the same apostle says, "established by the Holy Spirit
to govern *(regere)* the Church of the Lord" (*cf. Acts 20.28 Vulg.);*
that they are superior to priests, confer the sacrament of confirmation, ordain ministers of the Church, and can perform most of the
other functions over which those of a lower Order have no power (*cf.
n. 1720).*

1712 The holy Council teaches, furthermore, that in the ordination
1769 of bishops, of priests and of other grades, the consent, call or
mandate, neither of the people nor of any civil power or
authority , is necessary to the extent that without it the ordination
would be invalid. Rather it decrees that all those who ascend to the
exercise of these ministries, being called and installed only by the
people or by the civil power or authority, and those who in their
rashness assume them on their own, are not to be regarded as
ministers of the Church (*cf. n. 1721),* but "as thieves and robbers,
who have not entered by the door" *(cf. Jn 10.1).*

1713 Such are the main points which the Council wanted to teach
1770 the faithful regarding the sacrament of Order. It was decided
to condemn the contrary propositions with definite and spe-

cial canons in the way that follows, so that all those who with Christ's help observe the rule of faith may more easily discern and hold the Catholic truth amid the darkness of so many errors.

Canons on the sacrament of Order

1714 1. If anyone says that there is in the New Testament no
1771 visible and external priesthood, or that there is no power
of consecrating and offering the true body and blood of the Lord and of remitting and retaining sins, but only the office and bare ministry of preaching the Gospel; or that those who do not preach are not priests at all, *anathema sit (cf. nn. 1707, 1710).*

1715 2. If anyone says that besides the priesthood there are in the
1772 Catholic Church no others Orders, major and minor, by
which, as by various steps, one advances towards the priesthood, *anathema sit (cf. n. 1708).*

1716 3. If anyone says that Order or sacred ordination is not truly
1773 and properly a sacrament instituted by Christ the Lord, or
that it is a kind of human invention devised by men inexperienced in ecclesiastical matters, or that it is only a kind of rite by which are chosen the ministers of the word of God and of the sacraments, *anathema sit (cf. n. 1709).*

1717 4. If anyone says that by sacred ordination the Holy Spirit is
1774 not given and that, therefore, the bishops say in vain:
"Receive the Holy Spirit"; or if he says that no character is imprinted by ordination; or that he who has once been a priest can again become a layman, *anathema sit (cf. n. 1710).*

1718 5. If anyone says that the sacred anointing which the
1775 Church uses at holy ordination not only is not required
but is despicable and pernicious, and so are also the other ceremonies, *anathema sit.*

1719 6. If anyone says that in the Catholic Church there is no
1776 hierarchy instituted by divine ordinance, which consists of
bishops, priests and ministers, *anathema sit (cf. n. 1711).*

1720 7. If anyone says that bishops are not superior to priests; or
1777 that they do not have the power to confirm and ordain, or
that the power they have is common both to them and to priests; or if he says that Orders conferred by them without the

consent or call of the people or of the civil power are invalid; or that those who have neither been rightly ordained by ecclesiastical and canonical authority nor sent by it, but come from some other source, are lawful ministers of the word and of the sacraments, *anathema sit (cf. n. 1711f)*.

1721 8. If anyone says that that bishops chosen by the authority of
1778 the Roman Pontiff are not true and legitimate bishops but a human invention, *anathema sit*

LEO XIII

BULL *APOSTOLICAE CURAE* ON ANGLICAN ORDINATIONS (1896)

In the Edwardine Ordinal (1552) the rites of ordination of the Roman Pontifical were changed by Cranmer acting under the influence of Bucer. The Anglican ordinations performed with the new rite were already considered invalid from the Catholic stand-point by Pope Julius III in a letter to Card. Reginald Pole (1554) and by two letters of Pope Paul IV (Jan. 20 and Oct. 30, 1555).

The Bull Apostolicae Curae *of Pope Leo XIII declared them invalid because of a double defect of form and intention: the new rites did not mention adequately the offices of bishops and priests; the changes had been introduced with the explicit intention of excluding the idea of a sacrificial ministerial priesthood exercised in the Eucharist. More than a century later, the rites of ordination of bishops and priests were amended, but by then the Anglican hierarchy validly ordained according to the Roman Pontifical was already extinguished. In a letter to Cardinal Richard, Archbishop of Paris (1896), Pope Leo XIII stated that by issuing the bull* Apostolicae Curae *he intended to give "a final judgment and to completely settle the matter", his decision "being definitively fixed, valid and irrevocable". The Pope did not, however, intend to give to this decision the value of an infallible pronouncement.*

In the new ecumenical climate created in recent years, it is felt that the question of the value of orders derived from the Anglican hierarchy should once more be re-examined. Several Catholic bishops have expressed the desire that a mixed commission of Anglican and Catholic historians make an impartial examination of the facts with a view to clarifying the issue and dispelling misunderstandings. Independently of the historical facts, a further question has arisen of late, concerning the possibility of a Catholic recognition of the ministry of Christian Churches living outside the apostolic succession as traditionally understood, provided the integrity of the faith has been restored. This intricate question, which is at the centre of the ecumenical problem, is today the object of a new theological reflection.

(Defect of form)

1722 The words which, until quite recent times, have been
3316 generally held by Anglicans to be the proper form of priestly ordination: "Receive the Holy Spirit", certainly do not signify

definitely the Order of the priesthood or its grace and power, which is pre-eminently the power "to consecrate and offer the true body and blood of the Lord" *(cf. n. 1714)* in that sacrifice which is no "mere commemoration of the sacrifice accomplished on the Cross" *(cf. n. 1557)*.

It is true that this form was subsequently amplified by the addition of the words: "for the office and work of a priest"; but this proves, rather than anything else, that the Anglicans themselves had recognised that the first form had been defective and inadequate. Even if this addition could have lent the form a legitimate signification, it was made too late, when a century had already elapsed since the adoption of the Edwardine Ordinal and when, consequently, with the hierarchy now extinct, the power of ordaining no longer existed.

1723 Of late, some have sought an argument for their case in other prayers of the same Ordinal, but in vain. To say nothing of other reasons which show such prayers to be inadequate, when occuring in the Anglican rite, for the purpose suggested, let this one argument serve for all: namely, these prayers have been deliberately stripped of everything which in the Catholic rite clearly sets forth the dignity and functions of the priesthood. It is, then, impossible for a form to be suitable and sufficient for a sacrament if it suppresses that which it ought distinctively to signify.

1724 The case is the same with episcopal consecration.... It fol-
3317 lows that, since the sacrament of Order and the true priest-hood of Christ has been totally expunged from the Anglican rite, and since accordingly the priesthood is in no way conferred in the episcoral consecration of the same rite, it is equally impossible for the episcopate itself to be truly and properly conferred thereby; the more so because a chief function of the episcopate is that of ordaining ministers for the Holy Eucharist and for the sacrifice....

1725 ...Hence not only is there in the whole Ordinal no clear
3317a mention of sacrifice, of consecration, of priesthood, of the power to consecrate and offer sacrifice, but, as we have already indicated, every trace of these and similar things found in the prayers of the Catholic rite which were not completely rejected, was purposely removed and obliterated.

3317b The original character and spirit of the Ordinal, as one might say, is thus objectively evident....

(Even the amended form remains invalid)

1726 The efforts (made to vindicate the validity of the amended
3317b form) have been, we say, and remain fruitless. And they are
fruitless for this reason also, that, even though some words of
the Anglican Ordinal as it now stands may present the possiblity of
ambiguity, they cannot bear the same meaning as they have in the
Catholic rite. For, as we have seen, when once a new rite has been
introduced denying or falsifying the sacrament of Order and repudiating any notion whatsover of consecration and sacrifice, then the
formula: "Receive the Holy Spirit"—the Spirit, namely, who is
infused into the soul with the grace of the sacrament—is deprived of
its force; nor have the words "for the office and work of a priest" or
"of a bishop" and similar expressions any longer their force, being
now mere names, voided of the reality which Christ instituted.

The strength of this argument is felt by many Anglicans themselves who interpret the Ordinal more accurately than others; and
they use it openly against those who are vainly attempting, by a new
interpretation of the rite, to attach to the Orders conferred by this
rite a value and efficacy which they do not possess....

(Defect of intention)

1727 Then with this intrinsic defect of form has been combined a
3318 defect of intention—of that intention which is equally
necessary for the existence of the sacrament.... If the rite is
changed with the manifest purpose of introducing another rite which
is not accepted by the Church, and of repudiating what in fact the
Church does and by Christ's institution belongs to the nature of the
sacrament, then it is evident, not only that the intention necessary
for a sacrament is lacking, but even that an intention is present which
is adverse to, and incompatible with the sacrament....

(The decision)

1728 Therefore, adhering entirely to the decrees of the Pontiffs
3319 our Predecessors on this subject, and fully ratifying and
renewing them by our own authority, on our own initiative
and with sure knowledge, We pronounce and declare that ordinations performed according to the Anglican rite have been and are
absolutely null and utterly void.

PIUS X

DECREE *LAMENTABILI* OF THE HOLY OFFICE (1907)
ARTICLES OF MODERNISM CONDEMNED

On this document, see n. 1326i.

(Modernist errors on the origin of priesthood condemned)

[1729/49]   As the Christian Supper little by little took on the nature
3449   of a liturgical action, those who had been usually presid-
            ing over it acquired the priestly character.

[1729/50]   The elders, who discharged the function of overseers in
3450   the Christian communities, were established by the
            apostles as presbyters and *episkopoi* in order to see to
the good order made necessary by the growth of the communities;
not properly in order to perpetuate the apostolic mission and power.

PIUS XII

APOSTOLIC CONSTITUTION *EPISCOPALIS CONSECRATIONIS*
(1944)

The Constitution authoritatively decrees that the two bishops who assist the main consecrator in an episcopal ordination are really co-consecrators and must act as such. The text is found in AAS 37 (1945) 131ff.

(Ministers of the ordination of a bishop)

1730   With the fulness of the apostolic power we declare, decree
         and lay down the following. Though one bishop is necessary
and sufficient for the validity of an episcopal consecration, since he
performs the essential rites, nevertheless the two bishops who,
according to the Roman Pontifical, assist at the consecration as
stated by the ancient rule, must not only touch with both hands the
head of the bishop elect together with the consecrator while saying:
"Receive the Holy Spirit", but also recite the prayer: "Be propitious"
with the entire Preface that follows, after having duly made their
mental intention of conferring the episcopal consecration together
with the consecrating bishop. For they are themselves consecrators
and, therefore, they must henceforward be called co-consecrators.

ENCYCLICAL LETTER *MEDIATOR DEI* (1947)

Pope Pius XII's encyclical on the sacred liturgy (cf. nn. 1216ff) contains an extensive treatment on the priesthood. It shows that the foundation of the Church's priesthood lies in the priesthood of Christ Himself. It distinguishes clearly the ministerial priesthood (based on the sacrament of Order) from the common priesthood of the faithful, and shows how both are differently exercised in the eucharist sacrifice. The text is found in AAS 39 (1947) 521-595.

(Priesthood of Christ and priesthood of the Church)

1731 The divine Redeemer wished that the priestly life begun by Him in His mortal body by His prayers and His sacrifice should continue unceasingly through the centuries in His mystical Body which is the Church; and therefore He instituted a visible priesthood to offer everywhere a "pure oblation" (cf. Mal. 1.11), so that all men all over the world, being freed from sin, might serve God conscientiously and of their own free will.

(There follows the text quoted under n. 1216).

(The ministerial priesthood)

1732 The Church is a society, and, therefore, must have its own authority and hierarchy. Although it is true that all members of the mystical Body share the same benefits and tend to the same end, this does not mean that they all enjoy the same powers or are competent to perform the same actions. The divine Redeemer has established His Kingdom upon the stable foundation of a sacred order; and that order is a kind of reflection of the heavenly hierarchy.

Only the apostles and those who since have duly received from them and their successors the imposition of hands possess that priestly power in virtue of which they stand before their people as Christ's representatives and similarly before God as the representatives of the people. This priesthood is not transmitted by heredity or blood relationship; nor does it originate in the Christian community, nor is it derived by delegation from the people. Before acting in God's sight on behalf of the people, the priest is the ambassador of the divine Redeemer; and because Jesus Christ is the Head of that Body of which Christians are members, the priest is God's representative for the people entrusted to his care. The power committed to him, therefore, has by nature nothing human; it is supernatural and comes from God: "As the Father has sent me, even so I send you" (Jn 20.21)....

Therefore, the visible and external priesthood of Jesus Christ is not given in the Church universally, generally, or indeterminately; it is imparted to chosen men and constitutes a sort of spiritual birth which takes place in one of the seven sacraments, holy Order.

(Effects of the sacrament of Order)

1733   This sacrament not only confers the grace proper to this particular function and state of life; it also confers an indelible character which conforms the sacred ministers to Christ the Priest, and enables them lawfully to perform the acts of religion by which men are sanctified and God duly glorified according to the divine ordinance.

(The exercise of the ministerial priesthood and of the common priesthod in the eucharist sacrifice)

1734 It is therefore important, venerable brethren, for all the faith-
3849 ful to understand that it is their duty and highest privilege to take part in the eucharist sacrifice...with such active devotion as to be in the closest union with the High Priest... and to offer it together with Him, and with Him to surrender themselves....

But the fact that the faithful take part in the eucharistic sacrifice does not mean that they also possess the power of the priesthood....

3850   There are some who, holding a view not far removed from
  .   errors that have been already condemned (*cf.nn.1710ff*), teach that the New Testament knows of no priesthood other than that which is common to all the baptised; that the command which Jesus Christ gave to His apostles at the Last Supper, to do what He Himself had done, was addressed directly to the whole community of the faithful; and that thence and only later the hierarchical priesthood took its rise. They therefore maintain that the people possess the true priestly power, and that the priest acts only in virtue of a function delegated to him by the community....

It is necessary to show how plainly these captious errors contradict the truths we asserted above, in speaking of the special position that the priest holds in the mystical Body of Jesus Christ. One thing we think it advisable to repeat: that the priest acts in the name of the people precisely and only because he represents the person of our Lord Jesus Christ, considered as Head of all the members and offering Himself for them; that the priest, therefore, approaches the altar as Christ's minister, lower than Christ, but higher than the people; that the people, on the other hand, because it in no way represents the person of the divine Redeemer and is not mediator between itself and God, can in no way possess the priestly right.

All this is certain with the certainty of faith. Yet, it must be said that the faithful do also offer the divine victim, though in a different way.

(The faithful offer through the priest and with him)

1735 "Not only do priests offer", wrote Pope Innocent III, "but all
3851 the faithful offer too; what is performed in a special way by
the ministry of the priest is done in a universal manner by the
votive offering of the faithful."[1]...The rites and prayers of the Mass
show no less clearly that the offering of the victim is made by the
priest and the people together....

And there is no wonder that the faithful are accorded that privilege; for, by reason of their baptism Christians become by a common
title members of the Body of Christ the Priest; by the character that
is as it were engraved upon their soul, they are appointed to the
worship of God, and therefore, according to their condition, they
share in the priesthood of Christ Himself....

1736 To avoid any mistake in this very important matter, we must
3852 clearly define the exact meaning of the word 'offer'. The
unbloody immolation by which, after the words of consecration have been pronounced, Christ is rendered present on the altar
in the state of victim, is performed by the priest alone, and by the
priest in so far as he acts in the name of Christ, not in so far as he
represents the faithful. But, precisely because the priest places the
divine Victim on the altar he presents it as an oblation to God the
Father for the glory of the Blessed Trinity and for the benefit of the
whole Church. Now, understood in this restricted sense, the oblation is in their own way shared by the faithful, on a twofold ground;
for they do not only offer the sacrifice through the hands of the priest,
but also, in a certain sense, together with him. In virtue of this
participation, the people's offering also pertains to liturgical worship.

That the faithful offer that sacrifice through the hands of the
priest is clear from the fact that the minister at the altar acts in the
person of Christ considered as Head, and as offering in the name of
all the members; this is why it is true to say that the whole Church
makes the offering of the Victim through Christ. But when the people
are said to offer with the priest, this does not mean that all the
members of the Church, like the priest himself, perform the visible
liturgical rite; this is done only by the minister divinely appointed for
the purpose. Rather they are said to offer with him inasmuch as they
unite their votive offerings of praise, entreaty , expiation and thanks-

---

1. INNOCENT III, *De Sacro Altaris Mysterio,* 3, 6.

giving with the votive offering or mental intentions of the priest, indeed with those of the High Priest Himself, in order that they may be presented to God the Father in the external rite itself performed by the priest offering the victim. The external rite of sacrifice must, indeed, of its very nature, be a sign of internal worship; and what is signified by the sacrifice of the New Law is that supreme homage by which Christ, the principal offerer, and with Him and through Him all his mystical members, pay to God due honour and veneration....

APOSTOLIC CONSTITUTION *SACRAMENTUM ORDINIS* (1947)

By this Constitution Pope Pius XII determined the matter and form of the ordinations to the diaconate, the presbyterate and the episcopate. By authoritatively restating the doctrine of the ancient tradition, he brought to a conclusion the controversy of past centuries (cf. n. 1705i). Without pronouncing on the historical question whether the rite did in fact undergo a susbstantial change in the Western Church, the Pope, in virtue of his supreme apostolic authority, makes a practical declaration and decision for the future: henceforth for all three ordinations the matter is the imposition of hands alone, and the form the words determining its meaning. This is first stated for all three ordinations in general, and then for each in particular. The Pope's decision is based on the Church's power to determine the sacramental rites, provided that the "substance" of the sacrament—which is here very accurately defined (cf. n. 1324i)—be preserved. Noteworthy is the fact that the Constitution considers the three orders as sacramental: they produce a sacramental effect, which includes the power of Order and the grace of the Holy Spirit.

(Matter and form of diaconate, presbyterate and episcopate)

1737   3. ...Even according to the mind of the Council of Florence
3858   itself (*cf. n. 1705*), the handing over of the instruments (*traditio instrumentorum*) was not required for the substance and validity of this sacrament in virtue of the will of our Lord Jesus Christ Himself. If the same handing over of the instruments has at some time been necessary, even for validity, in virtue of the will and precept of the Church, all know that the Church has the power to change and abrogate what she has determined.

3859   4. By virtue of our supreme apostolic authority we declare with sure knowledge and, as far as it may be necessary, we determine and ordain: the matter of the holy orders of diaconate, presbyterate and episcopate is the laying on of hands alone, and the sole form is the words determining the application of the matter, words by which the effects of the sacrament—that is, the power of Order and the grace of the Holy Spirit—are unequivocally signified, and which for this reason are accepted and used by the Church. This leads us to declare, and, if other provisions have been legitimately made in the past at any time, we now determine that, at least in future, the handing over of the instruments is not necessary for the validity of the holy Orders of the diaconate, the presbyterate and the episcopate.

THE SECOND VATICAN GENERAL COUNCIL

The Council first dealt with the sacrament of Order when in the Constitution Lumen Gentium *it spoke of the hierarchical structure of the Church (chapter 3). It devoted a decree to the pastoral office of bishops (CD) and another to the priestly ministry and life (PO).*

The more characteristic points of doctrine in the conciliar documents are the following:

1. The ministerial priesthood in the context of the Church

LG speaks first of Christ's unique priesthood which is communicated by Him to His Church and is shared by the entire people of God (LG 10-13). Its function is to make Christ's unique priesthood present in the world. The basic priestly function is exercised differently by the Church's various members, laity and ministers (LG 18), but, in the context of the Church's fundamental priestly reality, the ministerial priesthood which differs from the common priesthood "in essence and not only in degree" (LG 10) is essentially related to it; it is viewed as a service to the people of God, the powers which it confers being ordained to that service. It consists of three degrees: the episcopate conferred on the bishops as successors of the apostles (LG 20-27; cf. 18-19), the presbyterate (LG 28) and the diaconate (LG 29).

2. The three degrees of the ministerial priesthood

The episcopte

One of the most important doctrinal points made by the Council is its clear affirmation of the sacramentality of the episcopate. The episcopal consecration confers the fulness of the sacrament of Order (LG 21); this is why it is mainly through the bishops that Christ, the supreme High Priest, is present in the midst of His people (LG 21). The bishops are the successors of the apostles and continue Christ's work (CD 2); to them is entrusted the care of that portion of God's people which is the diocese, a charge which they must exercise in communion with the Supreme Pontiff who is the centre of unity of the whole Church (LG 21). United with their head, the supreme Pontiff, the bishops constitute an apostolic college (LG 22), and share in his solicitude for the whole Church (LG 23-24).

The presbyterate

The presbyterate confers a specific degree of participation in the ministerial priesthood possessed in its fulness by the episcopal college (LG 28). Thus the priests are united with the bishops in priestly dignity (LG 28). Their ordination enables them to act in the person of Christ (LG 28) and to represent Him among their flock as Head of His Body, the Church (PO 2). They are established in the order of the presbyterate as collaborators of the bishop (LG 28; CD 29-30) and his necessary helpers and counsellors (PO 7). Together with him and around him they constitute "one college of priests" (unum presbyterium) (LG 28) and, in a sense, make him present in the local congregations entrusted to their care (LG 28). The sacrament of Order creates a bond of union between bishop and priests as well as between the priests themselves as co-members of the priestly college (LG 28).

The diaconate

It is a sacramental degree of Order (LG 29) and makes the deacon participate in his own degree in the function of the hierarchy. The Council determines the ministerial functions exercised by the deacons in communion with the bishops and the priestly college (LG 29). It recommends the restoration of the permanent diaconate in the Western Church (LG 29).

3. The twofold perspective of consecration and mission

In its teaching the Council synthesises two aspects of the ministerial priesthood: consecration to God and mission to the Christian community and to the world. Both are inseperable and complementary; if the priest is a man "set apart", he is so "within the fold of the people of God" (PO 3), not in order to be "separated from it or from any man", but to be fully engaged in the service of the community (PO 3). In order to exercise his ministerial function, he must live in contact with men; he cannot remain a stranger to their life (PO 3).

4. The threefold function of the ministerial priesthood

Christ's unique priesthood has a threefold function: He is at once Teacher, High Priest and Shepherd. These three functions of Christ's unique mediation are continued in the Church; hence the Church's threefold function, prophetic, sanctifying and pastoral. These three functions are shared by the entire people of God; the laity exercise them in their own way (LG 34-36). The same three functions are indissolubly linked in the ministerial priesthood and exercised in various degrees by bishops, presbyters and deacons. Going beyond the problematic of post-Tridentine theology, the Council links up here with the early Tradition to give to the priestly ministry its full significance. It cannot be reduced to the cultic function exercised mostly in the offering of the sacrifice of the Mass; its prophetic and pastoral aspects too are derived from the sacramental ordination. The bishops have the fulness of the threefold priestly function (LG 20). Their primary function is to preach the Gospel (LG 25), as authentic teachers of the faith (CD 2). The bishops are also the principal dispensers of the means of grace (LG 26) and the shepherds of their flock (LG 27; CD 16-19). Presbyters share in their own degree in the three functions attached to the priestly ministry (PO 2); as helpers of the bishops their first duty is to preach the Gospel to all men and to be the educators of the faith (PO 4); their prophetic function is oriented to their sanctifying function (PO 5) which finds its climax in the eucharistic celebration (PO 5; LG 28), centre of the life of the Christian community; they shepherd the community entrusted to them and thus build up the Body of Christ which is the Church (PO 6). Deacons too, in union with bishops and *priests, share in their own way in the threefold function of the ministry, in preaching, liturgy and the exercise of charity (LG 29).*

DOGMATIC CONSTITUTION *LUMEN GENTIUM* (1964)

(The common priesthood and the ministerial priesthood)

1738 10. The Lord Christ, High Priest taken from among men *(cf. Heb. 5.1-5),* made this new people into "a new Kingdom, priests to his God and Father" *(Rev. 1.6; 5.9-10).* For they who are regenerated by baptism and anointed by the Holy Spirit, are consecrated to be a spiritual household and a holy priesthood, so that in all their actions as Christians they may offer spiritual oblations and proclaim the marvels of Him who has called them out of darkness into His admirable light *(cf. 1 Pet. 2.4-10).* Therefore, all Christ's disciples must, in persevering prayer and praise of God *(cf. Acts 2.42-47),* show themselves living victims, holy and pleasing to God *(cf. Rom. 12.1);* they must bear witness to Christ throughout the world and give an answer to those who seek an account of that hope of eternal life which is in them *(cf. 1 Pet. 3.15).*

Though the common priesthood of the faithful and the ministerial or hierarchical priesthood do, indeed, differ from one another in essence and not only in degree, they are nonetheless ordained to each other; for both, in their respective manner, share in the one priesthood of Christ. In virtue of the sacred power with which he is endowed, the ministerial priest instructs and rules the priestly people, performs in the person of Christ the eucharistic sacrifice and offers it to God in the name of all the people; while the faithful on their part, in virtue of their royal priesthood, join in the eucharistic offering, and exercise their priesthood in receiving the sacraments, in prayer and thanksgiving, in the witness of a holy life, in self-denial and active charity.

(The episcopate as a sacrament)

1739 21. Thus in the bishops, who are assisted by priests, the Lord Jesus Christ, the Supreme High Priest, is present in the midst of those who believe. For, while He is sitting at the right hand of God the Father, He is not absent from the communtiy of His high priests; it is mainly through their signal service that He preaches the word of God to all nations and ceaselessly adminsters the sacraments of the faith to the believers; through their paternal action *(cf. 1 Cor. 4.15),* He incorporates new members into His Body by divine regeneration; through their wisdom and prudence, He directs and guides the People of the New Testament during their pilgrimage towards eternal happiness. These pastors, chosen to be shepherds of the Lord's flock, are servants of Christ and stewards of the mysteries of God (*cf. 1. Cor. 4.1*); to them has been entrusted the task of bearing witness to the good tidings of God's grace *(cf. Rom. 15.16; Acts 20.24)*, and the ministration of the Spirit and of justice in glory (*cf. 2 Cor. 3.8-9*).

In view of carrying out these lofty functions, the apostles were enriched by Christ with a special outpouring of the Holy Spirit (*cf. Acts 1.8; 2.4; Jn 20.22-23)*; this spiritual gift they passed on to their fellow-labourers by the imposition of hands (*cf. 1 Tim. 4.14; 2 Tim. 1.6-7)*, and it has come down to us in the episcopal consecration. This holy Council teaches that, through the episcopal consecration, the fulness of the sacrament of Order is conferred, that fulness, namely, which both in the Church's liturgical practice and in the language of the early Fathers is truly called the high priesthood and the apex of the sacred ministry. The episcopal consecration bestows, together with the function of sanctifying, the funtions also of teaching and governing, though these functions, of their very nature, can be exercised only in hierarchical communion with the Head and the members oif the College. For, from Tradition, as expressed chiefly both in the East and in the West, it is clear that through the imposition of hands and the words of consecration the grace of the Holy Spirit is so conferred and the sacred character so impressed that the bishops continue in an eminent and visible way Christ's own roles of Teacher, Shepherd and High Priest, and that they act in His person. It belongs to the bishops to admit new members into the episcopal body by means of the sacrament of Order.

(The Presbyterate)

1740 28. Christ, whom the Father sanctified and sent into the world (*cf. Jn 10.36)*, made His apostles partakers of His consecration and mission, and through them their successors the bishops. The bishops, in turn, legitimately handed on to different members of the Church various degrees of participation in their ministry. Thus, the divinely established ecclesiastical ministry is exercised in different ranks by those who from early times have been called bishops, presbyters, deacons. Although the presbyters do not possess the highest degree of the priesthood and depend on the bishops in the exercise of their power, they are nevertheless united with the bishops in sacerdotal dignity. By the power of the sacrament of Order they are, after the image of Christ, the supreme and eternal Priest (*cf. Heb. 5.1-10; 7.24; 9.11-28*), consecrated true priests of the New Testament, to preach the Gospel, to shepherd the faithful and to celebrate the divine worship. Sharing, according to their degree of the ministry, in the function of Christ, the sole Mediator (*cf. 1 Tim. 2.5*), they announce the word of God to all. They exercise their sacred function especially in the eucharistic liturgy or synaxis. In the sacrifice of the Mass, acting in the person of Christ and proclaiming His mystery, they join the offerings of the faithful to the sacrifice of their Head and, until the coming of the Lord (*cf. 1 Cor. 11.26*), represent and apply the one sacrifice of the New Testament, namely, the sacrifice of Christ offering Himself, once and for all, to the Father as a spotless victim (*cf. Heb. 9.14-28*). For the benefit of the sinners and the sick among the faithful, they exercise in a special manner the ministry oif reconciliation and of alleviation. They lay before God the Father the needs and prayers of the faithful (*cf. Heb. 5.1-4*). By performing within the limits of their authority the function of Christ, Shepherd and Head, they gather together the family of God as a brotherhood that has but one heart and one soul, and lead them through Christ in the Spirit to God the Father....

(The diaconate and its restoration)

1741 29. At a lower level of the hierarchy stand the deacons, upon whom hands are imposed "not unto the priesthood, but unto a ministry (of service)".[1] Indeed, strengthened with the sacramental grace, they serve the people of God in the service (*diakonia*) of the liturgy, of the word and of charity, in communion with the bishop and his priestly college (*presbyterium*)....

Since the present discipline of the Latin Church makes it difficult, in many regions, to fulfil these functions so necessary in the life of the Church, the diaconate can in the future be restored as a proper and permanent rank in the hierarchy. It is left to the various competent territorial bodies of bishops, with the approval of the Supreme Pontiff, to decide whether and where it is opportune to introduce permanent deacons for the care of souls....

---

1. *Constitutiones Ecclesiae Aegyptiacae*, III, 2.

DECREE *AD GENTES* (1965)

(Restoration of the diaconate in mission countries)

1741a 16. Where the bishops' conferences deem it opportune, the order of diaconate should be restored as a permanent state of life, as laid down in the Constitution "On the Church" (*n. 1741*). For it is beneficial that men who are really performing diaconal functions, whether preaching the word of God as catechists, or ruling remote Christian communities in the name of the parish priest or the bishop, or exercising charity in social and charitable works, should be strengthened and more closely joined to the altar by the imposition of hands, as handed down by the Apostles. They will more efficaciously fulfil their ministry through the sacramental grace of the diaconate.

PAUL VI

MOTU PROPRIO *SACRUM DIACONATUS ORDINEM* (1967)

(1742) *The Second Vatican Council had made the restoration of the permanent diaconate in the Latin Church possible. In this Motu Proprio Paul VI promulgates the general rules that govern this restoration. He determines the procedure; the choice of candidates: either young men who will be bound to celibacy, or older men, either unmarried or married; their training; their upkeep; their functions and spiritual life; th special case of religious deacons; the rite of their ordination. The text is found in AAS 59 (1967) 697-704.*

ENCYCLICAL LETTER *SACERDOTALIS COELIBATUS* (1967)

Till the third century, bishops and priests were mostly married men. As a result of the growing awareness of a close bond between priesthood and celibacy, by the fourth century the unmarried clergy became the majority; by then too, ordained ministers were forbidden to enter the married state. Celibacy, however, was not imposed as a rule, but continence in marriage was gradually required from the married clergy of the Western Church. The first document which witnesses to this is found in the Council of Elvira, Spain (c. 300-303) (cf. DS 119). In the sixth century continence became a clear obligation for the clergy of the Western Church. Recent Popes have reaffirmed that, though there is no bond of necessity between ministry and celibacy, as is made clear by the practice of the Eastern Church, there exists nevertheless a clear harmony between the two which recommends that the long tradition of the Western Church be preserved. The Second Vatican Council spoke in the same line (PO 16). A major document on the subject is the Encyclical Letter of Pope Paul VI. Aware of the recent questioning to which the law of clerical celibacy has been subjected and of the difficulties met by priests in the modern world, the Pope considers that, nevertheless, the impressive testimony of the past and the present in favour of celibacy cannot be wiped out and that the law must be maintained. In a doctrinal part, the Pope states the reasons in favour of priestly celibacy: celibacy has a Christological, an ecclesial and an eschatological meaning; he further shows the place of celibate ministry in the life of the Church and its relation to human values. The second part deals with practical questions such as the priestly life and training, priests abandoning the ministry, and the relations of priests with their bishops and the people (cf. AAS 59 (1967) 657-696).

1743 We consider then that the law of celibacy actually in force must still in our time, and firmly, be linked to the ecclesiastical ministry; it must sustain the minister of the Church in his choice, exclusive, definitive and total, of the one and sovereign love of Christ, of dedication to the worship of God and the service of the Church; and it must be the mark of his state of life, both in the community of the faithful and in secular society.

APOSTOLIC CONSTITUTION *PONTIFICALIS ROMANI* (1968)

(1744) *The Second Vatican Council had prescribed a revision of the rites of ordination (SC 76). In this Apostolic Constitution the Pope approves and promulgates the new rites of ordination to the diaconate, the presbyterate and the episcopate, prepared by the Consilium for the implementation of the Council's Constitution on the Sacred Liturgy (SC). The rites have been simplified, unified and given a richer doctrinal content. Since changes are introduced into the essential rites decreed by Pius XII (cf. n. 1738), the Pope uses his supreme authority to decree the new rites. For each order, the entire "consecratory prayer" which follows the laying on of hands is considered as the sacramental "form", but in each of the consecratory prayer one passage is singled out, which the Pope declares to be required for the validity of the ordination. In the ordination to the episcopate the consecratory prayer borrows from the* Apostolic Tradition *of Hippolytus; this is done in order that the meaning of the episcopal function, as "apex of the sacred ministry" (cf. n. 1739) in the apostolic succession, may be expressed more clearly than it was in the former Roman Pontifical. The new rite no longer limits the number of "consecrating bishops"; they not only lay on their hands on the bishops elect (cf. SC 76), but recite together with the "principal consecrator" the essential part of the consecratory prayer. The text is found in AAS 60 (1968) 369-373.*

THE THIRD SYNOD OF BISHOPS IN ROME

DE SACERDOTIO MINISTERIALI (1971)

The recent questioning on the ministerial priesthood, including the question of the specific character which distinguishes it from the common priesthood of the faithful, has led to the topic of the priestly ministry being introduced for discussion at the Third Synod of bishops in Rome. The official Synodal document, submitted to the Pope for his consideration, has been published by him in Dec. 1971. The text is made up of two parts, one stating doctrinal principles, the other proposing guide-lines for the priestly life and ministry. The doctrinal part points to the newness of the priesthood which Christ has brought to the world and which remains present in the Church; it goes on to show, along the lines of the Second Vatican Council (cf. n. 1738), the mutual link between flock and pastors which is inscribed in the very constitution of the Church. It is in this context that the specific function of the hierarchical ministry must be understood. The text is found in AAS 63 (1971) 898ff.

(The priesthood of Christ)

1745 ...Exercising a supreme and unique priesthood... He (Christ) surpassed, by fulfilling them, all the ritual priesthoods and holocausts of the Old Testament and indeed of the nations.... When therefore we speak of the priesthood of Christ, we should have before our eyes a unique, incomparable reality, which includes the prophetic and royal office of the Incarnate Word of God.

(The origin and nature of the hierarchical ministry)

1746 The Church, which through the gift of the Spirit is built up organically, participates in different ways in the functions of Christ as Priest, Prophet and King, in order to carry out her mission of salvation in His name and by His power, as a priestly people (cf. n. 1738).

It is clear from the New Testament writings that an apostle and a community of faithful united with one another by a mutual link under Christ as Head and the influence of His Spirit belong to the original inalienable structure of the Chruch....

This essential structure of the Church—consisting of a flock and of pastors appointed for this purpose (cf. 1 Pet. 5.1-4)—according to the tradition of the Church herself was always and remains the norm. Precisely as a result of this structure, the Church can never remain closed in on herself and is always subject to Christ as her origin and Head.

Among the various charisms and services, the priestly ministry of the New Testament, which continues Christ's function as mediator, and which differs from the common priesthood of all the faithful in essenece and not only in degree (cf.n. 1738), alone perpetuates the essential work of the apostles: by effectively proclaiming the Gospel, by gathering together and leading the community, by remitting sins, and especially by celebrating the Eucharist, it makes Christ, the Head of the community, present in the exercise of His work of redeeming mankind and glorifying God perfectly.

APOSTOLIC LETTER *MINISTERIA QUAEDAM*
(15 August 1972)

By this Apostolic Letter Pope Paul VI decrees the reform of the minor orders and of the subdiaconate in the Latin Church. The Council of Trent had considered those orders as "various steps" by which "one advances towards the priesthood" (n. 1715; cf. n. 1708). The reform suppresses the subdiaconate and restores lay ministries in the Latin Church. These are not called orders but "ministries"; they are not conferred through ordination but by "installation". Thus they are clearly distinguished from the sacramental orders of the diaconate, the presbyterate and the episcopate conferred through ordination. Belonging also to the laity, they do not introduce into the clerical state; the tonsure being suppressed, it is henceforward the ordination to the diaconate that introduces into that state.

The Apostolic Letter establishes two lay ministries, those of lector and acolyte, by which the part in the service of the word and of the altar open to lay people is officially sanctioned in view of its stable exercise. It also foresees that, besides these two lay ministries which are of value for the universal Church, episcopal conferences may request the creation of others, among which the ministry of catechist is mentioned. Thus the possibility of a certain diversification of lay ministries and of their adaptation to circumstances of place and time is recognised. The official installation in the lay ministries of lector and acolyte is reserved to men. The text is found in AAS 64 (1972) 529ff.

1747 Among the special offices to be preserved and adapted to contemporary needs, there are those which are especially connected with the ministries of the word and of the altar and in the Latin Church are called the offices of lector and acolyte, and the subdiaconate. It is fitting to preserve and adapt these in such a way that, from this time on, there will be two offices: that of lector and that of acolyte, which will include the functions of the subdiaconate....

It is in accordance with the reality itself and with the contemporary outlook that the above-mentioned ministries should no longer be called minor orders; their conferring should not be called 'ordination' but 'installation'; it is also proper that only those who have received the diaconate be considered as clerics. Thus there will better appear the distinction between clergy and laity, between what is proper and reserved to the clergy and what can be entrusted to the laity; thus there will appear more clearly their mutual relationship in so far as "the common priesthood of the faithful and the ministerial or hierarchical priesthood, though they differ in essence and not only in degree, are nonetheless ordained to each other; for both, in their respective manner, share in the one priesthood of Christ" *(cf. n. 1738).*

APOSTOLIC LETTER *AD PASCENDUM* (15 August 1972)

(1748) *Issued on the same day as the previous document, this* Motu Proprio *fixes precise norms concerning the diaconate. These norms partly complete the general rules promulgated earlier by Pope VI for the restoration of the parmanent diaconate (cf. n. 1742); their scope, however, is broader, for they also extend to the "transitional" diaconate of the candidates to the order of presbyters. Some of the new rules are suggested by the restoration of lay ministries. Aspirants to the permanent or transitional diaconate must, during their formation, be officially received among the candidates for that order by a rite of admission which is the first public manifestation of their vocation and of its recognition by the bishop. They must be installed in the ministries of lector and acolyte and exercise them as a preparation for their ministry of the word and of the altar in the sacrament of Order. They are introduced into the clerical state by the ordination to the diaconate. In the case of candidates for the presbyterate and of unmarried candidates for the permanent diaconate the consecration to a celibate life and its obligation are linked with the ordination to the diaconate. The text is found in* AAS *64 (1972) 534ff.*

DECLARATION *MYSTERIUM ECCLESIAE* OF THE
S. CONGREGATION FOR THE DOCTRINE OF THE FAITH
(11 May 1973)

This Declaration on the mystery of the Church devotes a section to the priestly ministry, in which it intends to clarify the nature and especially the permanent character of the priestly ministry. Repeating the doctrine of the Second Vatican Council and of the Third Synod of Bishops in Rome (cf. nn. 1745-1746), the document begins by situating the Church's priesthood in relation to Christ's perfect priesthood. The Church's share in the priesthood of Christ "consists of the common priesthood of the faithful and the ministerial and hierarchical priesthood, both of which, though they differ from one another in essence and not only in degree, are nonetheless ordained to each other within the communion of the Church" (cf. nn. 1738,1746). The document proceeds to show the origin in the Church of the priestly ministry derived from the apostolic succession. It shows how the permanent "character" of the ministry came progressively to be recognised in the Church. Though its nature is explained in different ways by theologians, the "permanent existence" or the "enduring nature of the priestly character through life" has traditionally been considered as "pertaining to the doctrine of faith" and must continue to be so considered. The text is found in AAS *65 (1973) 405-407.*

(The origin of the priestly ministry in the Church)

1749 Christ, the Head of the Church which is His Mystical Body, appointed as ministers of His priesthood His apostles and through them their successors, that they might act in His person within the Church (*cf. n. 1738; PO 2*) and also in turn legitimately hand on to priests in a subordinate degree the sacred ministry which they had received (cf. n. 1740). Thus there arose in the Church the apostolic succession of the ministerial priesthood for the glory of God and for the service of His people and of the entire human family which must be converted to God.

(Ordination to the ministry confers a permanent character)

1750   The Church has ever more closely examined the nature of the ministerial priesthood, which can be shown to have been invariably conferred from apostolic times (cf. 1 Tim. 4.15; 2 Tim. 1.6). By the assistance of the Holy Spirit, she recognised more clearly as time went on that God wished her to understand that this rite conferred upon priests not only an increase of grace for carrying out ecclesiastical duties in a holy way, but also a permanent disignation by Christ, or character, by virtue of which they are equipped for their work and endowed with the necessary power that is derived from the supreme power of Christ.

APOSTOLIC EXHORTATION *EVANGEL II NUNTIANDI* (1975)

By the Apostolic Letter Ministeria Quaedam *(1972) Pope Paul VI restored lay ministries in the Latin Church (cf. n. 1747). These have developed since and new lay ministries have been created, especially in some local Churches, to the benefit of the Church's mission of evangelisation. The 1974 Synod of Bishops on Evangelisation encouraged the installation of lay people in ministries by which their participation in the Church's mission is officially recognised. The Apostolic Exhortation on Evangelisation of Paul VI gives new impetus to lay ministries, while clearly distinguishing them from the ordained ministries. The Pope explains what is the specific role of all the laity in the Church's evangelising mission; in this context he shows the special contribution which lay ministries make to the Church's mission. The text is found in* AAS 68 (1976) 61-63.

(Lay ministries)

1751   73. The laity can also feel themselves called, or be called, to work with their pastors in the service of the ecclesial community, for its growth and life, by exercising a great variety of ministries according to the grace and charisms which the Lord is pleased to give them.

We cannot but experience a great inner joy when we see so many pastors, religious and lay people, fired with their mission to evangelize, seeking ever more suitable ways of proclaiming the Gospel effectively. We encourage the openness which the Church is showing today in this direction and with this solicitude. It is an openness to meditation first of all, and then to ecclesial ministries capable of renewing and strengthening the evangelizing vigour of the Church.

It is certain that, side-by-side with the ordained ministries, whereby certain people are appointed pastors and consecrate themselves in a special way to the service of the community, the Church recognises the place of non-ordained ministries which are able to offer a particular service to the Church.

A glance at the origins of the Church is very illuminating, and gives the benefit of an early experience in the matter of ministries. It was an experience which was all the more valuable in that it enabled the Church to consolidate herself and to grow and spread. Attention to the sources, however, has to be complemented by attention to the present needs of mankind and of the Church. To drink at these ever inspiring sources without sacrificing anything of their values, and at the same time to know how to adapt oneself to the demands and needs of today—these are the criteria which will make it possible to seek wisely and to discover the ministries which the Church needs and which many of her members will gladly embrace for the sake of ensuring greater vitality in the ecclesial community. These ministries will have a real pastoral value to the extent that they are established with absolute respect for unity and adhering to the directives of the pastors, who are the ones who are responsible for the Church's unity and the builders thereof.

These ministries, apparently new but closely tied up with the Church's living experience down the centuries—such as catechists, directors of prayer and chant, Christians devoted to the service of God's Word or to assisting their bethren in need, the heads of small communities, or other persons charged with the responsibility of apostolic movements—these ministries are valuable for the establishment, life, and growth of the Church, and for her capacity to influence her surroundings and to reach those who are remote from her. We owe also our special esteem to all the lay-people who accept to consecrate a part of their time, their energies, and sometimes their entire lives, to the service of the missions.

DECLARATION OF THE SACRED CONGREGATION FOR THE DOCTRINE OF THE FAITH, *INTER INSIGNIORES,* ON THE QUESTION OF THE ADMISSION OF WOMEN TO THE MINISTERIAL PRIESTHOOD

(15th October 1976)

The question of the possibility of admitting women to the priestly ministry has been asked in recent years and has become a theological, pastoral and ecumenical problem. It has led to this declaration by the Sacred Congregation for the Doctrine of the Faith which, though dated 15 October, 1976, was made public only on 27 January, 1977. In an introduction the document points to the increasing role played by women both in society and the Church's apostolate in modern times, including, in some Christian Churches, the admission of "women to the pastoral office on a par with men". To the question whether the Catholic Church too could consider admitting women to the priestly ministry, the Document answers: "The Church, in fidelity to the example of the Lord, does not consider herself authorized to admit women to priestly ordination" (Introduction). The Document proceeds to justify its negative answer with dogmatic and theological reasons, not all of which have the same weight and value. Six considerations are made: 1) The Church's constant tradition has been to ordain only men to the priestly ministry; 2) Jesus did not call any women to be members of the Twelve; 3) the apostles did not include any women in the apostolic group; 4) the practice of Christ and the apostles in this regard is permanently normative; 5) the priest must have a "natural resemblance" to Christ, and the male sex is constitutive of this resemblance; 6) the issue of equality in the Church and of human rights is irrelevant to the question of priestly ministry for women. The most weighty among these arguments, and, in the mind of the S. Congregation, the decisive one, is the dogmatic value which it attributes to the Church's constant tradition, based on the practice of Jesus himself and of the apostles: the exclusion of women from priestly ordination is considered as belonging to the substance of the sacrament which the Church has no power to change (cf. nn. 1324i; 1737i). The text is found in AAS 69 (1977) 98-116.

(The tradition of ordaining only men to the priestly ministry is normative)

1752 4. Could the Church today depart from the attitude of Jesus and the Apostles, which has been considered as normative by the whole of tradition up to our own day ?...

...The priestly ministry is not just a pastoral service; it ensures the continuity of the functions entrusted by Christ to the Apostles and the continuity of the powers, related to those functions. Adaptation to civilizations and times therefore cannot abolish, on essential points, the sacramental reference to the constitutive events of Christianity and to Christ Himself.

In the final analysis, it is the Church, through the voice of her Magisterium, that, in these various domains decides what can change and what must remain immutable. When she judges that she cannot accept certain changes, it is because she knows that she is bound by Christ's manner of acting. Her attitude, despite appearances, is therefore not one of archaism but of fidelity; it can be truly understood only in this light. The Church makes pronouncements in virtue of the Lord's promise and the presence of the Holy Spirit, in order to proclaim better the mystery of Christ and to safeguard and manifest the whole of its rich content.

This practice of the Church therefore has a normative character: in the fact of confering priestly ordination only on men, it is a question of a unbroken tradition throughout the history of the Church, universal in the East and in the West, and alert to repress abuses immediately. This norm, based on Christ's example, has been and is still observed because it is considered to conform to God's plan for his Church.

JOHN PAUL II

LETTER TO ALL THE PRIESTS OF THE CHURCH ON THE OCCASSION OF HOLY THURSDAY 1979
(9 April 1979)

The Pope's Letter is directly concerned with strengthening priests in their priestly vocation; it has no intention to develop at length a theology of the priestly ministry. It is a direct an unambiguous appeal for "fidelity to Christ", including fidelity to the commitment to celibacy freely entered upon by ordination. Though priestly ministry and celibacy are distinct charisms, the Latin Church has a long tradition of linking the latter to the former. Like Pope Paul VI (cf. n. 1743), Pope John Paul II considers that this link must be preserved. The reason is that celibacy is not only an eschatological sign, but has also a social meaning in the present life as a sign of freedom for service of the people of God. Once freely assumed, it becomes a matter of fidelity to Christ and His Church. No allusion is made in the letter to the possibility, often advocated in recent years, of admitting married men to priestly ordination, where the pastoral care of Christian communities would seem to demand it. The text is found in Osservatore Romano *(English Edition), 17 April 1979, pp. 6-9.*

(On priestly celibacy)

1753 8. The Latin Church has wished, and continues to wish, referring to the example of Christ the Lord Himself, to the apostolic teaching and to the whole Tradition that is proper to her, that all those who receive the sacrament of Orders should embrace this renunciation (of marriage) "for the sake of the kingdom of heaven". This tradition, however, is linked with respect for different traditions of other Churches. In fact, this tradition constitutes a characteristic, a peculiarity and a heritage of the Latin Catholic Church, a tradition to which she owes much and in which she is resolved to persevere, in spite of all the difficulties to which such fidelity could be exposed.

Why does the Latin Catholic Church link this gift (of celibacy) not only with the life of those who accept the strict programme of the evangelical counsels in Religious Institutes, but also with the vocation to the hierarchical and ministerial priesthood ? She does it because celibacy "for the sake of the kingdom" is not only an eschatological sign; it also has a great social meaning, in the present life, for the service of the People of God. Through his celibacy, the priest becomes the "man for others".... Celibacy is a sign of a freedom that exists for the sake of service. According to this sign, the hierarchical or "ministerial" priesthood is, according to the tradition of our Church, more strictly "ordered" to the common priesthood of the faithful.

HOMILY AT THE CONCLUSION OF THE
PARTICULAR SYNOD OF THE DUTCH BISHOPS IN ROME
(31 January 1980)

A particular Synod of the Dutch Bishops with Pope John Paul II was held in Rome, January 14-31, 1980. It was convoked in order that, together with the Pope, the bishops might take collegial decisions on problems affecting the life and pastoral activity of the Church in Holland. One of the problems discussed at the Synod was that of the concrete forms of activity open to lay "pastoral workers" and the limits to be imposed on them. The distinction between the common priesthood and the ministerial priesthood may not be obscured as would be the case if a "parallel" ministry by lay people were to operate as an alternative for the ordained ministry of presbyter and deacon. In his homily on the last day of the Synod the Pope made special reference to this point. The text is found in Osservatore Romano *(English Edition), 11 February 1980, p.3.*

(Pastoral tasks of lay people may not obscure the priestly ministry)

1754 4. Allow me to stress a special point which turned out to be at the centre of all the other questions raised and which will have a very great impact on the future of the Church. I am referring here to the true ministerial priesthood of priests, in its nature as well as in its relations with the bishops and in its relationship to the commitment of lay people in the mission of the Church.

The building up of the ecclesial community and the implementation of its mission are entrusted to the whole community, but, as the Dogmatic Constitution *Lumen Gentium* says *(cf. LG 30-38)*, this responsibility is exercised in harmony with the charism and the place of each one in the Body of Christ. All vocations, all services, all charisms are ordained to mainfesting in their variety the riches of the

Church and to serving her unity. The Church must be able to express the fulness of her life through the riches of vocations and charisms, in the ministerial priesthood as well as in the apostolate of the laity, and also in religious consecration according to the spirit and the specific purpose of every Institute.

But each of these ministries and these services has its own specific character, and they all complete one another without merging.... It is important... to safeguard, in the attribution of tasks and in the delimitation of responsibilities, the distinction between the contribution of the laity and the tasks entrusted to priests and deacons.

CHAPTER XVIII

MATRIMONY

All peoples have recognised a sacred character in the marriage union. In the Old Testament the sanctity of marriage is clearly attributed to the will of the Creator; marriage becomes, moreover, a prophetic symbol of the union of God with His people. St Paul shows how this union is fully realised in the mystical bond between Christ and the Church, of which Christian marriage is an image and reflection. Thus, Christian marriage is one of the means by which the mystery of the Church is actualised, for in the marriage coven-ant of her members she manifests herself as the mystery of the union of Christ with humanity. The Christian family is a fundamen-tal expression of the mystery of the Church, the most incarnate form of her charity; hence it is rightly called the "Church in miniature".

It is only in this perspective that the Christian doctrine of mar-riage can be fully understood. Its direct object is not the fundamental properties of marriage, its unity and indissolubility, as already inscribed in nature; it is rather the new significance which the institution of marriage takes on in the context of the Christian mystery, in which it is raised by Christ to the dignity of a sacrament.

The Christian dignity of marriage explains why the Church has from the earliest times vindicated its goodness against dualistic and rigoristic errors; why she upheld its sacred character against all tendencies to reduce it to a merely profane reality; why again she has claimed for herself the right to legislate in matrimonial matters.

The Church, however, has grown in the explicit awareness of Christian marriage as an effective sharing in the mystery of Christ's union with her, and hence as an efficacious sign of grace. Implicitly contained in the early tradition and practice, this doctrine could only be clearly formulated when the Church came to the explicit posses-sion of her sacramental doctrine. It was then clearly recognised that if Christian marriage endows the natural bond of marriage with new compelling force and firmness, this is precisely due to the participa-tion in the Christian mystery which the sacrament confers. Moreover, the sacrament also gives the spouses the grace neces-sary to foster indefectible fidelity and to achieve the ends of mutual union and of fruitfulness which in the supernatural order results in the increase of the People of God. Traditionally, the stress has been laid on the end of procreation, consonant with the institutional aspect of marriage. The aspect of partnership, however, has recently found increasing recognition and is clearly brought out in the Pastoral Constitution Gaudium et Spes of the Second Vatican Council.

·Long before the sacramental doctrine of marriage was explicitly formulated, the Church had alreay stated that the constitutive element of Christian marriage is the mutual consent of the partners. This forcibly brings out the fact that in Christian marriage it is the human reality of marriage itself which has been raised by Christ to the dignity of a sacrament: contract and sacrament are inseperable. This is also why the Church has claimed the right to determine the "canonical form" under which the contract must be made and to subject it to various conditions of validity.

Thus the Church documents uphold the dignity of the human reality of marriage and its place in her sacramental economy. At the same time, they show that the doctrine on marriage reflects in a particular manner the developments characteristic of the doctrine on the sacraments and on the Church herself. Against the denial of the Reformers the Council of Trent exposed clearly the sacramentality of Christian marriage and the consequences derived from it. Pope Leo XIII exphasised the intrinsic relation between the marriage contract and the sacrament. Pope Pius XI explained how Christian marrriage and family life are a way to Christian perfection. Lately, the Second Vatican Council has stressed the central role which conjugal love plays in Christian marriage; it has shown how the covenant relationship between the spouses reflects the union of Christ with the Church.

*   *   *

The moral aspects of conjugal life are dealt with in chapter XXII. The main doctrinal points treated in this chapter are the following:

Marriage is willed by God: 1824, 1835.
It has been raised by Christ to the dignity of a sacrament: 28, 32, 1305, 1311, 1803, 1806, 1807, 1808, 1820, 1822, 1823, 1824, 1830, 1834, 1836, 1843.
Marriage is good: 21, 402/11-12, 1802.
It may not be considered superior to the state of virginity: 1817.
Christian marriage is a sharing in the mystery of Christ and the Church: 1803, 1806, 1820, 1823, 1831, 1834, 1836, 1843.

The essential rite of the sacrament is the mutual consent of the spouses: (1801), 1803, 1823, 1825, 1835.

Contract and sacrament are inseparable: 1822, 1823.

Marriage comes under the legal competence of the Church: 1821.

The Church can establish impediments: 1810, 1811, 1816.

Vasectomy does not invalidate marriage: 1842.

The Church may determine the rite to be observed: 1818.

Matrimonial cases are in the competence of ecclesiastical courts: 1819.

The essential laws of marriage are not subject to human will: 1824, 1825.

The marital bond is exclusive: 28, 1805, 1809.

It is indissoluble: 1802, 1803, 1804, 1805, 1813, 1831, 1835, 1836, 1844.

It cannot be dissolved because of adultery: 1814.

Its indissolubility is perfected by the sacrament: 1806, 1820, 1844.

Marriage which has not been consummated can be dissolved in certain circumstances: 1812.

Marriage is a partnership of love in fidelity: 1803, 1804, 1828, 1830, 1835, 1837, 1839, 1841.

This partnership is uniquely expressed through the conjugal act: 1837, 1838.

The conjugal act is by its nature ordained to procreation resulting in the increase of the People of God: 1306, 1803, 1826, 1827, 1834, 1841.

Union between the spouses is intimately linked with the end of procreation: 1840, 1841.

The sacrament sanctifies the spouses and gives them graces necessary for their state: 1806, 1807, 1808, 1820, 1823, 1832, 1833, 1836.

Christian marriage is a way to perfection: 1834, 1836.

The Christian family is the primary cell of the Church: 1834.

ALEXANDER III (1159-1181)

LETTER TO THE ARCHBISHOP OF SALERNO (time unknown)

(1801)   *In answer to the inquiry made by the emperor of the Bulgarians,*
755   *converted to Christianity, as regards the essence of Christian*
756   *marriage, Pope Nicholas 1, in a Letter to the Bulgarians (866) had*
declared that the consent of the partners is as in the Roman law
the essential element of Christian marriage (cf. DS 643). But in the early
Middle Ages a controversy arose between those who, basing their doctrine
on the Germanic law, held that the conjugal act is necessary for the
'formation' of marriage and those who with Peter Lombard held the tradi-
tional view that the consent is sufficient. Alexander III settled the issue by
declaring that mutual consent makes the marriage, but the bond is per-
fected and becomes absolutely indissoluble through consummation. Pre-
vious to consummation, marriage can be dissolved by solemn religious
profession.

INNOCENT III

PROFESSION OF FAITH PRESCRIBED TO THE WALDENSIANS
(1208)

In the early times the main controversy on marriage centred on its
recognititon as a true human value. Dualistic tendencies, advocating two
principles, one of good and one of evil, attributed marriage to the principle of
evil. The Manichaean and Priscillianist denigration of marriage had been
condemned by the first Council of Toledo (400) (cf. DS 206) and by the
Council of Braga (561) (cf. nn. 402/11-12). The goodness of marriage is
again affirmed in the profession of faith prescribed by Innocent III to the
Waldensians who, like the Albigensians, held Manichaean views (cf. n.
403i), and forbade marriage to the 'perfect'.

1802   We do not deny that marriage can be contracted as the
794   apostle says *(cf. 1 Cor. 7);* but we strictly forbid that those
rightly contracted be broken. We believe and confess that man can
be saved even if he has a wife, and we do not condemn a second
marriage or even subsequent marriages.

THE GENERAL COUNCIL OF FLORENCE
DECREE FOR THE ARMENIANS (1439)

After affirming the sacramentality of marriage, the Decree for the
Armenians exposes the triple good of marriage according to the patristic
tradition. For the value of this document, see n. 1305i.

1803   The seventh is the sacrament of matrimony which is the sign
1327   of the union of Christ and the Church according to the saying
of the apostle: "This is a great mystery, and I mean in reference to Christ and the Church" *(Eph. 5.32).* The efficient cause of

matrimony is the mutual consent duly expressed in words relating to the present. A triple good is found in Matrimony. The first is the begetting of children and their education to the worship of God. The second is the faithfulness which each spouse owes to the other. Third is the indissolubility of marriage, inasmuch as it represents the indissoluble union of Christ and the Church. But, although it is permitted to separate on account of adultery, nevertheless it is not permitted to contract another marriage since the bond of a marriage legitimately contracted is perpetual.

THE GENERAL COUNCIL OF TRENT
TWENTY-FOURTH SESSION
DOCTRINE ON THE SACRAMENT OF MATRIMONY (1563)

The Reformers upheld the sacredness of marriage in the order of creation, but denied that it belongs to the order of grace as a Christian sacrament in the strict sense. Consequently, they rejected the Church's juridical function in matrimonial matters. They admitted the legitimacy of divorce because of adultery and other causes; some also held lenient opinions on bigamy. Besides, Luther's conception was not free from Augustinian pessimism. Hence the Council sought to defend the supernatural character of matrimony as a sacrament, giving new firmness to the bond of Christian marriage; it also defended the Church's claim to be competent in matrimonial matters. After a short exposition of the main doctrinal points concerning the sacrament, there follow the canons directed against the errors of the time.

In the second canon, the Council has specifically in mind the compliance of the Reformers in the case of Philip of Hesse's bigamous marriage. Canons 3 and 4 affirm the competence of the Church in matrimonial matters since the sacraments are entrusted to the Church. Canon 5 is categorical in rejecting the grounds for divorce, other than adultery, which were accepted by the Reformers, while Canon 6 defends the traditional view that marriage is dissolved by religious profession. Canon 7 deals with adultery as a ground for divorce. Tradition on this point was not absolutely clear and the Council did not wish to give offence to the Orientals among whom remarriage was allowed in such cases. The Canon is, therefore, carefully worded so as to demand acceptance of the Latin doctrine without expressly condemning the Oriental standpoint. Hence it does not seem to imply a dogmatic definition.[1] In the encyclical Casti Connubii *(1930), however, Pope Pius XI will take a more definite standpoint: "The Church was not, and is not now, in error when she taught and still teaches this doctrine; consequently, it is certain that the marriage bond cannot be dissolved even on the grounds of adultery"* (AAS 22 (1930) 574). *Canon 9 is so framed as not to include in the condemnation the Oriental custom of marriage before ordination to the*

---

1. Cf. P. F. FRANSEN, "Réflexions sur l'anathème du Concile de Trente", *Ephemerides Theologicae Lovanienses* 29 (1953) 657-672.

priesthood. Canon 10 affirms the excellence of virginity as compared to marriage; this is stated against the Protestant depreciation of virginity. Canon 12 carefully asserts the competence of ecclesiastical tribunals in matrimonial cases, without entirely excluding that of the State regarding certain matters. Later Church Law has interpreted this in such a way as to leave only the civil effects of marriage to the responsibility of the State.

1804 The first father of the human race, inspired by the divine
1797 Spirit, proclaimed the perpetual and indissoluble bond of matrimony when he explained: "This at last is bone of my bones and flesh of my flesh.... Therefore a man leaves his father and his mother and cleaves to his wife, and they become one flesh" (*Gen. 2.23f*).

1805 But that only two are united and joined together by this bond,
1798 Christ the Lord taught more clearly when, referring to these words as having been uttered by God, He said: "So they are no longer two but one" (*Mt. 19.6*), and immediately confirmed the stability of the bond which was proclaimed long ago by Adam in these words: "What therefore God has joined together, let no man put asunder" (*Mt. 19.6; Mk 10.9*).

1806 Christ Himself, who instituted the holy sacraments and
1799 brought them to perfection, merited for us by His passion the grace which perfects that natural love, confirms the indissoluble union and sanctifies the spouses. St Paul suggests this when he says: "Husbands, love your wives, as Christ loved the Church and gave Himself up for her" (*Eph. 5.25*), adding immediately: "This is a great mystery, I mean in reference to Christ and the Church" (*Eph. 5.32*).

1807 Since, because of the grace of Christ, matrimony under the
1800 Law of the Gospel is superior to the marriage unions of the old Law, the holy Fathers, the Councils and the tradition of the universal Church have with good reason always taught that it is to be numbered among the sacraments of the New Law. Contrary to this teaching, ungodly and foolish men of this age, not only have entertained false ideas concerning this holy sacrament but, in their usual way, under the pretext of the Gospel they have given freedom to the flesh, and, by word and writing, they have asserted—not without great harm to Christ's faithful—many things alien to the understanding of the Catholic Church and to customs approved since the apostolic times. Wishing to counteract their temerity, this holy ecumenical Council...declares as follows the condemnation of these heretics and of their errors.

Canons on the sacrament of matrimony

1808 1. If anyone says that matrimony is not truly and properly
1801 one of the seven sacraments of the Law of the Gospel,
instituted by Christ the Lord, but that it was devised in the
Church by men and does not confer grace, *anathema sit (cf. n.
1807).*

1809 2. If anyone says that it is lawful for Christians to have
1802 several wives at the same time and that this is not forbidden
by any divine law (*Mt. 19.9ff), anathema sit.(cf. n. 1805).*

1810 3. If anyone says that only those degrees of consanguinity
1803 and affinity which are mentioned in *Leviticus (18.6ff)*
can impede contracting marriage and invalidate the contract;
and that the Church cannot dispense from some of them or declare
other degrees impedient and diriment, *anathema sit.*

1811 4. If anyone says that the Church did not have the power to
1804 establish diriment impediments for marriage or that she has
erred in establishing them, *anathema sit.*

1812 5. If anyone says that the marriage bond can be dissolved
1805 because of heresy, or irksome cohabitation, or because of
the wilful desertion of one of the spouses, *anathema sit.*

1813 6. If anyone says that marriage contracted but not con-
1806 summated is not dissolved by the solemn religious profession of one of the spouses, *anathema sit.*

1814 7. If anyone says that the Church is in error for having taught
1807 and for still teaching that in accordance with the evangelical
and apostolic doctrine (*cf. Mk 10; 1 Cor. 7),* the marriage
bond cannot be dissolved because of adultery on the part of one of
the spouses, and that neither of the two, not even the innocent one
who has given no cause for infidelity, can contract another marriage
during the lifetime of the other; and that the husband who dismisses
an adulterous wife and marries again and the wife who dismisses an
adulterous husband and marries again are both guilty of adultery,
anathema sit.

1815 8. If anyone says that the Church errs when she declares
1808 that for many reasons separation may take place between
husband and wife with regard to bed and board or cohabitation for a definite period or even indefinitely, *anathema sit.*

1816 9. If anyone says that clerics in sacred orders or regulars
1809 who have made solemn profession of chastity can contract
marriage, and that one so contracted is valid despite the
ecclesiastical law or the vow; and that the contrary opinion is nothing
but a condemnation of marriage; and that all those who feel that they
do not have the gift of chastity, even though they have vowed it, can
contract marriage, *anathema sit*. For God does not refuse that gift to
those who ask for it rightly, and "He will not let you be tempted
beyond your strength" (*1 Cor. 10.13*).

1817 10. If anyone says that the married state surpasses that of
1810 virgintiy or celibacy, and that it is not better and happier to
remain in virginity or celibacy than to be united in matrimony
(*cf. Mt. 19.11f; 1 Cor. 7.25f, 38, 40), anathema sit*.

1818 11. If anyone says that the prohibition of the solemnisation of
1811 marriages at certain times of the year is a tyrannical superstition derived from pagan superstition; or condemns the
blessing and other ceremonies which the Church uses in solemn
nuptials, *anathema sit*.

1819 12. If anyone says that matrimonial cases do not belong to
1812 ecclesiastical judges, *anathema sit*.

LEO XII

ENCYCLICAL LETTER *ARCANUM DIVINAE SAPIENTIAE* (1880)

*After explaining the Tridentine doctrine on matrimony, Leo XIII strongly
vindicates the Church's authority over the marriages of Christians, which
he derives from the fact that the marriage contract and the sacrament are
inseparable. The fact that with some previous Popes (cf. DS 2598, 2990) he
claims exclusive jurisdiction for the Church over the marriage contract, can
in the historical context be understood as a reaction against various secula-
rist tendencies which tried to deny the Church all right over it. Hence this
teaching does not exclude the possiblity of an amicable agreement between
the Church and the civil power.*

(Marriage is a sacrament)

1820 Christ the Lord raised matrimony to the dignity of a sacra-
3142 ment and at the same time provided that the spouses, shelte-
red and strengthened by the grace which His merits have
won, should attain sanctification in marriage itself; and in it, marvellously modelled on the pattern of His mystical marriage with the
Church, He has both perfected the love proper to human nature and
by the bond of divine love strenghtened the naturally indissoluble
partnership of man and woman.

(The Church's authority over marriage)

1821 When Christ, therefore, renewed matrimony and raised it to
3144 such a great excellence, He gave and confided to the
Church the entire legislation in the matter. And the Church
has at all times and in all places exercised this power over the
marriages of Christians in such a manner that it appeared clearly as
something proper to her, not a concession sought from men but a
right granted to her by the will of her divine Founder.

(The marriage contract and the sacrament are inseparable)

1822 Let no one be misled by the distinction which supporters of
3145 the civil power try to make, whereby they separate the
marriage contract from the sacrament so that, leaving the
sacramental aspects to the Church, the contractual element
becomes subject to the power and judgment of the civil power. For
there is no basis for such a distinction, or rather such a disruption,
since it is clear that in Christian marriage the contract cannot be
dissociated from the sacrament; thus there can be no true legitimate
contract which is not also a sacrament. For Christ the Lord raised
matrimony to the dignity of a sacrament, and matrimony is the
contract itself provided it is legally made.

(Internal proof that the contract itself is the sacrament)

1823 Further, matrimony is a sacrament because it is a sacred and
3146 efficient sign of grace and the image of the mystical marriage
of Christ with the Church. This image and figure are
expressed by the bond of most intimate union by which man and
woman bind themselves together, which bond is nothing other than
matrimony itself. Hence it is clear that every valid marriage between
Christians is, in and of itself, the sacrament; and nothing is further
from the truth than to say that the sacrament is a sort of ornament
superadded, or an extrinsic property that can be dissociated and
separated from the contract by the will of men.

PIUS XI

ENCYCLICAL LETTER *CASTI CONNUBII* (1930)

*This is a complete exposition of the Catholic teaching on marriage. It
elaborately deals with the divine institution and sacramentality of marriage,
its laws and properties, the three "goods" of marriage, as exposed by the
Fathers of the Church, and the errors contrary to the Christian ideal of
marriage. Though the stress is somewhat on the institutional aspect, the
encyclical also brings out many personal elements. While, according to the*

prevailing view, it calls the procreation and education of offspring the primary end of marriage, it also refers to mutual union as "primary cause and reason" of marriage looked at, not as an institution, but as a partnership, according to the Catechism of the Council of Trent.

(Marriage as a divine institution)

1824　... Matrimony was not instituted or restored by man, but by
3700　　God; not man, but God, the Author of nature and Christ our
　　　　Lord, the restorer of nature, provided marriage with its laws, confirmed it and elevated it; and consequently those laws can in no way be subject to human wills or to any contrary pact made even by the contracting parties themselves.

(Divine order and human freedom)

1825　But, although matrimony by nature is of divine institution,
3701　　yet the human will has a part, and a very important part, to
　　　　play in it. Each marriage, in so far as it is a conjugal union between a particular man and a particular woman, arises solely out of a free consent of the two partners; and this free act by which each yields and receives the specifically marital right is so necessary for the constitution of marriage that it cannot be supplied by any human power. But the only role of this human freedom is to decide that each of the partners in fact wishes to enter the state of matrimony, and to marry this particular person. The freedom of man has no power whatever over the nature of matrimony itself, and, therefore, when once a person has contracted marriage, he becomes subject to its essential laws and properties....

(The Goods of marriage: offspring)

1826　... The Creator of the human race Himself, who in His
3704　　goodness has willed to use human beings as His ministers in
　　　　the propagation of life, taught us this truth when in instituting matrimony in the Garden of Eden He bade our first parents, and through them all married persons who should come after: "Be fruitful and multiply" (Gen. 1.28)...

1827　Christian parents should, moreover, understand that their
3705　　duty is not only to propagate and maintain the human race on
　　　　earth; it is not even merely to rear any sort of worshippers of the true God. They are called to provide children to the Church, to beget "fellow citizens with the saints and members of the household of God" (Eph. 2.19), in order that the people dedicated to the worship of our God and Saviour may increase from day to day....

(The Goods of marriage: conjugal fidelity)

1828 The second blessing of marriage...is fidelity, that is the
3706 mutual faithfulness of husband and wife in observing the
marital pledge. This implies that the right, which in virtue of
this divinely ratified agreement belongs to each spouse, will neither
be denied to the other nor be granted to any third party....

1829 This mutual interior conformation of husband and wife, this
3707 perservering endeavour to bring each other to the state of
perfection, may in a true sense be called, as the Roman
Catechism calls it,[1] the primary cause and reason of matrimony, so
long as marriage is considered, not in its stricter sense as the institution destined for the procreation and education of children, but in the
wider sense as a complete and intimate life-partnership and
association.

(The Goods of marriage: the sacrament)

1830 But the complement and crown of all is the blessing of
3710 Christian marriage which...we have called the sacrament. It
denotes both the indissolubility of the matrimonial bond, and
the consecration of this contract by Christ who elevated it to the
rank of a sign which is a cause of grace....

(The supernatural Mystery of marriage)

1831 If we seek with reverence to discover the intrinsic reason of
3712 this divine ordinance (the indissolubility of marriage)...we
shall easily find it in the mystical signification of Christian
wedlock, the full perfection of which is realised in consummated
marriage between the faithful. The apostle in the epistle to the
Ephesians... tells us that Christian wedlock signifies that most perfect union which exists between Christ and the Church: "This is a
great mystery, and I mean in reference to Christ and the Church"
(Eph. 5.32); and this is a union which, certainly, as long as Christ lives
and the Church lives by Him, can never cease and be dissolved....

(Graces of the sacrament)

1832 ...This sacrament, in those who do not, as is said, place
3714 an obstacle, not only increases in the soul sanctifying grace,

---

1. Cf. *Roman Catechism,* II, 8, 13.

the permanent principle of supernatural life; but also adds special gifts, good impulses and seeds of grace, amplifying and perfecting the power of nature and enabling the recipients, not only to understand with their minds, but also to relish immediately, grasp firmly, will effectively and fulfil in deed all that belongs to the state of wedlock and its purpose and duties; it also gives them the right to obtain the help of actual grace whenever they need it for the discharge of their duties belonging to the married state.

(An abiding sacrament)

1833 Let them constantly be mindful that they have been consecrated and strengthened for the duties and the dignity of their state by a sacrament whose efficacy, though it does not confer a character, remains nonetheless permanently.

THE SECOND VATICAN GENERAL COUNCIL

In comparsion with earlier documents, the Second Vatican Council adopts a striking personalistic standpoint. In the Dogmatic Constitution Lumen Gentium *(11), the ecclesial character of the sacrament of matrimony is explained, the family being called "the domestic church". It is meant to perpetuate the people of God.*

Marriage is a path to holiness (LG 11). It is the "primary form of interpersonal communion" (GS 12). It is of the highest importance for the well-being of the individual, and of the human and Christian society (GS 47). The pastoral Constitution Gaudium et Spes *vindicates the sanctity and indissolubility of marriage and insists on the personal nature of married love which pervades the whole of marital life and is uniquely expressed through the conjugal act (GS 48-49). Husband and wife are equal in pesonal dignity (GS 49). By cultivating constancy of love, they give witness to faithfulness, and thus help to bring about a renewal of marriage and the family (GS 49).*

The same Constitution Gaudium et Spes *has deliberately refrained from determining the 'hierarchy' of the ends of marriage; but it has clearly shown how the ends of mutual love and procreation are intimately linked together (GS 50). The importance of sexual intimacy for the total marital relationship is also pointed out (GS 49).*

DOGMATIC CONSTITUTION *LUMEN GENTIUM* (1964)

1834 11. Christian spouses, in virtue of the sacrament of matrimony, signify and share in the mystery of that union and fruitful love which exists between Christ and the Church (*cf. Eph. 5.32*). They help each other to attain to holiness in their married life and by the rearing and education of their children. And thus, in their state and way of life, they have their own special gift among the people of

God (cf. 1 Cor. 7.7). For their union gives rise to a family where new citizens are born to human society, and in baptism these are made into children of God by the grace of the Holy Spirit, for the perpetuation of God's People throughout the centuries. Within the family, which is, so to speak, the "domestic church", the parents should be the first to preach the faith to their children by word and example....

PASTORAL CONSTITUTION *GAUDIUM ET SPES* (1965)

(Sacredness of marriage and the family)

1835 48. The intimate partnership of life and conjugal love has been established by the Creator and provided by Him with its own laws. It has its beginning in the marriage convenant, that is, in an irrevocable personal consent. Thus, from the human act by which the spouses mutually give and accept each other, there arises, also in the eyes of society, that institution whose firmness stems from God's disposition.... Man and woman who by the marriage convenant "are no longer two but one" *(Mt. 19.6)*, render one another help and service by the intimate union of their persons and activities. They experience a sense of their oneness, and deepen it day by day. Being a mutual self-gift of two person, this intimate union demands, as indeed does the good of the children, the complete fidelity of the spouses and their indissoluble unity.

1836 Christ the Lord has bestowed abundant blessings on this many-faceted love, which springs from the divine fount of charity, and is formed after the model of His own union with the Church. For just as of old God went out to meet His People in a covenant of love and fidelity, so now the Saviour of men and the Spouse of the Church comes to meet the Christian spouses in the sacrament of matrimony. And He remains with them in order that, just as He Himself loved the Church and gave Himself up for her *(cf. Eph. 5.25)*, so the spouses also may, in mutual self-surrender, love one another with perpetual fidelity. Authentic married love is taken up into divine love and is ruled and enriched by the redemptive power of Christ and the salvfic action of the Church, so that the spouses may be effectively led to God and given help and courage in their sublime function as father and mother. That is why Christian spouses are strengthened and as it were consecrated for the duties and the dignity of their state by a special sacrament. When with the help of the sacrament they fulfil the duties of marriage and family life—animated by the Spirit of Christ which imbues their whole life with faith, hope and charity—they gradually realise their personal perfection and mutual sanctification, and thus jointly contribute to God's glorification.

(Marital love)

1837   49. The Word of God repeatedly invites the betrothed and the married to nourish and strengthen their engagement by chaste affection and their wedlock by an undivided love.... Since that love is directed from one person to another by an affection of the will, it is eminently human; it involves the good of the whole person, and so is able to bestow a special dignity on its bodily and spiritual expressions and to ennoble these as elements and special signs of conjugal friendship....

1838   This affection finds its special expression and its perfection in the act proper to marriage. And so the acts which realise the intimate and chaste union of the spouses are worthy and noble acts. When exercised in a manner that is truly human, they signify and foster the mutual self-gift by which the spouses enrich each other in joy and gratitude....

1839   The equal personal dignity of woman and man which must be recognised in their mutual and total love, clearly manifests the unity of marriage, a unity ratified by the Lord.

(Fecundity of Marriage)

1840   50. Marriage and conjugal love are by their nature ordained to the begetting and educating of children . Moreover, children are the supreme gift of marriage and they contribute greatly to the well-being of the parents themselves. God Himself who said: "It is not good that the man should be alone" *(Gen. 2.18)* and who "from the beginning made them male and female" *(Mt. 19.4),* wished to give man a special share in His own creative work, and so He blessed man and woman with the words: "Be fruitful and multiply" *(Gen. 1.28).* Hence, while not making the other ends of marriage of less account, the true practice of conjugal love, and the whole tenor of family life resulting from it, tend to dispose the spouses to cooperate generously with the love of the Creator and Saviour who through them day by day expands and enriches His family.

PAUL VI

ENCYCLICAL LETTER *HUMANAE VITAE* (1968)

The encyclical situates the problem of planned parenthood in the frame-work of a total vision of man and his vocation. The love of the spouses has its origin in God, who is Love. It must be fully human, faithful and exclusive, fruitful and suscitating new human lives. Responsible parenthood is deeply related to the moral order established by God; it requires that the finality of the conjugal act ordained to the union of the spouses and to procreation be respected. The Pope shows the intimate union of these two aspects. See also n. 2220i. The text is found in AAS 60 (1968) 481ff.

1841 12. This doctrine, often set forth by the teaching authority, is founded upon the inseparable connection, willed by God and which man cannot break on his own initiative, between the two meanings of the conjugal act: union and procreation. For, by its intimate structure, the conjugal act, while most closely uniting the spouses, enables them to procreate new lives according to laws inscribed in the very being of man and woman. It is by safeguarding these two essential aspects, union and procreation, that the conjugal act preserves in its fulness the sense of true mutual love and its ordination towards man's most high calling to parenthood. We believe that the men of our day are particularly capable of under-standing the deeply reasonable and human character of this funda-mental principle.

DECREE *CIRCA IMPOTENTIAM* OF THE

S. CONGREGATION FOR THE DOCTRINE OF THE FAITH

(13 May 1977)

In this decree, the S. Congregation settles a long standing doubt regard-ing the requirement of male conjugal potency for valid marriage. The text is found in AAS 69(1977) 426.

1842 The S. Congregation for the Doctrine of the Faith has always held that persons who have undergone vasectomy and others in similar conditions are not to be prevented from marriage, inas-much as their impotence is not certainly proved.

Now, however, after examining this practice and after renewed studies done by this S. Congregation and by the Commission for the Revision of the Code of Canon Law the Fathers...deemed that the following response should be given to questions proposed to them:

1. Whether impotence which invalidates marriage consists in the

incapacity, antecedent and permanent, whether absolute or relative, of completing conjugal copulation.

2. If *affirmative*, whether ejaculation of semen elaborated in the testicles is necessarily required for conjugal copulation.

To the first, *affirmative*. To the second, *negative*.

JOHN PAUL II

APOSTOLIC EXHORTATION *FAMILIARIS CONSORTIO* (1981)

As a follow-up of the Synod of Bishops, 1980, on the Family, the Pope issued an elaborate exhortation regarding the Role of the Christian Family in the Modern World. He points out that an evangelical discernment on the subject is to be practised in relation to the sense of faith of all the faithful. Marriage like celibacy is a way of expressing and living the one mystery of the covenant of God with His people. It is a sacrament or real symbol of the event of salvation in Christ, from which flow the unity and indissolubility of the marriage bond. The Pope strongly defends the sanctity and the indissolubility of Christian marriage. He reaffirms the teaching of the Church regarding responsible transmission of human life and asks that its practice be helped by proper sex education and research into human fertility (see n. 2236). The family as the first vital cell of society must be the prime concern of the whole of the society. It has a share in the life and mission of the Church. It is a community in dialogue with God through worship and prayer. The Pope emphasizes the need for pastoral care of the family. The text is found in Osservatore Romano *(English Edition), 21-28 December, 1981, pp. 1-9.*

(Sacramentality of Marriage)

1843 13. Like each of the seven sacraments, so also marriage is a real symbol of the event of salvation, but in its own way. The spouses participate in it as spouses, together, as a couple, so that the first and immediate effect *(res et sacramentum)* of marriage is not supernatural grace itself, but the Christian bond, a typically Christian communion of two persons which represents the mystery of Christ's incarnation and the mystery of His covenant. The participation in Christ's life which it confers is also specific: conjugal love involves a totality, in which all the elements of the person enter—the appeal of the body and instinct, the power of feeling and affectivity, the aspiration of the spirit and the will. It aims at deeply personal unity, the unity that, beyond union in the flesh, leads to forming one heart and soul; it demands indissolubility and faithfulness in definitive mutual self-giving; and it opens to fertility.

(Indissolubility of marriage)

1844 20. It is a fundamental duty of the Church to reaffirm strongly, as the Synod Fathers did, the doctrine of the indissolubility of marriage. To all those who, in our times, consider it too difficult, or indeed impossible, to be bound to one person for the whole of life, and to those who are caught up in a culture that rejects the indissolubility of marriage and openly mocks the commitment of spouses to fidelity, it is necessary to reaffirm the good news of the definitive nature of that conjugal love that has its foundation and strength in Christ.

Being rooted in the personal and total self-giving of the couple, and being required by the good of the children, the indissolubility of marriage finds its ultimate truth in the plan that God has manifested in His revelation; He wills and He communicates the indissolubility of marriage as a fruit, a sign and a requirement of the absolutely faithful love that God has for man and that the Lord Jesus has for the Church.

CHAPTER XIX

THE LIFE OF GRACE

The life of grace has its source in Christ's Paschal Mystery and its immediate principle in the person of the Holy Spirit dwelling in the heart of the justified man. In virtue of this twofold relationship to the Risen Lord and the Holy Spirit, man becomes son of the Father. Thus the Christian life consists in an intimate relationship with the three divine persons. All the gifts of the supernatural life flow from this Trinitarian centre: the infused supernatural virtues, the gifts of the Holy Spirit, and especially sanctifying grace. Configured to Christ, acted upon by His indwelling Spirit, endowed with a new life, man lives as a son of God.

The divine life is God's gratuitous self-gift to man. This gift must, however, be freely accepted by man through his self-commitment to God in faith and love. Hence the life of grace implies man's personal response to God's self-communication and demands his coopera-tion. It can be lost through grievous sin and restored through a new conversion. When it is allowed to unfold according to God's plan, it grows through the reception of the sacraments and the inner docility to the promptings of the Holy Spirit, and is destined to find its last fulfilment in the heavenly glory.

The life of the Spirit is not only imparted to individual Christians for their sanctification; it belongs to the whole Church. The Holy Spirit has been poured upon the community of the faithful to com-municate to them His manifold charisms for the benefit of the entire People of God.

A collection of Church documents on grace cannot adequately express the riches of the divine life offered to men. Not only do they not exhaust the treasures of Scripture and of the Christian Tradi-tion; but, calculated as they are to meet historical situations, they often limit themselves to highlighting those aspects of the divine life which were seriously threatened by opposite errors. Their value consists precisely in the firmness and clarity with which specific questions arising in the course of time were settled in the light of the Christian message.

Historically the doctrine of grace revolved around two main controversies: the Pelagian crisis in the 5th century and that initiated by the Reformers in the 16th century. Till the 5th century the doctrine of man's divinisation through Christ in the Spirit had been tranquilly possessed by the Church, though never articulated in official documents. Pelagius questioned its very essence. Eager to arouse the Church from a state of spiritual lethargy, he so stressed human freedom and the role of man's moral effort as to underestimate the need for God's grace and lead to a closed system in which man is made self-sufficient. Against this tendency towards complete self-reliance the necessity of grace in every man's life had to be affirmed by the Church. The crisis of the Reformation came from the opposite direction. The Reformers considered human nature as so damaged by original sin that it is intrinsically incapable of any good action. Against this pessimism, the Council of Trent asserted the intrinsic nature of man's justification in Christ. Thus the documents of the Church steer the middle course between two extremes.

During the post-Tridentine period the attention centred on actual grace and on the problem of human freedom, with little advertence, however, to the broad biblical perspective of man's inner renewal through the indwelling Spirit and his personal union with the Risen Christ.

At the end of the last century Pope Leo XIII began to reverse the trend by a deliberate return to the scriptural and patristic data. This renewal has been followed up by Pope Pius XII and the Second Vatican Council.

*   *   *

The Church's teaching on grace covers the following points:

Man, the new creation

In justification sins are forgiven: 1923, 1927, 1931f, 1934, 1943, 1961.

The Holy Spirit dwells in the justified: 1624, 1932f, 1993-1995, 1997, 1998.

The justified becomes a living member of Christ's body: 1618, 1934, 1995.

He becomes a son of the Father: 1928, 1932, 1946, 1997.

Eternal life is bestowed on him: 1927f, 1932-1934, 1960f, 1985.

Aided by grace, he must prepare himself for justification: 1914, 1929f, 1954-1959.

Faith is necessary for justification: 118, 122, 1918, 1930, 1935.

Faith alone without conversion is not sufficient: 1935f, 1939, 1959, 1962-1964, 1969-1971.

Grace is gratuitous and supernatural: 1925, 1929, 1935f, 1984, 1988, 1996.

With justification, the virtues of faith, hope and charity are infused: 1933f, 1961.

The life of grace increases through the fulfilment of the commandments and good works: 1937, 1939f, 1969-1971, 1974f, 1981f.

The justified man merits eternal life through his deeds done in grace: 1914, 1946-1948, 1976, 1981f, 1985/13.

Grace is lost through every mortal sin: 1425, 1943, 1945, 1973, 1977.

Actual grace

Already before justification man is able to perform good actions: 1923, 1940, 1957, 1986/20, 1988, 1990f.

Only through grace do human actions receive supernatural value: 1908, 1910f, 1913f, 1917, 1921f, 1925, 1951-1953.

The first impulse to justification comes from grace: 1911, 1913-1915, 1921, 1929, 1951-1953.

Man must respond to grace actively and freely: 120, 1914, 1929, 1954f, 1987, 1989, 1992.

Grace is necessary to persevere in avoiding grievous sin: 1901-1903, 1909, 1972.

Everyone receives the grace necessary to keep the commandments: 1922, 1938, 1968, 1972f, 1986/54, 1989;

but not to avoid all venial sins: 1904-1906, 1938, 1973.

Final perseverance is a special grace: 1942, 1966, 1972.

God's universal salvific will

God desires the salvation of all men: 1922, 1989/5.

No one is predestined to evil: 1922, 1956, 1967.

No one can with absolute certainty affirm that he is predestined to eternal life: 1941, 1965-1967

THE SIXTEENTH COUNCIL OF CARTHAGE (418)

Since Constantine had made Christianity the State religion, worldliness and laxity had crept into the Church. By the beginning of the fifth century the British monk Pelagius came to Rome where he expounded the strict demands of Christianity in the midst of general moral decay. Law, nature and especially man's freedom and acquired virtue are the watchwords of Pelagius' austere moral preaching, later organised into a system by his disciple Celestius.

The Pelagian heresy is a mentality rather than a logically structured body of doctrine. Its kernel is the assumption of the complete freedom of man, who in his free choice of good and evil can achieve salvation by his own unaided powers. Several errors followed from this assertion of man's self-sufficiency; human liberty essentially consists in the absence of all compelling force bending man towards good or evil; original sin as a natural inclination towards evil must be denied; therefore Adam's sin is reduced to a bad example set by him to his descendants and freely followed by them in their own personal decisions; baptism of children is not necessary, since no original sinfulness needs to be remitted. Christ's redemption is confined to the forgiveness of personal sins; His grace, moreover, is not absolutely necessary to avoid them. The contrary would be derogatory to the intrinsic dignity of man's self-sufficient nature. Impoverishing greatly the Christian message according to which our sufficiency comes from Christ alone, this system left no room for trust in God and personal commitment to His action.

The main condemnation of Pelagius is that of the Council of Carthage, a city where he had spent some time after Alaric's conquest of Rome. The sentence of the two hundred Bishops gathered at Carthage was soon confirmed by Pope Zosimus, at least in part. The Pope's Epistola tractoria addressed to all the Churches, explicitly confirms canons 3-5, those namely which were also included later in the Indiculus *(cf. n. 1912); no similar papal confirmation is however extant as regards the other canons, which, nevertheless, have always been held in great esteem by the later Magisterium, as containing the doctrine of faith. For canons 1-2 on original sin, cf. nn. 501-502.*

1901 3. Likewise it has been decided: Whoever says that the
225 grace of God by which man is justified through Jesus Christ
our Lord serves only for the remission of sins already committed, and is not also a help not to commit them, *anathema sit*.

1902 4. Again: Whoever says that this same grace of God through
226 our Lord Jesus Christ helps us not to sin solely because
through it an understanding of the commandments is
revealed and opened to us that we may know what we should seek
and what we should avoid, but not because through it is given to us
the love and the strength to do what we have recognised to be in our
duty, *anathema sit*. For, since the apostle says: "Knowledge puffs
up, but love builds up" (*1 Cor. 8.1*), it would be very wrong to believe

that we have the grace of Christ for knowledge which puffs up and not for love which builds up; for both are the gift of God: the knowledge of what we should do and the love to do it, so that built up by love we may not be puffed up by knowledge. Just as it is written of God: "He teaches men knowledge" *(Ps. 94 (93)10)*, so too it is written: "love is of God" *(1 Jn 4.7)*.

1903 5. Likewise it has been decided: Whoever says that the grace
227   of justification is given to us so that we may do more easily with grace what we are ordered to do by our free will, as if even without grace we were able, though without facility, to fulfil the divine commandments, *anathema sit*. For when the Lord spoke of the fruits of the commandments, He did not say that apart from Him we could do things with greater difficulty, but rather: "Apart from me you can do nothing" *(Jn 15.5)*.

1904 6. Likewise it has been decided: When St John the apostle
228   says: "If we say we have no sin we deceive ourselves, and the truth is not in us" *(1 Jn 1.8)*, whoever takes this to mean that we must say we have sin out of humility, not because it is true, *anathema sit*. For the apostle continues: "If we confess our sins, He is faithful and just, and will forgive our sins and cleanse us from all unrighteousness" *(1 Jn 1.9)*. From this passage it is quite clear that that is not said only out of humility, but also in truth. For the apostle could have said: "If we say that we have no sin, we are boasting and humility is not in us." But since he says: "We deceive ourselves and the truth is not in us", he clearly shows that anyone who says he has no sin is not speaking truly but falsely.

1905 7. Likewise it has been decided: Whoever says that the
229   reason why the saints say in the Lord's prayer: "Forgive us our debts" *(Mt. 6.12)* is not that they are saying this for themselves—for such a petition is no longer necessary for them— but for others among their people who are sinners, and that this is why none of the saints says: "Forgive me my debts", but: "Forgive us our debts", so that the just man is understood to pray for others rather than for himself, *anathema sit*. For the apostle James was a holy and just man when he said: "We all offend in many things" *(James 3.2 Vulg.)*. Why was the word "all" added, if not to bring the expression into agreement with the Psalm where we read: "Enter not into judgment with thy servant, for no man living is righteous before thee" *(Ps. 143 (142) 2)*? And in the prayer of Solomon, the wise man, (we read): "There is no man who does not sin" *(1 Kings 8.46)*; and in

the book of the holy man Job: "He seals up the hand of every man, that every man may know his weakness" (*cf. Job 37.7, old mistranslation*). Even the holy and just Daniel used the plural form in his prayer, when he said: "We have sinned, we have done wickedly" (*Dan. 9.5, 15*), and other things which he there truly and humbly confesses. And lest anyone should think , as some do, that he was not speaking of his own sins, but of those of his people, he said further: "While I was...praying and confessing my sin and the sin of my people" (*Dan. 9.20*) to the Lord my God. He would not say "our sins", but he spoke of the sins of his people and of his own sins, for as a prophet he foresaw that in the future there would be some who would badly misunderstand him.

1906 8. Likewise it has been decided: Whoever holds that the
230   words of the Lord's prayer where we say: "Forgive us our
     debts" (*Mt. 6.12*) are said by the saints out of humility but not truthfully, *anathema sit*. For who could tolerate that a man who prays be lying not to men but to the Lord Himself, by saying with his lips that he wishes to be forgiven while in his heart he denies that he has any debts to be forgiven?

THE *INDICULUS* (between 435 and 442)

In his constant struggle with the Pelagians, particularly with Julian of Eklanus, Augustine focused his attention on the relationship between human freedom and divine grace, between God's universal saving will and the divine predestination of the elect. Fierce controversies followed. The strongest oppostition came from Southern France, where a group of monks led by Cassian (ob. 435) opposed certain aspects of the Augustinian teaching. According to these monks (later called Semi-Pelagians), all men, being equal before God, receive from Him an equal measure of grace; any difference in the bestowal of grace comes solely from the difference in men's dispositions; man needs grace to perform good works, but the beginning of conversion (or the 'beginning of faith', as it was technically called) is his own doing for which grace is not required; after this foundation has been laid by man's own strength, God will grant him a further increase of faith. The conception of man's salvation by God as a transaction between equal partners at least in its initial stage implied a practical denial of the supremacy of grace.

It is in the midst of the semi-Pelagian controversy that the Indiculus *was composed. Redacted probably by Prosper of Aquitaine (c. 390-460), a disciple of St Augustine and Cassian's strongest opponent, this document is a summary of the doctrine of grace, based on papal pronouncements, the decrees of African Councils which had subsequently received papal approval, and the Church's faith as expressed mainly in her liturgy. By the end of the fifth century it was already accepted as the standard exposition of the Church's doctrine of grace, and gradually acquired great authority, due mainly to its tacit approval by the universal Church. For chapter 1 on original sin, cf. n. 503.*

1907 Some people who pride themselves on the name of
238 Catholics, still remain, either through malice or through
ignorance, under the sway of opinions condemned as heretical and have the presumption to contradict the most holy defenders (of the faith). While these men do not hesitate to condemn Pelagius and Celestius, still they oppose our teachers as though they had gone beyond the necessary bounds. Since they profess to follow and approve only what the most Holy See of the blessed apostle Peter has sanctioned and taught through the ministry of its bishops against the enemies of the grace of God, it has been necessary to make a diligent investigation as to what judgment the rulers of the Roman Church passed on the heresy that arose during their time and what opinion they thought should be held about the grace of God against the dangerous upholders of free will. We are also adding some sentences of the African Councils which the apostolic bishops certainly made their own when they approved them. In order therefore that those who are in doubt about some point may be more fully instructed, we are publishing in this short catalogue (*Indiculus*) the constitutions of the holy Fathers. Thus, if a person is not too contentious, he will admit that the conclusion of all these discussions is contained in the brief statements of the authorities adduced, and that there is no ground left for asserting the contrary, if with Catholics he believes and professes the following:

(Papal condemnation of errors on grace)

1908 2. No one is good of himself unless He who alone is good
240 makes him share in Himself. This is what the same pontiff
declares in the same letter where he says: "Can we henceforth expect anything good from men who think they can attribute to themselves the fact that they are good, without considering Him whose grace they receive every day, and who trust that without Him they are able to achieve so much ?"[1]

1909 3. Nobody, not even he who has been renewed by the grace
241 of baptism, is capable of overcoming the snares of the devil
and of conquering the concupiscence of the flesh, unless he

---

1. This refers to the *Epistola In Requirendis,* 3, addressed by Pope Innocent I to the Council of Carthage, already mentioned in chapter 1 of the *Indiculus (cf. n. 503).*

receives perseverance in good conduct through the daily help of God. This truth is confirmed by the doctrine of the same pontiff in the above quoted letter: "For although He redeemed man from his past sins, still, knowing that man could sin again, He kept many means whereby He could restore him and set him straight thereafter, offering him those daily remedies upon which we must always rely with confidence and trust; for by no other means shall we ever be able to overcome our human errors. For it is inevitable that, as with His help we conquer, without His help we are conquered."[1]

1910   5. All the efforts and all the works and merits of the saints
243   must be referred to the praise and glory of God, for no one
           can please Him except by what He Himself has given....

(*Are quoted as autnorities one passage of the* Epistola tractoria *of Pope Zosimus and its specific approval by the African bishops.*)

1911   6. God so works in the hearts of men and in the free will itself
244   that a holy thought, a good counsel and every movement of a
           good will come from God, because it is through Him that we can do any good, without whom we can do nothing (*cf. Jn 15.5*). The same teacher Zosimus instructed us to profess this doctrine when, speaking to the bishops of the whole world about the assistance of divine grace, he said: "Is there ever a time when we do not need His help ? Therefore in all our actions and affairs, in all our thoughts and inclinations, we must pray to Him as to our helper and protector. For it is pride on the part of human nature to arrogate anything to itself, when the apostle proclaims: "We are not contending against flesh and blood, but against the principalities, against the powers, against the world rulers of this present darkness, against the spiritual hosts of wickedness in the heavenly places" (*Eph. 6.12*). And as he says elsewhere: "Wretched man that I am ! Who will deliver me from the body of death ? The grace of God through our Lord Jesus Christ" (*Rom. 7.24 Vulg.*). And again: "By the grace of God I am what I am, and this grace towards me was not in vain. On the contrary, I worked harder than any of them, though it was not I but the grace of God which is in me" (*1 Cor. 15.10*)."[2]

(*Pontifical approval of the decrees of the Council of Carthage*)

1912   7. We likewise uphold as the teaching proper to the Holy

---

1. *Epistola In Requirendis*, 7.

2. *Epistola tractoria.*

245   See what was laid down in the decrees of the Council of
       Carthage; namely, what was defined in the third chapter
(there follows the text quoted in n. 1901), and again in the fourth
chapter *(n. 1902)*, and similarly in the fifth chapter *(n. 1903)*.

(The Liturgy and the necessity of grace)

(1913)   *(The necessity of grace is further established from the liturgy, the*
246   *many prayers offered for the conversion of people, so that "the*
             norm of prayer may establish the norm of belief".)

1914   9. ...Therefore, with the help of the Lord, we are so strength-
248   ened by these Church norms and these documents derived
           from divine authority that we acknowledge God as the
author of all good desires and deeds, of all efforts and virtues by
which from the beginning of faith man tends towards God. And we
do not doubt that all human merits are preceded by the grace of Him
through whom it is that we begin to will and to do any good work *(cf.
Phil. 2.13)*. By this help and gift of God, free will is assuredly not
destroyed but liberated, so that from darkness it is brought to light,
from evil to rectitude, from sickness to health, from imprudence to
circumspection. For such is God's goodness towards all men that
He wants His own gifts to be our merits and that He will give us an
eternal reward for what He has bestowed upon us. Indeed God so
acts in us that we both will and do what He wills; He does not permit
to lie idle in us what He has given us to be employed, not neglected,
so that we may be cooperators with the grace of God. And if we
notice that something is slackening in us because of our negligence,
we should earnestly have recourse to Him, who heals all our diseases and redeems our life from destruction *(cf. Ps. 103 (102) 3f)*, and
to whom we say daily: "Lead us not into temptation but deliver us
from evil" *(Mt. 6.13)*.

249   ...Whatever is contrary to the above statements we clearly
       consider as not being Catholic.

THE SECOND COUNCIL OF ORANGE (529)

*The Semi-Pelagian conflict continued well into the sixth century, and
was finally settled by the Council of Orange in 529, nearly a hundred years
after St Augustine's death. Caesarius of Arles, disciple of Augustine, sent to
Pope Felix IV nineteen chapters on grace culled from Augustine's works.
The Pope accepted eight and added others taken from a list drawn up by
Prosper of Aquitaine. It is this complex document which was accepted by*

the local Council of Orange and later approved by Felix's successor, Boniface II. In general, therefore, it can be said that the Council reflects a moderate Augustinianism, without upholding each one of Augustine's propositions. As for its doctrinal authority, the precise nature and the extent of the Pope's approval remain doubtful; the decrees of the Council soon fell into oblivion, which lasted until the sixteenth century. However, the Council was later explicitly quoted by both Vatican I (cf. n. 120) and Vatican II (cf. n. 152). For the canons on original sin, cf. nn. 504-505.

Canons on grace

1915 3. If anyone says that the grace of God can be conferred
373   because of human prayer, and not rather that it is grace itself
         that prompts us to pray, he contradicts the prophet Isaiah, or the apostle who says the same thing: "I have been found by those who did not seek me; I have shown myself to those who did ask for me" (Rom. 10.20; cf. Is. 65.1).

1916 4. If anyone contends that God awaits our will before cleans-
374   ing us from sin, but does not confess that even the desire to
         be cleansed is aroused in us by the infusion and action of the Holy Spirit, he opposes the Holy Spirit Himself speaking through Solomon: "The will is prepared by the Lord" (Prov. 8.35 Septuag.), and the apostle's salutary message: "God is at work in you, both to will and to work for His good pleasure" (Phil. 2.13).

1917 5. If anyone says that the increase as well as the beginning of
375   faith and the very desire of faith—by which we believe in Him
         who justifies the sinner and by which we come to the regeneration of holy baptism—proceeds from our own nature and not from a gift of grace, namely from an inspiration of the Holy Spirit changing our will from unbelief to belief and from godlessness to piety, such a man reveals himself in contradiction with the apostolic doctrine, since Paul says: "I am sure that He who began a good work in you will bring it to completion at the day of Christ Jesus" (Phil. 1.6); and again: "It has been granted to you that for the sake of Christ you should not only believe in Him but also suffer for His sake" (Phil. 1.29); and also: "By grace you have been saved, through faith; and this is not your own doing, it is the gift of God" (Eph. 2.8). For those who say that the faith by which we believe in God is natural, declare that all those who are strangers to the Church of Christ are, in some way, believers.

1918 6. If anyone says that mercy is ·divinely conferred upon us
376   when, without God's grace, we believe, will, desire, strive,
         labour, pray, keep watch, endeavour, request, seek, knock.

but does not confess that it is through the infusion and inspiration of the Holy Spirit that we believe, will or are able to do all these things as is required; or if anyone subordinates the help of grace to humility or human obedience, and does not admit that it is the very gift of grace that makes us obedient and humble, he contradicts the apostle who says: "What have you that you did not receive ?" *(1 Cor. 4.7);* and also: "By the grace of God I am what I am" *(1 Cor. 15.10).*

1919 7. If anyone asserts that by his natural strength he is able
377   to think as is required or choose anything good pertaining to
       his eternal salvation, or to assent to the saving message of the Gospel without the illumination and inspiration of the Holy Spirit, who gives to all ease and joy in assenting to the truth and believing it, he is deceived by the heretical spirit and does not understand the word said by God in the Gospel: "Apart from me you can do nothing" *(Jn 15.5),* nor the word of the Apostle: "Not that we are sufficient of ourselves to claim anything as coming from us; our sufficiency is from God" *(2 Cor. 3.5).*

1920 8. If anyone maintains that some are able to come to the
378   grace of baptism through (God's) mercy, but others through
       their own free will—which, it is clear, is wounded in all those who are born from the transgression of the first man—he shows that he has departed from the orthodox faith. For he does not acknowledge that free will has been weakened in all by the sin of the first man, or at least he holds that free will has been wounded only in such a way that some are still able to attain to the mystery of eternal salvation by themselves without divine revelation. Yet that the opposite is true is proved by the Lord Himself, who does not testify that some can come to Him, but that nobody can, unless he is drawn by the Father *(cf. Jn 6.55),* as He also says to Peter: "Blessed are you, Simon Bar Jona! For flesh and blood has not revealed this to you, but my Father who is in heaven" *(Mt. 16.17).* And the apostle too says: "No one can say: 'Jesus is the Lord', except by the Holy Spirit" *(1 Cor. 12.3).*

Conclusion redacted by Caesarius of Arles

(The teaching of Tradition on grace)

1921 Thus, according to the texts of Holy Scripture and the expla-
396   nations of the early Fathers quoted above, we must with
       God's help preach and believe the following: free will has

been so distorted and weakened by the sin of the first man, that thereafter no one could love God as was required, or believe in God, or perform for the sake of God what is good, unless the grace of the divine mercy first attained him. Therefore we believe that that excellent faith, so highly proclaimed to their praise by St Paul (*Heb. 11*), which was given to the just Abel, to Noah, to Abraham, Isaac and Jacob, and to that vast multitude of saints of old, was conferred through the grace of God, and not through the natural goodness which had first been given to Adam. And we know and believe that, even after the coming of the Lord, for all those who desire to be baptised this grace (of faith) is not found in their free will, but is conferred by the generosity of Christ, according to what has been repeatedly said above and which the apostle Paul preaches: "It has been granted to you that for the sake of Christ you should not only believe in Him but also suffer for His sake" (*Phil 1.29*); and also: "He who began a good work in you will bring it to completion at the day of Jesus Christ" (*Phil. 1.6*); and again: "By grace you have been saved through faith; and this is not your own doing, it is the gift of God" (*Eph. 2.8*). And of himself the apostle says: "I have obtained mercy that I might be faithful" (*1 Cor. 7.25 Vulg.*); where he does not say: "because I was faithful", but rather: "that I might be faithful." And again: "What have you that you did not receive ?" (*1 Cor. 4.7*); and again: "Every good endowment and every perfect gift is from above, coming down from the Father of lights" (*James 1.17*); and again: "No one can receive anything except what is given him from heaven" (*Jn 3.27*). There are innumerable passages of Sacred Scripture that could be adduced as testimonies in favour of grace, but they have been omitted for the sake of brevity. For, indeed, more texts will not help anyone for whom a few do not suffice.

(The teaching of Tradition on predestination)

1922 According to the Catholic faith we also believe that after
397 grace has been received through baptism, all the baptised, if
they are willing to labour faithfully, can and ought to accomplish with Christ's help and cooperation what pertains to the salvation of their souls. Not only do we not believe that some are predestined to evil by the divine power, but if there are any who wish to believe such an enormity, we with great abhorrence anathematise them. We also believe and profess for our salvation that in every good work it is not we who begin and afterwards are helped by God's mercy, but He Himself who, without any previous merits on our part,

first instils in us faith in Him and love for Him, so that we may faithfully seek the sacrament of baptism and, after baptism, we may with His help accomplish what is pleasing to Him. Therefore we must clearly believe that the wonderful faith of the thief whom the Lord called to His home in paradise (cf. Lk. 23.43), of Cornelius the centurion to whom an angel of the Lord was sent (cf. Acts 10.3) and Zacchaeus who merited to receive the Lord Himself (cf. Lk. 19.6) did not come from nature but was a gift from the bounty of divine grace.

LEO X

BULL *EXSURGE DOMINE* (1520)

The protracted controversies on grace which shook the Church from the time of Augustine onwards had undoubtedly the salutary effect of focussing the theological attention on, and throwing into bold relief, such important doctrines as the necessity of grace, the gratuitousness of faith as the initial step on the way to salvation, the right understanding of God's universal saving will, of divine predestination, original sin and the necessity of baptism. But there were liabilities as well, for there resulted a gradual departure from the biblical and patristic viewpoint. The theology of grace was no longer centred on the person of the Spirit dwelling in the justified man but rather on the created reality of grace. An effort made by Peter Lombard to stress the role of the Holy Spirit proved unsuccessful in so far as he wrongly identified created grace with the divine person of the Spirit. Hence it happened that in their zeal to vindicate the reality of created grace as distinct from the indwelling Spirit, medieval theologians began so to stress sanctifying grace as to almost entirely overlook the place of the Spirit in the mystery of grace. The description of the reality of created grace and of its action in terms of Aristotelian categories further contributed to separate the theological language from the biblical sources.

The Reformers reacted sharply against too juridical and metaphysical a conception of grace. Their reaction, however, was marred by an extreme pessimism and an extrinsic conception of man's justification. Luther's teaching on grace can be summarised as follows: original sin has so deeply affected human nature that, steeped in sinfulness, man sins in every action he does. He finds salvation through total faith in Jesus Christ which gives him the assurance that his sins are forgiven. He is thus justified before God; yet, inwardly, because of his concupiscence, he remains a sinner. His justification consists in the fact that God in His mercy no longer imputes sin to him. Thus, he is at once and simultaneously just on account of Christ's justice, and sinner by his own ineradicable sinfulness. In spite of the ambiguity of some of his expressions, Luther holds man to be radically transformed by a gratuitous justification which is deeply Christological. For, according to him the righteousness of Christ is not merely attributed to the justified legally and externally, but is rather Christ's presence in him through faith and the Holy Spirit. Thus justified, man is bound to perform good works, which are the external signs of his justification; but these works cannot cause in him an increase in grace.

Among Luther's proposition condemned by Pope Leo X in the Bull Exsurge Domine *(cf. n. 1309i), some pertaining to grace are quoted here.*

(Errors of Luther condemned)

[1923/2]   To deny that sin remains in a child after baptism is to
1452   disregard both Paul and Christ alike.

[1923/3]   The seed of sin *(fomes peccati)* hinders a soul departing
1453   from the body from entering into heaven, even though
             there is no actual sin.

[1923/31]   In every good work the just man sins.
1481

[1923/32]   A good work perfectly performed is a venial sin.
1482

[1923/36]   After sin, free will is an empty concept; and when it does
1486   what is in its power, it sins mortally.

THE GENERAL COUNCIL OF TRENT

SIXTH SESSION

DECREE ON JUSTIFICATION (1547)

The preparatory work for this most important decree of the Council took seven months. Its purpose was not only to reject the objectionable teaching of the Reformers, but to give a coherent exposition of the Catholic doctrine on grace. The Decree steers a middle course between the two extremes of Pelagian self-sufficiency and of the Protestant diffidence regarding the capabilities of man's wounded nature. The Decree is not concerned with the justification of children, who receive the grace of justification by baptism without their personal cooperation, but exclusively with that of adults. The entire document is built on the conception of a triple justification: the moment when justification is first attained; the preservation and increase of this justification; and the recovery of justification after it has been lost through sin.

Chapter I-III offer an overall view of God's plan of salvation: man is unable to justify himself (chapter I), but, thanks to the divine dispensation manifested in Christ (chapter II), he attains justification through Him (chapter III). Chapters IV-IX deal with the first justification as the concrete realisation of the divine plan of salvation: a brief outline of this first justification (chapter IV) is followed by the conciliar exposition of the necessity of preparing for it (chapter V) and the manner of this preparation (chapter VI). The causes of justification are briefly stated within the framework of the categories of scholastic theology then prevalent (chapter VII). The two concluding chapters of this section explain the correct understanding of the Pauline formula stressed by Luther, according to which the sinner is justified through faith (chapter VIII), and the reasons for rejecting Luther's conception of the certainity of justification through faith (chapter IX). Chapters

X-XIII deal with the second justification, the preservation and the increase of grace; man's justice can and ought to increase (chapter X) through the observance of the commandments, which bind also the justified (chapter XI). No one should rashly consider himself among the predestined (chapter XII), for final perseverance remains a gratuitous gift of God (chapter XIII).

Finally, chapters XIV-XV treat the possibility of recovering justification (chapter XIV), if it has been lost through sin (chapter XV), while the last chapter is devoted to merit (chapter XVI) as the fruit of justification; this chapter, completely biblical in conception, is one of the most satisfactory of the entire decree. To the chapters are appended corresponding canons, where the same doctrine is found in the form of the condemnation of opposite errors.

Foreword

1924 Since at this time a certain erroneous doctrine about justifica-
1520 tion is being disseminated not without the loss of many souls
and serious damage to Church unity, this holy, ecumenical and general Council of Trent, lawfully assembled in the Holy Spirit for the praise and glory of almighty God, for the tranquility of the Church and for the salvation of souls... intends to set forth for all the faithful of Christ the true and sound doctrine of justification which the "Sun of justice" (*Mal. 4.2*), Jesus Christ, "the pioneer and perfecter of our faith" (*Heb. 12.2*), has taught, which the apostles have handed down and which the Catholic Church, under the inspiration of the Holy Spirit, has always preserved. The Council strictly forbids that henceforth anyone dare to believe, preach or teach anything contrary to what is determined and declared in this Decree.

Chapter 1: The inability of nature
and the law to justify man

1925 First the holy Council declares that for a correct and clear
1521 understanding of the doctrine of justification if is neces-
sary that each one admits and confesses that all men, having lost innocence through the sin of Adam (*cf. Rom. 5.12; 1 Cor. 15.22*), "became unclean" (*Is. 64.6*) and, according to the apostle, were "by nature children of wrath" (*Eph. 2.3*), as the Council taught in its decree on original sin. So completely were they the slaves of sin (*cf. Rom. 6.20*) and under the power of the devil and of death, that not only the gentiles by means of the power of nature (*cf. n. 1951*) but even the Jews by means of the letter of the Law of Moses were unable to liberate themselves and to rise from that state, even though their free will, weakened and distorted as it was, was in no way extinct (*cf. n. 1955*).

Chapter II: The divine dispensation and the mystery of Christ's coming

1926 And so it came to pass that, when the blessed "fulness of
1522 time" (*Eph. 1.10; Gal. 4.4*) had come, the heavenly Father,
"the Father of all mercies and God of all comfort" (*2 Cor. 1.3*)
sent to men His own Son Jesus Christ (*cf. n. 1951*), who had been
announced and promised to many holy fathers before the Law and
during the time of the Law (*cf. Gen. 49.10, 18*). He was sent that the
Jews, who were under the Law, might be redeemed, and that the
Gentiles "who were not pursuing righteousness" (*Rom. 9.30*) might
attain it, and that all "might receive adoption as sons" (*Gal. 4.5*). God
has "put Him forward as an expiation by His blood, to be received by
faith" (*Rom. 3.25*), for our sins and "not for our sins only, but also for
the sins of the whole world" (*1 Jn 2.2*).

Chapter III: On those who are justified through Christ

1927 But even though "Christ died for all" (*2 Cor. 5.15*), still not all
1523 receive the benefit of His death, but only those to whom the
merit of His passion is imparted. For, as truly as men would
not be born unrighteous if they were not born children of Adam's
seed, since it is because of their descent from him that in their
conception they contract unrighteousness as their own, likewise
they would never be justified if they were not reborn in Christ (*cf. nn.
1952, 1960*), for it is this rebirth that bestows on them, through the
merit of His passion, the grace by which they become just. It is for
this favour that the apostle exhorts us always to give thanks to the
Father, "who has qualified us to share in the inheritance of the saints
in light" (*Col. 1.12*) and "has delivered us from the dominion of
darkness and transferred us to the kingdom of His beloved Son in
whom we have redemption, the forgiveness of sins " (*Col. 1.13f*).

Chapter IV: A brief description of the sinner's justification: its manner under the dispensation of grace

1928 In these words a description is outlined of the justification of
1524 the sinner as being a transition from the state in which man is
born a son of the first Adam, to the state of grace and
adoption as sons of God (*cf. Rom. 8.15*) through the second Adam,
Jesus Christ our Saviour. After the promulgation of the Gospel, this
transition cannot take place without the bath of regeneration (*cf. n.*

1424) or the desire fot it, as it is written: "Unless one is born of water and the Spirit, he cannot enter the kingdom of God"(Jn 3.5).

Chapter V: The necessity for adults to prepare themselves for justification and the origin of this justification

1929 The Council moreover declares that in adults the beginning
1525   of justification must be attributed to God's prevenient grace
through Jesus Christ (cf. n. 1953), that is, to His call addressed to them without any previous merits of theirs. Thus, those who through their sins were turned away from God, awakened and assisted by His grace, are disposed to turn to their own justification by freely assenting to and cooperating with that grace (cf. nn. 1954-1955). In this way, God touches the heart of man with the illumination of the Holy Spirit, but man himself is not inactive while receiving that inspiration, since he can reject it; and yet, without God's grace, he cannot by his own free will take one step towards justice in God's sight (cf. n. 1953). Hence, when it is said in sacred Scripture: "Return to me and I will return to you" (Zech. 1.3), we are reminded of our freedom; but when we reply: "Restore us to Thyself, O Lord, that we may be restored" (Lam. 5.21), we acknowledge that God's grace precedes us.

Chapter VI: The manner of preparation

1930 Adults are disposed for that justice (cf. nn. 1957, 1959) when,
1526   awakened and assisted by divine grace, they conceive faith
from hearing (cf. Rom. 10.17) and are freely led to God, believing to be true what has been divinely revealed and promised (cf. nn. 1962-1964), especially that the sinner is justified by God's grace "through the redemption which is in Christ Jesus" (Rom. 3.24); when, understanding that they are sinners and turning from the fear of divine justice—which gives them a salutary shock (cf. n. 1958)—to the consideration of God's mercy, they are aroused to the confident hope that God will be propitious to them because of Christ; when they begin to love God as the source of all justice and are thereby moved by a certain hatred and detestation for sin (cf. n. 1959), that is, by that repentance that must be practiced before baptism (cf. Acts 2.38); when, finally, they determine to receive baptism, to begin a new life and to keep the divine commandments.

1931   Scripture says about this disposition: "Whoever would
1527   draw near to God must believe that He exists and that He
        rewards those who seek Him" (*Heb. 11.6*); and: "Take heart,
my son, your sins are forgiven" (*Mt. 9.2; Mk 2.5*); and: "The fear of
the Lord drives out sin" (*Sir. 1.27 Vulg.*); and: "Repent and be
baptised everyone of you in the name of Jesus Christ for the forgiveness of sins; and you shall receive the gift of the Holy Spirit" *(Acts
2.38)*; and: "Go therefore and make disciples of all nations, baptising
them in the name of the Father, and of the Son and of the Holy Spirit,
teaching them to observe all that I have commanded you" (*Mt.
28.19*); and finally: "Direct your heart to the Lord" (*1 Sam. 7.3*).

Chapter VII: The nature and the causes
of the sinner's justification

1932   This disposition or preparation is followed by justification
1528   itself, which is not the remission of sins (*cf. n. 1961*) but the
        sanctification and renewal of the interior man through the
voluntary reception of grace and of the gifts, whereby from unjust
man becomes just, and from enemy a friend, that he may be "an heir
in hope of eternal life" (*Tit. 3.7*).

1529   The causes of this justification are the following: the final
        cause is the glory of God and of Christ, and life everlasting.
The efficient cause is the merciful God who gratuitously washes and
sanctifies (*cf. 1 Cor. 6.11*), sealing and anointing "with the promised
Holy Spirit, who is the guarantee of our inheritance" (*Eph. 1.13*). The
meritorious cause is the beloved only-begotten Son of God, our Lord
Jesus Christ who, "while we were sinners" (*Rom. 5.10*), "out of the
great love with which He loved us" (*Eph. 2.4*) merited for us justification by His most holy passion on the wood of the Cross (*cf. n. 1960*)
and made satisfaction for us to God the Father. The instrumental
cause is the sacrament of baptism which is the 'sacrament of faith',
without which (faith) no one has ever been justified. Finally, the single
formal cause is "the justice of God, not that by which He Himself is
just, but that by which He makes us just"[1] (*cf. nn. 1960-1961*), namely
the justice which we have as a gift from Him and by which we are
spiritually renewed. Thus, not only are we considered just, but we

---

1. Cf. St Augustine, *De Trinitate*, XIV, 12, 15.

are truly called just and we are just, each one receiving within himself his own justice, according to the measure which "the Holy Spirit apportions to each one individually as He wills" (1 Cor. 12.11), and according to each one's personal disposition and cooperation.

1933 For although no one can be just unless the merits of the
1530 passion of our Lord Jesus Christ are imparted to him, still this communication takes place in the justification of the sinner, when by the merit of the same most holy passion, "God's love is poured through the Holy Spirit into the hearts" (Rom. 5.5) of those who are being justified and inheres in them (cf .n. 1961). Hence, in the very act of justification, together with the remission of sins, man receives through Jesus Christ, into whom he is inserted, the gifts of faith, hope and charity, all infused at the same time.

1934 For faith without hope and charity neither unites a man
1531 perfectly with Christ, nor makes him a living member of His body. Therefore it is rightly said that "faith by itself, if it has no works, is dead" (James 2.17) and unprofitable (cf. n. 1969), and that "in Christ Jesus neither circumcision nor uncircumcision is of any avail, but faith working through love" (Gal 5.6; 6.15). This is the faith which, in keeping with apostolic tradition, the catechumens ask of the Church before the reception of baptism when they ask for "the faith that gives eternal life",[1] a life which faith without hope and charity cannot give. Hence they immediately hear Christ's words: "If you would enter life, keep the commandments" (Mt. 19, 17; cf. nn. 1968-1970). Accordingly, while they receive the true Christian justice, as soon as they have been reborn, they are commanded to keep it resplendent and spotless, like their "best robe" (Lk. 15.22) given to them through Jesus Christ in place of the one Adam lost for himself and for us by his disobedience, so that they may wear it before the tribunal of our Lord Jesus Christ and have eternal life.

Chapter VIII: The correct understanding of the sinner's gratuitous justification through faith

1935 When the apostle says that man is justified "through faith" (cf.
1532 n. 1959) and "gratuitously" (Rom. 3.22, 24), those words are to be understood in the sense in which the Catholic Church

---

1. *Roman Ritual,* Order of Baptism, 1.

has held and declared them with uninterrupted unanimity, namely, that we are said to be justified through faith because "faith is the beginning of man's salvation",[1] the foundation and root of all justification, "without which it is impossible to please God" (*Heb. 11.6*) and to come into the fellowship of His sons. And we are said to be justified gratuitously because nothing that precedes justification, neither faith nor works, merits the grace of justification; for "if it is by grace, it is no longer on the basis of works; otherwise (as the same apostle says) grace would no longer be grace" (*Rom. 11.6*).

Chapter IX: Against the vain confidence of heretics

1936 It is necessary to believe that sins are not forgiven and have
1533 never been forgiven except gratuitously by the divine mercy on account of Christ. And yet it must not be said that sins are forgiven or have been forgiven to anyone who boasts of his confidence and certainty that his sins are forgiven and who relies upon this confidence alone. This vain confidence which is foreign to all piety may exist and actually exists in our times among heretics and schismatics and is preached very vigorously against the Catholic Church (*cf. n. 1962*).

1534 Moreover it must not be asserted that those who are truly justified should unhesitatingly determine within themselves that they are justified, and that no one is absolved from his sins and justified unless he believes with certainty that he is absolved and justified, and that absolution and justification are brought about by this faith alone (*cf. n. 1964*), as if whoever lacks this faith were doubting God's promises and the efficacy of Christ's death and resurrection. For just as no devout man should doubt God's mercy, Christ's merit and the power and efficacy of the sacraments; so also, whoever considers himself, his personal weakness and his lack of disposition, may fear and tremble about his own grace (*cf. n. 1963*), since no one can know with a certitude of faith which cannot be subject to error, that he has obtained God's grace.

Chapter X: The increase of justification in the justified

1937 In this way therefore the justified become both "friends of

---

1. FULGENTIUS OF RUSPA, *De fide liber ad Petrum*, prologue, 1.

1535   God" and "members of His household" *(Jn 15.15; Eph. 2.19);*
"they go from strength to strength" *(Ps. 84 (83) 7),* "renewed
(as the apostle says) every day" *(2 Cor. 4.16),* that is "by putting to
death the members of their flesh" *(Col. 3.5 Vulg.)* and using them "as
instruments of righteousness" *(Rom. 6.13, 19)* unto sanctification by
observing the commandments of God and of the Church. When
"faith is active along with works" *(James 2.22),* they increase in the
very justice they have received through the grace of Christ, and are
further justified *(cf. nn. 1974, 1982),* as it is writtten: "Let the holy still
be holy" *(Rev. 22.11);* and again: "Fear not to be justified until you
die" *(Sir. 18.22 Vulg.);* and again: "You see that a man is justified by
works and not by faith alone" *(James 2.24).* It is this increase in faith
that the holy Church asks for when she prays: "Give us, O Lord, an
increase of faith, hope and charity."[1]

Chapter XI: The observance of the commandments; its necessity and possibility

1938   No one, however much he be justified, should consider him-
1536   self exempt from the observance of the commandments *(cf.
n. 1970);* and no one should say that the observance of God's
commandments is impossible for the man justified—a rash statement censured by the Fathers with anathema *(cf. nn. 1968, 1972).*
"For God does not command the impossible, but when He commands He admonishes you to do what you can and to pray for what
you cannot do",[2] and He helps you to be able to do it. "His commandments are not burdensome" *(1 Jn 5.3);* His "yoke is easy and His
burden light" *(Mt. 11.30).* For those who are sons of God love Christ,
and those who love Him keep His words, as He Himself testifies *(cf.
Jn 14.23),* and this they certainly can do with God's help.

1537   For although in this mortal life men, however just and holy
they may be, fall, sometimes at least, into those slight and
daily sins which are also called venial *(cf. n. 1973),* they do not on that
account cease to be just. For the petition of the just: "forgive us our
debts" *(Mt. 6.12),* is both humble and true. Hence the just themselves should feel all the more obliged to walk in the way of justice
because, having been "set free from sin and become the slaves of

---

1. *Roman Missal,* Thirteenth Sunday after Pentecost.
2. St Augustine, *De natura et gratia,* 43, 50.

God" *(Rom. 6.22)*, they can, by living "sober, upright and godly lives" *(Tit. 2.12)*, progress through Jesus Christ, through whom "they have obtained access to this grace" *(Rom. 5.2)*. For God "does not desert" those who have been once justified by His grace "unless they desert Him first".[1]

1939 Therefore nobody should flatter himself with faith alone *(cf.
1538* nn. 1959, 1969, 1970)*, thinking that by faith alone he is made an heir and will obtain the inheritance, even if he does not "suffer with Christ in order that he may also be glorified with Him" *(Rom 8.17)*. For even Christ Himself, as the apostle says, "although He was a Son, learned obedience through what He suffered, and, being made perfect, He became the source of eternal salvation to all who obey Him" *(Heb. 5.8f)*. That is why the apostle himself admonishes the justified, saying: "Do you not know that in a race all the runners compete, but only one receives the prize? So run that you may obtain it.... Well, I do not run aimlessly, I do not box as one beating the air; but I pommel my body and subdue it, lest after preaching to others I myself should be disqualified" *(1 Cor. 9.24-27)*. Similarly Peter the prince of the apostles says: "Be the more zealous to confirm your call and election through good works; for if you do this you will never sin" *(2 Pet. 1.10 Vulg.)*.

1940 Hence it is clear that those are opposed to the orthodox
1539 doctrine of religion who maintain that the just man sins at least venially in every good work *(cf. n. 1975)*, or (what is even more intolerable) that he merits eternal punishment. They too are opposed to it who assert that the just sin in all their works if in those works, while overcoming their sloth and encouraging themselves to run the race, they look for an eternal reward in addition to their primary intention of glorifying God *(cf. nn. 1976, 1981)*. For it is written: "I have disposed my heart to perform your statutes for the sake of the reward *(Ps. 119 (118) 112 Vulg.)*; and speaking of Moses the apostle says that "he looked to the reward" *(Heb. 11.26)*.

*Chapter XII: Rash presumption of one's own
predestination must be avoided*

1941 Furthermore, no one, so long as he lives in this mortal

---

1. ST AUGUSTINE, *De natura et gratia*, 26, 29.

1540   condition, ought to be so presumptuous about the deep mystery of divine predestination as to determine with certainty
that he is definitely among the number of the predestined (*cf. n.
1965*), as if it were true either that the one justified cannot sin
anymore (*cf. n. 1973*) or that, if he sins, he should promise himself an
assured repentance. For without special revelation it is impossible to
know whom God has chosen for Himself (*cf. n. 1966*).

Chapter XIII: The gift of perseverance

1942   The same is to be said of the gift of perseverance (*cf. n. 1966*),
1541   about which it is written: "He who endures to the end will be
saved"(*Mt. 10.22; 24.13*). This gift can be had only from Him
who has the power to uphold him who stands that he may stand with
perseverance (*cf. Rom. 14.4*) and who can lift him who falls. Let no
one promise himself any security about this gift with absolute certitude, although all should place their firmest hope in God's help. For,
unless they themselves are unfaithful to His grace, God, who began
the good work, will bring it to completion, effecting both the will and
the execution (*cf. Phil. 2.13; n. 1972*). Yet "let anyone who thinks that
he stands take heed lest he fall" (*1 Cor. 10.12*) and let him "work out
his salvation with fear and trembling" (*Phil. 2.12*), in labours, in vigils,
in almsgiving, in prayers and offerings, in fastings and chastity (*cf. 2.
Cor. 6.3ff*). Knowing that they are reborn unto the hope of glory (*cf.
1. Pet. 1.3*) and not yet unto glory, they should be in dread about the
battle they still have to wage with the flesh, the word and the devil, in
which they cannot be the winners unless with God's grace they obey
the apostle who says: "We are debtors, not to the flesh to live
according to the flesh, for if you live according to the flesh you will
die, but if by the Spirit you put to death the deeds of the body, you will
live" (*Rom. 8.12f*).

Chapter XIV: Those who sin after justification and
their restoration to grace

1943   Those who through sin have forfeited the grace of justifica-
1542   tion they had received, can be justified again (*cf. n. 1979*)
when, awakened by God, they make the effort to regain
through the sacrament of penance and by the merits of Christ the
grace they have lost. This manner of justification is the restoration of

the sinner which the holy Fathers aptly called "the second plank after the shipwreck of the loss of grace".[1] For Christ Jesus instituted the sacrament of penance for those who fall into sin after baptism, when He said: "Receive the Holy Spirit. If you forgive the sins of any, they are forgiven; if you retain the sins of any, they are retained" *(Jn 20.22f)*.

1944　Hence it must be taught that the repentance of a Christian
1543　after his fall into sin differs vastly from repentance at the time
　　　　of baptism. If includes not only giving up sins and detesting them, or "a broken and contrite heart" *(Ps. 51 (50) 17)*, but also their sacramental confession or at least the desire to confess them when a suitable occasion will be found, and the absolution of a priest; it also includes satisfaction by fasts, almsgiving, prayer and other pious exercises of the spiritual life, not indeed for the eternal punishment which, together with the guilt, is remitted by the reception or the desire of the sacrament, but for the temporal punishment *(cf. n. 1980)* which, as sacred Scripture teaches, is not always entirely remitted, as is done in baptism, to those who, ungrateful to the grace of God they have received, have grieved the Holy Spirit *(cf. Eph. 4.30)* and have not feared to violate the temple of God *(cf. 1. Cor. 3.17)*. Of this form of repentance it is written: "Remember from what you have fallen, repent and do the works you did at first" *(Rev. 2.5)*; and again: "Godly grief produces a repentance that leads to salvation" *(2 Cor. 7.10)*; and again: "Repent" *(Mt. 3.2; 4.17)*; and: "Bear fruit that befits repentance" *(Mt. 3.8)*.

　　　　Chapter XV: By every mortal sin grace is lost,
　　　　　　　　　but not faith

1945　It must also be asserted against the cunning wits of some
1544　who "by fair and flattering words deceive the hearts of the
　　　　simple-minded" *(Rom. 16.18)*, that the grace of justification, once received, is lost not only by unbelief *(cf. n. 1977)* which causes the loss of faith itself, but also by any other mortal sin, even though faith is not lost *(cf. n. 1978)*. Thus is defended the teaching of divine law that excludes from the kingdom of God not only unbelievers, but also the faithful who are "immoral, adulterers, homosexuals, thieves,

---

1. See for instance, Tᴇʀᴛᴜʟʟɪᴀɴ, *De paenitentia*, 4, 2; Sᴛ Jᴇʀᴏᴍᴇ, *Epistola* 84 *ad Pammachium et Oceanum*, 6; *Epistola* 130 *ad Demetriadem*, 9....

greedy, drunkards, revilers, robbers" (1 Cor. 6.9f), and all others who commit mortal sins which they can avoid with the help of divine grace and which seperate them from the grace of Christ (cf. n. 1977).

Chapter XVI: The merit of good works as a result of justification and the nature of merit

1946 Therefore, it is with this in mind that the men justified, 1545 whether they have continuously kept the grace they have once received or have lost it and recovered it, should be asked to consider the words of the apostle: "Abound in the good work of the Lord, knowing that in the Lord your labour is not in vain" (1 Cor. 15.58); "God is not so unjust as to overlook your work and the love which you showed for His sake" (Heb. 6.10); and: "Do not throw away your confidence, which has a great reward" (Heb. 10.35). And eternal life should therefore be set before those who persevere in good works "to the end" (Mt. 10.22) and who hope in God, both as a grace mercifully promised to the sons of God through Jesus Christ, and "as a reward"[1] which, according to the promise of God Himself, will faithfully be given them for their good works and merits (cf. nn. 1976, 1982). For this is the crown of justice which the apostle says is laid up for him after the fight and the race; the crown that will be given him by the just Judge, and not to him alone but to all who love His coming (cf. 2 Tim. 4.7f).

1947 For Jesus Christ Himself continuously infuses strength into 1546 the justified, as the head into the members (cf. Eph. 4.15) and the vine into the brances (cf. Jn 15.5); this strength always precedes, accompanies and follows their good works which, without it, could in no way be pleasing to God and meritorious (cf. n. 1952). Therfore, we must believe that nothing further is wanting to the justified for them to be regarded as having entirely fulfilled the divine law in their present condition by the works they have done in the sight of God; they can also be regarded as having truly merited eternal life, which they will obtain in due time, provided they die in the state of grace (cf. Rev. 14.13; n. 1982), since Christ our Saviour says: "Whoever drinks of the water that I shall give him will never thirst; the water that I shall give him will become in him a spring of water welling up to eternal life" (Jn 4.14).

---

1. ST AUGUSTINE, *De gratia et libero arbitrio*, 8, 20.

1547 Thus, neither is our justice considered as coming from us, nor is God's justice disregarded or denied (cf. Rom. 10.3); for the justice which is said to be ours because we become just by its inherence in us (cf. nn. 1960, 1961) is that of God Himself, since it is infused in us by God through the merit of Christ.

1948 Nor should this be overlooked: although in Holy Scripture
1548 such a high value is placed on good works that Christ prom-
ises that the person "who gives to one of His little ones even a cup of cold water shall not lose his reward" (Mt. 10.42) and the apostle testifies that "this slight momentary affliction is preparing for us an eternal weight of glory beyond all comparison" (2 Cor. 4.17), nevertheless, a Christian should never rely on himself or glory in himself instead of in the Lord (cf. 1 Cor. 1.31; 2 Cor. 10.17), whose goodnes towards all men is such that He wants His own gifts to be their merits (cf. n. 1982).

1949 And since "we all offend in many things" (James 3.2 Vulg; cf.
1549 n. 1973), everyone ought to keep in mind not only God's
mercy and goodness but also His severity and judgment. Neither should anyone pass judgment on himself, even if he is conscious of no wrong, because the entire life of man should be examined and judged, not by human judgment but by the judgment of God, "who will bring to light the things now hidden in darkness and will disclose the purposes of the heart. Then every man will receive his commendation from God" (1 Cor. 4.5) who, as it is written, "will render to every man according to his works" (Rom. 2.6).

1950 No one can be justified unless he faithfully and firmly accepts
1550 this Catholic doctrine on justification (cf. n. 1983), to which
the holy Council has decided to add the following canons, so that all may know, not only what they should hold and follow, but also what they should shun and avoid.

Canons on justification

1951 1. If anyone says that, without divine grace through Jesus
1551 Christ, man can be justified before God by his own works,
whether they be done by his own natural powers or through the teaching of the Law, anathema sit (cf. n. 1925).

1952 2. If anyone says that divine grace is given through Jesus

1552 Christ only in order that man may more easily live justly and merit eternal life, as if by his free will without grace he could do both, although with great difficulty, *anathema sit (cf. nn. 1928f)*.

1953 3. If anyone says that without the prevenient inspiration of
1553 the Holy Spirit and without His help, man can believe, hope and love or be repentant, as is required, so that the grace of justification be bestowed upon him, *anathema sit (cf. n. 1929)*.

1954 4. If anyone says that the free will of man, moved and
1554 awakened by God, in no way cooperates by an assent to God's awakening call, through which he disposes and prepares himself to obtain the grace of justification; and that man cannot refuse his assent if he wishes, but that like a lifeless object he does nothing at all and is merely passive, *anathema sit (cf. n. 1929)*.

1955 5. If anyone says that after Adam's sin the free will of man is
1555 lost and extinct, or that it is an empty concept, a term without real foundation, indeed a fiction introduced by Satan into the Church, *anathema sit (cf. nn. 1925, 1929)*.

1956 6. If anyone says that it is not in man's power to make his
1556 ways evil, but that God performs the evil works just as He performs the good, not only by allowing them but properly and directly, so that Judas' betrayal no less than Paul's vocation was God's own work, *anthema sit*.

1957 7. If anyone says that all works performed before justifica-
1557 tion, no matter how they were performed, are truly sins or deserve God's hatred; or that the more earnestly one tries to dispose himself for grace, the more grievously he sins, *anathema sit (cf. n. 1930)*.

1958 8. If anyone says that the fear of hell, which makes us turn to
1558 the mercy of God in sorrow for our sins, or which makes us avoid sin, is a sin or that it makes sinners worse, *anathema sit (cf. n. 1930)*.

1959 9. If anyone says that the sinner is justified by faith alone in
1559 the sense that nothing else is required by way of cooperation in order to obtain the grace of justification, and that it is not at all necessary that he should be prepared and disposed by the movement of his will, *anathema sit (cf. nn. 1935, 1939)*.

1960 10. If anyone says that men are justified without the justice of

1560   Christ, by which He merited for us, or that they are formally just by His own justice, *anathema sit* *(cf. nn. 1927, 1932).*

1961   11. If anyone says that men are justified either by the imputa-
1561   tion of Christ's justice alone, or by the remission of sins alone, excluding grace and charity which is poured into their hearts by the Holy Spirit and inheres in them, or also that the grace which justifies us is only the favour of God, *anathema sit (cf. nn. 1932f, 1946f).*

1962   12. If anyone says that justifying faith is nothing else than
1562   confidence in the divine mercy that remits sins on account of Christ, or that it is this confidence alone that justifies us, *anathema sit (cf. n. 1936).*

1963   13. If anyone says that, to attain the remission of sins, eve-
1563   ryone must believe with certainity and without any hesitation based on his own weakness and lack of disposi-tion, that his sins are forgiven, *anathema sit (cf. n. 1936).*

1964   14. If anyone says that man is absolved from his sins and
1564   justified because he believes with certainty that he is absolved and justified; or that no one is truly justified except he who believes he is justified, and that absolution and justification are effected by this faith alone, *anathema sit (cf. n. 1936).*

1965   15. If anyone says that a man who has been reborn and
1565   justified is bound by faith to believe that he is certainly among the number of the predestined, *anathema sit (cf. n. 1941).*

1966   16. If anyone says that he has absolute and infallible certi-
1566   tude that he will surely have the gift of final perseverance, unless he has learned this by a special revelation, *anathema sit (cf. n. 1941f).*

1967   17. If anyone says that the grace of justification is given ony
1567   to those who are predestined to life, and that all the others who are called, are called indeed, but do not receive grace, as they are predestined to evil by the divine power, *anathema sit.*

1968   18. If anyone says that the commandments of God are
1568   impossible to observe even for a man who is justified and established in grace, *anathema sit (cf. n. 1938).*

1969   19. If anyone says that nothing is commanded in the Gos-

1569   pels except faith, and that everything else is indifferent, neither prescribed nor prohibited, but free; or that the ten commandments in no way concern Christians, *anathema sit (cf. n. 1938).*

1970   20. If anyone says that a justified man, however perfect he
1570   may be, is not bound to observe the commandments of God and of the Church, but is bound only to believe, as if the Gospel were merely an absolute promise of eternal life without the condition that the commandments be observed, *anathema sit (cf. n. 1938).*

1971   21. If anyone says that Jesus Christ was given by God to
1571   men as a redeemer in whom they are to trust, but not also as a law-giver whom they are to obey, *anathema sit.*

1972   22. If anyone says that without God's special help a justified
1572   man can persevere in the justice he has received, or that with it he cannot persevere, *anathema sit (cf. n. 1942).*

1973   23. If anyone says that a man once justified cannot
1573   sin again and cannot lose grace and that therefore the man who falls and sins was never truly justified; or, on the contrary, says that a man once justified can avoid all sins, even venial ones throughout his entire life, unless it be by a special previlege of God as the Church holds of the Blessed Virgin Mary, *anathema sit (cf. nn. 1938, 1949).*

1974   24. If anyone says that the justice received is not preserved
1574   and even increased before God through good works, but that such works are merely the fruits and the signs of the justification obtained, and not also the cause of its increase, *anathema sit (cf. n. 1937).*

1975   25. If anyone says that the just man sins at least venially
1575   in every good work or (what is even more intolerable) that he sins mortally, and therefore merits eternal punishment, and that the only reason why he is not damned is that God does not impute those works unto damnation, *anathema sit (cf. n. 1940).*

1976   26. If anyone says that for the good works peformed in God
1576   the just ought not to expect and hope for an eternal reward from God through His mercy and the merits of Jesus Christ,

if they persevere to the end in doing good and in keeping the divine commandments, *anathema sit (cf. nn. 1939f)*.

1977 27. If anyone says that there is no mortal sin except that of
1577 unbelief, or that grace, once received, cannot be lost by any other sin, no matter how grievous and great, except that of unbelief, *anathema sit (cf. n. 1945)*.

1978 28. If anyone says that with the loss of grace through sin faith
1578 is also always lost, or that the faith which remains is not true faith, granted that it is not a living faith; or that the man who has faith without charity is not a Christian, *anathema sit (cf. n. 1945)*.

1979 29. If anyone says that the man who has fallen after baptism
1579 cannot rise again through God's grace; or that he can indeed recover the justice lost, but by faith alone without the sacrament of penance, contrary to what the holy Roman and universal Church, instructed by Christ the Lord and His apostles, has always professed, observed and taught, *anathema sit (cf. nn. 1943f)*.

1980 30. If anyone says that after the grace of justification has
1580 been received the guilt is so remitted and the debt of eternal punishment so blotted out for any repentant sinner, that no debt of temporal punishment remains to be paid, either in this world or in the other, in purgatory, before access can be opened to the kingdom of heaven, *anathema sit (cf. n. 1944)*.

1981 31. If anyone says that the justified man sins when he per-
1581 forms good works with a view to an eternal reward, *anathema sit (cf. n. 1940)*.

1982 32. If anyone says that the good works of the justified man
1582 are the gifts of God in such a way that they are not also the good merits of the justified man himself; or that by the good works he performs through the grace of God and the merits of Jesus Christ (of whom he is a living member), the justified man does not truly merit an increase of grace, eternal life and, provided he dies in the state of grace, the attainment of this eternal life, as well as an increase of glory, *anathema sit (cf. nn. 1948, 1946f)*.

1983 33. If anyone says that this Catholic doctrine of justification,
1583 expounded by the holy Council in the present decree, is in any way derogatory to the glory of God or to the merits of Jesus Christ our Lord, and does not rather manifest the truth of our faith and ultimately the glory of God and of Jesus Christ, *anathema sit*.

PIUS V

BULL *EX OMNIBUS AFFLICTIONIBUS* (1567)

CONDEMNED PROPOSITIONS OF MICHAEL DE BAY

Even after the Reformation the relationship between nature and grace remained one of the principal concerns of the Church's teaching on grace. In 1551 Michael de Bay, professor of theology at Louvain began, under Protestant influence, to spread erroneous opinions which were subsequently condemned by three Popes: by Pius V in 1567, by Gregory XIII in 1579, and by Urban VIII in 1641.

According to de Bay grace, immortality and freedom from concupiscence were not gratuitous gifts of God to Adam; they were due to man and given to him in creation. Concupiscence, which is a wrong attitude of the will is a continual transgression of the law: "you shall not covet". Human freedom consists only in the absence of external coercion; it does not necessarily imply the possibility of choosing between good and evil. Grace is not a supernatural, gratuitous gift of God; it consists rather in the capability of fulfilling God's commandments. Justification is accompanied by pure love, the opposite of concupiscence, which alone can be the principle of morally good actions.

The condemnation by Pope Pius V extends to 79 propositions culled from de Bay's works and listed without systematic order. The most important ones concerning grace are given below; they are grouped after the main lines of his system. For the propositions on original sin. cf. nn. 514/26ff.

(On man's original state)

[1984/21] The sublimation of human nature and its elevation to
1921   participation in the divine nature was due to the integrity
              of man in his first state, and is therefore to be called
natural, not supernatural.

[1984/23] It is absurd to hold that from the beginning man was
1923   raised above his own natural condition through a certain supernatural and gratuitous gift so that he might
worship God supernaturally with faith, hope and charity.

[1984/55] God could not have created man from the beginning in
1955   the condition in which now he is born.

[1984/78] The immortality of the first man was not a gift of grace
1978   but a natural condition.

[1984/79] The opinion of those doctors is wrong who hold that
1979   God could have created and constituted man without
              natural justice.

(On justification and merit)

[1985/13]   The good works performed by the sons of adoption are
1913   meritorious, not because they are done through the
                Spirit of adoption dwelling in the hearts of the sons of
God, but only because they conform to the law and because through
them man shows obedience to the law.

[1985/42]   The justice by which the sinner is justified through
1942   faith consists formally in the observance of the com-
                mandments; it is the justice of works. It does not consist
in any sort of grace infused in the soul by which man becomes God's
adopted son, is internally renewed and is made a sharer in the divine
nature so that, renewed in this way through the Holy Spirit, he may
henceforward lead a good life and obey the commandments of God.

[1985/63]   The distinction of a twofold justice must also be rejec-
1963   ted: one which is effected through the indwelling of
                the spirit of charity; the other which consists in the
inspiration of the Holy Spirit, who awakens the heart to repentance
but does not yet dwell in the heart nor diffuse in it the charity by
which the observance of the divine law can be fulfilled.

(On sin and concupiscence)

[1986/20]   No sin is of its nature venial, but every sin deserves
1920   eternal punishment.

[1986/50]   Evil desires to which reason does not consent and
1950   which man experiences against his will, are forbidden by
                the commandment: "You shall not covet" *(Ex. 20.17)*.

[1986/54]   The proposition that God has not commanded man to
1954   do the impossible is falsely attributed to Augustine,
                since it belongs to Pelagius.

[1986/67]   Man sins and even merits damnation in that which he
1967   does of necessity.

[1986/74]   In baptised persons who have fallen back into mortal
1974   sin and in whom concupiscence holds sway, concupis-
                cence, like the other evil habits, is sin.

(On the concept of freedom)

[1987/27]   Without the help of God's grace free will can do nothing
1927   but sin.

[1987/28] It is a Pelagian error to say that free will is capable of
1928 avoiding any sin.

[1987/39] What is done voluntarily, even if done of necessity, is
1939 nevertheless a free action.

[1987/40] In all his actions a sinner is the slave of a passion that
1940 overpowers him.

[1987/41] In the Scriptures the term 'freedom' does not mean
1941 freedom from necessity, but only freedom from sin.

[1987/66] The only thing opposed to man's natural freedom is
1966 violence.

(On love and the fulfilment of the Law)

[1988/16] Without charity, obedience to the Law is not true
1916 obedience.

[1988/34] The distinction of a twofold love of God, namely a
1934 natural love whose object is God as the author of
nature, and a gratuitous love whose object is God as
beatifying, is meaningless and imaginary; it has been devised as a
mockery of the sacred Scriptures and of the numerous testimonies of
ancient authors.

[1988/38] All love of a rational creature is either vicious cupidity
1938 by which the world is loved, which is forbidden by John,
or that praiseworthy charity which, "poured into the
hearts by the Holy Spirit" (*cf. Rom. 5.5),* makes them love God.

INNOCENT X

CONSTITUTION *CUM OCCASIONE* (1653)

ERRORS OF CORNELIUS JANSEN CONDEMNED

*Jansenism is but a further development of Baianism. Cornelius Jansen,
bishop of Ypres, after an exhaustive study of St Augustine's works, wrote
his famous Augustinus with the purpose of restoring to its place of honour
the African doctor's teaching on grace and free will. Jansen's work was
published posthumously, after its author had submitted in advance to the
decision of the Holy See. The work met with considerable success but was
condemned by Pope Urban VIII in 1642. Despite this papal condemnation,
however, the work of Jansen continued to spread until finally Innocent X
codemned again five propositions from Augustinus, dealing with the possibility of keeping the divine commandments and of resisting grace, the*

concept of freedom and predestination. The first four propositions are condemned as heretical, the fifth one as false and scandalous, and, if understood in the sense that Christ died only for the predestined, heretical. The prolonged Jansenist controversies were centred around these propositions.

[1989/1] Some of God's commandments cannot be observed by
2001 just men with the strength they have in the present
state, even if they wish and strive to observe them; nor do
they have the grace that would make their observance possible.

[1989/2] In the state of fallen nature interior grace is never re-
2002 sisted.

[1989/3] In order to merit or demerit in the state of fallen nature, it
2003 is not necessary for man to have freedom from necessity, but freedom from coercion suffices.

[1989/4] The Semi-Pelagians admitted the necessity of a preve-
2004 nient interior grace for every act, even for the beginning
of faith; and their heresy consisted in this, that they held
this grace to be such that the human will could either resist it or
submit to it.

[1989/5] It is Semi-Pelagian to say that Christ died or shed His
2005 blood for all men without exception.

CLEMENT XI

CONSTITUTION *UNIGENITUS DEI FILIUS* (1713)

PROPOSITIONS OF PASQUIER QUESNEL CONDEMNED

In spite of repeated papal condemnations, Jansenism continued to spread. Quesnel (1634-1719), relying exclusively on the unchallenged authority of St Augustine, brought out a new conception of grace as the principle of man's renewal. Without this grace man was wholly corrupt, but grace itself was irresistible; it endowed man with pure charity, the only moral motive for action. In the dogmatic Constitution Unigenitus, the last and most thorough rebuttal of Jansenism, Pope Clement XI condemned 101 propositions extracted from Quesnel's works.

(Errors concerning the necessity of grace)

[1990/1] What else is left in the soul that has lost God and His
2401 grace except sin and its effects, proud poverty and slug-
gish indigence, that is, a general inability to work, to pray
and to do any good work ?

[1990/38] Without the grace of the Redeemer the sinner is not
2438   free except for evil.

[1990/39] The will that is not preceded by grace has no light
2439   except to go astray, no eagerness except for self-
         destruction, no strength except to wound itself; it is
capable of all evil and incapable of any good.

[1990/40] Without grace we cannot love anything except to our
2440   own condemnation.

[1990/41] Any knowledge of God, even natural, even among hea-
2441   then philosophers, can only come from God; and with-
         out grace it produces nothing but presumption, vanity
and opposition to God Himself instead of a sense of adoration,
gratitude and love.

[1990/59] The prayer of sinners is a new sin and what God grants
2459   them is a new judgment against them.

(Propositions on the two loves)

[1991/44] There are only two loves that are the sources of all
2444   our volitions and actions: the love of God that does
         everything for the sake of God and which God rewards;
and the love by which we love ourselves and the world, and which,
because it does not refer to God what ought to be referred to Him,
becomes evil.

[1991/45] When the love of God no longer reigns in the heart
2445   of sinners, it is inevitable that carnal desires reign in
         it and corrupt all its actions.

[1991/46] It is covetousness or charity that makes the use of
2446   senses good or evil.

[1991/47] Obedience to the Law ought to flow from a source, and
2447   this source is charity. When the love of God is the inte-
         rior principle of this obedience and the glory of God its
end, then its exterior manifestation is pure; otherwise it is nothing
but hyprocrisy or false righteousness.

(Propositions on the compelling force of divine grace)

[1992/10] Grace is the working of the omnipotent hand of God
2410   which nothing can hinder or retard.

[1992/11]   Grace is nothing but the omnipotent will of God, com-
2411   manding and doing what He commands.

[1992/23]   God Himself has taught us the notion of the omnipotent
2423   working of His grace, signifying it by the operation
                 which produces creatures out of nothing and restores
life to the dead.

LEO XIII

ENCYCLICAL LETTER *DIVINUM ILLUD* (1897)

*After the Council of Trent, due largely to the subsequent controversies
De auxiliis between the followers of Báñez and Molina, and to the diffusion
and official condemnation of the systems of de Bay and Jansen, theological
attention became narrowly focussed on the nature of actual grace. The
doctrine of the indwelling of the Spirit in the justified, with which the Pauline
epistles and the Greek tradition were deeply imbued, had receded to the
background. Pope Leo XIII's encyclical Divinum Illud (1897) tries to restore
this prominent biblical theme to the place of honour due to it. Although
epoch-making because of the central role it attributes to the person of the
Holy Spirit, the encyclical is influenced almost exclusively by the Western
Fathers, while the rich theology of the Spirit, characteristic of the Eastern
tradition, is hardly represented in it. With regard to the mode of presence of
the Spirit in the justified, the Pope adopts the classical theory of appropriation, prevalent at that time.*

(The indwelling of the Holy Spirit)

1993   It is indeed certain that also in the just men who lived before
3329   Christ the Holy Spirit resided by grace, as we read in the
            Scriptures concerning the prophets, Zachary, John the Bap-
tist, Simeon and Anna. Thus, the self-communication of the Holy
Spirit at Pentecost was not such that "then for the first time He would
have begun to dwell in the saints, but that He was poured on them
more abundantly; crowning, not beginning His gifts; not commenc-
ing a new work, but giving more abundantly...."[1]

1994   The beginning of this regeneration and renovation of man
3330   takes place at baptism. In this sacrament...the Holy Spirit for
            the first time enters it (the soul) and makes it like to Himself.
"That which is born of the Spirit is spirit" (*Jn 3.6*). The same Spirit
gives Himself more abundantly in holy confirmation for the steadfast-
ness and the strength of the Christian life.... He not only brings to us

---

1. St Leo the Great, *Sermo*, 77, 1.

divine gifts, but is the author of them and is Himself the supreme gift, who, proceeding from the mutual love of the Father and the Son, is rightly considered and called "the gift of the most high".... Besides, by grace God abides in the just soul as in a temple, in a most intimate and singular manner. From this follows that bond of charity by which the soul adheres most closely to God, more than it could adhere to the most loving and beloved friend, and enjoys God in all fulness and sweetness.

3331   Now this wonderful union, which is properly called in-
        dwelling and differs only by reason of our condition or state
from that in which God embraces and beatifies the citizens of heaven, is most certainly produced by the divine presence of the whole Trinity: "We will come to him and make our home with him" *(Jn 14.23)*; nevertheless it is attributed in a particular manner to the Holy Spirit. For, whilst traces of the divine power and wisdom appear even in a sinful man, only the just man shares in charity, which is, as it were, the special mark of the Holy Spirit.

PIUS XII

ENCYCLICAL LETTER *MYSTICI CORPORIS* (1943)

This encyclical, devoted to the nature of the Church as the mystical Body of Christ (cf. n. 847i), contains some notable passages on the union of the justified with the risen Christ, and especially on the indwelling of the Holy Spirit. As the encyclical Divinum Illud *of Leo XIII, it centres the mystery of man's transformation in justification on the person of the Holy Spirit, rather than on the created reality of sanctifying grace. But Pius XII goes beyond the doctrine of Leo XIII.* Mystici Corporis *is based not exclusively on the Western Fathers, but integrates to a large extent the views of the Eastern tradition. The mode of the divine indwelling is not reduced to mere appropriation, though its precise nature is ultimately left undecided. Clear norms are laid down for a balanced presentation of this doctrine that will avoid all danger of pantheistic interpretations.*

(Union of the justified with Christ and the indwelling of the Holy Spirit)

1995   Whereas in a physical body the principle of unity joins the
3810   parts together in such a way that each of them completely
        lacks a subsistence of its own, on the contrary in the mystical
Body the cohesive force, intimate though it is, unites the members with one another in such a way that each of them wholly retains his own personality....

3811 Comparing now the mystical Body with a moral body, we must also notice between these a difference which is by no means slight but, on the contrary, of the very highest importance. For in a moral body the only principle of unity is a common end, and a common aspiration of all to that end by means of the social authority. But in the mystical Body, with which we are concerned, there is in addition to this common aspiration another internal principle, really existing and operative both in the whole structure and in each of its parts, and this principle is of such surpassing excellence that by itself it immeasurably transcends all the bonds of unity by which any physical or moral body is knit together. It is, as we have said above, something not of the natural, but of the supernatural order; indeed, in itself it is infinite and uncreated, namely the divine Spirit, who, in the words of the Angelic Doctor, "numerically one and the same, fills and unifies the whole Church."[1]

3813 Christ is in us through His Spirit, whom He imparts to us and through whom He so acts within us that any divine effect operated in our souls by the Holy Spirit must be said to be operated in us also by Christ. "Anyone who does not have the Spirit of Christ", says the apostle, "does not belong to Him. But if Christ is in you, ... your spirits are alive because of righteousness" (*Rom. 8.9f*). It is due also to this communication of the Spirit of Christ that all the gifts, virtues and miraculous powers which are found eminently, most abundantly and fontally in the Head, stream into all the members of the Church and in them are perfected daily according to the place of each in the mystical Body of Jesus Christ.....

(Warning against misunderstandings)

1996 Under pain of departing from pure doctrine and from the true
3814 teaching of the Church, all must hold this as quite certain: that any explanation of this mystical union is to be rejected if it makes the faithful in any way pass beyond the order of created things, and so trespass upon the divine sphere that even one single attribute of the eternal God could be predicted of them in the proper sense. Moreover, this certain truth must be firmly borne in mind, that in these matters all things are to be held common to the Blessed

---

1. St Thomas Aquinas, *De Veritate*, 29, 4c.

Trinity, so far as the same relate to God as the supreme efficient cause. It must also be remembered that we are dealing with a hidden mystery which during our exile on earth can never be completely unveiled, never altogether understood, nor adequately expressed in human language.

(The indwelling of the divine Persons)

1997 The divine Persons are said to indwell inasmuch as, being
3815 present in a mysterious way to living intellectual creatures, they are attained by these through knowledge and love, but in a manner which transcends all nature and is quite intimate and unique. If we would reach some little understanding of this, we shall do well to use the method recommended by the Vatican Council in such matters, the method by which light is successfully sought for some partial perception of God's hidden truths in a comparison of mysteries with one another and with the last end to which they are directed (*cf. n. 132*). Thus, when our wise predecessor of happy memory, Leo XIII, was treating of this union of ours with Christ and the indwelling of the divine Paraclete within us, he appropriately turned his gaze to that beatific vision wherein one day in heaven this mystical union will find its perfect consummation. "This wonderful union", he wrote, "which is properly called indwelling, differs only by reason of our condition or state from that in which God embraces and beatifies the citizens of heaven" (*cf. n. 1994*). In that vision it will be granted to the eyes of the mind, its powers augmented by supernatural light, to contemplate the Father, the Son and the Holy Spirit, for all eternity to witness closely the processions of the divine Persons, and to enjoy a beatitude very similar to that with which the most holy and undivided Trintiy is blessed.

THE SECOND VATICAN GENERAL COUNCIL

The doctrine of grace in Vatican II consists in passing references scattered in the Council's doctrinal documents. As compared with earlier declarations of the Church's teaching office, Vatican II lays greater emphasis on the ecclesial aspect of grace, which concerns not only the individual Christian, but affects the entire life of the Church. Along with this communitarian aspect of grace, the personal dimension comes strongly to the fore. During the Council sessions the Oriental bishops repeatedly voiced the complaint that full justice was not being done to the Eastern tradition with regard to the role of the Holy Spirit. In order to comply with their request, and also in keeping with modern theological trends in the West, greater stress is put on the action of the Spirit than in previous documents.

The sanctifying action of the Holy Spirit is described in two brief but dense passages in the frame-work of the Trinitarian structure of the Church and the Trinitarian origin of her mission (LG 2-4; AG 2-4). It is the Holy Spirit who guarantees the genuineness of the Church Tradition (DV 7-10, 19); He is the agent of biblical inspiration (DV 12, 18, 20). He is especially the principle of Christian unity (UR 2), whose influence extends outside the visible boundaries of the Catholic Church (UR 3-4; cf. LG 15); union can only be realised through the obedience of the Church to the promptings of the Spirit (UR 24).

Possibly one of the most important contributions made by the Council to the teaching on grace is the liberating paragraph on charisms (LG 12). According to St Paul they are not peripheral to the life of the Church, but as essential an element of its structure as the institutional element. Two norms for the discernment of true charisms are mentioned: their orientation to the service of the Church, and the proper balance between their rich variety and the necessary unity. The Holy Spirit distributes these gifts to the faithful of every rank; but charismatics are also subject to the Church authority (LG 7).

The Holy Spirit arouses in the Christian the faith in divine revelation (DV 5), which is the beginning of justification. He is the principle of life, dwelling in the Christian as in a temple, making him a son of God in worship and service. The sanctifying work of the Spirit renews the whole man, not only the soul (GS 22; cf. 41). The Council echoes the Eastern Fathers when it asserts that it is the Spirit Himself who makes us partakers of the divine nature (UR 15).

DOGMATIC CONSTITUTION *LUMEN GENTIUM* (1964)

(The Sanctifying Spirit)

1998 4. When the Son had accomplished on earth the task entrusted to Him by the Father, the Holy Spirit was sent on Pentecost day that He might for ever sanctify the Church. Thus, all who believe have access to the Father, through Christ, in one Spirit (*cf. Eph. 2.18*). He is the Spirit of life, the fountain of water springing up to life everlasting (*cf. Jn 4.14; 7.38f*); it is through Him that the Father gives life to men who were dead through sin; till at last, in Christ, He raises even their mortal bodies (*cf. Rom. 8.10f*). The Spirit dwells in the Church and in the hearts of the faithful as in a temple (*cf. 1 Cor. 3.16; 6.19*); He prays in them and bears witness to the fact that they are adopted sons (*cf. Gal. 4.6; Rom. 8.15f, 26*). He guides the Church into the fulness of truth (*cf. Jn 16.13*); He unites her in mutual communion and in service; He teaches and directs her through His hierarchic and charismatic gifts, and adorns her with His fruits (*cf. Eph. 4.11f; 1 Cor. 12.4; Gal. 5.22*). By the power of the Gospel, He preserves the Church's youthfulness, renews her incessantly and leads her to perfect union with her spouse. Together, the Spirit and the Bride say to the Lord Jesus: "Come" (*Rev. 22.17*). Thus the universal Church is clearly a "people whose unity is derived from the unity of the Father, the Son and the Holy Spirit".[1]

(The charisms of faith and of Christian life)

1999 12. God's holy people shares also in Christ's prophetic function when radiating His living testimony, mainly by a life of faith and charity, and offering to God a sacrifice of praise, the tribute of lips confessing His name (*cf. Heb. 13.15*). Because they are anointed by the Holy One (*cf. 1 Jn 2.20, 27*), the faithful as a body cannot err in their belief. They manifest this special prerogative of theirs by means of a supernatural sense of faith that belongs to the people as a whole, when "from the bishops down to the last lay believer",[2] they show universal agreement in matters of faith and morals. It is the Spirit of truth who awakens and sustains that sense of faith which enables the People of God, led by and obedient to the teaching authority of the Church, to accept not the word of men but the very word of God (*cf. 1 Thes. 2.13*), to cling unfailingly to the faith once communicated to the saints (*cf. Jude 3*), to penetrate more deeply into it and to live it more fully.

Further , the same Holy Spirit does not only sanctify the People of God, lead it and enrich it with virtues by means of the sacraments and the ministers of the Church, but he "apportions to each one individually as He wills" (*1 Cor. 12.11*), He distributes among the faithful of every rank special graces that make them fit and ready to undertake various tasks and functions conducive to the renewal and further development of the Church; for, so writes the Apostle, "to each is given the manifestation of the Spirit for the common good" (*1 Cor. 12.7*)....

---

1. ST CYPRIAN, *De Orat. Dom.*, 23.

2. ST AUGUSTINE, *De Praed. Sanct.* 14, 27; *PL* 44, 980.

CHAPTER XX

PRINCIPLES OF CHRISTIAN LIFE

In baptism the Christian has been sacramentally conformed to the mystery of Christ's death and resurrection and dedicated to God as a member of the Church. Christian living must carry out day by day this fundamental consecration. The Christian life consists essentially in the following of Christ through the perfection of charity. Each Christian lives this life not as an isolated indivudual person but as a member of the Christian community which constitutes the People of God willed by Him and established by Christ to act in the human race as a leaven, to be the living sign of God's kindness towards men and to witness to men's divine destiny. Hence, the Christian life is by nature a testimony; it implies for all Christians a call to perfection and holiness to which each must respond, according to his own charism, in the state of life God has destined for him, either lay or religious. This is to say that in Christian morality there is no minimum standard laid down; rather, every Chrstian is by his calling summoned to grow daily in the life of God and in the love of men, and to unify these two lives.

Though the Christian life is based on fundamental principles which go far beyond the natural demands of morality, it builds upon these demands which it brings to their perfection. This is why the Church has always been concerned with upholding the existence of a natural law, based on the dignity of the human person and inscribed in his heart by God, his Creator and last end. She has stressed man's responsibility to obey this law in a free assent and according to the dictates of his conscience; she has through the centuries explained the implications of this law in the various spheres of human life. In this process, the Church has often been led to react against two opposite extreme tendencies: on the one hand, a pessimistic and rigorist conception of human life, denying men the ability to do good; on the other hand, liberalism and laxism, emancipating man from law and objective norms of moral conduct. Thus, the Church has greatly contributed to defend and preserve the most fundamental human values. If her official documents often present a negative form, the reason is that they are directly intended to meet concrete threats to the moral and spiritual order and to man's dignity. It must, however, be admitted that the Church documents are not always free of a certain legalistic approach which has long charaterised the elaboration of moral doctrine.

As to the specifically Christian principles of human conduct, they are poorly represented in official documents which deal with Christian morality in a general way. Intimately connected as these principles are with life itself, they have often been taken for granted rather than explicitly stated by the Church's teaching office. Besides the life of the Church, the main source for her teaching on Christian living remains her doctrinal documents on the Christian faith itself, especially her doctrine on man's salvation through Christ, on the life of grace and on the sacraments, the Eucharist in particular, which have been dealt with in previous chapters.

In recent decades, however, papal encyclicals have brought out more explicitly the implications of the faith for the Christian life. These documents witness to the fact that legalism in Christian morality has largely been overcome and that a return to the radical demands of the Gospel is felt as a pressing need. The doctrine of the Second Vatican Council reflects this new spirit, its moral teaching being characterised by a positive appeal to all Christians as members of the People of God to live up to their high calling in all the spheres of human life.

*   *   *

The main points dealt with in this chapter are the following:

Man has a unique dignity shared by all: 2011, 2027, 2051, 2056f.
This dignity brings with it rights and duties: 2028-2042.
Man is social by nature: 2054.
His social character also entails rights and obligations: 2055, 2058.
Man's dignity is shown mostly in the exercise of his moral freedom: 2053.
Though impaired by sin, man's freedom is not destroyed: 1929, 1954-1957, 1987/27ff, 1989/1ff, (2002).
Man as individual and in groups has a right to religious liberty: 2048-2050.
In the exercise of his moral freedom man must obey the dictates of his conscience: 2052.
Man's conscience reveals to him the natural law, inscribed by God in his nature, which he must obey: 2008/2, 2012, 2020, 2022-2025, 2026, 2059.

Invincible error is possible: 2009/2.

It is licit to follow a probable opinion, though not a tenuous one:
2006/3, 2009/3.

*Human laws made by a legitimate authority in conformity with the
natural law must be obeyed:* 2005, 2010/56.63, 2013.

Moral evil can be tolerated but not willed: 2014.

All Christians, sharing the same dignity, are called to perfection:
2044, 2045.

Charity is the essence of and the way to perfection: 2001, 2046,
2060;

it includes the love of God and the love of men: 2021;

it goes beyond the demands of justice: 2019, 2161.

Active supernatural virtues must be practised: 2007/1ff, 2015-2018.

*The laity must seek Christian perfection according to their specific
vocation:* 2043;

they are called to moral responsibility: 2061.

*The religious profession is a specific vocation in the Church implying
a special call to holiness:* 2047.

A fundamental option defines a person's moral disposition: 2062.

Mortal sin is a serious violation of the order of love: 2063.

JOHN XXII

BULL *AD CONDITOREM* (1322)

In his Bull Ad Conditorem to the Friars Minor on their poverty, Pope John XXII has this incidental sentence which seems to be the first expression, in an official document, of the essential role of charity in Christian perfection.

(Charity is the essence of perfection)

2001 ...The perfection of Christian life consists principally and essentially in charity, which is called by the apostle the bond of perfection (*cf. Col. 3.14*) and somehow unites or joins man with his end....

THE GENERAL COUNCIL OF TRENT

SIXTH SESSION

DECREE ON JUSTIFICATION (1547)

(2002) *In its decree on justification, the Council of Trent has defined the existence and reality of human liberty. In the process of his justification man freely assents to, and cooperates with grace and thus disposes and prepares himself to obtain justification. He can also dissent and refuse grace and is thus responsible for making his ways evil (cf. text in nn. 1929, 1954, 1956). Man's free will was not destroyed by original sin (cf. text in nn. 1925, 1929, 1955); the moral acts that a man performs before his justification are not necessarily sinful (cf. text in n. 1957).*

ALEXANDER VII

ERRORS OF LAXIST MORALITY CONDEMNED

BY THE HOLY OFFICE (1605)

Among other propositions condemned as at least causing scandal, one is concerned with obedience to civil law.

(Obedience to civil law)

[2005] People do not sin even if, without any reason, they do not
2048 accept the law promulgated by the ruler.

INNOCENT XI

ERRORS OF LAXIST MORALITY CONDEMNED

BY THE HOLY OFFICE (1679)

The following proposition is condemned as at least causing scandal and harmful in practice.

(On probabilism)

[2006/3] Speaking in general, we are always acting prodently
2103   whenever we do something relying on an intrinsic or ex-
              trinsic probability, tenuous as this may be, provided we do
not go beyond the limits of what is probable.

CONSTITUTION *CAELESTIS PASTOR* (1687)

PROPOSITIONS OF MICHAEL MOLINOS CONDEMNED

*By this Constitution, Pope Innocent XI confirmed the condemnation of
68 propositions of M. Molinos, already condemned the same year by a
decree of the Holy Office. All the condemned propositions are related to
Molinos' false quietism which excluded from the spiritual life every moral
effort. For the propositions quoted below, the highest censures affixed by
the theologians of the Holy Office are as follows: 14 is condemned as
heretical; 2, 4, 5 as smacking of heresy.*

(On quietism)

[2007/1] It is necessary that [man] reduce [his] powers to nothing-
2201   ness and in this consists the interior way.

[2007/2] The will to work actively is an offence to God, who wishes
2202   to be Himself the sole agent; and, therefore, one must
              totally abandon one's whole self in God and thereafter
remain like a lifeless body.

[2007/4] Natural activity is the enemy of grace and it hinders
2204   God's action and true perfection, because God wishes
              to act in us without us.

[2007/5] By doing nothing the soul annihilates itself and returns to
2205   its principle and to its origin, which is the essence of
              God, in which it remains transformed and divinised, and
God then remains in Himself; because then there are no longer two
things which are united but only one, and in this way, God lives and
reigns in us and the soul annihilates itself as far as its active being is
concerned.

[2007/14] For one who is resigned to the divine will it is not proper
2214   to ask anything from God; because asking is an imper-
               fection, since it is an act of one's own will and choice,
and it is to wish that the divine will be conformed to our own, and not
our own to the divine will; and the passage of the Gospel saying: "Ask
and you will receive" *(Jn 16.24)* was not said by Christ for interior

souls who refuse to have a will; moreover, these kinds of souls reach the point when they cannot ask anything from God.

ALEXANDER VIII

DECREE OF THE HOLY OFFICE (24 August 1690)

Of the two propositions condemned in this decree, the following is considered as causing scandal and erroneous.

(On philosophical sin)

[2008/2] A philosophical or moral sin is a human act which does
2291 not agree with rational nature and the right reason; a theological and mortal sin is the free transgression of the divine law. A philosophical sin, however grievous it may be, if committed by one who either does not know God, or does not actually think of God, is a grievous sin but not an offence against God; nor is it a mortal sin which breaks off the friendship with God and deserves eternal punishment

DECREE OF THE HOLY OFFICE (7 December 1690)

This other decree of the Holy Office condemned, under the same Pope Alexander VIII, a number of Jansenist errors. The censure attached to those propositions, among which two are quoted here, varies from temerarious to heretical.

(On conscience in invincible ignorance about the natural law)

[2009/2] Although there is such a thing as invincible ignorance
2302 about the natural law, this, in the state of fallen nature, does not excuse from formal sin anyone acting out of ignorance.

(On probable opinion)

[2009/3] It is not licit to follow a (probable) opinion, even the most
2303 probable among the probable ones.

PIUS IX

SYLLABUS OF CONDEMNED ERRORS (1864)

On this document, cf. n. 1013i. Among the errors condemned some are concerned with matters of morality, natural and Christian, notably the following three.

(On moral and human laws)

[2010/56] The moral laws do not need a divine sanction, and it is
2956 not in the least required that human laws conform to
the natural law, or receive from God their binding force.

(On the nature of right)

[2010/59] Right consists in a material fact; all the duties of men
2959 are an empty name, and all human deeds have the force
of right.

(On submission to authority)

[2010/63] It is licit to withhold obedience to, or even to rebel
2963 against, the legitimate rulers.

LEO XIII

ENCYCLICAL LETTER *LIBERTAS PRAESTANTISSIMUM* (1888)

*In this encyclical, the Pope exposes the meaning of true freedom against
the doctrine of a certain liberalism according to which liberty consists in
freedom from law, with the result that every man has the right to believe and
do what he pleases.*

(Dignity of man as free)

2011 Liberty, the highest of human endowments, being the por-
3245 tion only of intellectual or rational natures, confers on man
this dignity, that he is in the hand of his counsel and has
power over his actions....

Such, then, being the condition of human liberty, it necessarily
stands in need of light and strength to direct its actions towards good
an to restrain them from evil. Without this the freedom of our will
would be our ruin. First of all there must be law; that is, a fixed rule of
teaching what must be done and what must be avoided.... In man's
free will, therefore, or in the moral necessity for our voluntary acts to
be in accordance with reason lies the very root of the necessity of
law. Nothing more foolish can be said or conceived than the idea
that, because man is free by nature, he is exempt from law. Were this
the case, it would follow that in order to be free we must be without
reason; whereas the truth is that we are bound to submit to law
precisely because we are free by our very nature. For law is the guide
of man's actions....

(Nature of law)

2012   ...First among all (laws) is the natural law, which is written
3247   and engraved in the mind of every man; for it is the human
reason itself, commanding to do right and forbidding sin.
Nevertheless all prescriptions of human reason can have force of law
only inasmuch as they are the voice and the interpreter of some
higher power on which our reason and liberty necessarily depend.
For, since the force of law consists in the imposing of obligations and
the granting of rights, it is wholly founded on authority, that is, on a
true power to fix duties and define rights, as also to assign the
necessary sanctions of reward and punishment for each and all of its
commands. But all this, clearly, cannot be found in man, as if, being
his own supreme legislator, he himself was laying down the norm for
his actions. It follows, therefore, that the law of nature is the eternal
law itself, implanted in rational creatures and inclining them to the
right course of action and to their end; it is the eternal reason of God,
the Creator and Ruler of the whole world....

(Human law)

2013   What reason and natural law do for individual men, human
3248   law, promulgated for the common good of citizens, does
for men in society. Among the laws established by men, some
are concerned with what is good or bad by its very nature....But such
decrees by no means derive their origin from society; because just as
society did not create human nature, so neither does it depend on
society whether something is a good which befits human nature or an
evil which is contrary to it. Rather, laws precede human society itself,
and have their origin in the natural, and consequently in the eternal
law....There are other enactments of the civil authority, which do not
follow immediately and directly, but somewhat remotely and indirectly, from the natural law; these determine many issues for which
nature provides only in a general and indefinite way.... It is in the
constitution of these particular rules of life, suggested by reason and
prudence, and put forth by competent authority, that human law,
properly so called, consists, and in so far as human law is in conformity with the dictates of the natural law, it leads to what is good and
deters from evil. From this it is manifest that the norm and rule of
freedom lies entirely in the eternal law of God, not only for each
individual man, but also for the community and human society.

(Tolerance)

2014 While the Church does not concede any right to anything
3251 save what is true and honest, she does not object to public
authority tolerating what is at variance with truth and justice,
for the sake of avoiding some greater evil or of obtaining or preserving some greater good. God Himself, in His providence, though
infinitely good and all-powerful, permits evil to exist in the world,
partly in order that greater good may not be impeded, and partly that
greater evil may not ensue. In the government of states it is sound to
imitate the Ruler of the world; moreover, since human authority is
powerless to prevent every evil, it has, as St Augustine says, "to
tolerate and leave unpunished many things which are rightly punished by divine Providence".[1] But if, under such circumstances, for
the sake of the common good—and this is the ony legitimate
reason—human law may or even must tolerate evil, it may not and
must not approve or will evil in itself *(per se)*, for evil, of itself, being
the privation of good, is opposed to the common welfare which every
legislator is bound to seek and defend to the best of his ability. In this
too, human law must endeavour to imitate God, who, in allowing evil
to exist in the world, "neither wills evil to be done, nor wills evil not to
be done, but wills to allow evil to be done, and this is good".[2] This
sentence of the angelic Doctor contains in brief the doctrine concerning the permission or evil.

LETTER *TESTEM BENEVOLENTIAE* TO CARDINAL GIBBONS, ARCHBISHOP OF BALTIMORE (1899)

On the occassion of the publication of a life of Fr I.T. Hecker by Fr W. Elliot, in which ways of adapting Catholicism to modern conditions were proposed, a controversy arose, chiefly in Europe, about what was called "Americanism". It is to end this controversy that Pope Leo XIII wrote this letter to Cardinal Gibbons. It mostly condemns unsafe or false doctrinal trends bearing on Christian morality, without however disapproving either Fr Hecker himself or his writings.

(On the contempt for supernatural and so called "passive" virtues)

2015 It is chiefly in the practice of virtues that the help of the Holy
3343 Spirit is absolutely required. But those who are enthusiastic

---

1. St Augustine, *De libero arbitrio*, 1, 41.

2. St Thomas Aquinas, *Summa theologica*, I, 19, 9, ad 3.

about following the new trends exalt beyond measure the natural virtues as though these suited more aptly the manners and the needs of the present times, and as if it was preferable to possess them, because they render a man more fit and more vigorous for action. It is hard to understand that those who are imbued with Christian wisdom could prefer natural virtues to supernatural ones and ascribe to them a greater efficacy and fruitfulness....

2016 Intimately connected with this opinion about natural virtues is
3344 another one according to which the Christian virtues as a
whole are divided, as it were, into two classes: the passive ones, as they say, and the active ones; and they add that, while the former were more suited for the past ages, the latter agree better with the present times.... Now, that some Christian virtues are more appropriate to one time and some to another will only be held by a man who does not remember the words of the apostle: "Those whom He foreknew He also predestined to be conformed to the image of His Son" (*Rom. 8.29*). The teacher and the model of all holiness is Christ; all those who wish to be admitted in the home of the blessed must be adapted to that rule. Now Christ does not change in the course of centuries, but He remains the same yesterday and today and for ever (*cf. Heb. 13.8*). Hence the saying applies to men of all ages: "Learn from me; for I am gentle and lowly in heart" (*Mt. 11.29*); and there is no period when Christ does not present Himself to us made "obedient unto death" (*Phil 2.8*); and this saying of the apostle is valid for all times: "Those who belong to Christ Jesus have crucified the flesh with its passions and desires" (*Gal. 5.24*).

2017 From this kind of contempt for the evangelical virtues,
3345 wrongly called passive, it was likely to follow that a disregard
for the religious life would also gradually pervade the minds. And that this is commonly the case with the champions of the new opinions, we gather from some of their sayings about the vows which are pronounced in religious orders. For they say that these vows are very remote from the spirit of our time inasmuch as they restrict the field of liberty; that they are suited to the weak souls rather than to the strong ones; and that they have absolutely no value to foster Christian perfection and the good of human society, but are rather an obstacle and a hindrance to both....

2018 From what we have dealt with up to now, it is clear that those
3346 opinions which, taken as a whole, some designate as "Americanism", cannot have our approval.

PIUS XI

ENCYCLICAL LETTER *QUADRAGESIMO ANNO* (1931)

In this encyclical on the social order (cf. nn. 2106ff), Pope Pius XI shows, in connection with social justice, the relationship which exists between the virtues of justice and charity: charity supposes that the demands of justice be respected, but it goes beyond them; the observance of justice does not by itself fulfil the Christian ideal.

(Justice and charity)

2019   ...Charity which is "the bond of perfection" (*cf. Col. 3.14*) must always play a leading part. How completely deceived are those rash reformers who, satisfied with enforcing commutative justice, proudly disdain the help of charity ! Certainly the practice of charity cannot be considered as taking the place of justice unfairly withheld. But, even though a state of things be pictured in which every man receives at last all that is his due, a wide field will always remain open for charity. For justice alone, however faithfully observed, though it can indeed remove the cause of social strife, can never by its own power bring about a union of hearts and minds. Yet this spiritual bond which unites the members together is the main principle of stability in all institutions, no matter how perfect they may seem, which aim at establishing social peace and promoting mutual help among men. In its absence, as repeated experience proves, the wisest regulations come to nothing. Then only will it be possible to unite all in harmonious striving for the common good, when all sections of society have the intimate conviction that they are members of one great family, and children of the same heavenly Father, and further, that they are "one body in Christ, and individually members one of another" (*Rom. 12.5*), so that, "if one member suffers, all suffer together" (*1 Cor. 12.26*).

PIUS XII

ENCYCLICAL LETTER *SUMMI PONTIFICATUS* (1939)

In this first encyclical of his pontificate, Pope Pius XII deplores the evils that flow from the growth of secularism. He considers their root to be the rejection of the natural law, of which he re-states the doctrine.

(Natural law)

2020   It is certain that the first and deeper source from which
3780   derive the evils which afflict today's society is the strong
          denial and rejection of a universal norm of morality in the

private life of individuals, as well as in public life and in the mutual relationships between peoples and nations; namely, the natural law is being undermined through criticism and disregard.

3781 This natural law has as its foundation God, the almighty Creator and Father of all, the supreme and perfect law-giver, the most wise and just judge of human actions. When the eternal will is rashly denied, the foundation of all moral honesty crumbles, the voice of nature becomes silent and grows faint, that voice which teaches even the unlearned or those to whom civilisation has not yet penetrated, what is right and what is wrong, what is allowed and what is forbidden, and gives them awareness that one day they will have to give to the supreme Judge an account of their good and evil deeds.

ENCYCLICAL LETTER *MYSTICI CORPORIS* (1943)

In his great Encyclical Letter on the mystery of the Church as the mystical Body of Christ (cf. nn. 847ff), Pope Pius XII shows the supreme role of the virtue of charity which surpasses faith and hope in creating ties between the members of the Church. He also shows how the love of God and of men are inseparable.

(Charity surpasses all other virtues)

2021 ...Charity, more than any other virtue, unites us closely with Christ....Therefore our divine Saviour earnestly exhorts us: "Abide in my love." And because charity is a poor thing unless it is shown and as it were put into practice by good works, He immediately adds: "If you keep my commandments, you will abide in my love, just as I have kept my Father's commandments and abide in His love" (*Jn 15.9-10*).

But our love of God, our love of Christ, must be accompanied by a corresponding charity towards our neighbour. How can we say that we love the divine Redeemer if we hate those He has redeemed with His precious blood to make them members of His mystical Body? ...Indeed it must be said that our union with God, our union with Christ, will become proportionately closer as we become more and more members one of another (*cf. Rom. 12.5*), more and more mutually careful one for another (*cf. 1 Cor. 12.25*); and, similarly, our union with each other by charity will become more intimate as we cleave more ardently to God and our divine Head.

INSTRUCTION OF THE HOLY OFFICE ON "SITUATION ETHICS"
(1956)

As explained in this document and as the name suggests, "Situation Ethics" rejects the absolute value of objective norms and places the ultimate criterion of morality in each man's personal intuitive judgment exercised in his concrete situation. Fundamentally it is based on the tenets of some currents of existentialist philosophy. It represents a reaction against too legalistic an approach which has often prevailed in matters of morality. At present it must be understood in the light of the current discussion on Moral Absolutes.

2022 Contrary to the moral doctrine and its application which is
3918 traditional in the Catholic Church, there has begun to be
spread abroad in many regions even among Catholics an ethical system which generally goes by the name of a certain "Situation Ethics". This ethics, they say, does not depend on the principles of objective ethics (which is ultimately based on ontological categories); nor it is merely put on the same plane as objective ethics, but it is ranked above it.

The authors who follow this system hold that the decisive and ultimate norm of conduct is not the objective right order, determined by the law of nature and known with certainty from that law, but a certain intimate judgment and light of the mind of each individual, by means of which, in the concrete situation in which he is placed, he learns what he ought to do. And so, according to them, this ultimate decision a man makes is not, as the objective ethics handed down by authors of great weight teaches, the application of the objective law to a particular case, which at the same time takes into account and weighs according to the rules of prudence the particular circumstances of the "situation", but that immediate, internal light and judgment. Ultimately, at least in many matters, this judgment is not measured, must not and cannot be measured, as regards its objective rectitude and truth, by any objective norm situated outside man and independent of his subjective persuasion, but is entirely self-sufficient.

2023 According to these authors, the traditional concept of
3919 "human nature" does not suffice; but recourse must be had
to the concept of "existent" human nature which in many respects does not have absolute objective value, but only a relative and, therefore, changeable value, except, perhaps, for those few factors and principles which pertain to metaphysical (absolute and

unchangeable) human nature. Of the same merely relative value is the traditional concept of the "law of nature". Thus, many things which are commonly considered today as absolute postulates of the natural law, according to their opinion and doctrine rest upon...the aforesaid concept of existent nature, and are, therefore, but relative and changeable; they can always be adapted to every situation.

2024 Having accepted these principles and put them into practice,
3920 they assert and teach that men are preserved or easily liberated from many otherwise insoluble ethical conflicts when each one judges in his own conscience, not primarily according to objective laws, but by means of that internal, individual light based on personal intuition, what he must do in a concrete situation.

2025 Many of the things set forth in this system of "Situation
3921 Ethics" contradict the truth of the matter and the dictates of sound reason, betray traces of relativism and modernism, and wander far from the Catholic doctrine handed down through the centuries. In not a few assertions they are akin to various systems of non-Catholic ethics.

Having considered all this, in order to avert the danger of the "New Morality" of which the Supreme Pontiff Pope Pius XII spoke in the Allocutions delivered on March 23 and April 18, 1952,[1] and in order to safeguard the purity and safety of Catholic doctrine, this supreme Congregation of the Holy Office forbids and prohibits this doctrine of "Situation Ethics", by whatever name it be designated, to be taught or approved in universities, academies, seminaries and houses of formation of religious, or to be propagated and defended in books, dissertations, assemblies or, as they are called, conferences, or in any other manner whatever.

JOHN XXIII

ENCYCLICAL LETTER *PACEM IN TERRIS* (1963)

In this encyclical, Pope John XXIII reminds all men of good will that peace in the world can be established only if the moral order laid down by God is respected. The encyclical comprises four parts: 1) the rights and duties of the human person; 2) the relations between persons and the State; 3) the relations between States; 4) the relations between States and the world community. The document belongs to the series of great social

---

1. Cf. *AAS* 44 (1952) 270ff, 413ff.

encyclicals. The first part, however, dealing with the fundamental rights and duties of man, comes under the scope of general principles of morality; quotations from this part are given here. For the application of these fundamental principles to the social order, cf. nn. 2124ff.

(Order imposed by God on men)

2026   ...The Creator of the world has imprinted in man's heart an
3956   order which his conscience reveals to him and strongly en-
          joins him to obey: "They show that what the law requires is
written on their hearts, while their conscience also bears witness"
(*Rom. 2.15*).

(Dignity of the person)

2027   The foundation of a well ordered and prosperous society lies
3957   in the principle that every man is a person endowed by
          nature with intelligence and free will. Hence he has rights and
duties of his own, flowing directly and simultaneously from his very
nature and, therefore, universal, inviolable and inalienable.

   If we look upon the dignity of the human person in the light of the
divinely revealed truth, we cannot help but esteem it far more highly.
For men are redeemed by the blood of Jesus Christ; they are by
grace the children and friends of God and heirs of eternal glory.

(Human rights)

2028   ... Every man has the right to life, to bodily integrity and to the
3958   means necessary and suitable for a decent way of life. These
          are primarily food and clothing, shelter, rest, medical care and
finally the necessary services which the State must provide for all.
Therefore man also has the right to security in case of sickness or
inability to work, of widowhood or old age, of unemployment, or in
any other case in which he is deprived of the means of subsistence
through no fault of his.

2029   By the natural law, every man has also the right to respect for
3959   his person and to his good reputation, to freedom in his quest
          for truth, in the expression and communication of his opin-
ions and in the pursuit of art, within the limits of the moral order and
the common good; the right also to truthful information about public
events.

2030   Again, natural law gives man the right to share in the benefits

3960   of culture and, hence, the right to a basic education and
         technical and professional training in keeping with the stage
of educational development of his country. Efforts must be made to
enable men, on the basis of their ability, to go on to higher studies, so
that, as far as possible, they may occupy posts and assume responsibilities in human society in accordance with their natural gifts and
the skills they have acquired.

2031   Among men's rights must also be counted that to honour
3961   God according to the norm of a right conscience and to
         profess one's religion privately and publicly....

2032   Moreover, men have the right to choose freely the state of
3962   life which they prefer, and, therefore, either to set up a family
         with equal rights and duties for man and woman, or to follow
a vocation to the priesthood or to the religious life.
    The family, based on marriage freely contracted, monogamous
and indissoluble, must be considered as the first and natural cell of
human society. Hence the need to provide for it with the greatest
care in the economic, social, cultural and moral fields, so as to
strengthen its stability and facilitate the fulfilment of its specific
mission. The right to see to the upkeep and the education of children
belongs, however, primarily to the parents.

2033   ...It is clear that men have the natural right not only to get an
3693   opportunity for work but also to choose their work freely.
    Indissolubly linked with these is the right to demand working
conditions in which physical health is not endangered, moral integrity is not threatened and the normal development of young people is
not impaired. As for women, they have the right to work in such
conditions as are in accordance with their needs and duties as wives
and mothers.

2034   From the dignity of the human person there also arises the
3964   right to exercise economic activities duly and with a proper
         sense of personal responsibility. Hence there is also—and
this must not be overlooked—the right to a wage, detemined
according to criteria of jusice, and therefore sufficient, in proportion
to the available resources, to give the worker and his family a
standard of living in keeping with the dignity of the human person....

2035   From the nature of man derives also the right to private

3965   property, even of productive goods....Finally—and this must be pointed out—the right of private property entails a social duty.

2036 From the fact that men are by nature social, they have the
3966 right of assembly and association, the right to give their associations the form they consider more conducive to the end they have in view, and to act in those societies on their own initiative and responsibility in order to achieve their desired objectives.... Such intermediate groups and societies (between State and family) must be considered as indispensable means of safeguarding the dignity and liberty of the human person, without interference with his sense of responsibility.

2037 Every man has the right to freedom of movement and of
3967 residence within the boundaries of his own country, and, when there are just reasons for it, to emigrate to other countries and take up residence there....

2038 The dignity of the human person involves further the right to
3968 take an active part in public affairs and to contribute to the common good of the citizens....

2039 The human person is also entitled to a legal protection of his
3969 rights, a protection that should be efficacious, impartial and in conformity with the true norm of justice....

(Duties)

2040 The natural rights with which we have been dealing are,
3970 however, inseparably connected, in the person who is their subject, with just as many respective duties; and rights as well as duties find their source, their sustenance and their inviolability in the natural law which grants or enjoins them.

For example, the right to life is correlative with the duty to preserve it; the right to a decent standard of living with the duty of living becomingly; the right to investigate the truth freely with the duty of seeking it ever more deeply and completely.

... In human society, to each particular right of one man there corresponds a duty in the other persons, the duty namely of acknowledging and respecting that right.... Those, therefore, who claim their own rights, yet altogether forget or neglect to carry out their respective duties, are like people who build with one hand and destroy with the other.

2041   ...A well-ordered human society requires that men recognise
3971   their mutual rights and discharge their mutual duties. By so
        doing they also contribute generously to the etablishment of
a civic order in which rights and duties are progressively more
diligently and more effectively observed.

It is not enough, for example, to acknowledge every man's right to
the necessary means of subsistence; we must also seek according to
our means to provide him with adequate food and nourishment.

Moreover, the society of men must not only be organised, but
must also provide them with abundant resources. This...also
requires that all join for combined action in the many enterprises
which modern civilisation either allows, or encourages or demands.

2042   The dignity of the human person also requires that every
3972   man enjoy the right to act freely and responsibly.

THE SECOND VATICAN GENERAL COUNCIL

*The Second Vatican Council has called for a renewal in the teaching of
moral theology: "Its scientific exposition should lean more on the teaching
of Sacred Scripture and set out the loftiness of the Christian vocation and
the obligation of the faithful to bear fruit in charity for the life of the world"
(OT 16). This teaching programme reflects the Council's conception of the
Christian life which theology is meant to articulate, and sums up the
fundamental principles which, according to the Council, constitute its
foundation. Because of the Council's primarily pastoral orientation, all the
concilar documents are concerned with various aspects of the Christian
life; its basic principles, however, are mostly expounded in the Dogmatic
Constitution* Lumen Gentium *and in the Pastoral Consitution* Gaudium et
Spes.
    *The Council's approach to Christian living is essentially positive in
character; going straight to the essentials, it proposes lofty Christian ideals
beyond all juridical attitudes. It is also universal in so far as these ideals are
proposed to all Christians without distinction. Thus, in the Constitution*
Lumen Gentium, *the conception of the Christian life is essentially based on
the theology of the Church as the People of God (LG 9ff); from this follows
the common call to holiness addressed to all the members of the Church
(LG 40). This fulness of the Christian life consists in the following of Christ
(LG 41) which leads to the perfection of charity (LG 42)—a charity which
does not separate the love of God from the love of men (GS 24). Applying
this to the laity, the Constitution explains their specific vocation (LG 31),
their dignity (LG 32) and their participation in the Church's mission (LG 33;
AA; AG 21, 41). Against this background, it is clear that the profession of
the evangelical counsels in the religious life does not give to the religious an
exclusive claim to Christian perfection. The religious life entails nevertheless a special call to holiness (LG 42), which summons a Christian to follow
Christ more closely and to live the baptismal consecration in a more radical
manner (LG 44) by the practice of the evangelical councils (LG 43; PC 1,*

12-14). The Council shows the ecclesial significance of the religious life and its eschatological dimension as a sign of the Kingdom (LG 44). The Decree Perfectae Caritaris *is chiefly concerned with its renewal and adaptation to the modern world. It states as the main principles of renovation a double faithfulness: to the sources, namely the Gospel and the inspiration of the founder, and to the demands of our time (PC 2).*

Another general feature of the moral doctrine of the Council is its social character. Here too the Constitution Lumen Gentium *sets the scene with its doctrine of the Church as the People of God, and the Body of Christ in which all members are mutually dependent. In a diversity of vocations and charisms, of functions and ministries, all share a common responsibility to build up the Church into God's holy people and the sign of the salvation He has wrought for all men in Jesus Christ. But to this common Christian calling, the Constitution* Gaudium et Spes *on the Church in the Modern World opens even broader perspectives. This vast document which embodies best the new spirit of the Church's openness to the world contains also its most far-reaching moral teaching. It gives to the Christian life its full dimension by bringing out its implications not only for the Christian community but for the world at large. It shows that Christian morality cannot remain centred on the individual, or even on the life of the Church; it must have in view the common good of the world community (GS 30).*

The first part of the Constitution Gaudium et Spes *deals with the Church and man's calling; four chapters treat of the dignity of the human person, the community of men, man's activity in the world, and the role of the Church in the modern world, respectively. This part lays down the basic principles of a broad-based Christian morality which the second part of the document applies to specific problems: marriage and the family, the development of culture, socio-economic life, the political community, peace and the building up of the community of nations.*

Among the fundamental principles the Constitution stresses first of all the dignity of the human person created in God's image (GS 12), the dignity and primacy of the moral conscience (GS 16), and the excellence of freedom (GS 17). This doctrine does not overlook the reality of sin (GS 13) and the consequent possibility for man of misusing his freedom (GS 17); but the light of faith also allows it an optimistic view of concrete man: marred by sin, Christian activity has been redeemed by Christ (GS 37), who through His Paschal Mystery has opened the way to true freedom (GS 38).

Secondly the Constitution stresses the essentially social character of man and his destiny in the plan of God (GS 24). Emphasis is laid on the fact that person and society are interdependent: man realises his personality through an interpersonal exchange with others; he fulfils his destiny in the context of a human society (GS 26).. Hence the need to promote the common good, which, however, is always ordained to the welfare of the persons (GS 26). Respect for the person and for all persons (GS 27), who all are equal (GS 29), is a supreme norm; it is in particular the norm on which social justice must be based (GS 29). Redeemed by Christ, human activity is at all levels a positive value (GS 34), willed by God for the full development of persons and the realisation of their divine destiny (GS 35). In this context the Constitution explains the rightful autonomy of secular realities (GS 36; cf. n. 423). Against this general background it goes on to expose the role of the Church in the world of today (GS 40ff). The laity are called upon to exercise moral responsibility (GS 43). The Constitution suggests a more personalistic understanding of the natural law (GS 51).

Insistence on the value of human freedom led the Council to make a special Declaration on religious liberty, the highest level at which man is called to exercise his freedom. The Declaration Dignitatis Humanae *shows the foundation of religious liberty to lie in the dignity of the person itself (DH 2). Man must be able to search for truth according to the dictates of his conscience (DH 3) and allowed to practise his religion, both interiorly and exteriorly, according to the same dictates (DH 3). Since in the practice of his religion too man is a social being, this liberty applies not only to individual persons but to groups (DH 4), among which the Declaration singles out the family (DH 5). Religious liberty being man's highest endowment, to protect it is the common responsibility of all men and of society (DH 6); at the same time, it is each man's and each group's responsibility to exercise it rightly and in keeping with the common good (DH 7). Here most of all education in the correct use of freedom is required (DH 8). To this freedom the Church herself claims an inalienable right (DH 13) for the exercise of her divine mission (DH 14).*

DOGMATIC CONSTITUTION *LUMEN GENTIUM* (1964)

(The vocation of the laity)

2043 31. ...It is the special vocation of the laity to seek the Kingdom of God engaging in temporal affairs and ordering them according to the mind of God. They live in the world, that is , in the various secular professions and occupations and in the ordinary circumstances of family and social life, from which the web of their existence is woven. There they are called by God to work for the sanctification of the world like a leaven, from within, by exercising their proper function according to the spirit of the Gospel. Especially by the testimony of their lives, by the radiance of their faith, hope and charity, they are to manifest Christ to others. It is their specific task to shed light upon and to order all the temporal affairs with which they are closely connected, in such a way that these may constantly be carried on and develop in keeping with the spirit of Christ, to the praise of the Creator and the Redeemer.

(The common dignity of all the members of the Church)

2044 32. ...Thus, the chosen people of God is one: "one Lord, one faith, one baptism" *(Eph. 4.5)*. As members, they share a common dignity from their rebirth in Christ; they have the same grace of sonship, the same call to perfection; they share in common one salvation, one hope and one undivided charity. In Christ, therefore, and in the Church there is no inequality on the basis of race or nationality, of social condition or sex, because "there is neither Jew nor Greek, there is neither slave nor free man; there is neither male nor female. For you are all 'one' in Christ Jesus" (*Gal. 3.28; cf. Col. 3.11*)....

(Universal call to holiness)

2045 40. ...Thus it is evident that all the faithful, whatever their station or rank, are called to the fulness of Christian life and to the perfection of charity—a holiness which promotes even in the earthly society a more human manner of life....

(Charity is the way to holiness)

2046 42. ...Charity, as the bond of perfection and the fulness of the law (*cf. Col. 3.14*), directs all the means that lead to holiness, animates them and makes them reach their end. Hence it is love for God and the neighbour that distinguishes the true disciple of Christ....

(The religious: their triple function in the Church)

2047 44. ...By his vows...a Christian takes upon himself the obligation of observing the three above-mentioned evangelical counsels. Thereby he dedicates himself totally to God, whom he loves above all things, and thus is ordained to the service and honour of God under a new and special title. By baptism he has already died to sin and has been consecrated to God; but, in order to draw more abundant fruit from the baptismal grace, he seeks by the profession of the evangelical counsels in the Church to free himself from impediments that could withdraw him from the fervour of charity and from the perfection of divine worship; and so he is more intimately consecrated to the service of God.....

It is clear that the evangelical counsels, through the charity which they develop, unite their followers in a special way with the Church and her mystery; therefore, the spiritual life of religious should also be dedicated to the welfare of the whole Church. Hence their duty of labouring for the implantation and strengthening of Christ's Kingdom in souls and for its extension to all regions....

The profession of the evangelical counsels, then, stands out as a standard that can and should effectively stimulate all the members of the Church to fulfil courageously the duties attached to their Christian vocation.... It manifests also more clearly to all believers the heavenly goods already present in this world; it bears a clearer witness to the new and eternal life which Christ's passion has won for us, and it foreshadows more directly the future resurrection and the glory of the heavenly kingdom....

Thus, the state of life which is constituted by the profession of the evangelical counsels, though it is not part of the hierarchical structure of the Church, decidedly belongs to her life and holiness.

DECLARATION *DIGNITATIS HUMANAE* (1965)

(Object and foundation of religious liberty)

2048 2. This Vatican Council declares that the human person has a right to religious freedom. This freedom means that all men are to be immune from coercion on the part of individuals or of social groups and of any human power, in such wise that in religious matters no one is to be forced to act against his conscience, or is, within just limits, to be hindered from acting in conformity with his conscience, whether privately or publicly, whether alone or in association with others. The Council further declares that the right to religious freedom has its foundation in the very dignity of the human person, as this dignity is known through the revealed word of God and by reason itself. This right of the human person to religious freedom must be recognised in the constitutional law governing society in such a way that it becomes a civil right.

(Freedom of external religious practice)

2049 3. ...The practice of religion, of its very nature, consists above all in those internal, voluntary and free acts whereby man sets the course of his life direct towards God; such acts can be neither commanded nor forbidden by any merely human authority. But the social nature of man requires him to give external expression to his internal acts of religion, to communicate with others in religious matters and profess his religion in community.

Injury is done, therefore, to the human person and to the very order established by God for men, if the free exercise of religion is denied to man in society when the just preservation of public order does not so require....

(Freedom of religious groups)

2050 4. The freedom or immunity from coercion in religious matters, which is the endowment of persons as individuals, is also to be recognised as their right when they act in community. For religious communities are a requirement of the social nature both of man and of religion itself.

Hence, provided the just demands of public order are observed, immunity is due by right to these communities in order that they may govern themselves according to their own norms, honour the Supreme Being in public worship, assist their members in the practice of their religious life, strengthen them by instruction, and promote institutions in which they may work together for the purpose of ordering their own lives in accordance with their religious principles....

PASTORAL CONSTITUTION *GAUDIUM ET SPES* (1965)

(Dignity of the human person: man made in God's image)

2051   12. Believers and non-believers alike generally agree to say that all things on earth must be ordained to man as their centre and crown.... Sacred Scripture teaches that man was created "in God's image", capable of knowing and loving his Creator, appointed by Him lord of all creatures on earth (*cf. Gen. 1.26; Wis. 2.23*), to rule over them and use them while giving glory to God (*cf. Sir. 17.3-10*).... But God did not create man as a solitary being; from the beginning "male and female He created them" *(Gen. 1.27)*; their companionship constitutes the primary expression of interpersonal communion. For man is in the depth of his nature a social being: he can neither live nor develop his talents except through relationships with others....

(Dignity of the moral conscience)

2052   16. In the depths of his conscience man detects a law which he does not make for himself but which he must obey. Its voice always summons him to love and to do what is good and to shun what is evil. At the right moment it resounds in the secrecy of his heart: do this, avoid that. For there is in man's heart a law written by God. His dignity lies in obeying it; and according to this law he will be judged *(cf. Rom. 2.14-16)*. Conscience is the most secret core and sanctuary of man. There he is alone with God, there in his innermost self he perceives God's voice. Through conscience man comes to know, in a wonderful manner, that law whose fulfilment consists in the love of God and neighbour (*cf. Mt. 22.37-40; Gal. 5.14*). In loyalty to their conscience, Christians join with the rest of men in the search for truth and for a true solution to the many moral problems arising in the life of both individuals and society. The more a right conscience holds sway, the more do persons and groups abandon arbitrary decisions and endeavour to conform to the objective norms of morality. However, it often happens that conscience errs through invincible ignorance; yet it does not on that score lose its dignity. This, however, cannot be said when a man cares little to seek for what is true and good, and when, through a habit of sin, his conscience little by little becomes practically blind.

(Excellence of freedom)

2053   17. But it is only as a free being that man can turn to what is good. Our contemporaries set a high store on this freedom and pursue it eagerly; and rightly so, to be sure. Often, however, they foster it in a perverse manner, as a licence to do anything they please, even what is evil. But genuine freedom is a striking sign of God's image in man; for God was pleased to "leave man in the hand of his own counsel" *(cf. Sir. 15.14),* so that man may seek his Creator of his own accord, and by adhering to Him reach in freedom to full perfection and happiness. Man's dignity, then, demands that he should act with deliberate and free choice. He must be led and guided from within by a personal decision, and not by a blind inner impulse or by mere external pleasure. Man attains this dignity when, freeing himself from all slavery of passion, he pursues his goal by the free choice of what is good and with intelligent application effectively procures for himself the means to that goal. However, as man's freedom is wounded by sin, he can make his Godward orientation fully effective only with the help of God's grace. And before the judgment seat of God each one will have to render an account of his life, of the good and of the evil he has done *(cf. 2 Cor. 5.10).*

(The community of men: interdependence of person and society)

2054   25. The social nature of man makes it evident that the development of the human person and the progress of society are mutually dependent. The principle, subject and goal of all social institution is and must be the human person who, by his very nature, has an absolute need of social life. Life in society is not something accidental to man; hence, by his dealings with other men, by mutual services and by fraternal dialogue, he develops all his personal gifts and is enabled to respond to his calling.

Among the social ties which man needs for his development some, like the family and the political community, answer more immediately his intimate nature, while others originate rather from his own free will.

(Promoting the common good)

2055   26. Human interdependence is increasing daily and is gradually spreading to the entire world. Hence it follows that the common good—or the sum total of those conditions of social life which allow groups and each of their members as well to attain their own perfection more fully and more readily—is today taking on a more universal dimension, involving rights and duties with regard to the whole of mankind. Every group has to take into account the needs and lawful aspirations of other groups and even the common good of the entire human family.

At the same time, however, there is a growing awareness of the exalted dignity of the human person, who is superior to all things and whose rights and duties are universal and inviolable. There must, therefore, be made available to man all that he is in need of to live a truly human life....

The social order and its development must result unceasingly in the good of the persons, since the order of things must be made subject to the order of persons, and not inversely....

(Respect for the human person)

2056   27. To come now to practical and particularly urgent applications, the Council insists on respect for man: everyone should consider his neighbour, no one excepted, as 'another self', take into account first of all his existence and the means necessary for him to live his life worthily, and beware not to imitate the rich man who did not care for the poor Lazarus (*cf. Lk. 16.19-31*).

In our days especially, the duty is more binding than ever to make ourselves neighbours to absolutely every man and give active help to anyone crossing our path....

(Essential equality of men)

2057   29. All men, endowed with a rational soul and created in the image of God, have the same nature and the same origin; redeemed by Christ, they all enjoy the same divine calling and divine destiny. Hence the basic equality of all men must increasingly be recognised.

(Going beyond an individualistic ethics)

2058   30. The profound and rapid changes now taking place demand more urgently than ever that no one should rest content with merely individualistic ethics for lack of attention to present day trends or out of inertia. Nowadays justice and charity demand more and more that every man contribute to the common good, according to his own abilities and taking into account the needs of others, and that he promote and help public or private institutions which serve to improve the living conditions of men. But there are people who, while making profession of lofty and generous ideas, continue to live as if they did not care at all for the needs of society.... Let all consider it a sacred duty to count social obligations among the primary duties of man today and to heed to them.

(Norm of human activity)

2059   35. This, therefore, is the norm of human activity: according to God's design and will, it must be in coformity with the genuine good of mankind and allow man, both as individual and as a member of society, to pursue and fulfil his total vocation.

(Human activity brought to perfection in the Paschal Mystery)

2060   38. For the Word of God, through whom all things were made, was Himself made flesh and dwelt on the earth of men *(cf. Jn 1.3, 14)*. Thus He entered the world's history as the perfect man, taking up into Himself and recapitulating that history *(cf. Eph. 1.10)*. He it is who reveals to us that "God is love" *(1 Jn 4.8)* and who teaches us at the same time that the basic law of man's perfection and hence of the transformation of the world is the new commandment of love. To those who believe in God's love, He thus brings the certainty that the way of love lies open to all men and that the efforts made to built up a universal brotherhood are not wasted....Constituted Lord by His resurrection and having been given all power in heaven and on earth *(cf. Acts 2.36; Mt. 28.18)*, Christ is now at work in the hearts of men through the power of His Spirit.

(The laity called to exercise moral responsibility)

2061   43. It pertains to their (the laity's) conscience, properly formed, to write the law of God into the life of the earthly city. From priests, the laity should look for light and spiritual energy. However, they should not imagine that their pastors are always such experts that they can give an immediate and concrete answer for every problem, however complicated, that arises, or even that such is their mission. Rather, enlightened by Christian wisdom and paying careful attention to the authoritative teaching of the Church, the layman should assume his own responsibilities.

PAUL VI

DECLARATION *DE PERSONA HUMANA* OF THE
S. CONGREGATION FOR THE DOCTRINE OF THE FAITH
(29 December 1975)

For the first time, in this Declaration on Sexual Ethics, the concept of 'fundamental option' is adopted by the Magisterium, although its excesses are rejected. Mortal sin is described as the violation of the order of love which is equivalent to a change in the fundamental option. The text is found in Osservatore Romano *(English Edition), 22 January, 1976, pp. 5, 11-12.*

(Fundamental option and particular acts)

2062 10. In reality, it is precisely the fundamental option which in the last resort defines a person's moral disposition. But it can be completely changed by particular acts, especially when, as it happens, these have been prepared for by previous more superficial acts.

(Mortal sin, serious violation of the order of love)

2063 10. A person, therefore, sins mortally not only when his action comes from direct contempt for love of God and neighbour, but also when he consciously and freely, for whatever reason, chooses something which is seriously disordered. For in this choice, ...there is already included contempt for the divine commandment: the person turns himself away from God and loses charity.

JOHN PAUL II

ENCYCLICAL LETTER *REDEMPTOR HOMINIS* (1979)

In his first Encyclical Letter on Christ, Redeemer of Man, Pope John Paul II shows the value which man acquires in the eyes of God through the mystery of redemption; see n. 2172i. In this context he stresses the values of love and freedom based on truth. The text is found in AAS 71 (1979) 280-281.

(Freedom founded on truth)

2064 12. Jesus Christ meets the man of every age, including our own, with the same words: "You will know the truth and the truth will make you free" *(Jn 8.32)*. These words contain both a fundamental requirement and a warning: the requirement of an honest relationship with regard to truth as a condition for authentic freedom, and the warning to avoid every kind of illusory freedom, every freedom that fails to enter into the whole truth about man and the world. Today also, even after two thousand years, we see Christ as the one who brings man freedom based on truth, frees man from what curtails, diminishes and as it were breaks off this freedom at its root, in man's soul, his heart and his conscience.

CHAPTER XXI

THE SOCIAL DOCTRINE OF THE CHURCH

Man is by nature a social being whose personality develops in the context of human society. The Christian message shows the deepest roots of the social character of man: all men are created by God as members of one human race in which all have the same rights and must live in a universal brotherhood. It also points to the divine destiny which all men are ordained by God to share in common: Christ has died that all men may be united with God and among themselves. Union of men with God and among themselves are two inseparable aspects of the Christian message. This vocation which will be fulfilled in the other world is in the process of realisation here on earth. Nor is the union between men to be conceived as a purely spiritual one. Christianity has always reacted against a pure spiritualism which would not do justice to man's true nature. It is man's entire person which must be able to grow in society to full liberation and development. It is in this context that the social order is for the Church a primary concern; the same opportunities must be offered to all to be fully human and so to attain to their divine destiny.

This preoccupation has always been present in the Church's consciousness. In early Christianity it found expression in the Church's condemnation of the practice of slavery which was in flagrant contradiction with the Christian ideal. But it is the deep changes brought about in society by the quick evolution of the modern world since the last century that have given rise in the Church to an elaborate social doctrine. This doctrine has developed gradually through an impressive series of documents, each of which attempts to apply the Christian social ideal to new problems arising from fast evolving situations.

The phenomenon of intensive industrialisation created the problem of the working class. The liberal individualistic theory of free competition, regardless of moral considerations, led to treating labour as a mere commodity; this resulted in allowing sub-human conditions for the workmen. Reacting on behalf of the working classes, opposite extremist theories arose which advocated the abolition of private property to allow the same opportunities for all. Striking a middle course between these opposite excessive tenden-

cies, the Church proclaimed the right of the worker to a living wage and worthy human conditions while defending the right of private property as flowing from natural law and necessary for all.

In rapidly evolving social conditions, further precisions were required as regards the nature of wages and the right of private property; the Church proclaimed the doctrine of family wage and advised that the wage contract be supplemented by a contract of partnership by which the workers be made sharers in the ownership of the enterprise; as to the right of private ownership, it is secondary, compared to the universal destination of material goods, and hence subordinate to the fundamental right of every man to make use of the goods of the earth.

Thus, the social doctrine gradually evolved from the questions of justice between man and man to the idea of true partnership between men in rights, duties and responsibilities, at the level of the enterprise and the nation. In recent years, due to the developing consciousness of the international community, the social doctrine of the Church has taken on a new dimension and broadened its scope so as to consider the various problems on a world-wide scale. Without neglecting the problems of social justice within a given community, the social principles are now extended to the relations between nations; special attention is given to the rights and needs of the developing nations and to the creation of supranational and world organisations endowed with proper authority to ensure equality between nations, and justice and peace in the world at large. This cannot be achieved without faith in God, the common Father of all, and without imitating His mercy.

*   *   *

The vast and rich material of these documents must be studied in the texts themselves ; here only some key-texts are quoted, in which the main elements of doctrine are found. They fall under the following headings:

Human Society

The social teaching of the Church is not monolithic: 2183a.
The right social order has its ultimate source in God: 2124.
Every man has the right and duty to self-fulfilment : 2145.
This must be achieved in society and respect the scale of human values: 2146, 2174.

Social progress must accompany economic development: 2116.
The aim is integral humanism open to God: 2146, 2149.
Women have equal rights with men: 2153b, 2179, 2181.
Racial discrimination is to be condemned: 2153c.
The right of migrants have to be defended: 2153d.
Mass media are to be used responsibly: 2153e.
The nature of society demands authority: 2125.
Authority is ultimately based on God: 2126.
Civil authority must respect the moral order: 2127.
Men have a right to choose their form of government: 2128.
Civil authority must promote the common good in its entirety: 2129.
In particular, it must defend and promote personal rights and duties:
    2130f, 2173.
The principle of subsidiarity between State and private initiative
    must regulate the economic order: 2113.
Socialism, a characterstic of present time: 2114.
Wider sharing of responsibility is to be fostered: 2156d.

Right of Ownership

The universal destination of earthly goods is primary: 2141, 2147.
Ownership has a double character, individual and social: 2106.
The right to private ownership is a natural right: 2101, 2119.
It is subordinated to the fundamental right of every man to use the
    goods of the earth: 2112, 2147, 2147a.
Radical reforms are needed to ensure this fundamental right: 2148.
Rules for the use of private ownership: 2103, 2108.
The limits in the use of ownership must be defined by the State in
    view of the common good: 2107, 2147a.
The right of the State to possess productive goods: 2121.
The Church condemns liberal capitalism and total collectivism:
    2147b.

Labour and Wages

Work is sharing in creation and redemption in Christ: 2180.
Labour has a personal and necessary character: 2104.
The subjective meaning of work has primacy over the objective:
    2175.
Labour has primacy over capital: 2176.
Work founds a right to ownership: 2177.
It has a double aspect, individual and social: 2110.

Both aspects must be considered in fixing wages: 2111/1-3.

Norms of a just wage: 2105, 2115, 2178.

Wage-contracts should be qualified by contracts of partnership: 2109.

Shared responsibility must be granted to workers: 2117/1-3, 2177.

Relations between States

They must be governed by respect of rights and acknowledgment of equality: 2132-2133.

War of self-defence can be justified as a last means: 2142.

In war international laws and agreements must be observed: 2142.

Total warfare is condemned: 2143.

Arms race is to be abandoned and disarmament to be fostered: 2134, 2144.

Peace is to be built on the order willed by God and justice among men: 2153.

Neocolonialism is to be condemned: 2147b, 2160.

World Community

Complete development of man includes the development of all humanity: 2150.

Developing countries have a right to full development: 2160.

Solidarity between rich and poor nations is needed: 2122, 2150.

It must be expressed in help given to poorer nations: 2151.

This help must be disinterested and given in mutual appreciation: 2123, 2133

In international transactions justice and charity are required: 2150, 2152.

The world community requires a supra-national authority: 2135-2137.

The principle of subsidiarity must regulate the relations between world authority and State Governments: 2138.

Duties of Catholics in Public Life

Catholics must take an active part in it: 2061, 2139, 2157.

Their collaboration with movements originating from non-Christian ideologies is subject to conditions: 2140/1-2, 2154-2156, 2158.

The Church has a specific role to play to bring about justice in the world: 2159, 2161.

Action for the liberation of men is part of the Church's mission: 2159, 2161, 2166, 2167, 2168.

The Church must witness to justice in her life: 2162.

The Church's mission may not be reduced to a temporal project: 2170.

Development and Liberation

The Christian vision of integral development: 2145.

Evangelisation is necessarily linked with human advancement: 2169.

The contribution of human sciences is to be positively evaluated: 2156a.

Mere human progress is ambiguous: 2156b, 2172.

Preferential respect is to be shown to the poor: 2153f.

The Gospel is a message of total liberation: 2167, 2168.

True liberation involves conversion: 2171.

The obstacles to the right development of nations must be overcome: 2160.

Violence is illegitimate except in extreme cases: 2147c, 2156c.

There is need for education to justice: 2163.

Liturgy can have a formation value for justice: 2164.

The Holy Year is the year of the poor, of redistribution of goods: 2165.

Justice needs to be imbued with mercy: 2174.

LEO XIII

ENCYCLICAL LETTER *RERUM NOVARUM* (1891)

This is the first in the series of the great Encyclical Letters on social questions. Confronted with the phenomenon of growing industrialisation, it is mostly concerned with the problems of ownership and wages. The right to private ownership is founded both at the individual and at the family level. The social aspect of the question manifests itself in the use one must make of one's property. In the determination of a just wage the personal and the necessary character of labour must be taken into account; this determination should not be left to the mere play of economic laws.

(Right and use of private property)

2101 Every man has by nature the right to possess property as his
3265 own.... For God has granted the earth to mankind in general,
not in the sense that all without distinction can deal with it as they like, but rather that no part of it was assigned to anyone in particular, and that the limits of private possession have been left to be fixed by man's own industry and by the laws of individual races.... Truly, that which is required for the preservation of life and for its well-being is produced in great abundance from the soil, but not until man has brought it into cultivation and exercised upon it his solicitude and skill. Now, when man thus turns the activity of his mind and the strength of his body towards procuring the fruits of nature, by such industry he makes his own that portion of nature's field which he cultivates—that portion on which he leaves, as it were, the impress of his individuality; and it cannot but be just that he should possess that portion as his own, and have the right to hold it—a right which no one is justified in violating.

2102 The rights here spoken of, belonging to each individual man,
3266 are seen in a much stronger light when considered in relation
to man's social and domestic obligations.... That right to property, therefore, which has been proved to belong naturally to individual persons, must likewise belong to man in his capacity of head of a family; nay, that right is all the more valid in proportion as human personality in the life of the family takes various forms. For it is a most sacred law of nature that a father should provide food and all necessities for those whom he has begotten, and, similarly, it is natural that he should wish that his children, who reproduce, so to speak, and prolong his personality, should be by him provided with all that is needed to enable them to keep themselves decently from want and misery amid the uncertainties of this mortal life. Now, in no

other way can a father effect this except by the ownership of productive property, which he can transmit to his children by inheritance....

2103 It is one thing to have a right to the possession of money, and
3267 another to use one's money rightly. Private ownership, as we
have seen, is the natural right of man; and to exercise that right, especially as members of society, is not only lawful, but absolutely necessary....But if the question be asked: How must one's possession be used?, the Church replies without hesitation in the words of St Thomas Aquinas: "Man should not consider his material possessions as his own, but as common to all, so as to share them without hesitation when others are in need. Hence the apostle says: 'As for the rich of this world, charge them...to be generous and willing to share' (*1 Tim. 6.17*)."[1] True, no one is commanded to distribute to others that which is required for his own needs and those of his household; nor even to give away what is reasonably required to keep up becomingly his condition in life....But when what necessity demands has been supplied and one's standing fairly provided for, it becomes a duty to give to the needy out of what remains over. "Of that which remains, give alms" (*Lk. 11.41 Vulg.*). It is a duty, not of justice (save in extreme cases), but of Christian charity—a duty not to be enforced by law. But the laws and judgment of men must yield to the law and judgment of Christ our God, who in many ways urges on His followers the practice of almsgiving....

(Rights arising from labour: A just wage)

2104 To labour is to exert oneself for the sake of procuring what is
necessary for the various purposes of life, and above all for
self-preservation.

3268 ...Hence a man's labour necessarily bears two notes or
characters. First of all, it is personal, inasmuch as the force which acts is bound up with the personality and is the exclusive property of him who acts, and further, was given to him for his benefit. Secondly, man's labour is necessary; for without the result of labour a man cannot live, and self-preservation is a law of nature, which it is wrong to disobey.

2105 Now, were we to consider labour merely in so far as it is

---

1. *Summa theologica,* II, II, 66, 2.

3269   personal, doubtless it would be within the workman's right to
        accept any rate of wages whatsoever; for in the same way as
he is free to work or not, so is he free to accept a small wage or even
no wage at all.

3270   But our conclusion must be very different if together with the
        personal element in a man's work we consider the fact that
work is also necessary for him to live; these two aspects of his work
are separable in theory, but not in reality. The preservation of life is
the bounden duty of one and all, and to be wanting therein is a crime.
It necessarily follows that each one has a natural right to procure for
himself what is required in order to live; and the poor can procure
that in no other way than by what they earn through their work. Let
then the working man and the employer make free agreements, and
in particular let them agree freely as to the wages; nevertheless,
underlying such agreements there is always a dictate of natural
justice more imperious and ancient than any bargain between man
and man, namely, that wages ought not to be insufficient to support a
frugal and well-behaved wage-earner. If through necessity or fear of a
worse evil the workman accepts harder conditions, forced on him
against his will, because an employer or contractor will give him no
better, he is made the victim of force and injustice....

PIUS XI

ENCYCLICAL LETTER *QUADRAGESIMO ANNO* (1931)

In this encyclical which celebrates the fortieth anniversary of Rerum
Novarum *the social aspect is stressed more than in the previous document,
both as regards the question of ownership and in the matter of wages. To
attain a more perfect balance and social harmony, the Pope says, it is
advisable to add to the wage contract a contract of partnership.*

(Ownership or right of property: individual and social character)

2106   The right to own private property has been given to man by
3726   nature, or rather by the Creator Himself, not only in order
        that individuals may be able to provide for their own needs
and those of their families, but also that, by means of it, the goods
which the Creator has destined for the human race may truly serve
this purpose. Now these ends cannot be secured, unless some
definite and stable order is maintained. There is therefore a double
danger to be avoided. On the one hand, if the social and public aspect
of ownership be denied or minimised, the logical consequence is

what is called "individualism" or something approaching it; on the other hand, the rejection or toning down of its private and individual character necessarily leads to "collectivism" or at least to some of its tenets....

(The State and ownership)

2107 If follows from the twofold character of ownership which we
3728 have termed individual and social, that men must take into account in this matter, not only their own advantage, but also the common good. To define in detail these duties, when the need occurs and when the natural law does not do so, is the function of the Government. Provided that the natural and divine law be observed, the public authority, in view of the common good, may specify more accurately what is licit and what is illicit for property owners in the use of their possessions....

(Use of superfluous income)

2108 At the same time a man's superfluous income is not left
3729 entirely to his own discretion.... On the contrary, the grave obligations of charity, beneficence and liberality, which rest upon the wealthy are constantly insisted upon in telling words by Holy Scripture and the Fathers of the Church.

However, the investment of superfluous income in securing favourable opportunities for employment, provided such employment be directed to the production of useful goods, is to be considered, according to the teaching of the angelic Doctor,[1] an act of real liberality, particularly appropriate to the needs of our time.

(A just wage)

2109 First of all, those who hold that the wage-contract is essen-
3733 tially unjust, and that in its place must be introduced a contract of partnership, are certainly in error.... In the present state of human society, however, we deem it advisable that the wage-contract should, when possible, be qualified somewhat by a contract of partnership, as is already being tried in various ways with no small gain both to the wage-earners and to the employers. In this way wage-earners and employers participate in the ownership or the management, or in some way share in the profits.

---

1. St Thomas Aquinas, *Summa theologica*, II, II, 134, 3.

In estimating a just wage, not one consideration alone but many must be taken into account....

(Labour's double aspect)

2110 The obvious truth is that in labour, especially hired labour, as
3734   in ownership, there is a social as well as a personal or individual aspect to be considered. For unless human society forms a truly social and organic body; unless labour be protected in the social and juridical order; unless the various forms of human endeavour, dependent one upon the other, are united in mutual harmony and mutual support; unless, above all, intelligence, capital and labour combine together for a common effort, man's toil cannot produce due fruit. Hence, if the social and individual character of labour be overlooked, it can neither be justly valued nor equitably retributed.

From this double aspect, growing out of the very notion of human labour, follow important conclusions for the regulation and fixing of wages.

(a. Support of the working man and his family)

2111/1 In the first place, the wage paid to the working man must be
3735   sufficient for his own support and that of his family....

Every effort must therefore be made that fathers of families receive a wage sufficient to meet adequately ordinary domestic needs. If in the present state of society this is not always feasible, social justice demands that reforms be introduced without delay which will guarantee such a wage to every adult working man....

(b. State of business)

2111/2 The condition of any particular business and of its owner
3736   must also come into consideration for settling the scale of wages; for it is unjust to demand wages so high that an employer cannot pay them without ruin, and without consequent distress amongst the working people themselves. If the business makes too little profit on account of bad management, want of enterprise or out-of-date methods, this is not a just reason for reducing the working men's wages. If, however, the business does not make enough money to pay the workman a just wage, either because it is overwhelmed with unjust burdens, or because it is compelled to sell its products at an unjustly low price, those who thus injure it are guilty of grievous wrong; for it is they who deprive the

working men of the just wage, and force them to accept lower terms....

(c. Demands of the common good)

2111/3 Finally, the wage-scale must be regulated with a view to the
3737   economic welfare of the whole people. We have already
shown how conducive it is to the common good that
wage-earners of all kinds be enabled, by economising that portion of
their wage which remains after necessary expenses have been met,
to attain to the possession of a certain modest fortune. Another
point, however, of no less importance must not be overlooked, in
these our days especially, namely, that opportunities for work be
provided for those who are willing and able to work. This depends
in large measure upon the scale of wages which multiplies opportunities for work as long as it remains within proper limits, and reduces
them if allowed to depart from these limits....To lower or raise wages
unduly, with a view to private profit, and with no consideration for
the common good, is contrary to social justice which demands that,
by union of effort and good will, such a scale of wages be set up, if
possible, as to offer to the greatest number opportunities of employment and of securing for themselves suitable means of livelihood....

PIUS XII

DISCOURSE ON THE FIFTIETH ANNIVERSARY OF

RERUM NOVARUM (1941)

*In this discourse Pope Pius XII clearly states the primacy of everyone's
right to make use of the goods of the earth. The text is found in AAS 33
(1941) 195ff.*

(Use of material goods)

2112 ...Every man, as a living being gifted with reason, has in fact
from nature the fundamental right to make use of the material goods of the earth, while it is left to the will of man and to the
juridical statutes of nations to regulate in greater detail the exercise
of this right. This individual right cannot in any way be suppressed,
even by other clear and undisputed rights over material goods.
Undoubtedly the natural order, deriving from God, also demands
private property and the free reciprocal commerce of goods by
interchange and gift, as well as the function of the State to control
both of these institutions. But all this remains subordinated to the

natural end of material goods and cannot be emancipated from the first and fundamental right which concedes their use to all men; it should rather serve to make possible the exercise of this right in conformity with its end....

JOHN XXIII

ENCYCLICAL LETTER *MATER ET MAGISTRA* (1961)

In the last decades the socio-economic conditions have changed considerably. The life of the individual is involved in complex social structures as a result of the development of social legislation and independent bodies, such as insurance-societies, etc.... In many countries the status of industrial workers has improved considerably while agricultural workers are often handicapped. Besides, the social problem has acquired world dimensions due to the vastly different conditions in prosperous and developing countries. This encyclical touches on all these problems. On the question of private ownership a new note is struck. It is not so much the question of subsistence that is stressed—this is often sufficiently provided for by the various social securities—but the element of freedom and the exercise of personal responsibility.

(Private initiative and State intervention in the economy)

2113   ...It should be affirmed that in the economy the first place
3943   must be given to the personal initiative of private citizens, working as individuals or in various associations for the pursuit of common interests.

But in this area, for reasons pointed out by our predecessors, authorities also must play an active role in duly promoting increased productivity with a view to social progress and the welfare of all citizens. This activity of public authority, which encourages, stimulates, co-ordinates, supplements and completes, is based on the principle of subsidiarity....

...This principle must always be retained: that State activity in the economic field, no matter what its reach or extent may be, ought not to be exercised in such a way as to curtail an individual's freedom of action, but rather to increase it, provided the essential rights of each individual person are duly safeguarded....

(Socialisation)

2114   One of the characteristic features of our epoch is socialisation. By this term is meant the growing interdependence of men in society, giving rise to various patterns of group life and activity and in many instances to social institutions established on a juridical basis....

It is clear that many benefits and advantages flow from socialisation thus understood....At the same time, however, it multiplies institutional structures and extends more and more to minute details the juridical control of human relations in every walk of life.... We consider that socialisation can and ought to be brought about in such a way as to maximise its advantages and eliminate or minimise its negative cosequences.

(Remuneration of work: standards of justice and equity)

2115   ...It not infrequently happens that in economically advanced countries great, and sometimes very great, reward is paid for the performance of some small task, or one of doubtful value. At the same time, however, the diligent and profitable toil of whole classes of decent, hard-working men receives a recompense that is too small, or even totally insufficient. Moreover, it may in no way correspond to their contribution to the good of the community, to the profit of the enterprises they are employed in or to the national economy.

3944   We judge it, therefore, to be our duty to reaffirm that just as the remuneration of work cannot be left entirely to the laws of the market, so too it cannot be fixed by an arbitrary decision. It must rather be determined according to justice and equity. This requires that workers should be paid a wage which allows them to live a truly human life and requires, too, that in the assessment of a fair wage for labour regard be had for the following: the contribution of individual workers to production; the economic health of the enterprise in which they are engaged; the demands of the national interest, especially with regard to any impact on employment of the total labour force; and finally the requirements of the universal common good, that is, of international communities of different nature and scope.

It is clear that these standards of judgment are valid always and everywhere. However, the degree to which they are applicable to concrete cases cannot be determined without reference to the available wealth....

(Balancing economic development and social progress)

2116   Since the economies of various nations are evolving rapidly,... we consider it opportune to call attention to a fundamental principle of social justice, namely, that social progress should accompany and be adjusted to economic development in such a way that all classes of citizens can participate in the increased productivity.

(Shared responsibility)

2117/1 Justice is to be observed not only in the distribution of
3947   wealth acquired by production but also with respect to the
            conditions under which production is achieved. For there
is an innate demand in human nature that when men engage in
productive activity, they should have the opportunity of exercising
responsibility and of perfecting their personalities....

2117/2 ...We uphold the desire of employees to participate
3948   actively in the management of enterprises in which they are
            employed....

2117/3 ...We cannot fail to emphasise how imperative it is or at
            least highly opportune that the workers should be able
freely to make their voices heard, and listened to, beyond the
confines of their individual productive units and at every level of
society....It is not the decisions made within each individual productive unit which have the greatest bearing (on the economic and social
complex); instead it is those made by public authorities or by institutions that function on a worldwide or national scale in regard to some
economic sector or category of production....

(Private property: changed conditions)

2118 ...There are many citizens today—and their number is on the
3949   increase—who through belonging to insurance groups or
          through social security, can afford to face the future with
serenity. Formerly such serenity depended on the ownership of
property, however, modest.... It is noted that today men strive to
acquire professional skills rather than to become owners of property. They have greater confidence in income derived from work or
rights founded on work than in income derived from capital or rights
founded on capital....
        The aspects of the economy just alluded to have certainly con-
tributed to spreading a doubt whether, in the present state of affairs,
a principle of the socio-economic order consistently taught and
defended by our predecessors has diminished in or lost its importance. The principle in question is that of the natural right of private
ownership, including ownership of productive goods.

(Confirmation of the right of private ownership)

2119 There is no reason for such a doubt to persist. The right of
          private ownership of goods, including productive goods, has

a permanent validity. This is so because it is a part of the natural law, which teaches us that individuals are prior to society and that society has as its purpose the service of man.

Moreover, it would be useless to insist on free, private initiative in the economic field, if the same initiative did not include the power to dispose freely of the means indispensable to its exercise. Further, history and experience testify that where governments fail to recognize the right to private ownership of goods, productive goods included, the fundamental manifestations of freedom are suppressed or stifled. Hence one may justifiably conclude that the exercise of freedom finds in the right of ownership both a guarantee and an incentive.

(Effective distribution)

2120 It is not enough to assert the natural character of the right of
3951 private property, including productive property; strenuous
efforts must be made to see that the ability to exercise this is extended to all social classes.

(Public ownership)

2121 The doctrine that has been set forth above obviously does not prohibit the State and other public agencies from lawfully possessing productive goods, particularly when they carry with them an opportunity for domination that is so great that it cannot be left in the hands of private individuals without injury to the community at large.... But in this matter also the principle of subsidiarity stated above is to be faithfully observed. Accordingly, the State and other agencies of public law should not extend their ownership except where evident and real needs of the common good dictate it; and they should be on their guard against extending it to the point where private property is excessively reduced or, even worse, abolished.

(Just relations between nations in different stages of economic development: emergency aid is not enough)

2122 One of the most difficult problems facing the modern world concerns the relations between nations that are economically advanced and those in the earlier stages of development.... The solidarity which binds all men and makes them, as it were, members of the same family requires that nations enjoying an abundance of material goods should not remain indifferent to those nations whose citizens suffer from internal problems that result in poverty, hunger and an inability to enjoy even the more elementary human rights. This obligation is all the more urgent since, given the growing interdependence among nations, it is impossible to preserve a lasting and beneficial peace while glaring socio-economic inequalities persist between them....

...Emergency aid, though a duty imposed by humanity and justice, will not suffice to eliminate or even reduce the permanent factors which in not a few nations bring about misery, hunger and want.... Part of the answer is to make available the capital needed to step up the economic development of these nations with the help of modern methods and techniques.

(Disinterested aid and cooperation on a world scale)

2123   ...The more highly developed nations face one very great temptation. They must take care lest, while giving technical and financial help to less developed nations, they turn the political situation that prevails there to their own profit or imperialistic aggrandizement.... Necessity and justice alike demand that technical and financial aid be given with sincere political disinterestedness and for the purpose of bringing those nations on the way to economic development, to the point where they can achieve themselves their economic and social growth....

... It can be said that contemporary problems of any importance, whatever their object may be—scientific, technical, economic, social, political or cultural—today commonly present supranational and often world dimensions.... Hence, mutual understanding and cooperation are a prime necessity. Individuals, and even all peoples, grow more and more convinced of this every day. Nevertheless, it seems that men, especially those entrusted with greater responsibility, are unable to achieve the understanding and cooperation which the general public desires. The root of such inability is not to be sought in any shortage of scientific knowledge, technical skill or economic proficiency, but in the absence of mutual trust.... As a consequence, vast human energies and gigantic resources are employed for destructive rather than constructive purposes....

Mutual trust among men and among States cannot stand firm and become deep-rooted without initial recognition of and respect for a just moral order on both sides. The moral order, however, cannot be built except on God.

ENCYCLICAL LETTER *PACEM IN TERRIS* (1963)

The first part of this other encylical of Pope John XXIII treats of the rights and duties of the human person; it has been dealt with in the chapter on the principles of the Christian life (cf. nn. 2028-2042). From this part, only one quotation is given here, which is more directly relevant to the social order (n. 2124). The other passages are taken from parts two, three and four, which deal with the relations between persons and State, between States, and finally between States and the world community. In the pastoral directives given at the end of the encyclical, the Pope encourages Catholics to work in harmony with other groups; he points out that a distinction must be made between error and the person who professes it, as well as between philosophical theories and the social movements that have arisen from them. This open and positive attitude, characterstic of Pope John, has paved the way for the Church's new approach to the modern world, officially stated in the Pastoral Constitution Gaudium et Spes *of the Second Vatican Council.*

(God and the moral order of society)

2124 The right order in human society is by nature spiritual.
3973 Founded as it is in truth, it must function according to the
norms of justice; it should be inspired and perfected by mutual love; and, finally, while preserving freedom, it should be brought to an ever more humane equitableness. This order, the principles of which are universal, absolute and unchangeable, has its ultimate source in the one true God, who is personal and transcends human nature. Inasmuch as God is the first truth and the supreme good, He alone is the deepest source from which society can draw its vitality....

(The citizen and the State: State authority)

2125 Human society would not be well ordered and prosperous
3979 without men lawfully vested with authority, who safeguard its
institutions and see to the common good. They derive their authority from God, as St Paul teaches: "For there is no authority except from God" *(Rom. 13.1)*.... This authority, no less than society itself, has its source in nature, and has, consequently, God for its author.

2126 Authority, however, is not without its own law. Being the
3980 power to command according to right reason, it derives its
binding force from the moral order and from God.... Thus, human authority can bind men in conscience only when it rests upon and shares in the authority of God.

2127   ... Since the right to command is required by the moral order
3981   and has its source in God, it follows that, if civil authorities
      make laws or command anything contrary to that order and,
therefore, contrary to the will of God, neither the laws made nor the
powers granted can be binding on the consciences of the citizens,
since "we must obey God rather than men" (*Acts 5.29*)....

2128   At the same time, the divine origin of authority does not take
3982   away from men the right to choose their rulers and form of
      government, and to determine both the way in which author-
ity is to be exercised and its limits. This doctrine, then, is consonant
with every form of truly democratic regime.

(The common good)

2129   ... Since the civil authority is entirely ordained to the com-
3983   mon good of all, its holders, while pursuing the common
      good, must respect its true nature; they must also adapt the
exercise of their authority to present conditions....

3984   Besides, the very nature of the common good requires that
      all citizens should share in it, in different ways according to
each one's task, merits and circumstances.... The common good
concerns the whole man, the needs both of his body and soul. Hence
it follows that the civil authorities must undertake to procure it by
ways and means proportionate to it: while respecting the hierarchy
of values, they should promote simultaneously both the material and
the spiritual welfare of the citizens.

(Responsibilities of the public authority)

2130   Contemporary thought holds that the common good lies
3985   chiefly in maintaining the rights and duties of the human
      person. Civil authorities therefore must ensure that these
rights be acknowledged and respected, mutually coordinated,
defended and promoted; then each one will be able to carry out his
duties more easily.... When civil authorities disown or violate the
rights of man, they not only fail in their duty, but their orders are
without binding force.

      One of the fundamental duties of civil authorities, therefore, is to
coordinate social relations in such fashion that the exercise of one
man's rights does not threaten others in the exercise of their own
rights nor hinder them in the fulfilment of their duties. Finally, the

rights of all should be effectively safeguarded and, if they have been violated, completely restored.

(Participation of citizens in public life)

2131 Citizens have the right, by virtue of their dignity as persons, to take an active part in government, although the manner in which they share in it will depend on the level of development of the political community....

(Relations between States: Mutual rights and duties)

2132 States have mutual rights and duties, as our predecessors taught repeatedly and we here reaffirm. Their relationships must be harmonised in truth, in justice, in active solidarity, and in liberty. The same natural law which governs the relations between man and man must also rule the relations between State and State....

2133 Truth must govern the relations between nations. This calls for the elimination of every trace of racialism and for the recognition of the principle that all nations are by nature equal in human dignity. Each of them accordingly is vested with the right to existence, to self-development, to the means necessary to achieve that development, and to the primary responsibility for that achievement. Each one may rightfully claim due consideration and respect.... Dealings between States must also be ruled by justice. This requires the recognition of their mutual rights and the fulfilment of their respective duties.... Relations between nations should further be animated by an active solidarity shown by mutual cooperation in many spheres, such as, in our times, has already taken place with laudable results in the economic, social, political and educational spheres, in health and sport....

(Disarmament)

2134 Justice, right reason and humanity urgently demand that the
3991 arms race should cease; that the stockpiles which exist in various countries should be reduced equally and simultaneously; that nuclear arms should be banned, and a general agreement reached for a progressive disarmament with an effective method of control. All must realise that there is no hope of putting an end to the building up of armaments,... unless the process is complete and thorough and unless it proceeds from an inner conviction; unless, that is, everyone sincerely cooperates to banish the fear and anxious expectations of war with which men are oppressed....

Men are becoming more and more convinced that conflicts which arise between States should not be resolved by recourse to arms, but rather through negotiation....

(The World Community: Interdependence of political communities)

2135   Recent progress in science and technology has deeply
3992   affected men; it has determined a world-wide movement
for cooperation and union.... The unity of the human family can never be destroyed, because it is made of members who share with equal rights in the same natural dignity. Hence it will always be a pressing need, arising from human nature itself, to attend seriously to the universal good, which bears on the entire human family....

As a result of the far-reaching changes which have taken place in the relations within the human community, the universal common good gives rise to problems that are very grave, complex and extremely urgent, especially as regards world security and peace. On the other hand, the public authorities of the individual nations— all of whom have equal rights—no matter how often they meet and how much ingenuity they display in an effort to draw up new and more adequate juridical instruments, do not find satisfactory solutions....

Yet, if serious consideration is given to the nature of the common good on the one hand, and, on the other, to the nature and function of public authority, it is clear that there exists between both a necessary connection.

(Universal common good and political authority)

2136   Today the universal common good poses problems of world-
3993   wide dimensions, which cannot adequately be tackled or
solved except by a public authority with adequate power, juridical status and means enabling it to operate in an effective manner on a world-wide basis. It follows then that the moral order itself demands that such a universal public authority be established.

This universal authority, with world-wide power and endowed with the proper means to pursue the universal common good, must be set up by the common agreement of all nations, and not imposed by force....

(Universal common good and personal rights)

2137   Because the universal common good, just as the national

3994   common good, is to be determined with reference to human
            persons, the world public authority must have as its funda-
mental objective the recognition, due respect, safeguard and promotion of personal rights....

(Principle of subsidiarity and world authority)

2138   Within each country, relations between the government and
3995   the citizens, families and intermediate societies, are gov-
            erned by the principle of subsidiarity.The same principle
must rule the relations between the world public authority and the
State governments. It belongs to the world authority to tackle and
solve problems posed by the universal common good in the economic, social, political and cultural fields, which State governments
are not equipped to solve adequately by themselves because of their
complexity, vastness or urgency.

   The world authority is not intended to curtail the sphere of action
proper to the State governments or to replace them. Rather, it must
aim at the creation in all countries of such conditions as will facilitate,
not only for the governments, but also for the citizens and the
intermediate societies, the fulfilment of their duties and the exercise
of their rights.

(Pastoral directives)

2139   ... We deem it opportune to remind our children of their duty
            to take an active part in public life and to contribute towards
the attainment of the common good of the entire human family and of
their own country....

3996   (These social principles) provide Catholics, therefore, with a
            vast field in which they can collaborate both with Christians
separated from the apostolic See and with men alien to the Christian
faith who are perceptive and whose dispositions are morally upright.
"On such occasions those who make profession of Catholicism must
take special care to be consistent and not to compromise in matters
wherein the integrity of religion or morals would suffer harm...."[1]

2140/1 Moreover, one must always distinguish error and the per-
             son who errs, even in the case of persons falling into error
or lacking sufficient knowledge in matters pertaining to the religious

---

1. JOHN XXIII, *Encyclical Letter Mater et Magistra, AAS* 53 (1961) 456.

and moral fields. The person who errs always remains a human being and he retains in every case his dignity as a human person; this dignity must always be taken into account....

2140/2   Similarly, one must clearly distinguish false philosophical
3997   theories on the nature, origin and destiny of the world and
              of man, from historical movements with economic or social, cultural or political objectives, even if the latter owe their origin and inspiration to the former. For, while a doctrine, once fixed and definitively fromulated, does not change, movements, concerned as they are with concrete and changing conditions, cannot but be influenced by that evolution....

THE SECOND VATICAN GENERAL COUNCIL
PASTORAL CONSTITUTION *GAUDIUM ET SPES* (1965)

The general moral teaching of the first part of the Constitution has been dealt with in the previous chapter (cf. nn. 2051ff). In its second part the Constitution turns its attention to urgent problems of the present time (cf. n. 2043i). Among these the topics relevant to this chapter are "the socio-economic and political life, the solidarity of the family of nations, and peace" (46). The Constitution reaffirms the principles laid down in the previous encyclicals, notably in Mater et Magistra *and* Pacem in Terris. *It takes a clear stand on the matter of war and especially of total warfare. It also gives directives for the cooperation between rich and developing nations.*

The main doctrinal points are as follows.Chapter III on "the socio-economic life" shows that economic development is at the service of the whole man (64). It explains the meaning of work, affirms man's right to work, treats of just wages and working conditions and of the opportunities due to man to develop his talents (67). It defends participation by the workers in management and their right to form labour unions (68). It completely reverses the perspective regarding earthly goods, first stressing the patristic doctrine of the universal destination of property (69), and only in this context affirming the right to private ownership (71). Chapter IV on "the life of the political community" explains its nature and goal (74) and advocates cooperation of all in public life (75). Chapter V on "fostering peace and building the community of nations" affirms that the pursuit of the universal common good requires that the community of nations be organised (84). It stresses international cooperation in the economic field (85) and lays down norms for this cooperation (86).

(Universal destination of created goods)

2141   69.   God has intended the earth and all that it contains for the
              use of all men and all peoples. Hence justice, accompanied by charity , must so regulate the distribution of created goods that they are actually available to all in an equitable measure. Whatever may

be the different forms of ownership, adapted to the legitimate local usages according to diverse and changeable circumstances, this universal destination of earthly goods must always be heeded. Therefore, in his use of them every man should consider his legitimate possessions not only as his own but also as common property, in the sense that they should be able to profit not only himself but other people as well. Moreover, all have the right to possess a share of earthly goods sufficient for themselves and their families. This is what the Fathers and Doctors of the Church had in mind when teaching that men are obliged to come to the aid of the poor, and to do so not merely out of their superfluous goods. A man who is in extreme necessity has the right to procure for himself what is necessary from the riches of other people.

(Avoidance of war: Curbing the savagery of war)

2142 79. ...The Council intends before all else to recall the permanent binding force of the natural rights of nations and of their universal principles.... Actions that deliberately violate them, and orders that command such actions are criminal; nor can blind obedience excuse people who carry out such orders. Among these actions must be reckoned first of all those which, for whatever reason or by whatever method, tend to the extermination of an entire people, nation or ethnic minority; such actions must be vehemently condemned as heinous crimes....

In matters of war, there exist various international agreements which a number of nations have signed, aimed at making military action and its consequences less inhuman.... Agreements of this kind must be observed.... Moreover, it seems right that laws should make humane provisions for the case of those who for reasons of conscience refuse to bear arms, provided they agree to serve the human community in some other way.

Certainly, war has not been eradicated from human affairs. And, as long as the danger of war remains and there is no competent international authority with sufficient forces at its disposal, governments cannot be denied the right of legitimate self-defence, once every means for a peaceful settlement has been exhausted.... But it is one thing to go to war in just defence of the people, and another to seek to subjugate other nations. The possession of armaments does not make every military or political use of them lawful. Neither does the mere fact that war has unfortunately already broken out render everything permissible between the warring camps.

(Total warfare)

2143 80. ...The Sacred Synod makes its own the condemnations of total warfare pronounced already by recent Popes, and issues the following declaration:

Every act of war tending to indiscriminate destruction of entire towns or large areas along with their population is a crime against God and against man himself, which must be condemned with firmness and without hesitation.

(The arms race)

2144 81. To be sure, scientific weapons are not being stocked for the sole purpose of using them in time of war. Since the defensive strength of each party is held to depend on its capacity for immediate retaliation against an adversary, the accumulation of arms, which increases year by year, serves as an unprecedented deterrent to possible enemy attack....

Whatever be the case with this method of deterrence, men should be convinced that the arms race, in which quite a considerable number of nations are now engaged, is not a safe way to preserve a steady peace, and the so-called balance resulting from it is neither a stable nor a true peace. The causes of war are thereby far from being eliminated. Rather they threaten to be gradually aggravated. While extravagant sums are being spent in preparing ever new weapons, no adequate remedy can be found for so many present-day miseries in the world....

For that reason it must be stated again: the arms race is a most grievous plague for mankind, and it wrongs the poor in an intolerable manner. It is much to be feared that, if this race persists, it may some day spawn all the deadly disasters the means for which it is now making ready....

PAUL VI

ENCYCLICAL LETTER *POPULORUM PROGRESSIO* (1967)

The Pope proposes a Christian vision of development. He reaffirms more strongly the universal destination of created goods (cf. n. 2141) and severely condemns liberal capitalism. He notes that, though it is every man's right to make use of the goods of the earth, the gap is widening between the wealth of the privileged and the misery of others. To remedy this situation is a pressing need. But man's true welfare extends far beyond his economic needs: it includes all values inherent in his personality. The problem of human progress has world dimensions. Private initiative is not enough; the question has to be dealt with on an international basis; it is the strict duty of prosperous nations to help developing nations. Peace can only be obtained through a social order based on universal justice. The Pope warns against the temptation to violence, but concedes its possibility in extreme cases. The text is found in AAS 59 (1967) 257ff.

(Christian vision of development)

2145 14. Development cannot be limited to mere economic growth. In order to be authentic, it must be complete, integral; that is, it has to promote the good of every man and of the whole man.

15. In the design of God, every man is called upon to develop and fulfil himself, for every life is a vocation.... Endowed with intelligence and freedom, he is responsible for his fulfilment as he is for his salvation. He is aided, or sometimes impeded, by those who educate him and those with whom he lives, but each one remains, whatever be those influences affecting him, the principal agent of his own success or failure.

(Communal responsibility and scale of values)

2146 17. But each man is a member of society. He is part of the whole of mankind. It is not just individuals, but all men who are called to this fulness of development.

18. This personal and communal development would be threatened if the true scale of values were undermined. The desire for necessities is legitimate and work undertaken to obtain them is a duty.... But the acquiring of temporal goods can lead to greed, to the insatiable desire for more, and can make increased power a tempting objective.

19. Increased possession is not the ultimate goal of nations nor of individuals. All growth is ambivalent. It is essential if man is to develop as a man, but in a way it imprisons man if he considers it the supreme good and restricts his vision.... Both for nations and for individual men, avarice is the most evident form of moral underdevelopment.

20. If further development calls for the work of more and more technicians, even more necessary is the deep thought and reflection of wise men in search of a new humanism which will enable modern man to find himself anew by embracing the higher values of love and friendship, of prayer and contemplation. This is what will permit the

fulness of authentic development, a development which is for each and all the transition from less human conditions to those which are more human.

(The universal purpose of created things and right of property)

2147 22. "Fill the earth and subdue it" *(Gen. 1.28)*: the Bible, from the first page on, teaches us that the whole of creation is for man, that it is his responsibility to develop it by intelligent effort and by means of his labour to perfect it, so to speak, for his use. If the world is made to furnish each individual with the means of livelihood and the instruments for his growth and progress, each man has therefore the right to find in the world what is necessary for himself.... All other rights whatsoever, including those of property and of free commerce, are to be subordinated to this principle. They should not hinder but on the contrary favour its application. It is a grave and urgent social duty to redirect them to their primary finality.

(Right to private property not absolute)

2147a 23. "If any one has the world's goods and sees his brothers in need, yet closes his heart against him, how does God's love abide in him?" *(1 Jn 3.17)*. It is well known how strong were the words used by the Fathers of the Church to describe the proper attitude of persons who possess anything towards persons in need. To quote Saint Ambrose: "You are not making a gift of your possessions to the poor person. You are handing over to him what is his. For what has been given in common for the use of all, you have arrogated to yourself. The world is given to all, and not only to the rich."[1] That is, private property does not constitute for anyone an absolute and unconditional right. No one is justified in keeping for his exclusive use what he does not need, when others lack necessities.... If there should arise a conflict between acquired private rights and primary community exigencies, it is the responsibility of public authorities to look for a solution, with the active participation of individuals and social groups.

24. If certain landed estates impede the general prosperity because they are extensive, unused or poorly used, or because they bring hardship to people or are detrimental to the interests of the country, the common good sometimes demands their expropria-

---

1. *De Nabuthe,* c. 12, n. 53.

tion.... It is unacceptable that citizens with abundant incomes from the resources and activity of their country should transfer a considerable part of this income abroad purely for their own advantage, without care for the manifest wrong they inflict on their country by doing so.

(Liberal capitalism severely condemned)

2147b   26. ...It is unfortunate that on these new conditions of society a system has been constructed which considers profit as the key motive for economic progress, competition as the supreme law of economics, and private ownership of means of production as an absolute right that has no limits and carries no corrosponding social obligation. This unchecked liberalism leads to the dictatorship rightly denounced by Pius XI as producing "the international imperialism of money".[1] One cannot condemn such abuses too strongly by solemnly recalling once again that the economy is at the service of man.

(Violence illegitimate except in extreme cases)

2147c   30. There are certainly situations whose injustice cries to heaven. When whole populations, destitute of necessities, live in a state of dependence, barring them from all initiative and responsibility, and from all opportunity to advance culturally and share in social and political life, recourse to violence, as a means to right these wrongs to human dignity, is a grave temptation.

31. We know, however, that a revolutionary uprising—save where there is manifest, long-standing tyranny which would do great damage to fundamental personal rights and dangerous harm to the common good of the country—produces new injustices, throws more elements out of balance and brings new disasters. A real evil should not be fought at the cost of greater misery.

(Planning for reform)

2148   32. We want to be clearly understood: the present situation must be faced with courage and the injustices linked with it must be fought against and overcome. Development demands bold transformations, far-reaching innovations. Urgent reforms should be undertaken without delay. It is for each one to take his share in them

---

1. *Quadragesimo Anno, AAS* 23 (1931) 212.

with generosity, particularly those whose education, position and opportunities afford them wide scope for action....Individual initiative alone and the mere free play of competition could never assure successful development....

33. Hence programmes are necessary in order to encourage, stimulate, coordinate, supplement and integrate the activity of individuals and of intermediate societies. It pertains to the public authorities to choose, even to lay down the objectives to be pursued, the ends to be achieved, and the means for attaining these, and it is for them to stimulate all the forces engaged in this common action. But let them take care to associate private initiative and intermediate societies with this work. They will thus avoid the danger of complete collectivisation or of arbitrary planning, which, by denying liberty, would prevent the exercise of the fundamental rights of the human person.

(The aim is integral humanism)

2149　42. What must be aimed at is integral humanism. And what is that if not the fully-rounded development of the whole man and of all men? A humanism closed in on itself, and not open to the values of the spirit and to God who is their origin and source, can only achieve apparent success. It is true that man can organise the world apart from God; but without God man can organise it in the end only to his own detriment. An isolated humanism inevitably becomes inhuman. There is no true humanism but that which is open to the Absolute and is conscious of a vocation which gives human life its true meaning....

(The development of the human race in a spirit of solidarity)

2150　43. There can be no progress towards the complete development of man without the simultaneous development of all humanity in a spirit of solidarity....

44. This duty is the concern especially of the properous nations. Their obligations stem from a brotherhood that is at once human and supernatural, and take on a threefold aspect: the duty of human solidarity—the aid that rich nations must give to developing countries; the duty of social justice—the rectification of inequitable trade relations between powerful nations and weak nations; the duty of universal charity—the effort to bring about a world that is more human towards all, where all will be able to give and receive, without

one group making progress at the expense of the other. The question is urgent, for on it depends the future of the civilisation of the world.

(The duty of human solidarity binding on nations)

2151   48. The same duty of solidarity that rests on individuals exists also for nations.... Given the increasing needs of the developing countries, it should be considered quite normal for an advanced country to devote a part of its production to meet their needs, and to train teachers, engineers, technicians and scholars prepared to put their knowledge and their skill at the disposal of less fortunate peoples.

49. We must repeat once more that the superfluous wealth of rich countries should be placed at the service of poor nations....

50. In order to be fully effective, these efforts ought not to remain scattered or isolated, much less be in competition with one another for reasons of power or prestige; the present situation calls for concerted planning....

(Equity in trade relations)

2152   The teaching of our predecessor Leo XIII in his Encyclical Letter *Rerum Novarum* is always valid: if the position of the contracting parties are too unequal, the consent of the parties does not suffice to guarantee the justice of their contract, and the rule of free agreement remains subservient to the demands of the natural law.[1] What was true of the just wage for the individual is also true of international contracts: an economy of exchange can no longer be based solely on the law of free competition, a law which, in its turn, too often creates an economic dictatorship. Freedom of trade is fair only if it is subject to the demands of social justice.

(Development is the new name for peace)

2153   Excessive economic, social and cultural inequalities among peoples arouse tensions and conflicts, and are a danger to peace.... To wage war on misery and to struggle against injustice is to promote, along with improved conditions, the human and spiritual progress of all men, and therefore the common good of humanity. Peace cannot be limited to a mere absence of war, the result of an

---

1. LEO XIII, *Acta* XI (1892) 131.

ever precarious balance of forces. No, peace is something that is built up day after day, in the pursuit of an order intended by God, which implies a more perfect form of justice among men.

APOSTOLIC LETTER *OCTOGESIMA ADVENIENS* (1971)

On the occasion of the eightieth anniversary of the encyclical Rerum Novarum *the Pope addressed an apostolic letter to Cardinal Maurice Roy, president of the Council of the Laity and of the Pontifical Commission for Justice and Peace.*

The letter stresses the new dimensions and applications of social justice in the world today (3-7). Some of the problems mentioned are: urbanisation, youth, women, workers' unions, strikes, immigration, impact of mass media (8-21). In a following section, the Pope, while insisting on the duty of Christians to take part in political activities (24), states the limits within which they may collaborate with movements which have their origin in non-Christian ideologies but are in part distinct from them (26-41). The letter then restates the Christian principles that must guide men in their social and political attitudes (42-47). It ends with a call to action addressed to all Christians (48-52). The text is found in AAS 63 (1971) 401ff.

(Social teaching of the Church not monolithic)

2153a   4.   In the face of such widely varying situations it is difficult for us to utter a unified message and to put forward a solution which has universal validity. Such is not our ambition, nor is it our mission. It is up to the Christian communities to analyze with objectivity the situation which is proper to their own country, to shed on it the light of the Gospel's unalterable words and to draw principles of reflection, norms of judgment and directives for action from the social teaching of the Church.

(Role of women)

2153b   13.   ...In many countries a charter for women which would put an end to an actual discrimination and would establish relationships of equality in rights and of respect for their dignity is the object of study and at times of lively demands. We do not have in mind that false equality which would deny the distinction laid down by the Creator Himself and which would be in contradiction with woman's proper role, which is of such capital importance, at the heart of the family as well as within society. Developments in legislation should on the contrary be directed to protecting her proper vocation and at the same time recognizing her independence as a person, and her equal rights to participate in cultural, economic, social and political life.

(Racial discrimination condemned)

2153c 16. Racial discrimination possesses at the moment a character of very great relevance by reason of the tension which
it stirs up both within certain countries and on the international level.
Men rightly consider unjustifiable and reject as inadmissible the
tendency to maintain or introduce legislation or behaviour systematically inspired by racialist prejudice. The members of mankind share
the same basic rights and duties, as well as the same supernatural
destiny. Within a country which belongs to each one, all should be
equal before the law, find equal admittance to economic, civic, and
social life and benefit from a fair sharing of the nation's riches.

(Right of migrants)

2153d 17. We are thinking also of the precarious situation of a
great number of emigrant workers whose condition as for-
eigners makes it all the more difficult for them to make any sort of
vindication, in spite of their real participation in the economic effort
of the country that receives them. It is urgently necessary for people
to go beyond a narrowly nationalist attitude in their regard and to
give them a charter which will assure them a right to emigrate, favour
their integration, facilitate their professional advancement and give
them access to decent housing where, if such is the case, their
families can join them.

(Responsible use of the mass media)

2153e 20. Among the major changes of our times, we do not wish
to forget to emphasize the growing role being assumed by
the media of social communication and their influence on the transformation of mentalities, of knowledge, of organizations and of
society itself. Certainly they have many positive aspects. Thanks to
them news from the entire world reaches us practically in an instant,
establishing contacts which supersede distances and creating elements of unity among all men. A greater spread of education and
culture is becoming possible. Nevertheless, by this very action the
media of social communication are reaching the point of representing as it were a new power. One cannot but ask about those who
really hold this power, the aims that they pursue and the means they
use, and, finally, about the effect of their activity on the exercise of
individual liberty, both in the political and ideological spheres and in
social, economic and cultural life. The men who hold this power have

a grave moral responsibility with respect to the truth of the information that they spread, the needs and the reactions that they generate and the values which they put forward.

(Preferential respect for the poor)

2153f 23. In teaching us charity, the Gospel instructs us in the preferential respect for the poor and the special situation they have in society: the more fortunate should renounce some of their rights so as to place their goods more generously at the service of others. If, beyond legal rules, there is really no deeper feeling of respect and service of others, then even equality before the law can serve as an alibi for flagrant discrimination, continued exploitation and actual contempt.

(Attraction of socialist currents)

2154 31. Some Christians are today attracted by socialist currents and their various developments. They try to recognise therein some of the aspirations which they carry within themselves in the name of their faith. They feel that they are inserted in that historical current and wish to play a part within it. Now this historical current takes on, under the same name, different forms according to different continents and cultures, even if it drew its inspiration, and still does in many cases, from ideologies incompatible with the faith. Careful judgment is called for. Too often Christians attracted by socialism tend to idealise it, in general and without restriction, as a perfect good; socialism then simply means a will for justice, solidarity and equality. They refuse to recognise the limitations of the historical socialist movements, which remain conditioned by the ideologies from which they originated. Distinctions must be made to guide concrete choices between the various levels of expression of socialism: a generous aspiration and a seeking for a more just society; historical movements with a political organisation and aim; an ideology which claims to give a complete and self-sufficient picture of man. Nevertheless, these distinctions must not lead one to consider such levels as completely separated and independent. The concrete link which, according to circumstances, exists between them must be clearly marked out. This insight will enable Christians to see the degree of commitment possible along these lines, while safeguarding the values, especially those of liberty, responsibility and openness to the spiritual, which guarantee the integral development of man.

(Historical evolution of Marxism)

2155 32. Other Christians even ask whether an historical development of Marxism might not authorise certain concrete rapprochements. They note in fact a certain splintering of Marxism, which until now appeared as a unitary ideology claiming to offer an explanation of the totality of man and the world in its process of development, and consequently atheistic. Apart from the ideological confrontation officially separating the various champions of Marxism-Leninism in their individual interpretations of the thought of its founders, and apart from the open opposition between the political systems which make use of its name today, some people lay down distinctions between various levels of expression of Marxism....

2156 34. While, in the doctrine of Marxism as concretely put in practice, one can distinguish these various aspects and the questions they pose for the reflection and activity of Christians, it would be illusory and dangerous to reach the point of forgetting the intimate link which radically binds them together, to accept the elements of Marxist analysis without recognising their relationship with ideology, and to enter into the practice of class struggle and its Marxist interpretations, while failing to take note of the kind of totalitarian and violent society to which this process leads.

(Value of human sciences)

2156a 38. In this world dominated by scientific and technological change, which threatens to drag it towards a new positivism, another more fundamental doubt is raised. Having subdued nature by using his reason, man now finds that he himself is as it were imprisoned within his own rationality; he in turn becomes the object of science. The 'human sciences' are today enjoying a significant flowering. On the one hand, they are subjecting to critical and rational examination the hitherto accepted knowledge about man, on the grounds that this knowledge seems either too empirical or too theoretical. On the other hand, methodological necessity and ideological presuppositions too often lead the human sciences to isolate, in the various situations, certain aspects of man, and yet to give these an explanation which claims to be complete, or at least an interpretation which is meant to be all-embracing, from a quantitative or phenomenological point of view. This scientific reduction betrays a dangerous presumption. To give a privileged position in this way to such an aspect of analysis is to mutilate man and, under the pretext of a scientific procedure, to make it impossible to understand man in his totality.

39. One must be no less attentive to the action which the human sciences can instigate, giving rise to the elaboration of models of society to be subsequently imposed on men as scientifically tested types of behaviour. Man can then become the object of manipulations directing his desires and needs and modifying this behaviour and even his system of values.

40. (However), as in the case of the natural sciences, the Church has confidence in this research also and urges Christians to play an active part in it. Prompted by the same scientific demands and the desire to know man better, but at the same time enlightened by their faith, Christians who devote themselves to the human sciences will begin a dialogue which promises to be fruitful.

(Ambiguous nature of progress)

2156b   41. Since the nineteenth century, Western societies and, as a result, many others have put their hopes in ceaselessly renewed and indefinite progress.... Yet a doubt arises today regarding both its value and its result.... The quality and the truth of human relations, the degree of participation and of responsibility, are no less significant and important for the future of society than the quantity and variety of the goods produced and consumed....

Is not genuine progress to be found in the development of moral consciousness, which will lead man to exercise a wider solidarity and to open himself freely to others and to God?

(Renouncing force)

2156c   43. In international exchanges there is need to go beyond relationships based on force in order to arrive at agreements reached with the good of all in mind. Relationships based on force have never in fact established justice in a true and lasting manner, even if at times the alternation of positions can often make it possible to find easier conditions for dialogue. The use of force, moreover, leads to the setting in motion of opposing forces, and from this springs a climate of struggle which opens the way to situations of extreme violence and to abuses.

(Wider sharing of responsibility)

2156d   47. The passing to the political dimension also expresses a demand made by the man of today: a greater sharing in responsibility and in decision-making. This legitimate aspiration becomes more evident as the cultural level rises, as the sense of freedom develops and as man becomes more aware of how, in a world facing an uncertain future, the choices of today are already the condition of life for tomorrow.... In order to counterbalance increasing technocracy, modern forms of democracy must be devised, not only making it possible for each man to become informed and to express himself, but also by involving him in a shared responsibility.

(Need to become involved in action)

2157 48. Let each one examine himself, to see what he has done up to now, and what he ought to do. It is not enough to recall principles, state intentions, point to crying injustice and utter prophetic denounciations; these words will lack real weight unless they are accompanied in each individual by a livelier awareness of his personal responsibility and by effective action. It is too easy to throw back on others the responsibility for injustice, if at the same time one does not realise how one shares in it personally, and how personal conversion is needed first. This basic humility will rid action of all inflexibility and sectarianism; it will preclude discouragement in the face of a task which seems limitless in size....

2158 49. Thus, amid the diversity of situations, functions and organisations, each one must recognise his own responsibility and discern in his conscience what kind of action he should take part in. Surrounded by various currents into which, besides legitimate aspirations, there insinuate themselves more ambiguous tendencies, the Christian must make a wise and vigilant choice and avoid involving himself in an unconditional collaboration which would be contrary to the principles of a true humanism, even in the name of a genuinely felt solidarity....

THE THIRD SYNOD OF BISHOPS IN ROME
DE IUSTITIA IN MUNDO (1971)

After its discussion on the priestly ministry regarded as the primary problem posed to the Church's inner life (cf. n. 1745i), the third Synod of bishops turned its attention to the question of justice in the world, which is the most crucial problem of mankind today. The official Synodal document, submitted to the Pope for his consideration, has been published by him in Dec. 1971, together with the document on the priestly ministry. The text is made up of three parts: justice and world society; the Gospel message and the mission of the Church; the practice of justice. It looks realistically at the situation of a world in which, due to the present character of society, many are "silent, indeed voiceless, victims of injustice"; it confronts this situation with the Gospel message and reflects on the role of the Church in the struggle against injustice; it proposes lines of action as regards the Church's own witness, education for justice, cooperation between Churches and international action.

The document stresses the right of nations to full development. It shows that action on behalf of justice and for the liberation of men is part of the Church's mission. The text is found in AAS 63 (1971) 923ff.

(Action for man's liberation is part of the mission of the Church)

2159   5. ... We shared our awareness of the Church's vocation to be present at the heart of the world by proclaiming the good news to the poor, freedom to the oppressed, and joy to the afflicted....

6. Action on behalf of justice and participation in the transmission of the world fully appear to us as a constitutive dimension of the preaching of the Gospel, or, in other words, of the Church's mission for the redemption of the human race and its liberation from every oppressive situation.

(Overcoming obstacles to right development of nations)

2160   15. The right to development must be seen as a dynamic interpenetration of all those fundamental human rights upon which the aspirations of individuals and nations are based.

16. This desire, however, will not satisfy the expectations of our time if it ignores the objective obstacles which social structures place in the way of a conversion of hearts, or even of the realization of the ideal of charity. It demands on the contrary that the general condition of being marginal in society be overcome, so that an end will be put to the systematic barriers and vicious circles which oppose the collective advance towards enjoyment of adequate remuneration of the factors of production, and which strengthen the situation of discrimination with regard to access to opportunities and collective services from which a great part of the people are now excluded. If the developing nations and regions do not attain liberation through development, there is a real danger that the conditions of life created especially by colonial domination may evolve into a new form of colonialism in which the developing nations will be the victims of the interplay of international forces.

17. By taking their future into their own hands through a determined will for progress, the developing peoples—even if they do not

achieve the final goal—will authentically manifest their own personalization. And in order that they may cope with the unequal relationships within the present world complex, a certain responsible nationalism gives them the impetus needed to acquire an identity of their own.

(Justice and liberation in the work of Christ and in the Church's mission)

2161   31. By His action and teaching Christ united in an indivisible way the relationship of man to God and the relationship of man to other men. Christ lived His life in the world as a total giving of Himself to God for the salvation and liberation of men....

34. Man's... response to the love of God, saving us through Christ, is shown to be effective in his love and service of men. Christian love of the neighbour, however, cannot be separated from justice. For love implies an absolute demand for justice, namely a recognition of the dignity and rights of one's neighbour. Justice attains its inner fulness only in love....

35. ...The mission of preaching the Gospel dictates at the present time that we should dedicate ourselves to the liberation of man even in his present existence in this world....

36. The Church has received from Christ the mission of preaching the Gospel message, which contains a call to man to turn away from sin to the love of the Father, universal brotherhood and a consequent demand for justice in the world. This is the reason why the Church has the right, indeed the duty, to proclaim justice on the social, national and international levels, and to denounce instances of injustice, when the fundamental rights of man and his very salvation demand it. The Church, indeed, is not alone responsible for justice in the world; however, she has a proper and specific responsibility which is identified with her mission of giving witness before the world of the need for love and justice contained in the Gospel message....

Of itself it does not belong to the Church, in so far as she is a religious and hierarchical community, to offer concrete solutions in the social, economic and political spheres for justice in the world. Her mission involves defending and promoting the dignity and fundamental rights of the human person.

(Witness of justice in the life of the Church)

2162   40. While the Church is bound to give witness to justice, she recognizes that anyone who ventures to speak to people about justice must first be just in their eyes. Hence we must undertake an examination of the modes of acting and of the possessions and life-style found within the Church herself.

41. Within the Church rights must be preserved.... Those who serve the Church by their labour, including priests and religious, should receive a sufficient livelihood and enjoy that social security which is customary in the region. Lay people should be given fair wages and a system of promotion. We reiterate the recommendation that lay people should exercise more important functions with regard to Church property and should share in its administration.

(Education to justice)

2163   49. ...Educational method must be such as to teach men to live their life in its entire reality and in accord with the evangelical principles of personal and social morality which are expressed in the vital Christian witness of life.

50. ...The method of education very frequently still in use today encourages narrow individualism. Part of the human family lives immersed in a mentality which exalts possessions. The school and the communications media, which are often obstructed by the established order, allow the formation only of the man desired by that order, that is to say, man in its image, not a new man but a copy of man as he is.

51. But education demands a renewal of heart, a renewal based on the recognition of sin in its individual and social manifestations. It will also inculcate a truly and entirely human way of life in justice, love and simplicity. It will likewise awaken a critical sense, which will lead us to reflect on the society in which we live and on its values; it will make men ready to renounce these values when they cease to promote justice for all men. In the developing countries, the principal aim of this education for justice consists in an attempt to awaken the consciences to a knowledge of the concrete situation and in a call to secure a total improvement....

52. Since this education makes men decidedly more human, it will help them to be no longer the object of manipulation by communications media or political forces. It will instead enable them to take in hand their own destinies and bring about communities which are truly human.

(Liturgy and formation for justice)

2164   58. The liturgy..., which is the heart of the Church's life, can greatly serve education for justice. For it is a thanksgiving to the Father in Christ, which through its communitarian form places before our eyes the bonds of our brotherhood and again and again reminds us of the Church's mission. The liturgy of the word, catechesis and the celebration of the sacraments, have the power to help us to discover the teaching of the prophets, the Lord and the Apostles on the subject of justice. The preparation for baptism is the beginning of the formation of the Christian conscience. The practice of penance should emphasize the social dimension of sin and of the sacrament. Finally, the Eucharist forms the community and places it at the service of others.

PAUL VI

BULL OF INDUCTION OF THE HOLY YEAR 1975
(23 May 1974)

The Pope wanted the ensuing Holy Year to be an opportunity for universal spiritual renewal and reconciliation that would imply a commitment to social justice according to biblical tradition. The text is found in AAS 66 (1974) 289ff.

(The Jubilee calls for a new and just ordering of things)

2165   34. The ancient origins of the Jubilee as seen in the laws and institutions of Israel clearly show that this social dimension is part of its very nature. In fact, as we read in the book of Leviticus *(25.8ff)*, the Jubilee Year, precisely because it was dedicated in a special way to God, involved a new ordering of all things that were recognized as belonging to God: the land which was allowed to lie fallow and was given back to its former owners; economic goods, in so far as debts were remitted; and, above all, man, whose dignity and freedom were reaffirmed in a special way by the manumission of slaves. The Year of God, then, was also the Year of Man, the Year of the Earth, the Year of the Poor.

THE FOURTH SYNOD OF BISHOPS IN ROME

DE EVANGELIZATIONE MUNDI HODIERNI (1974)

In its concluding Message to the Church, the Synod confirms that the mandate to evangelise all men constitutes the essential mission of the

Church. However, it also points out that the salvation that Christ came to bring implies the complete liberation of man from every bondage, including unjust social structures.

(The evangelising mission of the Church includes the full liberation of man)

2166 12. Prompted by the love of Christ and illumined by the light of the Gospel, let us nurture the hope that the Church, in more faithfully fulfilling the work of evangelisation, will announce the total salvation of man or rather his complete liberation, and from now on will start to bring this about. The Church...must conform to Christ who explained his own mission in these words: "The Spirit of the Lord is upon me, because he has anointed me to preach good news to the poor. He has sent me to proclaim release to the captives and sight to the blind, to set at liberty those who are oppressed" (*Lk. 4.18*).

13. Faithful to her evangelising mission, the Church, as a truly poor, praying and fraternal community, can do much to bring about the integral salvation or the full liberation of men. She can draw from the Gospel the most profound reasons and ever new incentives to promote generous dedication to the service of all men—the poor especially, the weak and the oppressed—and to eliminate the social consequence of sin which are translated into unjust social and political structures.... The Church does not remain within purely social and political limits... but leads towards freedom under all its forms— liberation from sin, from individual or collective selfishness—and to full communion with God and with men who are like brothers. In this way, the Church, in her evangelical way, promotes the true and complete liberation of all men, groups and peoples.

PAUL VI

APOSTOLIC EXHORTATION *EVANGELII NUNTIANDI* (1975)

Elaborating the theme of the Fourth Synod of Bishops, the Pope renews the commitment of the Church to evangelisation which means "bringing the Good News into all the strata of humanity, and through its influence transforming humanity from within and making it new" (cf. nn. 1149-1152). Hence it is essentially linked with justice, liberation and human advancement. However, the mission of the Church cannot be reduced "to the dimensions of a simply temporal project". The Pope here condemns violence without the nuance of Populorum Progressio (cf. n. 2147c). He declares that the specific contribution of the Church towards liberation is the inspiration of faith and the motivation of love. The text is found in AAS 68 (1976) 5ff.

(The Gospel message touches life as a whole)

2167   29. ...Evangelisation would not be complete if it did not take
account of the unceasing interplay of the Gospel and of
man's concrete life, both personal and social. This is why evangelisation involves an explicit message, adapted to the different situations
constantly being realized, about the rights and duties of every human
being, about family life without which personal growth and development is hardly possible, about life in society, about international life,
peace, justice and development—a message especially energetic
today of liberation.

(A message of liberation)

2168   30. ...Numerous Bishops from all continents, especially the
Bishops from the Third World, spoke at the last Synod...of
peoples...engaged with all their energy in the effort and struggle to
overcome everything which condemns them to remain on the margin of life: famine, chronic disease, illiteracy, poverty, injustices in
international relations and especially commercial exchanges, situations of economic and cultural neo-colonialism, sometimes as cruel
as the old political colonialism. The Church...has the duty to proclaim the liberation of millions of human beings—many of whom are
her own children—the duty of assisting the birth of this liberation, of
giving witness to it, of ensuring that it is complete. This is not foreign
to evangelisation.

(Evangelisation necessarily linked with human advancement)

2169   31. Between evangelisation and human advancement—
development and liberation—there are in fact profound links.
These include links of an anthropological order, because the man
who is to be evangelised is not an abstract being but is subject to
social and economic questions. They also include links in the theological order, since one cannot dissociate the plan of Creation from
the plan of Redemption. The latter plan touches the very concrete
situations of injustice to be combatted and justice to be restored.
They include links of the eminently evangelical order, which is that of
charity: how in fact can one proclaim the new commandment without promoting in justice and peace the true, authentic adancement of
man?

(Church's mission not to be reduced to a temporal project)

2170   32. ... Many, even generous Christians who are sensitive to the dramatic questions involved in the problem of liberation, in their wish to commit the Church to the liberation effort, are frequently tempted to reduce her mission to the dimensions of a simply temporal project.... Her activity, forgetful of all spiritual and religious preoccupations, would become initiatives of the political or social order. But if this were so, the Church would lose her fundamental meaning. Her message of liberation would no longer have any originality and would easily be open to manipulation by ideological systems and political parties. She would have no more authority to proclaim freedom in the name of God.

(True liberation involves a necessary conversion)

2171   36. The Church considers it undoubtedly important to build up structures which are more human, more just, more respectful of the rights of the person and less oppressive and less enslaving, but she is conscious that the best structures and the most idealized systems soon become inhuman if the inhuman inclinations of the human heart are not made wholesome, if those who live in these structures or who rule them do not undergo a conversion of heart and outlook.

JOHN PAUL II

ENCYCLICAL LETTER *REDEMPTOR HOMINIS* (1979)

In his first encyclical, the Pope lays down that the redemption of man accomplished in Jesus Christ is the centre of the Church's proclamation and the mainspring of her activity. Redemption is understood as elevation of man to special communion with God (cf. n. 677); thereby man takes on a special value (cf. n. 678) which is the deepest foundation of human rights and true human progress. The Pope particularly stresses the values of love, truth and freedom (cf. n. 2064). He vividly describes the threat man suffers from his own works when he is alienated from God. He points out that even the so-called human rights can turn out oppressive if they are sought only in the 'letter' and not also the 'spirit'. The text is found in AAS 71 (1979) 257ff.

(Progress or threat?)

2172   15. The man of today seems ever to be under threat from what he produces.... All too soon, often in an unforeseeable way, what this manifold activity of man yields is not only subjected to 'alienation', in the sense that it is simply taken away from the person who produces it, but rather it turns against man himself.... Man therefore lives increasingly in fear.... Exploitation of the earth not only for industrial but also military purposes and the uncontrolled development of technology outside the framework of a long-range authentically humanistic plan often bring with them a threat to man's natural environment, alienate him in his relations with nature.... The development of technology and the development of contemporary civilization, which is marked by the ascendancy of technology, demand a proportional development of morals....

16. If therefore our time...shows itself a time of progress, it is also seen as a time of threat in many forms for man.... Man's situation in the modern world seems indeed to be far removed from the objective demands of the moral order, from the requirements of justice, and even more of social love.... Man cannot relinquish himself or the place in the visible world that belongs to him; he cannot become the slave of things, the slave of economic systems, the slave of his own products.... (The) difficult road of the indispensable transformation of the structures of economic life is one on which it will not be easy to go forward without the intervention of a true conversion of mind, will and heart.

(Exercise of power must respect human rights)

2173   17. ...The rights of power can only be understood on the basis of respect for the objective inviolable rights of man. The common good that authority in the State serves is brought to full realization only when all the citizens are sure of their rights. The lack of this leads to the dissolution of society, opposition by citizens to authority, or a situation of oppression, intimidation, violence, and terrorism, of which many examples have been provided by the totalitarianisms of this century. Thus the principle of human rights is of profound concern to the area of social justice and is the measure by which it can be tested in the life of political bodies.

ENCYCLICAL LETTER *DIVES IN MISERICORDIA* (1980)

As Jesus is the relevation of God's mercy, the Church is called upon to bring a message of mercy to the world. The Pope points out that justice, without the deeper power of love manifested in mercy, can deviate from its goal. The text is found in AAS 72 (1980) 1215-1216.

(Justice needs to be imbued with mercy)

2174   12. The Church shares with the people of our time this profound and ardent desire for a life which is just in every aspect.... And yet, it would be difficult not to notice that very often programmes which start from the idea of justice...in practice suffer from distortions. Although they continue to appeal to the idea of justice, nevertheless experience shows that other negative forces have gained the upper hand over justice, such as spite, hatred and even cruelty. In such cases, the desire to annihilate the enemy, limit his freedom, or even force him into total dependence, becomes the fundamental motive for action, and this contrasts with the essence of justice which by its nature tends to establish equality and harmony between the parties in conflict.... The experience of the past and of our time demonstrates that justice alone is not enough, that it can even lead to its own negation and destruction, if that deeper power, which is love, is not allowed to shape human life in all its dimensions.

ENCYCLICAL LETTER *LABOREM EXERCENS* (1981)

The encyclical develops the human aspect of work which it calls the fundamental dimension of human existence on earth. It stresses the primacy of the subjective meaning of work over the objective: it is an activity of the human person and not a mere factor of production. Work has a personal, familial and communitarian dimension. The document brings out the clear priority of work over capital which itself is the fruit of work. Once again it distinguishes the Church's stand on ownership from that of Marxist collectivism and liberal capitalism. It asks that the rights of workers be preserved in any system of ownership. The encyclical touches on the questions of employment, wages, unions, rights of agricultural workers, the disabled and migrant workers. Finally it outlines a spirituality of work in the light of creation and redemption in Christ. The text is found in AAS 73 (1981) 577-647.

(The subjective meaning of work has primacy over the objective)

2175 6. ...The basis for determining the value of work is not primarily the kind of work being done but the fact that the one who is doing it is a person. The sources of the dignity of work are to be sought primarily in the subjective dimension, not in the objective one.

Such a concept practically does away with the very basis of the ancient differentiation of people into classes according to the kind of work done.... This leads immediately to a very important conclusion of an ethical nature: however true it may be that man is destined for work and called to it, in the first place work is 'for man' and not man 'for work'.... Independently of the work that every man does, and presupposing that this work constitutes a purpose—at times a very demanding one—of his activity, this purpose does not possess a definitive meaning in itself. In fact, in the final analysis it is always man who is the purpose of the work, whatever work it is that is done by man—even if the common scale of values rates it as the merest 'service', as the most monotonous, even the most alienating work.

(Priority of labour over capital)

2176   12. The structure of the present-day situation is deeply marked by many conflicts caused by man, and the technological means produced by human work play a primary role in it.... In view of this situation we must first of all recall a principle that has always been taught by the Church: *the principle of the priority of labour over capital.* This principle directly concerns the means of production: in this process labour is always a primary *efficient cause,* while capital, the whole collection of means of production, remains a mere *instrument* or instrumental cause.

   .... Since the concept of capital includes not only the natural resources placed at man's disposal but also the whole collection of means by which man appropriates natural resources and transforms them in accordance with his needs (and thus in a sense humanizes them), it must immediately be noted that *all these means are the result of the historical heritage of human labour.*

(Work founds a right to ownership)

2177   14. From this point of view the position of 'rigid' capitalism continues to remain unacceptable, namely the position that defends the exclusive right to private ownership of the means of production as an untouchable 'dogma' of economic life....

   In the light of the above, the many proposals put forward by experts in Catholic social teaching and by the highest Magisterium of the Church take on special significance: proposals for *joint owner-ship of the means of work,* sharing by the workers in the management and/or profits of business, so-called share-holding by labour, etc.

   .... While the position of 'rigid' capitalism must undergo continual revision,... it must be stated that, from the same point of view, these many deeply desired reforms cannot be achieved by an *a priori elimination of private ownership of the means of production....*

   .... Merely converting the means of production into State property in the collectivist system is by no means equivalent to 'socializing' that property. We can speak of socializing only when the subject character of society is ensured, that is to say, when on the basis of his

work each person is fully entitled to consider himself a part-owner of
the great work-bench at which he is working with everyone else.

(Just wages are criterion of justice of a socio-economic system)

2178   19. It should also be noted that the justice of a socio-
          economic system and, in each case, its just functioning,
deserve in the final analysis to be evaluated by the way in which
man's work is properly remunerated in the system. Here we return
once more to the first principle of the whole ethical and social order,
namely, *the principle of the common use of goods.* In every system,
regardless of the fundamental relationships within it between capital
and labour, wages, that is to say *remuneration for work*, are still a
practical means whereby the vast majority of people have access to
those goods which are intended for common use: both the goods of
nature and manufactured goods.

(No discrimination against women)

2179   19. ...The whole labour process must be organized and
          adapted in such a way as to respect the requirements of the
person and his or her forms of life, above all life in the home, taking
into account the individual's age and sex. It is a fact that in many
societies women work in nearly every sector in life. But it is fitting
that they should be able to fulfil their tasks *in accordance with their
own nature*, without being discriminated against and without being
excluded from jobs for which they are capable, but also without lack
of respect for their family aspirations and for their specific role in
contributing, together with men, to the good of society. The *true
advancement of women* requires that labour should be structured in
such a way that women do not have to pay for their advancement by
abandoning what is specific to them and at the expense of the family,
in which women as mothers have an irreplaceable role.

(Work as sharing in creation and redemption in Christ)

2180   25. The word of God's revelation is profoundly marked by
          the fundamental truth that *man*, created in the image of God,
shares by his work in the activity of the Creator and that, within the
limits of his own human capabilities, man in a sense continues to
develop that activity, and perfects it as he advances further in the
whole of creation....

          26. The truth that by means of work man participates in the
activity of God Himself, his Creator, was *given particular promi-*

nence by Jesus Christ.... For Jesus not only proclaimed but first and foremost fulfilled by His deeds the 'Gospel', the word of eternal Wisdom, that had been entrusted to Him. Therefore this was also 'the gospel of work', because *He who proclaimed it was Himself a man of work,* a craftsman like Joseph of Nazareth.... It can indeed be said that *He looks with love upon human work* and the different forms that it takes, seeing in each one of these forms a particular facet of man's likeness with God, the Creator and Father....

27. The Christian finds in human work a small part of the Cross of Christ and accepts it in the same spirit of redemption in which Christ accepted His Cross for us. In work, thanks to the light that penetrates us from the Resurrection of Christ, we always find a *glimmer* of new life, of the *new good,* as if it were an announcement of "the new heavens and the new earth" *(cf. 2 Pet. 3.13; Rev. 21.1)....* On the one hand, this confirms the indispensability of the Cross in the spirituality of human work; on the other hand, the Cross which this toil constitutes reveals a new good springing from work itself, from work understood in depth and in all its aspects and never apart from work.

APOSTOLIC EXHORTATION *FAMILIARIS CONSORTIO* (1981)

While describing marriage as communion of persons, the Pope again upholds the dignity and rights of women. For an introduction to the document, see n. 1843i.

(Dignity and rights of women)

2181   22. Above all it is important to underline the equal dignity and responsibility of women with men. This equality is realized in a unique manner in that reciprocal self-giving by each one to the other and by both to the children, which is proper to marriage and the family. What human reason intuitively perceives and acknowledges is fully revealed by the word of God: the history of salvation, in fact, is a continuous and luminous testimony to the dignity of women.

23. There is no doubt that the equal dignity and responsibility of men and women fully justifies women's access to public functions. On the other hand the true advancement of women requires that clear recognition be given to the value of their maternal and family role, by comparison with all other public roles and all other professions. Furthermore, these roles and professions should be harmon-

iously combined if we wish the evolution of society and culture to be truly and fully human.

With due respect to the different vocations of men an women, the Church must in her own life promote as far as possible their equality of rights and dignity; an this for the good of all, the family, the Church and society.

But clearly all of this does not mean for women a renunciation of their feminity or an imitation of the male role, but the fulness of true feminine humanity which should be expressed in their activity, whether in the family or outside of it, without disregarding the differences of customs and cultures in this sphere.

CHAPTER XXII

SEXUAL ORDER AND RESPECT FOR LIFE

God has created the human race in the complementarity of the sexes so that man and woman may find their fulfilment through a mutual union ordained by the Creator to the generation of new human life. It is in this complementarity that man is created as the image of God. Human sexuality is not only a biological drive, but an emotional and spiritual potentiality which calls for free decision and personal commitment. In the Christian context, virginity and marriage, chastity and the sexual order, take on new dimensions: all are related to the mystery of Christ and of the Church.

Chastity is the progressive integration of human sexuality with love according to one's state, married or celibate; it implies a gradual spiritualisation of the sex instinct by true charity. Respect of the sexual order established by God and confirmed by Christ is part of the Christian's conformity to the ideal of Christian love.

The Church has been especially concerned with the respect due to the sexual order because of the important personal, social and Christian values involved in it. The earlier documents principally dealt with the right use of sexual pleasure and defended its legitimacy within the boundaries of that order. The moral teaching of the Church sought to avoid the excesses of rigorism on the one hand and hedonism on the other. The Christian attitude to sex has been reaffirmed in recent years in opposition to the strong erotic currents pervading modern society. While taking a firm stand against these currents which depersonalise the use of sex, the Church has stressed the potentiality of sexual intercourse in marriage for preserving and promoting conjugal love, provided its full significance as an act open to procreation be not contradicted.

New moral issues have been raised in recent years in the sexual sphere by the discovery of new means of controling the generative process. The Church has reacted against the unlawful practices which would amount to a sub-human manipulation of procreation. On this score, are condemned contraception on the one hand and the practice of artificial insemination on the other. At the same time, in view of the phenomenon of population explosion, the Church recommends planned parenthood in order that children born from wedlock may have the guarantee of such human conditions as are conducive to their full personal development and to the attainment of their divine calling. Even today, the Church remains engaged in a process of reflection as regards eugenic methods in keeping with the Christian law of love.

Human life is sacred, whatever its stage of development or condition. It is the most basic value upon which all other values depend. Hence the Church strongly condemns any violation of that right for any cause, by abortion, infanticide or euthanasia.

*   *   *

This doctrinal aspects of marriage have been treated in Chapter XVIII. The moral aspects of sex and the respect for life, considered in this chapter, fall under the following headings:

Right Ordering of Sexuality

A right order in the use of sex is needed: 2201/9, 2201/48, 2201/50, 2228.

Premarital intercourse is never justified: 2229.

In marriage, the enjoyment of sexual pleasure is legitimate: 2211; but just moderation is needed: 2212.

Sexual intimacy plays an important role in fostering marital love: 2204, 2215, 2217, 2219.

Masturbation is forbidden by the law of nature: 2201/49, 2231.

Homosexual acts are always illicit: 2230.

Need for sexual education: 2232

Responsibility in Procreation

Parenthood must be responsible and generous: 2214.

The decision regarding the number of children belongs to the spouses: 2214, 2219.

Conjugal love and respect for life must be harmonised: 1841, 2215.

The divine plan for the transmission of human life must be observed: 2220, 2236.

The morality of birth control methods is determined by objective criteria: 2217.

The use of infertile periods is licit: 2204, 2225, 2236.

Positive interference with the procreative effect is an intrisic disorder: 2202, 2209, 2222, 2223, 2236.

Direct sterilisation is unlawful: 2222;

but indirect sterilisation is permitted: 2224.

Artificial insemination does not fully accord with the personal nature of human procreation: 2210, 2213.

The State plays a role in population control provided personal rights are respected: 2218, 2219.

It has no right to impose sterilisation: 2208.

A eugenic programme should not be imposed by the State: 2207.

Demographic education and birth control information are needed: 2219.

Respect of Human Life

Abortion is a grave crime: 2205, 2216, 2221, 2226-2227.

Even therapeutic abortion is not lawful: 2206, 2221.

Mercy killing is forbidden: 2233-2235.

INNOCENT XI

ERRORS OF LAXIST MORALITY CONDEMNED BY

THE HOLY OFFICE (1679)

Among the errors of laxist morality condemned in this decree of the Holy Office (cf. nn. 2006/1ff), some are related to the sexual order. Pending further decision (cf. n. 2006/1i), the propositions are condemned as causing scandal and harmful in practice. It must be noted that the ninth proposition is condemned only in the sense given to it by laxist morality; this condemnation has wrongly been made use of by the rigorists to defend their own position.

[2201/9] The marriage act performed for pleasure alone is entirely
2109   free of all fault and venial defect.

[2201/48] It seems clear that fornication by itself implies no malice
2148   and is evil solely because it is forbidden, so that the
    contrary seems entirely in disagreement with reason.

[2201/49] Masturbation is not forbidden by natural law. Hence, if
2149   God had not forbidden it,it would often be good and at
    times even an obligation under pain of mortal sin.

[2201/50] Intercourse with a married woman, with the consent of
2150   the husband, is not adultery.

PIUS XI

ENCYCLICAL LETTER *CASTI CONNUBII* (1930)

After exposing the doctrine on Christian marriage (cf. nn. 1824-1833) the Pope condemns certain abuses which were becoming widespread. These include hedonism, trial marriages, marital infidelity and divorce. The condemnation is particularly firm as regards 'Onanism'. Perhaps the Pope had directly in mind only interrupted intercourse, though the document generally received a stricter interpretation, later favoured by Pius XII.[1] But the encyclical recognises the lawfulness of choosing the sterile period for intercourse, since the marital act is meant for fostering mutual love besides achieving the end of procreation. Sterilisation is condemned in particular when it is imposed by civil authority for eugenic reasons, in violation of the natural right to marry and beget children. Destruction of unborn life is condemned as a grave crime.

(Interference with the procreative effect of intercourse is always illicit)

2202 ... No reason whatever, even the gravest, can make what is

---

1. Cf. J. T. NOONAN, *Contraception* (Cambridge 1966) 429.

3716   intrinsically against nature become conformable with nature and morally good. The conjugal act is of its very nature designed for the procreation of offspring; and, therefore, those who in performing it deliberately deprive it of its natural power and efficacy, act against nature and do something which is shameful and intrinsically immoral....

3717   Wherefore,...the Catholic Church, to whom God has committed the task of teaching and preserving morality and right conduct in their integrity, standing firm amidst this moral ruin, raises her voice in sign of her divine mission to keep the chastity of the marriage contract unsullied by this ugly stain, and through our voice proclaims anew that any use of marriage in the exercise of which the act is deprived, by human interference, of its natural power to procreate, is an offence against the law of God and nature, and those who commit it are guilty of grave sin....

(The innocent partner is excused)

2203   Holy Church is also well aware that in many cases one of
3718   the partners is more sinned against than sinning, reluctantly allowing a violation of the right order for a truly grave reason. Such a partner is not guilty, so long as the law of charity even then is remembered and every effort made to dissuade and prevent the other partner from sinning.

(The use of infertile period is licit)

2204   Nor are husband and wife to be accused of acting against
3718   nature if they make use of their right in the proper and natural manner, even though natural causes, either circumstances of time or certain defects, render the origin of new life impossible. Both marriage and the use of marital rights have secondary ends—such as mutual help, the fostering of reciprocal love, and the abatement of concupiscence—which husband and wife are quite entitled to have in view, so long as the intrinsic nature of that act, and, therefore, its due ordination to its primary end, is safeguarded....

(Abortion is not justified on any ground)

2205   Another very grave crime is to be noted...which consists
3719   in the taking of the life of the offspring hidden in the mother's womb. Some want it to be allowed and left to the will of the father or mother; others say that it is lawful when there are

weighty reasons which they call medical, social, or eugenic "indications"....

2206 As for what they call "medical and therapeutic indications",
3720 we have much pity for the mother whose health and even
life is gravely imperilled in the performance of the duty allotted to her by nature; nevertheless, what valid reason could there be for excusing in any way the direct killing of the innocent? This is precisely what we are dealing with here. Whether inflicted upon the mother or upon the child, it is against the precept of God and the law of nature: "You shall not kill" (*Ex. 20.13*).The life of both is equally sacred, and no one, not even public authority, can ever have the power to destroy it. It is no use to appeal to the right of taking away life in punishment; for here we are dealing with the innocent, whereas that right applies only with regard to the guilty. Nor does the right to use violence in self-defence against an unjust aggressor apply here; for who would call the innocent child an unjust aggressor? Again, there is no question here of whast is called the "law of extreme necessity", as though this could extend even to the direct killing of the innocent. Upright and skilful doctors are, therefore, most praiseworthy for striving to safeguard and preserve the lives of both mother and child; on the contrary, those show themselves most unworthy of the noble medical profession who bring about the death of one or the other, under the pretence of practising medicine or out of misguided pity....

(Eugenics through legislation is not justified)

2207 There are some who, in their excessive preoccupation with
3722 eugenic considerations are not content to give salutary
advice for the improvement of the unborn child's health and strength, which is certainly quite reasonable. They want to set these considerations above all other ends, even those of a higher order, and would have the public authority forbid marriage to any persons, who, in the light of the laws and conjectures of eugenic science, are deemed likely, because of their heredity, to beget defective offspring, even though in themselves they are fit to marry. They even demand that legislation be passed to deprive such persons of that natural faculty by medical action, even against their will....

(The State has no right to impose sterilisation)

2208 Public authorities have no direct power over the bodily

3722   members of the citizens and, therefore, in the absence
of any crime or any cause calling for corporal punishment, they can never directly injure or attack the integrity of the body on any ground whatever, eugenic or otherwise....

PIUS XII

ALLOCUTION TO MIDWIVES (1951)

In this allocution, meant to exhort midwives to live up to their noble calling, Pius XII stronly reaffirms the Church's condemnation of contraception and points out the need for self-control in marriage. The text is found in AAS 43 (1951) 835ff.

2209   Our predecessor, Pius XI, of happy memory, in his encyclical
Casti Connubii of Dec. 31, 1930, once again solemnly proclaimed the fundamental law of conjugal relations; every attempt of either husband or wife in the performance of the conjugal act or in the development of its natural consequences which aims at depriving it of its inherent force and hinders the procreation of new life is immoral (*cf. n. 2202*); and no "indication" or need can turn an act which is intrinsically immoral into a moral and lawful one (*cf. nn. 2205f*). The precept is in full force today as in the past, and it will be so in the future as well and always, because it is not due to a simple human fancy but is the expression of a natural and divine law.

(Artificial insemination contradicts the personal nature of human procreation)

2210   To reduce the common life of husband and wife and the
conjugal act to a mere organic function for the transmission of seed would be to convert the domestic hearth, the family sanctuary, into a biological laboratory....The conjugal act, in its natural structure, is a personal action, in which husband and wife simultaneously and immediately cooperate; the very nature of the agents and the quality of the act make it to be the expression of a reciprocal gift, which, according to Holy Scripture, effects union "in one flesh" (*cf. Gen. 2.24*). This is more than the union of two genes, which can be effected even by artificial means, that is without the natural action of husband and wife. The conjugal act, ordained and desired by nature, is a personal cooperation, the right to which husband and wife confer on each other when contracting marriage.

(Just moderation in seeking pleasure)

2211 The same Creator, who in his bounty and wisdom willed to make use of the work of man and woman, by uniting them in matrimony, for the preservation and propagation of the human race, has also decreed that in this function the partners should experience pleasure and happiness of body and spirit, Husband and wife, therefore, by seeking and enjoying this pleasure do no wrong. They accept what the Creator has destined for them.

2212 Nevertheless, here also, husband and wife must know how to keep themselves within the limits of just moderation. As with the pleasure of food and drink, so with the sexual pleasure, they must not abandon themselves without restraint to the impulse of the senses. The correct rule is this: the use of the natural procreative process is morally lawful in marriage only, and in the service of, and in accordance with the ends of marriage itself. Hence it follows that only in marriage and in submission to this rule is the desire and enjoyment of this pleasure and satisfaction lawful. For the pleasure is subordinate to the law of the action whence it is derived, and not vice versa the action to the pleasure. Moreover, this law, so very reasonable, concerns not only the substance but also the circumstances of the action, so that, even when the substance of the act remains morally right, it is possible to sin in the way it is performed.

ALLOCUTION TO THE SECOND WORLD CONGRES OF FERTILITY AND STERILITY (1956)

Pope Pius XII again takes a stand against artificial insemination by bringing out the personal aspect of human generation according to the divine plan. The text is found in PIUS XII, Discorsi e Radiomessagi, *vol. 18, pp. 211-221.*

2213 The Church has likewise rejected the opposite asttitude which pretended to separate, in procreation, the biological activity from the personal relations of husband and wife The child is the fruit of the marriage union, when this union finds its full expression in the setting into motion of the functional organs, of the sensible emotions related to them, and of the spiritual and disinterested love which animates such a union. It is within the unity of this human act that the biological conditions of procreation must be viewed. It is never permitted to separate these different aspects to the point of excluding positively either the ordination to procreation or the conjugal relation.

THE SECOND VATICAN GENERAL COUNCIL

PASTORAL CONSTITUTION *GAUDIUM ET SPES* (1965)

In this Constitution the Council stresses the personal values of Christian marriage and conjugal life (cf. nn. 1834-1840). It declares that well ordered sexual intercourse is an important factor in fostering marital love. The parents are called upon to cooperate with the love of the Creator and Saviour, with a sense of human and Chrsitian responsibility which takes into account the interests of the family, of society and of the Church (50)

Because of the demographic pressure and other sociological factors of our time, the Council had to deal with the problem of reconciling marital love with the respect for life. It clearly states the need for responsible parenthood. In planning the size of the family, dishonourable practices like abortion and infanticide are excluded. The morality of the means employed does not depend only on subjective motivation, but must be determined by objective standards, based on the nature of the human person and of his actions. The full meaning of mutual self-giving and of human procreation in the context of true love render the use of some methods unlawful according to objective criteria followed by the Church's doctrine (51). But the Council has deliberately refrained from making a defenitive pronouncement on the morality of specific methods of birth regulation since the matter was being studied by a papal commission. Nevertheless, it states several principles which must guide the solution of specific questions.

The Council calls for a vigorous programme to promote the family which is the foundation of society (52). It also sets the limits of the competence of the public authorities with regard to population problems (87).

The Council upholds the values of life from the moment of conception. Abortion (after animation, the time of which however is uncertain) is considered as infanticide and, therefore, an abominable crime.

(Responsible parenthood)

2214 50. In their function of transmitting life and bringing up children, which must be regarded as their proper mission, the spouses know that they are cooperators with the love of God the Creator and, so to speak, its interpreters. Therefore, they will discharge their task with a sense of human and Christian responsibility; and, with docile reverence towards God, by common counsel and effort, they will endeavour to form a right judgment. In doing so, they will take into account their own good and that of the children, already born or to be born; they will consider carefully the material and spiritual conditions of their times and of their own situation, and, finally, they will consult the interests of their own family, of the temporal society, and of the Church herself. It is the spouses themselves who ultimately must make this judgment in the sight of God. In their way of acting, Christian spouses should be aware that they cannot proceed arbitrarily but must always be guided by their conscience, a conscience duly conformed to the divine law itself; and let them be docile towards the teaching authority of the Church which interprets the law authentically in the light of the Gospel. That divine law shows the full meaning of conjugal love; it protects this love and leads it on its true human fulfilment. When Christian spouses, trusting in divine Providence and fostering in themselves a spirit of sacrifice, assume their function of procreating children with a generous, human and Christian sense of responsibility, they give glory to the Creator and grow towards perfection in Christ. Among the spouses who thus fulfil their God-given task, those merit a special mention who, after prudent and common deliberation, magnanimously accept to bring up, as far as their means allow, even a large number of children.

(Conjugal intimacy and respect for human life)

2215   51.   The Council realises that couples who wish to organise their married life harmoniously are often hindered by certain modern conditions of life, and that they may happen to be in circumstances in which they cannot increase the number of their children, at least for the time being. As a result, the faithful exercise of love and full community of life are difficult for them to maintain. But when the intimacy of married life is broken off, faithfulness can often be imperilled and the offspring can suffer: for, then, the education of the children and the courage to accept more children are both in danger.

There are people who venture to offer to these problems dishonourable solutions and who do not even draw back from the taking of life. But the Church reminds them that there can be no real contradiction between the divine law of transmitting life and that of fostering genuine conjugal love.

(Abortion is immoral)

2216   51.   For God, the Master of life, has entrusted to men the noble ministry of safeguarding life—a ministry to be discharged in a manner worthy of man. Therefore, life must be guarded with great care from the moment of conception; abortion and infanticide are heinous crimes.

(The morality of methods of birth regulation is based on objective criteria)

2217   51.   Human sexuality and man's faculty of generating surpass in a wonderful way all that is found in the lower degrees of life;

hence the acts proper to married life, when performed in keeping with man's true dignity, must be surrounded with great reverence. Therefore, when there is question of harmonising conjugal love with a responsible transmission of life, the morality of any way of acting does not depend only on the sincerity of the intention and on the evaluation of the motives; it must be determined by objective criteria, based on the nature of the person and of his acts. Such criteria respect the full meaning of mutual self-gift and human procreation, in a context of true love. This is impossible unless the virtue of conjugal chastity is sincerely practised. On the strength of these principles, the sons of the Church are not allowed, in the matter of regulating procreation, to adopt methods which are reproved by the teaching authority of the Church interpreting the divine law.

(The role of the State in the population problem)

2218 87. ...Within the limits of their competence, governments have rights and duties with regard to the population problem in their own nation, for instance, in the matter of social and family legislation, of migration of rural people to the cities, of information concerning the situation and needs of the country....

2219 Many people assert that the growth of the world population, or at least that of some countries, must be radically reduced, by every means and by every kind of government intervention. Hence this Council exhorts all to beware of solutions, advocated privately or publicly, and sometimes even imposed, which are contrary to the moral law. For, in view of man's inalienable right to marry and to beget children, the decision concerning the number of children they should have depends on the honest judgment of the parents, and may not be committed in any way to the decision of public authority. As this judgment presupposes a rightly formed conscience, it is important that all should be given the possibility of exercising their responsibility in an upright and truly human manner which, while taking into account the circumstances and times, is ever mindful of the law of God. This requires that education and social conditions in various places be improved, and especially that the possibility be offered of a religious formation or at least a complete moral training. Furthermore, people should be judiciously informed of the progress of science in the study of the methods by which married people can be helped in regulating births, when the reliability of these methods has been adequately tested and their harmony with the moral law established.

PAUL VI

ENCYCLICAL LETTER *HUMANAE VITAE* (1968)

Since 1965 the difficult question of birth-regulation was studied, on the Pope's request, by a commission of experts. The Second Vatican Council left it to the Pope to pronounce on the legitimacy of methods of birth-control in the light of the findings of this special commission (cf. n. 2214i). Having personally examined the data contained in the report of the commission, the Pope took position in 1968.

The encyclical first exposes the positive values attached to the conjugal love as cooperation with the Creator in the transmission of new life. It calls for responsible parenthood in the light of an integral vision of man and his vocation (cf. n. 1841i), along the lines of the teaching of Vatican II (cf. n. 2214). It shows the intimate connection which exists between the two aspects of the conjugal act (n. 1841), whose finality must be respected. On the strength of these doctrinal principles, the encyclical declares that "each and every marriage act" (quilibet matrimonii usus) must be open to the transmission of life (11). Various means of birth-regulation are therefore excluded, notably those by which the working of the natural process of generation would be prevented. Contraception and direct sterilisation are an intrinsic disorder, while recourse to infecund periods is always licit. The principle of totality according to which a conjugal act in which conception is voluntarily prevented could be considered lawful in the context of the totality of a fecund marital life is declared erroneous. After considering the serious consequences deriving from artificial birth-control, the encyclical ends with a pastoral exhortation: married couples are called to generosity and trust in God; educators are asked to create an atmosphere favourable to chastity; pastors are invited to expound the Church's teaching faithfuly, and at the same time to treat people with kindness and understanding.

Though the encyclical is a clear papal statement, commanding a corresponding assent, it is not an infallible document. While explaining it, several national hierarchies have introduced nuances in its teaching and made suggestions for its pastoral application. Thus, the French bishops do not exclude a recourse to other means, considered as a lesser evil, when periodic continence is not possible and a person is in a 'perplexed conscience' or faced with a conflict of duties.[1] The text is found in AAS 60 (1968) 481ff.

(The divine plan for the transmission of human life)

2220   13. It is in fact justly observed that a conjugal act imposed upon one's partner without regard for his or her condition and lawful desires is not a true act of love, and, therefore, denies an exigency of right moral order in the relationship between husband and wife. Hence, one who reflects well must also recognise that a reciprocal act of love, which jeopardises the potentiality to transmit

---

1. Cf. *The Catholic Mind*, 1969, 47ff.

life which God the Creator, according to particular laws, inserted therein, is in contradiction with the innate design of marriage, and with the will of the Author of life. To use this divine gift while destroying, even if only partially, its true meaning and its purpose is to contradict the nature both of man and woman and of their most intimate relationship, and, therefore, it is to contradict also the plan of God and His will. On the other hand, to make use of the gift of conjugal love while respecting the laws of the generative process means to acknowledge oneself not to be the arbiter of the sources of human life, but rather the minister of the design established by the Creator. In fact, just as a man does not have unlimited dominion over his body in general, so also, with particular reason, he has no such dominion over his generative faculties as such, because of their intrinsic ordination towards raising up life, of which God is the principle....

(Contraception is intrinsically a disorder)

2221 14. In conformity with these landmarks in the human and Christian vision of marriage, we must once again declare that the direct interruption of the generative process already begun, and above all, directly willed and procured abortion, even if for therapeutic reasons, are to be absolutely excluded as licit means of regulating birth.

2222 Equally to be excluded, as the teaching authority of the Church has frequently declared, is direct sterilisation, whether permanent or temporary, whether of the man or of the woman. Similarly excluded is every action which either in anticipation of the conugal act, or in its accomplishment, or in the development of its natural consequences, proposes, whether as an end or as a means, to render procreation impossible.

2223 To justify conjugal acts made intentionally infecund, one cannot invoke as valid reasons the lesser evil, or the fact that such acts would constitute a totality together with the fecund acts already performed or to follow later, and hence would share in one and the same moral goodness. In truth, if it is something licit to tolerate a lesser evil in order to avoid a greater evil or to promote a greater good, it is not licit, even for the gravest reasons, to do evil so that good may follow therefrom; that is, to make into the object of a positive act of the will something which is intrinsically a disorder, and hence unworthy of the human person, even when the intention is to safeguard or promote individual, family or social well-being. Consequently it is an error to think that a conjugal act which is deliberately made infecund and so is intrinsically dishonest could be made honest and right by the ensemble of a fecund conjugal life.

(Indirect sterilisation is not unlawful)

2224 15. The Church, on the contrary, does not at all consider illicit the use of therapeutic means truly necessary to cure diseases of the organism, even if an inpediment to procreation, which may be foreseen, should result therefrom, provided such impediment is not, for whatever motive, directly willed.

(The use of the sterile period is permissible)

2225 16. ...If there are serious motives to space out births, which are derived from the physical or psychological conditions of husband and wife, or from external conditions, the Church teaches that it is then licit to take into account the natural rhythms immanent in the generative functions, for the use of marital rights in the infecund periods only, and in this way to regulate birth without offending against the moral principles which we have recalled earlier.

The Church is coherent with herself when she considers recourse to the infecund periods to be licit, while at the same time condemning, as being always illicit, the use of means directly contrary to fecundation, even if such use is inspired by reasons which may appear honest and serious. In reality, there are essential differences between the two cases: in the former, the married couple make legitimate use of a natural disposition; in the latter, they impede the development of natural processes.

DECLARATION *DE ABORTU PROCURATO* OF THE
S. CONGREGATION FOR THE DOCTRINE OF THE FAITH
(28 June 1974)

The widespread evil of abortion, the increasing permissive attitude towards it and the trend to its legalization have prompted the S. Congregation to recall the essential elements of the Church's doctrine in the matter. This doctrine is primarily based on the value and respect due to human life in the light of reason and of faith. The Document explicitly grants that the moment of animation is under dispute. But even when the presence of the soul is only probable, the taking of life would involve incurring the risk of killing a human person. As life is the most basic value, procured abortion would never be justified by the intention of protecting any other value. The right of the unborn person to live calls for protection on the part of society and public authority. The Document also declares: "Never, under any pretext, may abortion be resorted to, either by a family or political authority, as a legitimate means of regulating births" (cf. n. 2221). The Document points out that it is not enough to condemn abortion, but there is also the need for tackling the causes that lead to it. However, it does not answer questions like: 1) what would be the moral evaluation of expelling the zygote before nidation if the absence of human personhood could be shown with moral certainty at that stage?; 2) when the death of the mother would also entail the death of the fetus, would not intervention be a lesser evil? The text is found in AAS 66 (1974) 730-747.

(Abortion never licit)

2226   12. Any discrimination based on the various stages of life is no more justified than any other discrimination. The right to life remains complete in an old person, even one greatly weakened; it is not lost by one who is incurably sick. The right to life is no less to be respected in the small infant just born than in the mature person. In reality, respect for human life is called for from the time that the process of generation begins. From the time that the ovum is fertilized, a life is begun which is neither that of the father nor of the mother; it is rather the life of a human being with its own growth. It would never be made human if it were not human already.

13. To this perpetual evidence—perfectly independent of the discussions on the moment of animation—modern genetic science brings valuable confirmation. It has demonstrated that, from the first instant, there is established the programme of what this living being will be: this individual man with his characteristic aspects already well determined.... Moreover, it is not up to biological sciences to make a definitive judgment on questions which are properly philosophical and moral such as the moment when a human person is constituted or the legitimacy of abortion. From a moral point of view this is certain: even if a doubt existed concerning whether the fruit of conception is already a human person, it is objectively a grave sin to dare to risk murder.

(Combatting the causes of abortion

2227   26. ... One can never approve of abortion; but it is above all necessary to combat its causes. This includes political action, which will be in particular the task of the law. But it is necessary at the same time to influence morality and to do everything possible to help families, mothers and children. Considerable progress in the service of life has been accomplished by medicine.

One can hope that such progress will continue, in accordance with the vocation of doctors, which is not to suppress life but to care for it and favour it as much as possible. It is equally desirable that, in suitable institutions, or, in their absence, in the outpouring of Christian generosity and charity, every form of assistance should be developed.

DECLARATION *DE PERSONA HUMANA* OF THE
S. CONGREGATION FOR THE DOCTRINE OF THE FAITH
(29 December 1975)

The increasing breakdown of sexual morality as well as questioning of the traditional doctrine of the Church on the matter has led the S. Congregation to reaffirm the basic principles of sexual ethics.

Although the doctrine is present in the traditional natural law perspective, there are some new openings. There is emphasis on the dignity and values of the human person as well as on relationships. The basic principle that every genital act must be within the marital framework is defended by an appeal to the meaning of sexuality as an expression of inter-personal relationship. At the same time, the need for pastoral understanding is stressed. Modern psychology is credited with much value in formulating a more equitable judgment on moral responsibility and in orienting pastoral action. Although it is reaffirmed that masturbatory acts are in the objective order seriously evil, the importance of considering the totality of the individual's practice of charity and justice or his fundamental option (cf. n. 2062) is also recognized. The Document also calls for a healthy sex education in the context of total education. The text is found in AAS 68 (1976) 77-96).

(Basic principle of sexual ethics)

2228 5. This same principle which the Church holds from divine Revelation and from her authentic interpretation of the natural law, is also the basis of her traditional doctrine, which states that the use of the sexual function has its true meaning and moral rectitude only in true marriage.

(Premarital intercourse never justified)

2229 7. However firm the intention of those who practise such premature sexual relations may be, the fact remains that these relations cannot ensure, in sincerity and fidelity, the inter-personal relationship between a man and a woman, nor especially can they protect this relationship from whims and caprices.

Experience teaches us that love must find its safeguard in the stability of marriage, if sexual intercourse is truly to respond to the requirements of its own finality and to those of human dignity. These requirements call for a conjugal contract sanctioned and guaranteed by society—a contract which establishes a state of life of capital importance both for the exclusive union of man and woman and for the good of their family and of the human community. Most often, in fact, premarital relations exclude the possibility of children. What is represented to be conjugal love is not able to develop into paternal and maternal love. Or, if it does happen to do so, this will be to the detriment of the children, who will be deprived of the stable environment in which they ought to develop in order to find in it the ways and means of their insertion into society as a whole.

(Homosexual acts always illicit)

2230 8. In the pastoral field, these homosexuals must certainly be treated with understanding and sustained in the hope of overcoming their personal difficulties and their inability to fit into society. Their culpability will be judged with prudence. But no pastoral method can be employed which would give moral justification to these acts, on the ground that they would be consonant with the condition of such people. For according to the objective moral order, homosexual relations are acts which lack an essential and indispensable finality. In Sacred Scripture they are condemned as a depravity and even presented as the sad consequence of rejecting God. This judgment of Scripture does not of course permit us to conclude that all those who suffer from this anomaly are personally responsible for it, but it does attest to the fact that homosexual acts are intrinsically disordered and can in no case be approved of.

(Masturbation intrinsically evil)

2231 9. Whatever the force of certain arguments of a biological and philosophical nature, which have sometimes been used by theologians, in fact both the Magisterium of the Church—in the constant tradition—and the moral sense of the faithful have declared without hesitation that masturbation is an intrinsically and seriously disordered act. The main reason is that, whatever the motive for acting in this way, the deliberate use of the sexual faculty outside normal conjugal relations essentially contradicts the finality of the faculty. For it lacks the sexual relationship called for by the normal order, namely the relationship which realises "the full communion of mutual self-giving and human procreation in the context of true love" (GS 51).

In the pastoral ministry, in order to form an adequate judgment in concrete cases, the habitual behaviour of people will be considered in its totality, not only with regard to the individual's practice of charity and of justice, but also with regard to the individual's care in observing the particular precepts of chastity. In particular one will have to examine whether the individual is using the necessary means, both natural and supernatural, which Christian asceticism from its long experience recommends for overcoming the passions and progressing in virtue.

(Need for sex education)

2232 13. Parents, in the first place, and also teachers of the young must endeavour to lead their children and their pupils by way of a complete education, to the psychological, emotional and moral maturity befitting their age. They will therefore prudently give them information suited to their age; and they will assiduously form their wills in accordance with Christian morals, not only by advice but above all by the example of their own lives, relying on God's help, which they will obtain in prayer. They will likewise protect the young from many dangers of which they are quite unaware.

DECLARATION ON EUTHANASIA OF THE
S. CONGREGATION FOR THE DOCTRINE OF THE FAITH
(5 May 1980)

As a sequel to the document on Procured Abortion (cf. nn. 2226-2227), in which the principle of the inviolability of human life at any stage or in any condition was upheld, this document again clarifies that the right to life extends to all, whether the sick or the unborn. Recent advances in medicine have increased immensely the capacity to prolong life, which gives rise to a double problem: a) would it be permissible at some stage to provide an 'easy death' in order to put an end to the suffering of the patient and anxiety of the family?; b) to what extent is one obliged to use the life-prolonging procedures now available? While the Declaration answers a resolute 'no' to the first question, it adopts a new way of speaking regarding the use of therapeutic means in terminal illness, namely the distinction between 'proportionate' and 'disproportionate' means. It clarifies the meaning of 'right to die' and explains the Christian meaning of suffering and death. The text is found in AAS 72 (1980) 542-552.

(Direct killing of an innocent never permissible)

2233 It is necessary to state firmly once more that nothing and no one can in any way permit the killing of an innocent human being, whether a fetus or an embryo, an infant or an adult, an old person or one suffering from an incurable disease, or a person who is dying. Furthermore, no one is permitted to ask for this act of killing, either for himself or for another person entrusted to his or her care, nor can he or she consent to it, either explicitly or implicitly; nor can any authority legitimately recommend or permit such an action. For it is a question of the violation of the divine law, an offence against the dignity of the human person, a crime against life and an attack on humanity.

The pleas of gravely ill people who sometimes ask for death are not to be understood as implying a true desire for euthanasia; in fact, it is almost always a case of an anguished plea for help and love. What a sick person needs, besides medical care, is love, the human and supernatural warmth with which the sick person can and ought to be surrounded by all those close to him or her, parents and children, doctors and nurses.

(Right to die with dignity)

2234   Today it is very important to protect at the moment of death, both the dignity of the human person and the Christian concept of life, against a technological attitude that threatens to become an abuse. Thus some people speak of a 'right to die', which is an expression that does not mean the right to procure death either by one's own hand or by means of someone else's as one pleases, but rather the right to die peacefully with human and Christian dignity.

(No obligation to use 'disproportionate' means)

2235   However, is it necessary in all circumstances to have recourse to all possible remedies?

In the past, moralists replied that one is never obliged to use 'extraordinary' means. This reply, which as a principle still holds good, is perhaps less clear today, by reason of the imprecision of the term and the rapid progress made in the treatment of sickness. Thus, some people prefer to speak of 'proportionate' means. In any case, it will be possible to make a correct judgment as to the means by studying the type of treatment to be used, its degree of complexity or risks, its cost and the possibilities of using it, and comparing these elements with the result that can be expected, taking into account the state of the sick person and his or her physical and moral resources.

JOHN PAUL II

APOSTOLIC EXHORTATION *FAMILIARIS CONSORTIO* (1981)

While reaffirming the basic stand of Humane Vitae *(nn. 2220-2225), the Pope brings out more clearly the ethical differences between suppression of fertility and respecting the same through natural family planning. As was the case in* Humanae Vitae, *here too the Pope does not say how one should proceed in conflict situations. For an introduction to the document, see n. 1843i.*

(Ethical differences between contraception and natural family planning)

2236 32. When couples, by means of recourse to contraception, separate these two meanings (unitive and procreative, of the conjugal act) which God the Creator has inscribed in the being of man and woman, and in the dynamism of their sexual communion, they act as 'arbiters' of the divine plan and they 'manipulate' and degrade human sexuality—and with it themselves and their married partner—by altering its value of 'total' self-giving. Thus the innate language that expresses the total reciprocal self-giving of husband and wife is overlaid, through contraception, by an objectively contradictory language, namely, that of not giving oneself totally to the other. This leads not only to a positive refusal to be open to life but also to a falsification of the inner truth of conjugal love, which is called upon to give itself in personal totality.

When, instead, by means of recourse to periods of infertility, the couple respect the inseparable connection between the unitive and procreative meanings of human sexuality, they are acting as 'ministers' of God's plan and they 'benefit from' their sexuality according to the original dynamism of 'total' self-giving, without manipulation or alteration.

In the light of the experience of many couples and of the data provided by the different human sciences, theological reflection is able to perceive and is called to study further *the difference, both anthropological and moral,* between contraception and recourse to the rhythm of the cycle: it is a difference which is much wider and deeper than is usually thought, one which involves in the final analysis two irreconcilable concepts of the human person and of human sexuality. The choice of the natural rhythms involves accepting the cycle of the person, that is the woman, and thereby accepting dialogue, reciprocal respect, shared responsibility and self-control.

CHAPTER XXIII

CHRISTIAN FULFILMENT

Salvation history, which began with creation and culminated in Christ's Paschal Mystery, moves on gradually towards its consummation: God's full glorification in His ultimate self-gift to men at the end of time. The time of the Church extends between the two poles of Christ's glorification establishing Him as the Lord and of His final epiphany at the parousia. During this entire period, the pilgrim People of God, by responding freely to God's communication of Himself through His Son in the Spirit, advances through its final fulfilment, awaiting in hope the transfiguration of the world. When the Lord of glory will be revealed at the end of time, He will confront all men in judgment to make the elect share, in soul and body, in His own fulness.

Thus, the Church's doctrine on men's ultimate destiny is entirely centred on Jesus Christ, the Eschaton. Its dimension is essentially ecclesial and even cosmic. The eternal fate of the individual Christian must be viewed in this perspective. The final encounter with Christ in death, which for the elect is the decisive conformation to the Paschal Mystery,is the moment of truth in which each man's eternal fate is fixed. Cleansed from all stain of sin under the impact of Christ's purifying light, those who have responded to God's saving love enter into eternal glory, while those who have definitely closed themselves to it are irremediably lost. The heavenly bliss of the elect looks towards the completion of the Church in the Kingdom of God and to the final transformation of the world.

In the course of the centuries the Church's eschatological doctrine has passed through two main phases of development. In the early centuries the communal dimension predominated, with Christ's parousia as its pivotal point; the eternal fate of the individual Christian, which received much less attention, was viewed within the context of the completion of the ecclesial community. The Middle Ages brought about a shift from the communitarian to the individual aspect. Theological thought then focussed on the moment of death on which hinges man's eternal destiny, while the social events of parousia and the resurrection, now receding into the background, were considered primarily as the final stage of man's personal destiny, and certain doctrines like that of purgatory came to be stressed. It is the task of a well-poised Christian eschatology harmoniously to combine its ecclesial and individual dimensions. Moreover, the eschatological hope does not merely consist in the expectation of things to come. For the Church as for the individual Christian it is a reality already present and operative: the Christian life and the Church's pilgrimage on earth are a progressive growth into the fulness of Christ, a path leading to the final encounter with the Lord.

The Church documents on eschatology are comparatively few in number. Belonging as they do for the most part to the Middle Ages, they reveal an individual rather than an ecclesial perspective, and deal primarily with purgatory, the vision of God and the resurrection of individual bodies. While they clarify doubts and reject errors originating from Orthodoxy and the Reformation, they do not convey the full richness and complexity of the Christian message on the fulfilment of all things in God. It is in the Second Vatican Council that the Christian fulfilment has once again been presented in its universal significance for the life of the Church and of the world.

*   *   *

These, then, are the doctrinal points contained in the following documents:

The Church is the eschatological community, awaiting Christ's second coming and the fulfilment of all creation: 2311, 2316.

Death is the punishment for sin which will be destroyed in Christ's second coming: 39/21, 508-509, 2312, 2315, 2316.

Those who depart from this life free from sin go to eternal happiness: 5, 10, 17, 20, 25, 26, 39/21, (2303), 2305, 2309, 2317.

Heaven consists in the vision of God: 39/22, 1997, 2305f, 2309.

Those who are subject to temporal punishment are to be purified: 26, 35, 39/21, 1980, (2304), 2308, 2310, 2317.

They are helped by the acts of intercession and the good works of the faithful: 26, 35, 1548, 1557, 1685/22, 1689, (2304), 2308, 2310, 2317.

Those who die in mortal sin are condemned: 17, 20, 26, 506, (2303), 2307, 2317.

Their punishment is eternal: 17, 20, 506, 2301, (2303), 2317.

In the end of times all rise in their bodies: 5, 10, 12, 17, 20, 25, 27, 2302, (2303), 2307, 2317.

They will be judged by Christ: 5, 7, 10, 12, 17, 20, 23, 27, 2302, (2303), 2307.

The communion of saints comprises the pilgrim Church, those who are purified and the blessed in heaven: 39/23, 2312, (2313f).

THE COUNCIL OF CONSTANTINOPLE

ANATHEMATISMS AGAINST THE ORIGENISTS (543)

Emperor Justinian drew up a series of canons against the Origenists which were subsequently promulgated at the Provincial Council of Constantinople in 543. On the basis of Platonic philosophy the Origenists attempted to explain the creation and the end of the world by laws by inner necessity. According to them human souls pre-existed to their infusion in the body (cf. n. 401), and all would one day be freed from the imprisonment of the body to recover their pristine spiritual state. Consequently, the punishment of hell was only temporary; it was to be followed by the general restoration of all souls to their former state (apokatastasis). This document of condemnation seems to have been signed by all the Eastern Patriachs and possibly was confirmed by Pope Vigilius.

2301   9.   If anyone says or holds that the punishment of the demons
411   and of impious men is temporary, and that it will have an end
             at some time, or that there will be a complete restortion
(*apokatasasis)* of demons and impious men, *anathema sit.*

THE ELEVENTH COUNCIL OF TOLEDO

SYMBOL OF FAITH (675)

A Creed or profession of faith, prepared by Quiricius, archbishop of Toledo, was approved at the beginning of this provincial Council by the seventeen bishops present. Besides a long elaboration on the mysteries of the Trinity (cf. nn. 308ff) and of the Incarnation and Redemption (cf. nn. 628ff), it contains a much shorter treatment of Christian eschatology. Though never approved by a Pope, this document, always held in high regard by the Church, is among the important formulas of doctrine; most of its contents belong to the doctrine of faith (cf. n. 18). Its doctrine is partly inspired by the Pseudo-Athanasian Symbol Quicumque *(cf. nn. 16f), partly by the great Latin doctors, especially St Augustine and St Hilary.*

(On the fate of man after death)

2302   Thus, according to the example of our Head, we confess that
540   there is a true resurrection of the body for all the dead. And
             we do not believe that we shall rise in an ethereal body or in
any other body, as some foolishly imagine, but in this very body in
which we live and are and move. After having given an example of
this holy resurrection, our Lord and Saviour by His ascension
returned to the throne of His Father from which in His divine nature
He had never departed. There, seated at the right hand of the Father,
He is awaited till the end of time as judge of all the living and the dead.
From there He shall come with all the holy [angels and men] to pass
judgment and to render to each one the reward due to him, accord-

ing to what each one has done while he was in the body, whether good or evil (cf. 2 Cor. 5.10).

We believe that the holy Catholic Church, which He purchased at the price of His own blood, will reign with Him forever. Taken up into her bosom, we believe in and profess one baptism for the remission of all sins. By this faith we truly believe in the resurrection of the death and look forward to the joys of the world to come. This only must we pray and beg for, that when the Son, having completed the judgment, will have delivered the kingdom to God the Father (cf. 1 Cor. 15.24), He may make us sharers in His kingdom, so that through this faith by which we have adhered to Him, we may reign with Him forever.

THE FOURTH LATERAN GENERAL COUNCIL

SYMBOL OF LATERAN (1215)

(2303) *The twelfth general Council was held at the Lateran in 1215, under Pope Innocent III. Before the decrees concerning the recovery of the Holy Land and the general reform of the Church, the Council issued a profession of the Catholic faith directly intended against the errors of the Albigensians and the Cathars (cf. n. 19i). The Albigensian system was in certain respects the upshot of the previous Manichaean heresy, which held matter to be intrinsically evil as proceeding from an eternal evil principle. Imprisoned in the bodies, human souls were to undergo a gradual purification through a process of transmigration till their final restoration to their original heavenly state; consequently the punishment of hell was not considered as eternal. Against these heretical tendencies, the Council's profession of faith declares the Catholic doctrine of creation according to which all things, spiritual and corporeal, are created by God, and naturally good (cf. n. 19). It goes on to express the Christian faith as regards the resurrection of the bodies, the judgment of all men according to their deeds, and the subsequent eternal reward or punishment. The text is found in n. 20.*

THE SECOND GENERAL COUNCIL OF LYONS

"PROFESSION OF FAITH OF MICHAEL PALAEOLOGUS" (1274)

(2304) *Among the points of dissent between the Latin and the Greek Churches which the Second General Council of Lyons attempted to suppress several were related to Christian eschatology. The profession of faith proposed by Pope Clement IV to emperor Michael Palaeologus as early as 1267 as pre-required condition for union was read at the Council convened by Pope Gregory X in 1274, but was neither discussed at the Council nor accepted by the Greeks as a basis for a doctrinal agreement with the Latins (cf. n. 22i). The eschatological doctrine is treated in the second part of the "Profession of Faith of Michael Palaeologus". In the context of a complete doctrine of individual eschatology, which will be* *taken up later by the Council of Florence (cf. nn. 2308f), it lays stress on the immediate retribution and on purgatory, the two main points on which Latins and Greeks were at variance in current controversies; it also affirms the efficacy of prayer for the dead. A clause on the general judgment is added to mark the agreement between Greeks and Latins on this point. The text is found under nn. 25-27.*

BENEDICT XII

CONSTITUTION *BENEDICTUS DEUS* (1336)

The common teaching of the Church on immediate retribution after death held that the blessed on entering the heavenly state were introduced to the immediate and eternal vision of God. Departing from this traditional opinion, Pope John XXII, in a series of sermons which he preached in Paris in 1331, asserted, as a private theologian, that soon after death the blessed enjoy only the vision of Christ's glorified humanity, while the access to the vision of the Triune God will be opened to them only after the resurrection, on the day of judgment. The following year he adapted this opinion of a progressive retribution to the condition of the damned. The Pope's opinion led to a fierce controversy, notably between the Franciscans who supported the Pope and the Dominicans who opposed him. The University of Paris requested the Pope to settle the dispute authoritatively. Though he intended to heed the request, John XXII was able only to retract his own former opinion on the eve of his death and to submit personally to the traditional doctrine of the Church. His successor Benedict XII, after a thorough enquiry, issued in 1336 the Constitution Benedictus Deus *by which he meant to bring the controversy to an end. According to this Constitution the souls of the blessed departed see the Triune God face to face immediately after death and prior to the resurrection. But the nature of their intermediate state between death and resurrection, which is conceived as that of bodiless souls, is presupposed by the Constitution rather than directly taught.*

(On the beatific vision of God)

2305 By this Constitution which is to remain in force for ever, we,
1000 with apostolic authority, define the following: According to the general disposition of God, the souls of all the saints who departed from this world before the passion of our Lord Jesus Christ and also of the holy apostles, martyrs, confessors, virgins and other faithful who died after receiving the holy baptism of Christ—provided they were not in need of any purification when they died, or will not be in need of any when they die in the future, or else, if they then needed or will need some purification, after they have been purified after death—and again the souls of children who have been reborn by the same baptism of Christ or will be when baptism is conferred on them, if they die before attaining the use of free will: all these souls, immediately (*mox*) after death and, in the case of those

in need of purification, after the purification mentioned above, since the ascension of our Lord and Saviour Jesus Christ into heaven, already before they take up their bodies again and before the general judgment, have been, are and will be with Christ in heaven, in the heavenly kingdom and paradise, joined to the company of the holy angels. Since the passion and death of the Lord Jesus Christ, these souls have seen and see the divine essense with an intuitive vision and even face to face, without the mediation of any creature by way of object of vision; rather the divine essence immediately manifests itself to them, plainly, clearly and openly, and in this vision they enjoy the divine essence . Moreover, by this vision and enjoyment the souls of those who have already died are truly blessed and have eternal life and rest. Also the souls of those who will die in the future will see the same divine essence and will enjoy it before the general judgment.

2306   Such a vision and enjoyment of the divine essence do away
1001   with the acts of faith and hope in these souls, inasmuch as
        faith and hope are properly theological virtues. And after such intuitive and face-to-face vision and enjoyment has or will have begun for these souls, the same vision and enjoyment has continued and will continue without any interruption and without end until the last Judgment and from then on forever.

(On hell and the general judgment)

2307   Moreover we define that according to the general disposition
1002   of God, the souls of those who die in actual mortal sin go
        down into hell immediately *(mox)* after death and there suffer the pain of hell. Nevertheless, on the day of judgment all men will appear with their bodies "before the judgment seat of Christ" to give an account of their personal deeds, "so that each one may receive good or evil, according to what he has done in the body" *(2 Cor. 5.10)*.

THE GENERAL COUNCIL OF FLORENCE
DECREE FOR THE GREEKS (1439)

The reunion with the Orientals, attempted by the second Council of Lyons in 1274, did not materialise in practice. A new and more successful attempt at reconciliation, the results of which, however, were also short-lived, was made at the Council of Florence under Pope Eugene IV. Besides the sections on the procession of the Holy Spirit (cf. nn. 322ff), on the

Eucharist (cf. n. 1508), and on the Roman primacy (cf. n. 809), the Decree for the Greeks contains a section on Christian eschatology. As regards the doctrine of purgatory, the Orientals admitted its existence as well as the efficacy of prayers offered for the dead. But, while the Latin Church explained its nature with the help of the juridical concept of satisfaction, the East conceived it in a more mystical manner, as a process of maturation and spiritual growth. With regard to the beatific vision, the Orientals denied its immediate possibility and held that it would begin only after the general resurrection. In settling this double issue, the Council repeats almost verbatim the previous decree of Lyons (cf. nn. 26-27), with an important addition, however, concerning the various degrees of intensity of the vision which depend on the diversity of merits. The section on purgatory strikes a careful balance between the Western conception of satisfaction-expiation and the Oriental insistence on purification. Moreover, out of consideration for the Oriental position, the Council deliberately omits all allusion to fire and carefully avoids whatever could lead to the concept of purgatory as a place.

(On the eternal fate of the dead)

2308 And, if they are truly penitent and die in God's love before
1304 having satisfied by worthy fruits of penance for their sins of commission and omission, their souls are cleansed after death by purgatorial penalties. In order that they be relieved from such penalties, the acts of intercession (*suffragia*) of the living faithful benefit them, namely the sacrifices of the Mass, prayers, alms and other works of piety which the faithful are wont to do for the other faithful according to the Church's practice.

2309 The souls of those who, after having received baptism, have
1305 incurred no stain of sin whatever, and those souls who, after having contracted the stain of sin, have been cleansed, either while in in their bodies or after having been divested of them as stated above, are received immediately (*mox*) into heaven, and see clearly God Himself, one and three, as He is, though some more perfectly than others, according to the diversity of merits.

1306 As for the souls of those who die in actual mortal sin or with original sin only, they go down immediately (*mox*) to hell *(in infernum),* to be punished however with different punishments.

THE GENERAL COUNCIL OF TRENT

TWENTY-FIFTH SESSION

DECREE ON PURGATORY (1563)

Luther had rejected the doctrine of indulgences in 1517. Soon after, he took objection to the doctrine of purgatory. In his first writings, however, he attacked this doctrine only indirectly, denying its scriptural foundation and raising doubts as regards the state of souls in purgatory and the possibility for them of expiation for sins. This first position of Luther is reflected in four propositions condemned by Pope Leo X in the Bull Exsurge Domine (1520) (cf. DS 1487-1490). Later on, as his position gradually hardened, Luther denied the existence of purgatory. This denial was in the logic of the system; expiation for sins contradicted the fundamental principles of the Reformation on salvation sola gratia.

The question of purgatory was on the agenda of the Council already in 1547. It was touched upon during the sixth session in the decree on justification (cf. n. 1980), and again during the twenty-second session in the doctrine on the sacrifice of the Mass (cf. nn. 1548, 1557). But, its explicit discussion was postponed till the last session which took place in 1563. At that moment, various reasons forced the Council fathers to wind up hurriedly the Council work. Several questions left pending were thus examined more at the disciplinary than at the doctrinal level. Before treating of the cult of saints (cf. nn. 1255ff) and of indulgences (cf. n. 1686), the twenty-fifth session devoted a decree to the question of purgatory, based on the Council's previous doctrine on the subject. This decree is notable for its sobriety. Though disciplinary rather than doctrinal in nature, it teaches again the existence of purgatory and the usefulness of prayers offered for the dead, as belonging to the Catholic faith; but it remains silent as regards the nature of purgatory.

2310 The Catholic Church, instructed by the Holy Spirit and in
1820 accordance with sacred Scripture and the ancient Tradition of the Fathers, has taught in the holy Councils and most recently in this ecumenical Council that there is a purgatory (cf. n. 1980), and that the souls detained there are helped by the acts of intercession (suffragia) of the faithful, and especially by the acceptable sacrifice of the altar (cf. nn. 1548, 1557). Therefore this holy Council commands the bishops to strive diligently that the sound doctrine of purgatory, handed down by the Holy Fathers and the sacred Councils, be believed by the faithful and that it be adhered to, taught and preached everywhere. But let the more difficult and subtle questions which do not make for edification and, for the most part, are not conducive to an increase of piety (cf. 1 Tim. 1.4), be excluded from the popular sermons to uneducated people. Likewise they should not permit opinions that are doubtful and tainted with error to be spread and exposed. As for those things that belong to the realm of curiosity or superstition, or smack of dishonourable gain, they should forbid them as scandalous and injurious to the faithful.

THE SECOND VATICAN GENERAL COUNCIL

The eschatological character of the Church comes to the foreground in the Second Vatican Council more than in earlier documents. This is due to the fact that the Church is conceived no longer primarily as an institution with static structures, but as the pilgrim People of God moving towards its heavenly destiny, and as the sacrament of salvation (LG 1, 9,48),containing already and effectively communicating God's saving grace, while still awaiting its last manifestation.

According to Vatican II, man can be understood only in relation to the final destiny of his whole being: made up of a body which "is to be raised again on the last day" and of a "spiritual and immortal" soul, he is one (GS 14) (cf. n. 421). Similarly, the whole of human history is considered as tending to its final goal which it will reach "in the Holy City, whose light shall be the glory of God, when the nations will walk in His light" (NA 1) (cf. n. 1019). Again, human solidarity and all human activity will attain their final destiny in Christ's heavenly kingdom (GS 32, 39). For Christ is not only the Alpha, but also the Omega, the fulfilment of all creation (GS 45) (cf. n. 669). It is in this cosmic perspective that the life of the Church herself is viewed as oriented towards the kingdom. The main eschatological text of the Council is chapter VIII of the Constitution Lumen Gentium on the eschatological nature of the Church (48-51). Unlike the original draft which was more individualistic, the final text is fully ecclesial. It pictures the entire pilgrim Church on its way to its final cosummation. Other texts corroborate the same approach. The earthly liturgy makes the Church "share in foretaste in that heavenly liturgy which is celebrated in the Holy City of Jersalem" (SC 8). The time of her missionary activity "lies between the first coming of the Lord and the second", and "tends towards the eschatological fulfilment (AG 9). Thus the eschatological doctrine of Vatican II opens up for the world and the Church the grandiose horizon of a final transfiguration into Christ's glory.

Symptomatic of the Council's approach is the meaning given to the mystery of death in the Constitution Gaudium et Spes. Death is the most anguishing question that is put to man: "It is in the face of death that the riddle of human existence becomes most acute" (GS 18). But, when the Council explains its meaning in the plan of God, it does not merely repeat the traditional doctrine of death as the punishment for sin (GS 18), but rather insists on its positive significance: in the light of the word of God, death is for man the decisive conformation to Christ's Paschal Mystery, associating him intimately with Christ's own death and resurrection (GS 22). Already defeated by Christ on the cross, the last enemy will be definitively vanquished by Him in the end of times (GS 39; cf. LG 49).

DOGMATIC CONSTITUTION *LUMEN GENTIUM* (1964)

(Eschatological character of our vocation in the Church)

2311   48. The Church, to which all of us are called in Christ Jesus and in which, through God's grace, we acquire holiness, will reach her consummation only in the glory of heaven, when the time will come for the restoration of all things *(cf. Acts 3.21)*, when, along with mankind, the whole universe—which is intimately related to man and achieves its goal through him—will be established in Christ *(cf. Eph. 1.10; Col. 1.20; 2 Pet. 3.10-13)*.

... The promised restoration which we are awaiting has already begun in Christ; it is carried on in the mission of the Holy Spirit, and through Him it continues in the Church in which faith teaches us the meaning also of our temporal existence....

Therefore, the final stage of time has already come upon us (*cf. 1 Cor. 10.11*). The renewal of the world is irrevocably determined and, in some real manner, it is anticipated in the present era.... However, until there will be the new heavens and the new earth in which justice will dwell (*cf. 2. Pet. 3.13*), the pilgrim Church, in her sacraments and institutions, which belong to the present era, bears the image of this world which is passing away, and she has her abode among the creatures who groan and are still in travail, awaiting the manifestation of the sons of God (*cf. Rom. 8.19-22*).

(Communion between the Church of heaven and the Church on earth)

2312 49. ...Until the Lord shall come in His majesty, and all His angels with Him (*cf. Mt. 25.31*), and, death having been destroyed, all things shall be subject to Him (*cf. 1 Cor. 15.26-27*), some of His disciples are pilgrims on earth, while others have died and are being purified, and still others are glorified, seeing "clearly God Himself, one and three, as He is" (*cf. n. 2309*). We all, however, in various ways and degrees share in the same love of God and neighbour, and we all sing the same hymn of glory to our God.

(The text continues as under n. 1689.)

(Relations between the pilgrim Church and the heavenly Church)

(2313) 50. *(In the life of the Church on earth the communion of saints is expressed by the intercessory prayers for the dead and in the veneration of the saints. The Church prays for the intercession of the saints, proposes them to the imitation of the faithful, derives from their lives, which show a secure path to perfect union with Christ, new inspiration for seeking the City that is to come. The veneration of the saints by the Church on earth and their intercession in heaven for the wayfarers manifests the bond of charity that unites all in Christ. This communion finds expression primarily in the sacred liturgy.)*

(Pastoral directives)

(2314) 51. *(The cult of the saints should be fostered according to the ancient tradition; yet, abuses and excesses must be avoided. The true cult of the saints consists not so much in the multiplicity of external acts, but rather in the intensity of an active love.)*

PASTORAL CONSTITUTION *GAUDIUM ET SPES* (1965)

(Death according to Christian faith)

2315 18. While in the face of death all imagination fails, the Church, taught by divine revelation, states that man was created by God for a happy goal beyond the reach of the miseries of this earthly life. In addition, our Christian faith teaches that bodily death—from which man would have been preserved had he not sinned (*cf. Wis. 1. 13; 2.23f; Rom. 5.21; 6.23; James 1.15*)—will be overcome by the all-powerful mercy of the Saviour, when man will be restored to the salvation lost through his own fault. God has called and still calls man to be united to Him with his whole being by an everlasting sharing in a divine life beyond all decay. Christ achieved this victory when, liberating man from death, He rose again to life (*cf. 1. Cor. 15.56f*). Thus, to any thoughtful man, the faith, when presented with its solid foundations, offers an answer to his anxiety about what the future holds for him. At the same time it offers him the possibility of being united in Christ with his loved ones who have already died, and gives him hope that they have already attained to true life with God.

(New earth and new heaven)

2316 39. We do not know the time for the consummation of the earth and of mankind (*cf. Acts 1.7*), nor do we know the manner in which the universe will be transformed. The form of this world, deformed by sin, passes away (*cf. 1 Cor. 7.31*); but we are taught that God is preparing a new dwelling place and a new earth, where justice will reign (*cf. 2 Cor. 5.2; 2 Pet. 3.13*) and whose happiness will fulfil and surpass all the longings for peace that arise in the hearts of men (*cf. 1 Cor. 2.9; Rev. 21.4-5*). Then, with death defeated, the sons of God will be raised up in Christ. What had been sown in weakness and corruption will be clothed with incorruptibility (*cf. 1 Cor. 15.42, 53*); charity and its works will remain (*cf. 1 Cor. 13.8; 3.14*), and this whole creation made by God for man's sake will be freed from the bondage of vanity (*cf. Rom 8.9-21*)...

For those values of human dignity, brotherly fellowship and freedom, all these noble fruits of nature and of our effort, which we shall spread over the earth in the Spirit of the Lord and according to His command, we shall find again later, cleansed of all stain, illuminated and transfigured, when Christ will hand over to the Father an eternal and universal Kingdom, "a kingdom of truth and life, of holiness and grace, of justice, love and peace."[1] Here on earth the kingdom is present already in mystery; at the coming of the Lord it will be brought to completion.

JOHN PAUL II

LETTER OF THE S. CONGREGATION FOR THE DOCTRINE OF THE FAITH ON CERTAIN QUESTIONS CONCERNING ESCHATOLOGY
(17 May 1979)

This document is concerned with the problems of eschatology arising mostly from new anthropological perspectives. While firmly insisting on the substance of the Christian doctrine on life after death, the resurrection of the whole person, the purification of the elect, and eternal reward or punishment, the document remains silent about modern controversies, e.g., the possibility of man's purification at the moment of his death or the eventual salvation of all men out of God's infinite mercy.

There is a noteworthy discrepancy between the text of the Osservatore Romano *(23 July 1979, pp. 7-8) and of the* Acta Apostolicae Sedis *(71 (1979) 939). N. 3 speaks about the personal subsistence of the "soul" after death, leaving open, according to the text in O.R., the possibility of an immediate "resurrection" of the whole person. The official text in* AAS, *however, qualifies the "human self" that lives on beyond death as "deprived for the present of the complement of its body" (interim tamen complemento sui corporis carens), thus maintaining the traditional view that the wholeness of the person after death, which includes the bodily existence, is delayed, presumably till the end of time. This change in the official text may point to an insecurity about the degree to which modern anthropology should be allowed to affect traditional theological thinking.*

(Man's condition after death)

2317 The Sacred Congregation, whose task is to advance and protect the doctrine of the faith, here wishes to recall what the Church teaches in the name of Christ, especially concerning what happens between the death of the Christian and the general resurrection.

1. The Church believes (cf. the Creed) in the resurrection of the dead.

2. The Church understands this resurrection as referring to the whole person; for the elect it is nothing other than the extension to human beings of the resurrection of Christ Himself.

3. The Church affirms that a spiritual element survives and

---

1. *Roman Missal,* Preface of the feast of Christ the King.

subsists after death, an element endowed with consciousness and will, so that the "human self" subsists, *though deprived for the present of the complement of its body.* To designate this element, the Church uses the word "soul", the accepted term in the usage of Scripture and Tradition. Although not unaware that this term has various meanings in the Bible, the Church thinks that there is no valid reason for rejecting it; moreover she considers that the use of some word as a vehicle is absolutely indispensable in order to support the faith of Christians.

4. The Church excludes every way of thinking or speaking that would render meaningless or unintelligible her prayers, her funeral rites and religious acts offered for the dead. All these are, in their substance, *loci theologici*.

5. In accordance with the Scriptures, the Church looks for "the glorious manifestation of Our Lord Jesus Christ" *(DV 4)*, believing it to be distinct and deferred with respect to the situation of people immediately after death.

6. In teaching her doctrine about man's destiny after death, the Church excludes any explanation that would deprive the Assumption of the Virgin Mary of its unique meaning, namely the fact that the bodily glorification of the Virgin is an anticipation of the glorification that is the destiny of all the other elect.

7. In fidelity to the New Testament and Tradition, the Church believes in the happiness of the just who will one day be with Christ. She believes that there will be eternal punishment for the sinner, who will be deprived of the sight of God, and that this punishment will have a repercussion on the whole being of the sinner. She believes in the possibility of a purification for the elect before they see God, a purification altogether different from the punishment of the damned. This is what the Church means when speaking of Hell and Purgatory.

When dealing with man's situation after death, one must especially beware of arbitrary imaginative representations: excess of this kind is a major cause of the difficulties that Christian faith often encounters. Respect must, however, be given to the images employed in the Scriptures. Their profound meaning must be discerned, while avoiding the risk of over-attenuating them, since this often empties of substance the realities designated by the images.

Neither Scripture nor theology provides sufficient light for a proper picture of life after death. Christians must firmly hold the two following essential points: on the one hand, they must believe in the fundamental continuity, thanks to the power of the Holy Spirit, between our present life in Christ and the future life (charity is the law of the Kingdom of God and our charity on earth will be the measure of our sharing in God's glory in heaven); on the other hand, they must be clearly aware of the radical difference between the present life and the future one, due to the fact that the economy of faith will be replaced by the economy of fulness of life; we shall be with Christ and "we shall see God" (cf. 1 Jn 3.2), and it is in these promises and marvellous mysteries that our hope essentially consists. Our imagination may be incapable of reaching these heights, but our heart does so instinctively and completely.

TABLES AND INDICES

CHRONOLOGICAL TABLE OF DOCUMENTS

(Figures refer to the numbers of the volume.)

c. 96	CLEMENT I, Letter to the Corinthians: 1701
?	The Dêr-Balizeh papyrus: 1
c. 215-217	The Apostolic Tradition of Hippolytus: 2
?	The Symbol of the Roman Order of baptism: 5
256	STEPHEN I, Letter to Cyprian, bishop of Carthage: 1401
262	DIONYSIUS, Letter to Dionysius of Alexandria: 301-303
c. 300-303	THE COUNCIL OF ELVIRA: 1402
325	The Symbol of Eusebius: 6
325	THE FIRST GENERAL COUNCIL OF NICAEA Symbol of Nicaea: 7-8, (304), (601) Canons: 1101, 1403, 1601-1602
c. 348	The Symbol of Cyril of Jerusalem: 9
360?	THE COUNCIL OF LAODICEA: (201)
374	The Symbol of Epiphanius: 10-11
381	THE FIRST GENERAL COUNCIL OF CONSTANTINOPLE Symbol of Constantinople: 12-13, 305, (602)
382	THE COUNCIL OF ROME, "Tome of Damasus": 306/1-24, 603/6-14
385	SIRICIUS, Letter to Himerius, bishop of Tarragona: 1404-1405
?	The Symbol of St Ambrose (*ob.* 397): 3
?	The "Faith of Damasus": 14-15
c. 404	The Symbol of Rufinus: 4
405	INNOCENT I, Letter *Consulenti Tibi* to Exsuperius, bishop of Toulouse: (202)
416	id., Letter to Decentius, bishop of Gubbio: 1406, 1603
417	id., Letter *In Requirendis* to the African bishops: 801
418	THE SIXTEENTH COUNCIL OF CARTHAGE: 501-(502), (1407), 1901-1906
428	CELESTINE I, Letter to the bishops of Vienna and Narbonne: 1604
431	THE GENERAL COUNCIL OF EPHESUS Second letter of Cyril of Alexandria to Nestorius: 604-605, (701) The Twelve Anathematisms of Cyril against Nestorius: 606/1-12

433	The formula of union between Cyril of Alexandria and the bishops of Antioch: 607-608
435-442?	The *Indiculus:* 503, 1907-1914
449	LEO THE GREAT, Letter to Flavian of Constantinople: 609-612
451	THE GENERAL COUNCIL OF CHALCEDON Symbol of Chalcedon: 613-616
452	LEO THE GREAT, Letter to Theodore, bishop of Frejus: 1605
459	id., Letter to the bishops of Roman rural districts: 1606
?	The Pseudo-Athanasian Symbol *Quicumque:* 16-17, (307)
?	GELASIUS I, Decree of Gelasius: 203
529	THE SECOND COUNCIL OF ORANGE: 504-505, 1915-1922
534	JOHN II, Letter to the Senate of Constantinople: 617, (702)
543	THE COUNCIL OF CONSTANTINOPLE, Anathematisms against the Origenists: 401/1-8, 618/2-3, 2301
553	VIGILIUS, *Constitutum I:* 619/1-5
553	THE SECOND GENERAL COUNCIL OF CONSTANTINOPLE Profession of faith: 204 Anathematisms against the three chapters: 620/1-10, 621-623
561	THE COUNCIL OF BRAGA, Anathematisms against the Priscillianists: 402/5-13
589	THE THIRD COUNCIL OF TOLEDO: 1607
590-604?	GREGORY THE GREAT, Letter to Abbot Mellitus: 1102
600	id., Letter to Eulogius, Patriarch of Alexandria: 624-626
c. 601	id., Letter to the bishops of Georgia: 1702
649	THE COUNCIL OF LATERAN: 205, 627/1-16, 703
675	THE ELEVENTH COUNCIL OF TOLEDO, Symbol of faith: (18), 308-316, 628-634, 2302
681	THE THIRD GENERAL COUNCIL OF CONSTANTINOPLE Defenition on the two wills and actions in Christ: 635-637
787	THE SECOND GENERAL COUNCIL OF NICAEA Definition on sacred images: 1251-1252 Anathematisms and canons: 206, 1001
793	HADRIAN I, Letter *Si Tamen Licet* addressed to the Spanish bishops: 638
796-797?	THE COUNCIL OF FRIULI, Profession of faith: 639

870	THE FOURTH GENERAL COUNCIL OF CONSTANTINOPLE Canon: 1253
1053	LEO IX, Letter *Congratulamini Vehementer* to Peter, patriarch of Antioch: 207
1076	GREGORY VII, Letter to Anzir, king of Mauritania: 1002
1079	THE COUNCIL OF ROME, Oath of Berengar of Tours: 1501
1130-43?	INNOCENT II, Letter to the bishop of Cremonia: 1408
1159-81?	ALEXANDER III, Letter to the archbishop of Salerno: (1801)
1201	INNOCENT III, Letter to Humbert, archbishop of Arles: 506, 1409-1410
1202	id., Letter *Cum Marthae Circa* to John, former archbishop of Lyons: 1502-1503
1208	id., Profession of faith prescribed to the Waldensians: 403, 640, 1301, 1411, 1504, 1703, 1802
1215	THE FOURTH LATERAN GENERAL COUNCIL Symbol of Lateran: 19-21, (404), (641), (802), (1505), (2303) Other chapters: 317-320, 1103, 1201-1202, 1609
1274	THE SECOND GENERAL COUNCIL OF LYONS Constitution on the Blessed Trinity and the Catholic faith: 321 "Profession of faith of Michael Palaeoiogus": 22-29, (642), (803), (1302), (2304)
1302	BONIFACE VIII, Bull *Unam Sanctam:* 804
1312	THE GENERAL COUNCIL OF VIENNA Constitution *Fidei Catholicae:* 405 Decree: 1104
1322	JOHN XXII, Bull *Ad Conditorem:* 2001
1327	id., Condemnation of errors of Marsilius of Padua on the Constitution of the Church: 805/2-4
1329	id., Errors of Eckhart on the relation between God and world and man: 406/1-28
1336	BENEDICT XII, Constitution *Benedictus Deus:* 2305-2307
1341	id., Libellus *Cum Dudum:* 407
1343	CLEMENT VI, Jubilee Bull *Unigenitus Dei Filius:* 634, 1681-1683
1400	BONIFACE IX, Bull *Sacrae Religionis:* 1704
1415	THE GENERAL COUNCIL OF CONSTANCE Decree *Haec Sancta:* 806 Condemnation of the errors of Wyclif and Hus: 807/8-37, 808/1-15, 1303, 1610

Decree on communion under the species of bread alone: 1506

1418   MARTIN V, Bull *Inter Cunctas:* 1254, 1304, 1507/16-17, 1611/20-25, 1684/26-27

1434   THE GENERAL COUNCIL OF BASEL
Decree on Jews and neophytes: 1105

THE GENERAL COUNCIL OF FLORENCE
1439   Decree for the Greeks: 322-324, 809, 1508, 2308-2309

1439   Decree for the Armenians: 1305-1308, 1412-1418, 1509-1511, 1612-1613, 1705, 1803

1442   Decree for the Jacobites: 208, 325-326, 408-409, 644-646, 810, 1003-1005, 1419

1477   SIXTUS IV, Constitution *Cum Praeexcelsa:* 704

1513   THE FIFTH LATERAN GENERAL COUNCIL
Bull *Apostolici Regiminis:* 410

1520   LEO X, Bull *Exsurge Domine.* Errors of Luther condemned: (811), 1309, 1614/5-14, 1685/17-22, 1923/2-36

1528   THE COUNCIL OF PARIS (Senonense): 209

THE GENERAL COUNCIL OF TRENT
1546   Session IV:
Decree on sacred books and on traditions to be received: 210-215

1546   Session V:
Decree on original sin: 507-513, 705
Decree on teaching and preaching the word of God: 1203-1205

1547   Session VI:
Decree on justification: 647, 706, 1924-1983, (2002)

1547   Session VII:
Decree on the sacraments: 1310-1323
Canons on the sacrament of baptism: 1420-1433
Canons on the sacrament of confirmation: 1434-1436

1551   Session XIII:
Decree on the most holy Eucharist: 1512-1536

1551   Session XIV:
Doctrine on the sacrament of penance: 1615-1634
Doctrine on the sacrament of extreme unction: 1635-1640
Canons on the sacraments of penance and extreme unction: 1641-1655, 1658-1659

1555   PAUL IV, Constitution *Cum Quorumdam Hominum:* 648, 707

THE GENERAL COUNCIL OF TRENT

1562   Session XXI:
        Doctrine on communion under both species and on
        communion of little children: 1324, (1537-1540),
        1541-1544

1562   Session XXII:
        Doctrine on the most holy sacrifice of the Mass:
        1545-1563

1563   Session XXIII:
        Doctrine on the sacrament of Order: 1706-1721

1563   Session XXIV:
        Doctrine on the sacrament of matrimony: 1804-1819

1563   Session XXV:
        Decree on purgatory: 2310
        Decree on the invocation, the veneration and the
        relics of saints and on sacred images: 1255-1257
        Decree on indulgences: 1686

1564   PIUS IV, Bull *Iniunctum Nobis,* Profession of faith: 30-38

1567   PIUS V, Bull *Ex Omnibus Afflictionibus.* Condemned
        propositions of Michael de Bay: 514/26-49, 708,
        1984/21-79, 1985/13-63, 1986/20-74, 1987/27-66,
        1988/16-38

1653   INNOCENT X, Constitution *Cum Occasione.* Errors of
        Cornelius Jansen condemned: 1989/1-5

1659   Instruction of the S. Congregation *de Propaganda Fide*
        to the Vicars apostolic of Tonkin and Cochinchina:
        1106-1110

1665   Errors of Laxist morality condemned by the Holy Office:
        2005

1679   Errors of Laxist morality condemned by the Holy Office:
        2006/3, 2201/9-50

1687   INNOCENT XI, Constitution *Caelestis Pastor,* Propositions
        of Michael Molinos condemned: 2007/1-14

1690 Aug.   Decree of the Holy Office: 2008/2

1690 Dec.   Decree of the Holy Office, Jansenist errors condemned:
             1325, 2009/2-3

1713   CLEMENT XI, Constitution *Unigenitus Dei Filius.* Propositions
        of Pasquier Quesnel condemned: 1990/1-59, 1991/44-47

1794   PIUS VI, Constitution *Auctorem Fidei:* 649, (812)

1824   LEO XII, Encyclical Letter *Ubi Primum:* 1006

1832   GREGORY XVI, Encyclical Letter *Mirari Nos Arbitramur:*
        1007

1844	Promise signed by L.E. Bautain: 101-105
1846	Pius IX, Encyclical Letter *Qui Pluribus:* 106-111, 1008
1854	id., Bull *Ineffabilis Deus:* 709
1854	id., Allocution *Singulari Quadam:* 813, 1009-1011
1855	The fourth proposition signed by A. Bonnetty: 105
1862	Pius IX, Encyclical Letter *Amantissimus:* 1206
1863	id., Encyclical Letter *Quanto Conficiamur Moerore:* 814, 1012
1864	id., Encyclical Letter *Quanta Cura:* 815-816
1864	id., *Syllabus* of condemned errors: 112/2-11, 411/1-2, 1013/15-79, 2010/56-63
1868	id., Letter *Iam vos Omnes* to Protestants and other non-Catholics: 901-902

THE FIRST VATICAN GENERAL COUNCIL

1870	Session III: Dogmatic Constitution *Dei Filius* on the Catholic faith: 113-140, 216-219, 327-331, 412-418, (817)
1870	Session IV: Dogmatic Constitution *Pastor Aeternus* on the Church of Christ: 818-840
1873	Pius IX, Encyclical Letter *Quartus Supra* to the Armenians: 903
1875	Collective Declaration of the German Hierarchy: 841
1880	Leo XIII, Encyclical Letter *Arcanus Divinae Sapientiae:* 1820-1823
1885	id., Encyclical Letter *Mortale Dei:* 1014-1015
1887	Errors of A. Rosmini-Serbati condemned by the Holy Office: 141-142
1888	Leo XIII; Encyclical Letter *Libertas Praestantissimum:* 2011-2014
1891	id., Encyclical Letter *Rerum Novarum:* 2101-2105.
1891	id., Encyclical Letter *Octobri Mense:* 710
1893	id., Encyclical Letter *Providentissimus Deus:* 220-227
1894	id., Encyclical Letter *Praeclara Gratulationis:* 904-906
1894	id., Constitution *Orientalium Dignitas:* 1207
1896	id., Bull *Apostolicae Curae* on Anglican Ordinations: 1722-1728
1897	id., Encyclical Letter *Divinum Illud:* 1993-1994
1899	id., Letter *Testem Benevolentiae* to Cardinal Gibbons, archbishop of Baltimore: 2015-2018

1903	Pius X, Motu Proprio *Tra le Sollecitudini:* 1208
1904	id., Encyclical Letter *Ad Diem Illum:* 712
1905	id., Decree *Sacra Tridentina:* 1209/1-4
1907	Decree *Lamentabili* of the Holy Office. Articles of Modernism condemned: 228/1-24, 650/27-38, 846/6-56, 1326/39-41, 1437/42-44, 1660/46-48, 1729/49-50
1907	Pius X, Encyclical Letter *Pascendi:* 1327
1910	Oath against the errors of Modernism: 143, 143/1-13
1912	Pius X, Apostolic Constitution *Tradita Ab Antiquis:* 1210
1918	Decree of the Holy Office: 651/1-3
1919	Benedict XV, Apostolic Letter *Maximum Illud:* 1111-1114
1920	id., Encyclical Letter *Spiritus Paraclitus:* 229-231
1921	id., Apostolic Letter *Sodalitatem Nostrae Dominae:* 1661
1925	Pius XI, Encyclical Letter *Quas Primas:* 652-653, 1211
1926	id., Encyclical Letter *Rerum Ecclesiae:* 1115-1118
1928	id., Encyclical Letter *Mortalium Animos:* 907
1928	id., Encyclical Letter *Miserentissimus Redemptor:* 654-659
1928	**id., Apostolic Constitution** *Divini Cultus:* 1212
1930	id., Encyclical Letter *Casti Connubii:* 1824-1833, 2202-2208
1931	id., Encyclical Letter *Quadragesimo Anno:* 2019, 2106-2111/3
1937	id., Letter *Missionalium Rerum:* 1213
1939	Pius XII, Encyclical Letter *Summi Pontificatus:* 1119-1121, 2020
1941	id., Discourse on the fiftieth anniversary of *Rerum Novarum:* 2112
1943	id., Encyclical Letter *Mystici Corporis:* 660-661, 847-853, 1214-1215, 1328-1330, 1564-1565, 1662, 1995-1997, 2021
1943	id., Encyclical Letter *Divino Afflante Spiritu:* 232-236
1944	id., Address to the directors of Pontifical Mission Works: 1122-1123
1944	id., Apostolic Constitution *Episcopalis Consecrationis:* 1730
1945	id., Christmas Message: 1124-1125
1946	id., Decree *Spritus Sancti Munera* on the minister of confirmation: (1438)
1947	id., Encyclical Letter *Mediator Dei:* 1216-(1226), 1331-1333, 1566-1570, 1731-1736
1947	id., Apostolic Constitution *Sacramentum Ordinis:* 1737
1948	Letter of the Biblical Commission to Cardinal Suhard, archbishop of Paris: 237

| 1949 | Letter of the Holy Office to the archbishop of Boston: 854-857 |

| 1949 | Instruction *Ecclesia Catholica* of the Holy Office: 908 |

| 1950 | THE FIRST PLENARY COUNCIL OF INDIA: 1016-1017 |

| 1950 | PIUS XII, Encyclical Letter *Humani Generis:* 144-148, 238-239, 419-420, 858-859, 1571 |

| 1950 | id., Apostolic Constitution *Munificentissimus Deus:* 713-715 |

| 1951 | id., Encyclical Letter *Evangelii Praecones:* 1126-1129 |

| 1951 | id., Encyclical Letter *Sempiternus Rex:* 662-663 |

| 1951 | id., Allocution to midwifes: 2209-2212 |

| 1955 | id., Encyclical Letter *Musicae Sacrae Disciplina:* 1227 |

| 1956 | Instruction of the Holy Office on "Situation Ethics": 2022-2025 |

| 1956 | PIUS XII, Encyclical Letter *Haurietis Aquas:* 664-667 |

| 1956 | id., Allocution to the Second World Congress of fertility and sterility: 2213 |

| 1956 | id., Discourse at the International Congress on pastoral liturgy: 1228, 1572-1573 |

| 1957 | id., Encyclical Letter *Fidei Donum:* 1130-1131 |

| 1958 | Instruction of the S. Congregation of rites on sacred music and the sacred liturgy: 1229-1230 |

| 1959 | JOHN XXIII, Encyclical Letter *Princeps Pastorum:* 1132-1135 |

| 1961 | id., Encyclical Letter *Mater et Magistra:* 2113-2123 |

| 1963 | id., Encyclical Letter *Pacem in Terris*: 2026-2042, 2124-2140/2 |

	THE SECOND VATICAN GENERAL COUNCIL
1963	Session II:
	Constitution *Sacrosanctum Concilium:* 1231-1234, 1258, 1334-1335, 1574-1575, 1663-1666

| 1964 | Instruction of the Biblical Commission *Sancta Mater Ecclesia:* 240-245 |

| 1964 | PAUL VI, Encyclical Letter *Ecclesiam Suam:* 155-159, 1029-1030 |

	THE SECOND VATICAN GENERAL COUNCIL
1964	Session III:
	Dogmatic Constitution *Lumen Gentium:* 716-718, (860-882), 1018, 1136, 1439, 1576, 1667, 1738-1741, 1834, 1998-1999, 2043-2047, 2311-(2314)
	Decree *Orientalium Ecclesiarum* : 1235
	Decree *Unitatis Redintegratio:* 909-914

| 1964 | PAUL VI, Address to representatives of various religions: 1031-1032 |

1965   id., Encyclical Letter *Mysterium Fidei:* 1577-1580

THE SECOND VATICAN GENERAL COUNCIL
1965   Session IV:
     Declaration *Nostra Aetate:* 424, 1019-1022
     Dogmatic Constitution *Dei Verbum:* 149-(153), 246-257
     Decree *Apostolicam Actuositatem:* 1440
     Declaration *Dignitatis Humanae:* 2048-2050
     Decree *Ad Gentes:* 1023-1026, 1137-1144, 1741a
     Pastoral Constitution *Gaudium et Spes:* (154), 421-423, 668-669, 1027-1028, 1145, 1835-1840, 2051-2061, 2141-2144, 2214-2219, 2315-2316

1966   PAUL VI, Address to theologians at the Symposium on original sin: 516

1967   id., Apostolic Constitution *Indulgentiarum Doctrina:* 1687-1689, 1690/1-5

1967   id., Encyclical Letter *Populorum Progressio:* 2145-2153

1967   Directory Concerning Ecumenical Matters, Part I, *Ad Totam Ecclesiam:* 1440a-1440b

1967   Instruction *Eucharisticum Mysterium* of the S. Congregation of Rites: 1581-1587

1967   PAUL VI, Motu Proprio *Sacrum Diaconatus Ordinem:* (1742)

1967   id., Encyclical Letter *Sacerdotalis Coelibatus:* 1743

1967   id., Letter *Africarum Terrarum* to the hierarchy and the peoples of Africa: 1033-1034

1968   id., Apostolic Constitution *Pontificalis Romani:* (1744)

1968   id., Profession of faith: 39/1-23

1968   id., Encyclical Letter *Humanae Vitae:* 1841, 2220-2225

1970   General Instruction on the Roman Missal of the S. Congregation for divine worship: 1588-1589

1970   PAUL VI, Mission Sunday Message: 1146-1148

1970   id., Radio Message to the governments and peoples of Asia: 1035

1971   id., Apostolic Letter *Octogesima Adveniens:* 2153a-2158

1971   id., Apostolic Constitution *Divinae Consortium Naturae:* 1441-1442

1971   THE THIRD SYNOD OF BISHOPS IN ROME
     De Sacerdotio Ministeriali: 1745-1746
     De Iustitia in Mundo: 2159-2164

1972   Declaration *Mysterium Filii Dei* of the S. Congregation for the doctrine of the faith: 333, 670-671

1972   Statement by the Secretariat for Promoting Christian Unity, *In Quibus Rerum Circumstantiis:* 915

1972	PAUL VI, Apostolic Letter *Ministeria Quaedam:* 1747
1972	id., Apostolic Letter *Ad Pascendum:* (1748)
1972	id., Apostolic Constitution *Sacram Unctionem Infirmorum:* 1668
1973	‹Declaration *Mysterium Ecclesiae* of the S. Congregation for the doctrine of the faith: 160-162, 883, 1749-1750
1973	The New *Ordo Paenitentiae:* 1669-1671
1974	PAUL VI, Apostolic Exhortation *Marialis Cultus:* 719-720
1974	id., Bull of Induction of the Holy Year 1975: 2165
1974	Declaration *De Abortu Procurato* of the S. Congregation for the doctrine of the faith: 2226-2227
1974	THE FOURTH SYNOD OF BISHOPS IN ROME *De Evangelizatione Mundi Hodierni:* 2166
1975	PAUL VI, Apostolic Exhortation *Evangelii Nuntiandi:* 672-673, 884-885, 1036, 1149-(1157), 1259, 1336, 1751, 2167-2171
1975	Declaration *De Persona Humana* of the S. Congregation for the doctrine of the faith: 2062-2063, 2228-2232
1976	S. Congregation for Catholic Education on Theological Formation of Future Priests: 258
1976	Declaration of the S. Congregation for the doctrine of the the faith, *Inter Insigniores:* 1752
1977	Decree *Circa Impotentiam* of the S. Congregation for the doctrine of the faith: 1842
1979	JOHN PAUL II, Address to the Third General Assembly of Latin American Bishops: 425-426, 674-676
1979	id., Eycyclical Letter *Redemptor Hominis:* 427-430, 517, 677-679, 886, 1037-1039, 1672, 2064, 2172-2173
1979	id., Letter to All Priests of the Church: 1753
1979	id., Apostolic Constitution *Sapientia Christiana:* 163
1979	Letter of the S. Congregation for the doctrine of the faith on Certain Questions Concerning Eschatology: 2317
1979	JOHN PAUL II, Discourse at the Liturgy in St George's at Phanar: 916-921
1980	id., Homily at the Conclusion of the Particular Synod of the Dutch Bishops in Rome: 1754
1980	id., Letter to All the Bishops of the Church, *Dominicae Cenae:* 1590
1980	id., Address to the Bishops of Zaïre: 1237-1239
1980	Declaration on Euthanasia of the S. Congregation for the doctrine of the faith: 2233-2235

1980	JOHN PAUL II, Address to Workmen in São-Paulo: 1158-1159
1980	id., Homily at the Inaugural Mass of the National Eucharistic Congress at Fortaleza: 1591
1980	Instruction on Infant Baptism, *Pastoralis Actio,* of the S. Congregation for the doctrine of the faith: 1443-1446
1980	JOHN PAUL II, Address to Scientists: 164-170
1980	id., Homily to the Diaspora Catholics of Osnabrück: 922
1980	id., Address to the Evangelical Church Council of Germany: 923-926
1980	id., Address to the German Episcopal Conference: 927
1980	id., Encyclical Letter *Dives in Misericordia:* 2174
1981	id., Message to the People of Asia: 1040
1981	id., Encyclical Letter *Laborem Exercens:* 2175-2180
1981	id., Apostolic Exhortation *Familiaris Consortio:* 1843-1844, 2181, 2236

BIBLICAL INDEX

(For the scriptural texts mentioned in the documents, references indicate in ordinary characters the marginal numbers of the documents. For scriptural texts mentioned in the introductions, the references indicate the page numbers; these are printed here in italics.)

Genesis (Gen)

1.26	427,677,2051
1.26-30	517
1.27	2051
1.28	428, 1826, 1840, 2147
2.18	1840
2.23f	1804
2.24	2210
3.6-13	677
3.15	150, 1637
3.16ff	1630
3.22	617
4.4	1547
8.20	1547
12.2	150
12.8	1547
14.18	1546
22	1547
22.12	624
49.10	1926
49.18	1926

Exodus (Ex)

3.14	39/2
12.1ff	1546
20.13	2206
20.17	1626
33.11	149

Leviticus (Lev)

18.6ff	1810

Numbers (Num)

12.14f	1630
20.11f	1630

Deuteronomy (Deut)

22.11	1103
28.66	617

Ruth (Ruth)

1.16	317

1 Samuel (1 Sam)

2.3	135
7.3	1931

2 Samuel (2 Sam)

12.13f	1630

1 Kings (1 Kings)

8.46	1905
19.8	1524

Job (Job)

37.7	1905

Psalms (Ps)

2.8	1144
8.6	677
30(29)10	1115
33(32)6	14
36(35)6	1009
45(44)13f	1207
51(50)4	1672
51(50)17	1944
78(77)25	1524
84(83)7	1937
94(93)10	1902
97(96)7	1520
103(102)3f	1914
103(102)14	1615

104(103)30 . | 14
110(109)4 | 1546
111(110)4 | 1515
119(118)112 | 1940
135(134)15ff | 1257
143(142)2 | 1905
147(146)5 | 313

Proverbs (Prov)

8.35 (Sept) | 1916
9.1 | 609

Song of Solomon (Song)

6.3 | 1710

The Wisdom of Solomon (Wis)

1.13 | 2315
2.23 | 2051
2.23f | 2315
7.14 | 1681
7.26 | 315
8.1 | 413, 424, 1019

Sirach (Sir)

1.27 | 1931
2.12 | 1103
15.14 | 2053
17.3-10 | 2051
18.22 | 1937

Isaiah (Is)

1.6 | 1681
11.12 | 123, 1574
38.15 | 1645
40.8 | 257
48.16 | 633
53.4f | 1687
59.1 | 1011
64.6 | 1925
65.1 | 1915

Lamentations (Lam)

4.4 | 1554

5.21 | 1929

Baruch (Bar)

3.38 | 149

Ezekiel (Ez)

18.20 | 504
18.30 | 1616
18.31 | 1622
33.12 | 1604
33.16 | 1604

Daniel (Dan)

7.13f | 652
9.5 | 1905
9.15 | 1905
9.20 | 1905

Jonah (Jonah)

3 | 1624

Zechariah (Zech)

1.3 | 1929

Malachi (Mal)

1.11 | 657, 1547, 1564, 1731
3.8 | 617
4.2 | 1924

Matthew (Mt)

2.11 | 1520
3.2 | 1631, 1944
3.8 | 1631, 1944
4.4 | 1202
4.8 | 675
4.17 | 1631, 1944
5.17 | 253
5.28 | 1626
5.48 | 39/6, 320
6.11 | 1524
6.12 | 1905, 1906, 1938
6.13 | 1656, 1914
7.1f | 1027
7.14 | 1002

9.2	1931
9.11	1662
10.22	122, 1942, 1946
10.42	1948
11.21	1631
11.25	131
11.29	2016
11.30	110, 1938
13.25	1512
15.11	1004
16.16	674, 819, 917
16.17	1920
16.17-19	819
16.18	832
16.19	1614/11, 1625, 1633, 1686, 1708
18.17	849
18.18	1625, 1627, 1633, 1650, 1686
18.20	1331, 1334
19.4	1840
19.6	1805, 1835
19.9ff	1809
19.11ff	1817
19.17	1934
22.11ff	1523
22.21	675
22.29	1502
22.37-40	2052
24.13	122, 1942
24.36	672
25.31	2312
25.41	810, 1005
26.26	1515, 1517
26.26ff	1514, 1519, 1520
28.17	1520
28.18	2060
28.19	1, 67, 854, 301, 1931
28.19f	1
28.20	818

Mark (Mk)

1.10	400
2.5	1672, 1931
2.16	1662
6.13	1636
10	1814
10.9	1805
12.17	675
13.32	624
14.22	1517
14.22ff	1514, 1519
16.15	1018, 1236
16.20	301

Luke (Lk)

1.28	716
1.38	716, 719
1.78	1524
2.19	246
2.51	246
4.5	675
4.17-21	400
4.18	2166
4.43	1149
6.37f	1027
10.16	853, 858, 884
11.41	2103
13.5	1616
15.2	1662
15.22	1934
16.19-31	2056
19.6	1922
20.22f	1708
22.19	1546, 1556, 1581, 1708
22.19f	1514, 1519
22.32	836, 917
23.43	1922
24.19	1202
24.27	253

John (Jn)

1.1	626
1.1-18	151
1.3	150, 626, 2060
1.9	1002
1.14	302, 610, 629, 2060
1.14-16	660

1.17	131, 710	15.15	1937
1.29	510	15.26f	*400*
1.42	819	16.13	677, 1998
2.26	1039	'16.24	39/23, 2007/14
3.5	511, 1412, 1421, 1443, 1928	17.2	660
3.6	1994	17.3	*xxvii*, 95
3.8	1039	17.4	151
3.16	517	17.18	1330
3.27	1921	17.20ff	818
3.34	151, 851	17.22	320
4.14	1947, 1998	17.22f	317
4.24	1115	17.23	658, 908
5.36	151	18.36	39/20, 675
6.24	1034	19.34	1509
6.28f	*31*	20.21	818, 853, 1330, 1732
6.38	635	20.22	621, 851, 853
6.48ff	1524	20.22f	1617, 1643, 1739, 1943
6.52	(1537)	20.23	1625, 1627, 1633, 1650
6.54	(1537)	20.28	621
6.55	(1537), 1920	21.15	819
6.57	1515, (1537)	21.17	804, 819
6.59	(1537)		
7.38f	1998	*Acts of the Apostles (Acts)*	
8.11	1672	1.7	672, 1024, 2316
8.32	2064	1.8	*400*, 1739
10.1	1712	2	*400*
10.16	804, 1574	2.4	1104, 1739
10.29	319	2.14-39	*1*
10.30	303	2.33	*1*
10.36	1740	2.36	*1*, 2060
11.52	1574	2.38	1616, 1930, 1931
13.3	626	2.42-47	1738
13.35	1115, 1590	2.43	1138
14.6	617, 1021	3.12-26	*1*
14.9	151	3.15	617
14.10f	302	3.21	2311
14.11	303	4.8-12	*1*
14.14	1215	4.12	510
14.23	1938, 1994	4.32	317
14.26	1512	5.29	2127
15.5	1329, 1903, 1919, 1947	5.29-32	*1*
15.9f	2021	6.5	1708
15.12	1115	8.14-17	1406, 1417
15.14f	149	9.1	659

9.5	659	5.20	39/10
9.20	1	5.21	2315
10.3	1922	6.4	512, 1150
10.34-43	1	6.4f	656
10.36	1	6.9	1517, 1566
10.38	1333	6.12ff	512
13.16-41	1	6.13	1937
13.33	1	6.16	504
14.17	424, 1019	6.19	1937
15.28	921	6.20	1925
15.29	1004	6.22	1938
17.22-31	1039	6.23	2315
17.25-28	1018	7.7	512
17.26	424, 1019	7.14-20	512
17.27	1023	7.24	1911
17.28	1632	8.1	512
20.24	1739	8.4	512
20.28	617, 827, 1711	8.9	851
		8.9f	1995
Romans (Rom)		8.9-21	2316
		8.10f	1998
1.4	1	8.12f	1942
1.5	152	8.14-17	851
1.16	673, 1150	8.15	1928
1.19f	150	8.15f	1998
1.20	113, 131, 143/1	8.17	512, 1631, 1667, 1939
1.21	1018	8.19	517
1.25	1018	8.19-22	517, 2311
2.1-11	1027	8.22	517
2.5	1631, 2026	8.26	1040, 1998
2.6	1949	8.29	2016
2.6f	150, 424, 1019	8.29-30	677
2.14-16	2052	9.4f	1018
3.22	1935	9.30	1926
3.23	923	10.3	1947
3.24	1930, 1935	10.9	1
3.25	1926	10.17	1930
5.2	1938	10.20	1915
5.5	1933	11.6	1935
5.10	647, 1631, 1932	11.28f	1018
5.11	677	12.1	109, 119, 656, 1728
5.11-21	517	12.5	317, 847, 2019, 2021
5.12	505, *137*, 509, 511, 1412, 1925	13.1	2125
5.12-19	420	14.4	1942

14.10-12	27, 1027	9.22	1213
14.13	923	9.24-27	1939
14.19	926	10.11	2311
15.16	1739	10.12	1942
16.17f	1006	10.13	1816
16.18	1945	10.21	1547
16.25f	253	10.22	1004
16.26	152, 883	11.3	1515
		11.23	1546

1 Corinthians (1 Cor)

		11.23ff	1514
1.10	1515	11.24	1515, 1546, 1556
1.18	1150	11.24ff	1519
1.23	1418	11.26	1515, 1581, 1740
1.24	302	11.28	1332, 1522
1.30	510, 643, 1681	11.29	1522
1.31	1632, 1948	11.34	1324
2.4	1150	12.3	1, 1920
2.7-10	131	12.4	1998
2.8	617	12.7	1999
2.9	114, 2316	12.11	1932, 1999
3.8	317	12.12	1618
3.14	2316	12.12-27	1689
3.16	1256, 1998	12.13	849
3.17	1631, 1944	12.25	2021
4.1	1324, 1739	12.26	659, 2019
4.5	1949	12.27	659
4.7	1918, 1921	12.29	1710
4.15	1759	12.30	1104
5.12	1618	13.8	2316
6.9f	1945	15.3f	1
6.11	1932	15.3-6	1
6.12	1004	15.10	1911, 1918
6.17	317	15.22	1925
6.19	1256, 1998	15.24	2302
7	1802, 1814	15.26f	2312
7.7	1834	15.42	2316
7.25	1921	15.53	2316
7.25f	1817	15.56	2315
7.31	39/20, 2316	15.58	1946
7.38	1817		
7.40	1817		

2 Corinthians (2 Cor)

8.1	1902	1.3	1926
8.6	5, 7, 617	3.5	1631, 1919
9.16	1139, 1149	3.8f	1739

3.14-16	253
3.17	851
3.18	851
4.10	656
4.16	1937
4.17	1948
5.2	2316
5.6f	132
5.8	1689
5.10	2053, 2302, 2307
5.15	1927
5.17	1150
5.18f	1021
5.21	634
6.3ff	1942
6.16	1256
7.10	1944
10.5f	152
10.17	1632, 1948
12.14f	1213
13.13	1

Galatians (Gal)

1.8	674
2.20	668, 1669
3.27	510, 1619
3.28	2044
4.4	620/3, 1926
4.5	1926
4.6	851, 1998
4.6f	851
5.1	430
5.6	120, 1523, 1934
5.13	430
5.14	2052
5.22	1998
5.24	656, 2016
6.14	1632
6.15	1150, 1934

Ephesians (Eph)

1.3-14	*1, 2*
1.8	677, 851

1.9	149
1.10	*115*, 669, 1926, 2060, 2311
1.13	1932
2.3	1626, 1925
2.4	647, 1615, 1932
2.8	673, 1917, 1921
2.14	1002
2.18	149, 1998
2.19	1827, 1937
3.8	1036
3.15	308
3.19	921
4.4-6	*5, 7*
4.5	804, 849, 1010, 2044
4.7	851
4.11	1710
4.11f	1998
4.13	1574
4.14	507
4.15	1947
4.15f	658
4.16	1684
4.22f	512
4.23-24	1150
4.30	1631, 1944
5.2	606/10
5.23	1515
5.25	884, 1669, 1806, 1836
5.31	621
5.32	1803, 1806, 1831, 1834
6.12	1911

Philippians (Phil)

1.1	1708
1.6	1917, 1921
1.29	1917, 1921
2.6-11	*1*
2.7	603/14, 630, 662
2.8	853, 2016
2.11	*1*
2.12	1942
2.13	1914, 1916, 1942
4.13	1632

Colossians (Col)

1.10	1012
1.12	124, 1927
1.13	853, 1546
1.13f	1927
1.15	149, 668
1.15f	115
1.16	679
1.18	847
1.19	660
1.20	677, 2311
1.24	654, 1667, 1689
2.3	660
2.6	1
2.8	134
2.13	654
3.5	1937
3.9	1103
3.9f	512, 1150
3.11	2044
3.14	2001, 2019
3.16	246

1 Thessalonians (1 Thes)

2.13	1999
5.1-2	672

1 Timothy (1 Tim)

1.4	2310
1.17	149, 713
2.4	124, 424, 1002, 1018, 1019, 1115
2.5	611, 273, 1215, 1255, 1605, 1689, 489, 1740
3.6f	1101
3.8ff	1708
3.15	1514
3.16	1
4.4	1004
4.14	1638, 1709, 1739
4.15	1750
5.22	1633
6.14	151
6.16	39/2
6.17	2103
6.20	134

2 Timothy (2 Tim)

1.6	1750
1.6f	1709, 1739
2.5	512
2.11f	1667
3.5	1630
4.7f	1946

Titus (Tit)

1.15	1004
2.12	1938
2.13	151
3.6	1669
3.7	1932

Hebrews (Heb)

1.1f	113, 151
1.6	1520
2.14	**508**
2.21f	**1574**
3.1	606/10
4.13	413
4.14	1
4.15	614
4.16	1548
5.1	656, 657
5.1-4	1740
5.1-5	1738
5.1-10	1740
5.3	657
5.7	619/5
5.8	619/5
5.8f	1939
6.10	1946
7.11	1546
7.12ff	1707
7.24	1546, 1740
7.27	1546
9.11-28	1740
9.12	643, 1681

9.14	1548
9.14-28	1740
9.27	1548
10.14	1546
10.23	124
10.29	1631
10.35	1946
11	1921
11.1	118
11.6	122, 507, 857, 1139, 1931, 1935
11.26	1940
12.2	124, 1924
13.8	2016
13.14	39/20, 1574
13.15	1999

James (James)

1.15	2315
1.17	1921
2.17	1934
2.22	1937
2.24	1937
3.2	1905, 1949
5.3	1631
5.14	1656
5.14f	19 n.1, 446, 1603, 1613, 1636, 1660/48
5.14-16	1667
5.15	1637
5.16	1625

1 Peter (1 Pet)

1.3	1942
1.18f	643, 1681
1.23	1138
1.23-25	257
2.2-9	1441
2.4-10	1440, 1738
2.9	124, 657, 489
2.21	1105
2.21f	1687
2.25	818
3.15	1738

4.13	1667
5.1-4	1746
5.8	1635

2 Peter (2 Pet)

1.4	149, 656
1.10	1939
1.19	119
2.19	504
3.10-13	2311
3.13	2180, 2311, 2316

1 John (1 Jn)

1.8	1904
1.9	1625, 1904
1.10	911
2.1f	1631
2.2	1926
2.20	1999
2.27	1999
3.2	39/22, 1010, 2317
4.7	1902
4.8	39/2, 2060
4.14	883
4.19	1669
5.3	1938
5.7	317
5.8	317

Jude (Jude)

3	917, 1999

Revelation (Rev)

1.6	1738
2.5	1944
5.9f	1738
12.21f	669
14.13	1947
17.15	1509
21.1	2180
21.4f	2316
21.5	1150
21.23f	424, 1019
22.11	1937
22.17	1998

ANALYTICAL AND ONOMASTIC INDEX

(For the main topics this index refers in bold characters to the page numbers of the analytical tables of the various chapters. Italics indicate page numbers of the volume and ordinary characters its marginal numbers.)

Aachen, Synod of—:*9*
ABELARD: *176*
abortion: **661**
absolution: **447**
Acacian Schism:*216*
acculturation, cf. adaptation
activity, human—: *422,* 2059f
Acts of the Apostles: 621, 301, 1417
Adam: *39/9,* 420, **134,** *135,* 501, 503, 504, 505, 516, 668, 708, 716, 1129, 1805, 1927, 1934, 1955
adaptation, liturgical—: *336,* **336,** *352;* missionary—: *302,* **303**
adoptionism: *147, 176,* Spanish—: *173f,* 638, *174f,* 639
adultery: **525**
Africa: *216,* 1029, *294,* 1033, *320*
African tradition: 1033f
AGATHO, Pope: *172*
Agnoetes: *144, 164,* 626
ALARIC: *544*
ALBERT THE GREAT: *62*
Albigensians: *14, 106, 119, 120, 217, 367, 453, 526, 683*
ALEXANDER III, pope: *526,* (1801)
ALEXANDER VII, pope: *204, 308, 586*
ALEXANDER VIII, pope: *588*
Alexandria: *6;* patriarchate of—: 809
Alexandrian tradition: *143, 154*
Altzelle in Saxony: *493*
Amalricians: *13*
AMBROSE OF MILAN: *1, 4,* 3, *718, 823,* 1408, 2147a
"Americanism": *591,* 2018
Anabaptists: *393*
analogy of faith: 132, 143/9, 221, *90,* 250
ANASTASIUS II, pope: *122*
ANASTASIUS, priest: *147*
Ancyra, Council of—: *449*

angles: 19, *39/1,* 402/5, 407, 412
Anglican,—hierarchy: *499;* —orders: *499,* 1722-1728;—rite: 1722-1728
Anglicans: *499,* 1722-1728
animism: 1033
anointing of the sick: *446,* **447**
ANSELM, ST: *110,* 325
ANZIR, king of Mauritania: *276*
Antioch, patriarchate of—: 809
Antiochian tradition: *143, 147, 151, 154*
anti-Semitism: *288f*
apokatastasis: 682, 2301, *683*
APOLLINARIS OF LAODICAEA: *146,* 620/4, *158,* 623
Apollinarism, Apollinarists: 13, *147*
apostles: 204, 210, 246, (863), 1739
Arabs: *288*
Arianism, Arians: *5, 7, 8,* 13, *98, 99, 253,* 1404
Aristotelianism, Aristotelians: 108, *123, 553*
ARISTOTLE: *218*
ARIUS: *5, 96, 99,* 306/3, *146*
Arles, Council of—: *386, 449*
Armenians: *122,* 407, *221, 257, 368f,* 1305, *390, 392, 411,* 1509, *427, 454, 494, 526*
Asia: 1029, *296, 299*
Assisi: *350,432*
assumption: *200,* **200**
ATHANASIUS OF ALEXANDRIA: 11, *161,* 635
atheism: **33f**
ATHENAGORAS I, patriarch: *265, 268*
attrition: **447**
Augsburg Confession: *370, 395*
AUGUSTINE, ST: *11, 13,* 222, 223, *91, 107,* 624, *169,* 659, 711, *221,* 1015, *359,* 1408, 1444, 1516, 1524, 1549, 1662, *527, 546, 549f, 553,* 1932, 1938, 1946, 1986/54, *573,* 1999, 2014, *682*

AUGUSTINE OF CANTERBURY: *304*, 1102
authority, Church—: **214f**; civil—: **584, 612**
Avignon: *217, 219*

Baianism: 573
BAIUS, cf. DE BAY, M.
BAÑEZ,D.: *576*
Bangalore: *285*
baptism: **134**, *383f*, **384**; liturgy of—: *2, 2, 4f*
Basel: *221, 307*
Basel, General Council of—: *307,* 1105
Basel, Council of—: *202*
BASIL, ST: 1252
BAUTAIN, L.E.: *35,* 101-104
beatific vision: *136,* 506, *679f,* **680**
BENEDICT VIII, pope: *9*
BENEDICT XII, pope: *122,* 407, *684,* 2305-2307
BENEDICT XIII, pope of Avignon: *219*
BENEDICT XIV, pope: *315*
BENEDICT XV pope: 80, 229-231, *181, 310,* 1111-1114, *313, 321, 472,* 1661
BERENGAR OF TOURS: *407;* Oath of—: 1501
BERTOLIUS OF METZ: *388*
Bible: **69**; cf. Scripture
Biblical Commission: *84, 237, 86,* 240-245, *91*
biblical criticism: *180*
birth regulation: **660f**
bishops: **215, 490f**;—successor apostles: 247 **(863),** 1739
BISMARK: *234*
body, creation of—: **116**; resurrection of —:**680**
Bohemia: *220, 368*
Bombay: *293*
BONAVENTURE: 105
BONIFACE II, pope: *550*
BONIFACE VIII, pope: *217,* 804, *482*
BONIFACE IX, pope: *493,* 1704
Bonn: *35*
BONNETTY, A.: *35,* 105
Boston: *240*
BOTTE, B.: *3*
Braga, Council of—: *118,* 402/5-13, *526*

Brazil: *332, 443*
Brest-Litovsk: *254*
BUCER, M.: *393, 499*
Buddhism: *286, 288, 295*
Bulgarians: *526*
Byzantine tradtion: *359, 399*

CAESARIUS OF ARLES: *549,* 1921-1922
CALVIN, J.: *361, 395, 413, 423, 470*
CAMELOT, P.T.: *148, 152, 154*
canon of Scripture: **69**
capitalism: **613**
CAPELLE, B.: *3*
Capharnaitic eating: *410*
Carthage: *386*
Carthage, Council of 251-252: *449*
Carthage, Council of 416: *135*
Carthage, Sixteenth Council of—: *135,* 501-(502), *137, 388,* (1407), *544,* 1901-1906, *547*
CASEL, O.: *377*
CASSIAN: *546f*
catechists: *323*
Cathars: *14, 217,* 1601, *683*
Catholic action: 1128
Catholic Church: 36, 39/2, 847, 856, (860); cf. Church
CELESTINE I, pope: *148,* 1212, *450,* 1604
CELESTIUS: *544,* 1907
celibacy, priestly—: *512,* 1743
Chalcedon, General Council of—: *8, 14, 16, 151,* 609-612, *153f,* 613-616, *155, 156, 160, 163, 172, 176, 180, 186f, 189, 201, 253, 368*
Chaldeans: *221*
Chapters, "Three Chapters": *157, 158,* 621-623, *165*
character, sacramental—: **366, 384f, 490f**
charismatic element of the Church: **215**
charisms: *541, 580*
charity: **584**; cf. virtues, theological
chastity: *659f,* **660f**
China: *308, 315*
Chinese rites: *315*
Christianity, uniqueness of—: *274,* **275**; —, fulfilment of all human values: **275, 303**

Church: *213f*, **214f, 255**; —and Holy Scripture: **69**; missionary activity: **215**, *301f*, **303**; universality and catholicity: **215, 303**; —and sacraments: *365f*, **366**; —and Eucharist: *403f*, **404f**; —and Churches: *253–255*, **255f**; eschatological nature of the —: **215, 680f**; —cf. local

Cistercians: *493f*

Citeaux: *494*

CLEMENT I, pope: *492*, 1701

CLEMENT IV, pope: *16f, 217, 683*

CLEMENT V, pope: 410

CLEMENT VI, pope: *176f*, 643, 390, *482*, 1681

CLEMENT XI, pope: *271, 574*, 1990/1-59, 1991/44-47, 1992/10-23

clergy, cf. Order

Cochinchina: *308*

COGGAN, D., Archbishop of Canterbury: *266*

collectivism: **613**

collegiality, cf. bishops

commandments, divine—: **543**, 1902f, 1938, 1968, 1969, 1970, 1992/11

communicatio in sacris: 912

communion, cf. meal, eucharistic; daily—: *341*, 1209/1-4

communion of saints: *363*, 1687, **681**

community, human—, cf. race

concelebration: **405**

conciliarism: *213, 218f*

concupiscence: **134**

Confessio Augustana: 271f

confession: **447**

confirmation: *383f*, **384f**

CONFUCIUS: *315*

CONGAR, Y.: *xxix*

Congregation, S.C. of the Holy Office: *48*, 141f, 79, 228/1-24, *180*, 650/27-38, *181*, 651/1-3, *235*, 846/6-56, *240f*, 854-857, *260f*, 908, 373, 1325, *374f*, 1326/39-41, *395*, 1437/42-44, *432*, 471, 1660/46-48, *502*, 1729/49-50, *586*, 2005, 2006/3, *587, 588*, 2008/2, *588*, 2009/2-3, *595*, 2022-2025, *622*, 2201/9-

50; S.C. for the Doctrine of the Faith: *59*, 160-162, *113*, 333, *192*, 670f; *247f*, 883, *400*, 1443-1446, *518f*, 1752; *537*, 1842, *609*, 2060-2063, *672f*, 2226-2227, *674*, 2228-2232, *676*, 2233-2235, *691*, 2317; S.C. of Rites: *350*, 1229f, *355f*, *438*, 1581-1587; S.C. for Divine Worship: *356, 399, 441f, 476*, 1669-1671; S.C. for Catholic Education: *92f*, 258; S.C. *de Propaganda Fide: 308*, 1106-1110, *315*; S.C. of the Index: *35, 48*

conscience: **584**

Constance, General Council of—: *213, 219f*, 806, *219f*, 807/8-37, 808/1-15, *367*, 1303, *409f*, 1506, *453*, 1610

CONSTANS II, emperor: *165*

CONSTANTINE I, emperor: *5, 544*

CONSTANTINE IV, emperor: 172, 276

Constantinople: *359*; partiarachate of—: *809, 268*

Constantinople, First General Council of —: *7, 8, 12f, 14, 20f, 99*, 305, *146f*, (602), *174, 368*

Constantinople, Second General Council of —: *70, 204, 158f*, 620/1-10, 621-623; *173*

Constantinople, Third General Council of —: *166, 172*, 635-637

Constantinople, Fourth General Council of —: *216, 232, 360*, 1253

Constantinople, Council of 448: *152*

Constantinople, Council of 543: *118*, 401/1-8, *156*, 618/2-3, *682*, 2301

Constitutiones Ecclesiae Aegyptiacae: 511, 1741

consubstantial: 19, 22, 23, 319, 325, 333, 625, 627/1; cf. *homoousios*

contraception: **660f**

contrition: **447**

Copts: *221*

Corinth; *492*

Councils, ecumenical—: *xxvi-xxviii*, **69**, 829

CRANMER, T.: *499*

creation: 115, **116**

Creeds, cf. Symbols of Faith

Cremenia: *388*

criticism, biblical —: 143/9, *68*, 223, 228/1, *82*

cult, cf. liturgy

CYPRIAN OF CARTHAGE: *15*, *112*, 656, *216*, *386*, 1998

Cyprus: *221*

CYRIL OF ALEXANDRIA: *148f*, 604f, 606/1-12, *151f* 155, 617, *158*, 161, 622, 623, *166*, 636, 653, *201*

CYRIL OF JERUSALEM: 6, 9, *9*

DAMASUS I, pope: 8, *10f*, 70, *146f*; *Tome of*—: *100*, 306/1-24, *147*, 603, 6-14

death: **134**, *679*, **680**, *688*

DE BAY, M.: *140*, *204*, *571f*, 576

DE BONALD. L.: 35

DECENTIUS OF GUBBIO: *387*, 449

DECIUS: *449*

deism: *123*

DE LAMENNAIS, F.: *35*, *280*

DE LA MOTTE, L.: *308*

demons: 2301

Dêr-Balizeh papyrus: *1*, *3*, 1

DESCARTES, R.: *279*

descent to hell: 4, 5, 17, 20, 23

development, human—: **303**, **615**;—of nations: **614**

devil: 402/7.8.12, 508

diaconate: **491**

diakonos: 1701

dialogue, ecumenical—: **256**; religious— *274*, **275**, 287, 288, 291, 292, 298, 1037, *299f*, 1040, **303**

Didachê: 1565

DIMITRIOS I, patriarch: *266*, *268*

diocese: 1201; cf. bishops; Church, local—

DIOCLETIAN, emperor: *449*

DIODORUS OF TARSUS: *147*

DIONYSIUS, pope: *98*, 301-303

DIONYSIUS OF ALEXANDRIA: *98*

DIOSCORUS OF ALEXANDRIA: *151f*, *153*

divorce: *662*; cf. marriage, properties of—, indissolubility of—

Djakarta: *293*

docetism: *146, 175, 662*

dogma: *xxvi-xxviii;* development of —: 136; evolution of —: 143/4, 846/54; immutability of—: 1207; irreformability of—: 162, *226;* conditioning and interpretation of—: 160-161; cf. pluralism, dogmatic—

DOMINIC, ST: *367*

Dominicans: *202*, *684*

Donatism: *253*

dualism: *95, 115, 118, 119, 120, 122, 174f, 523, 526*

Eastern Churches: *207*, *221*, **255f**, 1207, *367*, *397*, *411*, 1508, *512*

Eastern Tradition: *576*, *577*, *579f*, *686*

ECKHART, J.: *121*, 406/27

ecumenism: *208f*, 253-255, **255f**

Edwardine Ordinal: 499, 1722-1728

efficacy, — of liturgy: 318; — of sacraments: *365f*, **366**

Egypt: *3*, 221, 253

ELIPANDUS OF TOLEDO: *174*

ELLIOT, W., *591*

Elvira, Council of —: *386*, 1402, *449*, 512

emanationism: *115*

England: *186, 220, 304, 452*

Ephesus, General Council of—: 8, *14*, *147f*, 604f, *151*, 155, 157, *163f*, *176*, *180*, *187*, *189*, *201*, (701), *216*

Ephesus, Council of 449: *153f*

epiclesis: *411*

Epicureans: 621

EPICURIUS: 621

EPHIPHANIUS OF SALAMIS: 7, *10f*, *8*

episcopate: **490**; cf. bishops

episkopos: 1701, 1729/50

Epistola ad Diognetum: 151

ERASMUS, D.: *72*, 137

eschatology: *679f*, **680**; cf. Church, eschatological nature of the—

Ethiopia: *253*

Eucharist: *403f*, **404f**

Eudoxians: 13

EUGENE IV, pope: *221*, *307*, *368f*, 685

EULOGIUS OF ALEXANDRIA: *164*

Eunomians: 13

Eunomius: 8, 306/3

EUSEBIUS OF CAESARAEA:: 5, 6, *6f*, 1018, 1036

EUSEBIUS OF VERCELLI: *13*
EUTYCHES: *152, 153,* 617, 620/4
Eutychianism, Eutychians: *154*
evangelisation: *301f,* **303**
evil: 402/7
evolutionism: *115, 125,* 419, *134,* 516
ex cathedra: 39/13, 839
exegesis: **69**
existentialism: 147, *595*
ex opere operato: 1209/4, 1221, 1222,
   366, 1318, *374, 379*
ex opere operantis: 1221, 1222
EXSUPERIUS OF TOULOUSE: *70*
"extreme unction", cf. anointing of the
   sick

faith: *31f,* **33**;—and reason: *34;*— and
   justification: **543**;— and science: *62,*
   164-170
"Faith and Order": *259*
family: **525**
Father, God the—: **96f**
Fathers of the Church: **69**, 627/1-16
FARVACQUES, F.: *374*
Febronianism: *223*
FEENEY, L.: *240*
FELIX IV, pope: *549*
Ferrara: *221, 307*
fideism: *32, 35, 40, 279*
filioque: 9, 10, 100, 321, *110,* 322, 324,
   254, 368
FLANNERY, A.: *265, 356*
FLAVIAN OF CONSTANTINOPLE: *151f*
Florence: *307*
Florence, General Council of—: *xxix, 9,*
   17, 71, 72, 208, 79, 109f, 322-326, *122f,*
   408f, *177,* 644-646, *221,* 809f, *230, 232,*
   253f, 277, 1003-1005, *341f, 368f,* 1305-
   1308, *390,* 1412-1418, *392,* 1419, *411,*
   1508-1511, *427, 454,* 1612f, *494,* 1705,
   506, 526, 1803, *684, 685,* 2308f
FOREVILLE, R.: *14*
form-criticism: *82, 86, 245*
Fortaleza: *443*
France: *51, 119, 120, 304, 453*
Franciscans: *120, 202, 683*
FRANCIS OF ASSISI: *367*
Frankfurt, Council of—: *174*

FRANZEN, P.F.: *528*
freedom, human: **134**; moral—: **584**;
   religious—: *274,* **275**, 1030, **584**
French hierarchy: *670*
Friars Minor: *586*
Friuli, Council of—: *174,* 639
FULGENTIUS OF RUSPA: 326, *221,* 810, 277,
   1005, 1935
FUMASONI-BIONDI, Card.: *343*

Gaul: *9, 10, 16*
Gelasian Sacramentary: 407
GELASIUS I, pope: *70,* (203)
Genesis, Book of—:134, 237, 239
Georgia: *493*
German hierarchy: *234f,* 841, *272*
Germany: *9, 62* 186, *270, 271, 483*
GIBBONS, Card.: *591*
GILROY, Card.: *285*
gnosticism- *68, 72, 146*
God natural knowledge of—: **33f**;
   Christian concept of—: *95,* **96**;—
   creator: **116**; Triune—: *95,* **96f**
goods of marriage: *526,* 1803, *531,* 1826-
   1830
Gospel, formation of—: 241-245;
   apostolic origin of—: 254
grace: **134**; life of—: *541f,* **542f**;
   sanctifying and actual—: *541f,* **542f**
   life of—and baptism: **384**; life of—and
   Eucharist: **405**; life of—and
   reconciliation: **447**
Greeks: *16f, 110, 217,* 804, *221, 222,*
   337, 368, 395, 411, 576, 683f
GREGORY I, pope: *164,* 624-626, 827, 850,
   304, 1102, *386, 493,* 1702
GREGORY II pope: *386*
GREGORY VII, pope: *276f,* 1002
GREGORY IX, pope: *494*
GREGORY X, pope: *16, 683*
GREGORY XII, pope: *219*
GREGORY XIII, pope: *571*
GREGORY XVI, pope: *280,* 1007
GREGORY OF NAZIANZEN: 319, 635, 1619

HADRIAN I, pope: *173f,* 638, 276
HANEBERG, D.: *75*
heaven: **680**

Hebrews, Epistle to the—: 619/5
HECKER, I.T.: *591*
hell: 679, **680;** cf. descent to—
HERACLIUS, emperor: *165*
HERMAS: *452*
HERMES, G.: *35f*
hierarchy, Church—: 205f, **215, 490f;** cf. local—
hierarchy of truths: *xxvii, 262, 912*
hierocratic theory: *217*
HILARY OF POITIERS: *682*
HIMERIUS OF TARRAGONA: *387*
Hinduism: *286, 288, 294*
Hippo, Council of—:*344*
HIPPOLYTUS, *Apostolic Tradition: 1, 3,* 2, 513
history,—and Scripture: **69;**— and faith: **34;** cf. salvation, history of—; dogma, development of—
Holand: *521*
HOLSTEIN, H.: *17*
homoousios: 7, 6, 10, 8, 12, 39/4, 99, 309, 614, 620/1.8; cf. consubstantial
HONORIUS I, pope: *165, 172*
hope: *1942, 1976, 2306;* cf. virtues, theological
HORMISDAS, pope: *155, 216*
HUMBERT OF ARLES: *136, 389*
hupostasis: 7, 301, 606/3f, 615, 617, 619/2, 620/1ff, 637; *kath' hupostasin:* 605, 606/2, 619/1f, 620/4.5.7, 622
HUS, J.: *219, 220f, 223, 361, 368, 409, 410, 421, 453, 483*
hypostatic union: *144,* **145**

IBAS OF EDESSA: *154, 156f, 163, 623*
iconoclasm: *276, 359, 360, 361;* cf. images, sacred—
idealism: 147
idolatry: *359, 361,* 1255
IGNATIUS OF ANTIOCH: 1579
ignorance, invincible—: *813, 282,* 1010
images, sacred—: **358**
immaculate conception: *199f,* **200**
immanentism: 147
incarnation: *143f,* **144f**
India, Plenary Council of—: *285,* 1016f
Indian heritage: 1031
Indiculus: 135, 503, *546f,* 1907-1914

indifferentism: *224, 259f, 274,* **275**
individualism: 2106
Indochina: *308*
indulgences; *480f,* **481**
indwelling, divine—: **542**
inerrancy of Scripture; **69**
infallibility: **215**
infant baptism: **384**
INNOCENT I, pope: *70,* (202), *503, 216,* 801, *386, 387, 388,* 1406, *449f,* 1603, 1908f
INNOCENT II, pope: *388,* 1408
INNOCENT III, pope: *13, 106, 119f,* 403, *136f,* 506, *175f, 640, 337, 367,* 1301, 389, 1409-1411, *390, 407f,* 1502f, *409,* 1504, *493,* 1703, 1735, *526,* 1802, *683*
INNOCENT IV, pope: *390*
INNOCENT VIII, pope: *494*
INNOCENT X, pope: *573,* 1989/1-5
INNOCENT XI, pope: *586, 587,* 2007/1-14, *662*
inspiration of Scripture: **69**
intercession,—for the dead: **680;**—of the saints: *358,* **358**
intercommunion: 915
international,—community: *614,* **614f;**— authority: **614**
inter-ritualism: *341f,* 1210
Ireland: *452*
IRENAEUS OF LYONS: 716, 823
IRENE, empress: *276, 359*
Islam: *273, 286, 288;* cf. Muslims
Italy: *120, 223, 282f*

Jacobites: *71, 72, 109, 122, 221f, 222, 277,* 392
JAHN, J.: *74f*
James, Epistle of—: 1603, 1636, 1637, 1660/48
JANSEN, C.: *573,* 576
Jansenism, Jansenists: *179f, 204, 223, 274, 374, 573, 574, 588*
Japan: *315*
JEROME, ST: *10, 80, 229,* 1626, *564*
Jerusalem, patriarchate of—: 809
JESUS CHRIST, God and man, person and work: *143f,* **144f;**—, founder of the Church: **214f;** —, present in the liturgy:

336;— and the sacraments: 365f, 366;— and the Eucharist: 403f, 404f

Jews: 273f, 275, 1018, 288, 305f, 1103, 307, 1105; cf. Judaism

JOACHIM OF FIORE: 13, 107, 317, 320

JOHN II, pope: 155, 617, 201, (702)

JOHN XXII, pope: 121, 406/1-28, 218, 805/2-4, 586, 2001, 684

JOHN XXIII, pope: xxvi, 261, 287, 320f, 1132-1135, 596, 2026-2042, 622, 2118-2123, 627, 2124-2140/2, 631

JOHN PAUL II, pope: 61, 163, 62, 164-170, 128, 425-426, 129, 427-430, 141, 517, 194f, 674-676, 197, 677-679, 250, 886, 268, 916-921, 270, 922, 271, 923-926, 272, 927, 298, 1037-1039, 299f, 1040, 332, 1158-1159, 356, 1237-1239, 442, 1590, 443, 1591, 478, 1672, 520, 1753, 521, 1754, 538, 1843-1844, 609, 2064, 652, 2172-2173, 653, 2174, 654, 2175-2180, 657, 2181, 678, 2236

JOHN XXIII of PISA: 219

JOHN OF ANTIOCH: 151

JOHN CHRYSOSTOM: 110, 90

JOHN OF JANDUN: 219

JOHN OF LYONS: 407

JOHN PARASTRON: 18, 26

Judaism: 275, 286, 288f, 305f, 1103, 307; cf. Jews

judgement, general—: 681

JULIAN II, pope: 483

JULIAN OF EKLANUS: 546

JULIUS III, pope: 499

jurisdiction, Church—: 215; power of—: 447

justice; 584; social—: 611f, 612-614

justice, original—: 133, 134

justification: 542f

JUSTINIAN, emperor: 155, 617, 156, 157, 682

KANT, E.: 32, 35

KELLY, J.N.D.: 11

kenosis: 90, 190

kenotic theory: 187, 662

Khristotokos: 147

Kingdom of God: 39/5.12.20, 244, (860), 2302, 2315

Kingship of Christ: 145; feast of the—: 342

labour: 611f, 613f

laity,—in the Church: (864);— in the missions: 303; call to perfection of—: 585; cf. People of God

Laodicea, Council of—: 70, (201)

Last Supper: 404

Latin Church, cf. Western Church

Lateran, Fourth General Council of—: 13f, 19-21, 106, 317-320, 120, (404), 124, 176, (641), 217, (802), 305, 1103, 337, 1201f, 338f, 409, (1505), 413, 446, 453, 1608f, 462, 469, 683, (2203)

Lateran, Fifth General Council of—: 46, 122, 410

Lateran, Council of 649: 71, 205, 165, 627/1-16, 172, 201, 703

latria: 664, 359, 1252, 1520, 1531

Lausanne: 259

law, natural: 583, 584f; human—: 585; international —: 614; Roman and Germanic—: 526

laxism: 583, 586, 662

lay ministries: 491

legalism: 584, 595

Leninism: 2155

LEO I, pope: 151f, 609-612, 153f, 617, 172, 636, 663, 823, 286, 368, 387, 451, 1605, 451, 1606, 1993

LEO II, pope: 172

LEO III, pope: 9

LEO IX, pope: 16, 71, 207, 174

LEO X, pope: 223, (811), 370, 1309, 455, 1614/5-14, 483, 1685/17-22, 553, 1923/2-36, 687

LEO XII, pope: 279, 1006

LEO XIII, pope: 71, 76, 220-227, 80, 81, 200, 205, 710, 237, 240, 258, 904f, 284, 1014f, 339, 1207, 342, 429, 499f, 1722-1728, 524, 530f, 1820-1823, 542, 576, 1993, 577, 1977, 589, 2011-2014, 591, 2015f, 616, 2101-2105, 639

LEO III, emperor: 359

lex orandi, lex credendi: 336

liberalism: 274, 280, 284, 583, 589

liberation, man's—: 303, 611, 615; cf. salvation

liberty, cf. freedom
life, respect of human—: **661**
literary genres: **69**
liturgical,—cycle: **336**, 1258;—
  participation: 335f, **336**, 352; —
  renewal: 335f, 351-353
liturgy: 335, **336**;— of the hours: 1225,
  352; cf. liturgical
local,—Church: **215**, 302, **303**, 323;—
  clergy: 302, **303**;—hierarchy: 302,
  303;— language: 1104, 1114
Lombards: 119
London: 493
LUTHER, M.: 73, 133, 137, 218, 223, 270,
  271, 361, 370, 393, 395, 413, 423, 455,
  457, 465, 470, 483, 527, 553f, 554, 686
Lyons, Second General Council of : 9,
  16f, 22-29, 71, 109f, 321, 176, (642)
  217, (803), 232, 253, 367, (1302), 409,
  683f, (2304) 686

MACARIUS OF CONSTANTINOPLE: 172
Macedonianism, Macedonians: 8
Magisterium: 213f, **215**;—and Scripture:
  xxv-xxvii, **68**; —and dogma: 161;
  and theology: xxv-xxix, 163, 243, 858-
  859
Malankara Catholics: 253
man, created: **116**;—, body and soul:
  116; —'s dignity: **584**; —'s rights and
  duties: **584**, **612f**; —'s social
  character: **584**, **612f**; —'s eternal
  destiny: 679f, **680**
MANES: 402/5.7.11.12.13, 621
Manichaeism and Manicheans: 115, 118,
  119, 122, 409, 137, 175, 359, 393, 526, 683
Manila: 296, 299
Marcellians: 13
MARCIAN, emperor: 154
MARCION: 71, 301, 621
Marcionites: 621
Maria Laach: 377
MARIS THE PERSIAN: 623
marriage, properties of : **524**; indissolubility of—:**524f**; use of—:659f, **660f**;
  —bond: **524f**; —contract—: **524f**; —
  ends: **524f**; —impediments: **524f**; —
  laws: **524f**; cf. matrimony
Maronites: 221, 254

MARSILIUS OF PADUA: 218, 223
MARTIN I, pope: 165, 201
MARTIN V, pope: 218, 360, 1254 368,
  1304, 410, 1507/16-17, 454, 1611/20-
  25, 483, 1684/26-27, 493
Marxism: 2155f
MARY, —Virgin Mother of God: 199f,
  200; —and man's redemption: **200**; —
  and the Church: **200**
Mass, cf. sacrifice, eucharistic; meal,
  eucharistic
masturbation: **660**
materialism: 40, 112, 124, 125
matrimony: 523f, **524f**; cf. marriage
meal, eucharistic—: 403f, **404f**
Mediator, Christ the—: **145**
MEKHITAR, Catholicos of Armenia: 390
MELANCHTON, P.: 270, 370, 393, 395, 413,
  423, 470
MELLITUS, abbot: 304
membership, Church—: **215**, **384**
memorial, cf. Eucharist
MENAS OF CONSTANTINOPLE: 118, 682
merit: **543**
merits, —of Christ: **145**, **480f**; —of
  saints: **481**
MERSCH, E.: 236
Mesopotamia: 222
Messalians: 393
Mexico: 195
MICHAEL VIII PALAEOLOGUS: 16, 71, 109,
  176, 217, 253, 367, 683f
ministry, cf. Order
miracles: **33**
missiology: 1132
Missions: 301f, **303**
Mission Works: 317, 1123
Modalism: 96, 98
Modernism, Modernists: 20, 32, 48f, 79f,
  180, 182, 214, 235, 374f, 375, 1327, 395,
  417f, 502; Oath against—: 143/1-13,
  228/1-24
MOHAMMED : 305
MOLINA, L.: 576
MOLINOS, M.: 587
monarchia: 301, 303
Mono-energism: 165, 171
monogamy, cf. marriage, properties of—

monogenism: *125*
Monophysitism, Monophysitists: *143,*
149, 152, 153, 155, 156, 158, 164, 165,
173, 201, 253, 360
monotheism: 1029
Monothelitism, Monothelitists: *143, 165f,*
172, 173, 201
Montanism: *253*
motherhood, divine—of Mary: *199,* **200**
MUNIER, CH.: *16*
Muslims: *207, 273, 276,* 1002, 1018, *288,*
1029, *306;* cf. Islam
"Mysteric presence": *377*
mysterium fidei: 407, 1502
Mysteries: *xxvi, xxvii,* **33**; Christ's— in
the liturgy: **336**
Mystical Body: **215**
mythology: *95*

Narbonne: *450*
nations, relations between—: **614**; cf.
development of—
NAUTIN, P.: *3*
Neo-Chalcedonianism: *156*
Nestorianism, Nestorians: *143, 147f, 152,*
154, 156f, 158, 620/4, *626, 174, 179,*
201, 253, 493
NESTORIUS: 147f, 617, *157, 158,* 620/4.5,
622, 623, 201
"New Morality": 2025
Nicaea, First General Council of—: *5, 6,*
7, 7, 8, 9, 11, 14, 22, 99, (304), *146,*
(601), *155, 180, 189, 304,* 1101, *386,*
1403, *417, 449,* 1601f
Nicaea, Second General Council of—:
71, 206, *276,* 1001, *359,* 1251f, *360, 362*
NICHOLAS I, pope: *526*
Nouvelle Théologie: 52
Novatianism, Novatians: 1404, *449,*
1601, 1617

Oceania: *296*
OLIEU, P.J. (OLIVI) : *120,* 176
"Onanism": **662**
Orange, Second Council of—: *135, 136,*
504-505, 549f, 1915-1922
Order: 489f, **490**
orders, major and minor—: 1708, 1715,
515, 1747

Oriental Rites: **336,** *354f*
Orientals: 527f, *685f*
ORIGEN: 98, *118, 156*
Origenists: *118, 156, 682*
Orthodox Church: *681*
ORTIZ DE URBINA, I.: *6, 7, 9,*
Osith, St—in Essex: *493,* 1704

Padua: *123*
PALLU, F.: *308*
pantheism: *40,* 143/11, *95, 112, 115, 123,*
124, 577
papacy: *213f,* **215**
parenthood, responsible—: **660**
Paris,: *84, 684*
Paris, Council of—: *73,* 209
parousia: *679f,* **680.**
partnership: **613;** contract of—: *612,* **614**
Paschal Mystery: *143,* **144,** *403*
patriarchates: *221,* 809, **255f**
Patripassianism: *147*
PAUL IV, pope: *178,* 648, *203,* 707, *499*
PAUL VI, pope: *22,* 39/1-23, *57,* 155-159,
141, 190, 193f, 672-673, *210,* 719-720,
249, 884-885, *265f, 292,* 1029f, *294,*
1031f, *294f,* 1033f, *296,* 1035, *296f,*
1036, 328f, 1146-1148, *336,* 1149-
(1157), *355, 363,* 1259, *380,* 1336, *396,*
398, 1441, *436,* 1577-1580, *441, 476f,*
480, 485, 1687-1690/5, *512,* (1742),
512f, 1743, *513,* (1744), *515,* 1747, *516,*
(1748), *516,* 1749-1750, *517,* 1751, *537,*
1841, *634f,* 2145-2153, *640,* 2153a-
2158, *645, 649,* 2165, *650,* 2167-2171,
670, 2220-2225
PAUL IV OF CONSTANTINOPLE: *276*
PAUL OF SAMOSATA: *386*
Paulianists: *386,* 1403
PAULINUS OF AQUILEIA: *174*
peace: **614**
Pelagianism, Pelagians: *135, 137, 216,*
541, 544, 554, 1987/28
PELAGIUS: *133, 135,* 504, *542, 554,* 1907,
1986/54
penance, cf. reconciliation
Pentateuch: 84
People of God: *245,* (862)
perfection, Christian—: *583f,* **584f**

perseverance, final—: **542**
persons, divine—: **96f;** human—, cf man
PETER OF ANTIOCH: *16*
PETER CANISIUS: *20*
PETER LOMBARD: *107,* 317, 318, *527, 553*
PETER WALDO: *367*
PHILIP, Roman legate: 822
PHILIP THE FAIR: *217*
PHILIP OF HESSE: *527*
philosophy: **32f**
Photinians: 13
phusis: 608, 613
Pistoia, Jansenist Synod of—: *140, 179, 223*
PIUS IV, pope: *20f,* 30-38, *420, 486, 495*
PIUS V, pope: *140,* 514/26-49, *204,* 708, *335, 571f,* 1984/21-79, 1985/13-63, 1986/20-74, 1987/27-66, 1988/16-38
PIUS VI, pope: *179,* 649, *223,* (812)
PIUS VII, pope: *411*
PIUS IX, pope: *35f,* 106-111, *40, 123f,* 411/1-2, *204,* 709, *223,* 813-816, *234, 257,* 901f, *257f,* 903, *280,* 1008, *280,* 1009f,*282f,* 1012, 1013/15-79,*284, 339,* 1206, *588,* 2010/56-63
PIUS X, pope: *20, 48, 71, 79,* 228/1-24, *180, 205,* 711,*340,* 1208,*340,* 1209/1-4, *340f,* 1210, *343, 374,* 1327,*411, 471*
PIUS XI, pope: *182f,* 652f, *183,* 654-659, *259f,* 907,*260, 313,* 1115-1118,*318, 342,* 1211f, *343,* 1213, *472, 524, 527, 531,* 1824-1833, *593,* 2019, *618,* 2106-2111/3, *662.* 2202-2208, 2209
PIUS XII, pope: *52f,* 144-148,*82f,* 232-236, *85,* 238f, *125,* 419f, *185,* 660f,*186,* 662f, *187,* 664-667, *206,* 713-715, *214, 236f,* 847-853, 856f, *243,* 858f, *244f, 285,* 315f 1119-1121,*316,* 1122f,*317,* 1124f,*318,* 1126-1129,*320,* 1130f,*321, 344f,* 1214f, *345,* 1216-(1226), *349,* 1227f,*373, 375,* 1328-1330, *377f,* 1331-1333,*378f, 396,* (1438),*428,* 1564f,*430,* 1566-1570,*431,* 1571, *432,* 1572f,*472,* 1662,*494, 502,* 1730, 1731-1736, *506,* 1737, *513, 515,* 1747-(1748),*542, 577,* 1995-1997,*593,* 2020-2021, *596, 621,* 2112, *662, 665,* 2209-2212,*666,* 2213

PLATO: 621
Platonism, Platonists: 108,*118,* 621,*682*
pluralism, dogmatic—:*xxvii,* 912; liturgical—: *315, 339*

Pneumatomachs: 8, 13
POLE, R. Card.: *499*
polygenism: *125,* 420, 516
POMPONAZZI, P.: *122*
power, cf. authority
praeparatio evangelica: 1018, 1023
prayer, liturgical and private: **336**
preaching, cf. Word, liturgy of the—
predestination: *220,* 808/1-6, **543**
preexistence of souls: **116,** *682*
presbyterate; **490**
presence, eucharistic—: *403f,* **405**
preternatural gifts: **134**
priesthood,—of Christ: 1546, *489,* 1731, *507,* 1745
priesthood, common:*384,* **385,***489f,* **491**
priesthood, ministerial: *489f,* **490f;** threefold function of—: **490;**— and Eucharist: **404f, 490;** —and remission of sins: **447, 490**
primacy,—of Peter,—of the Roman Pontiff: *213f,* **215**
"primitive religions": *286, 288, 294,* 1033
PRISCILLIAN: *118,* 402/5-13, *137*
Priscillianism, Priscillianists: *118, 253,* 526
probabilism: **585**
processions, divine—: **97**
procreation: *659f,* **660f**
Professions of Faith, cf. Symbols of Faith
property, right of private—: *612,* **613**
prophecies: 110, 119, 143/2
proskunêsis: 359, 1252
prosôpon: 147, 604 608, 615, 620/1
PROSPER OF AQUITAINE: *546,* 549
Protestantism, Protestants: *133, 186, 203, 208, 254, 257, 270, 528, 554, 571*
Providence, divine—: **116**
PSEUDO—ALEXANDER I: 1509
PSEUDO—ATHANASIUS, Symbol: *11,* 16f, *13, 102, 169, 369, 682*
PSEUDO-DIONYSIUS: *166*
PSEUDO-JULIUS I: 1509

psychology, human—of Christ: **145**
public life, participation of Catholics in : **614**; participation of citizens in—: 2131
Puebla: *128, 194*
purgatory: *679f,* **680**

quaternity: 317, 318, *629*
QUESNEL, P.: *140, 574*
quietism: *587*
QUIRICIUS OF TOLEDO: *13, 682*

race, unity of the human—: **116**, 1119, *616*
RAHNER, K.: *414*
RAMSEY, M., Archbishop of Canterbury: *266*
rationalism, rationalists: *32, 35f,* 106-111, *39,* 112/2-11, 143/9, *178, 203, 224, 280, 281*
reason, cf. faith
rebirth, cf. baptism
reconciliation: *445f,* **446f**
redemption: *143f,* **145**; cf. salvation
Reformation and Reformers: *21, 68, 72, 73, 136, 203, 214, 219, 220, 224, 815, 254, 262, 338, 361, 367, 392, 403, 413, 420, 424, 433, 446, 456, 480, 484, 489, 495, 524, 526, 541f, 553, 554, 570, 682, 686*
Reims: *175*
relations, divine: **96**
relativism, dogmatic—: 148; cf. dogma, evolution of—
relics: **358**
religions, world—: *273f,* **274f**
religious life: *247,* **585**; —in ,the missions: **303**
reservation of cases: **447**
resurrection, —of Christ: **145**; —of the dead: *679f,* **680**
revelation: *31f;* **33**; —and reason **33**; —and science: **34**, *62,* 164-170; —and Church: **33**, **69**; —and tradition: **68f**
RICHARD, Card.: *499*
RICCI, SCIPIO: *179*
rigorism: *583, 659*
Rites, liturgical: **336**
ROBERTS, G.: *3*

Roman Breviary: 1575
Roman Missal: 1219, 1220, 1232, 1549, *441,* 1588, 1937, 2316
Roman Pontifical: 499, 1730, *513*
Roman Ritual: 1934
Rome: *3, 221, 307,* 1124; cf. S. Congregations, law, primacy
Rome, Council of 382: *100,* 306/1-24, *147,* 603/6-14
Rome, Council of 449: *154*
Rome, Council of 680: *172*
Rome, Council of 1059: *407*
Rome, Council of 1079; *407,* 1501
Rome, Symbol of —: *4f,* 5
ROSMINI-SERBATI, A.: *48*
ROY, M., Card.: *642*
RUFINUS OF AQUILAEA: *1, 4,* 4
RUNCIE, R., Archbishop of Canterbury: *266*

Sabellianism, Sabellians: *7, 13, 98*
SABELLIUS: *98,* 301, 306/2
sacraments: *365f,* **366**
sacred art: *344,* 1213, *352, 353*
Sacred Heart: **145**, *179, 183*
sacred music: *340, 343, 349,* 1227, *350, 351, 352*
sacrifice,—of Christ: *144,* **145**; *403f,* **404**; eucharistic—: *403f,* **404**
saints, cult of—: **358**
salvation, economy of—: *273,* **275**, 1018; history of—: **33**, *88, 91, 143, 365, 679;*— through Christ: **145**, --through the Church: **215**, *301,* **303**; —outside the Church: **215**, *273,* **273f**
salvific will, God's—: **542**
São-Paulo: *332*
Saracens: 305, 306
Satan, cf. devil
satisfaction: **447**
Schism, Eastern—: *253, 342;* Western—: *219*
Scholasticism: *408, 446, 472, 473, 482, 555*
science, sciences, cf. revelation, Scripture
Scotism: *454*
Scripture: **68f**; —and sciences; **69**; —and tradition: *xxv-xxvi, 67f,* **68f**;

interpretation of— by the Church: **69, 215;** —and theology: 258

Secretariat for Christian Unity: *261, 266, 267, 915 398,* 1440a-b

secularism: *56, 593;* —of State: *284,* 1014

seeds of the Word: **275**

semi-rationalism: *36*

Semi-Pelagianism, Semi-Pelagians: *546f, 549,* 1989/4f

Sens, Council of—: *176*

senses of Scripture: **68f**

SERGIUS OF CONSTANTINOPLE: *165, 172*

sexual order: *659f,* **660f**

sign, sacramental—: *366*

sin, original: *133,* **134, 384;** personal: **134, 384;** philosophical—: 2008/2; loss of grace by personal—: **542;** remission of— by baptism: **384;** remission of— by reconciliation: **446f**

SIRICIUS, pope: *387,* 1404

"Situation Ethics": *595,* 2022, 2025

Sitz im Leben: 86

SIXTUS III, pope: *151*

SIXTUS IV, pope: 513, *202f,* 704, 705

social order: *611f,* **612f**

socialisation: **613,** 2114

socialist ideologies: *627,* 2140/2, 2154

society, human—: *611f,* **612f**

Son,—of God: **96f, 144f,** cf. Jesus Christ

sonship, divine—: **542**

soul, created: **116;**—, form of body: **117**

Spain: *9, 10, 118, 174, 386, 452,* 1607

Spirit, Holy: *96,* **96f,** *100;* Holy—and grace: **542;** Holy—and the Church: **215;** Holy—and confirmation: **385;** cf. inspiration of Scripture

"Spirirituals": *120*

Spoleto, Council of—: *283*

state: **613**

states, relations between: **613f**

Statuta Ecclesiae Antiqua: 16, 71, 494

STEPHEN I, pope: *386,* 1401

sterilisation: **661**

Stoicism: 108

Strasburg: *35*

subdiaconate: 1708, *515,* 1747

subsidiarity, principle of—in the economic order: **613f**

subordinationism: *96, 99*

SUHARD, E. Card.: *84, 85*

supernatural: **134, 542f;** cf. grace

SYLVESTER I, pope: *6,* 1509

Symbols of faith: *xxviii, 1f,* 1-39/23, *95f*

"Symbol of the Apostles": *1f, 4,* 3f, *4f,* 5

syncretism: 1016, 1144

Synod, Particular Synod of Dutch Bishops in Rome: *521*

Synod, Third Synod of Bishops in Rome: *513f,* 1745f, *645,* 2159-2164

Synod, Fourth Synod of Bishops in Rome: *649,* 2166

Syrian Christians,: *110, 221*

TARASIUS OF CONSTANTINOPLE: *276*

temporal order, autonomy of—: 135, 423

temporal punishment, remission of—by the Church: **384, 447,** *480,* **480f;**—and purgatory: **680**

TERTULLIAN: 108, 143/12. *564*

Testament, Old and New—: **69**

TETZEL J.: *483*

THEODORA, empress: *360*

THEODORE OF FREJUS: *451*

THEODORE OF MOPSUESTIA: *157, 158f,* 620/4.5.6, 621, 622, 623

THEODORET OF CYRUS: *153f, 156f,* 622

THEODOSIUS I, emperor: 8

THEODOSIUS II, emperor: *148, 151, 154*

theology: *xxv, xxixf,* 112/8, 147f; cf. Magisterium, pluralism. dogmatic—

theotokos: 147, 605, 606/1, 607, *199, 201*

THOMAS AQUINAS: *xxvi,* 105, 710, *369, 370,* 1444, *407, 411,* 1578, *454, 494,* 1995, 2014, 2103, 2108

Toledo, First Council of—: *13,* 526

Toledo, Third Council of—: *9, 13, 100, 452,* 1607

Toledo, Fourth Council of—: *13, 169*

Toledo, Sixth Council of—: *13, 169*

Toledo, Eleventh Council of—: *13,* (18), *14, 102,* 308-316, *168,* 628-634, *682,* 2302

Toledo, Sixteenth Council of—: *13*

tolerance: **275**

tolerantism: 1006

Toscany: *179, 223*

Tradition,—and Scriputre: *xxv, xxvi, 67f,* **68f**

Traditionalism: *32, 35, 40*

Traducianism: *122*

transfinalisation: *436,* 1577, 1580

transignification: *436,* 1577, 1580

transmigration: *118,* 683

transubstantiation: **405**

treasury of the Church: *480,* **480**

Trent, General Council of—: *20f, 22, 25, 32, 68, 71, 72f,* 210–215, *75, 79, 82, 133, 135, 137,* 507–513, *176, 178,* 647, *202f,* 705f, *204, 223, 242, 338,* 1203–1205, *351,* 1255–1257, *362, 370f,* 1310–1323, *373,* 1324, *375, 378, 388, 392,* 1420–1433, *394,* 1434–1436, *409, 413f,* 1512–1536, *421f,* (1537)–(1540), 1541–1544, *423,* 1545–1563, *430, 432, 433, 436, 437, 446, 457,* 1615–1634, *465,* 1635–1640, 1641–1655, 1656–1659, *472, 484,* 1686, *485, 494, 495,* 1706–1721, *515, 524, 527f.* 1804–1819, *530, 542, 554f,* 1924- **1983** *576, 586, 686f,* 2310

Trinity: *95,* **96;**—Father, Son, Holy Spirit: **96f**

tritheism: *98*

TROMP, S.: *236*

Turks: *254*

Ukranians: *254*

Uniate Churches: *254, 258*

union of Churches: *253–255,* **255**

Upanisad: 1031

URBAN IV, pope: 1511

URBAN VIII, pope: *571, 573*

VASKEN I, patriarch of the Armenians: *266*

Vatican, First General Council of—*20, 22, 35, 40f,* 113–140, *52, 54, 56, 71, 75,* 216–219, *79, 85, 90, 111,* 327–331, *120, 124,* 412–418, *214, 216, 217, 223, 226,* (817), 818–839, *235, 245f, 248, 281, 576*

Vatican, Second General Council of—: *xxvii, xxxi, 22, 32, 40, 54,* 149–(153)

56, (154), *68, 71, 88,* 246–257, *112,* (332), *126,* 421–424, *140,* (515), *414,* 189–191, 668f, *199f,* 205, *207f,* 716–718, *213, 223, 226,* 244–247, *254, 261–262,* 909–913, *274, 276, 284, 285, 285–287,* 1018, *288f,* 1019–1026, *291,* 1027–1028, *292, 294, 302, 322–324,* 1136–1145, *335, 351–353,* 1231–1234, *354,* 1235f, *362,* 1258, *378f,* 1334f, *384, 396f,* 1439f, *404, 421, 423, 432, 433–435,* 1574–1576, *436, 438f, 439f, 446, 473f,* 1663–1667, *485, 486, 490,* 507–509, 1738–1741a, *512, 513, 514, 515f, 524, 534f,* 1834–1840, *542, 579f,* 1998–1999, *584,* 600–602, 2043–2047, 2048–2050, 2051–2061, *627, 632,* 2141–2144, *667,* 2214–2219, *670, 680, 687,* 2311–(2314), 2315–2316

Vienna: *450*

Vienna, General Council of—: *120,* 405, *123, 176, 306,* 1104

VIGILIUS, pope: *118, 156,* 619/1–5, *158f,* 682

VIGILIUS OF THAPSIS: 309

VINCENT OF LERINS: 136

virginity: **524;**—of Mary: **200**

virtues, theological—: **543,** 2306; moral—: **585**

vision, cf. beatific—

VOSTE, J.M.: *84,* 237

Vulgate: **69**

wages: *611f,* **613**

Waldensians: *14, 71, 119, 120, 175, 367, 389, 390, 409, 453, 493, 526*

war: **614**

Western Church: *411,* 1508, *506, 512,* 683f, *686*

Western Tradition: *576, 577, 686*

WOLTER, H.: *17*

women,—in Church ministry: **491;**—in society: **613**

Word of God, cf. Son of God, Jesus Christ

word of God, cf. Scripture

word, liturgy of the—: **336,** *352*

work: *446;* cf. labour

works, good—of the justified: **542;**
  good—of the faithful: **680**

world, created: **116;**—spiritual and
  material : **116;** new—:2316

worship, cf. liturgy

WYCLIF, J.: *219, 220f, 223, 361, 368, 410,*
  413, 454, 483

ZOSIMUS, pope: *544,* 1910f

ZWINGLI, U.: *361, 413*

CONCORDANCE WITH DENZINGER-SCHÖNMETZER

(This concordance leaves out the numbers referring to documents quoted elsewhere in the volume. Figures between brackets indicate texts not quoted but summarised.)

ND	DS	ND	DS
1	2	140	3044-3045
2	10	141-142	3201, 3205
3	13	143	3537
4	16	143/1-13	3538-3550
5	30	144-145	3875-3876
6	40	146	3876
7-8	125-126	147-148	3882-3883
9	41	149-(153)	—
10-11	42-43	(154)	—
12-13	150-151	155-159	—
14-15	71-72	160-162	—
16-17	75-76	163	—
19-21	800-802	164-170	—
22-25	851-855	(201)	—
26-29	855-861	(202)	213
30-38	1862-1870	(203)	179
39/1-23	—	204	—
101-104	2765-2768	205	517
105	2814	206	609
106	2775	207	685
107-111	2776-2780	208	1334
112/2	2902	209	—
112/3-5	2903-2905	210-213	1501-1504
112/6-7	2906-2907	214-215	1506-1507
112/8-9	2908-2909	216-217	3006-3007
112/10-11	2910-2911	218	3029
113-114	3004-3005	219	3011
115-117	3026-3029	220	—
118-122	3008-3012	221-222	3283-3284
123	3013	223-224	3286-3288
124	3014	225-227	3290-3293
125-130	3031-3036	228/1	3401
131-136	3015-3020	228/4	3404
137-139	3041-3043	228/9	3409

ND	DS	ND	DS
228/11	3411	405	902
228/14-16	3414-3416	406/1-3	951-953
228/23-24	3423-3424	406/26-27	976-977
229	3650	406/28	978
230-231	3652-3653	407	1007
232	—	408	1333
233-234	3825-3826	409	1336
235	3828	410	1440
236	3830	411/1-2	2901-2902
237	3864	412-413	3002-3003
238	3887	414-418	3021-3025
239	3898	419-420	3896-3897
240-245	—	421-423	—
246-257	—	424	—
258	—	425-426	—
		427-430	—
301	112		
302	113	501	222
303	115	(502)	223
305	150	503	239
306/1-3	153-155	504-505	371-372
306/10-13	162-165	506	780
306/16-24	168-177	507-513	1510-1516
308-316	525-532	514/26	1926
317	803	514/46-49	1946-1949
318-320	804-806	(515)	—
321	850	516	—
322-324	1300-1302	517	—
325-326	1330-1331		
327	3001	603/6-7	158-159
328-331	3021-3024	603/14	166
(332)	—	604-605	250-251
333	—	606/1-12	252-263
		607-608	272-273
401/1	403	609-610	291-292
401/8	410	611-612	293-294
402/5	455	613-616	300-303
402/6	456	617	401
402/7-8	457-458	618/2-3	404-405
402/9	459	619/1-5	416-420
402/11-13	461-463	620/1-10	421-432
403	790	621-623	434-437

ND	DS	ND	DS
624-626	474-476	715	3903-3904
627/1-16	501-516	716-718	—
628-634	533-539	719-720	—
635-637	556-558	801	217
638	610	804	870-875
639	619	805/2-4	942-944
640	791	806	—
643	1025-1027	807/8	1158
644-645	1337-1338	807/37	1187
646	1347	808/1	1201
647	1529	808/3	1203
648	1880	808/5-6	1205-1206
649	2661	808/10	1210
650/27-38	3427-3438	808/13	1213
651/1-3	3645-3647	808/15	1215
652	3675	809	1307-1308
653	3676	810	1351
654-659	—	813	2865i
660	—	814	2865-2867
661	3812	815	2893
662	—	816	2895
663	3905	818-840	3050-3075
664	3922	841	3115
665-667	3924-3925	846/6-7	3406-3407
668	—	846/52-56	3452-3456
669	—	847	—
670-671	—	848	3801
672-673	—	849	3802
674-676	—	850	3804
677-679	—	851	3807
703	503	852	3808
704	1400	853	—
705	1516	854-857	3866-3872
706	1573	858-859	3885-3886
707	1880	(860-882)	—
708	1973	883	—
709	2803-2804	884-885	—
710	3274	886	—
712	3370	901-902	2998-2999
713	3902	903	—
714	—	904-906	—

ND	DS	ND	DS
907	—	1111-1114	—
908	—	1115-1118	—
909-914	—	1119-1121	—
915	—	1122-1123	—
916-921	—	1124-1125	—
922	—	1126-1129	—
923-926	—	1130-1131	—
927	—	1132-1135	—
		1136-1145	—
1001	—	1146-1148	—
1002	—	1149-(1152)	—
1003	1348	1158-1159	—
1004	1350		
1005	1351	1201-1202	—
1006	2720	1203-1205	—
1007	2730	1206	—
1008	2785	1207	—
1009-1011	—	1208	—
1012	—	1209/1-4	3379-3382
1013/15-17	2915-2917	1210	—
1013/21	2921	1211	—
1013/77-79	2977-2979	1212	—
1014-1015	3176-3177	1213	—
1016-1017	—	1214-1215	3819-3820
1018	—	1216	—
1019-1022	—	1218	3841
1023-1026	—	1219-1220	3842
1027-1028	—	1221	3844
1029-1030	—	1222	3846
1031-1032	—	1223-1225	—
1033-1034	—	1227	—
1035	—	1228	—
1036	—	1229-1230	—
1037-1039	—	1231-1234	—
1040	—	1235-1236	—
		1237-1239	—
1101	—	1251-1252	600-601
1102	—	1253	653-654
1103	—	1254	1269
1104	—	1255-1257	1821-1823
1105	—	1258	—
1106-1110	—	1259	—

ND	DS	ND	DS
1301	793	1502-1503	782-783
1303	1154	1504	794
1304	1262	1506	1199
1305-1308	1310-1313	1507/16-17	1256-1257
1309	1451	1508	1303
1310-1323	1600-1613	1509-1511	1320-1322
1324	1728	1512-1520	1635-1643
1325	2328	1521-1522	1645-1646
1326/39-41	3439-3441	1523-1525	1648-1650
1327	3489	1526-1536	1651-1661
1328-1330	—	(1537-1540)	1726-1730
1331	3840	1541-1544	1731-1734
1332	—	1545-1554	1738-1749
1333	3855	1555-1563	1751-1759
1334-1335	—	1564-1565	—
1336	—	1566	3848
		1569	3853
1401	110	1570	3854
1402	120	1571	3891
1403	128	1572-1573	—
1404	183	1574-1576	—
1405	184	1577-1580	—
1406	215	1581-1587	—
1408	741	1588-1589	—
1409	780	1590	—
1410	781	1591	—
1411	794	1601	127
1412-1415	1314-1316	1602	129
1416-1418	1317-1319	1603	216
1419	1349	1604	236
1420-1433	1614-1627	1605	308
1434-1436	1628-1630	1606	323
1437/42-43	3442-3443	1607	—
1437/44	3444	1608	812
(1438)	—	1609	814
1439	—	1610	1157
1440	—	1611/20-21	1260-1261
1440a-1440b	—	1611/25	1265
1441-1442	—	1612	1323
1443-1446	—	1613	1324-1325
1501	700	1614/5-14	1455-1464

ND	DS	ND	DS
1615-1626	1668-1680	1743	—
1627-1629	1684-1686	(1744)	—
1630-1632	1689-1691	1745-1746	—
1633-1634	1692-1693	1747	—
1635-1637	1694-1696	(1748)	—
1638-1640	1697-1700	1749-1750	—
1641-1655	1701-1715	1751	—
1656-1659	1716-1719	1752	—
1660/46-47	3446-3447	1754	—
1660/48	3448	(1801)	755-756
1661	—	1802	794
1662	—	1803	1327
1663-1666	—	1804-1807	1797-1800
1667	—	1808-1819	1801-1812
1668	—	1820	3142
1669-1671	—	1821	3144
1672	—	1822-1823	3145-3146
1681-1683	1025-1027	1824-1825	3700-3701
1684/26-27	1266-1267	1826-1828	3704-3706
1685/17-22	1467-1472	1829	3707
1686	1835	1830	3710
1687-1690	—	1831	3712
1701	101	1832	3714
1702	478	1833	—
1703	794	1834	—
1704	1145	1835-1840	—
1705	1326	1841	—
1706	1763	1842	—
1707-1713	1764-1770	1843-1844	—
1714-1721	1771-1778	1901-1906	225-230
1722-1724	3316-3317	1907	238
1725-1726	3317ab	1908	240
1727-1728	3318-3319	1909	241
1729/1-2	3449-3450	1910-1914	243-249
1730	—	1915-1918	273-276
1731-1733	—	1919-1920	277-278
1734-1736	3849-3852	1921-1922	396-397
1737	3858-3859	1923/2-3	1452-1453
1738-1741	—	1923/31-32	1481-1482
1741a	—	1923/36	1486
(1742)	—	1924-1983	1520-1583

ND	DS	ND	DS
1984/21	1921	2010/56	2956
1984/23	1923	2010/59	2959
1984/55	1955	2010/63	2963
1984/78	1978	2011	3245
1984/79	1979	2012-2013	3247-3248
1985/13	1913	2014	3251
1985/43	1943	2015-2017	3343-3345
1985/63	1963	2018	3346
1986/20	1920	2019	—
1986/50	1950	2020	3780-3781
1986/54	1954	2021	—
1986/67	1967	2022-2025	3918-3921
1986/74	1974	2026-2042	3956-3972
1987/27-28	1927-1928	2043-2047	—
1987/39	1939	2048-2050	—
1987/40	1940	2051-2061	—
1987/41	1941	2062-2063	—
1987/66	1966	2064	—
1988/16	1916		
1988/34	1934	2101-2105	3265-3270
1988/38	1938	2106	3726
1989/1-5	2001-2005	2107-2108	3728-3729
1990/1	2401	2109-2111/3	3733-3737
1990/38-41	2438-2441	2112	—
1990/59	2459	2113	3943
1991/44-47	2444-2447	2114	—
1992/10-11	2410-2411	2115-2116	3944
1992/23	2423	2117/1-3	3947-3948
1993	3329	2118-2119	3949
1994	3330-3331	2120	3951
1995	3810-3813	2121-2123	—
1996-1997	3814-3815	2124	3973
1998-1999	—	2125-2130	3979-3985
		2131-2133	—
2001	—	2134-2140/2	3991-3997
2005	2048	2141-2144	—
2006/3	2103	2145-2153	—
2007/1-2	2201-2202	2153a-2158	—
2007/4-5	2204-2205	2159-2164	—
2007/14	2214	2165	—
2008/2	2291	2166	—
2009/2-3	2302-2303	2167-2171	—

ND	DS	ND	DS
2172-2173	—	2220-2225	—
2174	—	2226-2227	—
2175-2180	—	2228-2232	—
2181	—	2233-2235	—
2201/9	2109	2236	—
2201/48-50	2148-2150	2301	411
2202	3716-3717	2302	540
2203-2206	3718	2305-2307	1000-1002
2205-2206	3719-3720	2308-2309	1304-1306
2207-2208	3722	2310	1820
2209-2212	—	2311-2312	—
2213	—	(2313-2314)	—
2214-2219	—	2315-2316	—
		2317	—